SCOTT FORESMAN • ADDISON WESLEY

Mathematics

Authors

Randall I. Charles

Warren Crown

Francis (Skip) Fennell

Janet H. Caldwell
Mary Cavanagh
Dinah Chancellor
Alma B. Ramirez

Jeanne F. Ramos
Kay Sammons
Jane F. Schielack

William Tate
Mary Thompson
John A. Van de Walle

Consulting Mathematicians

Edward J. Barbeau
Professor of Mathematics
University of Toronto
Toronto, Ontario, Canada

David M. Bressoud
DeWitt Wallace Professor
of Mathematics
Macalester College
Saint Paul, Minnesota

Gary Lippman
Professor of Mathematics
and Computer Science
California State University Hayward
Hayward, California

Editorial Offices: Glenview, Illinois • Parsippany, New Jersey • New York, New York

Sales Offices: Parsippany, New Jersey • Duluth, Georgia • Glenview, Illinois
Coppell, Texas • Ontario, California • Mesa, Arizona

Teacher's Edition
Available online and on CD-ROM

Grade 6 • Volume 2 (Chapters 4–6)

Reading Consultants

Peter Afflerbach
Professor and Director of
The Reading Center
University of Maryland
College Park, Maryland

Donald J. Leu
John and Maria Neag
Endowed Chair in Literacy
and Technology
University of Connecticut
Storrs, Connecticut

ESL Consultant

Jim Cummins
Professor of Curriculum
Ontario Institute for Studies in Education
University of Toronto
Toronto, Ontario, Canada

Professional Development Consultant

David C. Geary
Chair and Middlebush Professor
Department of Psychological Sciences
University of Missouri
Columbia, Missouri

ISBN: 0-328-11736-6

2 3 4 5 6 7 8 9 10 V064 12 11 10 09 08 07 06 05 04

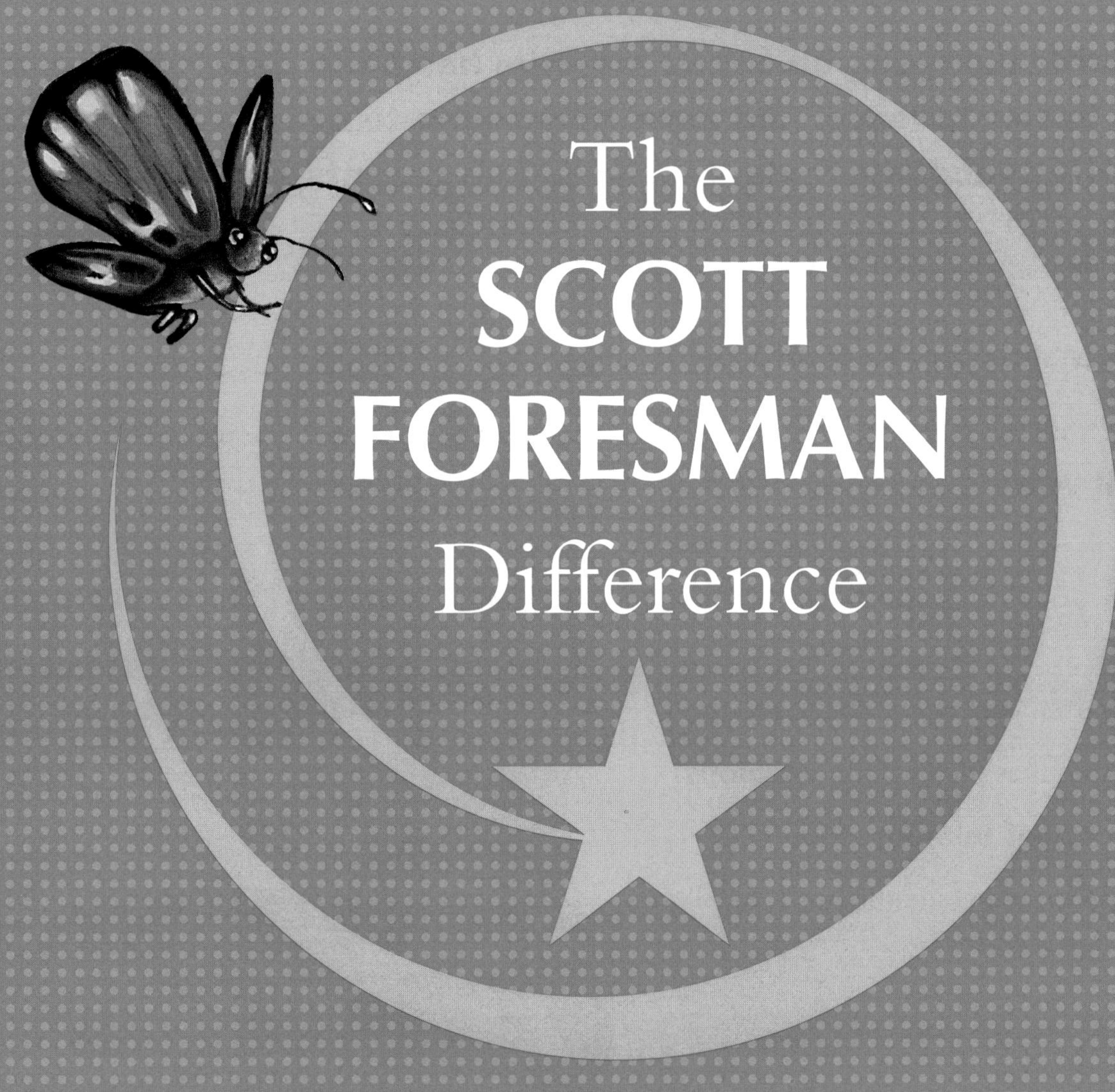

SCOTT FORESMAN • ADDISON WESLEY

Mathematics

You can count on us.

The difference that counts . . .

Our all-new scientifically research-based program has been designed to make math simpler to teach, easier to learn, and more accessible to every student. With the Scott Foresman Difference, students, teachers, and parents can all say: "I get it!"

Pre-Kindergarten

Count on our unique, **scientifically research-based** Pre-K math program to help early math learners bloom. **Field tested for eight years** in diverse classrooms, it has been proven to build essential math background.

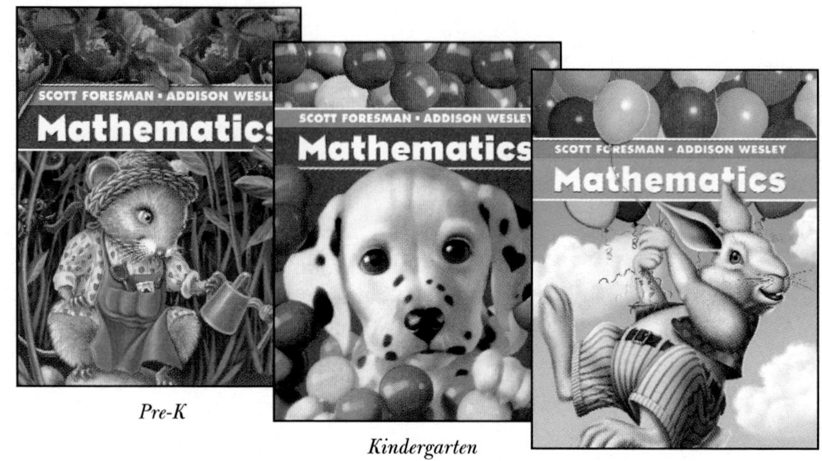

Pre-K *Kindergarten* *Grade 1*

Kindergarten

We follow up in Kindergarten with a flexible, **research-based,** full-day curriculum that successfully **develops and extends mathematical thinking.** Stories, games, and center activities teach your students basic math understandings.

Grade 2 *Grade 3* *Grade 4*

Grades 1 and 2

To help your students comprehend and successfully apply basic facts, our **research-based program** begins with an **understanding of number** and what the number sentence means. This leads to **algebra success.**

Grades 3 through 6

In the upper grades, the Scott Foresman Difference is evident from cover-to-cover. From **instruction right on the student page** to daily assessment and **customized intervention,** our **research-based program** ensures that your students **achieve progress and test success.**

Grade 5 *Grade 6*

and the research that proves it.

Completely planned, written, and reviewed by the authors, our program is backed by more than 100 years of research into what really works in the classroom. Four phases of research were integrated into the program's development by the authors, who are all recognized experts in the acquisition of mathematical learning.

1 Ongoing Research

The proven effectiveness of Scott Foresman, Addison Wesley, and Silver Burdett Ginn previous math programs provides a longitudinal research base that spans more than 100 years. Pretest and posttest results show that these programs improve students' math proficiency.

2 Scientific Research Base

An experienced authorship team provided expertise in synthesizing and contributing to a rich body of scientific evidence. Research-based techniques were embedded into the program's instructional materials, assessments, and professional development.

3 Formative Research

Classroom field studies, school administrators, mathematics teachers, and reviewers contributed valuable recommendations as the program was designed and written. Pretest and posttest scores were part of the information gathered during program development.

4 Summative Research

Scientific evidence, including longitudinal studies in the classroom, further validate the efficacy of our program. Control group research designs and test score data ensure that the program is of the highest quality and predictive of success.

Authors

Randall I. Charles
Professor Emeritus, Department of Mathematics and Computer Science
San Jose State University
San Jose, California

Warren Crown
Professor of Mathematics Education
Rutgers University
New Brunswick, New Jersey

Francis (Skip) Fennell
Professor of Education
McDaniel College
Westminster, Maryland

Janet H. Caldwell
Professor of Mathematics
Rowan University
Glassboro, New Jersey

Mary Cavanagh
Project Coordinator, Math, Science and Beyond
Solano Beach School District
San Diego County, California

Dinah Chancellor
Coordinator of Math, Science, Gifted/Talented, Title IV
Carroll ISD
Southlake, Texas

Alma B. Ramírez
Senior Research Associate, Mathematics
Case Methods Project
WestEd
Oakland, California

Jeanne F. Ramos
Administrative Coordinator, K–12 Mathematics
Los Angeles Unified School District
Los Angeles, California

Kay Sammons
Supervisor of Mathematics
Howard County Public Schools
Ellicott City, Maryland

Jane F. Schielack
Associate Professor of Mathematics
Texas A&M University
College Station, Texas

William Tate
Professor and Chair of the Department of Education
College of Arts and Sciences
Washington University
St. Louis, Missouri

Mary Thompson
Mathematics Instructional Specialist
New Orleans Public Schools Louisiana
New Orleans, Louisiana

John Van de Walle
Professor Emeritus of Mathematics Education/Consultant
Virginia Commonwealth University
Richmond, Virginia

Consulting Mathematicians

Edward J. Barbeau
Professor of Mathematics
University of Toronto
Toronto, Ontario, Canada

David M. Bressoud
DeWitt Wallace Professor of Mathematics
Macalester College
Saint Paul, Minnesota

Gary Lippman
Professor of Mathematics and Computer Science
California State University Hayward
Hayward, California

Reading Consultants

Peter Afflerbach
Professor and Director of the Reading Center
University of Maryland
College Park, Maryland

Donald J. Leu
John and Maria Neag Endowed Chair in Literacy and Technology
University of Connecticut
Storrs, Connecticut

ESL Consultant

Jim Cummins
Professor of Curriculum
Ontario Institute for Studies in Education
University of Toronto
Toronto, Ontario, Canada

Professional Development Consultant

David C. Geary
Chair and Middlebush Professor
Department of Psychological Sciences
University of Missouri
Columbia, Missouri

Reviewers

Mary Bacon
Mathematics Specialist
East Baton Rouge Parish School System
Baton Rouge, Louisiana

Cheryl Baker
Mathematics Teacher
Norton Middle School
Norton, Ohio

Marcelline A. Barron
Curriculum Leader Math and Science, Grades K–5
Fairfield Public Schools
Fairfield, Connecticut

Mary Connery-Simmons
Mathematics Specialist
Springfield Massachusetts Public Schools
Springfield, Massachusetts

Anthony C. Dentino
Supervisor of Curriculum
Brick Township Schools
Brick, New Jersey

Donna McCollum Derby
Teacher
Kernersville Elementary School
Kernersville, North Carolina

Dawn Evans
Mathematics Teacher
Bret Harte Elementary School
Chicago, Illinois

Terri Geaudreau
Title I Math Facilitator
Bemiss Elementary
Spokane, Washington

Sister Helen Lucille Habig, RSM
Assistant Superintendent of Catholic Schools
Archdiocese of Cincinnati
Cincinnati, Ohio

Sam Hanson
Teacher
Totem Falls Elementary
Snohomish, Washington

Allison Harris
Professional Development School Coach
Seattle Public Schools
Seattle, Washington

Kim Hill
Teacher
Hayes Grade Center
Ada, Oklahoma

Pamela Renee Hill
Teacher
Durham Public Schools
Durham, North Carolina

Martha Knight
Teacher
Oak Mountain Elementary
Birmingham, Alabama

Catherine Kuhns
Teacher
Country Hills Elementary
Coral Springs, Florida

Madeleine A. Madsen
District Curriculum Resource
District Community Consolidated School District 59
Arlington Heights, Illinois

Susan Mayberger
Supervisor of English as a Second Language/Director of Migrant Education
Omaha Public Schools
Omaha, Nebraska

Judy Peede
Elementary Lead Math Teacher
Wake County Schools
Raleigh, North Carolina

Lynda M. Penry
Teacher
Wright Elementary
Fort Walton Beach, Florida

Jolyn D. Raleigh
District Math Curriculum Specialist, Grades K–2
Granite School District
Salt Lake City, Utah

Deanna P. Rigdon
District Math Curriculum Specialist, Grades 3–4
Granite School District
Salt Lake City, Utah

Thomas Romero
Principal
Adams Elementary
Wapato, Washington

Wendy Siegel
Mathematics Coordinator, Grades K–12
Orchard Park Middle School
Orchard Park, New York

Sandra Smith
Teacher
Cheat Lake Elementary
Morgantown, West Virginia

Vickie H. Smith
Assistant Principal
Phoenix Academic Magnet Elementary School
Alexandria, Louisiana

Rochelle A. Solomon
Mathematics Resource Teacher
Cleveland Municipal School District
Cleveland, Ohio

Frank L. Sparks
Curriculum Design and Support Specialist, Secondary Mathematics
New Orleans Public Schools
New Orleans, Louisiana

Beth L. Spivey
Lead Teacher, Elementary Mathematics
Wake County Public School System
Raleigh, North Carolina

Paula Spomer
Teacher
Chisholm Elementary
Edmond, Oklahoma

Robert Trammel
Math Consultant
Fort Wayne Community Schools
Fort Wayne, Indiana

Annemarie Tuffner
Mathematics Lead Teacher, Grades K–12
Neshaminy School District
Langhorne, Pennsylvania

Ann Watts
Mathematics Specialist
East Baton Rouge Parish School System
Baton Rouge, Louisiana

Judy L. Wright
Curriculum and Staff Development Specialist
Columbus Public Schools
Columbus, Ohio

Theresa Zieles
Teacher
Indianapolis Public School #88
Indianapolis, Indiana

National Math Advisory Board

F. William Amorosi
Saugus Public Schools
Saugus, Massachusetts

Linda Bailey
Oklahoma City, Oklahoma

Mary Bording
Huntsville Public Schools
Huntsville, Alabama

Patti Bridwell
Austin, Texas

Merry Brown
Lake Jackson, Texas

Gayle D. Coleman
St. Louis Public Schools
St. Louis, Missouri

Steven T. Cottrell
Davis School District
Farmington, Utah

Brenda DeBorde
Grand Prairie ISD
Grand Prairie, Texas

Toni Lynn De Vore
Wood County Schools
Parkersburg, West Virginia

Sandra Eliason
Orland School District 135
Orland Park, Illinois

Larue Evans
Cherry Hill Elementary Schools
Cherry Hill, New Jersey

Ann R. Flanagan
Sachem Central School District
Holbrook, New York

Nancy C. French
Davenport Community School District
Davenport, Iowa

Marguerite Hart
Indianapolis, Indiana

Cathy Hutchins
Laird Elementary School
Tempe, Arizona

Nancy B. Knight
Mount Laurel Township Schools
Mount Laurel, New Jersey

Suzzanne Legg
Kansas City Public Schools
Kansas City, Kansas

Gale Levow
Community School District 8
Bronx, New York

Lynda M. Penry
Wright Elementary
Fort Walton Beach, Florida

Patricia Paluch Pockl
Ohio County Schools
Wheeling, West Virginia

Sylvia O. Reeder-Tucker
Prince George's County Public Schools
Capitol Heights, Maryland

Beverly Kendrick Ross
Kyrene School District
Tempe, Arizona

Kathy Ross
New Orleans, Louisiana

Edward J. Sahagian
North Bergen School District
North Bergen, New Jersey

Kathleen Savage
Mesa Public Schools
Mesa, Arizona

Beth Ann Schefelker
Henry David Thoreau Elementary
Milwaukee Public Schools
Milwaukee, Wisconsin

Dana Smith Simmons
Flint Community Schools
Flint, Michigan

Toni Vela
Laredo, ISD
Laredo, Texas

Julie Victory
Pocono Mountain School District
Swiftwater, Pennsylvania

Jesse Warren
South Bend Community School Corporation
South Bend, Indiana

Nancy Zirkelbach
Cloverdale Elementary
Bonneville School District #93
Idaho Falls, Idaho

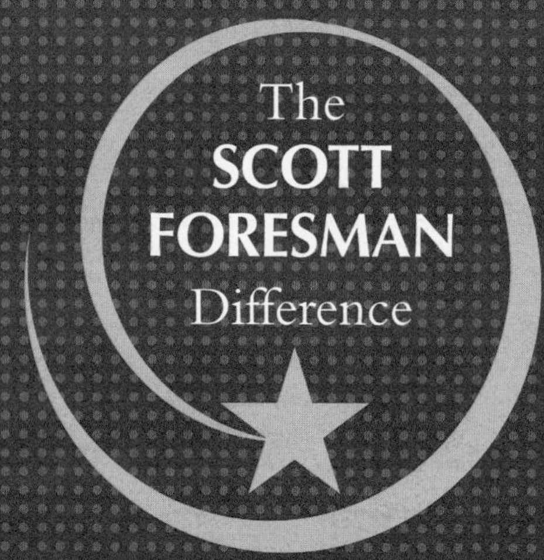

We truly teach for understanding.

Research shows that teaching for understanding is the best test prep you can provide. That's why every program claims to teach for understanding. But our program is different.

Includes instruction right on the student page

Everything your students need to "get it" is always accessible. Students are able to engage in deeper, independent learning while parents can help at home.

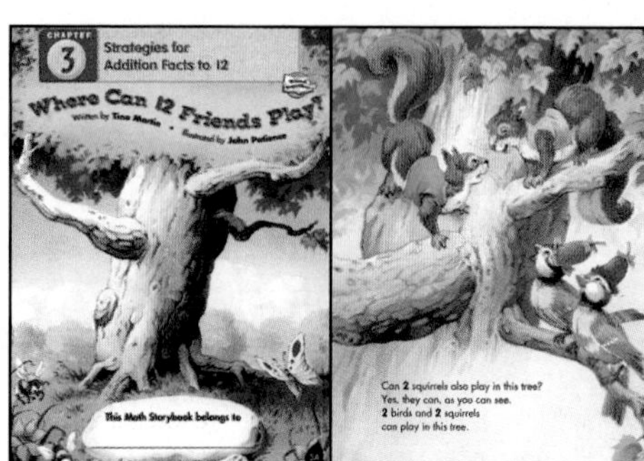

Instructional Stories

At the primary level, Read-Together Math Stories in the Student Edition and in Big Book format actually teach math concepts. Your students build math background while improving their reading fluency.

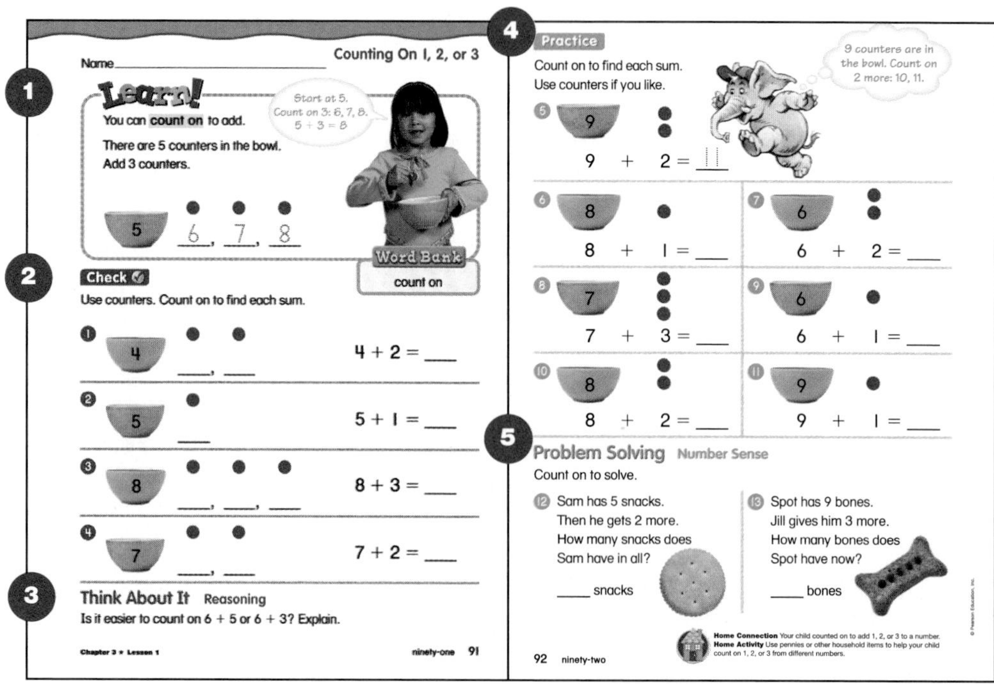

Name______ Counting On 1, 2, or 3

1 **Learn!**
You can **count on** to add.
There are 5 counters in the bowl.
Add 3 counters.

Start at 5. Count on 3: 6, 7, 8. 5 + 3 = 8

5 6, 7, 8

Word Bank
count on

2 **Check**
Use counters. Count on to find each sum.

1. 4 ___, ___ 4 + 2 = ___
2. 5 ___ 5 + 1 = ___
3. 8 ___, ___, ___ 8 + 3 = ___
4. 7 ___, ___ 7 + 2 = ___

3 **Think About It** Reasoning
Is it easier to count on 6 + 5 or 6 + 3? Explain.

Chapter 3 • Lesson 1 ninety-one 91

4 **Practice**
Count on to find each sum.
Use counters if you like.

9 counters are in the bowl. Count on 2 more: 10, 11.

5. 9 + 2 = 11
6. 8 + 1 = ___
7. 6 + 2 = ___
8. 7 + 3 = ___
9. 6 + 1 = ___
10. 8 + 2 = ___
11. 9 + 1 = ___

5 **Problem Solving** Number Sense
Count on to solve.

12. Sam has 5 snacks. Then he gets 2 more. How many snacks does Sam have in all? ___ snacks

13. Spot has 9 bones. Jill gives him 3 more. How many bones does Spot have now? ___ bones

Home Connection Your child counted on to add 1, 2, or 3 to a number. **Home Activity** Use pennies or other household items to help your child count on 1, 2, or 3 from different numbers.

92 ninety-two

1. Learn
Introduces concepts and vocabulary clearly

2. Check
Quickly assesses your students' grasp of the new concept before practice

3. Think About It
Gives your students a chance to verbalize and clarify understanding before practice begins

4. Practice
Provides instruction with more examples your students can explore with manipulatives

5. Problem Solving
Engages your students with daily problem-solving activities

6. Magnetic Manipulatives
Fun, no-mess manipulatives your students can hold up to display their work and help you check for understanding

Identifies explicitly what your students need to achieve

Lessons in the Student Edition clearly explain the mathematics your students need to understand and the skills they need to master. Step-by-step instruction guides their thinking when they need it most.

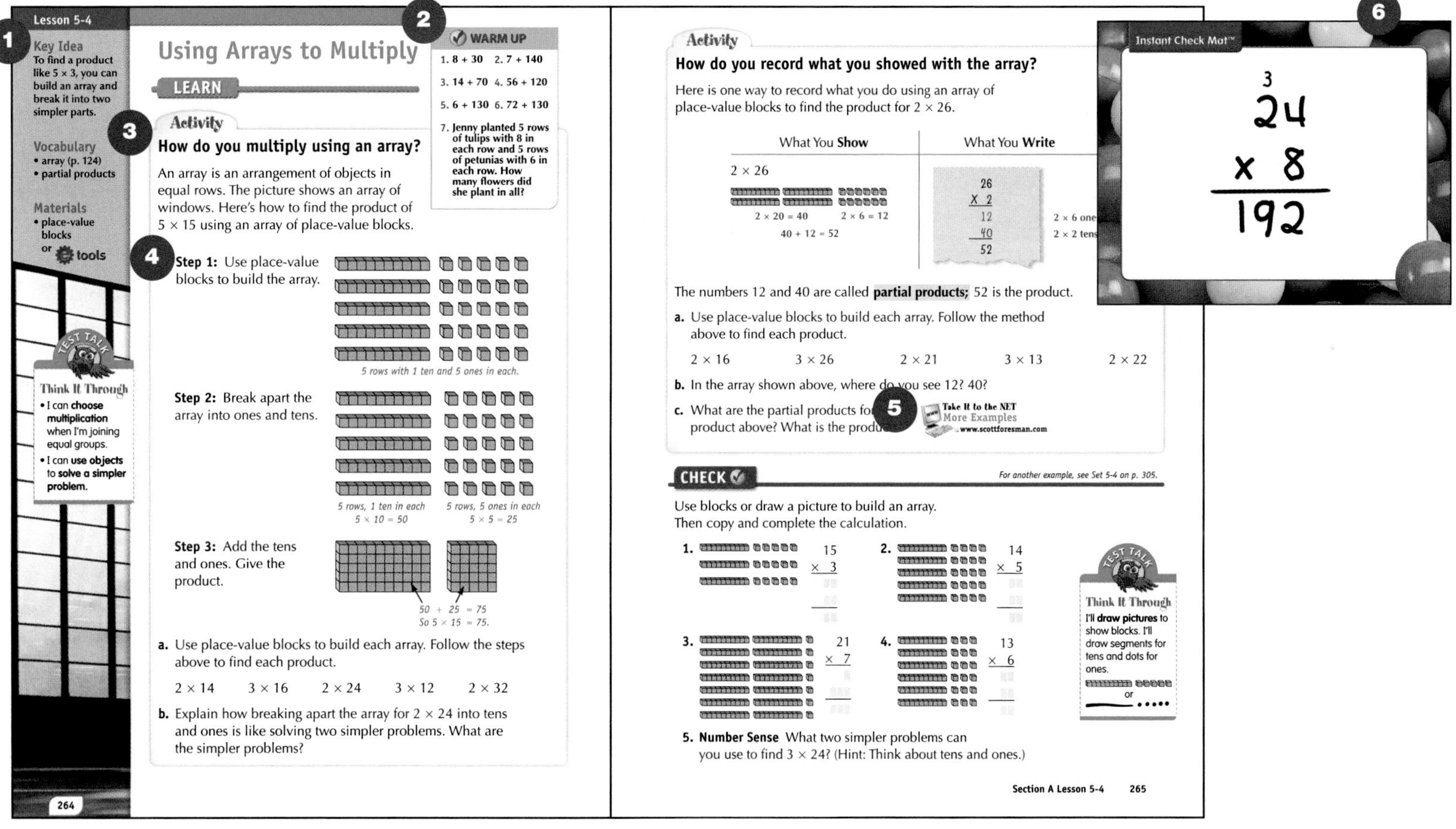

Lesson 5-4

Key Idea
To find a product like 5 × 3, you can build an array and break it into two simpler parts.

Vocabulary
• array (p. 124)
• partial products

Materials
• place-value blocks
or tools

Test Talk
Think It Through
• I can choose multiplication when I'm joining equal groups.
• I can use objects to solve a simpler problem.

Using Arrays to Multiply

LEARN

WARM UP
1. 8 + 30 2. 7 + 140
3. 14 + 70 4. 56 + 120
5. 6 + 130 6. 72 + 130
7. Jenny planted 5 rows of tulips with 8 in each row and 5 rows of petunias with 6 in each row. How many flowers did she plant in all?

Activity
How do you multiply using an array?

An array is an arrangement of objects in equal rows. The picture shows an array of windows. Here's how to find the product of 5 × 15 using an array of place-value blocks.

Step 1: Use place-value blocks to build the array.

5 rows with 1 ten and 5 ones in each.

Step 2: Break apart the array into ones and tens.

5 rows, 1 ten in each 5 × 10 = 50
5 rows, 5 ones in each 5 × 5 = 25

Step 3: Add the tens and ones. Give the product.

50 + 25 = 75
So 5 × 15 = 75.

a. Use place-value blocks to build each array. Follow the steps above to find each product.

2 × 14 3 × 16 2 × 24 3 × 12 2 × 32

b. Explain how breaking apart the array for 2 × 24 into tens and ones is like solving two simpler problems. What are the simpler problems?

264

Activity
How do you record what you showed with the array?

Here is one way to record what you do using an array of place-value blocks to find the product for 2 × 26.

What You Show	What You Write
2 × 26 2 × 20 = 40 2 × 6 = 12 40 + 12 = 52	26 × 2 12 2 × 6 ones 40 2 × 2 tens 52

The numbers 12 and 40 are called **partial products;** 52 is the product.

a. Use place-value blocks to build each array. Follow the method above to find each product.

2 × 16 3 × 26 2 × 21 3 × 13 2 × 22

b. In the array shown above, where do you see 12? 40?

c. What are the partial products for the product above? What is the product?

Take It to the NET
More Examples
www.scottforesman.com

CHECK

For another example, see Set 5-4 on p. 305.

Use blocks or draw a picture to build an array. Then copy and complete the calculation.

1. 15 × 3
2. 14 × 5
3. 21 × 7
4. 13 × 6

5. **Number Sense** What two simpler problems can you use to find 3 × 24? (Hint: Think about tens and ones.)

Test Talk
Think It Through
I'll draw pictures to show blocks. I'll draw segments for tens and dots for ones.

Section A Lesson 5-4 265

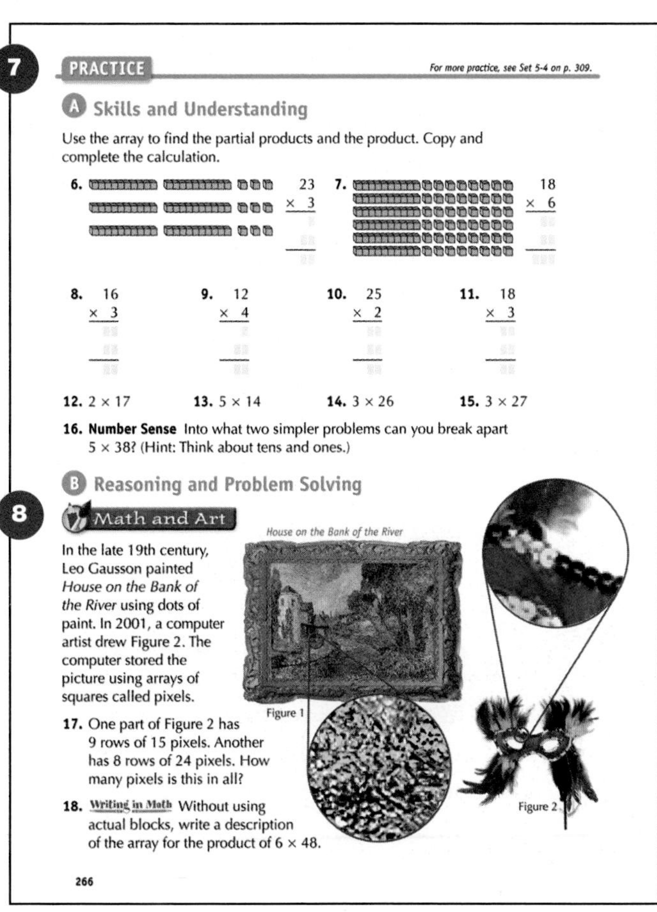

PRACTICE

For more practice, see Set 5-4 on p. 309.

A Skills and Understanding

Use the array to find the partial products and the product. Copy and complete the calculation.

6. 23 × 3
7. 18 × 6

8. 16 × 3 9. 12 × 4 10. 25 × 2 11. 18 × 3

12. 2 × 17 13. 5 × 14 14. 3 × 26 15. 3 × 27

16. **Number Sense** Into what two simpler problems can you break apart 5 × 38? (Hint: Think about tens and ones.)

B Reasoning and Problem Solving

Math and Art

In the late 19th century, Leo Gausson painted *House on the Bank of the River* using dots of paint. In 2001, a computer artist drew Figure 2. The computer stored the picture using arrays of squares called pixels.

House on the Bank of the River

Figure 1

Figure 2

17. One part of Figure 2 has 9 rows of 15 pixels. Another has 8 rows of 24 pixels. How many pixels is this in all?

18. Writing in Math Without using actual blocks, write a description of the array for the product of 6 × 48.

266

1. Key Idea
Identifies important mathematics concepts clearly right at the start

2. Warm Up
Activates prior knowledge of skills your students will need in the upcoming lesson

3. Focus Questions
Sets up instruction for your students' understanding

4. Guided Instruction
Makes concepts easier for your students to grasp with step-by-step instruction and clear models right on the student page

5. Take It to the Net
Provides online access to test prep, more practice, and more examples

6. Instant Check Mat™
See all your students' work at a glance and assess their understanding instantly

7. Built-in Leveled Practice
Allows you to customize instruction to match your students' abilities

8. Curriculum Connections
Encourages your students to transfer the concepts they acquire to other subject areas

Monitors understanding every step of the way

With embedded assessment opportunities right on the student page, it's easy to gauge your students' progress on an ongoing basis. This frees you to focus your time and energy on helping each student acquire the skills and understanding needed for test success.

Before the Lesson

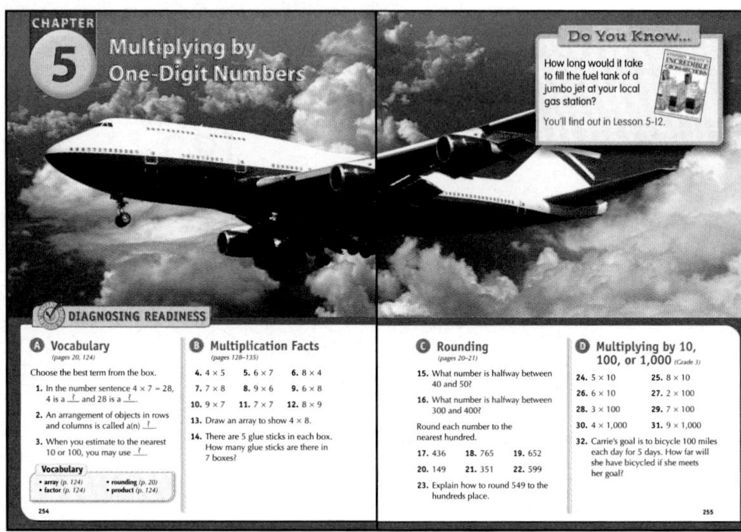

Diagnosing Readiness

Helps you assess your students' knowledge of vocabulary, skills, and concepts, and then prescribe individualized intervention prior to chapter lessons

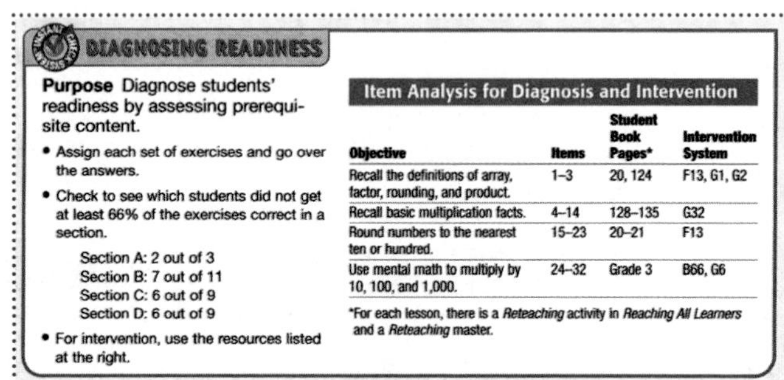

DIAGNOSING READINESS

Purpose Diagnose students' readiness by assessing prerequisite content.

- Assign each set of exercises and go over the answers.
- Check to see which students did not get at least 66% of the exercises correct in a section.
  - Section A: 2 out of 3
  - Section B: 7 out of 11
  - Section C: 6 out of 9
  - Section D: 6 out of 9
- For intervention, use the resources listed at the right.

Item Analysis for Diagnosis and Intervention

Objective	Items	Student Book Pages*	Intervention System
Recall the definitions of array, factor, rounding, and product.	1–3	20, 124	F13, G1, G2
Recall basic multiplication facts.	4–14	128–135	G32
Round numbers to the nearest ten or hundred.	15–23	20–21	F13
Use mental math to multiply by 10, 100, and 1,000.	24–32	Grade 3	B66, G6

*For each lesson, there is a *Reteaching* activity in *Reaching All Learners* and a *Reteaching* master.

Every assessment aligns with customized intervention in the Teacher's Edition

During the Lesson

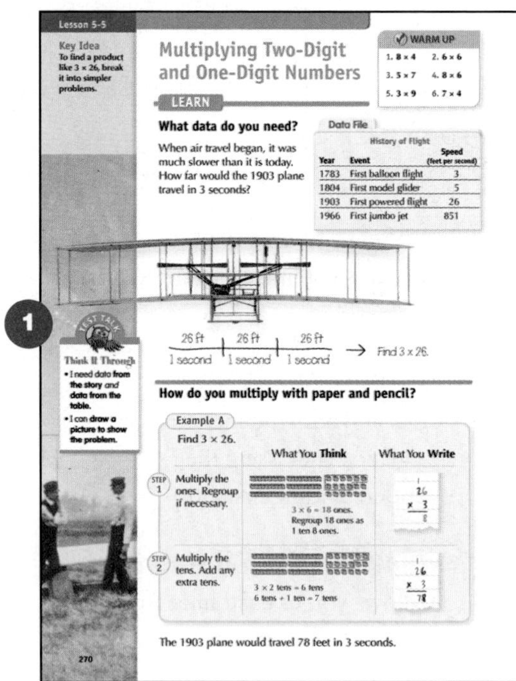

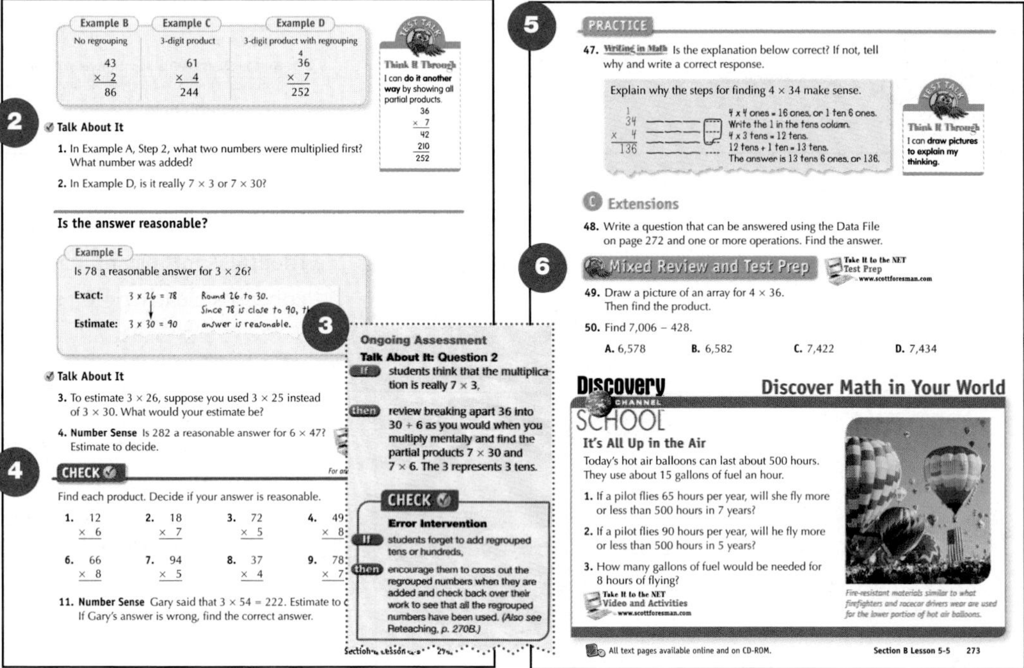

1. Test Talk—Think It Through
Gives your students practice in the type of thinking and problem-solving strategies they'll use on tests

2. Talk About It
Supplies your students with an informal assessment opportunity that lets them verbalize their understanding

3. If . . . Then
Provides instant intervention before your students get too far off track

4. Check
Sees if your students "get it" before beginning independent practice

5. Writing in Math
Prepares your students for open-ended and short- or extended-response questions on state and national tests

6. Mixed Review and Test Prep
Helps your students keep their test-taking skills sharp

Aligns all assessments with immediate and systematic remediation

Our unique Item Analysis for Diagnosis and Intervention in the Teacher's Edition lets you quickly assess your students' understanding of math concepts and prescribe individualized intervention.

After the Lesson *at the End of Each Section . . .*

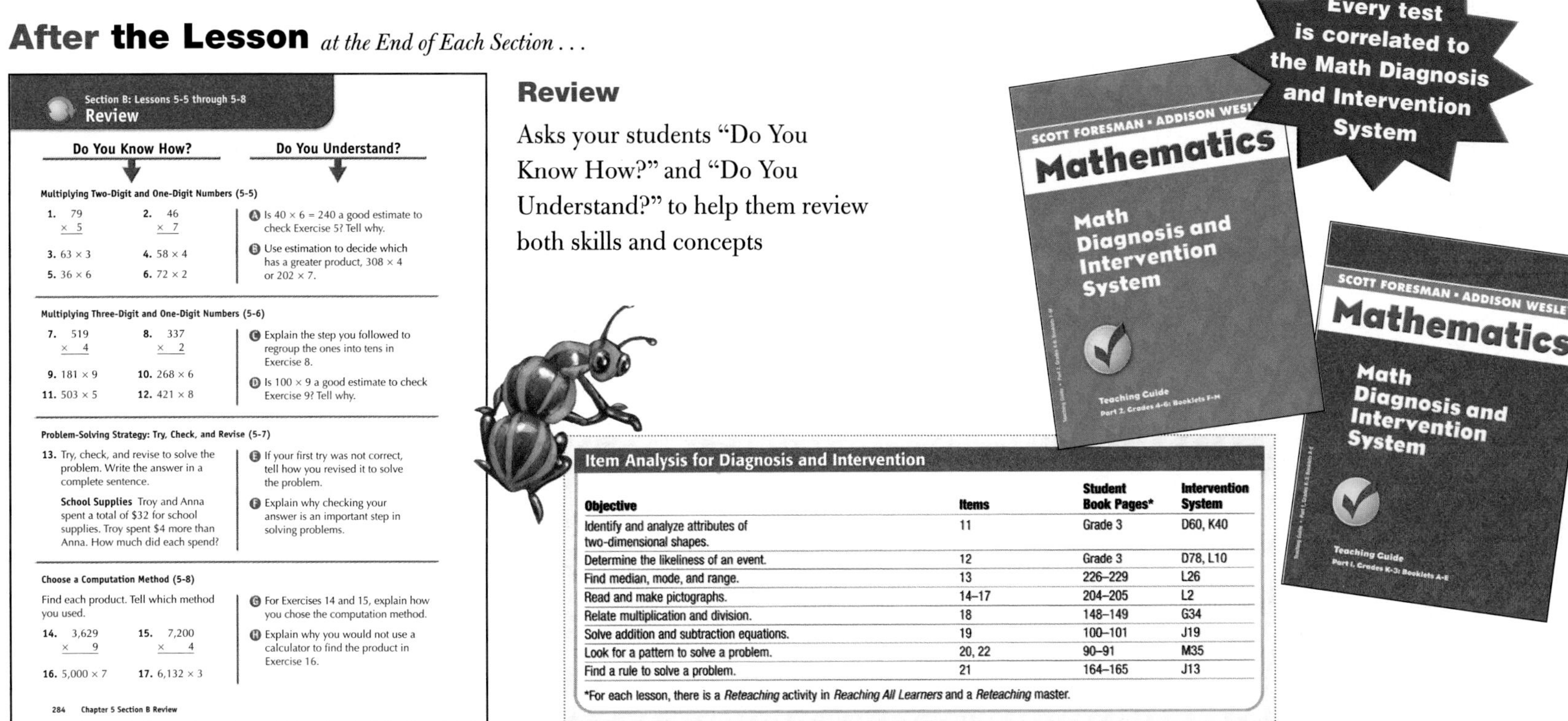
Section B: Lessons 5-5 through 5-8
Review

Do You Know How?	Do You Understand?
Multiplying Two-Digit and One-Digit Numbers (5-5)	
1. 79 × 5 2. 46 × 7	A Is 40 × 6 = 240 a good estimate to check Exercise 5? Tell why.
3. 63 × 3 4. 58 × 4	B Use estimation to decide which has a greater product, 308 × 4 or 202 × 7.
5. 36 × 6 6. 72 × 2	
Multiplying Three-Digit and One-Digit Numbers (5-6)	
7. 519 × 4 8. 337 × 2	C Explain the step you followed to regroup the ones into tens in Exercise 8.
9. 181 × 9 10. 268 × 6	D Is 100 × 9 a good estimate to check Exercise 9? Tell why.
11. 503 × 5 12. 421 × 8	
Problem-Solving Strategy: Try, Check, and Revise (5-7)	
13. Try, check, and revise to solve the problem. Write the answer in a complete sentence.	E If your first try was not correct, tell how you revised it to solve the problem.
School Supplies Troy and Anna spent a total of $32 for school supplies. Troy spent $4 more than Anna. How much did each spend?	F Explain why checking your answer is an important step in solving problems.
Choose a Computation Method (5-8)	
Find each product. Tell which method you used.	G For Exercises 14 and 15, explain how you chose the computation method.
14. 3,629 × 9 15. 7,200 × 4	H Explain why you would not use a calculator to find the product in Exercise 16.
16. 5,000 × 7 17. 6,132 × 3	

284 Chapter 5 Section B Review

Item Analysis for Diagnosis and Intervention

Objective	Items	Student Book Pages*	Intervention System
Identify and analyze attributes of two-dimensional shapes.	11	Grade 3	D60, K40
Determine the likeliness of an event.	12	Grade 3	D78, L10
Find median, mode, and range.	13	226–229	L26
Read and make pictographs.	14–17	204–205	L2
Relate multiplication and division.	18	148–149	G34
Solve addition and subtraction equations.	19	100–101	J19
Look for a pattern to solve a problem.	20, 22	90–91	M35
Find a rule to solve a problem.	21	164–165	J13

*For each lesson, there is a *Reteaching* activity in *Reaching All Learners* and a *Reteaching* master.

Review

Asks your students "Do You Know How?" and "Do You Understand?" to help them review both skills and concepts

After the Lesson *at the End of Each Chapter . . .*

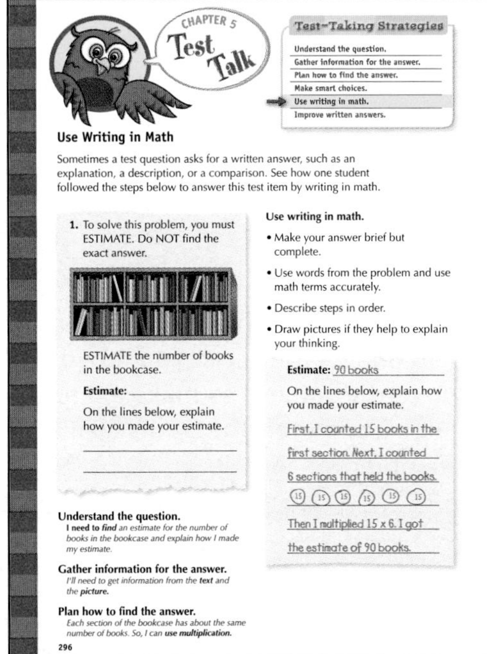
Chapter 5 Test Talk

Use Writing in Math

Sometimes a test question asks for a written answer, such as an explanation, a description, or a comparison. See how one student followed the steps below to answer this test item by writing in math.

1. To solve this problem, you must ESTIMATE. Do NOT find the exact answer.

ESTIMATE the number of books in the bookcase.

Estimate: 90 books

On the lines below, explain how you made your estimate.

First, I counted 15 books in the first section. Next, I counted 6 sections that held the books. Then I multiplied 15 x 6. I got the estimate of 90 books.

Use writing in math.
- Make your answer brief but complete.
- Use words from the problem and use math terms accurately.
- Describe steps in order.
- Draw pictures if they help to explain your thinking.

Understand the question.
I need to find an estimate for the number of books in the bookcase and explain how I made my estimate.

Gather information for the answer.
I'll need to get information from the text and the picture.

Plan how to find the answer.
Each section of the bookcase has about the same number of books. So, I can use multiplication.

296

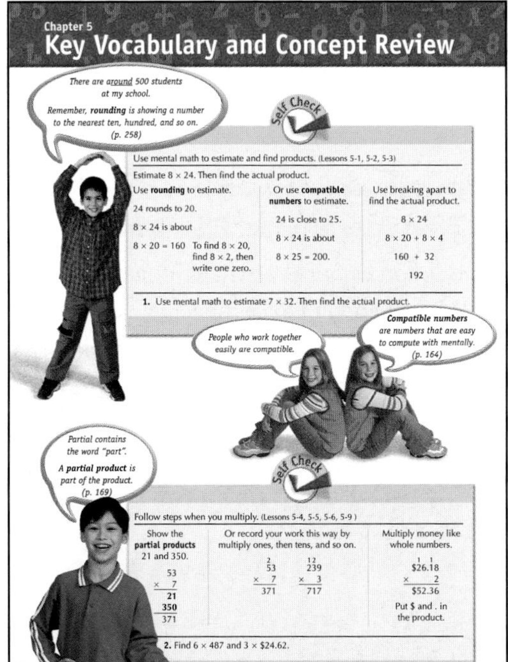
Chapter 5 Key Vocabulary and Concept Review

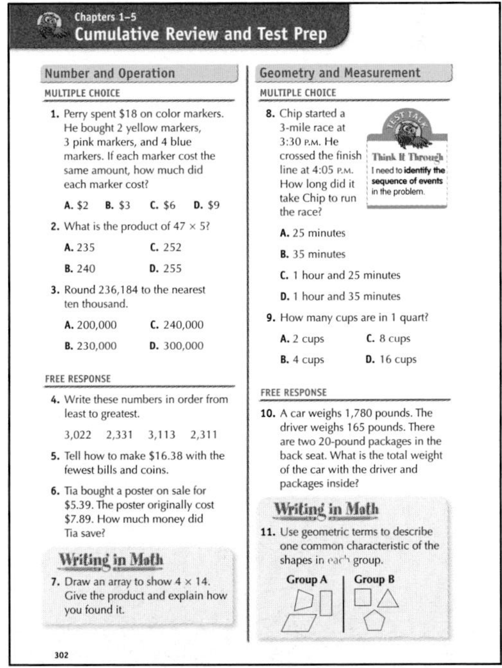
Chapters 1–5 Cumulative Review and Test Prep

Number and Operation

MULTIPLE CHOICE

1. Perry spent $18 on color markers. He bought 2 yellow markers, 3 pink markers, and 4 blue markers. If each marker cost the same amount, how much did each marker cost?
   A. $2 B. $3 C. $6 D. $9
2. What is the product of 47 × 5?
   A. 235 B. 240 C. 252 D. 255
3. Round 236,184 to the nearest ten thousand.
   A. 200,000 B. 230,000 C. 240,000 D. 300,000

FREE RESPONSE

4. Write these numbers in order from least to greatest.
   3,022 2,331 3,113 2,311
5. Tell how to make $16.38 with the fewest bills and coins.
6. Tia bought a poster on sale for $5.39. The poster originally cost $7.89. How much money did Tia save?

Writing in Math

7. Draw an array to show 4 × 14. Give the product and explain how you found it.

Geometry and Measurement

MULTIPLE CHOICE

8. Chip started a 3-mile race at 3:30 P.M. He crossed the finish line at 4:05 P.M. How long did it take Chip to run the race?
   A. 25 minutes B. 35 minutes C. 1 hour and 25 minutes D. 1 hour and 35 minutes

Think It Through: I need to identify the sequence of events in the problem.

9. How many cups are in 1 quart?
   A. 2 cups B. 4 cups C. 8 cups D. 16 cups

FREE RESPONSE

10. A car weighs 1,780 pounds. The driver weighs 165 pounds. There are two 20-pound packages in the back seat. What is the total weight of the car with the driver and packages inside?

Writing in Math

11. Use geometric terms to describe one common characteristic of the shapes in each group.
   Group A | Group B

302

Test Talk

Gives your students in-depth instruction and practice on the test-taking strategies introduced at the beginning of the Student Edition

Key Vocabulary and Concept Review

Checks your students' understanding of math concepts and provides them with real-world vocabulary connections

Cumulative Review and Test Prep

Provides ongoing assessment and practice of previously taught content

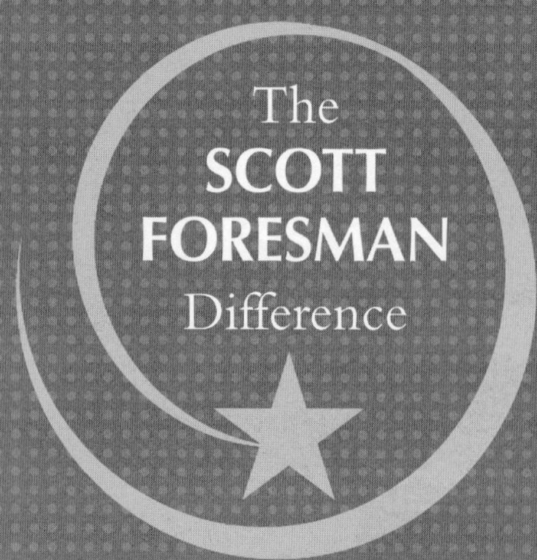
The
SCOTT
FORESMAN
Difference

We create better problem solvers.

Problem solving is incredibly important to math proficiency and test success. That's why every program has a problem-solving component. But our program is different.

Connects reading and writing to problem solving

Research shows math performance is often connected to literacy. We apply familiar reading and writing strategies to math and explain to your students how these strategies can help them become more successful problem solvers.

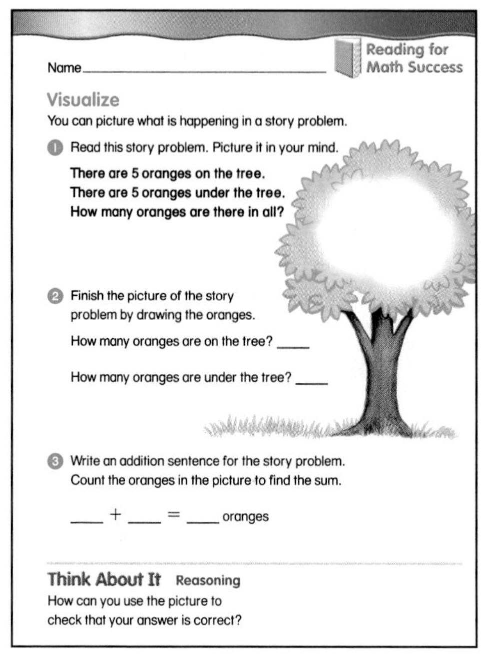

Name ______ Reading for Math Success

Visualize

You can picture what is happening in a story problem.

1. Read this story problem. Picture it in your mind.

There are 5 oranges on the tree.
There are 5 oranges under the tree.
How many oranges are there in all?

2. Finish the picture of the story problem by drawing the oranges.

How many oranges are on the tree? ____

How many oranges are under the tree? ____

3. Write an addition sentence for the story problem. Count the oranges in the picture to find the sum.

___ + ___ = ___ oranges

Think About It Reasoning
How can you use the picture to check that your answer is correct?

Reading for Math Success

Identifies a reading strategy your students already know and shows them how to apply the strategy to math word problems

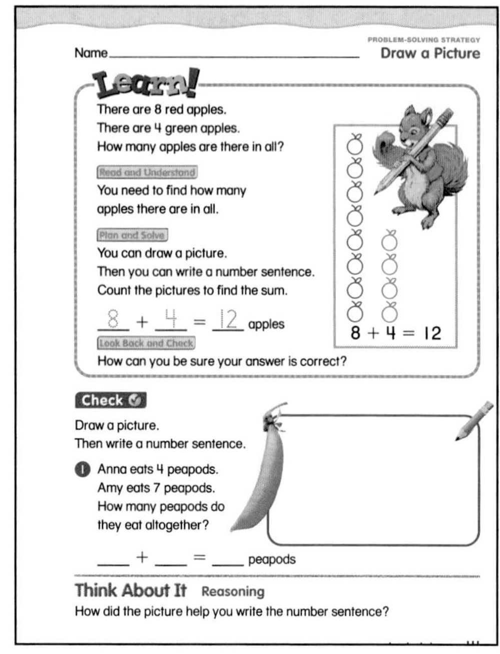

Name ______ PROBLEM-SOLVING STRATEGY Draw a Picture

Learn!

There are 8 red apples.
There are 4 green apples.
How many apples are there in all?

Read and Understand
You need to find how many apples there are in all.

Plan and Solve
You can draw a picture.
Then you can write a number sentence.
Count the pictures to find the sum.

8 + 4 = 12 apples

8 + 4 = 12

Look Back and Check
How can you be sure your answer is correct?

Check

Draw a picture.
Then write a number sentence.

1. Anna eats 4 peapods.
Amy eats 7 peapods.
How many peapods do they eat altogether?

___ + ___ = ___ peapods

Think About It Reasoning
How did the picture help you write the number sentence?

Problem-Solving Strategy

Teaches your students how and when to use the reading strategy to solve problems, and then provides an opportunity for them to demonstrate what they have learned

Problem of the Day Transparencies Flip Chart

Reinforces previously taught math content and enhances specific problem-solving skills and strategies each day for whole-class or small group problem-solving

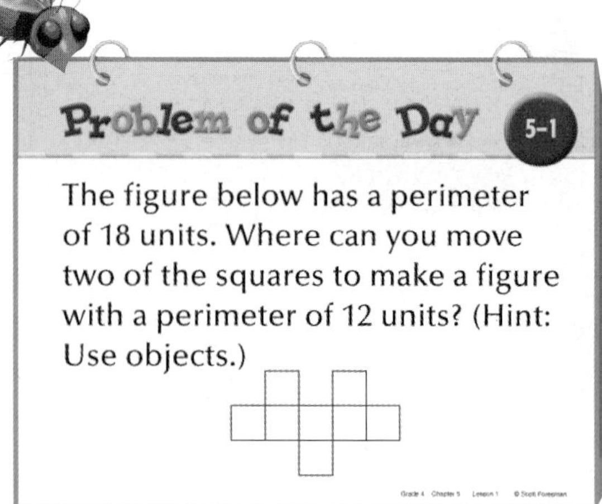
Problem of the Day
5-1
The figure below has a perimeter of 18 units. Where can you move two of the squares to make a figure with a perimeter of 12 units? (Hint: Use objects.)

Links techniques to understanding and solving word problems

By linking reading and writing to math, students become more adept at understanding word problems and identifying what they need to do. Your students will improve their abilities to recognize and organize the important details and learn how to describe their solutions by writing clear, concise, and accurate answers.

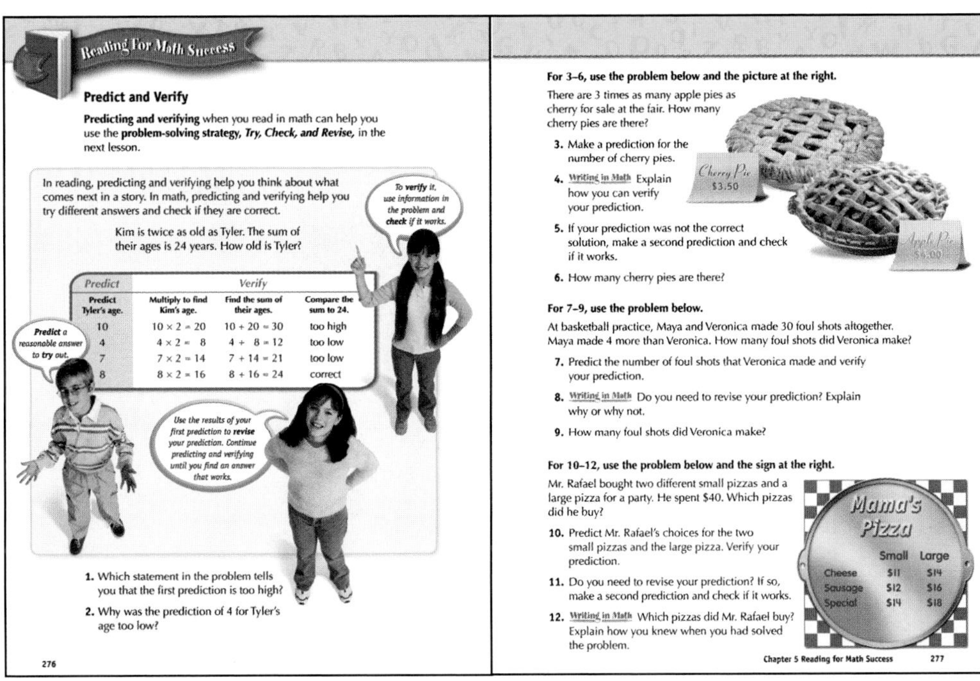

Reading For Math Success

Predict and Verify

Predicting and verifying when you read in math can help you use the **problem-solving strategy, *Try, Check, and Revise,*** in the next lesson.

In reading, predicting and verifying help you think about what comes next in a story. In math, predicting and verifying help you try different answers and check if they are correct.

Kim is twice as old as Tyler. The sum of their ages is 24 years. How old is Tyler?

Predict	Verify		
Predict Tyler's age.	Multiply to find Kim's age.	Find the sum of their ages.	Compare the sum to 24.
10	10 × 2 = 20	10 + 20 = 30	too high
4	4 × 2 = 8	4 + 8 = 12	too low
7	7 × 2 = 14	7 + 14 = 21	too low
8	8 × 2 = 16	8 + 16 = 24	correct

1. Which statement in the problem tells you that the first prediction is too high?
2. Why was the prediction of 4 for Tyler's age too low?

276

For 3–6, use the problem below and the picture at the right.

There are 3 times as many apple pies as cherry for sale at the fair. How many cherry pies are there?

3. Make a prediction for the number of cherry pies.
4. Writing in Math Explain how you can verify your prediction.
5. If your prediction was not the correct solution, make a second prediction and check if it works.
6. How many cherry pies are there?

For 7–9, use the problem below.

At basketball practice, Maya and Veronica made 30 foul shots altogether. Maya made 4 more than Veronica. How many foul shots did Veronica make?

7. Predict the number of foul shots that Veronica made and verify your prediction.
8. Writing in Math Do you need to revise your prediction? Explain why or why not.
9. How many foul shots did Veronica make?

For 10–12, use the problem below and the sign at the right.

Mr. Rafael bought two different small pizzas and a large pizza for a party. He spent $40. Which pizzas did he buy?

10. Predict Mr. Rafael's choices for the two small pizzas and the large pizza. Verify your prediction.
11. Do you need to revise your prediction? If so, make a second prediction and check if it works.
12. Writing in Math Which pizzas did Mr. Rafael buy? Explain how you knew when you had solved the problem.

Mama's Pizza

	Small	Large
Cheese	$11	$14
Sausage	$12	$16
Special	$14	$18

Chapter 5 Reading for Math Success 277

Reading for Math Success

Reviews reading comprehension skills and strategies and provides a clear connection to appropriate math strategies

Problem-Solving Strategy

Uses explicit and systematic instruction to focus your students' thinking on exactly **"How"** and **"When"** to use specific problem solving strategies in math

Problem-Solving Skill

Includes lessons that reinforce the Writing in Math exercises by teaching your students specific techniques for Writing to Explain, Writing to Describe, and Writing to Compare

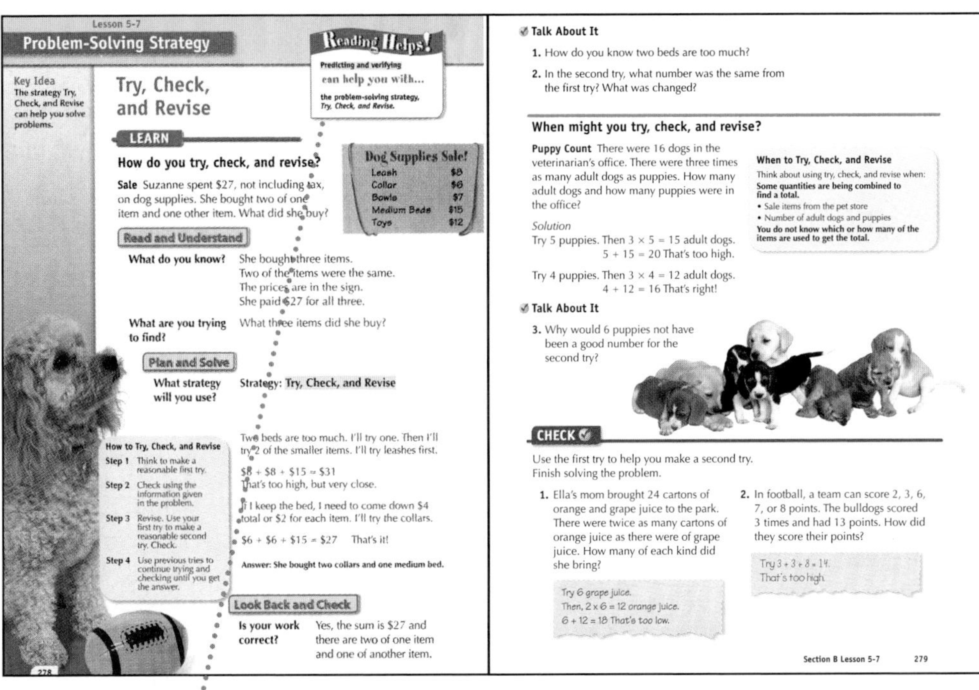

Lesson 5-7

Problem-Solving Strategy

Key Idea The strategy Try, Check, and Revise can help you solve problems.

Try, Check, and Revise

LEARN

How do you try, check, and revise?

Sale Suzanne spent $27, not including tax, on dog supplies. She bought two of one item and one other item. What did she buy?

Dog Supplies Sale!

Leash	$8
Collar	$6
Bowls	$7
Medium Beds	$15
Toys	$12

Read and Understand

What do you know? She bought three items. Two of the items were the same. The prices are in the sign. She paid $27 for all three.

What are you trying to find? What three items did she buy?

Plan and Solve

What strategy will you use? Strategy: Try, Check, and Revise

How to Try, Check, and Revise

Step 1 Think to make a reasonable first try.

Step 2 Check using the information given in the problem.

Step 3 Revise. Use your first try to make a reasonable second try. Check.

Step 4 Use previous tries to continue trying and checking until you get the answer.

Two beds are too much. I'll try one. Then I'll try 2 of the smaller items. I'll try leashes first.

$8 + $8 + $15 = $31

That's too high, but very close.

If I keep the bed, I need to come down $4 total or $2 for each item. I'll try the collars.

$6 + $6 + $15 = $27 That's it!

Answer: She bought two collars and one medium bed.

Look Back and Check

Is your work correct? Yes, the sum is $27 and there are two of one item and one of another item.

278

Talk About It

1. How do you know two beds are too much?
2. In the second try, what number was the same from the first try? What was changed?

When might you try, check, and revise?

Puppy Count There were 16 dogs in the veterinarian's office. There were three times as many adult dogs as puppies. How many adult dogs and how many puppies were in the office?

Solution

Try 5 puppies. Then 3 × 5 = 15 adult dogs. 5 + 15 = 20 That's too high.

Try 4 puppies. Then 3 × 4 = 12 adult dogs. 4 + 12 = 16 That's right!

When to Try, Check, and Revise

Think about using try, check, and revise when:

Some quantities are being combined to find a total.

- Sale items from the pet store
- Number of adult dogs and puppies

You do not know which or how many of the items are used to get the total.

Talk About It

3. Why would 6 puppies not have been a good number for the second try?

CHECK

Use the first try to help you make a second try. Finish solving the problem.

1. Ella's mom brought 24 cartons of orange and grape juice to the park. There were twice as many cartons of orange juice as there were of grape juice. How many of each kind did she bring?

Try 6 grape juice. Then, 2 × 6 = 12 orange juice. 6 + 12 = 18 That's too low.

2. In football, a team can score 2, 3, 6, 7, or 8 points. The bulldogs scored 3 times and had 13 points. How did they score their points?

Try 3 + 3 + 8 = 14. That's too high.

Section B Lesson 5-7 279

Reading Helps!

Predicting and Verifying

can help you with...

the problem-solving strategy, *Try, Check, and Revise.*

Reading Helps

Provides quick, memorable reminders that teach your students to recognize how reading skills and strategies connect with problem solving

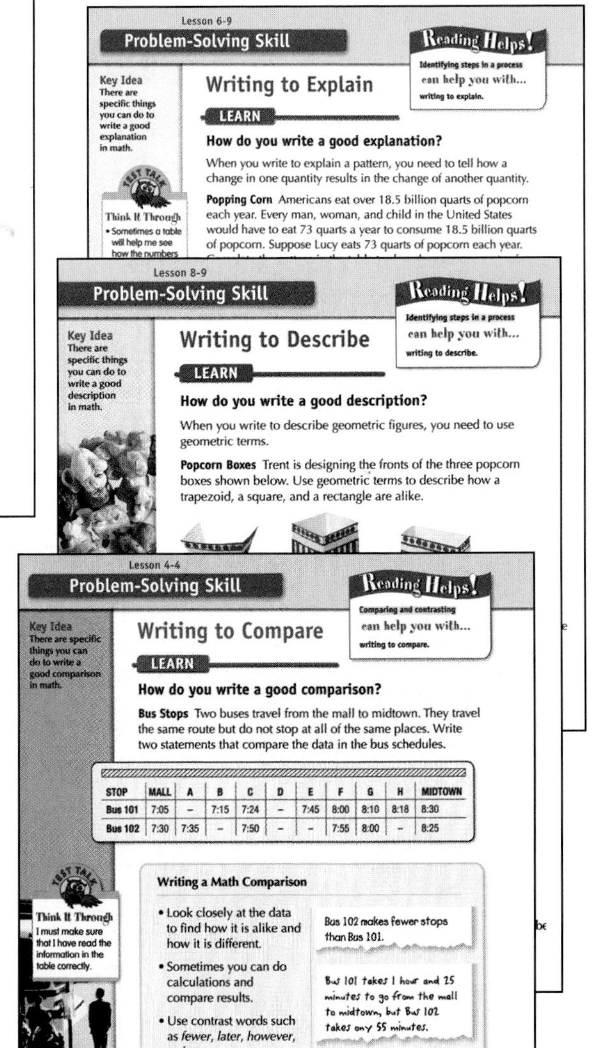

Lesson 6-9

Problem-Solving Skill

Key Idea There are specific things you can do to write a good explanation in math.

Writing to Explain

Reading Helps! Identifying steps in a process can help you with... writing to explain.

LEARN

How do you write a good explanation?

When you write to explain a pattern, you need to tell how a change in one quantity results in the change of another quantity.

Popping Corn Americans eat over 18.5 billion quarts of popcorn each year. Every man, woman, and child in the United States would have to eat 73 quarts a year to consume 18.5 billion quarts of popcorn. Suppose Lucy eats 73 quarts of popcorn each year.

Think It Through

- Sometimes a table will help me see how the numbers

Lesson 8-9

Problem-Solving Skill

Key Idea There are specific things you can do to write a good description in math.

Writing to Describe

Reading Helps! Identifying steps in a process can help you with... writing to describe.

LEARN

How do you write a good description?

When you write to describe geometric figures, you need to use geometric terms.

Popcorn Boxes Trent is designing the fronts of the three popcorn boxes shown below. Use geometric terms to describe how a trapezoid, a square, and a rectangle are alike.

Lesson 4-4

Problem-Solving Skill

Key Idea There are specific things you can do to write a good comparison in math.

Writing to Compare

Reading Helps! Comparing and contrasting can help you with... writing to compare.

LEARN

How do you write a good comparison?

Bus Stops Two buses travel from the mall to midtown. They travel the same route but do not stop at all of the same places. Write two statements that compare the data in the bus schedules.

STOP	MALL	A	B	C	D	E	F	G	H	MIDTOWN
Bus 101	7:05	–	7:15	7:24	–	7:45	8:00	8:10	8:18	8:30
Bus 102	7:30	7:35	–	7:50	–	–	7:55	8:00	–	8:25

Think It Through

I must make sure that I have read the information in the table correctly.

Writing a Math Comparison

- Look closely at the data to find how it is alike and how it is different.
- Sometimes you can do calculations and compare results.
- Use contrast words such as *fewer, later, however,* or *but.*

Bus 102 makes fewer stops than Bus 101.

Bus 101 takes 1 hour and 25 minutes to go from the mall to midtown, but Bus 102 takes only 55 minutes.

Provides real-world applications

Our unique partnerships with Discovery Channel School™ and Dorling Kindersley provide your students with rich real-world applications that answer the common question: "When am I ever going to use this?"

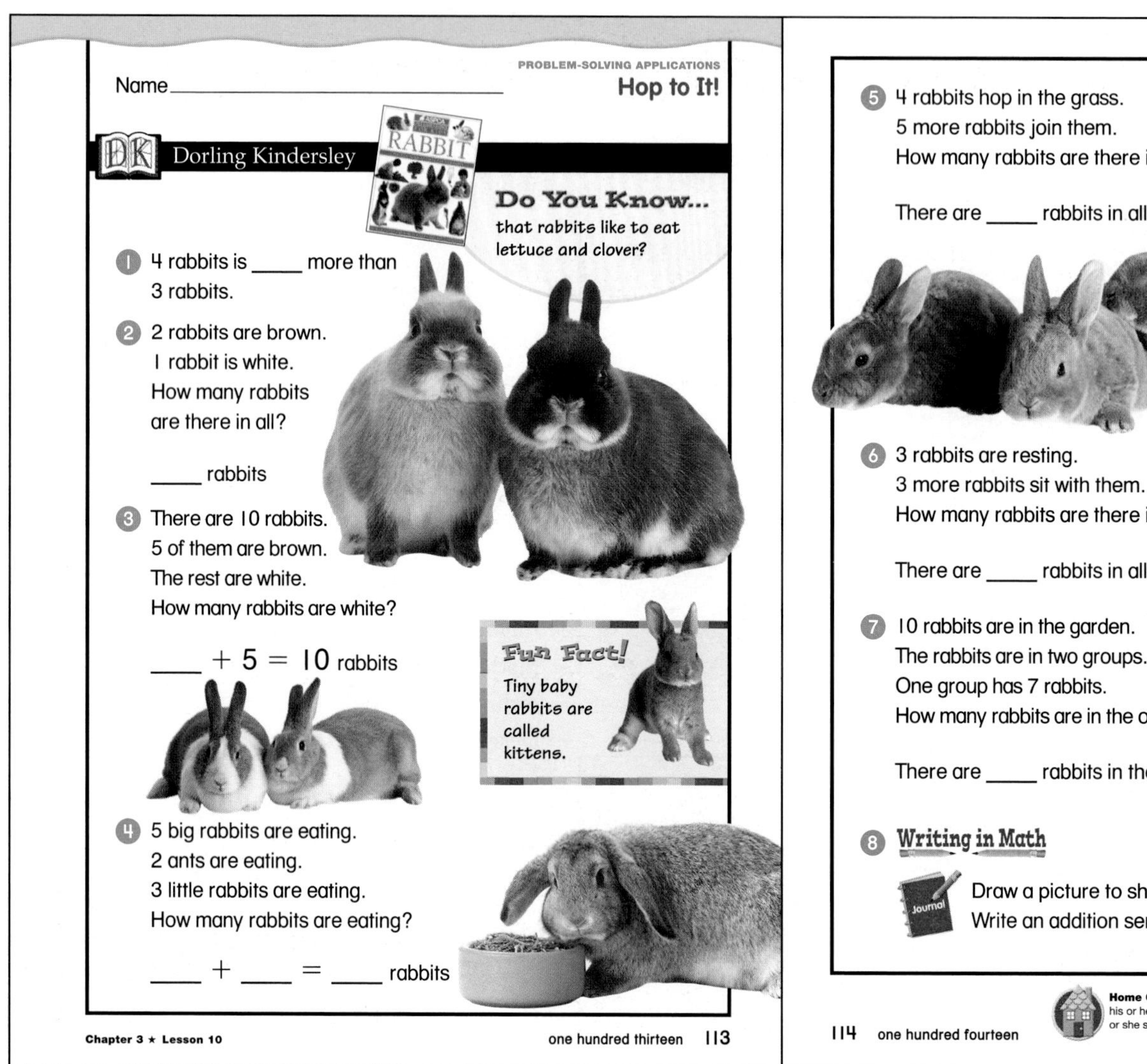

Name________________________

PROBLEM-SOLVING APPLICATIONS

Hop to It!

Dorling Kindersley

Do You Know... that rabbits like to eat lettuce and clover?

1. 4 rabbits is ____ more than 3 rabbits.
2. 2 rabbits are brown. 1 rabbit is white. How many rabbits are there in all?

   ____ rabbits
3. There are 10 rabbits. 5 of them are brown. The rest are white. How many rabbits are white?

   ____ + 5 = 10 rabbits

Fun Fact! Tiny baby rabbits are called kittens.

4. 5 big rabbits are eating. 2 ants are eating. 3 little rabbits are eating. How many rabbits are eating?

   ____ + ____ = ____ rabbits

Chapter 3 ★ Lesson 10 one hundred thirteen 113

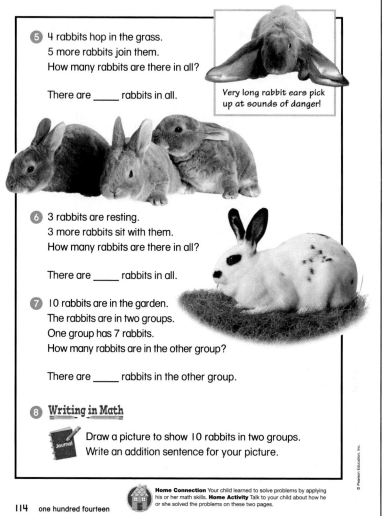

5. 4 rabbits hop in the grass. 5 more rabbits join them. How many rabbits are there in all?

   There are ____ rabbits in all.

Very long rabbit ears pick up at sounds of danger!

6. 3 rabbits are resting. 3 more rabbits sit with them. How many rabbits are there in all?

   There are ____ rabbits in all.
7. 10 rabbits are in the garden. The rabbits are in two groups. One group has 7 rabbits. How many rabbits are in the other group?

   There are ____ rabbits in the other group.
8. **Writing in Math**

   Draw a picture to show 10 rabbits in two groups. Write an addition sentence for your picture.

114 one hundred fourteen

Home Connection Your child learned to solve problems by applying his or her math skills. **Home Activity** Talk to your child about how he or she solved the problems on these two pages.

© Pearson Education, Inc.

Problem-Solving Applications

Dorling Kindersley provides visually stunning ways for your students to see how math concepts apply to the world around them.

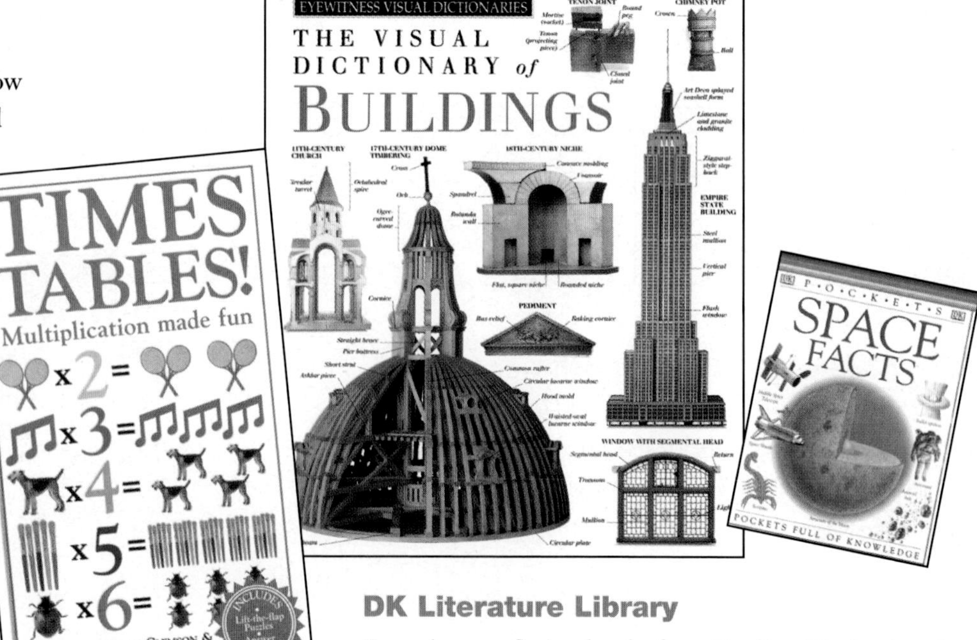

EYEWITNESS VISUAL DICTIONARIES
THE VISUAL DICTIONARY of BUILDINGS
TIMES TABLES!
Multiplication made fun
WENDY CLEMSON & DAVID CLEMSON
POCKETS
SPACE FACTS
POCKETS FULL OF KNOWLEDGE

DK Literature Library

Engaging nonfiction books from Dorling Kindersley, the world-famous publisher of the DK Eyewitness Books, provide real-world, high-interest data for problem solving.

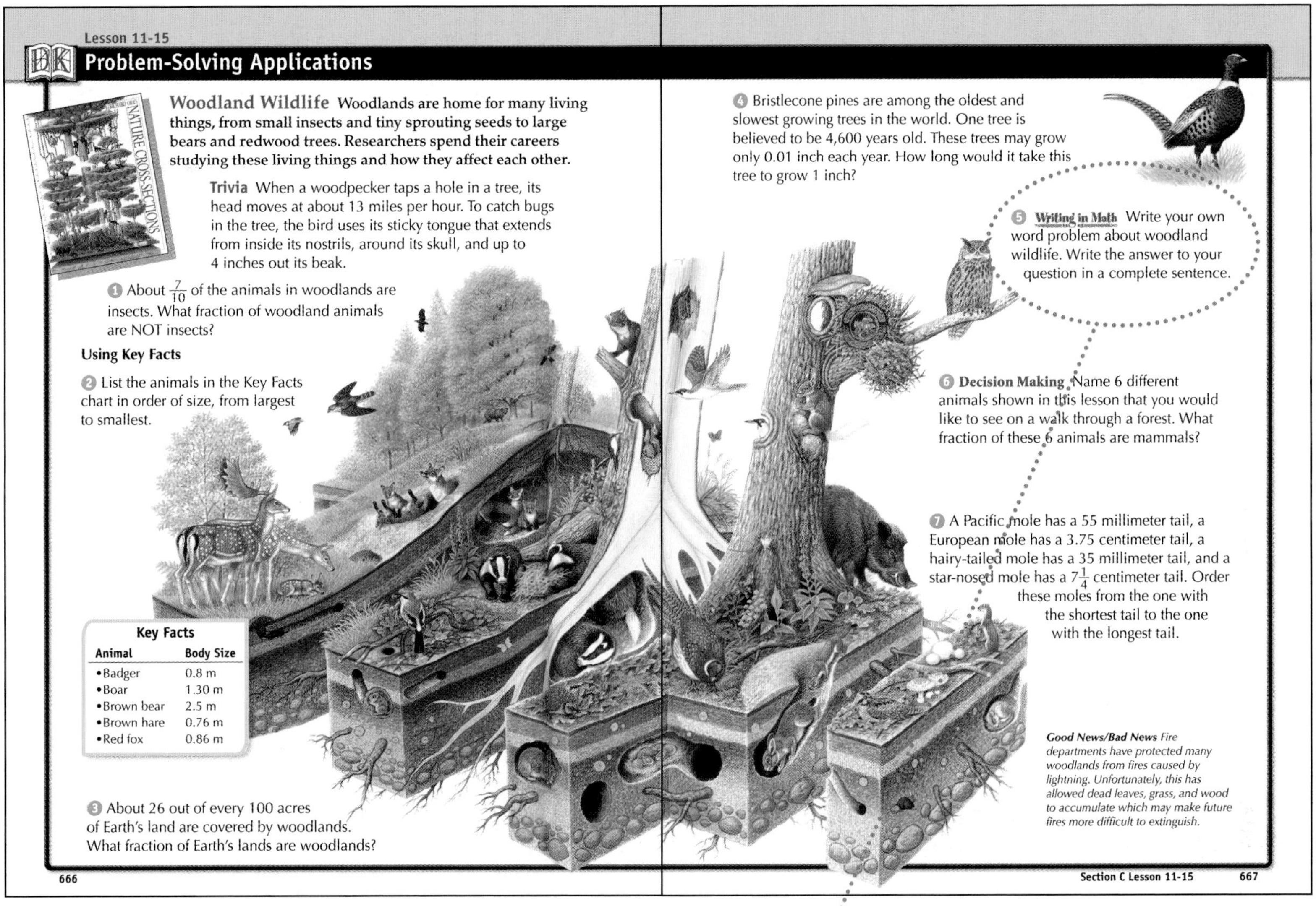

Lesson 11-15

Problem-Solving Applications

Woodland Wildlife **Woodlands are home for many living things, from small insects and tiny sprouting seeds to large bears and redwood trees. Researchers spend their careers studying these living things and how they affect each other.**

Trivia When a woodpecker taps a hole in a tree, its head moves at about 13 miles per hour. To catch bugs in the tree, the bird uses its sticky tongue that extends from inside its nostrils, around its skull, and up to 4 inches out its beak.

1. About $\frac{7}{10}$ of the animals in woodlands are insects. What fraction of woodland animals are NOT insects?

Using Key Facts

2. List the animals in the Key Facts chart in order of size, from largest to smallest.

Key Facts

Animal	Body Size
•Badger	0.8 m
•Boar	1.30 m
•Brown bear	2.5 m
•Brown hare	0.76 m
•Red fox	0.86 m

3. About 26 out of every 100 acres of Earth's land are covered by woodlands. What fraction of Earth's lands are woodlands?

4. Bristlecone pines are among the oldest and slowest growing trees in the world. One tree is believed to be 4,600 years old. These trees may grow only 0.01 inch each year. How long would it take this tree to grow 1 inch?

5. **Writing in Math** Write your own word problem about woodland wildlife. Write the answer to your question in a complete sentence.

6. **Decision Making** Name 6 different animals shown in this lesson that you would like to see on a walk through a forest. What fraction of these 6 animals are mammals?

7. A Pacific mole has a 55 millimeter tail, a European mole has a 3.75 centimeter tail, a hairy-tailed mole has a 35 millimeter tail, and a star-nosed mole has a $7\frac{1}{4}$ centimeter tail. Order these moles from the one with the shortest tail to the one with the longest tail.

Good News/Bad News Fire departments have protected many woodlands from fires caused by lightning. Unfortunately, this has allowed dead leaves, grass, and wood to accumulate which may make future fires more difficult to extinguish.

666 | Section C Lesson 11-15 667

Writing in Math

Gives your students a chance to explain their thinking and improve their writing skills and helps them become better problem solvers

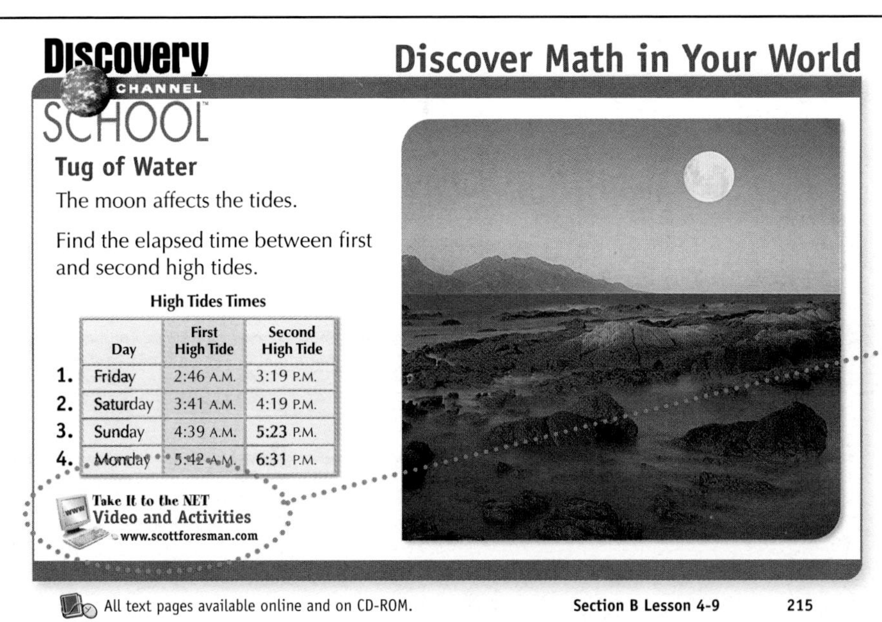
Discovery Channel School

Discover Math in Your World

Tug of Water

The moon affects the tides.

Find the elapsed time between first and second high tides.

High Tides Times

	Day	First High Tide	Second High Tide
1.	Friday	2:46 A.M.	3:19 P.M.
2.	Saturday	3:41 A.M.	4:19 P.M.
3.	Sunday	4:39 A.M.	5:23 P.M.
4.	Monday	5:42 A.M.	6:31 P.M.

Take It to the NET
Video and Activities
www.scottforesman.com

All text pages available online and on CD-ROM. Section B Lesson 4-9 215

Discovery Channel School™

Helps your students discover math in their world with engaging real-world applications in every chapter

Take It to the NET

Shows your students how math connects to the world outside the classroom with online real-world video links from Discovery Channel School

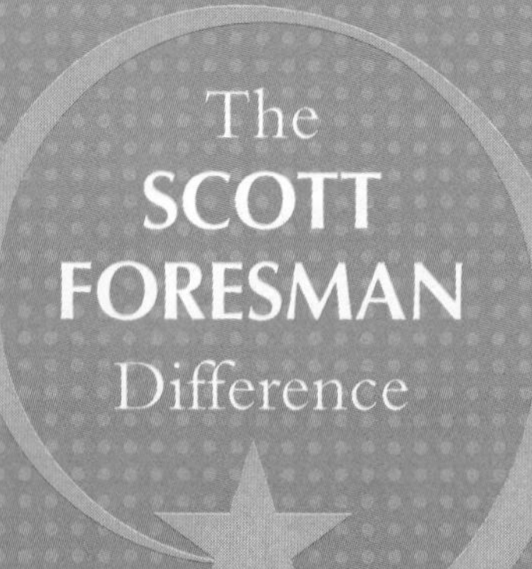

We meet the needs of all teachers.

Teachers need help simplifying the planning and instruction process and saving time. Every program offers teacher resources and classroom support for their materials. But our program is different.

Teaches important content before the test

Exclusive daily warm-up activities in Pacing for Test Success cover all the important content in later chapters and prepare your students for test success.

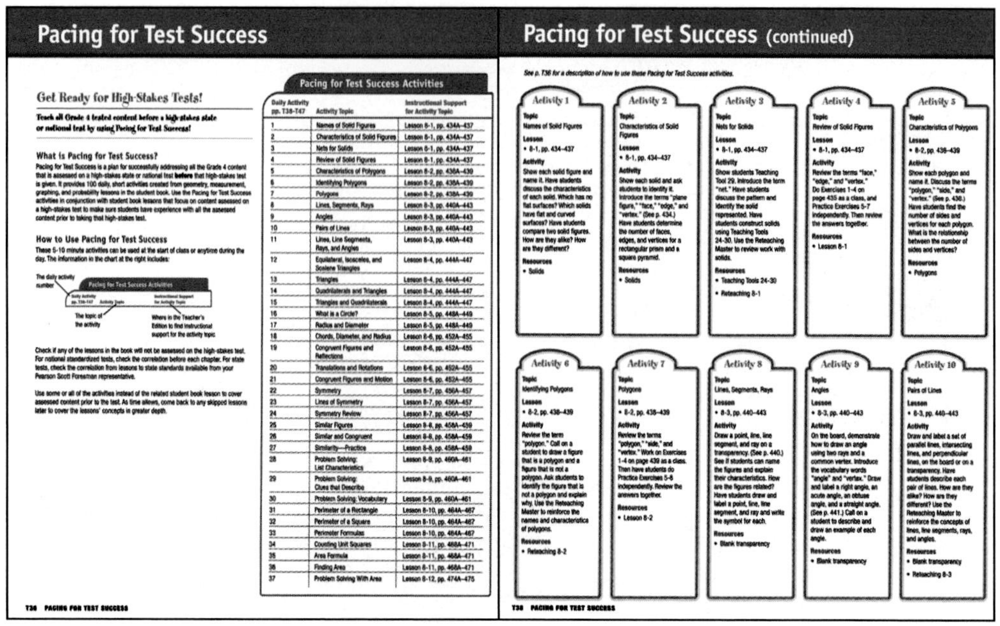
Pacing for Test Success

Get Ready for High-Stakes Tests!

What is Pacing for Test Success?

How to Use Pacing for Test Success

Pacing for Test Success Activities

Pacing for Test Success (continued)

Activity 1 · Activity 2 · Activity 3 · Activity 4 · Activity 5 · Activity 6 · Activity 7 · Activity 8 · Activity 9 · Activity 10

Simplifies the planning process

Everything you need to create effective lessons is organized into an easy-to-read Lesson Planner. From ongoing assessment opportunities to Student Edition resources, you'll always be completely prepared for every lesson.

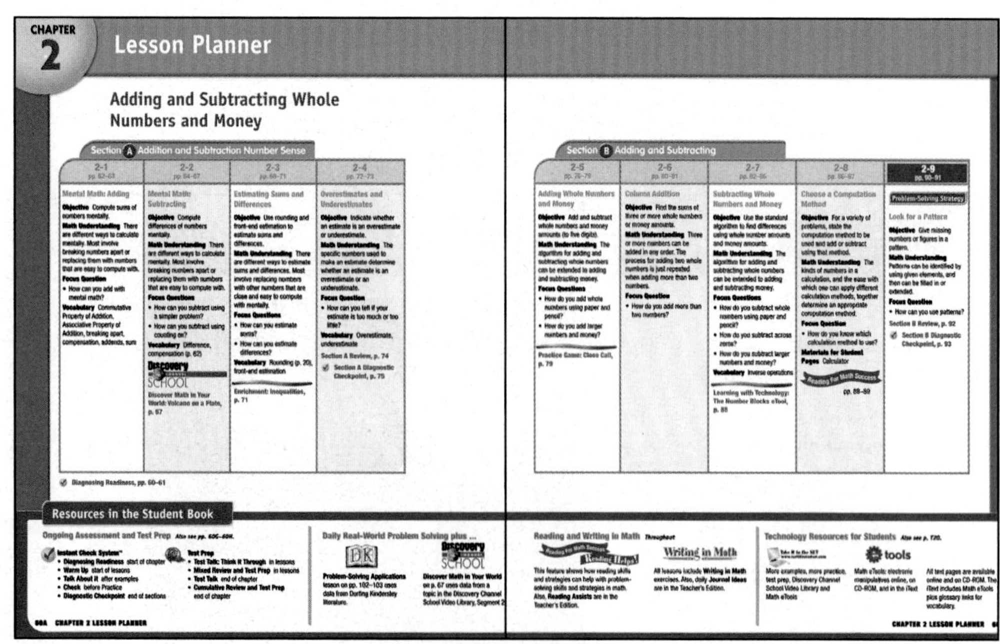
CHAPTER 2 Lesson Planner

Adding and Subtracting Whole Numbers and Money

Section A Addition and Subtraction Number Sense

Section B Adding and Subtracting

Resources in the Student Book

Reaches all learners with differentiated instruction options

Customize your instruction to meet the individual needs of all your students. Research-based suggestions for approaching lessons allow you to reach every child effectively and individually.

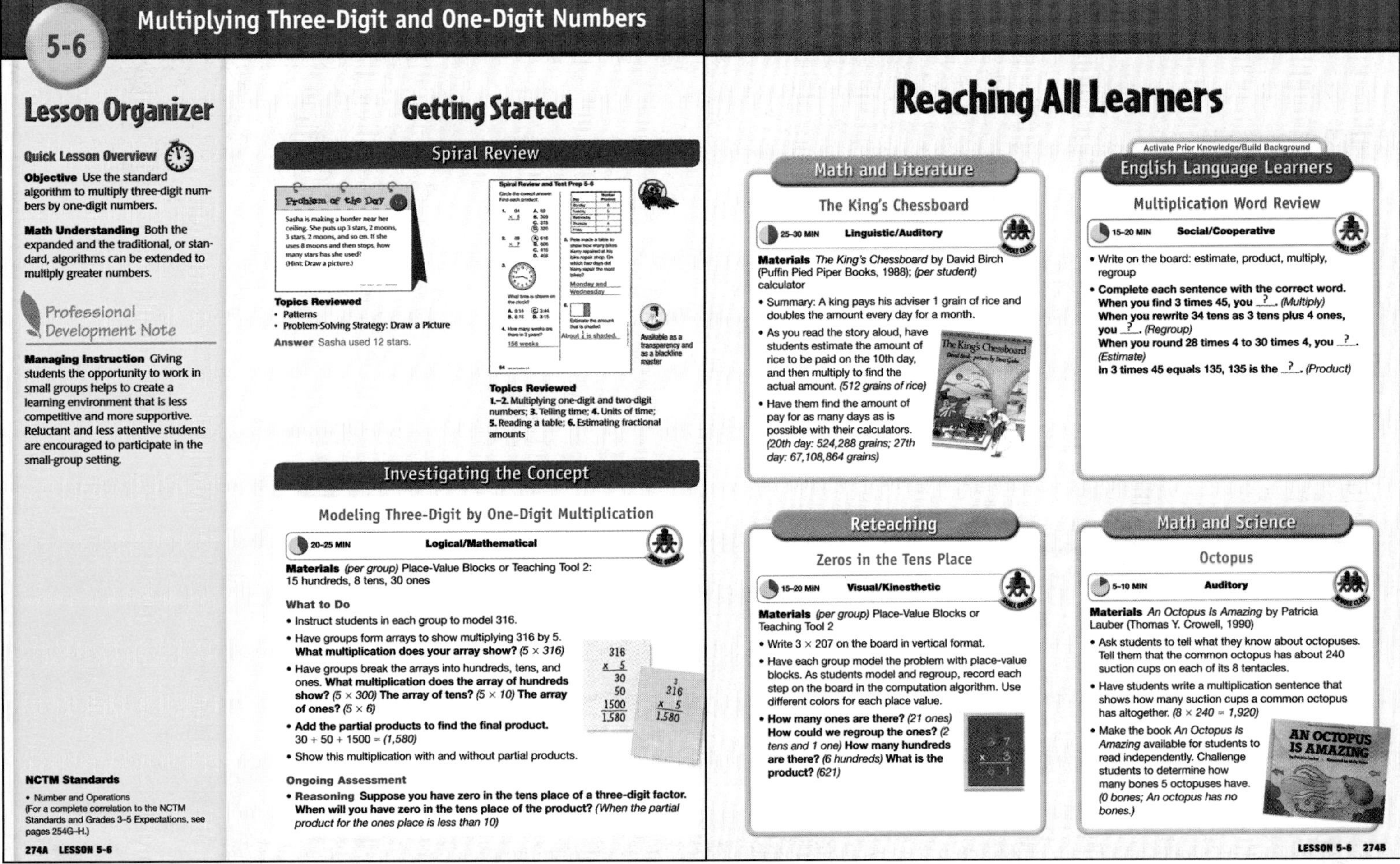

5-6 Multiplying Three-Digit and One-Digit Numbers

Lesson Organizer

Quick Lesson Overview

Objective Use the standard algorithm to multiply three-digit numbers by one-digit numbers.

Math Understanding Both the expanded and the traditional, or standard, algorithms can be extended to multiply greater numbers.

Professional Development Note

Managing Instruction Giving students the opportunity to work in small groups helps to create a learning environment that is less competitive and more supportive. Reluctant and less attentive students are encouraged to participate in the small-group setting.

NCTM Standards

- Number and Operations

(For a complete correlation to the NCTM Standards and Grades 3-5 Expectations, see pages 254G–H.)

Getting Started

Spiral Review

Problem of the Day

Sasha is making a border near her ceiling. She puts up 3 stars, 2 moons, 3 stars, 2 moons, and so on. If she uses 8 moons and then stops, how many stars has she used? (Hint: Draw a picture.)

Topics Reviewed

- Patterns
- Problem-Solving Strategy: Draw a Picture

Answer Sasha used 12 stars.

Spiral Review and Test Prep 5-6

Available as a transparency and as a blackline master

Topics Reviewed

1.–2. Multiplying one-digit and two-digit numbers; **3.** Telling time; **4.** Units of time; **5.** Reading a table; **6.** Estimating fractional amounts

Investigating the Concept

Modeling Three-Digit by One-Digit Multiplication

20–25 MIN **Logical/Mathematical**

Materials *(per group)* Place-Value Blocks or Teaching Tool 2: 15 hundreds, 8 tens, 30 ones

What to Do

- Instruct students in each group to model 316.
- Have groups form arrays to show multiplying 316 by 5. **What multiplication does your array show?** *(5 × 316)*
- Have groups break the arrays into hundreds, tens, and ones. **What multiplication does the array of hundreds show?** *(5 × 300)* **The array of tens?** *(5 × 10)* **The array of ones?** *(5 × 6)*
- **Add the partial products to find the final product.** 30 + 50 + 1500 = *(1,580)*
- Show this multiplication with and without partial products.

Ongoing Assessment

- **Reasoning Suppose you have zero in the tens place of a three-digit factor. When will you have zero in the tens place of the product?** *(When the partial product for the ones place is less than 10)*

274A LESSON 5-6

Reaching All Learners

Math and Literature

The King's Chessboard

25–30 MIN **Linguistic/Auditory**

Materials *The King's Chessboard* by David Birch (Puffin Pied Piper Books, 1988); *(per student)* calculator

- Summary: A king pays his adviser 1 grain of rice and doubles the amount every day for a month.
- As you read the story aloud, have students estimate the amount of rice to be paid on the 10th day, and then multiply to find the actual amount. *(512 grains of rice)*
- Have them find the amount of pay for as many days as is possible with their calculators. *(20th day: 524,288 grains; 27th day: 67,108,864 grains)*

English Language Learners

Activate Prior Knowledge/Build Background

Multiplication Word Review

15–20 MIN **Social/Cooperative**

- Write on the board: estimate, product, multiply, regroup
- **Complete each sentence with the correct word.**
  When you find 3 times 45, you __?__. *(Multiply)*
  When you rewrite 34 tens as 3 tens plus 4 ones, you __?__. *(Regroup)*
  When you round 28 times 4 to 30 times 4, you __?__. *(Estimate)*
  In 3 times 45 equals 135, 135 is the __?__. *(Product)*

Reteaching

Zeros in the Tens Place

15–20 MIN **Visual/Kinesthetic**

Materials *(per group)* Place-Value Blocks or Teaching Tool 2

- Write 3 × 207 on the board in vertical format.
- Have each group model the problem with place-value blocks. As students model and regroup, record each step on the board in the computation algorithm. Use different colors for each place value.
- **How many ones are there?** *(21 ones)* **How could we regroup the ones?** *(2 tens and 1 one)* **How many hundreds are there?** *(6 hundreds)* **What is the product?** *(621)*

Math and Science

Octopus

5–10 MIN **Auditory**

Materials *An Octopus Is Amazing* by Patricia Lauber (Thomas Y. Crowell, 1990)

- Ask students to tell what they know about octopuses. Tell them that the common octopus has about 240 suction cups on each of its 8 tentacles.
- Have students write a multiplication sentence that shows how many suction cups a common octopus has altogether. *(8 × 240 = 1,920)*
- Make the book *An Octopus Is Amazing* available for students to read independently. Challenge students to determine how many bones 5 octopuses have. *(0 bones; An octopus has no bones.)*

LESSON 5-6 274B

Lesson Organizer

Quick lesson overviews include math objectives and understanding while Professional Development Notes improve your teaching methods

Getting Started

Includes daily suggestions for spiral review and investigating the concept

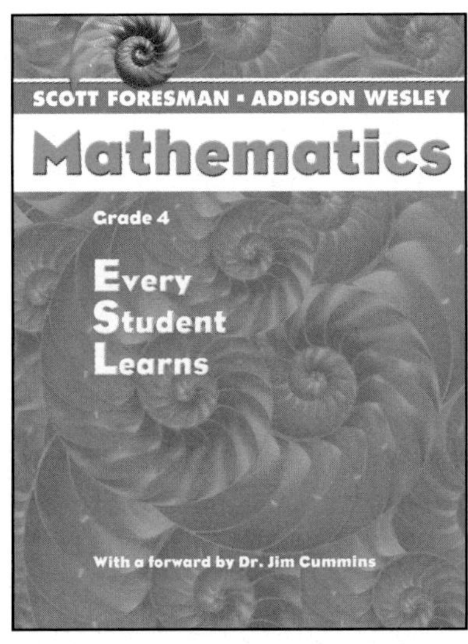

Reaching All Learners

Meet the diverse needs in your classroom with fun and stimulating activities that are easy to incorporate directly into your lesson plan

- Math Vocabulary
- Reading in Math
- Writing in Math
- Oral Language in Math
- Math and Literature
- English Language Learners
- Reteaching
- Math and Technology
- Advanced Learners
- Students with Special Needs
- Cross-Curriculum Connections

Every Student Learns

Lesson-specific suggestions help your students overcome language barriers to access math content

Simplifies the instruction process

Our lessons include all the resources you need right at the point of use to help you keep all your lessons on track.

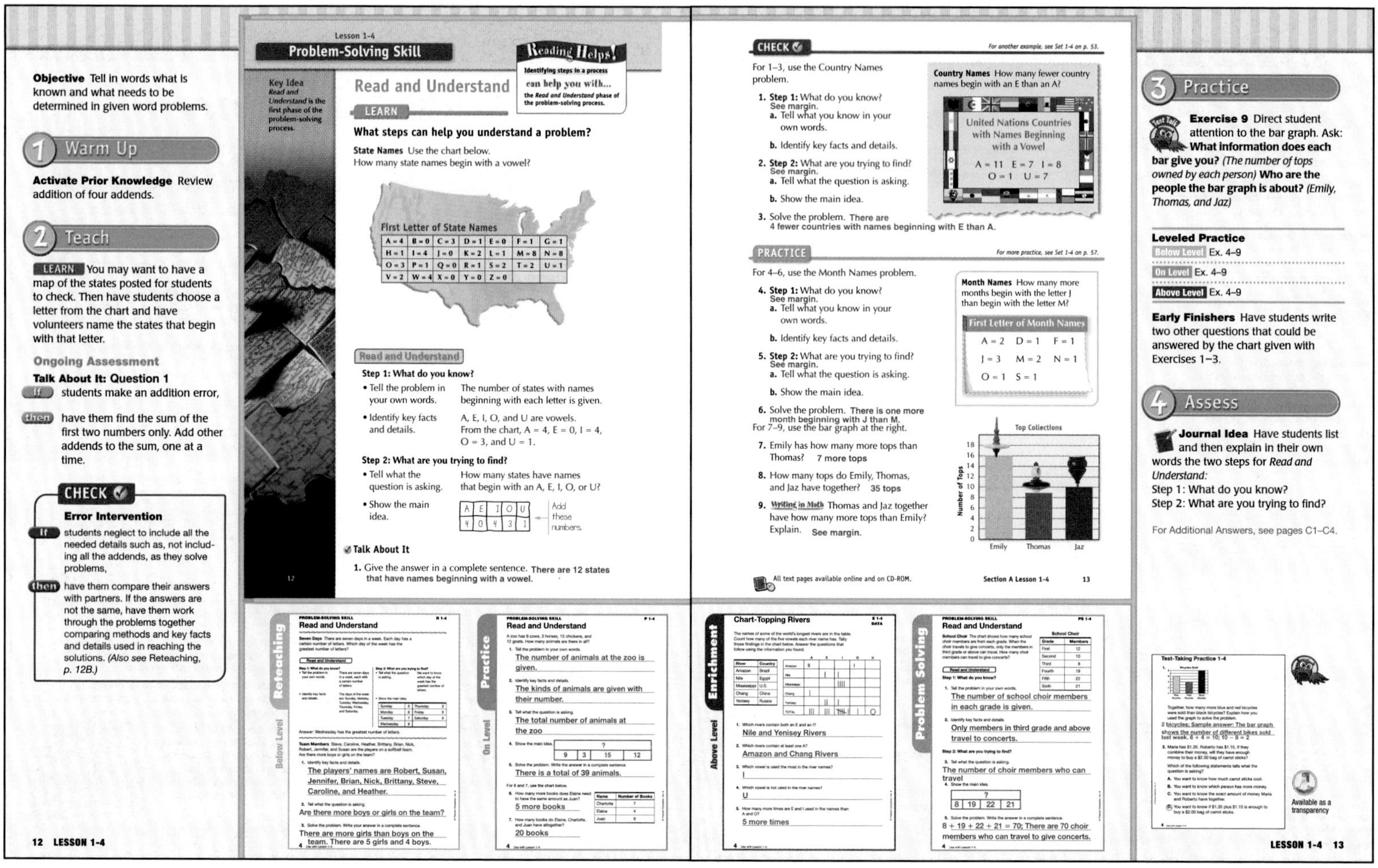

Objective Tell in words what is known and what needs to be determined in given word problems.

1 Warm Up

Activate Prior Knowledge Review addition of four addends.

2 Teach

LEARN You may want to have a map of the states posted for students to check. Then have students choose a letter from the chart and have volunteers name the states that begin with that letter.

Ongoing Assessment

Talk About It: Question 1

If students make an addition error,

then have them find the sum of the first two numbers only. Add other addends to the sum, one at a time.

CHECK

Error Intervention

If students neglect to include all the needed details such as, not including all the addends, as they solve problems,

then have them compare their answers with partners. If the answers are not the same, have them work through the problems together comparing methods and key facts and details used in reaching the solutions. *(Also see Reteaching, p. 12B.)*

Lesson 1-4

Problem-Solving Skill

Reading Helps! Identifying steps in a process can help you with... the *Read and Understand* phase of the problem-solving process.

Key Idea *Read and Understand* is the first phase of the problem-solving process.

Read and Understand

LEARN

What steps can help you understand a problem?

State Names Use the chart below. How many state names begin with a vowel?

First Letter of State Names

A = 4	B = 0	C = 3	D = 1	E = 0	F = 1	G = 1
H = 1	I = 4	J = 0	K = 2	L = 1	M = 8	N = 8
O = 3	P = 1	Q = 0	R = 1	S = 2	T = 2	U = 1
V = 2	W = 4	X = 0	Y = 0	Z = 0		

Read and Understand

Step 1: What do you know?

- Tell the problem in your own words. — The number of states with names beginning with each letter is given.
- Identify key facts and details. — A, E, I, O, and U are vowels. From the chart, A = 4, E = 0, I = 4, O = 3, and U = 1.

Step 2: What are you trying to find?

- Tell what the question is asking. — How many states have names that begin with an A, E, I, O, or U?
- Show the main idea. — A E I O U / 4 0 4 3 1 — Add these numbers.

Talk About It

1. Give the answer in a complete sentence. There are 12 states that have names beginning with a vowel.

12

CHECK For another example, see Set 1-4 on p. 53.

For 1–3, use the Country Names problem.

1. **Step 1:** What do you know? See margin.
   a. Tell what you know in your own words.
   b. Identify key facts and details.
2. **Step 2:** What are you trying to find? See margin.
   a. Tell what the question is asking.
   b. Show the main idea.
3. Solve the problem. There are 4 fewer countries with names beginning with E than A.

Country Names How many fewer country names begin with an E than an A?

United Nations Countries with Names Beginning with a Vowel

A = 11 E = 7 I = 8
O = 1 U = 7

PRACTICE For more practice, see Set 1-4 on p. 57.

For 4–6, use the Month Names problem.

4. **Step 1:** What do you know? See margin.
   a. Tell what you know in your own words.
   b. Identify key facts and details.
5. **Step 2:** What are you trying to find? See margin.
   a. Tell what the question is asking.
   b. Show the main idea.
6. Solve the problem. There is one more month beginning with J than M.

Month Names How many more months begin with the letter J than begin with the letter M?

First Letter of Month Names

A = 2 D = 1 F = 1
J = 3 M = 2 N = 1
O = 1 S = 1

For 7–9, use the bar graph at the right.

7. Emily has how many more tops than Thomas? 7 more tops
8. How many tops do Emily, Thomas, and Jaz have together? 35 tops
9. **Writing in Math** Thomas and Jaz together have how many more tops than Emily? Explain. See margin.

Top Collections (Number of Tops: Emily, Thomas, Jaz)

All text pages available online and on CD-ROM. Section A Lesson 1-4 13

3 Practice

Exercise 9 Direct student attention to the bar graph. Ask: **What information does each bar give you?** *(The number of tops owned by each person)* **Who are the people the bar graph is about?** *(Emily, Thomas, and Jaz)*

Leveled Practice

Below Level Ex. 4–9

On Level Ex. 4–9

Above Level Ex. 4–9

Early Finishers Have students write two other questions that could be answered by the chart given with Exercises 1–3.

4 Assess

Journal Idea Have students list and then explain in their own words the two steps for *Read and Understand:*
Step 1: What do you know?
Step 2: What are you trying to find?

For Additional Answers, see pages C1–C4.

Reteaching (Below Level) — Problem-Solving Skill: Read and Understand

Practice (On Level) — Problem-Solving Skill: Read and Understand

Enrichment (Above Level) — Chart-Topping Rivers

Problem Solving — Problem-Solving Skill: Read and Understand

Test-Taking Practice 1-4 — Available as a transparency

12 LESSON 1-4 — LESSON 1-4 13

Four manageable and familiar steps

1 Warm Up

Helps you activate prior knowledge

2 Teach

Suggests how to introduce the math concept, assess your students, and intervene if necessary

3 Practice

Uses leveled exercises to help you reach every student in your classroom

4 Assess

Provides specific strategies for checking your students' understanding before moving on

Ongoing Assessment

Provides multiple checkpoints in each lesson with immediate intervention for your students who may be struggling with the concept

Blackline Masters

Leveled Practice and Problem-Solving blackline masters are shown right at the point of use along with the Test-Taking Practice Transparencies.

Supports professional development every day

We include the professional development resources you need to be more effective and successful in the classroom, no matter what your experience level may be.

Successful Beginnings

Professional Development Needs Assessment

Shows your school how to interpret student achievement test scores, assess staff development needs, and implement a professional development program that incorporates research-based best practices

On-Site Inservice

Occurs at the beginning of the school year to introduce the program philosophy and explain the Teacher's Edition and program components

Chapter Facilitator Guides

Provides workshop or discussion-group leaders the support they need on content and instruction for every chapter

In the Teacher's Edition

Professional Development

Appears at the beginning of each chapter and includes a Skills Trace as well as Math Background and Teaching Tips for each section in the chapter

Professional Development Note

Provides insights for every lesson, every day, on Math Background, How Children Learn Math, Effective Questioning Techniques, Managing Instruction, or Research Base

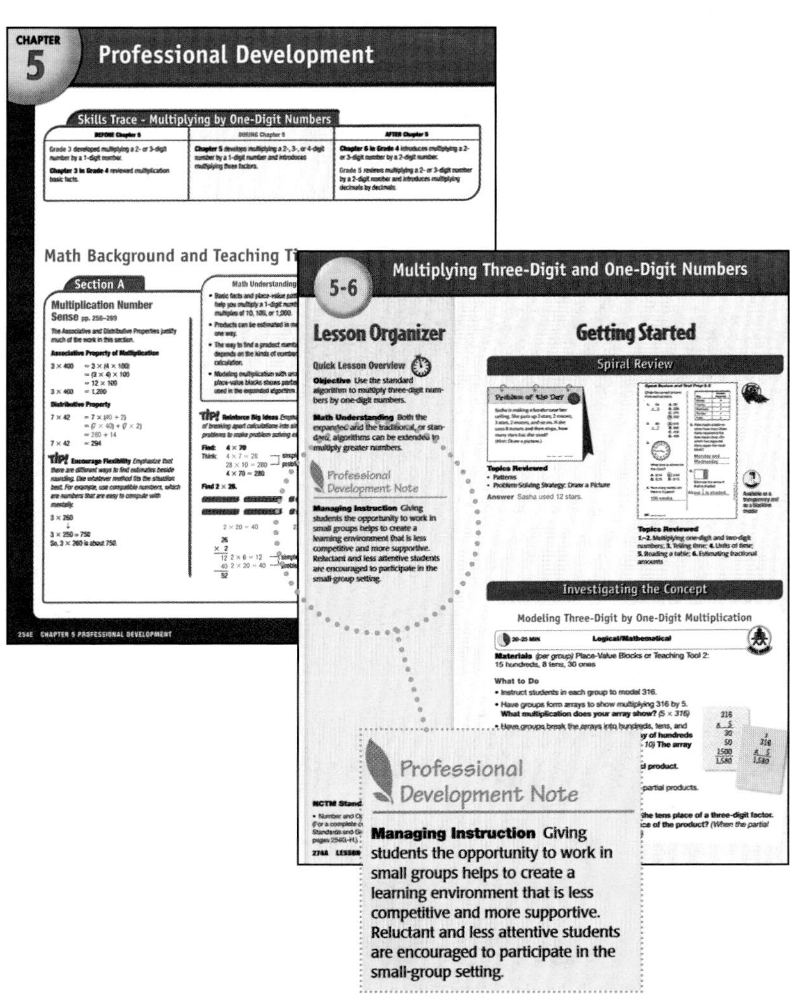

Ongoing Professional Development

Professional Development Series

Contains a set of three modules with videos of real classroom lessons and all the resources necessary for presenting a two- to three-hour workshop on specific math content or for doing independent study

Math Across the Grades

Gives you more in-depth math background for every strand

Look for **LessonLab BreakThrough™ Professional Development** on page T20.

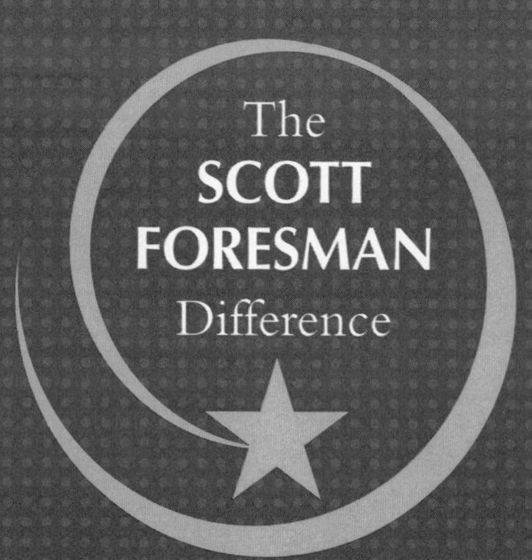

We offer integrated technology solutions.

Technology is not only changing the nature of mathematics, it also is changing students' needs for success in the 21st century. Most math programs feature technology. But our program is different.

Integrates technology with curriculum

We bring technology and curriculum together, providing technology solutions for all students, teachers, and parents that directly improve student learning and increase test success.

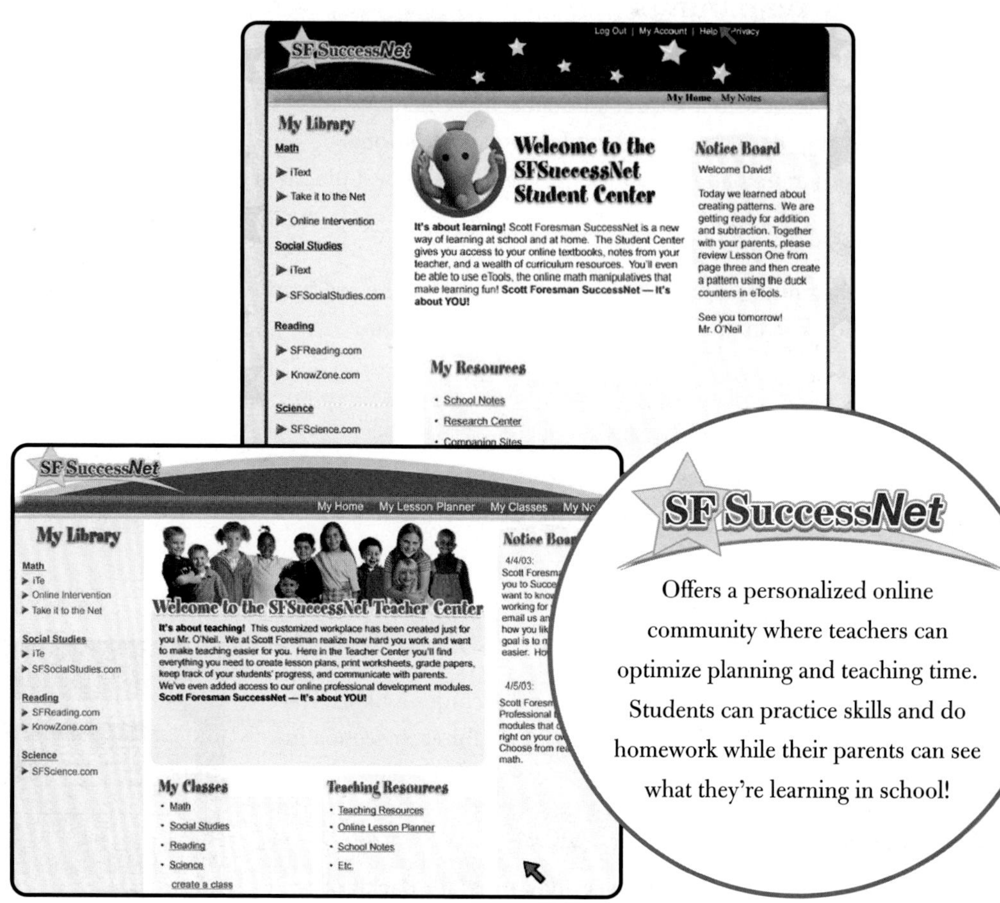

Professional Development

Professional Development Series

Enables you to grow as an educator and help all your students succeed with videos that show flexible ways to implement research-based best practices for instruction

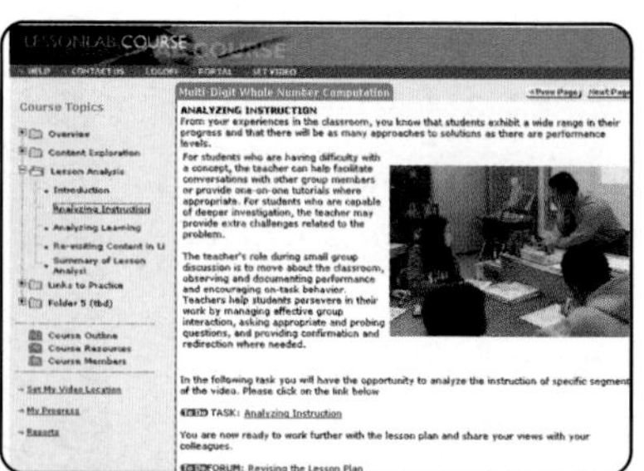

LessonLab BreakThrough™ Professional Development

Utilizes cutting-edge, interactive, online technology to provide facilitated professional development designed exclusively for our program

Teach and assess efficiently with versatile resources

Our technology options make it easy for you to monitor your students' progress and provide each of them with individualized intervention.

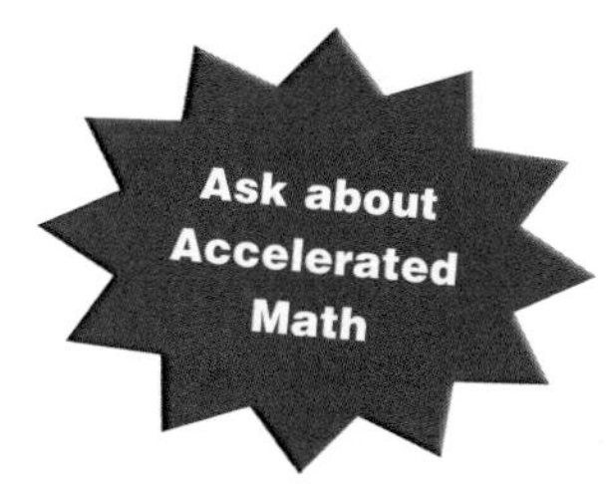

Teacher Resources

Student Resources

Math Online Intervention

Helps diagnose your entire class with online diagnostic tests that assess every student and prescribe individualized intervention with reports to monitor adequate yearly progress

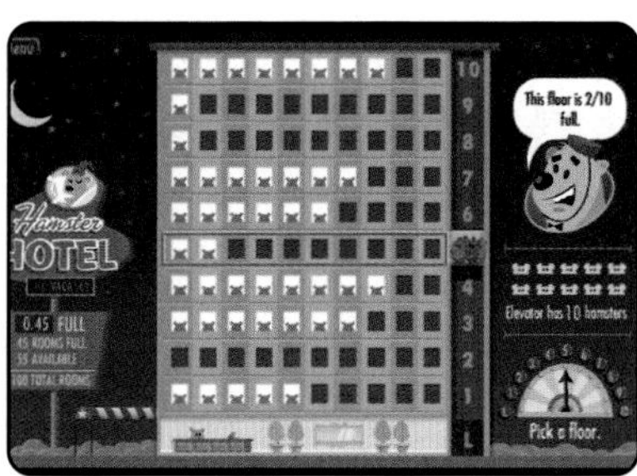

Scott Foresman's Web Site "Take It to the NET"

Provides your students with access to more examples, more practice, test prep, videos, and Math eTools tied directly to their lessons

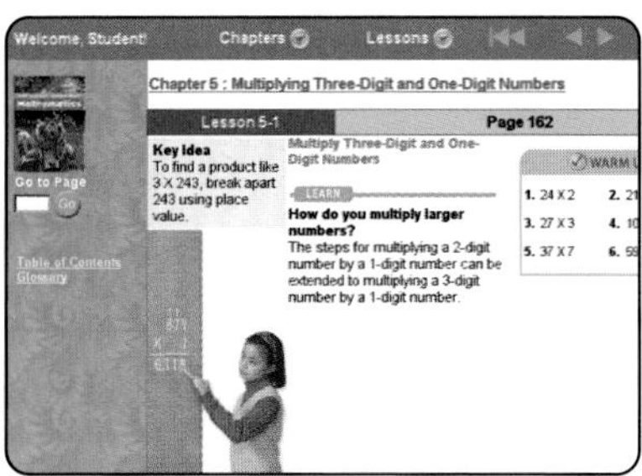

Online Student Edition

Gives your students easy access to their textbooks online or on CD-ROM from any home computer—a great solution to heavy backpacks!

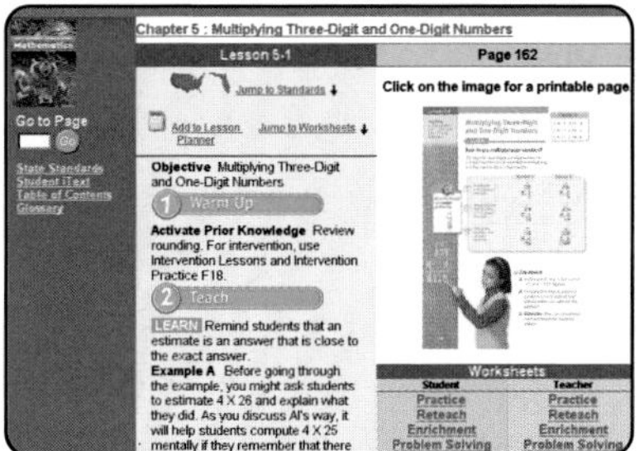

Online Teacher's Edition

Provides complete access to your entire Teacher's Edition, an online lesson planner, and selected ancillary pdf files online or on CD-ROM

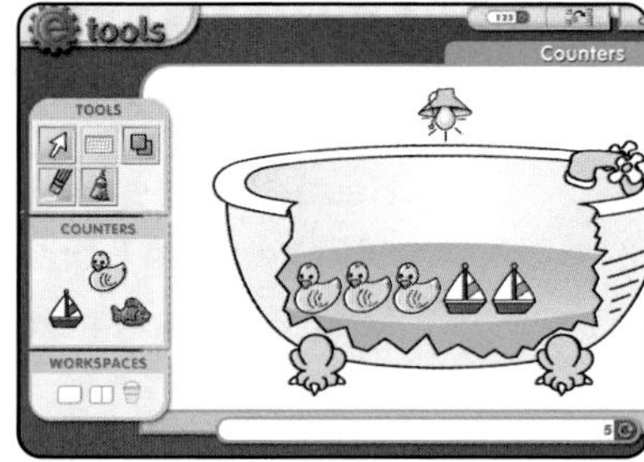

Math eTools

Helps your students grasp difficult math concepts with electronic manipulatives and software tools online or on CD-ROM

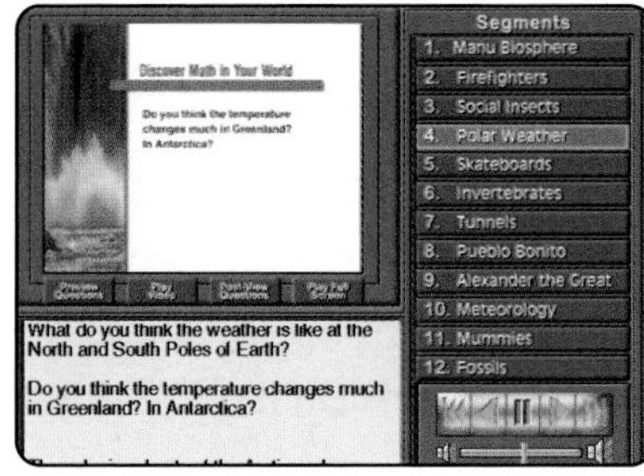

Discovery Channel School™ Video Library

Engages your students with online, CD-ROM, or videocassette segments for every chapter in the Student Edition, helping them discover math in their world

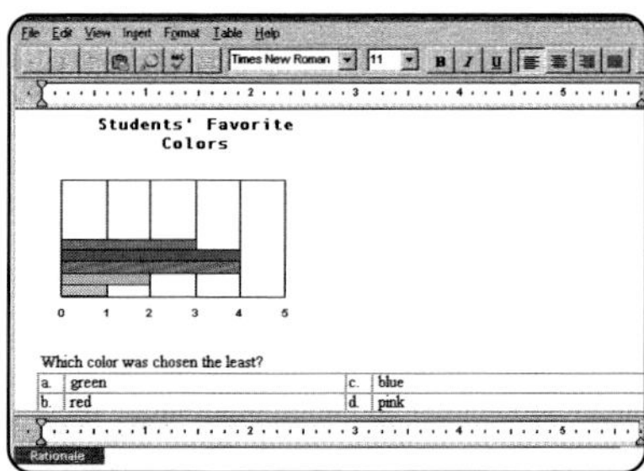

ExamView® Test Generator

Allows you to create and print customized tests quickly and easily with varied questions and test formats that assess your students' math understanding of key concepts and skills

MindPoint™ Quiz Show CD-ROM

Uses multiple-choice questions in a fun format to give your students additional math practice

Digital Learning CD-ROM powered by KnowledgeBox®

Supplies an interactive, completely customizable, educational multimedia center where your students can play games, watch videos, take tutorials, or participate in sing-alongs

SCOTT FORESMAN • ADDISON WESLEY

Mathematics

Components

Teaching for Understanding

Pre-K Program (Pre-K)
Student Big Book (K)
Student Edition Chapter Booklets (K)
Student Edition (K–6)
Practice Masters/Workbook (K–6)
Reteaching Masters/Workbook (1–6)
Enrichment Masters/Workbook (K–6)
Homework Workbook (1–6)
Instant Check Mat (K–6)
Workmats (K–2)
Assessment Sourcebook (K–6)
Test-Taking Practice Transparencies (1–6)
Spiral Review and Test Prep Masters/Workbook (1–6)
Spiral Review and Test Prep Transparencies (1–6)
Math Diagnosis and Intervention System (K–6)
SAT 9/10 Practice and Test Prep (1–6)
TerraNova Practice and Test Prep (1–6)
ITBS Practice and Test Prep (3–6)
Benchmark Tests (3–6)
Review from Last Year Masters (1–6)

Problem-Solving Connections

Problem-Solving Masters/Workbook (1–6)
Problem of the Day Transparencies/Flip Chart (K–6)
Math Vocabulary Kit (K–6)
Discovery Channel School™ Masters/Videos (1–6)
Read-Together Math Stories Big Books (K–2)
DK Literature Library (Pre-K–6)
Math Leveled Literature Library (K–6)

Teaching Support

Teacher's Edition (Pre-K–6)
Teaching Tool Masters (K–6)
Every Student Learns (K–6)
Home-School Connection (K–6)
Chapter File Folders (K–6)
Classroom Manipulatives Kit (Pre-K–6)
Overhead Manipulatives Kit (K–6)
Solution Manual (3–6)
Student Magnetic Manipulatives Kit (K–6)
Teacher Magnetic Manipulatives Kit (K–2)
Math Games (K–6)
Calendar Time Kit (K–5)
Professional Development Series (K–6)
Chapter Facilitator Guide (K–6)
Math Across the Grades (K–Algebra)

Technology

SuccessNet Portal (K–6)
Math eTools (Pre-K–6)
Digital Learning CD-ROM
powered by KnowledgeBox® (1–6)
Online Student Edition (1–6)
MindPoint™ Quiz Show (1–6)
Discovery Channel School™ Video Library (1–6)
www.scottforesman.com (K–6)
Online Teacher's Edition (K–6)
LessonLab's BreakThrough™ Mathematics (K–6)
Professional Development Series (K–6)
Math Online Intervention (1–6)
ExamView® Test Generator (1–6)

Table of Contents

Volume 1: Chapters 1–3

Volume 2: Chapters 4–6

Volume 3: Chapters 7–9

Volume 4: Chapters 10–12

** Shown in Volumes 1-4 of the Teacher's Edition*

*** Shown in Volume 1 of the Teacher's Edition*

Pacing Guide

The pacing suggested below assumes one day for most lessons plus time for assessment for a total of 180 days. You may need to adjust pacing to meet the needs of your students and your district curriculum.

Chapter 1....18 days
Chapter 2....16 days
Chapter 3....14 days
Chapter 4....10 days
Chapter 5....13 days
Chapter 6....12 days
Chapter 7....14 days
Chapter 8....16 days
Chapter 9....16 days
Chapter 10....19 days
Chapter 11....20 days
Chapter 12....12 days

CHAPTER 1

Table of Contents

Numbers, Expressions, and Equations

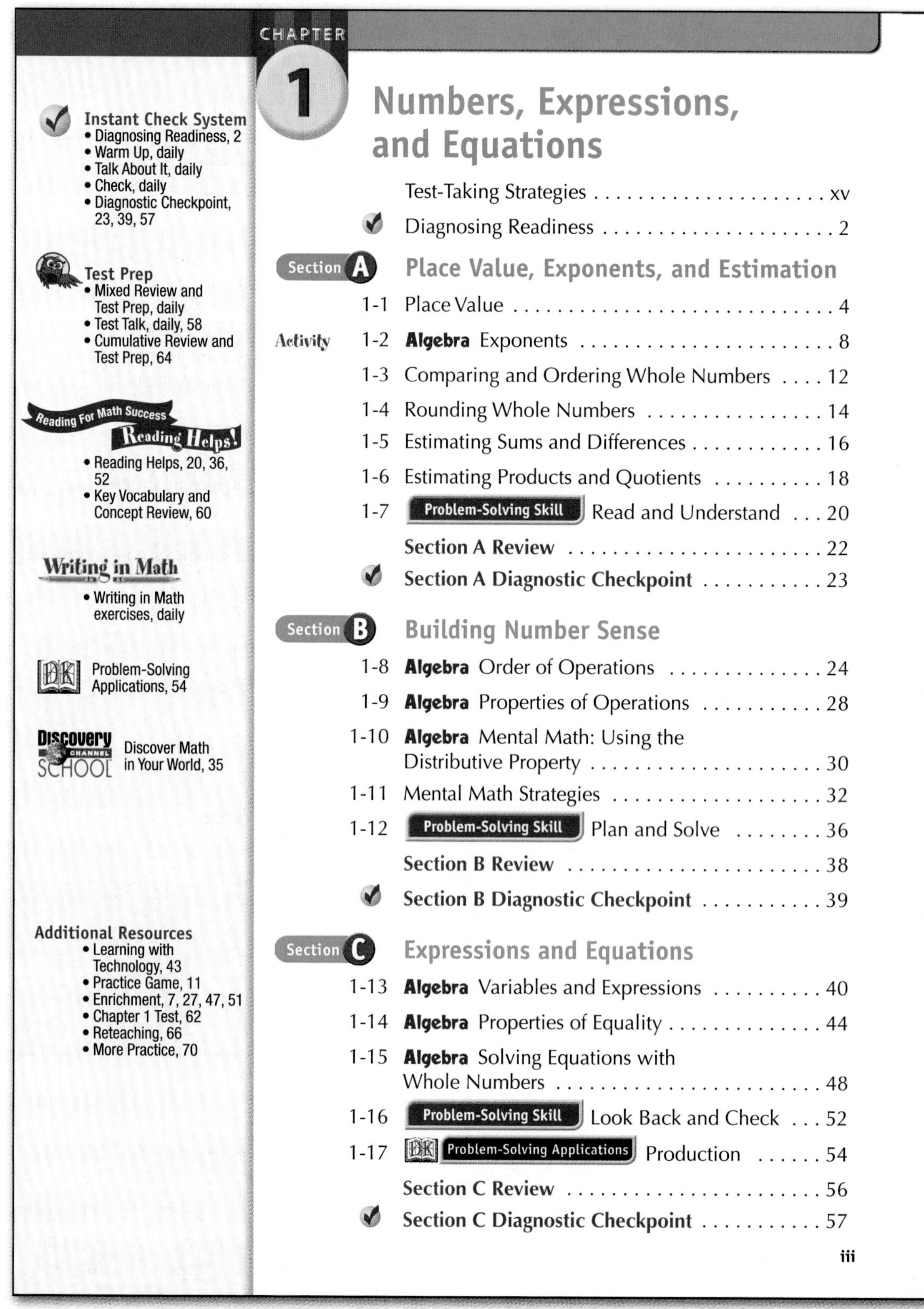

CHAPTER 1

Instant Check System
- Diagnosing Readiness, 2
- Warm Up, daily
- Talk About It, daily
- Check, daily
- Diagnostic Checkpoint, 23, 39, 57

Test Prep
- Mixed Review and Test Prep, daily
- Test Talk, daily, 58
- Cumulative Review and Test Prep, 64

Reading For Math Success
Reading Helps!
- Reading Helps, 20, 36, 52
- Key Vocabulary and Concept Review, 60

Writing in Math
- Writing in Math exercises, daily

DK Problem-Solving Applications, 54

Discovery Channel School Discover Math in Your World, 35

Additional Resources
- Learning with Technology, 43
- Practice Game, 11
- Enrichment, 7, 27, 47, 51
- Chapter 1 Test, 62
- Reteaching, 66
- More Practice, 70

Numbers, Expressions, and Equations

iii

 EC NTL 12 11 10 9 8 7 6 5 4 3 2

CHAPTER 2

Table of Contents

Decimals

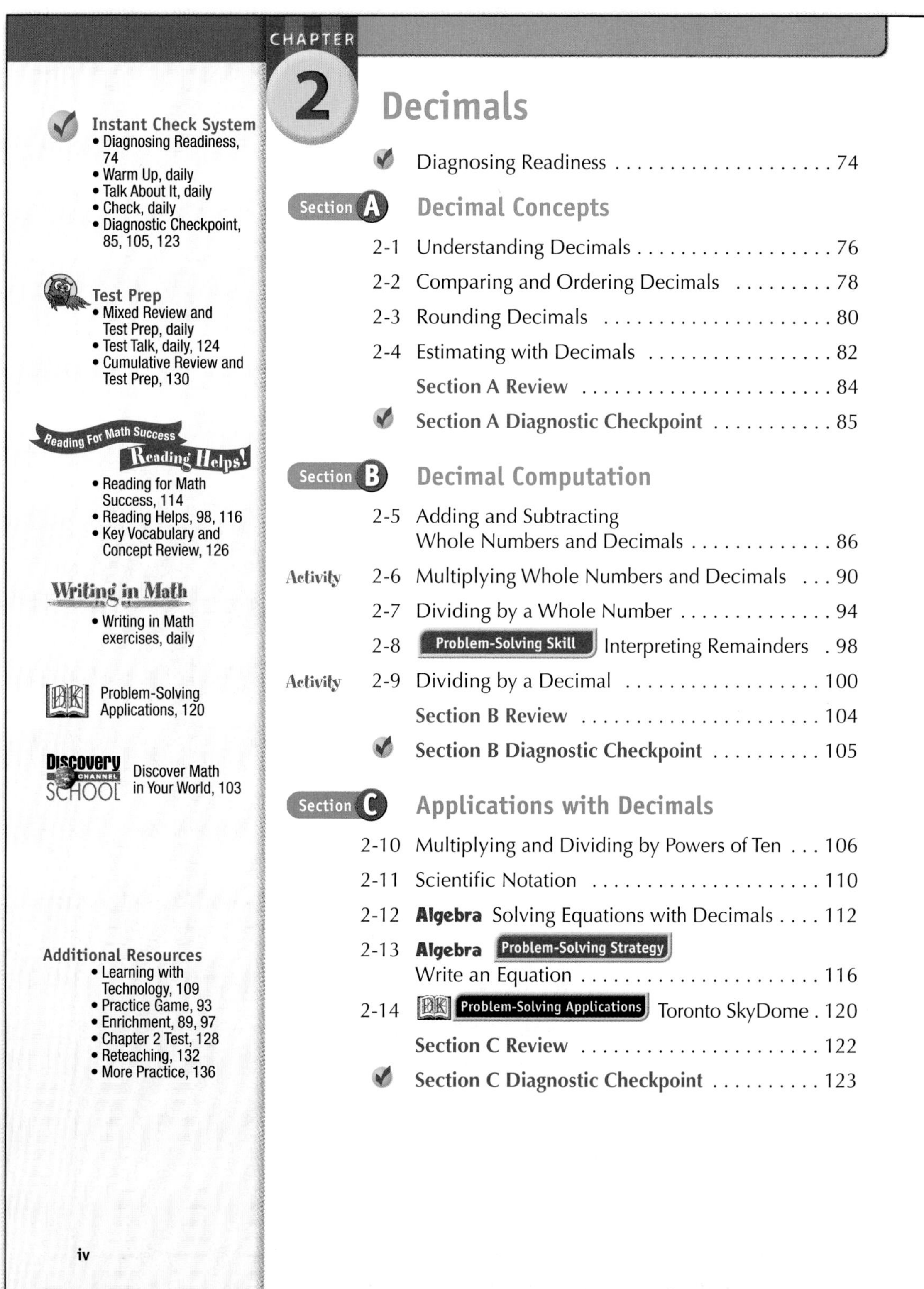

Instant Check System
- Diagnosing Readiness, 74
- Warm Up, daily
- Talk About It, daily
- Check, daily
- Diagnostic Checkpoint, 85, 105, 123

Test Prep
- Mixed Review and Test Prep, daily
- Test Talk, daily, 124
- Cumulative Review and Test Prep, 130

Reading For Math Success / Reading Helps!
- Reading for Math Success, 114
- Reading Helps, 98, 116
- Key Vocabulary and Concept Review, 126

Writing in Math
- Writing in Math exercises, daily

DK Problem-Solving Applications, 120

Discovery Channel School — Discover Math in Your World, 103

Additional Resources
- Learning with Technology, 109
- Practice Game, 93
- Enrichment, 89, 97
- Chapter 2 Test, 128
- Reteaching, 132
- More Practice, 136

iv

CHAPTER 2

Decimals

Table of Contents

CHAPTER 3

Number Theory and Fraction Concepts

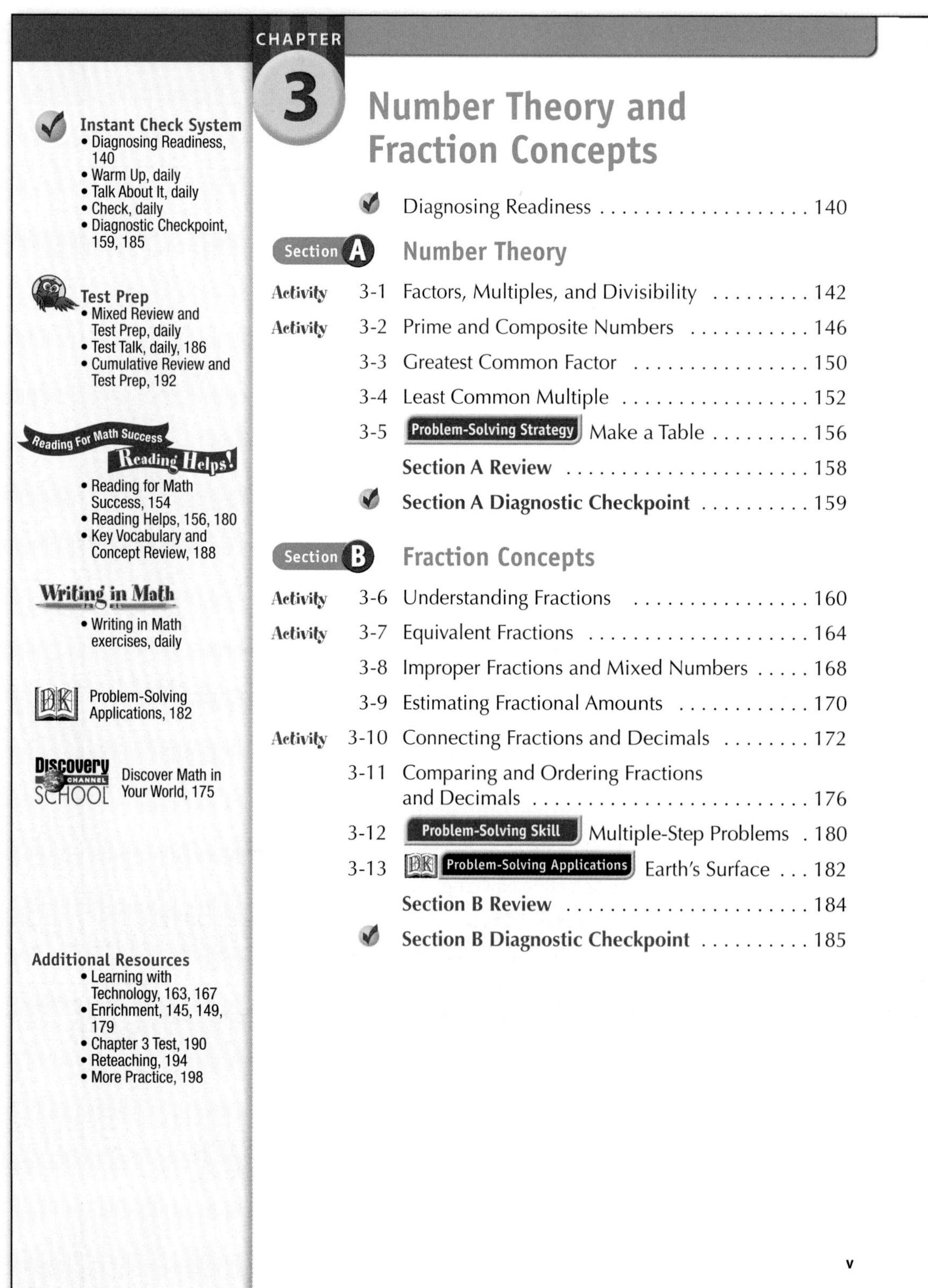

Instant Check System
- Diagnosing Readiness, 140
- Warm Up, daily
- Talk About It, daily
- Check, daily
- Diagnostic Checkpoint, 159, 185

Test Prep
- Mixed Review and Test Prep, daily
- Test Talk, daily, 186
- Cumulative Review and Test Prep, 192

Reading For Math Success / Reading Helps!
- Reading for Math Success, 154
- Reading Helps, 156, 180
- Key Vocabulary and Concept Review, 188

Writing in Math
- Writing in Math exercises, daily

DK Problem-Solving Applications, 182

Discovery Channel School — Discover Math in Your World, 175

Additional Resources
- Learning with Technology, 163, 167
- Enrichment, 145, 149, 179
- Chapter 3 Test, 190
- Reteaching, 194
- More Practice, 198

CHAPTER 3

Number Theory and Fraction Concepts

v

Table of Contents

Adding and Subtracting Fractions

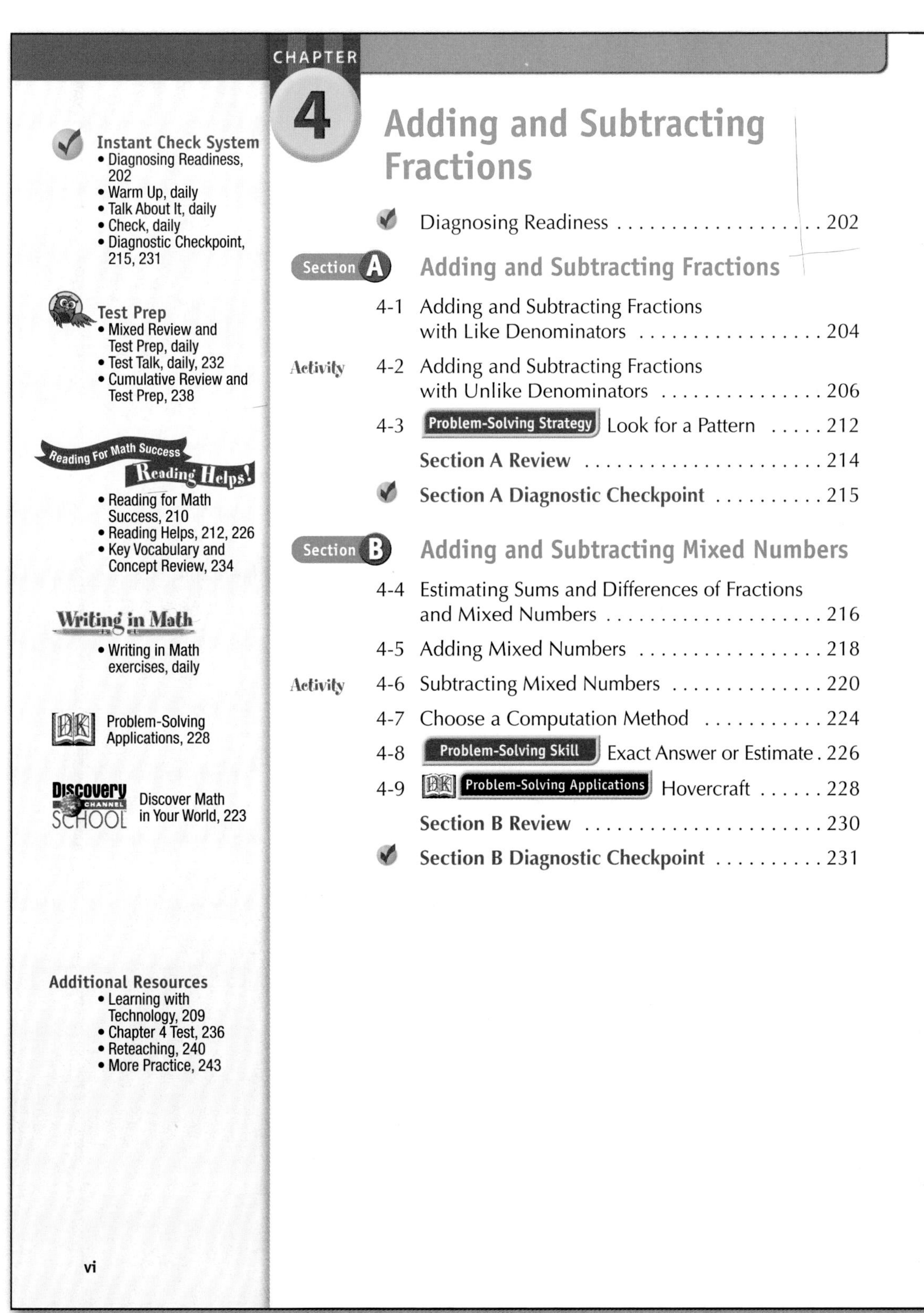

Instant Check System
- Diagnosing Readiness, 202
- Warm Up, daily
- Talk About It, daily
- Check, daily
- Diagnostic Checkpoint, 215, 231

Test Prep
- Mixed Review and Test Prep, daily
- Test Talk, daily, 232
- Cumulative Review and Test Prep, 238

Reading For Math Success
Reading Helps!
- Reading for Math Success, 210
- Reading Helps, 212, 226
- Key Vocabulary and Concept Review, 234

Writing in Math
- Writing in Math exercises, daily

DK Problem-Solving Applications, 228

Discovery Channel School Discover Math in Your World, 223

Additional Resources
- Learning with Technology, 209
- Chapter 4 Test, 236
- Reteaching, 240
- More Practice, 243

vi

CHAPTER 4

Adding and Subtracting Fractions

CHAPTER 5

Table of Contents

Multiplying and Dividing Fractions

CHAPTER 5

Multiplying and Dividing Fractions

Instant Check System
- Diagnosing Readiness, 246
- Warm Up, daily
- Talk About It, daily
- Check, daily
- Diagnostic Checkpoint, 261, 273, 283

Test Prep
- Mixed Review and Test Prep, daily
- Test Talk, daily, 284
- Cumulative Review and Test Prep, 290

Reading For Math Success / Reading Helps!
- Reading for Math Success, 262
- Reading Helps, 264, 278
- Key Vocabulary and Concept Review, 286

Writing in Math
- Writing in Math exercises, daily
- Writing to Explain, 278

DK Problem-Solving Applications, 280

Discovery Channel School — Discover Math in Your World, 269

Additional Resources
- Learning with Technology, 255
- Practice Game, 255
- Enrichment, 251
- Chapter 5 Test, 288
- Reteaching, 292
- More Practice, 295

vii

CHAPTER 6

Table of Contents

Ratio, Rates, and Proportion

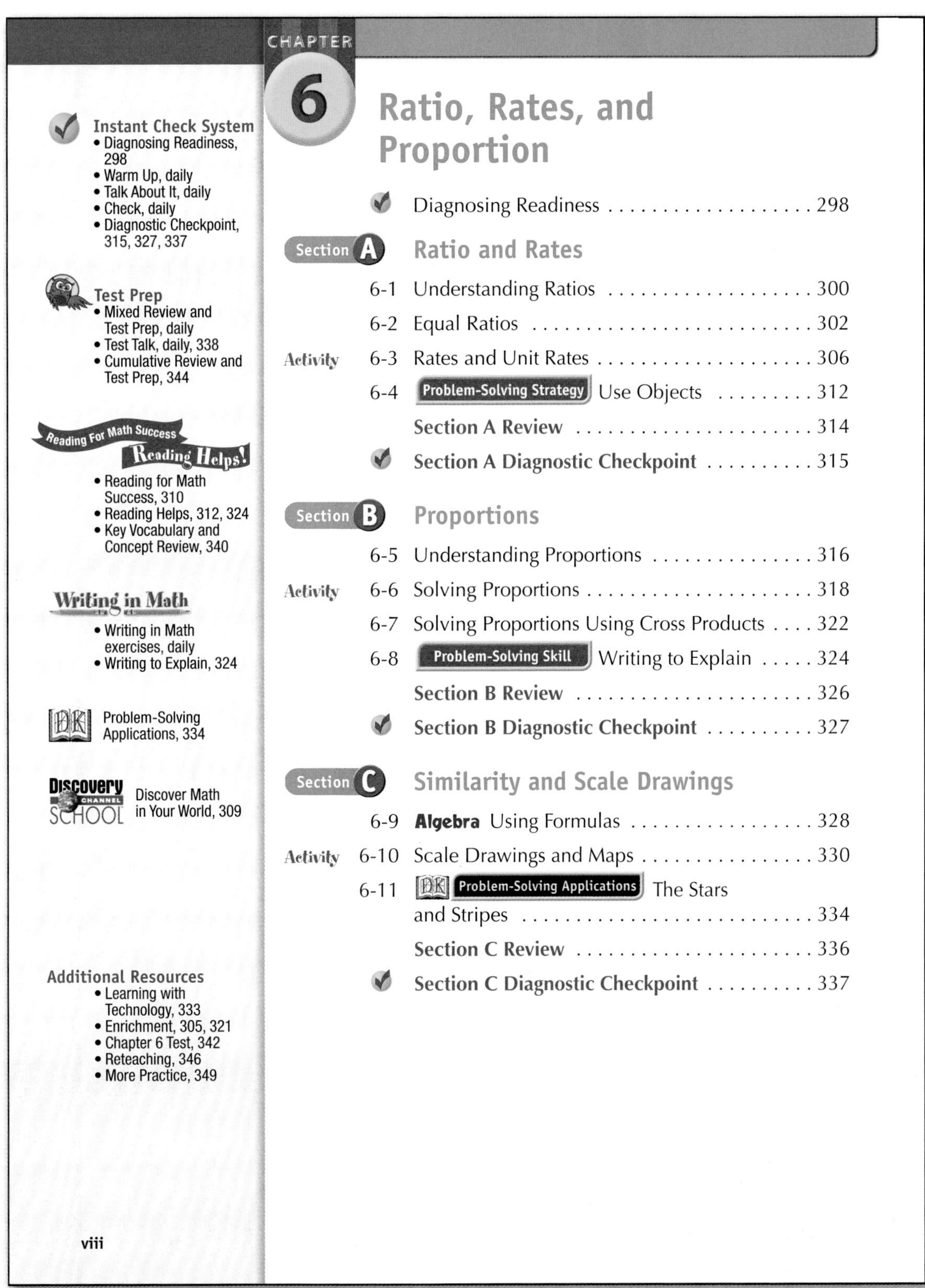

Instant Check System
- Diagnosing Readiness, 298
- Warm Up, daily
- Talk About It, daily
- Check, daily
- Diagnostic Checkpoint, 315, 327, 337

Test Prep
- Mixed Review and Test Prep, daily
- Test Talk, daily, 338
- Cumulative Review and Test Prep, 344

Reading For Math Success
Reading Helps!
- Reading for Math Success, 310
- Reading Helps, 312, 324
- Key Vocabulary and Concept Review, 340

Writing in Math
- Writing in Math exercises, daily
- Writing to Explain, 324

Problem-Solving Applications, 334

Discovery Channel School Discover Math in Your World, 309

Additional Resources
- Learning with Technology, 333
- Enrichment, 305, 321
- Chapter 6 Test, 342
- Reteaching, 346
- More Practice, 349

CHAPTER 6

Ratio, Rates, and Proportion

viii

CHAPTER 7 Table of Contents

Percent

Instant Check System
- Diagnosing Readiness, 352
- Warm Up, daily
- Talk About It, daily
- Check, daily
- Diagnostic Checkpoint, 365, 379, 391

Test Prep
- Mixed Review and Test Prep, daily
- Test Talk, daily, 392
- Cumulative Review and Test Prep, 398

Reading For Math Success / Reading Helps!
- Reading for Math Success, 372
- Reading Helps, 362, 374
- Key Vocabulary and Concept Review, 394

Writing in Math
- Writing in Math exercises, daily
- Writing to Explain, 362

DK Problem-Solving Applications, 388

Discovery Channel School: Discover Math in Your World, 383

Additional Resources
- Learning with Technology, 357
- Practice Game, 361
- Chapter 7 Test, 396
- Reteaching, 400
- More Practice, 403

CHAPTER 7

Percent

CHAPTER 8

Table of Contents

Algebra: Integers and Rational Numbers

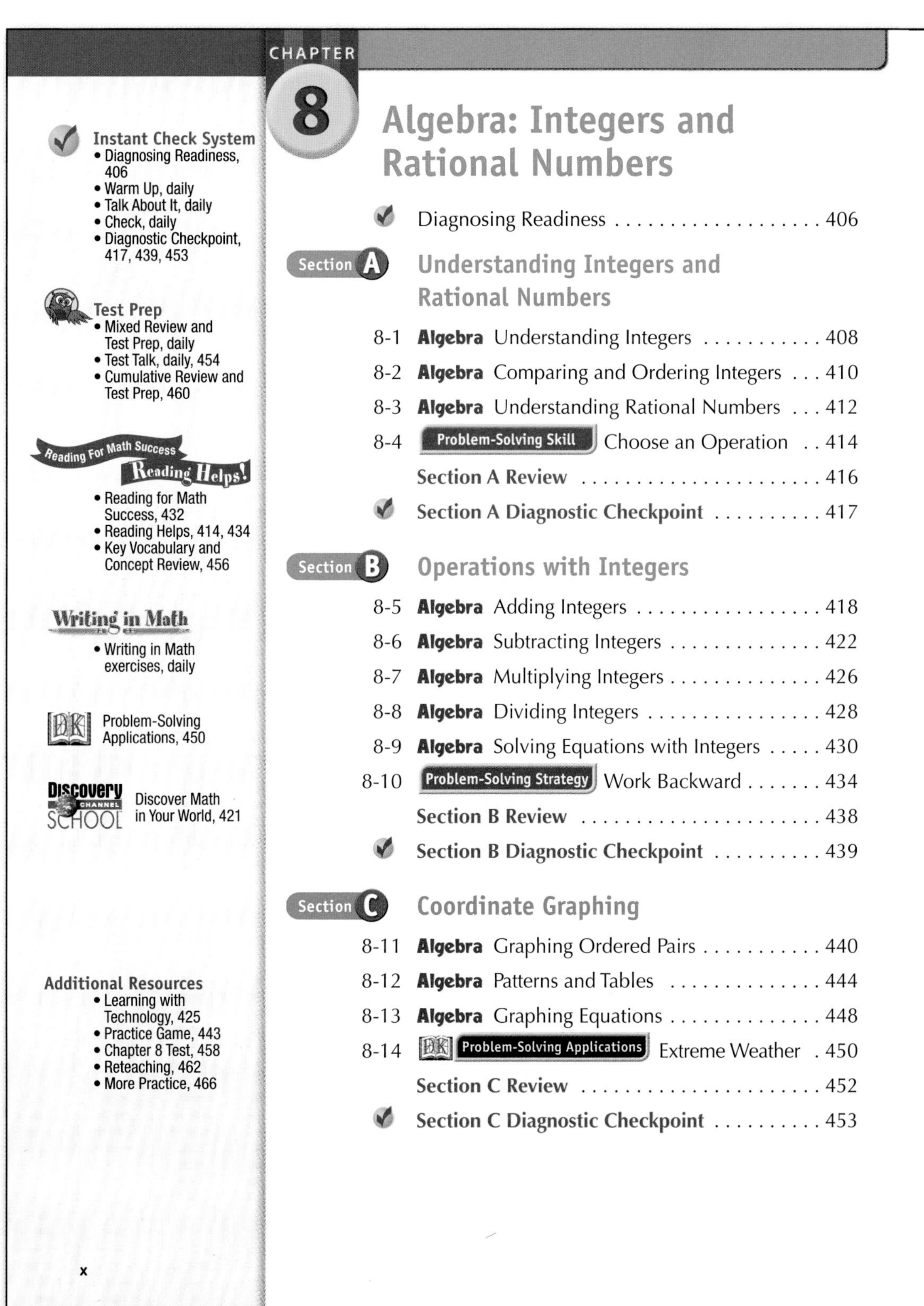

Instant Check System
- Diagnosing Readiness, 406
- Warm Up, daily
- Talk About It, daily
- Check, daily
- Diagnostic Checkpoint, 417, 439, 453

Test Prep
- Mixed Review and Test Prep, daily
- Test Talk, daily, 454
- Cumulative Review and Test Prep, 460

Reading For Math Success
Reading Helps!
- Reading for Math Success, 432
- Reading Helps, 414, 434
- Key Vocabulary and Concept Review, 456

Writing in Math
- Writing in Math exercises, daily

DK Problem-Solving Applications, 450

Discovery Channel School Discover Math in Your World, 421

Additional Resources
- Learning with Technology, 425
- Practice Game, 443
- Chapter 8 Test, 458
- Reteaching, 462
- More Practice, 466

x

CHAPTER 8

Algebra: Integers and Rational Numbers

CHAPTER 9

Table of Contents

Geometry

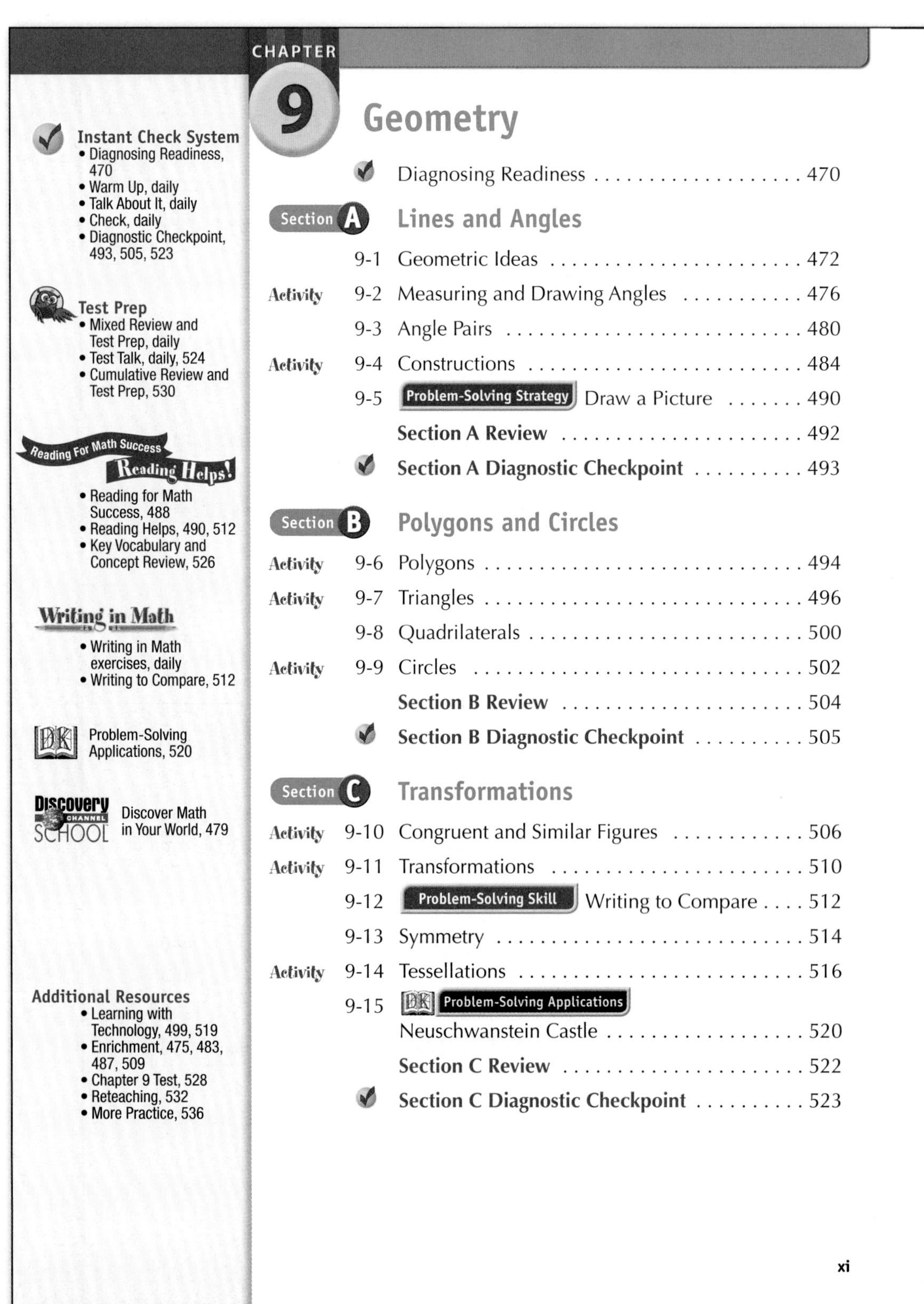

CHAPTER 9

Geometry

Instant Check System
- Diagnosing Readiness, 470
- Warm Up, daily
- Talk About It, daily
- Check, daily
- Diagnostic Checkpoint, 493, 505, 523

Test Prep
- Mixed Review and Test Prep, daily
- Test Talk, daily, 524
- Cumulative Review and Test Prep, 530

Reading For Math Success
Reading Helps!
- Reading for Math Success, 488
- Reading Helps, 490, 512
- Key Vocabulary and Concept Review, 526

Writing in Math
- Writing in Math exercises, daily
- Writing to Compare, 512

DK Problem-Solving Applications, 520

Discovery Channel School — Discover Math in Your World, 479

Additional Resources
- Learning with Technology, 499, 519
- Enrichment, 475, 483, 487, 509
- Chapter 9 Test, 528
- Reteaching, 532
- More Practice, 536

Measurement

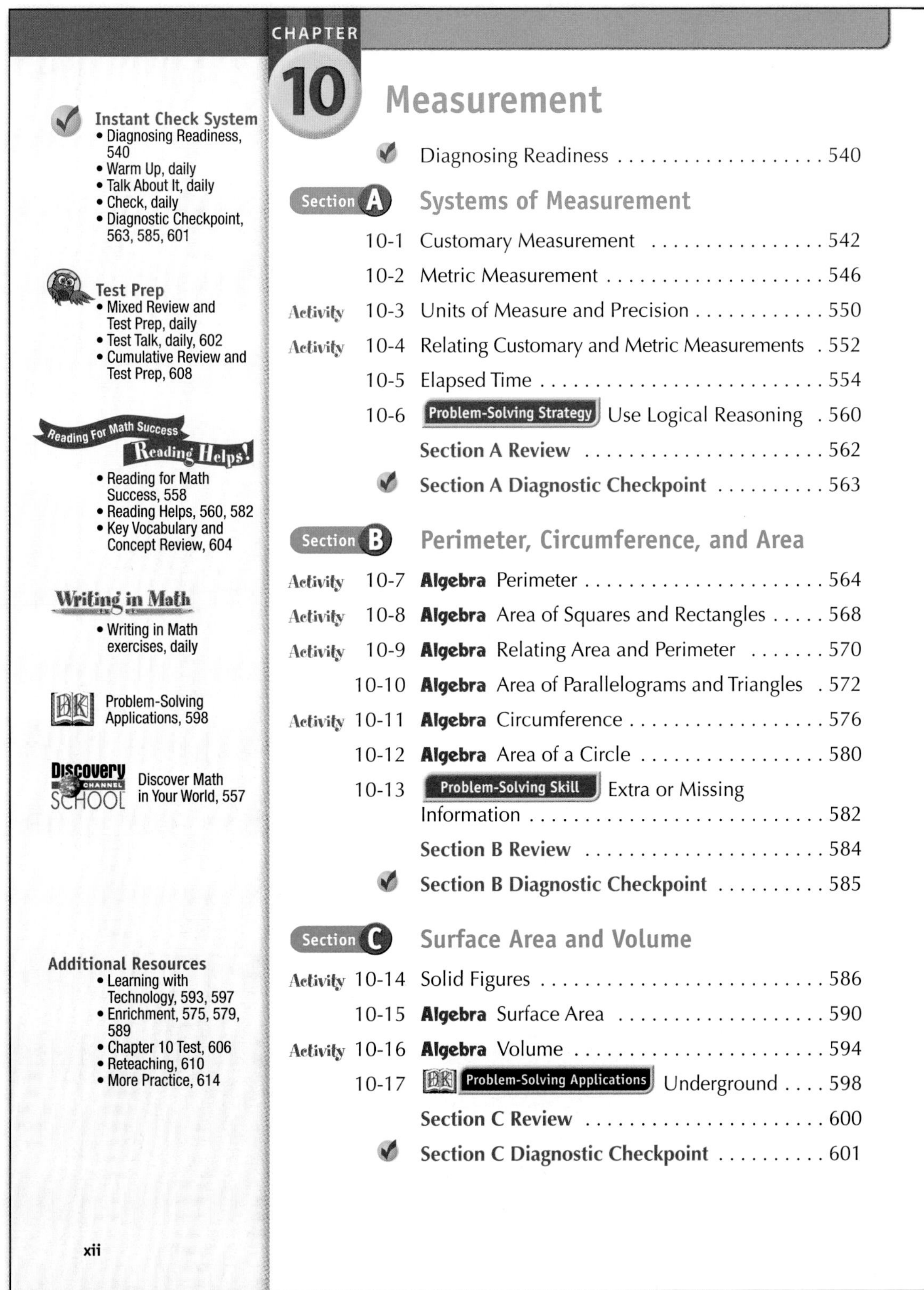

CHAPTER 10

Measurement

Instant Check System
- Diagnosing Readiness, 540
- Warm Up, daily
- Talk About It, daily
- Check, daily
- Diagnostic Checkpoint, 563, 585, 601

Test Prep
- Mixed Review and Test Prep, daily
- Test Talk, daily, 602
- Cumulative Review and Test Prep, 608

Reading For Math Success
Reading Helps!
- Reading for Math Success, 558
- Reading Helps, 560, 582
- Key Vocabulary and Concept Review, 604

Writing in Math
- Writing in Math exercises, daily

DK Problem-Solving Applications, 598

Discovery Channel School Discover Math in Your World, 557

Additional Resources
- Learning with Technology, 593, 597
- Enrichment, 575, 579, 589
- Chapter 10 Test, 606
- Reteaching, 610
- More Practice, 614

xii

CHAPTER 11

Table of Contents

Data, Graphs, and Probability

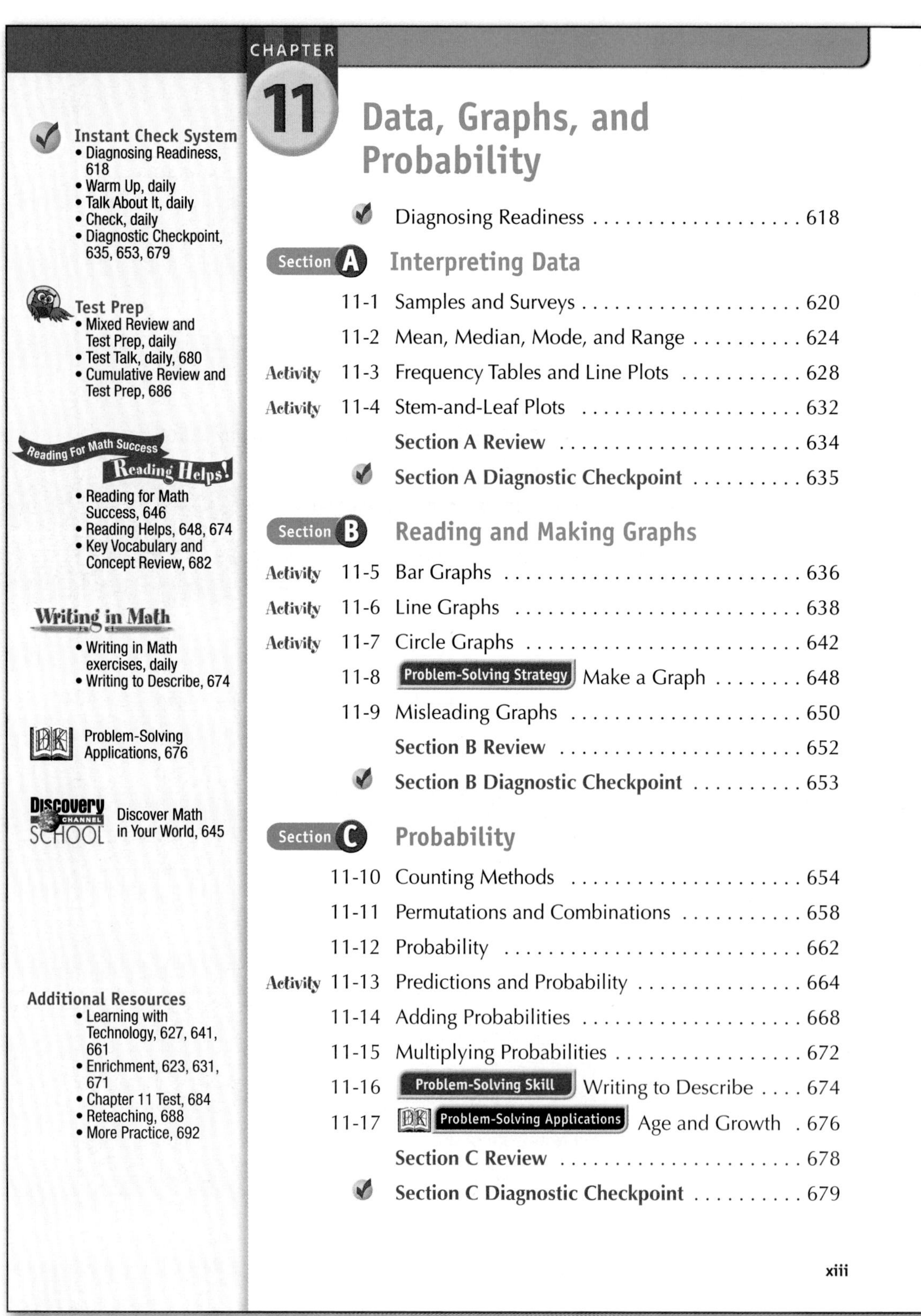

Instant Check System
- Diagnosing Readiness, 618
- Warm Up, daily
- Talk About It, daily
- Check, daily
- Diagnostic Checkpoint, 635, 653, 679

Test Prep
- Mixed Review and Test Prep, daily
- Test Talk, daily, 680
- Cumulative Review and Test Prep, 686

Reading For Math Success
Reading Helps!
- Reading for Math Success, 646
- Reading Helps, 648, 674
- Key Vocabulary and Concept Review, 682

Writing in Math
- Writing in Math exercises, daily
- Writing to Describe, 674

DK Problem-Solving Applications, 676

Discovery Channel School Discover Math in Your World, 645

Additional Resources
- Learning with Technology, 627, 641, 661
- Enrichment, 623, 631, 671
- Chapter 11 Test, 684
- Reteaching, 688
- More Practice, 692

CHAPTER 11

Data, Graphs, and Probability

xiii

Table of Contents

Algebra: Inequalities, Equations, and Graphs

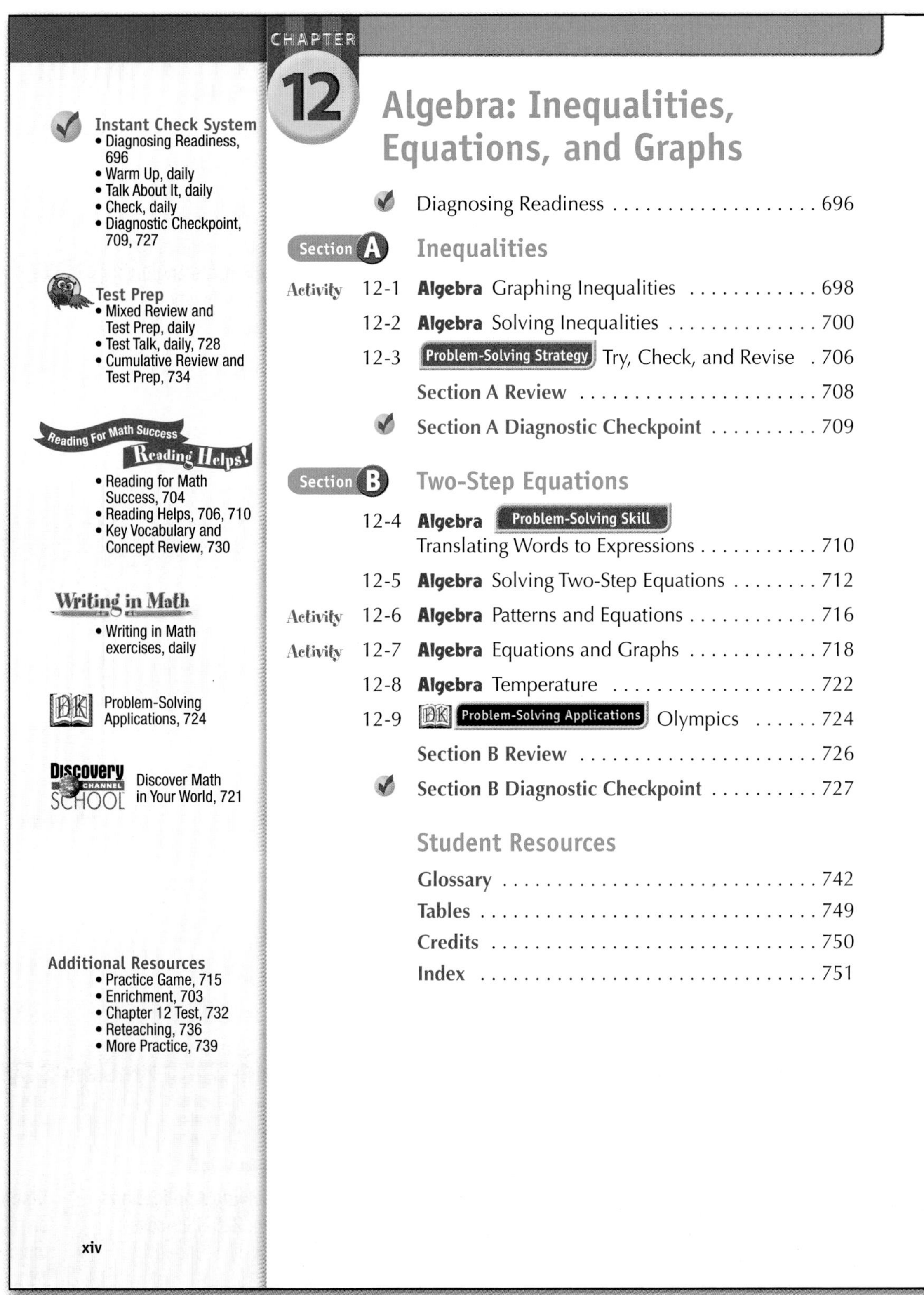

CHAPTER 12

Algebra: Inequalities, Equations, and Graphs

Instant Check System
- Diagnosing Readiness, 696
- Warm Up, daily
- Talk About It, daily
- Check, daily
- Diagnostic Checkpoint, 709, 727

Test Prep
- Mixed Review and Test Prep, daily
- Test Talk, daily, 728
- Cumulative Review and Test Prep, 734

Reading For Math Success — Reading Helps!
- Reading for Math Success, 704
- Reading Helps, 706, 710
- Key Vocabulary and Concept Review, 730

Writing in Math
- Writing in Math exercises, daily

DK Problem-Solving Applications, 724

Discovery Channel School — Discover Math in Your World, 721

Additional Resources
- Practice Game, 715
- Enrichment, 703
- Chapter 12 Test, 732
- Reteaching, 736
- More Practice, 739

xiv

CHAPTER 4

Lesson Planner

Adding and Subtracting Fractions

Suggested Pacing: 10 days

Section A Adding and Subtracting Fractions

4-1 pp. 204–205	4-2 pp. 206–209	4-2 (continued)	4-3 pp. 212–213
Adding and Subtracting Fractions with Like Denominators **Objective** Add and subtract fractions with like denominators, and simplify the answer if possible. **Math Understanding** When adding or subtracting fractions with like denominators, you are adding or subtracting pieces or portions of the same size, so you can add the numerators—the numbers of pieces or portions—without changing the denominator. **Focus Question** • How can you find sums and differences of fractions? **Vocabulary** Like denominators, common denominator	**Adding and Subtracting Fractions with Unlike Denominators** **Objective** Find common denominators for fractions, with unlike denominators, and find their sums and differences in simplest form. **Math Understanding** To obtain a sum or difference of fractions, they first must be expressed using equal-sized pieces or portions. The least common denominator represents the largest possible size of these pieces or portions. **Focus Questions** • *Activity* How can you use fraction strips to add? • *Activity* How can you use fraction strips to subtract? • How can you find sums and differences of fractions with unlike denominators? **Vocabulary** Unlike denominators, least common multiple (LCM) (p. 152), least common denominator (LCD) (p. 164)	**Materials for Student Pages** Fraction strips or tools **Learning with Technology: Fractions eTool: Strips and Wedges, p. 209** Reading For Math Success pp. 210–211	Problem-Solving Strategy **Look for a Pattern** **Objective** Give missing numbers or figures in a pattern. **Math Understanding** Patterns can be identified by using given elements and then can be filled in or extended. **Focus Question** • What is the pattern? **Section A Review, p. 214** **Section A Diagnostic Checkpoint, p. 215**

Diagnosing Readiness, pp. 202–203

Resources in the Student Book

Ongoing Assessment and Test Prep *Also see pp. 202G–202H.*

Instant Check System™
- **Diagnosing Readiness** start of chapter
- **Warm Up** start of lessons
- **Talk About It** after examples
- **Check** before Practice
- **Diagnostic Checkpoint** end of sections

Test Prep
- **Test Talk: Think It Through** in lessons
- **Mixed Review and Test Prep** in lessons
- **Test Talk** end of chapter
- **Cumulative Review and Test Prep** end of chapter

Daily Real-World Problem Solving plus ...

Problem-Solving Applications lesson on pp. 228–229 uses data from Dorling Kindersley literature.

Discover Math in Your World on p. 223 uses data from a topic in the Discovery Channel School Video Library, Segment 4.

Section B Adding and Subtracting Mixed Numbers

4-4 pp. 216–217

Estimating Sums and Differences of Fractions and Mixed Numbers

Objective Estimate sums and differences of fractions and mixed numbers using a number line, benchmark fractions, and rounding to the nearest whole number.

Math Understanding Mixed numbers can be expressed as improper fractions, or they can be broken apart into their whole-number and fractional parts. This provides a basis for estimating and doing operations with two mixed numbers, with a mixed number and a whole number, and with a mixed number and a fraction.

Focus Questions

- Do you need an exact answer or is an estimate enough?
- What are some ways to estimate?

Vocabulary Round (p. 14)

4-5 pp. 218–219

Adding Mixed Numbers

Objective Find sums of mixed numbers with and without renaming.

Math Understanding Mixed numbers can be expressed as improper fractions, or they can be broken apart into their whole-number and fractional parts. This provides a basis for estimating and doing operations with two mixed numbers, with a mixed number and a whole number, and with a mixed number and a fraction.

Focus Question

- How can you find the sum of mixed numbers?

Vocabulary Mixed number (p. 168)

4-6 pp. 220–223

Subtracting Mixed Numbers

Objective Find differences of mixed numbers with and without renaming.

Math Understanding Mixed numbers can be expressed as improper fractions, or they can be broken apart into their whole-number and fractional parts. This provides a basis for estimating and doing operations with two mixed numbers, with a mixed number and a whole number, and with a mixed number and a fraction.

Focus Questions

- *Activity* How can you model the difference of mixed numbers?
- How can you find the difference of mixed numbers?
- Do you always have to rename both mixed numbers before subtracting?

Vocabulary Mixed number (p. 168)

4-6 (continued)

Materials for Student Pages Fraction strips or eTools

Discovery Channel School

Discover Math in Your World: A Braking Event, p. 223

4-7 pp. 224–225

Choose a Computation Method

Objective For a variety of problems, state the computation method to be used and add or subtract using that method.

Math Understanding The kinds of numbers in a calculation, and the ease with which one can apply different calculation methods, together determine an appropriate computation method.

Focus Question

- What computation method should you use?

Materials for Student Pages Calculator

Reading and Writing in Math *Throughout*

This feature shows how reading skills and strategies can help with problem-solving skills and strategies in math. Also, **Reading Assists** are in the Teacher's Edition.

Writing in Math

All lessons include **Writing in Math** exercises. Also, daily **Journal Ideas** are in the Teacher's Edition.

Technology Resources for Students *Also see p. T20.*

More examples, more practice, test prep, Discovery Channel School Video Library, and Math eTools

Math eTools: electronic manipulatives online, on CD-ROM, and in the Online Student's Edition

All text pages are available online and on CD-ROM. The Online Student's Edition includes Math eTools plus glossary links for vocabulary.

Lesson Planner

Adding and Subtracting Fractions (continued)

4-8
pp. 226–227

Problem-Solving Skill

Exact Answer or Estimate?

Objective Obtain exact or estimated results to solve problems in real-world contexts.

Math Understanding Some problems require exact answers, while others need only an estimate.

Focus Question

- Do you always need an exact answer to a word problem?

4-9
pp. 228–229

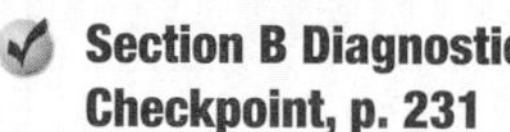

Hovercraft

Objective Review and apply key concepts, skills, and strategies learned in this and previous chapters.

Math Understanding Some real-world problems can be solved using known concepts, skills, and strategies.

Section B Review, p. 203

Section B Diagnostic Checkpoint, p. 231

Wrap Up
pp. 232–245

Test Talk: Make Smart Choices, pp. 232–233

Key Vocabulary and Concept Review, pp. 234–235

Chapter 4 Test, pp. 236–237

Cumulative Review and Test Prep, pp. 238–239

Reteaching, pp. 240–242

More Practice, pp. 243–245

Additional Resources for...

Reaching All Learners

- **Practice** Masters/Workbook, every lesson
- **Reteaching** Masters/Workbook, every lesson
- **Enrichment** Masters/Workbook, every lesson
- **Every Student Learns** A teacher resource with daily suggestions for helping students overcome language barriers to learning math
- **Spiral Review and Test Prep** Transparencies and Masters/Workbook, every lesson
- **Math Games** Use *Like and Unlike* anytime after Lesson 4-2.
- **Investigation** See pp. 202I–202J.

Problem Solving

- **Problem Solving** Masters/Workbook, every lesson
- **Problem of the Day** Flipchart/Transparencies, every lesson
- **Discovery Channel** Masters, follow-up to Segment 4 in the Discovery Channel School Video Library

Notes

Reading in Math
- **Vocabulary Kit** Word Cards plus transparencies and activities for instructional word walls and for small groups
- **Dorling Kindersley Literature Library** Books with interesting data

Assessment, Intervention, and Test Prep
- **Assessment Sourcebook** See pp. 202G–202H.
- **Diagnosis and Intervention System** See pp. 202G–202H.
- **Test-Taking Practice** Transparencies, every lesson
- **SAT 9, Terra Nova Practice** and **Test Prep Packages** include practice tests, correlations, and more.
- **Benchmark Tests** Multiple-choice tests on content in Chapters 1-2, 3-4, 5-6, 7-8, 9-10 and in the National Assessment of Educational Progress.

Teacher Support
- **Teaching Tools** Masters: paper manipulatives and more
- **Home-School Connection** Masters, use Chapter 4 Family Letter at the start of the chapter. Use Study Buddies 7 and 8 after Lessons 4-2 and 4-5.
- **Professional Development Resources** See p. T18.
- **Technology Resources** TE and more; see p. T20.

CHAPTER 4

Professional Development

Skills Trace - Adding and Subtracting Fractions

BEFORE Chapter 4	DURING Chapter 4	AFTER Chapter 4
Grade 5 reviewed adding and subtracting fractions, and introduced adding and subtracting mixed numbers. **Chapter 3 in Grade 6** reviewed fraction concepts that are needed for operating with fractions.	**Chapter 4** focuses on estimating and finding sums and differences of fractions and mixed numbers with and without regrouping, and applying these skills to complete number patterns and solve problems.	**Chapter 5 in Grade 6** focuses on multiplying and dividing fractions and applying these skills to evaluate expressions and solve equations. Grade 7 applies adding and subtracting fractions and mixed numbers to solving equations.

Math Background and Teaching Tips

Section A

Adding and Subtracting Fractions
pp. 204–215

Ideas related to addition and subtraction with whole numbers—joining, separating, and comparing—apply to real-world situations that involve fractions. A solid conceptual understanding of the meaning of fractions and equivalent fractions will help students add and subtract fractions.

Problems that involve adding or subtracting with like denominators can be solved by these general rules:

$\frac{a}{b} + \frac{c}{b} = \frac{a+c}{b}$ $\quad$ $\frac{a}{b} - \frac{c}{b} = \frac{a-c}{b}$

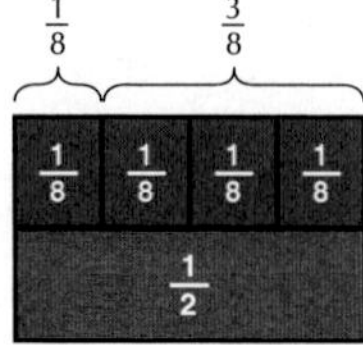

$\frac{1}{8} + \frac{3}{8} = \frac{1}{2}$

Developing algorithms for adding and subtracting fractions with unlike denominators takes longer. The main idea, however, is the same after the fractions have been renamed and have like denominators.

TIP! Use Representations *When students model adding and subtracting fractions with unlike denominators, they need to process a variety of situations that include exercises where one fraction needs to be renamed, where both need to be renamed, and where the sum or difference needs to be simplified. In the case of sums, the answer may need to be expressed as a mixed number.*

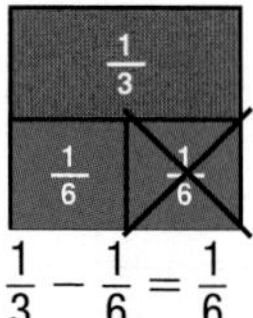

$\frac{1}{3} - \frac{1}{6} = \frac{1}{6}$

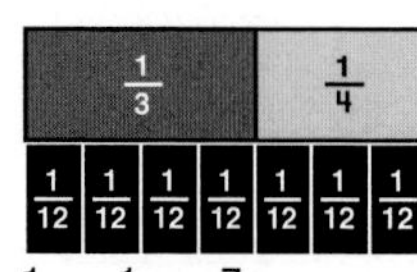

$\frac{1}{3} + \frac{1}{4} = \frac{7}{12}$

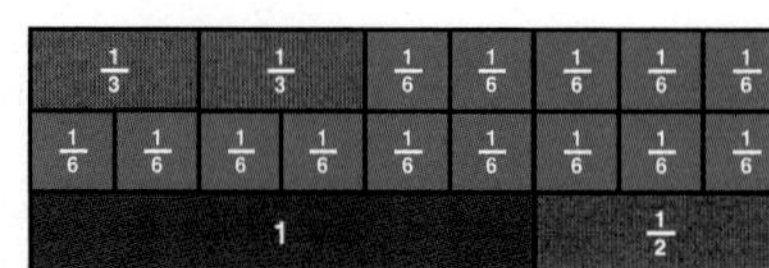

$\frac{2}{3} + \frac{5}{6} = \frac{9}{6} = 1\frac{3}{6} = 1\frac{1}{2}$

These alternate algorithms for adding or subtracting fractions use a shortcut method for writing each fraction with a common denominator:

$\frac{a}{b} + \frac{c}{d} = \frac{ad + bc}{bd}$ $\quad$ $\frac{a}{b} - \frac{c}{d} = \frac{ad - bc}{bd}$

Math Understandings

- Fractions with like denominators are easy to add and subtract because the denominators represent pieces or portions of the same size.
- Finding the least common denominator will allow you to add and subtract fractions with unlike denominators.
- Patterns can be identified by using given elements and then can be filled in or extended.

The alternate algorithms are based on the idea that the product of two denominators will always be a common denominator, although it may not be the least common denominator (LCD). In such cases, an additional step to simplify an answer may be necessary. A comparison of both algorithms is shown below.

Traditional Algorithm

$\frac{5}{6} + \frac{1}{9} = \frac{15}{18} + \frac{2}{18}$ $\quad$ Think: LCM = 18 Write both fractions with an LCD of 18.

$= \frac{17}{18}$

Alternate Algorithm

$\frac{5}{6} + \frac{1}{9} = \frac{(5 \times 9) + (1 \times 6)}{6 \times 9}$

$= \frac{51}{54}$

$= \frac{17}{18}$

Section B

Adding and Subtracting Mixed Numbers

pp. 216–231

The traditional paper-and-pencil algorithms for adding and subtracting mixed numbers are similar to those for adding and subtracting whole numbers in that they all operate from right to left, and any renaming is done as needed throughout the computation. When students add and subtract mixed numbers using models, however, they do not need to operate as if using a traditional algorithm.

Add: $1\frac{3}{4} + 1\frac{5}{8}$

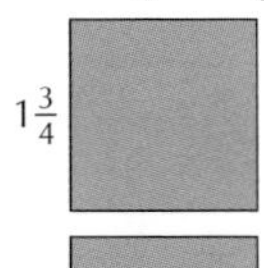

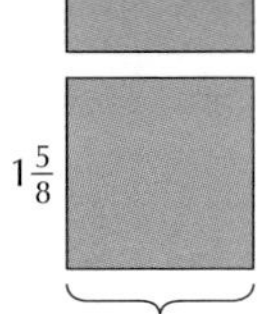

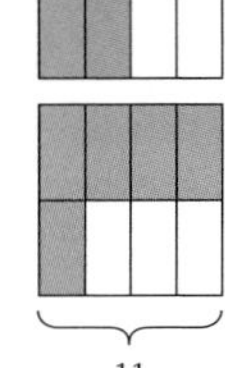

$1 + 1 = 2$

$\frac{3}{4} + \frac{5}{8} = \frac{6}{8} + \frac{5}{8} = \frac{11}{8}$

$\frac{11}{8} = 1\frac{3}{8}$

$2 + 1\frac{3}{8} = 3\frac{3}{8}$

So, $1\frac{3}{4} + 1\frac{5}{8} = 3\frac{3}{8}$.

Subtract: $3 - 1\frac{1}{4}$

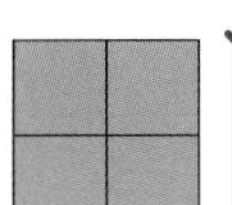
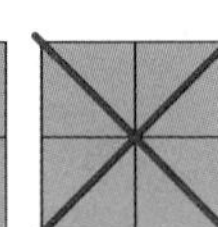
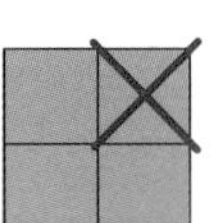

$3 - 1 = 2$

Since $\frac{4}{4} = 1, 2 = 1\frac{4}{4}$.

$1\frac{4}{4} - \frac{1}{4} = 1\frac{3}{4}$

So, $3 - 1\frac{1}{4} = 1\frac{3}{4}$.

The front-end approach used in solving these problems can be extended to making estimates. Front-end estimation is an especially effective technique when estimating sums and differences of mixed numbers.

TIP! Reinforce Big Ideas *Emphasize using whole-number parts first to estimate. Then use the fractional parts to adjust or refine the estimate.*

Estimate: $4\frac{3}{8} + 2\frac{7}{9} + 1\frac{1}{6}$

$4\frac{3}{8}$	$\frac{3}{8}$ is close to $\frac{1}{2}$.
$2\frac{7}{9}$	$\frac{7}{9}$ is close to 1.
$+ 1\frac{1}{6}$	$\frac{1}{6}$ is close to 0.
7 ← first estimate	

Adjusted estimate: $7 + 1\frac{1}{2} = 8\frac{1}{2}$

Math Understandings

- Mixed numbers can be expressed as improper fractions, or they can be broken apart into their whole-number and fractional parts. This provides a basis for estimating and doing operations with two mixed numbers, with a mixed number and a whole number, and with a mixed number and a fraction.
- The kinds of numbers in a calculation, and the ease with which one can apply different calculation methods, together determine an appropriate computation method.
- Some problems require exact answers, while others need only an estimate.

Estimate: $7\frac{1}{8} - 4\frac{2}{3}$

$7\frac{1}{8}$	$\frac{1}{8}$ is close to 0.
$- 4\frac{2}{3}$	$\frac{2}{3}$ is close to $\frac{1}{2}$.
3 ← first estimate	

Adjusted estimate: less than 3, since $\frac{1}{8} < \frac{2}{3}$

TIP! Teach for Understanding

A common error students make when subtracting mixed numbers occurs when they rename a whole number as a fraction. They incorrectly use a base-ten place-value idea (adding 10 to the numerator of the fraction), instead of correctly renaming the fraction to be able to subtract. An understanding of renaming fractions prevents this error.

$4\frac{1}{4}$	$3\frac{11}{4}$ ← incorrectly changed
$-2\frac{3}{4}$	$\frac{1}{4}$ to $\frac{11}{4}$.

Assessment, Intervention, Test Prep

Assessment Resources

DIAGNOSING READINESS

Start of Year Diagnosing Readiness for Grade 6, Assessment Sourcebook, pp. 43–46 and in Online Intervention

Start of Chapter Diagnosing Readiness for Chapter 4, Student Book pp. 202–203 and in Online Intervention

Start of Lesson Warm Up, Student Book pp. 204, 206, 216, 218, 220, 224

Instant Check System™

ONGOING ASSESSMENT

During Instruction Talk About It, Student Book, every lesson

Before Independent Practice Check, Student Book, every lesson

After a Section Diagnostic Checkpoint, pp. 215, 231 and in Online Intervention

Basic-Facts Timed Test 4 Assessment Sourcebook, p. 30

FORMAL EVALUATION

Chapter Tests Chapter 4 Test, Student Book pp. 236–237; Assessment Sourcebook Forms A and B pp. 69–74, Form C Performance Assessment p. 7; Multiple-Choice Chapter Test in Online Intervention

Cumulative Tests Chapters 1-3, 1-6, 1-9, 1-12; Assessment Sourcebook, pp. 65–68, 87–90, 109–112, 131–134; Online Intervention

Test Generator Computer-generated tests; can be customized

Correlation to Assessments, Intervention, and Standardized Tests

		Assessments		Intervention	Standardized Tests				
	Lessons	Diagnostic Checkpoint	Chapter Test	Math Diagnosis and Intervention System	SAT 9/10	ITBS	CTBS	CAT	MAT
4-1	Adding and Subtracting Fractions with Like Denominators	p. 215: Ex. 1, 3, 5, 9, 19	Ex. 1, 18	Booklet H: H29	•/•	•	•	•	•
4-2	Adding and Subtracting Fractions with Unlike Denominators	p. 215: Ex. 2, 4, 6–8, 10–14, 18, 20, 21	Ex. 2, 10, 17	Booklet H: H31	•/•	•	•	•	•
4-3	Problem-Solving Strategy: Look for a Pattern	p. 215: Ex. 15–17	Ex. 11, 22	Booklet M: M36	•/•	•	•		•
4-4	Estimating Sums and Differences of Fractions and Mixed Numbers	p. 231: Ex. 3–6	Ex. 3, 4, 15, 16	Booklet H: H33	/•	•	•	•	
4-5	Adding Mixed Numbers	p. 231: Ex. 2, 7, 9, 12, 13, 17	Ex. 5, 6, 19, 24	Booklet H: H34	•/	•	•	•	•
4-6	Subtracting Mixed Numbers	p. 231: Ex. 1, 8, 10, 11, 14, 18	Ex. 7–9, 20, 23	Booklet H: H35	•/	•	•	•	•
4-7	Choose a Computation Method	p. 231: Ex. 19	Ex. 21	Booklet H: H36	•/•	•	•	•	•
4-8	Problem-Solving Skill: Exact Answer or Estimate	p. 231: Ex. 15, 16	Ex. 12–14	Booklet M: M8	•/•	•	•		•

KEY: **SAT 9** Stanford Achievement Test; **SAT 10** Stanford Achievement Test; **ITBS** Iowa Test of Basic Skills; **CAT** California Achievement Test; **CTBS** Comprehensive Test of Basic Skills (TerraNova); **MAT** Metropolitan Achievement Test

Intervention and Test Prep Resources

INTERVENTION

During Instruction Helpful "If... Then..." suggestions in the Teacher's Edition in Ongoing Assessment and Error Intervention.

During Practice "Reteaching" and "More Practice" sets at the back of the chapter, referenced under "Check" and "Practice" in the lessons.

Math Diagnosis and Intervention System Diagnostic tests, individual and class record forms, two-page Intervention Lessons (example, practice, test prep), and one-page Intervention Practice (multiple choice), all in cross-grade strand booklets (Booklets A-E for Grades 1–3, Booklets F-M for Grades 4–6).

Online Intervention Diagnostic tests; individual, class, school, and district reports; remediation including tutorials, video, games, practice exercises.

TEST PREP

Test Talk: Think It Through within lessons and tests

Mixed Review and Test Prep end of lessons

Test Talk before the chapter test, pp. 232–233

Cumulative Review and Test Prep after each chapter, pp. 238–239

Test-Taking Strategies, pp. xv-xix before Chapter 1

Pacing for Test Success, pp. T36-T-47

Test-Taking Practice Transparencies for every lesson

Spiral Review and Test Prep for every lesson

SAT 9, SAT 10, ITBS, TerraNova Practice and Test Prep section quizzes, practice tests

Take It to the Net: Test Prep www.scottforesman.com, referenced in lessons

Correlation to NCTM Standards and Grades 6–8 Expectations

Number and Operations

Understand meanings of operations and how they relate to one another.

Grades 6–8 Expectations

- Understand the meaning and effects of arithmetic operations with fractions, decimals, and integers. *Lessons 4-1, 4-2, 4-5, 4-6, 4-9*
- Use the associative and commutative properties of addition and multiplication and the distributive property of multiplication over addition to simplify computations with integers, fractions, and decimals. *Lesson 4-5*

Compute fluently and make reasonable estimates.

Grades 6–8 Expectations

- Select appropriate methods and tools for computing with fractions and decimals from among mental computation, estimation, calculators or computers, and paper and pencil, depending on the situation, and apply the selected methods. *Lessons 4-7, 4-8*
- Develop and analyze algorithms for computing with fractions, decimals, and integers and develop fluency in their use. *Lessons 4-1, 4-2, 4-5, 4-6, 4-7*
- Develop and use strategies to estimate the results of rational-number computations and judge the reasonableness of the results. *Lessons 4-4, 4-8*

Algebra

Understand patterns, relations, and functions.

Grades 6–8 Expectations

- Represent, analyze, and generalize a variety of patterns with tables, graphs, words, and when possible, symbolic rules. *Lesson 4-3*

Represent and analyze mathematical situations and structures using algebraic symbols.

Grades 6–8 Expectations

- Use symbolic algebra to represent situations and to solve problems, especially those that involve linear relationships. *Lesson 4-9*

The NCTM 2000 Pre-K through Grade 12 Content Standards are Number and Operations, Algebra, Geometry, Measurement, and Data Analysis and Probability. The Process Standards (Problem Solving, Reasoning and Proof, Communication, Connections, and Representation) are incorporated throughout lessons.

CHAPTER 4

Investigation

Adding and Subtracting Fractions

Activity 1

Use in place of the Investigating the Concept activity before Lesson 4-2.

Adding Fractions with Unlike Denominators

Overview Students create and explain ways to add two fractions with unlike denominators, before learning the traditional algorithm in Lesson 4-2.

Materials (per small group) Centimeter Grid Paper (Teaching Tool 18); scissors

The Task

- Distribute materials.
- **Outline a 4-by-6 rectangle on the grid paper. Draw on the grid lines to divide the rectangle into at least three parts. Make each part a different size. Label each part with a fraction written in simplest form that describes the relation of the part to the whole rectangle. Cut out all the parts. Choose two parts and find their sum, or what part of the whole rectangle they represent. Write the sum in simplest form. Write the steps you followed.**
- **Repeat the task by drawing another 4-by-6 rectangle and dividing it into parts that are different sizes from what you used the first time.**

Observing and Questioning

- Observe how students find sums. If needed, ask the following questions:
- **Would it help to compare the total of the two small parts to the whole rectangle? How?**
- **How could the grid lines on each part help you?**
- Watch for students who are having difficulty writing equivalent fractions. Remind them that each small square on each part is $\frac{1}{24}$ of the whole rectangle.

Sharing and Summarizing

- After students show their work, summarize the different methods used. For example, below Maria compared the part of the rectangle covered by two parts to the whole rectangle. Tyler used the grid lines on two parts to write equivalent fractions with like denominators and then added.
- If no students used equivalent fractions with like denominators, ask, **How could what you know about adding fractions with like denominators help you add fractions with unlike denominators?**
- **Key Idea** As students share their work, summarize the different techniques used. Lesson 4-2 presents the traditional algorithm for adding fractions with unlike denominators which involves writing equivalent fractions with like denominators and writing the sum of the numerators over the common denominator.
- Have students find $\frac{1}{4} + \frac{2}{3}$, using a 4-by-6 rectangle if necessary.
- **Extension** Have students find $\frac{2}{3} - \frac{1}{4}$.

Maria

$\frac{1}{2} + \frac{3}{8}$

The whole rectangle is $\frac{8}{8}$.

Together, $\frac{1}{2}$ and $\frac{3}{8}$ are $\frac{1}{8}$ less than the whole rectangle.

$\frac{1}{2} + \frac{3}{8} = \frac{7}{8}$

Tyler

$\frac{1}{4} + \frac{1}{3}$

$\downarrow \quad \downarrow$

$\frac{6}{24} + \frac{8}{24} = \frac{14}{24} = \frac{7}{12}$

Activity 2

Use in place of the Investigating the Concept activity before Lesson 4-6.

Subtracting Mixed Numbers

Overview

Students create and find ways to subtract mixed numbers before learning the traditional algorithm in Lesson 4-6.

Materials

(per small group) Play money: 4 dollar bills, 2 half dollars, 8 quarters, 20 dimes, 20 nickels

The Task

- Write $1\frac{3}{4} - \frac{3}{10}$, $3 - 1\frac{3}{4}$, and $2\frac{1}{2} - \frac{7}{10}$ on the chalkboard, and distribute materials.
- Review with students what fraction of a dollar is represented by each type of coin.
- **Use dollar bills and coins to find each difference. Write to describe the steps you used to find each difference.**

Observing and Questioning

- Observe how students use the bills and coins to find the differences. If needed, ask the following questions to spur further thinking.
- **Will you subtract bills or coins first? Why?**
- **Can exchanging coins for an equivalent amount of money help you? How?**
- Watch for students who are having difficulty modeling subtraction. Ask, **How can you use bills and coins to model $1\frac{3}{4} - \frac{1}{4}$?**

Sharing and Summarizing

- After students show their work, summarize the steps used. For example, the student pictured below traded a half dollar for dimes and renamed $\frac{1}{2}$ as $\frac{5}{10}$, traded a dollar for dimes and renamed $2\frac{5}{10}$ as $1\frac{15}{10}$, and then subtracted. Ask, **How is subtracting mixed numbers like subtracting whole numbers? How is it different?**
- **Key Idea** Point out the steps needed to subtract mixed numbers. Rename if fractions do not have a common denominator and if more fractional parts are needed. Then subtract fractions and whole numbers. Lesson 4-6 presents this traditional algorithm.

Follow-Up

- Have students find the differences $4 - 2\frac{3}{10}$ and $2\frac{1}{4} - 1\frac{9}{10}$, using play money if needed.

I traded 1 half dollar for 5 dimes. Then I traded $1 bill for 10 dimes. I have $1 and 15 dimes. Now I can subtract 7 dimes.

$2\frac{1}{2} \rightarrow 2\frac{5}{10} \rightarrow 1\frac{15}{10}$

$-\frac{7}{10}$ $\quad$ $\frac{7}{10}$

$1\frac{8}{10} = 1\frac{4}{5}$

CHAPTER 4

Adding and Subtracting Fractions

The focus of Chapter 4 is adding and subtracting fractions and mixed numbers with like and unlike denominators. Problem-solving strategies and skills are also included.

Vocabulary

Also, see Glossary, *pp. 742–748.*

like denominators *(p. 204)*
common denominator *(p. 204)*
unlike denominators *(p. 207)*
least common multiple (LCM) *(p. 152)*
least common denominator (LCD) *(p. 164)*
round *(p. 14)*
mixed number *(p. 168)*

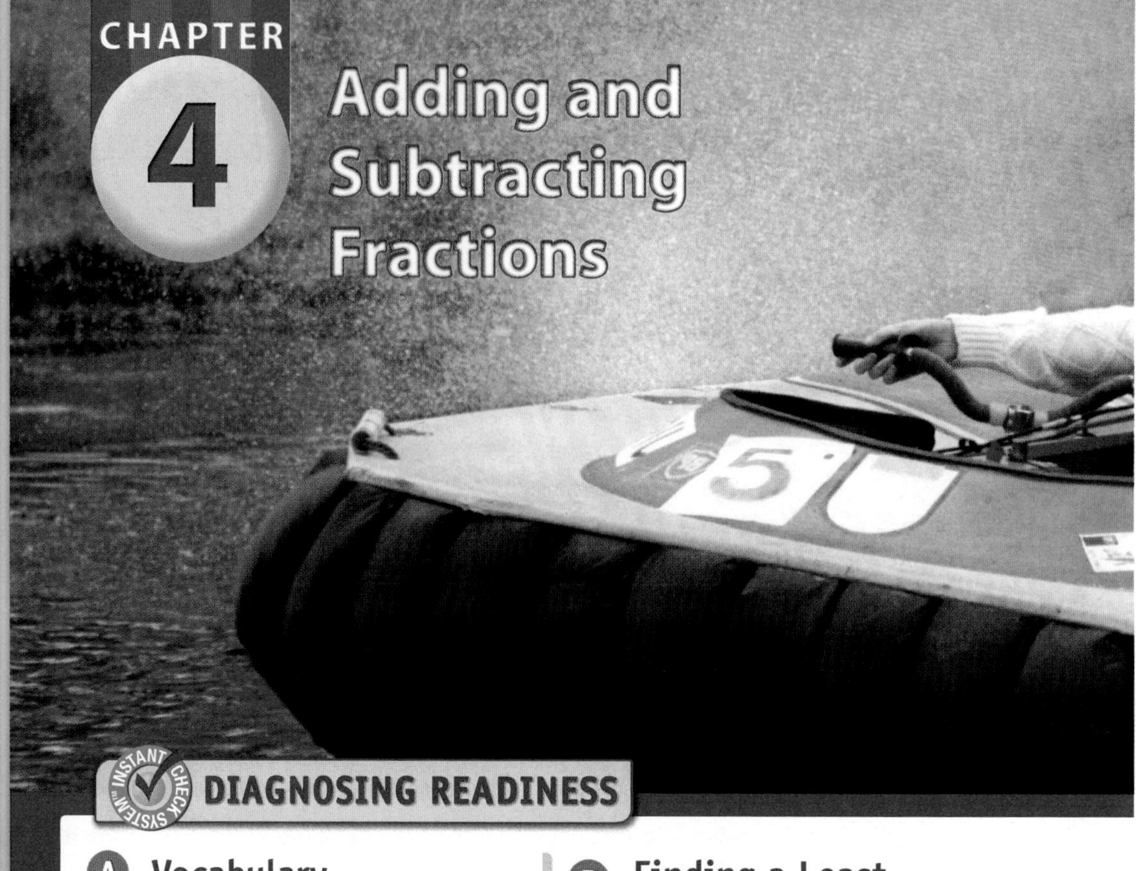

INSTANT CHECK SYSTEM DIAGNOSING READINESS

A Vocabulary
(pages 146, 164, 168)

Choose the best term from the box.

1. Numbers which contain a whole number and a fraction are called __?__. **mixed numbers**
2. __?__ have numerators greater than or equal to denominators. **Improper fractions**
3. Fractions that name the same part of a whole or a set are __?__. **equivalent fractions**
4. A fraction in __?__ has a numerator and denominator with no common factor. **simplest form**

Vocabulary
- **improper fractions** *(p. 168)*
- **equivalent fractions** *(p. 164)*
- **simplest form** *(p. 164)*
- **mixed numbers** *(p. 168)*
- **prime number** *(p. 146)*

B Finding a Least Common Multiple
(pages 152–153)

Find the least common multiple for each set of numbers.

5. 7, 21 **21**
6. 8, 12 **24**
7. 3, 9 **9**
8. 4, 10, 12 **60**
9. 12, 18 **36**
10. 16, 32, 48 **96**
11. 7, 5 **35**
12. 12, 20, 36 **180**
13. Rita wants to give her nieces her silver dollar collection. She plans to give Nicole $\frac{2}{5}$ the coins, Karen $\frac{1}{3}$ the coins, and Wendy $\frac{1}{4}$ the coins. What is the least number of silver dollars Rita could have in her collection for each niece to get the allotted share? **60 silver dollars**

202

Math Vocabulary Kit

Every vocabulary word is written on a card with the definition of the word printed on the back. Vocabulary activities are provided in the *Math Vocabulary Kit Teacher's Guide.*

Add the words from the *Vocabulary* list at the left to your Math Word Wall.

unlike fractions

least common denominator

mixed number

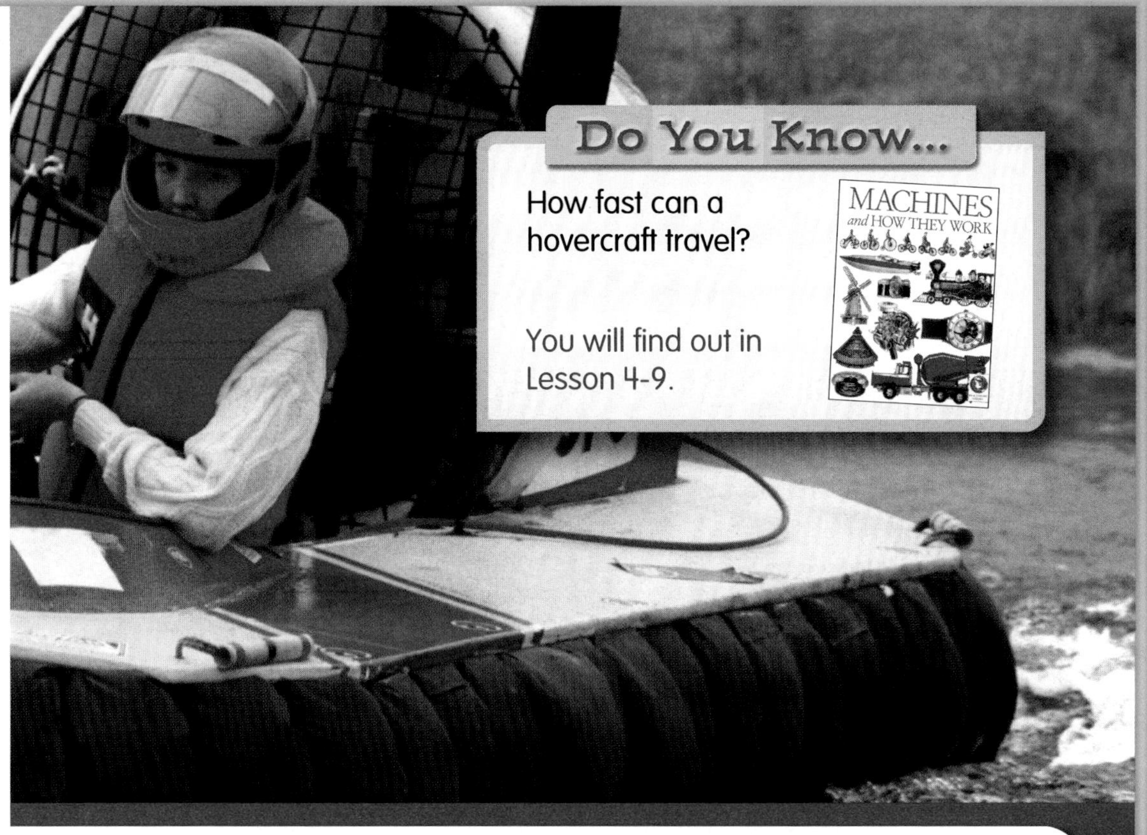

Do You Know...
How fast can a hovercraft travel?
You will find out in Lesson 4-9.
MACHINES
and HOW THEY WORK

C Relating Fractions and Mixed Numbers

(pages 168–169)

Find each missing number.

14. $\frac{18}{5} = 3\frac{\square}{5}$ **3**

15. $8 = 7\frac{5}{\square}$ **5**

16. $\frac{29}{6} = 4\frac{5}{\square}$ **6**

17. $\frac{7}{3} = \square\frac{1}{3}$ **2**

18. $9 = \square\frac{8}{8}$ **8**

19. $\frac{10}{5} = \square$ **2**

20. $5\frac{4}{9} = \frac{\square}{9}$ **49**

21. $\frac{23}{4} = \square\frac{3}{4}$ **5**

22. Cathy buys 18 inches of ribbon. How many feet is this? **$1\frac{1}{2}$ feet**

23. You have 5 oranges cut into thirds. How many friends could each be given 2 pieces if you save 1 piece for yourself? **7 friends**

D Adding and Subtracting Decimals

(pages 86–89)

Estimate each answer. Then find each answer. **Sample estimates are given.**

24. 5.63 + 17.89 **24; 23.52**

25. 40.89 + 7.27 **48; 48.16**

26. 56 − 42.52 **13; 13.48**

27. 23.5 − 5.88 **18; 17.62**

28. 9.15 + 0.352 **9; 9.502**

29. 10.66 − 9.6 **1; 1.06**

30. 15 − 14.38 **1; 0.62**

31. 62.5 + 3.89 **67; 66.39**

32. Dean bought a paintbrush for $7.98, a gallon of paint for $34.95, and a paint scraper for $2.49. What was the total of his bill, not including tax? **$45.42**

33. Cedric lives 1.87 miles from school and Sam lives 2.14 miles from school. How much farther does Sam live from school than Cedric? **0.27 miles**

203

Literature: Dorling Kindersley and Other Sources

Factastic Millennium Facts
Russell Ash. New York: Dorling Kindersley Publishing, Inc., 1999.

Use with Lesson 4-2 Packed with intriguing information and entertaining anecdotes, this book filled with facts from the last 1,000 years provides many opportunities for work with fractions.
Available in the Scott Foresman Dorling Kindersley Literature Library.

Insects (National Audubon Society First Field Guide)
New York: Scholastic, Inc., 1998.

Use with Lesson 4-6 Contains photographs, descriptions, lengths (given as mixed numbers), habits, and ranges of many insects.

The Olympic Summer Games
Caroline Arnold. New York: Franklin Watts, 1991.

Use with Lesson 4-7 Discusses the history and organization of the Olympics; describes individual sporting events of the summer Olympics.

INSTANT CHECK SYSTEM DIAGNOSING READINESS

Purpose Diagnose students' readiness by assessing prerequisite content.

- Assign each set of exercises and go over the answers.
- Check to see which students did not get at least 66% of the exercises correct in a section.

  Section A: 3 out of 4
  Section B: 6 out of 9
  Section C: 7 out of 10
  Section D: 7 out of 10

- For intervention, use the resources listed at the right.

Item Analysis for Diagnosis and Intervention

Objective	Items	Student Book Pages*	Intervention System
Recall the definitions of equivalent fractions, simplest form, improper fractions, and mixed numbers.	1–4	164, 168	H3, H15, H24
Find the least common multiple of two or more numbers.	5–13	152–153	H5
Relate fractions and mixed numbers.	14–23	168–169	H15
Add and subtract decimals.	24–33	86–89	I15–I16

*For each lesson, there is a *Reteaching* activity in *Reaching All Learners* and a *Reteaching* master.

Lesson Organizer

Quick Lesson Overview

Objective Add and subtract fractions with like denominators, and simplify the answer, if possible.

Math Understanding When adding or subtracting fractions with like denominators, you are adding or subtracting pieces or portions of the same size, so you can add the numerators—the number of pieces or portions—without changing the denominator.

Vocabulary Like denominators, common denominator

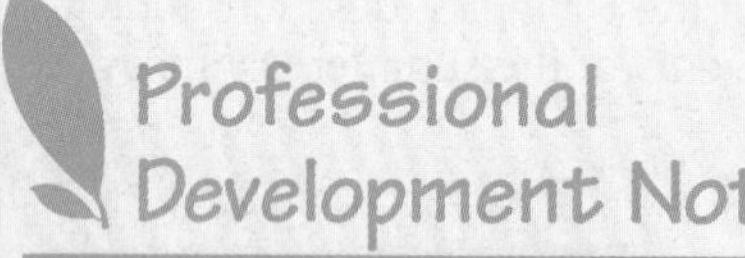

Research Base

Kieren's (1988) research has suggested that instruction with addition and subtraction of fractions should be built on intuitive ideas and the use of manipulatives or other models. In this lesson and the next, students will use the ideas they have previously developed about fractions to add fractions with either like or unlike denominators.

NCTM Standards

- Number and Operations

(For a complete correlation to the NCTM Standards and Grades 6–8 Expectations, see pages 202G–H.)

Getting Started

Spiral Review

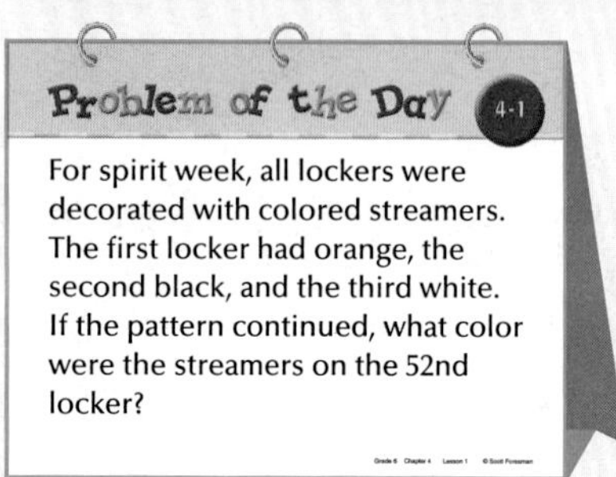

Problem of the Day 4-1

For spirit week, all lockers were decorated with colored streamers. The first locker had orange, the second black, and the third white. If the pattern continued, what color were the streamers on the 52nd locker?

Topics Reviewed

- Multiples and divisibility
- Problem-Solving Strategy: Solve a Simpler Problem

Answer The 52nd locker was decorated orange.

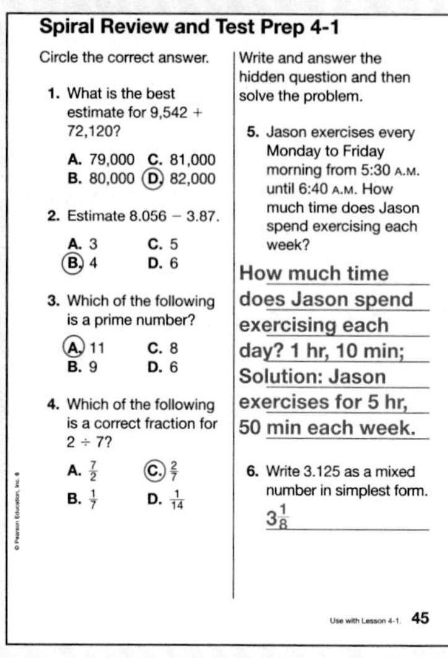

Spiral Review and Test Prep 4-1

Circle the correct answer.

1. What is the best estimate for 9,542 + 72,120?
   A. 79,000 C. 81,000
   B. 80,000 (D.) 82,000

2. Estimate 8.056 − 3.87.
   A. 3 C. 5
   (B.) 4 D. 6

3. Which of the following is a prime number?
   (A.) 11 C. 8
   B. 9 D. 6

4. Which of the following is a correct fraction for 2 ÷ 7?
   A. $\frac{7}{2}$ (C.) $\frac{2}{7}$
   B. $\frac{1}{7}$ D. $\frac{1}{14}$

Write and answer the hidden question and then solve the problem.

5. Jason exercises every Monday to Friday morning from 5:30 A.M. until 6:40 A.M. How much time does Jason spend exercising each week?
   How much time does Jason spend exercising each day? 1 hr, 10 min; Solution: Jason exercises for 5 hr, 50 min each week.

6. Write 3.125 as a mixed number in simplest form.
   $3\frac{1}{8}$

© Pearson Education, Inc. 6

Use with Lesson 4-1. 45

Available as a transparency and as a blackline master

Topics Reviewed

1.–2. Estimating sums; **3.** Prime and composite numbers; **4.** Understanding fractions; **5.** Multiple-step problems; **6.** Connecting decimals with fractions; **7.** Ordering fractions and decimals

Investigating the Concept

Add and Subtract Fractions Using Rectangles

 15–20 MIN **Visual/Spatial** 

Materials *(per student)* $\frac{1}{4}$-Inch Grid Paper (Teaching Tool 10); markers

What to Do

- Draw a 3-by-5 rectangular grid on the board. **How many squares are there? What fraction does each square show?** *(15 squares; $\frac{1}{15}$)* **Let's add $\frac{2}{15}$ and $\frac{7}{15}$.** Use two colors of chalk to show the addition. Write the equation $\frac{2}{15} + \frac{7}{15} = \frac{9}{15}$ under the model. **Is the answer in simplest form?** *(No)* **Why not?** *(3 is a factor of both 9 and 15.)* Have a volunteer simplify it. *($\frac{3}{5}$)* Repeat the discussion for the subtraction problem $\frac{11}{15} - \frac{6}{15} = \frac{5}{15}$. Have students use a color for the first fraction and Xs for the subtraction.
- **Use grid paper to make two more addition and two more subtraction models.**

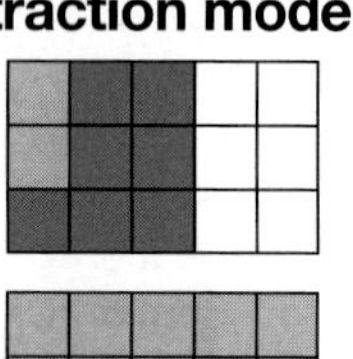

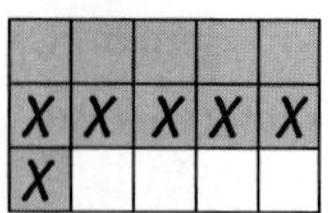

Ongoing Assessment

- **Reasoning When you add two fractions that are each greater than $\frac{1}{2}$, how does the sum compare to 1?** *(The sum is greater than 1.)*

 EC NTL 12 11 10 9 8 7 6 5 4 3 2

Reaching All Learners

Math and Literature

Recipes from the Past

 15–20 MIN **Linguistic** 

Materials *(per class)* Copies of recipes from *Samantha's Cookbook: A Peek at Dining in the Past with Meals You Can Cook Today (American Girls Collection)* by Jodi Evert, Terri Braun, et al (Pleasant Company Publications, 1994)

- Summary: Includes recipes for foods a young girl might have made one hundred years ago.
- Have students choose a recipe from the book and determine the amounts of ingredients for two batches.
- Students may also enjoy looking for recipes in *Strudel Stories* by Joanne Rocklin (Yearling Books, Random House, 2000)

Extend Language

English Language Learners

Naming Denominators

 10–15 MIN **Verbal** 

- Write *denominator* on the board. Circle *nomin*. ***Nomin*** **is an old word for *name*. In a math word problem, the number in the denominator names the total number of objects in the group.**
- Model giving names to denominators. **The 6 in $\frac{5}{6}$ can be 6 (equal) pieces of apple pie or 6 items of clothes.**
- Display $\frac{1}{8} + \frac{2}{8}$ on the board. Have students use complete sentences to tell what things the denominators might stand for.

Reteaching

Add and Subtract with Number Lines

 15–20 MIN **Logical/Mathematical** 

- Draw a number line showing ninths. Draw a segment above $\frac{1}{9}$. **How can I add $\frac{5}{9}$ to this?** *(Move 5 spaces to the right.)* Complete the model by drawing the arrow and a segment above $\frac{6}{9}$. Repeat with $\frac{5}{9} - \frac{2}{9}$ by starting at $\frac{5}{9}$ and moving 2 spaces to the left.
- Have partners agree on a denominator. Have Partner 1 show an addition model and Partner 2 shows a subtraction model. They trade papers and write the corresponding equations. Have them repeat the activity using three other denominators.

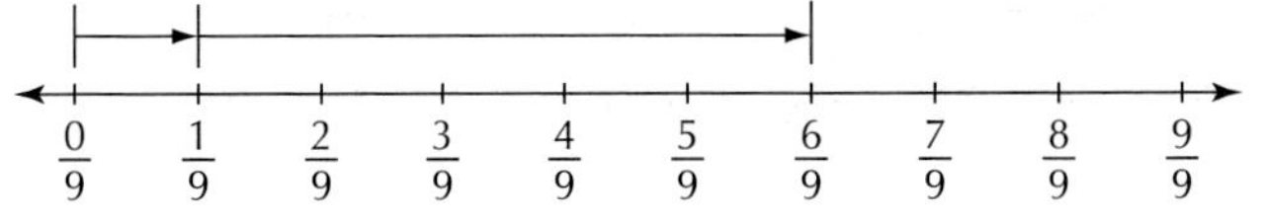

Math and Technology

Adding Fractions

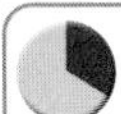 15–20 MIN **Visual** 

Materials Fraction eTool

- **Use the Fraction eTool to represent sums of fractions. Use the *Pieces* mode of the basic workspace.**
- Have students add wedges with the same denominator to represent sums less than one.
- Have students add wedges with the same denominator to represent sums greater than one.

Objective Add and subtract fractions with like denominators, and simplify the answer, if possible.

1 Warm Up

Activate Prior Knowledge Review writing proper fractions in simplest form and improper fractions as mixed numbers in simplest form.

2 Teach

LEARN The lesson uses square models. Have students also show the examples with Fraction Models: Circles and Number Lines (Teaching Tools 14, 2).

Ongoing Assessment

Talk About It: Question 1

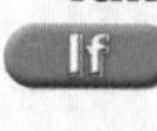

If students do not realize that the same number must be used for all three *x*s,

then ask:

What has happened to the numerators to get the sum? *(Five was added to three.)*

When can you add the numerators? *(Only when the denominators are the same)*

CHECK ✓

Error Intervention

If students forget to simplify answers,

then remind them to check if the numerator is greater than the denominator or if the numerator and denominator have any common factors. *(Also see* Reteaching, *p. 204B.)*

Lesson 4-1

Key Idea
Fractions with like denominators are easy to add and subtract because the denominators represent pieces of the same size.

Vocabulary
- like denominators
- common denominator

Think It Through
I can **use a picture** to help me find the answer.

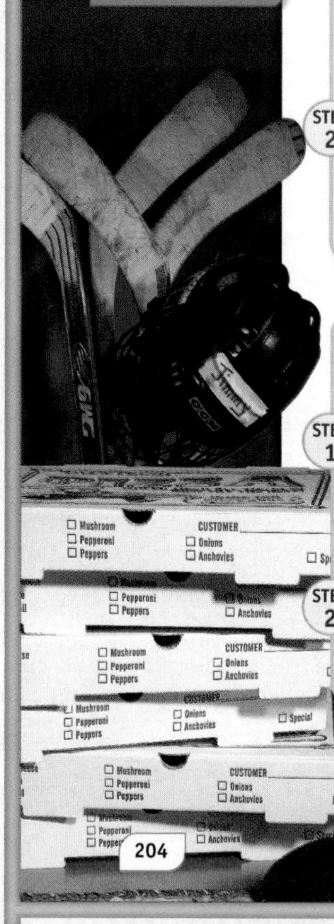

Adding and Subtracting Fractions with Like Denominators

✓ WARM UP

Simplify.

1. $\frac{9}{12}$ $\frac{3}{4}$
2. $\frac{12}{16}$ $\frac{3}{4}$
3. $\frac{12}{8}$ $1\frac{1}{2}$
4. $\frac{15}{9}$ $1\frac{2}{3}$

LEARN

How can you find sums and differences of fractions?

Example A

Darla's hockey team ordered different pizzas that were the same size and cut into 16 equal pieces. Darla ate $\frac{3}{16}$ of a veggie pizza, and $\frac{1}{16}$ of a cheese pizza. What fraction of a whole pizza did she eat in all?

Find $\frac{3}{16} + \frac{1}{16}$.	What You **Think**	What You **Write**
STEP 1 The fractions have **like denominators.** Add the numerators. Write the sum over the **common denominator.**	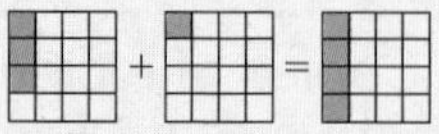 [square models]	$\frac{3}{16} + \frac{1}{16} = \frac{4}{16}$
STEP 2 Simplify if possible.	The GCF of 4 and 16 is 4. $\frac{4 \div 4}{16 \div 4} = \frac{1}{4}$	$\frac{3}{16} + \frac{1}{16} = \frac{4}{16} = \frac{1}{4}$

Darla ate $\frac{1}{4}$ of a whole pizza.

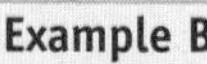

Example B

Find $\frac{8}{16} - \frac{6}{16}$.	What You **Think**	What You **Write**
STEP 1 The fractions have like denominators. Subtract the numerators. Write the difference over the common denominator.	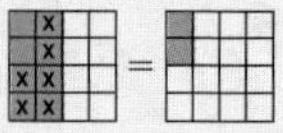 [square models]	$\frac{8}{16} - \frac{6}{16} = \frac{2}{16}$
STEP 2 Simplify if possible.	The GCF of 2 and 16 is 2. $\frac{2 \div 2}{16 \div 2} = \frac{1}{8}$	$\frac{8}{16} - \frac{6}{16} = \frac{2}{16} = \frac{1}{8}$

✓ Talk About It

1. Give 3 different values for x that make the equation $\frac{3}{x} + \frac{5}{x} = \frac{8}{x}$ true.
Sample answers: 10, 17, 20

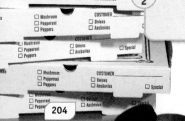

204

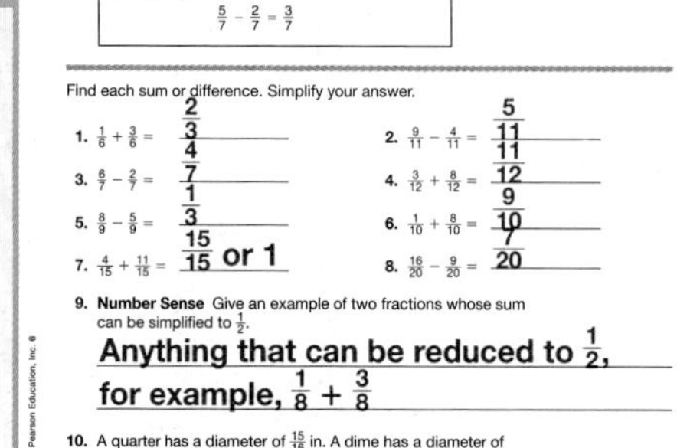

Reteaching — Below Level

Adding and Subtracting Fractions with Like Denominators R 4-1

How to find sums or differences of fractions with like denominators:

Find $\frac{2}{14} + \frac{6}{14}$. The fractions have like denominators, so you can just add the numerators.

$\frac{2}{14} + \frac{6}{14} = \frac{8}{14}$ Write the sum over the common denominator.

$\frac{8}{14} = \frac{4}{7}$ Simplify if possible.

Find $\frac{5}{7} - \frac{2}{7}$. The denominators are the same, so you can subtract the numerators.

$\frac{5}{7} - \frac{2}{7} = \frac{3}{7}$ $\frac{3}{7}$ cannot be simplified, so $\frac{5}{7} - \frac{2}{7} = \frac{3}{7}$

Find each sum or difference. Simplify your answer.

1. $\frac{1}{6} + \frac{3}{6} =$ **$\frac{2}{3}$**
2. $\frac{9}{11} - \frac{4}{11} =$ **$\frac{5}{11}$**
3. $\frac{6}{7} - \frac{2}{7} =$ **$\frac{4}{7}$**
4. $\frac{3}{12} + \frac{8}{12} =$ **$\frac{11}{12}$**
5. $\frac{8}{9} - \frac{5}{9} =$ **$\frac{1}{3}$**
6. $\frac{1}{10} + \frac{8}{10} =$ **$\frac{9}{10}$**
7. $\frac{4}{15} + \frac{11}{15} =$ **$\frac{15}{15}$ or 1**
8. $\frac{16}{20} - \frac{9}{20} =$ **$\frac{7}{20}$**
9. **Number Sense** Give an example of two fractions whose sum can be simplified to $\frac{1}{2}$.
Anything that can be reduced to $\frac{1}{2}$, for example, $\frac{1}{8} + \frac{3}{8}$
10. A quarter has a diameter of $\frac{15}{16}$ in. A dime has a diameter of $\frac{11}{16}$ in., and a nickel has a diameter of $\frac{13}{16}$ in. If you put each coin side by side, what is the combined width of the three coins?
$\frac{39}{16}$ in., or $2\frac{7}{16}$ in.

Use with Lesson 4-1. 45

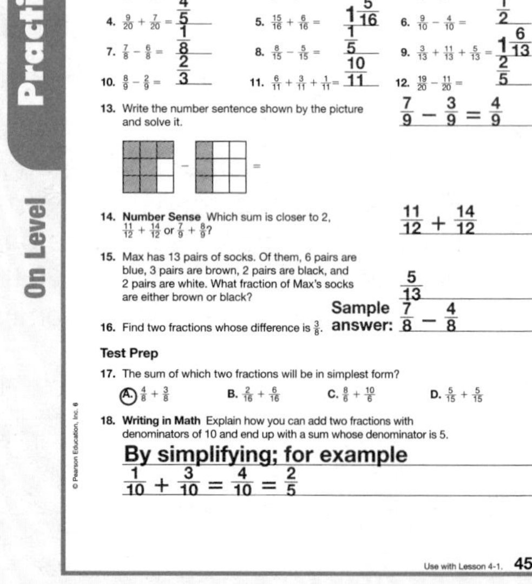

Practice — On Level

Adding and Subtracting Fractions with Like Denominators P 4-1

Find each sum or difference. Simplify your answer.

1. $\frac{6}{11} + \frac{4}{11} =$ **$\frac{10}{11}$**
2. $\frac{5}{9} - \frac{2}{9} =$ **$\frac{1}{3}$**
3. $\frac{5}{3} + \frac{4}{3} =$ **3**
4. $\frac{9}{20} + \frac{7}{20} =$ **$\frac{4}{5}$**
5. $\frac{15}{16} + \frac{6}{16} =$ **$1\frac{5}{16}$**
6. $\frac{9}{10} - \frac{4}{10} =$ **$\frac{1}{2}$**
7. $\frac{7}{8} - \frac{6}{8} =$ **$\frac{1}{8}$**
8. $\frac{8}{15} - \frac{5}{15} =$ **$\frac{1}{5}$**
9. $\frac{3}{13} + \frac{11}{13} + \frac{5}{13} =$ **$1\frac{6}{13}$**
10. $\frac{8}{9} - \frac{2}{9} =$ **$\frac{2}{3}$**
11. $\frac{6}{11} + \frac{3}{11} + \frac{1}{11} =$ **$\frac{10}{11}$**
12. $\frac{19}{20} - \frac{11}{20} =$ **$\frac{2}{5}$**
13. Write the number sentence shown by the picture and solve it. **$\frac{7}{9} - \frac{3}{9} = \frac{4}{9}$**
14. **Number Sense** Which sum is closer to 2, $\frac{11}{12} + \frac{14}{12}$ or $\frac{7}{9} + \frac{8}{9}$? **$\frac{11}{12} + \frac{14}{12}$**
15. Max has 13 pairs of socks. Of them, 6 pairs are blue, 3 pairs are brown, 2 pairs are black, and 2 pairs are white. What fraction of Max's socks are either brown or black? **$\frac{5}{13}$**
16. Find two fractions whose difference is $\frac{3}{8}$. **Sample answer: $\frac{7}{8} - \frac{4}{8}$**

Test Prep

17. The sum of which two fractions will be in simplest form?
(A.) $\frac{4}{8} + \frac{3}{8}$ B. $\frac{2}{16} + \frac{6}{16}$ C. $\frac{8}{6} + \frac{10}{6}$ D. $\frac{5}{15} + \frac{5}{15}$
18. **Writing in Math** Explain how you can add two fractions with denominators of 10 and end up with a sum whose denominator is 5.
By simplifying; for example $\frac{1}{10} + \frac{3}{10} = \frac{4}{10} = \frac{2}{5}$

Use with Lesson 4-1. 45

CHECK

For another example, see Set 4-1 on p. 240.

Find each sum or difference. Simplify your answer.

1. $\frac{6}{15}+\frac{3}{15}$ **$\frac{3}{5}$**
2. $\frac{10}{14}-\frac{3}{14}$ **$\frac{1}{2}$**
3. $\frac{11}{20}-\frac{3}{20}$ **$\frac{2}{5}$**
4. $\frac{5}{8}+\frac{1}{8}$ **$\frac{3}{4}$**
5. $\frac{5}{12}+\frac{11}{12}+\frac{1}{12}$ **$1\frac{5}{12}$**
6. **Number Sense** Is $\frac{4}{5}+\frac{3}{5}$ less than, equal to, or greater than 1? Without computing, how can you tell? **Greater than 1; Both $\frac{4}{5}$ and $\frac{3}{5}$ are greater than $\frac{1}{2}$, so adding them together will yield a number greater than 1.**

PRACTICE

For more practice, see Set 4-1 on p. 243.

A Skills and Understanding

Find each sum or difference. Simplify your answer.

7. $\frac{2}{15}+\frac{4}{15}$ **$\frac{2}{5}$**
8. $\frac{3}{9}+\frac{5}{9}$ **$\frac{8}{9}$**
9. $\frac{7}{16}-\frac{3}{16}$ **$\frac{1}{4}$**
10. $\frac{7}{12}+\frac{11}{12}$ **$1\frac{1}{2}$**
11. $\frac{5}{3}-\frac{2}{3}$ **1**
12. $\frac{9}{10}-\frac{3}{10}$ **$\frac{3}{5}$**
13. $\frac{9}{20}+\frac{6}{20}$ **$\frac{3}{4}$**
14. $\frac{12}{18}-\frac{9}{18}$ **$\frac{1}{6}$**
15. $\frac{7}{9}-\frac{4}{9}$ **$\frac{1}{3}$**
16. $\frac{3}{16}+\frac{9}{16}+\frac{11}{16}$ **$1\frac{7}{16}$**
17. **Number Sense** Give 2 fractions with like denominators whose sum is greater than 1. **Sample answer: $\frac{5}{7}+\frac{6}{7}$**

B Reasoning and Problem Solving

18. What is the total amount of garlic powder, dry mustard, and paprika? **$1\frac{1}{2}$ tsp.**
19. How much olive oil and sugar would you need to make 8 servings? **See above.**
20. **Writing in Math** Malcolm says, "Adding fractions is easier if you just add the numerators and then the denominators." Use an example to explain why Malcolm's idea doesn't work. **See below.**

19. $1\frac{1}{2}$ cup olive oil; $\frac{1}{2}$ tsp. sugar

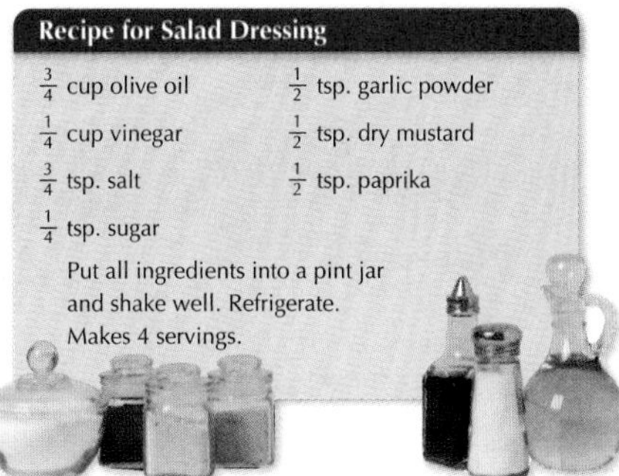
Recipe for Salad Dressing

$\frac{3}{4}$ cup olive oil	$\frac{1}{2}$ tsp. garlic powder
$\frac{1}{4}$ cup vinegar	$\frac{1}{2}$ tsp. dry mustard
$\frac{3}{4}$ tsp. salt	$\frac{1}{2}$ tsp. paprika
$\frac{1}{4}$ tsp. sugar	

Put all ingredients into a pint jar and shake well. Refrigerate. Makes 4 servings.

Mixed Review and Test Prep

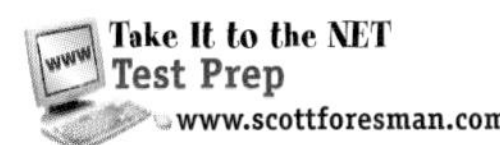

Copy and complete the following table.

21.

Fraction	$4\frac{3}{5}$	$\frac{9}{10}$	$\frac{2}{3}$	$\frac{1}{3}$	$\frac{5}{6}$
Decimal	4.6	0.9	**$0.\overline{6}$**	0.3	**$0.8\overline{3}$**

22. Order from least to greatest. 0.4, 1.6, $\frac{1}{5}$, $\frac{9}{15}$

A. $\frac{9}{15}$, 0.4, 1.6, $\frac{1}{5}$ B. $\frac{1}{5}$, $\frac{9}{15}$, 0.4, 1.6 C. $\frac{9}{15}$, $\frac{1}{5}$, 1.6, 0.4 **(D.)** $\frac{1}{5}$, 0.4, $\frac{9}{15}$, 1.6

20. Sample answer: $\frac{1}{2}+\frac{1}{4}\neq\frac{2}{6}$; you must have a common denominator to add fractions.

 All text pages available online and on CD-ROM.

3 Practice

Exercise 20 Remind students that they can draw models as part of their explanations of why Malcolm's idea does not work.

Leveled Practice

- **Below Level** Ex. 7–17, 20–22
- **On Level** Ex. 9–22
- **Above Level** Ex. 9–22

Early Finishers Have students use fractional parts of quarts to create a punch recipe with at least four different ingredients. Have them add to find the total number of quarts and then convert to 1-cup servings.

4 Assess

Journal Idea Have students shade a 4-by-4 square to show $\frac{5}{16}$ and add a fraction to $\frac{5}{16}$ so that the sum is greater than $\frac{1}{2}$. Then have them shade another 4-by-4 square to show $\frac{5}{16}$ and subtract a fraction so that the difference is less than $\frac{1}{4}$. Have them explain how they found their answers.

Enrichment — Above Level

Tri-Puzzling E 4-1 NUMBER SENSE

The sum of the fractions on each side of each triangle is the same. Complete each triangle by filling in the missing fractions.

Sample answers are given.

1. Top: $\frac{12}{32}$; left side: $\frac{8}{32}$; right side: **$\frac{4}{32}$**; bottom: **$\frac{6}{32}$**, **$\frac{10}{32}$**, $\frac{10}{32}$
2. Top: $\frac{11}{19}$; left side: **$\frac{3}{19}$**; right side: $\frac{1}{19}$; bottom: $\frac{4}{19}$, **$\frac{8}{19}$**, **$\frac{6}{19}$**
3. Top: **$\frac{14}{64}$**; left side: $\frac{37}{64}$; right side: $\frac{9}{64}$; bottom: $\frac{4}{64}$, **$\frac{19}{64}$**, **$\frac{32}{64}$**

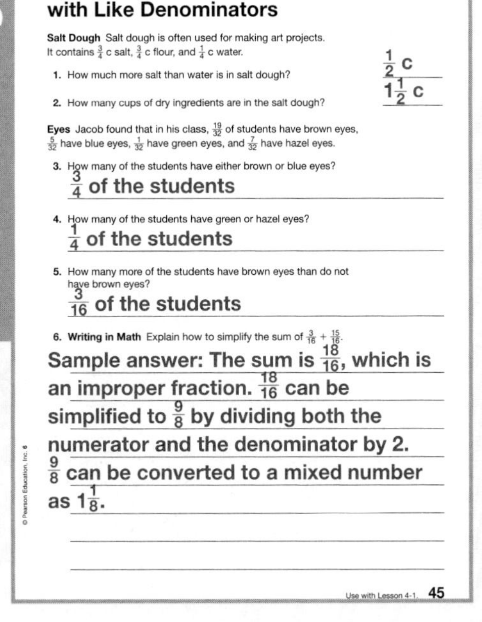
Problem Solving

Adding and Subtracting Fractions with Like Denominators PS 4-1

Salt Dough Salt dough is often used for making art projects. It contains $\frac{3}{4}$ c salt, $\frac{3}{4}$ c flour, and $\frac{1}{4}$ c water.

1. How much more salt than water is in salt dough? **$\frac{1}{2}$ c**
2. How many cups of dry ingredients are in the salt dough? **$1\frac{1}{2}$ c**

Eyes Jacob found that in his class, $\frac{19}{32}$ of students have brown eyes, $\frac{5}{32}$ have blue eyes, $\frac{3}{32}$ have green eyes, and $\frac{5}{32}$ have hazel eyes.

3. How many of the students have either brown or blue eyes? **$\frac{3}{4}$ of the students**
4. How many of the students have green or hazel eyes? **$\frac{1}{4}$ of the students**
5. How many more of the students have brown eyes than do not have brown eyes? **$\frac{3}{16}$ of the students**
6. **Writing in Math** Explain how to simplify the sum of $\frac{3}{16}+\frac{15}{16}$. **Sample answer: The sum is $\frac{18}{16}$, which is an improper fraction. $\frac{18}{16}$ can be simplified to $\frac{9}{8}$ by dividing both the numerator and the denominator by 2. $\frac{9}{8}$ can be converted to a mixed number as $1\frac{1}{8}$.**

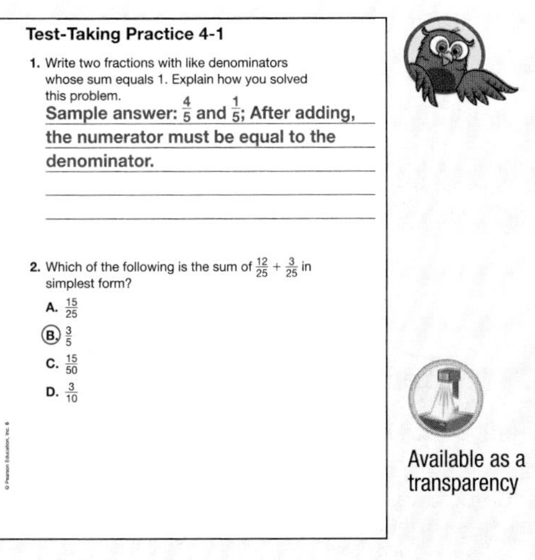
Test-Taking Practice 4-1

1. Write two fractions with like denominators whose sum equals 1. Explain how you solved this problem. **Sample answer: $\frac{4}{5}$ and $\frac{1}{5}$; After adding, the numerator must be equal to the denominator.**
2. Which of the following is the sum of $\frac{12}{25}+\frac{3}{25}$ in simplest form?
   A. $\frac{15}{25}$
   (B.) $\frac{3}{5}$
   C. $\frac{15}{50}$
   D. $\frac{3}{10}$

Available as a transparency

Lesson Organizer

Quick Lesson Overview

Objective Find common denominators for fractions with unlike denominators and find their sums and differences in simplest form.

Math Understanding To obtain a sum or difference of fractions, they first must be expressed using equal-sized pieces or portions. The least common denominator represents the largest possible size of these pieces or portions.

Vocabulary Unlike denominators, least common multiple (LCM) (p. 152), least common denominator (LCD) (p. 164)

Materials for Student Pages
Fraction Strips or Teaching Tool 15 or Fractions eTool

Professional Development Note

Effective Questioning Techniques
Students who persist in "adding the tops and adding the bottoms" when adding fractions with unlike denominators may need help in developing number sense for fractions. Showing both fractions as models will help. Ask estimation questions such as, Will the answer be more or less than $\frac{1}{2}$? More or less than 1 whole?

NCTM Standards

- Number and Operations

(For a complete correlation to the NCTM Standards and Grades 6–8 Expectations, see pages 202G–H.)

Getting Started

Spiral Review

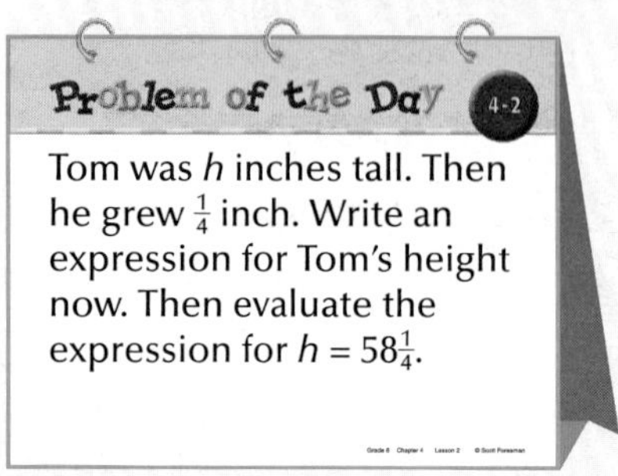

Problem of the Day 4-2

Tom was h inches tall. Then he grew $\frac{1}{4}$ inch. Write an expression for Tom's height now. Then evaluate the expression for $h = 58\frac{1}{4}$.

Topics Reviewed

- Adding mixed numbers; evaluating expressions
- Problem-Solving Skill: Translating Words into Expressions

Answer $h + \frac{1}{4}$; $58\frac{1}{2}$ in.

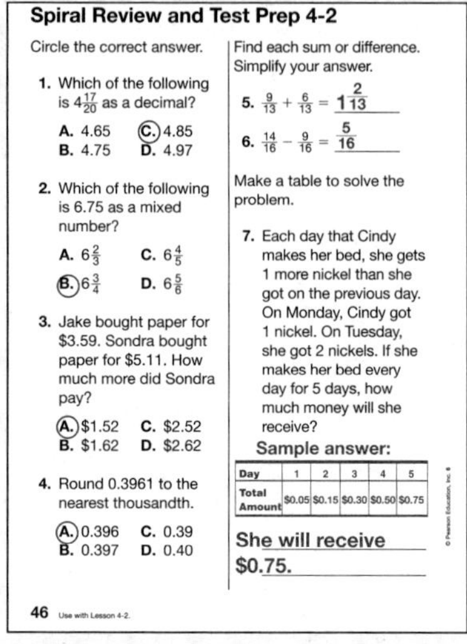

Spiral Review and Test Prep 4-2

Circle the correct answer.

1. Which of the following is $4\frac{17}{20}$ as a decimal?
   A. 4.65 (C.) 4.85
   B. 4.75 D. 4.97
2. Which of the following is 6.75 as a mixed number?
   A. $6\frac{2}{3}$ C. $6\frac{4}{5}$
   (B.) $6\frac{3}{4}$ D. $6\frac{5}{6}$
3. Jake bought paper for \$3.59. Sondra bought paper for \$5.11. How much more did Sondra pay?
   (A.) \$1.52 C. \$2.52
   B. \$1.62 D. \$2.62
4. Round 0.3961 to the nearest thousandth.
   (A.) 0.396 C. 0.39
   B. 0.397 D. 0.40

Find each sum or difference. Simplify your answer.

5. $\frac{9}{13} + \frac{6}{13} = 1\frac{2}{13}$
6. $\frac{14}{16} - \frac{9}{16} = \frac{5}{16}$

Make a table to solve the problem.

7. Each day that Cindy makes her bed, she gets 1 more nickel than she got on the previous day. On Monday, Cindy got 1 nickel. On Tuesday, she got 2 nickels. If she makes her bed every day for 5 days, how much money will she receive?

Sample answer:

Day	1	2	3	4	5
Total Amount	\$0.05	\$0.15	\$0.30	\$0.50	\$0.75

She will receive \$0.75.

46 Use with Lesson 4-2.

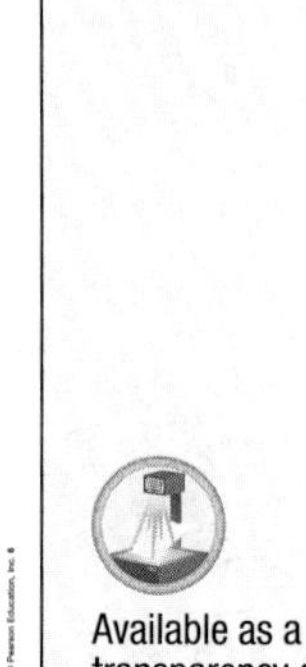

Available as a transparency and as a blackline master

Topics Reviewed
1.–2. Connecting fractions and decimals; **3.** Subtracting decimals; **4.** Rounding decimals; **5.** Adding fractions with like denominators; **6.** Subtracting fractions with like denominators; **7.** Make a table

Investigating the Concept

Adding with Fraction Strips

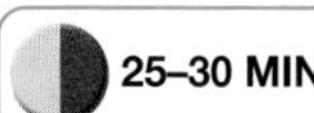

25–30 MIN **Kinesthetic** SMALL GROUP

Materials *(per group)* Fraction Strips or Teaching Tool 15; markers; scissors

What to Do

- Have groups agree on colors for the fractions—red for halves, orange for thirds, and so on—and then color and cut out the strips.
- **Show strips for $\frac{1}{2}$ plus $\frac{1}{6}$. We can add if the denominators are the same. Make a trade so the denominators are the same.** *($\frac{1}{2}$ for three $\frac{1}{6}$)* **The sum is $\frac{4}{6}$. Show in simplest form.** *(Trade four $\frac{1}{6}$ for two $\frac{1}{3}$.)*
- Record the addition on the board: $\frac{1}{2} + \frac{1}{6} = \frac{3}{6} + \frac{1}{6} = \frac{4}{6} = \frac{2}{3}$
- Have groups create, model, and record several more addition problems.

Ongoing Assessment

- **Number Sense Is $\frac{3}{4} + \frac{1}{6}$ greater than 1? Explain.** *(No; $\frac{1}{6}$ is less than $\frac{1}{4}$.)*

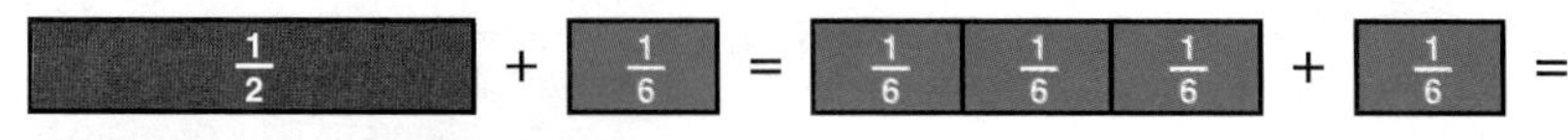

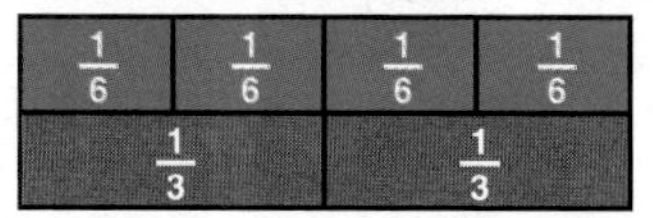

Reaching All Learners

Math Vocabulary

Name the Problem Parts

 10–15 MIN **Linguistic** 

- Write these terms on the board:

LCM	LCD
simplify	simplest form
numerator	denominator
improper fraction	mixed number
common denominator	equivalent fractions
like denominators	unlike denominators

- Write this problem on the board. Have students take turns coming to the board, choosing a term, and showing where it occurs in the problem.

$$\frac{7}{8} \rightarrow \frac{7\times 3}{8\times 3} \rightarrow \frac{21}{24}$$
$$+\frac{1}{6} \rightarrow \frac{1\times 4}{6\times 4} \rightarrow +\frac{4}{24}$$
$$\frac{25}{24} = 1\frac{1}{24}$$

Activate Prior Knowledge/Build Background

English Language Learners

Describing Denominators

 10–15 MIN **Verbal/Visual/Spatial** 

Materials *(per pair)* Classroom objects; fruit; bag

- Take objects, such as school supplies and pieces of fruit, out of a bag one by one. Ask each pair to group them by how they are alike.
- Write $\frac{1}{5}$, $\frac{2}{3}$, $\frac{2}{5}$ on the board. **Which fractions can be added as shown? How are they alike? Which fraction cannot be added as shown with the other fractions? Why?**
- Explain that these three fractions have a *common denominator;* they can all be changed to fifteenths. Demonstrate changing them to $\frac{3}{15}$, $\frac{10}{15}$, and $\frac{6}{15}$. Have partners talk through adding those fractions.

Reteaching

Adding with Circular Models

 15–20 MIN **Logical/Mathematical** 

Materials *(per student)* Fraction Models: Circles (Teaching Tool 14); markers

- Write $\frac{5}{6} + \frac{3}{4}$ in vertical form. **What is the product of 6 and 4?** *(24)* **This is a common denominator. Is there a common denominator that is less than 24?** *(12)* Write = and the denominator 12 next to each fraction. Have volunteers write equivalent fractions.
- Have students use 12-part circles to model the sum.
- Repeat with $\frac{1}{6} + \frac{1}{4}$ and $\frac{2}{3} + \frac{1}{4}$.

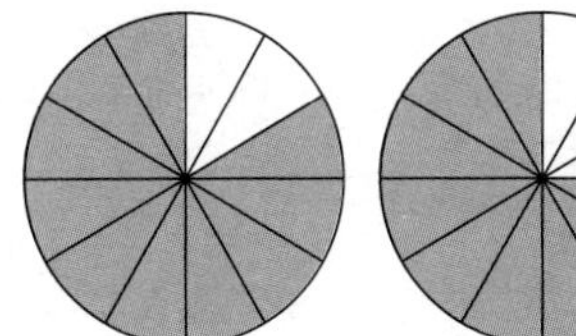

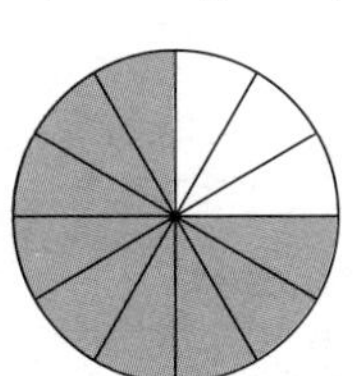

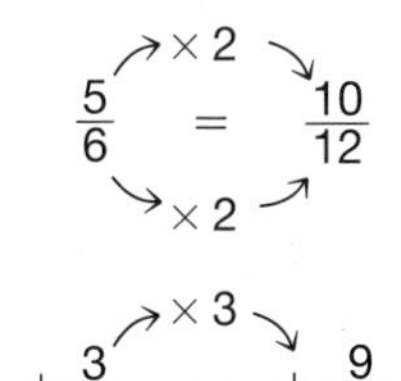

Math and Music

Fractions and Musical Notes

 15–20 MIN **Auditory**

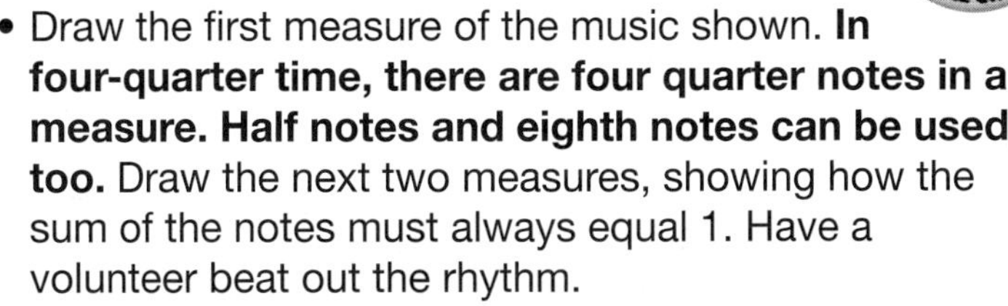

- Draw the first measure of the music shown. **In four-quarter time, there are four quarter notes in a measure. Half notes and eighth notes can be used, too.** Draw the next two measures, showing how the sum of the notes must always equal 1. Have a volunteer beat out the rhythm.
- Have students write other rhythms. If possible, include a student who is taking band lessons in each group.

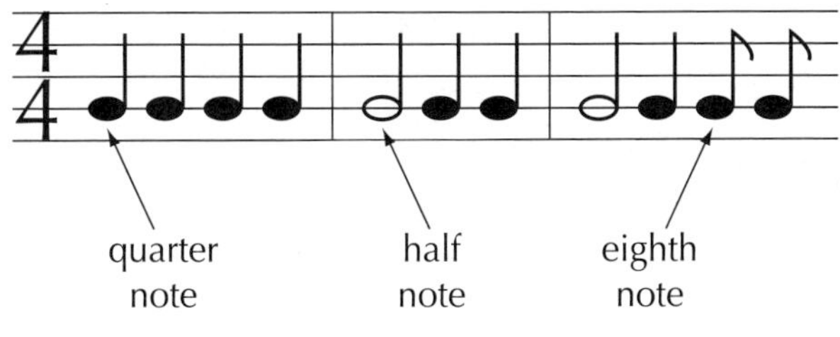

Objective Find common denominators for fractions with unlike denominators and find their sums and differences in simplest form.

1 Warm Up

Activate Prior Knowledge Review how to find the least common multiple for sets of numbers and how to find the least common denominator for pairs of fractions.

2 Teach

LEARN Tell students that this lesson combines four skills that they have already learned:

1. Finding the least common denominator for fractions
2. Writing fractions with a common denominator
3. Adding or subtracting fractions having the same denominator
4. Simplifying fractions

These four skills correspond to the steps shown in Examples A and B.

Examples A and B You may need to show the steps that occur before the stage shown in the lesson. Begin with this setup that uses empty square placeholders for the equivalent fractions.

$$\begin{array}{rcr} \frac{1}{2} & = & \frac{\square}{\square} \\ +\frac{1}{5} & = & +\frac{\square}{\square} \\ \hline \end{array}$$

Key Idea
Finding the least common denominator will allow you to add and subtract fractions with unlike denominators.

Vocabulary
- unlike denominators
- least common multiple (LCM) (p. 152)
- least common denominator (LCD) (p. 164)

Materials
- fraction strips or tools

Think It Through
I can **use objects** to **solve a simpler problem.**

Adding and Subtracting Fractions with Unlike Denominators

WARM UP

Find the least common multiple for each set of numbers.

1. 12 and 4 **12**
2. 9 and 2 **18**
3. 10 and 5 **10**
4. 8 and 6 **24**
5. 6 and 5 **30**
6. 3, 4 and 6 **12**

LEARN

Activity

How can you use fraction strips to add?

Find $\frac{1}{2} + \frac{1}{3}$.

Step 1 Use fraction strips to show both fractions.

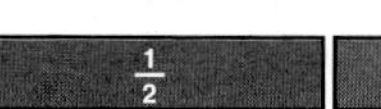

Step 2 Find a common denominator.

The least common denominator (LCD) of 2 and 3 is 6.

Step 3 Use fraction strips with the common denominator to represent each fraction.

$\frac{1}{2}$ | $\frac{1}{3}$
$\frac{1}{6}$ $\frac{1}{6}$ $\frac{1}{6}$ | $\frac{1}{6}$ $\frac{1}{6}$

Step 4 Write the sum.

$\frac{3}{6} + \frac{2}{6} = \frac{5}{6}$

Use fraction strips to find each sum.

a. $\frac{1}{4} + \frac{2}{3}$ $\frac{11}{12}$ **b.** $\frac{2}{5} + \frac{3}{10}$ $\frac{7}{10}$ **c.** $\frac{5}{8} + \frac{3}{4}$ $1\frac{3}{8}$ **d.** $\frac{1}{6} + \frac{1}{2}$ $\frac{2}{3}$

Activity

How can you use fraction strips to subtract?

Find $\frac{1}{2} - \frac{1}{3}$.

Step 1 Use fraction strips to show both fractions.

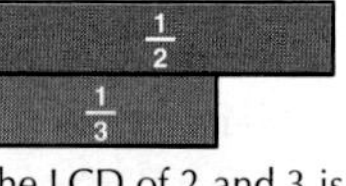

Step 2 Find a common denominator.

The LCD of 2 and 3 is 6.

Step 3 Find fraction strips with the common denominator to show the difference.

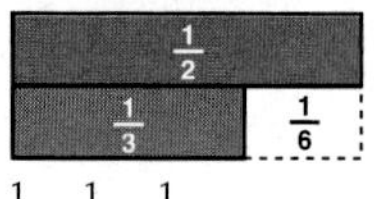

Step 4 Write the difference.

$\frac{1}{2} - \frac{1}{3} = \frac{1}{6}$

Use fraction strips to find each difference.

a. $\frac{2}{3} - \frac{1}{4}$ $\frac{5}{12}$ **b.** $\frac{9}{10} - \frac{2}{5}$ $\frac{1}{2}$ **c.** $\frac{7}{8} - \frac{1}{4}$ $\frac{5}{8}$ **d.** $\frac{5}{6} - \frac{1}{4}$ $\frac{7}{12}$

Below Level — Reteaching

Adding and Subtracting Fractions with Unlike Denominators

R 4-2

If you are adding or subtracting fractions and the denominators are not the same, the first thing to do is find a common denominator. The best common denominator to use is the least common multiple of the two denominators.

Step 1: Use the LCM to find a common denominator.	Find $\frac{2}{6} + \frac{1}{2}$. The LCM of 2 and 6 is 6. The least common denominator (LCD) is 6.	Find $\frac{3}{4} - \frac{1}{3}$. The LCD of 3 and 4 is 12.
Step 2: Write equivalent fractions.	$\frac{2}{6} = \frac{2}{6}$; $+\frac{1}{2} = +\frac{3}{6}$	$\frac{3}{4} = \frac{9}{12}$; $-\frac{1}{3} = -\frac{4}{12}$
Step 3: Add or subtract. Simplify if possible.	$\frac{2}{6} = \frac{2}{6}$; $+\frac{1}{2} = +\frac{3}{6}$; $\frac{5}{6}$	$\frac{3}{4} = \frac{9}{12}$; $-\frac{1}{3} = -\frac{4}{12}$; $\frac{5}{12}$

Find each sum or difference. Simplify your answer.

1. $\frac{3}{4} + \frac{5}{2} =$ $3\frac{1}{4}$
2. $\frac{11}{12} - \frac{1}{3} =$ $\frac{7}{12}$
3. $\frac{4}{15} + \frac{4}{5} =$ $\frac{16}{15}$, or $1\frac{1}{15}$
4. $\frac{5}{6} - \frac{4}{9} =$ $\frac{7}{18}$
5. $\frac{2}{3} + \frac{7}{10} =$ $\frac{41}{30}$, or $1\frac{11}{30}$
6. $\frac{2}{5} + \frac{2}{3} - \frac{6}{30} =$ $\frac{13}{15}$
7. **Number Sense** The least common denominator for the sum $\frac{3}{8} + \frac{5}{12}$ is 24. Name another common denominator that you could use.
   Sample answers: 48, 72
8. A recipe calls for $\frac{1}{2}$ cup of milk and $\frac{1}{3}$ cup of water. What is the total amount of liquid in the recipe?
   $\frac{5}{6}$ c

46 Use with Lesson 4-2.

On Level — Practice

Adding and Subtracting Fractions with Unlike Denominators

P 4-2

Find each sum or difference. Simplify your answer.

1. $\frac{5}{6} + \frac{4}{12} =$ $1\frac{1}{6}$
2. $\frac{4}{5} - \frac{1}{10} =$ $\frac{7}{10}$
3. $\frac{5}{12} + \frac{2}{3} =$ $1\frac{1}{12}$
4. $\frac{9}{20} + \frac{3}{5} =$ $1\frac{1}{20}$
5. $\frac{6}{16} - \frac{1}{4} =$ $\frac{1}{8}$
6. $\frac{19}{21} - \frac{2}{7} =$ $\frac{13}{21}$
7. $\frac{2}{5} + \frac{5}{20} =$ $\frac{13}{20}$
8. $\frac{8}{9} - \frac{5}{12} =$ $\frac{17}{36}$
9. $\frac{7}{8} + \frac{11}{24} - \frac{5}{6} =$ $\frac{1}{2}$
10. **Number Sense** Is $\frac{7}{8}$ or $\frac{11}{10}$ closer to 1? How did you decide?
    $\frac{11}{10}$ is closer to 1 because $\frac{1}{10} < \frac{1}{8}$, so $\frac{11}{10}$ is a shorter distance from 1.

Emma has a small garden. Emma's garden is $\frac{1}{5}$ beans, $\frac{1}{8}$ peas, and $\frac{1}{2}$ corn. The rest is planted with flowers.

11. What fraction of Emma's garden is planted with vegetables?
    $\frac{33}{40}$ of Emma's garden is planted with vegetables.
12. Are there more flowers or peas in Emma's garden?
    There are more flowers, because $\frac{7}{40}$ of the garden is flowers, and only $\frac{5}{40}$ is peas.

Test Prep

13. To solve the subtraction sentence $\frac{17}{10} - \frac{2}{5} = ?$, which common denominator is the best choice?
    (A.) 10 **B.** 15 **C.** 20 **D.** 50
14. **Writing in Math** To find the sum of $\frac{4}{9}$ and $\frac{7}{12}$, Mario rewrites the fractions as $\frac{8}{36}$ and $\frac{21}{36}$. His answer is $\frac{29}{36}$. Is Mario right? If not, show his error and correct it.
    Mario is wrong. $\frac{4}{9}$ should be rewritten as $\frac{16}{36}$. The correct answer is $\frac{37}{36}$.

46 Use with Lesson 4-2.

How can you find sums and differences of fractions with unlike denominators?

In order to add or subtract fractions that have different or **unlike denominators,** write them with the same denominator. That is, you need to find equivalent fractions.

	Example A	Example B
	Find $\frac{1}{2} + \frac{1}{5}$.	Find $\frac{5}{6} - \frac{1}{3}$.
STEP 1 Use the **least common multiple (LCM)** to find the **least common denominator.**	Since the LCM of 2 and 5 is 10, the **least common denominator (LCD)** is 10.	The LCD of 6 and 3 is 6.
STEP 2 Write equivalent fractions.	$\frac{1}{2} = \frac{5}{10}$ $+\frac{1}{5} = +\frac{2}{10}$	$\frac{5}{6} = \frac{5}{6}$ $-\frac{1}{3} = -\frac{2}{6}$
STEP 3 Add or subtract. Simplify if possible.	$\frac{1}{2} = \frac{5}{10}$ $+\frac{1}{5} = +\frac{2}{10}$ $\frac{7}{10}$	$\frac{5}{6} = \frac{5}{6}$ $-\frac{1}{3} = -\frac{2}{6}$ $\frac{3}{6} = \frac{1}{2}$

Think It Through
I'll try to **make a simpler problem.** I will write equivalent fractions with like denominators.

Talk About It

1. In Example A, explain how to find the equivalent fractions for $\frac{1}{2}$ and $\frac{1}{5}$. **The least common multiple of 2 and 5 is 10. For $\frac{1}{2}$, multiply both numerator and denominator by 5 to get $\frac{5}{10}$. For $\frac{1}{5}$, multiply both numerator and denominator by 2 to get $\frac{2}{10}$.**
2. **Reasoning** In Example B, would 18 have worked just as well as a common denominator? Explain. **Yes; 6 and 3 are both factors of 18, so $\frac{5}{6} = \frac{15}{18}$ and $\frac{1}{3} = \frac{6}{18}$; $\frac{15}{18} - \frac{6}{18} = \frac{9}{18} = \frac{1}{2}$.**
3. **Reasoning** Why would you use the least common denominator when adding or subtracting fractions with unlike denominators? **Using the LCM will minimize the time spent simplifying the sum or difference.**

Take It to the NET
More Examples
www.scottforesman.com

For another example, see Set 4-2 on p. 240.

Find each sum or difference. Simplify your answer.

1. $\frac{5}{6} - \frac{1}{2}$ **$\frac{1}{3}$**
2. $\frac{3}{4} + \frac{3}{5}$ **$1\frac{7}{20}$**
3. $\frac{7}{8} + \frac{1}{6}$ **$1\frac{1}{24}$**
4. $\frac{11}{12} + \frac{3}{4}$ **$1\frac{2}{3}$**
5. $\frac{4}{15} - \frac{1}{10}$ **$\frac{1}{6}$**
6. **Number Sense** Why is it necessary for fractions to have common denominators before you add or subtract them? **When you add and subtract fractions with like denominators, the denominator acts as a label. It tells you what size pieces you're using. Pieces and parts have to be the same when you add or subtract.**

Ongoing Assessment

Talk About It: Question 3

If students cannot explain the advantages of using a least common denominator,

then have them work Example A using 20 as the common denominator and Example B using 18. Any common denominator will give the correct answer, but the *least* common denominator is easier to work with and often more efficient because you may not have to simplify the result.

CHECK

Error Intervention

If students are making mistakes when forming equivalent fractions,

then make sure students are working the problems in vertical form as shown in the examples. Suggest that they write the factors under and over the equals signs. *(Also see* Reteaching, *p. 206B.)*

$$\frac{7}{8} \xrightarrow{\times 3} \frac{\square}{24}$$
$$+\frac{5}{6} \xrightarrow{\times 4} +\frac{\square}{24}$$

Enrichment — Above Level

What's in the Box?

E 4-2 REASONING

You can use multiplication to find sums and differences of fractions! Each of the examples below shows the same way to find $\frac{4}{5} - \frac{1}{3}$.

Find the cross products. Then write the sum or difference over the product of the denominators.

$$\frac{4}{5} - \frac{1}{3} = \frac{(4 \times 3) - (5 \times 1)}{5 \times 3} = \frac{12 - 5}{15} = \frac{7}{15}$$

This can be written algebraically as

$$\frac{a}{b} - \frac{c}{d} = \frac{(a \times d) - (b \times c)}{b \times d}$$

and

$$\frac{a}{b} + \frac{c}{d} = \frac{(a \times d) + (b \times c)}{b \times d}$$

Write the fractions in the boxes. Multiply the denominators of each fraction by the numerator of the other fraction.

So, $\frac{4}{5} - \frac{1}{3} = \frac{7}{15}$

12 − 5; 3 × 4; 5 × 1

12	5	
4	1	7
5	3	15

Subtract: 12 − 5
Multiply: 5 × 3

Subtract (or add) the products to find the numerator of the difference (or sum). Multiply the two denominators to find the denominator of the difference (or sum).

Use cross products or boxes to find each sum or difference. Simplify if necessary.

1. $\frac{7}{8} + \frac{1}{6} =$ **$1\frac{1}{24}$**
2. $\frac{11}{20} - \frac{1}{8} =$ **$\frac{17}{40}$**
3. $\frac{15}{16} + \frac{3}{10} =$ **$1\frac{19}{80}$**
4. $\frac{7}{25} - \frac{1}{12} =$ **$\frac{59}{300}$**

Complete the boxes and write the answer in the blank. Simplify if necessary.

5. $\frac{4}{7} + \frac{1}{3} =$ **$\frac{19}{21}$**

12	7	
4	1	19
7	3	21

6. $\frac{2}{9} - \frac{1}{16} =$ **$\frac{23}{144}$**

32	9	
2	1	23
9	16	144

Problem Solving

Adding and Subtracting Fractions with Unlike Denominators

PS 4-2

Flooring Pete is putting new wood flooring in his kitchen. He only has a small part to finish, but he wants to use all of the small pieces of flooring he has left.

1. On the first strip, Pete needs to have $\frac{3}{8}$ ft of flooring. He has a piece of flooring that measures $\frac{5}{16}$ ft. How much will he need to cut off? **$\frac{1}{16}$ ft**
2. Pete has a $\frac{1}{4}$ ft piece and a $\frac{1}{8}$ ft piece. How long will the two pieces be together? **$\frac{3}{8}$ ft**
3. The last two pieces Pete needs are $\frac{17}{18}$ ft and $\frac{2}{3}$ ft. What is the difference in size between the two pieces? **$\frac{5}{18}$ ft**

Exercise Tina spends at least 30 min exercising every evening.

4. One day, Tina spent $\frac{1}{2}$ hr jogging and $\frac{1}{8}$ hr walking. How much time did Tina spend on the two activities? **$\frac{5}{8}$ hr**
5. How much more time did Tina spend jogging than she did walking? **$\frac{3}{8}$ hr**
6. Another day, Tina spent $\frac{1}{4}$ hr jogging, $\frac{1}{6}$ hr walking, and $\frac{3}{8}$ hr swimming. How much time did Tina spend exercising altogether? **$\frac{19}{24}$ hr**
7. How much more time did Tina spend walking and jogging than swimming? **$\frac{1}{24}$ hr**
8. **Writing in Math** How can you find the least common denominator when subtracting $\frac{7}{8} - \frac{1}{3}$? Explain. **Sample answer: Find the prime factors of each denominator and multiply. 3 × 2 × 2 × 2 = 24. So, the LCD is 24.**

3 Practice

Exercises 7–16 Before students begin, have them identify exercises in which one denominator is a multiple of the other. Point out that the LCD is the greater denominator, so they need to convert only one fraction to an equivalent form.

Exercises 19–21 Put this drawing on the board to show students that the newspaper layout is based on a 12-part grid. Some students may need help seeing that the photo covers $\frac{1}{4}$ of the page. Point out that each box is $\frac{1}{12}$ of the page and $\frac{3}{12} = \frac{1}{4}$.

photo	photo	photo
		ad
		ad
	ad	ad

Exercise 23 Before students plan their paragraphs, have two volunteers show the work for the problem at the board using both methods. Title the two methods "Product of Denominators" and "LCD."

Reading Assist Use Picture Clues Before discussing the activities at the beginning of the lesson, ask students to describe what they think is happening using just the illustrations of the fraction strips. *(Sample answer: The strips, or bars, show the fractions $\frac{1}{2}$ and $\frac{1}{3}$. First, the strips are added; then they are subtracted.)*

23. Sample answer: Ramon's method is actually more efficient. Since Ramon uses the least common denominator when finding equivalent fractions, he won't have to simplify his answer as much as June will.

PRACTICE

For more practice, see Set 4-2 on p. 243.

A Skills and Understanding

Find each sum or difference. Simplify your answer.

7. $\frac{2}{5} + \frac{3}{8}$ **$\frac{31}{40}$** **8.** $\frac{5}{6} - \frac{1}{9}$ **$\frac{13}{18}$** **9.** $\frac{9}{10} + \frac{3}{5}$ **$1\frac{1}{2}$** **10.** $\frac{5}{8} - \frac{1}{3}$ **$\frac{7}{24}$** **11.** $\frac{7}{8} - \frac{5}{12}$ **$\frac{11}{24}$**

12. $\frac{7}{12} + \frac{2}{3}$ **$1\frac{1}{4}$** **13.** $\frac{4}{5} + \frac{11}{15}$ **$1\frac{8}{15}$** **14.** $\frac{2}{3} - \frac{5}{8}$ **$\frac{1}{24}$** **15.** $\frac{6}{7} + \frac{11}{14}$ **$1\frac{9}{14}$** **16.** $\frac{9}{10} - \frac{1}{4} + \frac{3}{8}$ **$1\frac{1}{40}$**

17. Convert the fractions in Exercises 7, 9, and 16 to decimals and find each answer. Does your decimal answer agree with your original answer? **0.775, 1.5, 1.025; yes**

18. Number Sense Is $\frac{15}{16} - \frac{4}{5}$ less than, equal to, or greater than $\frac{1}{2}$? How do you know without computing? **Less than $\frac{1}{2}$; I am subtracting nearly 1 from almost 1; 1 − 1 = 0**

B Reasoning and Problem Solving

Math and Social Studies

One page of the *Lydia Lake Reporter* newspaper has advertisements covering $\frac{1}{3}$ of the page and a photo covering $\frac{1}{4}$ of the page. The rest of the page is a news story.

ONLY $\frac{1}{3}$ ARE RESIDENTS!

Call now for a FREE estimate 555-5565 CABIN CARPENTRY

Bob's Clam House Voted "Best Clam Chowder" Daily Specials Present this coupon & receive $2 off purchase! $2 Off coupon

19. What fraction of the page contains ads and the photo? **$\frac{7}{12}$**

20. How much more of the page is covered by ads than by the photo? **$\frac{1}{12}$**

21. Reasoning What fraction of the page is a news story? Explain. **See above.**

21. $\frac{5}{12}$; It is the amount left over when I subtract $\frac{7}{12}$ from 1.

22. Suppose Wanda studied $\frac{3}{4}$ hour for the math quiz and Shantal studied $\frac{5}{6}$ hour. Who studied longer? How much longer? **Shantal; $\frac{1}{12}$ hour longer, or 5 minutes.**

23. Writing in Math Whose method do you prefer for finding $\frac{3}{8} + \frac{5}{6}$? Why?

June
I use the product of the denominators as my common denominator. It saves time and work.

Ramon
I find the least common denominator. It keeps me from making mistakes when I simplify my answer.

See margin.

Think It Through
I can **check how the denominators are related.** If they have common factors, their product will NOT be the least common denominator.

Test-Taking Practice

Test-Taking Practice, Item 1, p. 209
There are two parts to the problem; the difference and explanation are each worth two points. Remind students that they should answer as much as they can since partial credit is given for this type of problem.

Discuss the sample responses shown and compare them to papers produced by your students.

4-point answer Answer is correct; explanation shows complete understanding of subtracting fractions.

Find a common denominator.
$\frac{25}{50} \times \frac{2}{2} = \frac{50}{100}$. Subtract
$\frac{50}{100} - \frac{50}{100}$ mentally.

The difference is zero.

PRACTICE

C Extensions

24. Write two fractions with unlike denominators whose difference is $\frac{1}{2}$. **Sample answer: $\frac{7}{8} - \frac{6}{16}$**

25. Name 2 fractions with unlike denominators whose sum is greater than $1\frac{1}{2}$. **Sample answer: $\frac{7}{8} + \frac{15}{16}$**

Add each pair of fractions. Describe any pattern you see.

26. $\frac{1}{2} + \frac{1}{4}$ **$\frac{3}{4}$** **27.** $\frac{3}{4} + \frac{1}{8}$ **$\frac{7}{8}$** **28.** $\frac{7}{8} + \frac{1}{16}$ **$\frac{15}{16}$**

The numerator is 1 less than the denominator.

Mixed Review and Test Prep

Find each answer.

29. $\frac{3}{5} + \frac{2}{5}$ **1** **30.** $\frac{11}{12} + \frac{5}{12}$ **$1\frac{1}{3}$** **31.** $\frac{5}{6} - \frac{2}{6}$ **$\frac{1}{2}$** **32.** $\frac{7}{8} - \frac{1}{8}$ **$\frac{3}{4}$**

33. Which is the decimal equivalent for $\frac{1}{50}$?

A. 0.0150 **(B.)** 0.02 **C.** 0.15 **D.** 0.2

Learning with Technology

Fractions eTool: Strips and Wedges

You can use the Strips workspace to find sums of fractions. You can represent fractions by selecting pieces from the toolbar. You can also select a denominator to divide the strip into parts.

For 1–3, use the Strips workspace to find each sum.

1. $\frac{1}{8} + \frac{1}{3}$ **$\frac{11}{24}$** **2.** $\frac{3}{5} + \frac{4}{16}$ **$\frac{17}{20}$** **3.** $\frac{2}{3} + \frac{1}{12} + \frac{1}{16}$ **$\frac{13}{16}$**

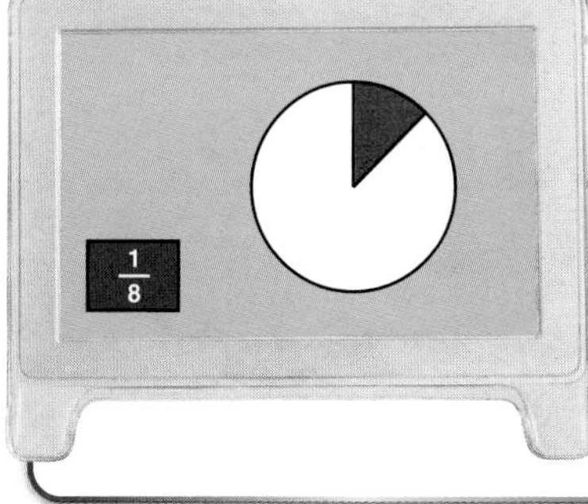

Use the Wedges workspace to find differences of fractions. Select pieces from the toolbar. To find $\frac{3}{4} - \frac{1}{8}$, select a $\frac{1}{8}$ wedge. Add other pieces until $\frac{3}{4}$ of the circle is filled.

For 4–6, use the wedges feature to find each difference.

4. $\frac{7}{8} - \frac{1}{2}$ **$\frac{3}{8}$** **5.** $\frac{1}{2} - \frac{5}{12}$ **$\frac{1}{12}$** **6.** $\frac{2}{3} - \frac{1}{12}$ **$\frac{7}{12}$**

Leveled Practice

Below Level Ex. 7–16, 18–20, 23, 29–33

On Level Ex. 7–17 odd, 18–25, 29–33

Above Level Ex. 10–16 even, 17, 21–33

Early Finishers Have students write a word problem that requires adding fractions with unlike denominators to solve. Have them exchange papers and solve each other's problems.

Learning with Technology Students need access to Fractions eTool.

The visual representations will help students understand the basis for adding and subtracting fractions with unlike denominators and also provide meaningful practice.

4 Assess

Journal Idea Have students solve the following problem and explain how they decided on their answer. Janet bought $\frac{7}{8}$ of a pound of cherries. Was her purchase closer to $\frac{1}{2}$ pound or 1 pound?

4-point answer Answer is correct; explanation shows complete understanding of subtracting fractions.

Change $\frac{25}{50}$ and $\frac{50}{100}$ to $\frac{1}{2}$.
Subtract $\frac{1}{2} - \frac{1}{2}$ mentally.
The difference is zero.

3-point answer Answer is correct; shows understanding of subtracting with fractions.

Change the fractions to the same denominator. Then subtract.
The difference is zero.

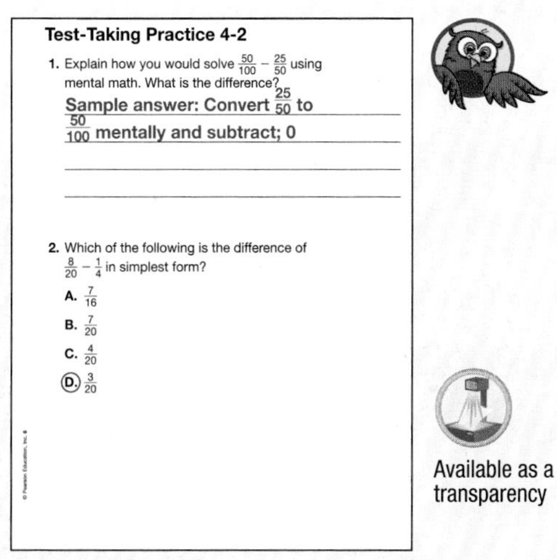
Test-Taking Practice 4-2

1. Explain how you would solve $\frac{50}{100} - \frac{25}{50}$ using mental math. What is the difference?
Sample answer: Convert $\frac{25}{50}$ to $\frac{50}{100}$ mentally and subtract; 0

2. Which of the following is the difference of $\frac{8}{20} - \frac{1}{4}$ in simplest form?
A. $\frac{7}{16}$
B. $\frac{7}{20}$
C. $\frac{4}{20}$
(D.) $\frac{3}{20}$

Available as a transparency

Reading for Math Success

Purpose Reinforce reading skills and strategies to use in math. *Predict and Generalize* helps prepare students for the problem-solving strategy lesson, *Look for a Pattern*, which follows.

Using Student Pages 210–211

In their reading classes, students frequently are asked to read a certain segment of a story or article and then use the information in it to predict what will happen next. Their prediction may end up being a generalization, a statement telling what several things have in common. In doing mathematics, students can apply generalizing and predicting skills to identify a pattern and the items that will complete it.

Model the Process Tell students that in order to predict what comes next in a pattern, they need to be able to generalize what the pattern is. The way to do this is to look for the relationship between the items in the pattern. Once they identify the pattern, they can predict any item in it. **When I see a pattern with missing numbers or geometric figures, I figure out how to get from the first item to the second, from the second to the third, and from the third to the fourth. Next, I state a generalization that describes the pattern. My generalization lets me predict what the missing numbers or geometric figures will be.**

Reading For Math Success

Predict and Generalize

Predicting and generalizing when you read in math can help you use the **problem-solving strategy, *Look for a Pattern,*** in the next lesson.

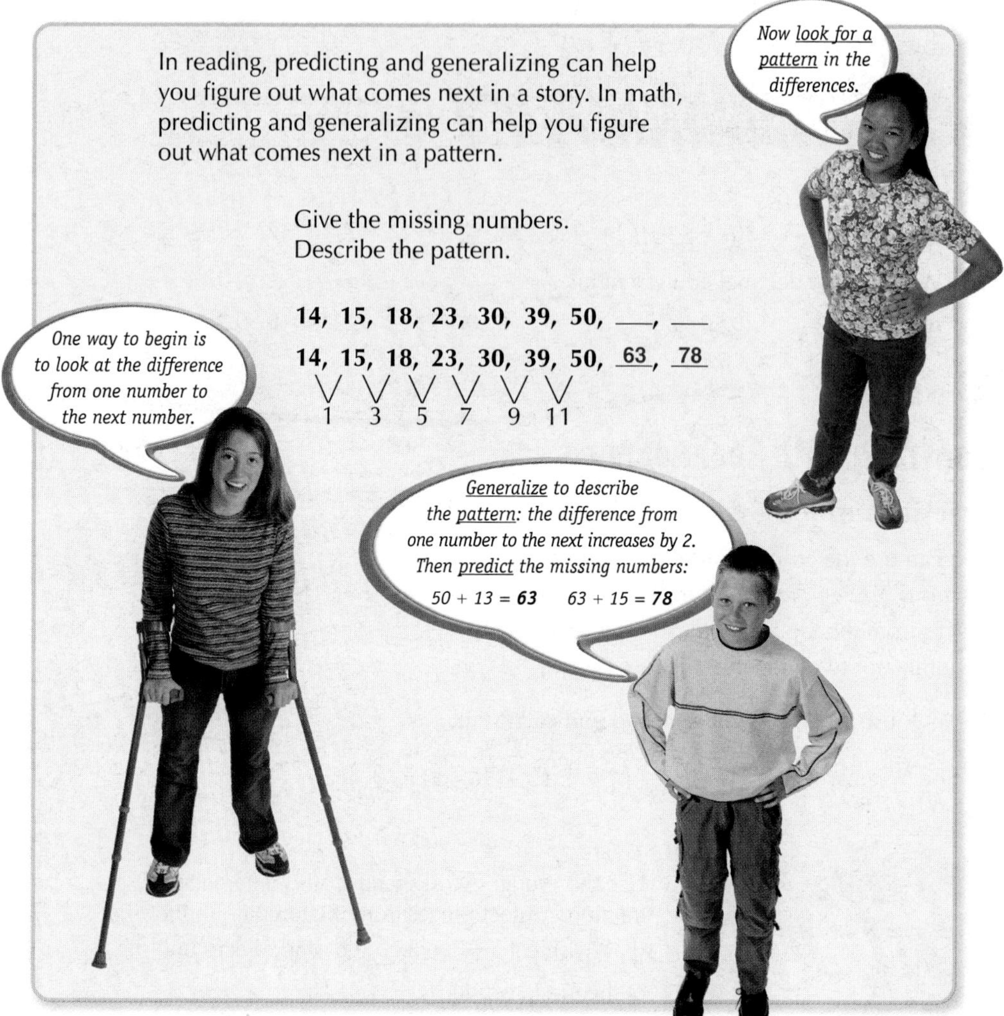

In reading, predicting and generalizing can help you figure out what comes next in a story. In math, predicting and generalizing can help you figure out what comes next in a pattern.
Now look for a pattern in the differences.
Give the missing numbers. Describe the pattern.
14, 15, 18, 23, 30, 39, 50, ___, ___
14, 15, 18, 23, 30, 39, 50, 63, 78
1 3 5 7 9 11
One way to begin is to look at the difference from one number to the next number.
Generalize to describe the pattern: the difference from one number to the next increases by 2. Then predict the missing numbers:
50 + 13 = 63 63 + 15 = 78

1. Predict the next number in the pattern after 78. 95
2. If the pattern stayed the same, but the first number was 8, what would the fourth number be? 17

210

For 3–6, use the number pattern at the right.

3. What is the difference between the first number and the second? between the second and the third? Find the rest of the differences.
2.5; 2.5; 2.5; 2.5; 2.5
4. Generalize by describing the pattern.
The difference from one number to the next is 2.5.
5. Predict the next number. **17.5**
6. Writing in Math How is this pattern different from the number pattern on page 210?
In this pattern, the differences are the same. On page 210, the differences increase.

2.5, 5, 7.5, 10, 12.5, 15

For 7–9, use the picture below.

7. What is the difference between the amount of money in the first purse starting at the left and the second purse? between the second and the third? Find the rest of the differences.
3; 6; 9; 12; 15
8. Generalize by describing the pattern.
The difference from one number to the next increases by 3.
9. Predict the amount of money in the next purse.
$69

11. The difference from one number to the next doubles.

For 10–13, use the picture at the right.

10. List the differences between consecutive pairs of locker numbers, starting at the left.
2; 4; 8; 16; 32
11. Generalize by describing the pattern.
See above.
12. If the pattern stayed the same, but the first locker number was 3, what would the fourth locker number be? **17**
13. Writing in Math Predict the next locker number. Explain how you made your prediction. **134; I added (2 × 32) to 70.**

Guide the Activity Direct students' attention to the pattern. **How do you get from the first number to the second number?** *(Add 1)* **How do you get from the second number to the third?** *(Add 3)* **How do you get from the third number to the fourth?** *(Add 5)* **What generalization can you make about this pattern?** *(It increases by two for every number.)* Have a volunteer read the next two numbers in the pattern; then have students do Exercises 1 and 2 orally. Assign Exercises 3–13, reminding students that the patterns in them may involve other operations besides addition.

Error Intervention

If students identify patterns incorrectly,

then point out that they may have to look for the relationship between several numbers or patterns, not just the first two or three.

Journal Idea Have students create a number pattern that uses a different operation from those in the exercises. Then have students write an explanation of how each pattern works.

Look for a Pattern

Lesson Organizer

Quick Lesson Overview

Objective Give missing numbers or figures in a pattern.

Math Understanding Patterns can be identified by using given elements and then can be filled in or extended.

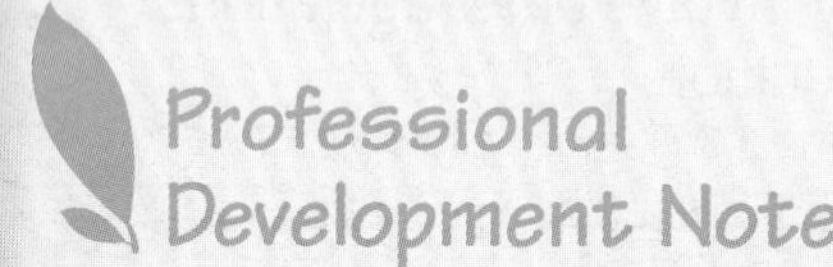

Math Background Identifying and exploring patterns in a sequence of numbers or figures introduces students to the algebraic concepts of function and variable.

NCTM Standards

- Algebra

(For a complete correlation to the NCTM Standards and Grades 6–8 Expectations, see pages 202G–H.)

Getting Started

Spiral Review

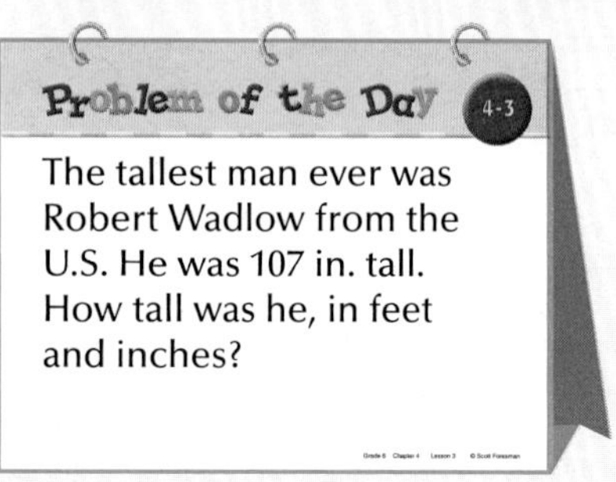

Problem of the Day 4-3

The tallest man ever was Robert Wadlow from the U.S. He was 107 in. tall. How tall was he, in feet and inches?

Topics Reviewed

- Dividing by whole numbers
- Problem-Solving Skill: Interpreting Remainders

Answer Robert Wadlow was 8 ft, 11 in. tall.

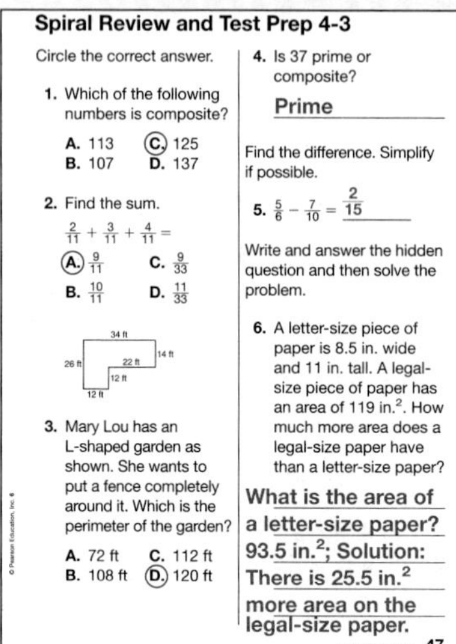

Spiral Review and Test Prep 4-3

Circle the correct answer.

1. Which of the following numbers is composite?
   A. 113 (C.) 125
   B. 107 D. 137

2. Find the sum.
   $\frac{2}{11} + \frac{3}{11} + \frac{4}{11} =$
   (A.) $\frac{9}{11}$ C. $\frac{9}{33}$
   B. $\frac{10}{11}$ D. $\frac{11}{33}$

3. Mary Lou has an L-shaped garden as shown. She wants to put a fence completely around it. Which is the perimeter of the garden?
   A. 72 ft C. 112 ft
   B. 108 ft (D.) 120 ft

4. Is 37 prime or composite? Prime

Find the difference. Simplify if possible.

5. $\frac{5}{6} - \frac{7}{10} = \frac{2}{15}$

Write and answer the hidden question and then solve the problem.

6. A letter-size piece of paper is 8.5 in. wide and 11 in. tall. A legal-size piece of paper has an area of 119 in.^{2}. How much more area does a legal-size paper have than a letter-size paper?
   What is the area of a letter-size paper? 93.5 in.^{2}; Solution: There is 25.5 in.^{2} more area on the legal-size paper.

Use with Lesson 4-3. 47

Available as a transparency and as a blackline master

Topics Reviewed

1., 4. Prime and composite numbers; **2.** Adding fractions with like denominators; **3.** Finding perimeter; **5.** Subtracting fractions with unlike denominators; **6.** Multiple-step problems

Investigating the Concept

Looking for Patterns

15–20 MIN **Visual/Spatial**

Materials *(per student)* $\frac{1}{4}$–Inch Grid Paper (Teaching Tool 10)

What to Do

- Begin the pattern shown below on a transparency of grid paper. Have students continue the pattern until they run out of space.
- **Write the side lengths of the squares.** *(Alternating, the lengths and widths of the figures are the Fibonacci sequence: 1, 1, 2, 3, 5, 8, 13, ...)* **How can you get the next number in the sequence?** *(Add the two previous numbers.)*

Ongoing Assessment

- **What is the next fraction in the pattern $\frac{1}{2}, \frac{2}{3}, \frac{3}{5}, \frac{5}{8}, \frac{8}{13}, \frac{13}{21}, \ldots$?** *($\frac{21}{34}$)* **How is this pattern formed?** *(Numerators are Fibonacci numbers beginning with 1; denominators are Fibonacci numbers beginning with 2.)*

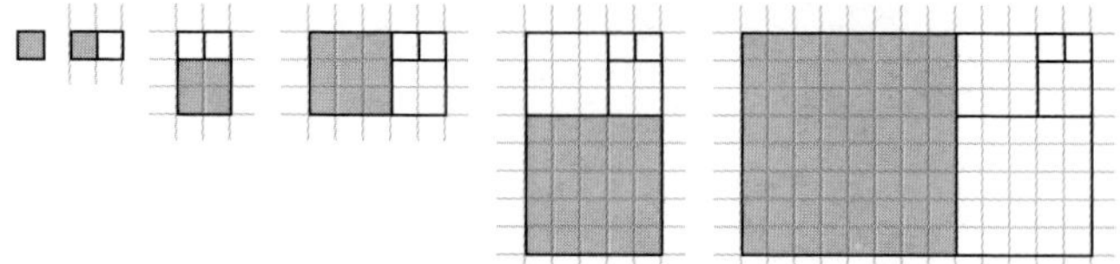

Reaching All Learners

Writing in Math

Talking About Number Patterns

 10–15 MIN **Social/Cooperative** 

- Have students create number patterns with three or more terms. Have volunteers share their patterns. Then ask students to identify various terms in the sequence and the pattern used. Have students extend the sequences.
- **In analyzing patterns, look for changes from the first to the second term, from the second to the third, and so on.**

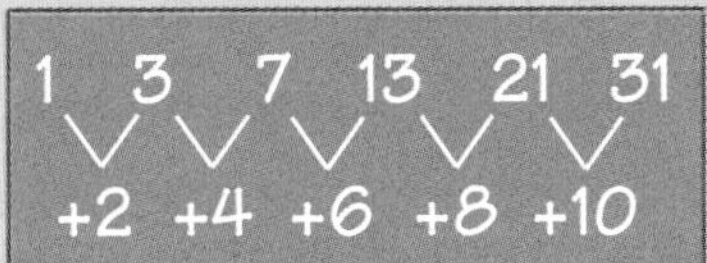

Access Content

English Language Learners

Creating Patterns

 15–20 MIN **Linguistic/Visual/Spatial** 

Materials *(per student)* Play Money or Teaching Tool 5 coins

- Have a volunteer read the lesson title *(Look for a Pattern)* and the first section on page 212. Discuss how a phase is a stage in something.
- Have students talk through drawing the diagram for phase 4. **What is the pattern?**
- Display a pattern with pennies and nickels. **How would the pattern continue?**
- Have pairs create their own patterns using combinations of pennies, nickels and dimes.

Reteaching

Two Views of One Pattern

 15-20 MIN **Social/Cooperative** 

- Draw 2 dots on the board. Have a volunteer connect the dots. **How many ways are there to connect the dots?** *(1 way)*
- Repeat with 3 through 6 dots, making sure that no 3 dots are on the same segment.
- Have students describe the pattern for the number of segments for each group of dots. *(Add 2, 3, 4, ...)*

 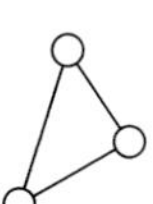 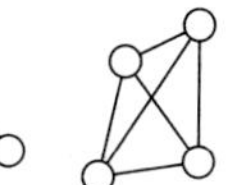 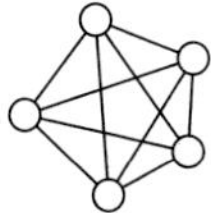 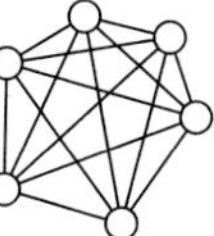

Math and Science

Radioactive Decay

 10–15 MIN **Logical/Mathematical** 

- **Radioactive substances disintegrate, or decay, at a steady rate. The length of time it takes for half the material to disintegrate is called a "half-life."**
- **Suppose you have 800 mg of a radioactive isotope. After one half-life, there will be 400 mg left.**
- For the isotope, have students show the number of milligrams at the start and after each half-life. *(800 mg, 400 mg, 200 mg, 100 mg, 50 mg, 25 mg, . . .)* **How do you get the next term in this pattern?** *(Divide by 2.)*

Objective Give missing numbers or figures in a pattern.

1 Warm Up

Activate Prior Knowledge Review sequences formed by adding or subtracting a constant number. Use examples with whole numbers, fractions, and decimals.

2 Teach

LEARN Explain the example on p. 212 or present the problem using these teaching actions.

BEFORE Read and Understand

Could you find the number of employees by making tree diagrams for Phases 4 and 5? Explain. *(Yes, but it would be difficult to read at a glance and easy to make an error.)*

DURING Plan and Solve

What do 2^2, 2^3, 2^4, and 2^5 represent? *(The difference between the number of people contacted during each phase of the emergency plan)*

AFTER Look Back and Check

What pattern was used to extend the table? *(The number of e-mails sent during each phase doubles.)*

For Additional Answers, see pages C1–C4.

Lesson 4-3

Problem-Solving Strategy

Reading Helps!

Predicting and generalizing can help you with... the problem-solving strategy, *Look for a Pattern.*

Key Idea
Learning how and when to look for a pattern can help you solve problems.

Look for a Pattern

LEARN

What is the pattern?

Emergency Plan The president of Best Idea has a 5-phase emergency plan.

Phase 1 — The president emails her 2 vice presidents.

Phase 2 — Each vice president forwards the email to 2 employees.

Phase 3 — Each employee who receives the email sends it to 2 employees. How many employees work for the company if everyone knows about the emergency in 5 phases?

Read and Understand

What do you know? Three employees know in Phase 1. In Phase 2, seven employees know. Fifteen employees know in Phase 3.

What are you trying to find? Find the number of employees in the company.

Plan and Solve

What strategy will you use? **Strategy: Look for a Pattern**

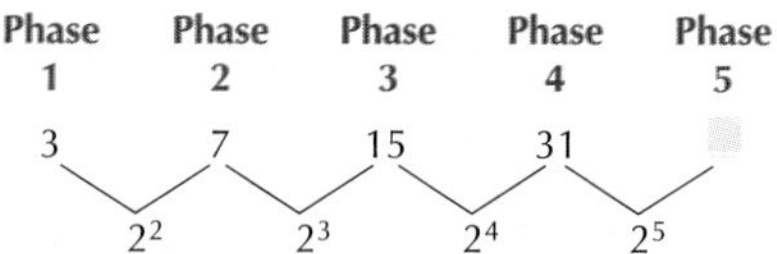

Answer: There are 63 employees in the company.

Look Back and Check

Is your answer reasonable? Yes, the difference from one phase to the next doubles.

Test Talk — Think It Through
Looking at how numbers or figures in a pattern compare can help you find the rule that creates the pattern.

✓ Talk About It

1. Do you see a relationship between the phase number and the exponent? Explain. **Yes: The phase number equals the exponent to which 2 is raised.**

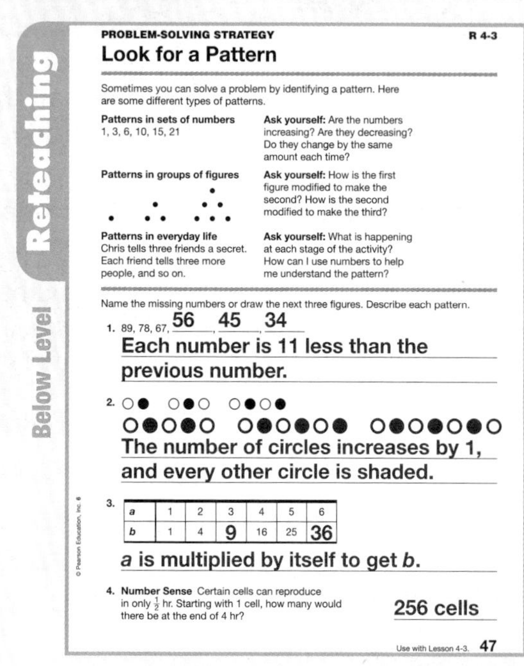

Reteaching — Below Level

PROBLEM-SOLVING STRATEGY — R 4-3

Look for a Pattern

Sometimes you can solve a problem by identifying a pattern. Here are some different types of patterns.

Patterns in sets of numbers
1, 3, 6, 10, 15, 21

Ask yourself: Are the numbers increasing? Are they decreasing? Do they change by the same amount each time?

Patterns in groups of figures

Ask yourself: How is the first figure modified to make the second? How is the second modified to make the third?

Patterns in everyday life
Chris tells three friends a secret. Each friend tells three more people, and so on.

Ask yourself: What is happening at each stage of the activity? How can I use numbers to help me understand the pattern?

Name the missing numbers or draw the next three figures. Describe each pattern.

1. 89, 78, 67, 56, 45, 34
Each number is 11 less than the previous number.

2. ○● ○●○ ○●○●
○●○●○ ○●○●○● ○●○●○●○
The number of circles increases by 1, and every other circle is shaded.

3.

a	1	2	3	4	5	6
b	1	4	9	16	25	36

a is multiplied by itself to get *b*.

4. **Number Sense** Certain cells can reproduce in only $\frac{1}{2}$ hr. Starting with 1 cell, how many would there be at the end of 4 hr? 256 cells

Use with Lesson 4-3. 47

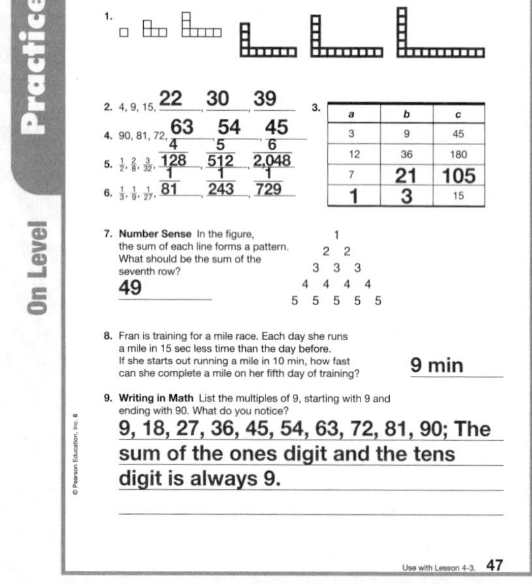

Practice — On Level

PROBLEM-SOLVING STRATEGY — P 4-3

Look for a Pattern

Name the missing numbers or draw the next three figures.

1.

2. 4, 9, 15, 22, 30, 39

3.

a	b	c
3	9	45
12	36	180
7	21	105
1	3	15

4. 90, 81, 72, 63, 54, 45

5. $\frac{1}{2}, \frac{2}{8}, \frac{3}{32}, \frac{4}{128}, \frac{5}{512}, \frac{6}{2,048}$

6. $\frac{1}{3}, \frac{1}{9}, \frac{1}{27}, \frac{1}{81}, \frac{1}{243}, \frac{1}{729}$

7. **Number Sense** In the figure, the sum of each line forms a pattern. What should be the sum of the seventh row? 49

1
2 2
3 3 3
4 4 4 4
5 5 5 5 5

8. Fran is training for a mile race. Each day she runs a mile in 15 sec less time than the day before. If she starts out running a mile in 10 min, how fast can she complete a mile on her fifth day of training? 9 min

9. **Writing in Math** List the multiples of 9, starting with 9 and ending with 90. What do you notice?
9, 18, 27, 36, 45, 54, 63, 72, 81, 90; The sum of the ones digit and the tens digit is always 9.

Use with Lesson 4-3. 47

CHECK ✓

For another example, see Set 4-3 on p. 240.

Name the missing numbers or draw the next three figures. Describe each pattern.

1. 0, 1, 3, 6, 10, ▒, ▒, ▒ **15 21 28** **See above.**
2. [figures] **See margin. Add 1 to each arm.**
3. 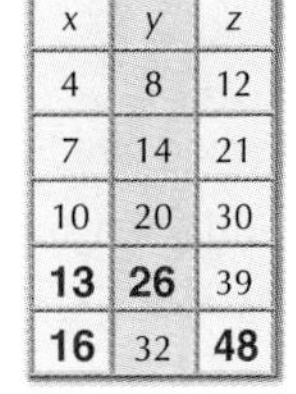

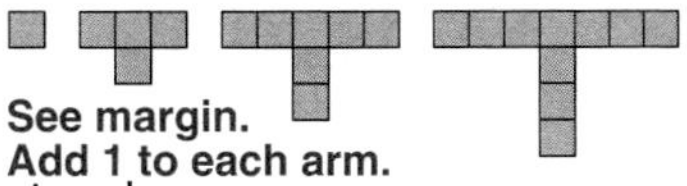

x	y	z
4	8	12
7	14	21
10	20	30
13	**26**	39
16	32	**48**

x: add 3, y: add 6, z: add 9

4. 2, 3, 5, 8, 12, ▒, ▒, ▒ **17 23 30** **Add 1, then 2, then 3...**
5. **Number Sense** Write an expression that you can use to find the number of right angles in the diagram below. Find the number of right angles. **Sample answer: 4 × 16 × 2 = 128**

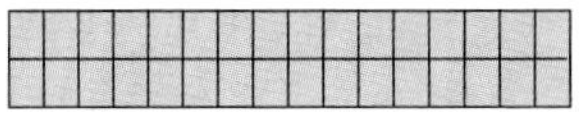

1. Add 1, then 2, then 3...

PRACTICE

For more practice, see Set 4-3 on p. 243.

Name the missing numbers or draw the next three figures. Describe each pattern.

6. 1, 3, 9, 27, ▒, ▒, ▒ **81 243 729** **Multiply by 3.**
7.  [figures] **See above.** **7. The number of circles increases by 3, 5, 7, 9, 11, and so on.**
8.

a	b	c
12	48	96
18	72	144
24	**96**	192
30	120	**240**

a: add 6, b: add 24, c: add 48

9. 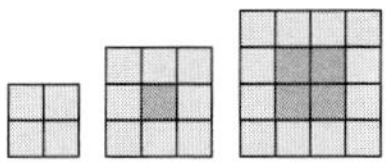 [figures] **The number of shaded squares increased by 3, 5, 7, 9, and so on.**
10. $\frac{2}{3}, \frac{4}{6}, \frac{6}{9}, \frac{8}{12}$, ▒, ▒, ▒ **$\frac{10}{15}$ $\frac{12}{18}$ $\frac{14}{21}$** **Numerator: add 2, denominator: add 3**
11. **Number Sense** Use the table below. Write an expression that you can use to find the total cost for 10 items. Find the total cost for 10 items.

Number of items	1	2	3	4	5	6
Total cost	\$1.38	\$2.76	\$4.14	\$5.52	\$6.90	\$8.28

10 × \$1.38 = \$13.80

Look for a pattern in each chart. Copy and write the missing numbers.

12.

1 × 8 + 1 =	9
12 × 8 + 2 =	98
123 × 8 + 3 =	987
1,234 × 8 + 4 =	9,876
12,345 × 8 + 5 =	? **98,765**
? **123,456** × 8 + 6 =	? **987,654**

13.

$\frac{1}{9}$ = 0.11111...	$\frac{1}{11}$ = 0.090909...
$\frac{2}{9}$ = 0.22222...	$\frac{2}{11}$ = 0.181818...
$\frac{3}{9}$ = 0.33333...	$\frac{3}{11}$ = 0.272727...
$\frac{4}{9}$ = ? **0.44444...**	$\frac{4}{11}$ = ? **0.363636...**
$\frac{5}{9}$ = ? **0.55555...**	$\frac{5}{11}$ = ? **0.454545...**

14. **Writing in Math** There are pairs of numbers that when squared, make an interesting pattern. One pair is 12^2 and 21^2; $12^2 = 144$ and $21^2 = 441$. Explain whether this pattern is the same for the pairs 13^2, 31^2 and 112^2, 211^2. **In each case, the numbers are repeated in reverse order.**

All text pages available online and on CD-ROM.

CHECK ✓

Error Intervention

If students have difficulty with the visual patterns,

then let them use counters to build each pattern from the previous one to help them focus on what is changing at each step. *(Also see* Reteaching, *p. 212B.)*

3 Practice

TEST TALK **Exercise 14** Allow students to use calculators to examine the pattern for 13^2 and 31^2. Explanations should include a description of the pattern.

Leveled Practice

Below Level Ex. 6–9, 11, 13–14

On Level Ex. 7–10, 12–14

Above Level Ex. 7–8, 10–14

Early Finishers Have students continue the patterns for the fractions in Exercise 13 through $\frac{8}{9}$ and $\frac{8}{11}$.

4 Assess

Journal Idea Have students solve this problem: Jake has \$45 in his savings account. He deposits \$60 every Monday and withdraws \$10 every Friday. Show this pattern with a list of numbers.

Enrichment — Above Level

Pick a Toothpick

E 4-3 VISUAL THINKING

Solve each toothpick puzzle.

1. Which 4 toothpicks could be removed to leave 4 congruent triangles? Draw an "X" through the toothpicks you would remove. **Sample answers are given.** 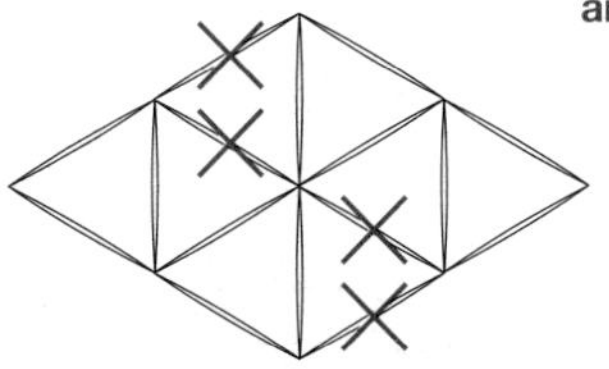
2. Move 2 toothpicks and add 1 more toothpick to make 2 diamonds. Draw an "X" through the toothpicks you would move and draw in the 2 moved toothpicks and the 1 added toothpick.

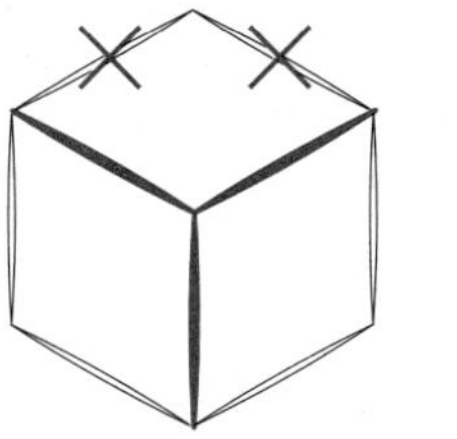

Use with Lesson 4-3. 47

Problem Solving

PROBLEM-SOLVING STRATEGY PS 4-3

Look for a Pattern

Salary Ted has been offered a new job contract. His starting salary is \$24,000 a year, and it will increase by \$3,000 a year for the next 5 years. How much will Ted be making during the fifth year?

Read and Understand

1. How much is Ted's starting salary? **\$24,000**
2. How much will Ted's salary increase each year? **\$3,000**
3. What are you trying to find? **Sample answers given for 3–7.** **How much Ted's salary will be after 5 years**

Plan and Solve

4. What strategies can you use to solve the problem? **Look for a pattern; Make a table**
5. Complete the table. What pattern repeats or changes?

Year	1	2	3	4	5
Pay	\$24,000	\$27,000	**\$30,000**	**\$33,000**	**\$36,000**

Ted's salary increases by \$3,000 each year.

6. Write the answer in a complete sentence. **Ted will be making \$36,000 during the fifth year.**

Look Back and Check

7. Explain how you can check your answer. **You can subtract \$3,000 from \$36,000 five times and find the starting salary of \$24,000.**

Use with Lesson 4-3. 47

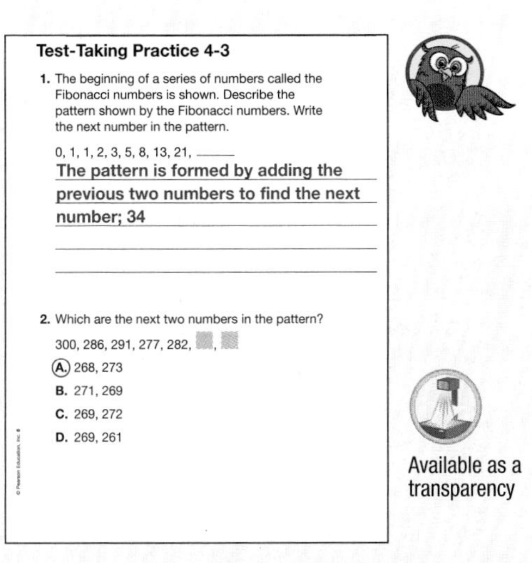
Test-Taking Practice 4-3

1. The beginning of a series of numbers called the Fibonacci numbers is shown. Describe the pattern shown by the Fibonacci numbers. Write the next number in the pattern.

   0, 1, 1, 2, 3, 5, 8, 13, 21, ____

   The pattern is formed by adding the previous two numbers to find the next number; 34

2. Which are the next two numbers in the pattern?

   300, 286, 291, 277, 282, ▒, ▒

   (A.) 268, 273
   B. 271, 269
   C. 269, 272
   D. 269, 261

Available as a transparency

Review

Purpose Help students review content learned in Section A.

Using Student Pages 214–215

Do You Know How? exercises are appropriate for written work.

Do You Understand? questions are designed for whole-class discussion or small-group discussion followed by a report to the whole class.

Vocabulary Review

You may wish to review these terms before assigning the page.

like denominators *(p. 204)*

common denominator *(p. 204)*

unlike denominators *(p. 207)*

least common multiple (LCM) *(p. 152)*

least common denominator (LCD) *(p. 164)*

Section A: Lessons 4-1 through 4-3

Review

Do You Know How?

Do You Understand?

Adding and Subtracting Fractions with Like Denominators (4-1)

Find each sum or difference. Simplify if possible.

1. $\frac{2}{3} + \frac{2}{3}$ $1\frac{1}{3}$
2. $\frac{7}{10} + \frac{1}{10}$ $\frac{4}{5}$
3. $\frac{5}{12} + \frac{11}{12}$ $1\frac{1}{3}$
4. $\frac{9}{10} - \frac{4}{10}$ $\frac{1}{2}$
5. $\frac{7}{8} - \frac{1}{8}$ $\frac{3}{4}$
6. $\frac{8}{9} - \frac{2}{9}$ $\frac{2}{3}$
7. $\frac{8}{6} - \frac{3}{6}$ $\frac{5}{6}$
8. $\frac{9}{16} + \frac{7}{16}$ 1

A Explain how you found each sum or difference. **See above.**

A. All exercises had like denominators so I added or subtracted the numerators as indicated, then simplified.

B Explain why you should add or subtract only numerators and not denominators.
The denominator indicates how many parts there are in the whole, while the numerator indicates the actual number of parts you have with which to add or subtract.

Adding and Subtracting Fractions with Unlike Denominators (4-2)

Find each sum or difference. Simplify if possible.

9. $\frac{3}{4} + \frac{1}{5}$ $\frac{19}{20}$
10. $\frac{5}{6} + \frac{7}{8}$ $1\frac{17}{24}$
11. $\frac{9}{10} + \frac{1}{2}$ $1\frac{2}{5}$
12. $\frac{11}{12} - \frac{3}{4}$ $\frac{1}{6}$
13. $\frac{2}{5} - \frac{1}{6}$ $\frac{7}{30}$
14. $\frac{7}{10} - \frac{1}{4}$ $\frac{9}{20}$
15. $\frac{7}{12} - \frac{3}{8}$ $\frac{5}{24}$
16. $\frac{3}{10} + \frac{3}{5}$ $\frac{9}{10}$

C Explain how you found the difference in Exercise 13. **See below.**

D Redo Exercises 11 and 12 using a different common denominator. Are your answers the same as your original ones? **Yes, they just needed to be reduced further.**

C. I chose the LCD of 30 and converted the fractions to $\frac{12}{30} - \frac{5}{30}$. Then I subtracted the numerators.

Problem Solving Strategy: Look for a Pattern (4-3)

17. The first three *rectangular numbers* are shown below. Look for a pattern to find the number of dots needed to represent the eighth rectangular number.

1st ●● 2nd ●●● / ●●● 3rd ●●●● / ●●●● / ●●●●

72 dots

Name the missing numbers.

18. 2, 4, 12, 48, ▪, ▪, ▪ **240; 1,440; 10,080**

E. Sample answer: I looked at how the numbers of rows and columns changed from the 1st to the 2nd, and the 2nd to the 3rd.

E Explain how you found the pattern for the rectangular numbers. **See above.**

F Which method do you think is easier for solving this problem, drawing a picture or making a table? Explain.
Sample answer: Making a table because there are so many dots to draw and count.

214 Chapter 4 Section A Review

Item Analysis for Diagnosis and Intervention

Objective	Review Items	Diagnostic Checkpoint Items	Student Book Pages*	Intervention System
Add and subtract fractions with like denominators.	1–8	1, 3, 5, 9, 19	204–205	H29
Add and subtract fractions with unlike denominators.	9–16	2, 4, 6–8, 10–14, 18, 20–21	206–209	H31
Look for patterns to solve problems.	17–18	15–17	212–213	M36

*For each lesson, there is a *Reteaching* activity in *Reaching All Learners* and a *Reteaching* master.

Chapter 4 Section A

Diagnostic Checkpoint

MULTIPLE CHOICE

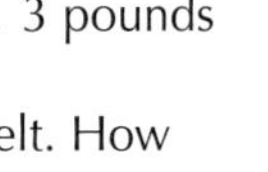

Think It Through
Be sure that you **know what operation to use** to solve the problem.

1. Juan bought $\frac{3}{4}$ pound of Delicious apples and $\frac{3}{4}$ pound of Granny Smith apples. How many pounds of apples did he buy in all? (4-1)

A. $\frac{3}{8}$ pounds **B.** $\frac{6}{8}$ pounds **(C.)** $1\frac{1}{2}$ pounds **D.** 3 pounds

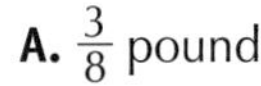

2. Ms. Chan had $\frac{1}{3}$ yard of red felt and $\frac{1}{2}$ yard of blue felt. How much more blue felt than red felt did she have? (4-2)

A. 2 yards **B.** $\frac{5}{6}$ yard **C.** $\frac{2}{5}$ yard **(D.)** $\frac{1}{6}$ yard

FREE RESPONSE

Find each sum or difference. Simplify if possible. (4-1, 4-2)

3. $\frac{5}{8} + \frac{5}{8}$ **$1\frac{1}{4}$** **4.** $\frac{4}{5} - \frac{3}{10}$ **$\frac{1}{2}$** **5.** $\frac{11}{12} + \frac{5}{12}$ **$1\frac{1}{3}$** **6.** $\frac{3}{4} + \frac{3}{6}$ **$1\frac{1}{4}$**

7. $\frac{3}{8} + \frac{3}{5}$ **$\frac{39}{40}$** **8.** $\frac{2}{3} - \frac{1}{6}$ **$\frac{1}{2}$** **9.** $\frac{7}{15} - \frac{2}{15}$ **$\frac{1}{3}$** **10.** $\frac{7}{8} + \frac{5}{12}$ **$1\frac{7}{24}$**

11. $\frac{4}{5} - \frac{1}{3}$ **$\frac{7}{15}$** **12.** $\frac{1}{6} + \frac{5}{9}$ **$\frac{13}{18}$** **13.** $\frac{5}{8} - \frac{1}{6}$ **$\frac{11}{24}$** **14.** $\frac{4}{21} + \frac{5}{7}$ **$\frac{19}{21}$**

George is to arrange oranges in a square pyramid in the produce section of his uncle's store. Use the information in the table at the right for Exercises 15–17. (4-3)

Oranges in Pyramid	
Layer	**Number**
Bottom	81
Second from bottom	64
Third from bottom	49
Fourth from bottom	36

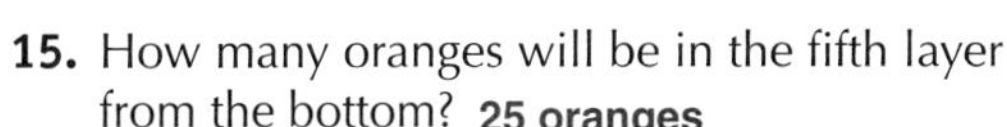

15. How many oranges will be in the fifth layer from the bottom? **25 oranges**

16. For which layer will George have 1 orange? **9th layer from bottom**

17. How many oranges will George use in all? **285 oranges**

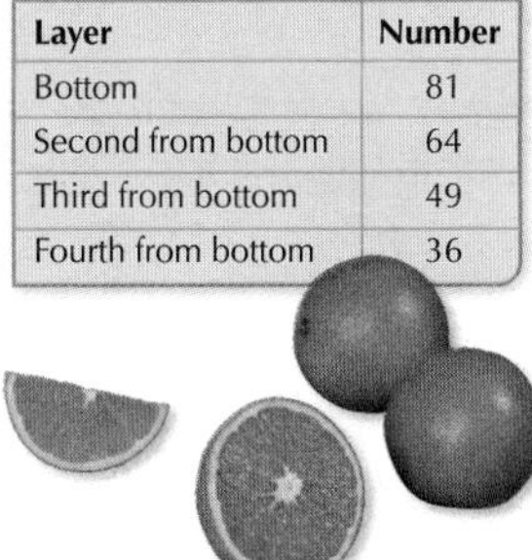

18. A recipe for muffins calls for $\frac{2}{3}$ cup granulated sugar and $\frac{3}{4}$ cup brown sugar. How much more brown sugar than granulated sugar is there in the muffins? (4-2) **$\frac{1}{12}$ cup more**

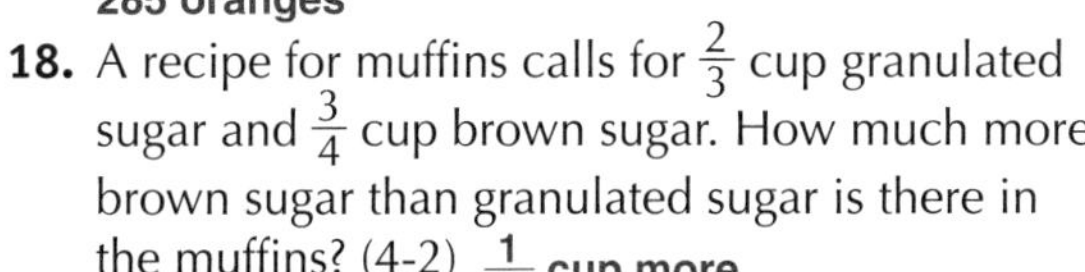

Writing in Math

19. Explain how to find $\frac{3}{8} + \frac{7}{8}$. (4-1) **Add the numerators, 3 + 7 = 10. Simplify by dividing 8 into 10 and reducing the remainder; $1\frac{1}{4}$.**

20. Explain how to find $\frac{5}{6} - \frac{1}{4}$. (4-2)
Using a common denominator of 12, write the fractions, $\frac{10}{12} - \frac{3}{12}$. Subtract numerators, 10 – 3 = 7; $\frac{7}{12}$.

21. Show how to find $\frac{3}{4} + \frac{1}{6}$ using 3 different common denominators. Are your answers the same? (4-2)
$\frac{9}{12} + \frac{2}{12} = \frac{11}{12}$, $\frac{18}{24} + \frac{4}{24} = \frac{22}{24} = \frac{11}{12}$, $\frac{36}{48} + \frac{8}{48} = \frac{44}{48} = \frac{11}{12}$; yes

Sample student work for Exercise 20

Find LCD for 6 and 4. Write equivalent fractions. Subtract the numerators. Simplify, if possible.

$\frac{5}{6} = \frac{10}{12}$

$-\frac{1}{4} = \frac{3}{12}$

$\frac{7}{12}$ ← simplest form

The rubric below is a scoring guide that shows how many points to give an answer to Exercise 20. Many teachers would assign a score of 4 points to this explanation. Discuss the sample response shown and compare it to papers produced by students.

Scoring Rubric

4 Full credit: 4 points
The answer is correct; can subtract fractions with unlike denominators; explanation is complete.

3 Partial credit: 3 points
The answer is correct; can subtract fractions with unlike denominators; explanation is incomplete.

2 Partial credit: 2 points
The answer is incorrect; can subtract fractions with unlike denominators; good explanation.

1 Partial credit: 1 point
The answer is correct; gives no explanation.

0 No credit
The answer is incorrect; can't subtract fractions with unlike denominators.

Lesson Organizer

Quick Lesson Overview

Objective Estimate sums and differences of fractions and mixed numbers using a number line, benchmark fractions, and rounding to the nearest whole number.

Math Understanding Mixed numbers can be expressed as improper fractions, or they can be broken apart into their whole-number and fractional parts. This provides a basis for estimating and doing operations with two mixed numbers, with a mixed number and a whole number, and with a mixed number and a fraction.

Vocabulary Round (p. 14)

Professional Development Note

Research Base

A clear message from the research is that students should estimate sums and differences of fractions and mixed numbers before developing algorithms and as a method of increasing their number sense with fractions (Smith, 2002). In this lesson, students learn to estimate fraction sums and differences as a readiness for working with addition and subtraction of mixed numbers in the lessons to follow.

NCTM Standards

- Number and Operations

(For a complete correlation to the NCTM Standards and Grades 6–8 Expectations, see pages 202G–H.)

Getting Started

Spiral Review

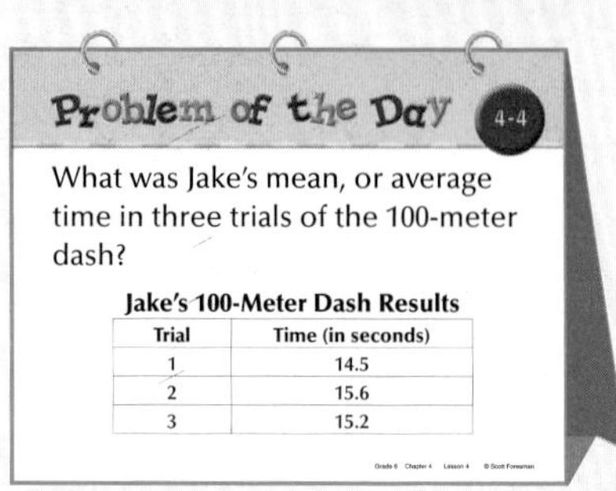

Problem of the Day 4-4

What was Jake's mean, or average time in three trials of the 100-meter dash?

Jake's 100-Meter Dash Results

Trial	Time (in seconds)
1	14.5
2	15.6
3	15.2

Topics Reviewed

- Mean
- Problem-Solving Skill: Multiple-Step Problem

Answer Jake's average time for the 100-meter dash was 15.1 sec.

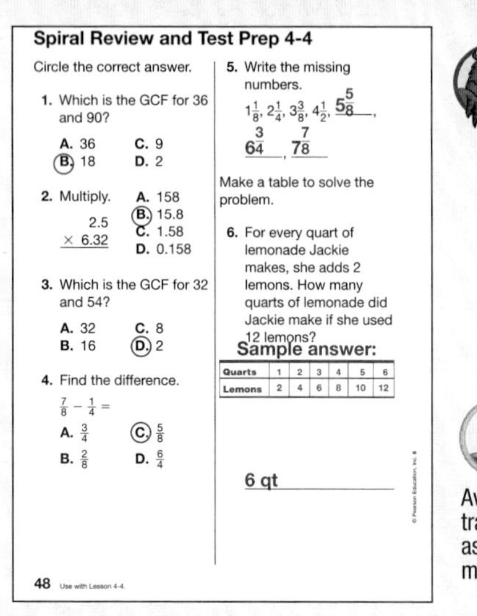

Spiral Review and Test Prep 4-4

Circle the correct answer.

1. Which is the GCF for 36 and 90?
   A. 36 (B.) 18 C. 9 D. 2
2. Multiply. 2.5×6.32
   A. 158 (B.) 15.8 C. 1.58 D. 0.158
3. Which is the GCF for 32 and 54?
   A. 32 B. 16 C. 8 (D.) 2
4. Find the difference. $\frac{7}{8} - \frac{1}{4} =$
   A. $\frac{3}{4}$ B. $\frac{2}{8}$ (C.) $\frac{5}{8}$ D. $\frac{6}{4}$
5. Write the missing numbers.
   $1\frac{1}{8}, 2\frac{1}{4}, 3\frac{3}{8}, 4\frac{1}{2}$, $5\frac{5}{8}$, $6\frac{3}{4}$, $7\frac{7}{8}$

Make a table to solve the problem.

6. For every quart of lemonade Jackie makes, she adds 2 lemons. How many quarts of lemonade did Jackie make if she used 12 lemons?

Sample answer:

Quarts	1	2	3	4	5	6
Lemons	2	4	6	8	10	12

6 qt

48 Use with Lesson 4-4.

Available as a transparency and as a blackline master

Topics Reviewed

1., 3. Greatest common factor; **2.** Multiplying decimals; **4.** Subtracting fractions with unlike denominators; **5.** Look for a pattern; **6.** Make a table

Investigating the Concept

Estimating with Centimeter Strips

20–25 MIN **Kinesthetic/Visual**

Materials *(per student)* Centimeter Grid Paper (Teaching Tool 18); markers; scissors

What to Do

- Have students cut the grids into strips of ten squares, marking a halfway point in each square.
- Write $5\frac{7}{8}$ and $3\frac{1}{3}$ on the board. **Shade a strip to show how to round each mixed number to the nearest whole number. What are the rounded numbers?** *(6, 3)*
- Have volunteers show how to use the strips to estimate the sum and difference.

Ongoing Assessment

- **Reasoning** **How can you decide if a fraction is greater than $\frac{1}{2}$?** *(If twice the numerator is greater than the denominator, the fraction is greater than $\frac{1}{2}$.)*

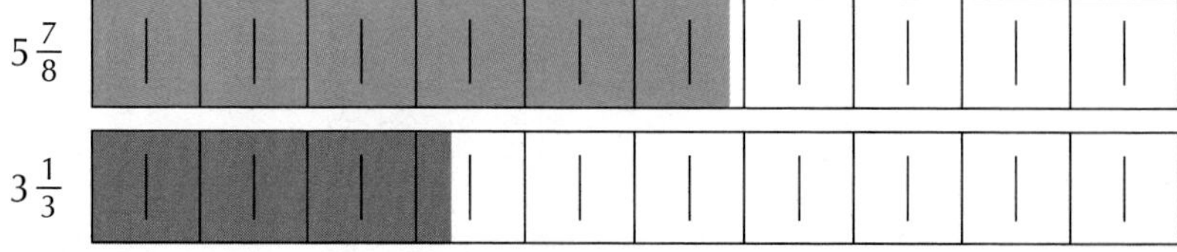

Reaching All Learners

Writing in Math

Are We There Yet?

 15–20 MIN **Linguistic** 

- Sketch a rough map on the board for students to copy. **Write a story using this map. Each distance must be a mixed number such as $1\frac{7}{8}$ miles or $2\frac{1}{4}$ miles.**
- Have students create names for the locations marked by circles and assign a distance in miles for each route.
- **Somewhere in your story, have your characters estimate the distance of a route on the map.**

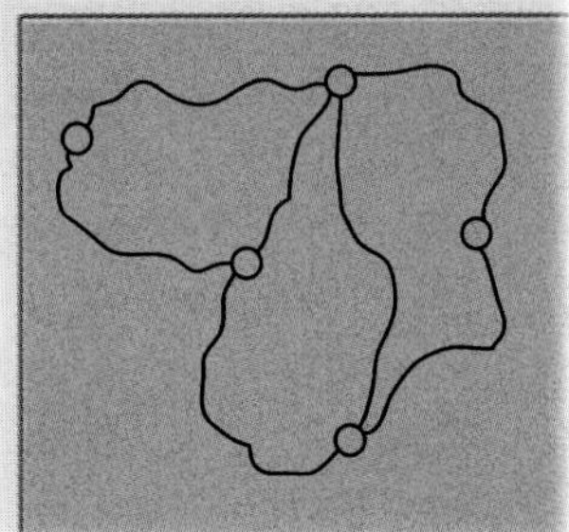

Access Content

English Language Learners

Estimating with Fractions

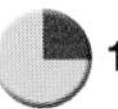 10–15 MIN **Linguistic/Verbal** 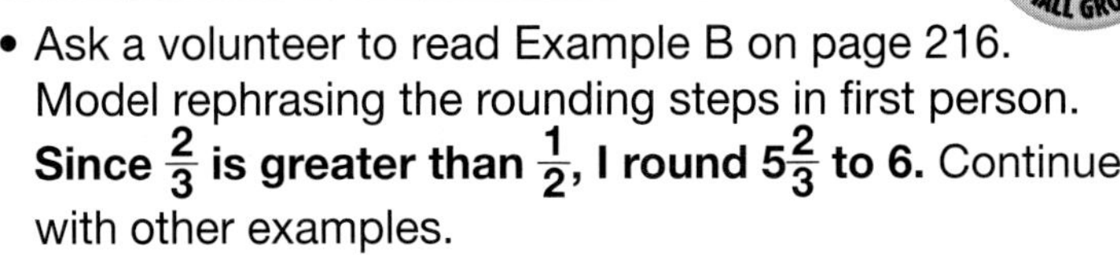

- Ask a volunteer to read Example B on page 216. Model rephrasing the rounding steps in first person. **Since $\frac{2}{3}$ is greater than $\frac{1}{2}$, I round $5\frac{2}{3}$ to 6.** Continue with other examples.
- Display mixed number addition and subtraction problems, such as $2\frac{2}{5} + 2\frac{1}{4}$. Have students explain in first person the steps involved in estimating by rounding.
- Have students discuss how estimating with fractions is similar to estimating with decimals.

Reteaching

Modeling Estimation with Circles

 15–20 MIN **Social/Cooperative** 

Materials *(per student)* Colored pencils

- On the board, model $4\frac{1}{3}$ and $2\frac{3}{4}$. **$4\frac{1}{3}$ rounds to 4, and $2\frac{3}{4}$ to 3. Why?** *($\frac{1}{3}$ is less than $\frac{1}{2}$; $\frac{3}{4}$ is greater than $\frac{1}{2}$.)*
- **To estimate the sum, add 4 and 3. To estimate the difference, subtract 3 from 4.**
- Have students model $3\frac{1}{4} + 1\frac{7}{8}$ and $3\frac{1}{4} - 1\frac{7}{8}$, and write the estimated sum and difference.

Students with Special Needs

Comparing Fractions to $\frac{1}{2}$

 15–20 MIN **Visual/Spatial** 

Materials *(per pair)* Colored pencils; 3 Copies of Fraction Models: Circles (Teaching Tool 14)

- Have partners color $\frac{1}{2}$ of each circle on the first sheet.
- On a second sheet, Partner 1 colors a circle to show a fraction greater than $\frac{1}{2}$. On the third sheet, Partner 2 finds the circle with the same number of parts and colors to show a fraction less than $\frac{1}{2}$.
- Have partners continue the activity until all the circles have been colored.

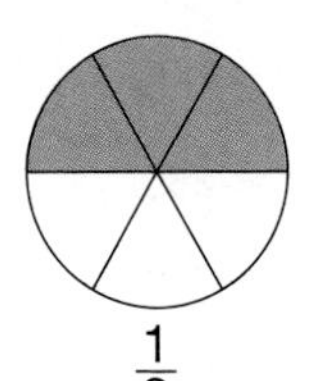
$\frac{1}{2}$

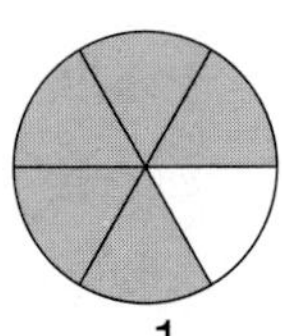
$> \frac{1}{2}$

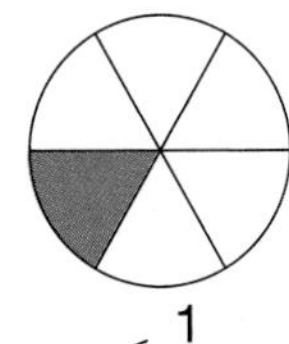
$< \frac{1}{2}$

Objective Estimate sums and differences of fractions and mixed numbers using a number line, benchmark fractions, and rounding to the nearest whole number.

1 Warm Up

Activate Prior Knowledge Review rounding decimals and writing fractions as decimals.

2 Teach

LEARN Some students will not know what a *bolt* of fabric is. Bring a sewing pattern to class to pass around so that students can see the yardage chart on the envelope and the layout showing how to position the pieces on fabrics of various widths.

Ongoing Assessment

Talk About It: Question 1

If students cannot decide how to round $5\frac{1}{2}$,

then suggest they think of rounding the decimal 5.5 to the nearest whole number. When the tenths digit is 5 or greater than 5, they should round up. One half equals 5 tenths, so one half is also rounded up.

CHECK

Error Intervention

If students are rounding incorrectly,

then they may need further practice deciding if a fraction is less than or greater than $\frac{1}{2}$. If twice the numerator is less than the denominator, the fraction is less than $\frac{1}{2}$.
(Also see Reteaching, *p. 216B.)*

Lesson 4-4

Key Idea
Estimating sums and differences of fractions and mixed numbers is similar to estimating with whole numbers, decimals, and benchmark fractions.

Vocabulary
• round (p. 14)

Think It Through
I need **data from the problem** and **data from the table.**

Estimating Sums and Differences of Fractions and Mixed Numbers

WARM UP

Estimate. Sample answers are given.
1. 3.55 + 7.3 11
2. 5 + 3.66 9
3. 0.8 − 0.25 0.5
4. 3 − 2.45 0.5

LEARN

Do you need an exact answer or is an estimate enough?

Ms. Patel wants to make a size 14 dress and a matching jacket. She has $4\frac{1}{2}$ yards of 45-inch wide fabric. Does she have enough to make the dress and jacket?

To decide if she has enough material, estimate $2\frac{7}{8} + 2\frac{1}{4}$.

Fabric Required (in yards)

	Bolt Width	Size 10	Size 12	Size 14
Dress	45 in.	$2\frac{1}{4}$	$2\frac{1}{2}$	$2\frac{7}{8}$
Dress	60 in.	$1\frac{5}{8}$	$1\frac{7}{8}$	$1\frac{7}{8}$
Jacket	45 in.	$1\frac{7}{8}$	2	$2\frac{1}{4}$
Jacket	60 in.	$1\frac{1}{2}$	$1\frac{5}{8}$	$1\frac{5}{8}$

What are some ways to estimate?

Example A

Estimate $2\frac{7}{8} + 2\frac{1}{4}$.

You can use a number line to **round** fractions and mixed numbers to the nearest whole number.

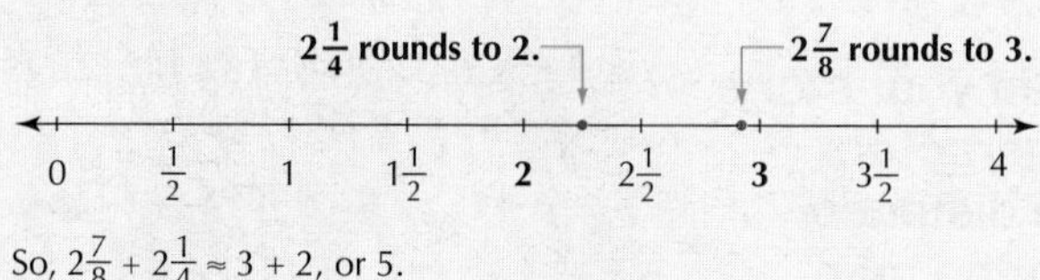

So, $2\frac{7}{8} + 2\frac{1}{4} \approx 3 + 2$, or 5.

Ms. Patel does not have enough fabric.

Example B

Estimate $5\frac{2}{3} - 2\frac{3}{8}$ by rounding to the nearest whole number.

$5\frac{2}{3} - 2\frac{3}{8} \approx 4$

Since $\frac{2}{3}$ is greater than $\frac{1}{2}$, $5\frac{2}{3}$ rounds to 6. Since $\frac{3}{8}$ is less than $\frac{1}{2}$, $2\frac{3}{8}$ rounds to 2. 6 − 2 = 4.

Talk About It

Take It to the NET
More Examples
www.scottforesman.com

1. How would you round $5\frac{1}{2}$?
Since $5\frac{1}{2}$ is halfway between 5 and 6 on a number line, it rounds to 6.

216

Reteaching — Below Level

Estimating Sums and Differences of Fractions and Mixed Numbers — R 4-4

You can use rounding to estimate sums and differences of fractions and mixed numbers.

How to round fractions:

If the fractional part is greater than or equal to $\frac{1}{2}$, round up to the next whole number.

Example: Round $3\frac{5}{7}$ to the nearest whole number.
$\frac{5}{7}$ is greater than $\frac{1}{2}$, so $3\frac{5}{7}$ rounds up to 4.

If the fractional part is less than $\frac{1}{2}$, drop the fraction and use the whole number you already have.

Example: Round $6\frac{1}{3}$ to the nearest whole number.
$\frac{1}{3}$ is less than $\frac{1}{2}$, so drop $\frac{1}{3}$ and round down to 6.

How to estimate sums and differences of fractions and mixed numbers:

Round both numbers to the nearest whole number. Then add or subtract.

Example: Estimate $4\frac{1}{8} + 7\frac{2}{3}$.
$4\frac{1}{8}$ rounds down to 4.
$7\frac{2}{3}$ rounds up to 8.
4 + 8 = 12
So, $4\frac{1}{8} + 7\frac{2}{3}$ is about 12.

Round to the nearest whole number.

1. $8\frac{6}{7}$ 9
2. $14\frac{2}{9}$ 14
3. $42\frac{4}{7}$ 43
4. $6\frac{51}{100}$ 7
5. $29\frac{4}{5}$ 30
6. $88\frac{2}{4}$ 89
7. $19\frac{3}{44}$ 19
8. $63\frac{41}{49}$ 64

Estimate each sum or difference.

9. $7\frac{2}{5} + 8\frac{1}{9}$ 15
10. $13\frac{5}{8} - 2\frac{7}{10}$ 11
11. $2\frac{1}{4} + 5\frac{1}{2} + 10\frac{3}{4}$ 19
12. $11\frac{3}{5} - 4\frac{1}{12}$ 8
13. $8 + 4\frac{11}{14} + 5\frac{1}{9}$ 18
14. $15\frac{6}{7} - 12\frac{2}{10}$ 4

48 Use with Lesson 4-4.

Practice — On Level

Estimating Sums and Differences of Fractions and Mixed Numbers — P 4-4

Round to the nearest whole number.

1. $3\frac{4}{9}$ 3
2. $5\frac{6}{7}$ 6
3. $2\frac{2}{5}$ 2
4. $11\frac{12}{15}$ 12

Estimate each sum or difference.

5. $2\frac{1}{4} + 3\frac{5}{6}$ 6
6. $5\frac{6}{9} - 1\frac{3}{4}$ 4
7. $8\frac{5}{13} + 5\frac{3}{5}$ 14
8. $11 - 6\frac{3}{7} + 2\frac{2}{5}$ 7

Rodrigo and Mel are competing in a track meet. The table at the right shows the results of their events.

Participant	Event	Results/Distance
Rodrigo	Long jump	1. $6\frac{3}{8}$ ft 2. $5\frac{5}{6}$ ft
Rodrigo	Softball throw	$62\frac{1}{5}$ ft
Mel	Long jump	1. $4\frac{7}{10}$ ft 2. $4\frac{3}{4}$ ft
Mel	Softball throw	$71\frac{7}{8}$ ft

9. Rodrigo claims his best jump was about 1 ft longer than Mel's best jump. Is he correct?
Yes, the difference is about 1 ft.

Test Prep

10. Use the table above. If the school record for the softball throw is 78 ft, about how much farther must Rodrigo throw the ball to match the record?
A. 15 ft (B.) 16 ft C. 18 ft D. 20 ft

11. **Writing in Math** Consider the sum of $\frac{3}{5} + \frac{3}{4}$. Round each fraction and estimate the sum. Add the two fractions using a common denominator and then round the result. Which estimate is closest to the actual answer?
$1 + 1 = 2$; $\frac{12}{20} + \frac{15}{20} = \frac{27}{20} = 1\frac{7}{20}$; This rounds to 1; The second estimate is closer to the actual answer.

48 Use with Lesson 4-4.

CHECK

For another example, see Set 4-4 on p. 241.

Round to the nearest whole number.

1. $5\frac{2}{7}$ **5** 2. $4\frac{5}{8}$ **5** 3. $2\frac{9}{16}$ **3** 4. $4\frac{9}{11}$ **5** 5. $8\frac{1}{8}$ **8**

Estimate each sum or difference. **Sample answers are given.**

6. $5\frac{2}{7} + 6\frac{8}{15}$ **12** 7. $4\frac{5}{8} - 3\frac{1}{3}$ **2** 8. $8\frac{6}{10} + 2\frac{1}{2}$ **12** 9. $7 - 5\frac{2}{3}$ **1** 10. $8\frac{2}{3} - 1\frac{4}{9}$ **8**

11. **Number Sense** The difference of two numbers is about 3. One of the numbers is $7\frac{9}{16}$. What might the other number be? Explain. **See below.**

PRACTICE

For more practice, see Set 4-4 on p. 244.

A Skills and Understanding

11. Sample answer: $5\frac{1}{4}$; When rounding, $7\frac{9}{16}$ is about 8; 8 − 3 is 5, so the other number rounds to 5; Since $5\frac{1}{4}$ rounds to 5, the difference of $7\frac{9}{16}$ and $5\frac{1}{4}$ is about 3.

Round to the nearest whole number.

12. $12\frac{1}{5}$ **12** 13. $6\frac{3}{5}$ **7** 14. $7\frac{4}{9}$ **7** 15. $71\frac{2}{96}$ **71** 16. $13\frac{61}{100}$ **14**

Estimate each sum or difference.

17. $10\frac{11}{20} - 3\frac{6}{25}$ **8** 18. $11\frac{5}{6} - 5\frac{12}{13}$ **6** 19. $10\frac{3}{5} + 2\frac{87}{100}$ **14** 20. $9 - 5\frac{3}{8}$ **4** 21. $3\frac{1}{5} + 6\frac{4}{7} + 5\frac{5}{9}$ **16**

22. **Number Sense** The sum of two numbers is about 5. One of the numbers is $3\frac{3}{7}$. What might the other number be? Explain. **Sample answer: $1\frac{5}{6}$; When rounding, $3\frac{3}{7}$ is about 3; 5 − 3 is 2, so the other number rounds to 2; Since $1\frac{5}{6}$ rounds to 2, the sum of $3\frac{3}{7}$ and $1\frac{5}{6}$ is about 5.**

B Reasoning and Problem Solving

For 23–24, use the table on page 216.

Elena wants to make a size 10 dress and matching jacket from 60-inch wide fabric.

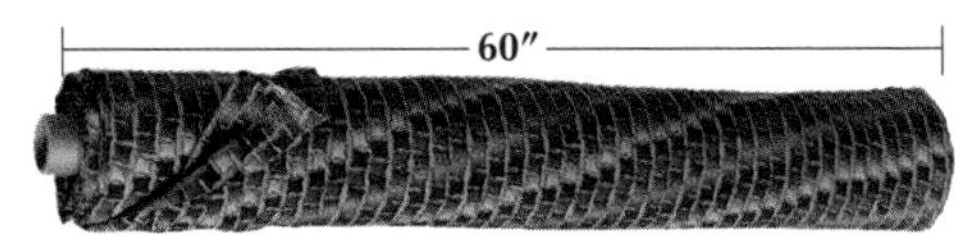

23. About how much fabric will Elena need altogether? **About 4 yards**

24. **Writing in Math** Will Elena need more fabric if she uses 45-inch wide fabric? Explain. **Yes; The amount of fabric Elena will need is closer to 4 yards.**

Mixed Review and Test Prep

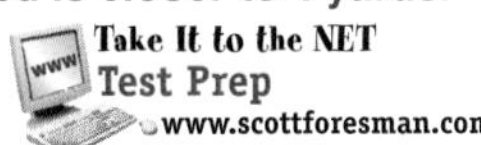

Find each answer.

25. $\frac{7}{10} + \frac{9}{10}$ **$1\frac{3}{5}$** 26. $\frac{11}{16} - \frac{7}{16}$ **$\frac{1}{4}$** 27. $\frac{5}{12} + \frac{7}{8}$ **$1\frac{7}{24}$** 28. $\frac{13}{15} - \frac{2}{5}$ **$\frac{7}{15}$**

29. **Algebra** In the equation $7\frac{1}{4} + x = 10\frac{1}{5}$, estimate the value of x. **$x \approx 3$**

30. What are the next 3 items in this pattern: 1, 5, 12, 22, 35, 51, ■, ■, ■?

A. 68, 86, 105 **(B.)** 70, 92, 117 C. 71, 94, 120 D. 83, 174, 275

All text pages available online and on CD-ROM.

3 Practice

Exercises 12–21 Before students begin, have them tell whether each fraction is less than or greater than $\frac{1}{2}$.

TEST TALK Exercise 24 Students will need to find the total yardage needed before they can make a comparison.

Leveled Practice

Below Level Ex. 12–20, 22, 24–30

On Level Ex. 14–30

Above Level Ex. 14–30

Early Finishers Have students estimate the amount of fabric needed for a dress and jacket in each of the six combinations of sizes and fabric widths. Have them show their answers in a chart.

4 Assess

Journal Idea Have students describe two situations: one in which they estimate the sum of $2\frac{1}{4}$ and $3\frac{7}{8}$ and another in which they estimate the difference of $3\frac{1}{8}$ and $1\frac{5}{6}$.

Enrichment — Above Level

Bake Sale E 4-4 DECISION MAKING

Gwen and her mother are going to prepare some foods for the school bake sale. They can choose to bake any of the foods in the chart. They can bake as many different things as they like. Use the chart to answer the questions.

Item	Sugar	Flour	Servings
Oatmeal cookies	$1\frac{1}{3}$ c	$2\frac{1}{4}$ c	18
Pound cake	$\frac{1}{2}$ c	$\frac{2}{3}$ c	12
Pumpkin bread	$1\frac{1}{2}$ c	$1\frac{3}{4}$ c	10
Apple cobbler	$\frac{3}{4}$ c	$1\frac{1}{2}$ c	8

1. Estimate to the nearest cup the amount of flour needed to make 4 loaves of pumpkin bread. **Sample answer: About 8 c**
2. Gwen wants to take at least two different items. If Gwen's mother has 2 c of sugar and 3 c of flour, name a combination of baked goods that they could prepare for the sale. **Sample answer: Oatmeal cookies and pound cake**
3. Which choice would be the best if Gwen wanted to make as many servings as possible? **Pound cake; 48 servings**
4. Would it take more sugar and flour combined to make the cookies or the pumpkin bread? **Cookies use the greater amount, $3\frac{7}{12}$ c.**
5. Gwen needs to take enough food to the bake sale for at least 30 servings. What are some different combinations of baked goods she could take? **Sample answers: 1 apple cobbler and 2 pound cakes; oatmeal cookies and 1 pound cake**
6. Estimate the amount of flour needed to bake everything listed in the chart. **Sample answer: About 7 c**

48 Use with Lesson 4-4.

Problem Solving

Estimating Sums and Differences of Fractions and Mixed Numbers PS 4-4

Window Box Jill needs to replace two pieces of wood on her window plant box. One piece is $12\frac{3}{4}$ in. long, and the other piece is $4\frac{3}{16}$ in.

1. About how much wood does Jill need? **About 17 in. of wood**
2. Jill has a board that is $16\frac{1}{2}$ in. long. Is her board long enough? **No**

Frog Jumping Mykayla's pet frog jumped $7\frac{5}{16}$ in. Then it jumped another $4\frac{3}{32}$ in.

3. About how far did Mykayla's frog jump altogether? **About 11 in.**
4. About how much farther did the frog jump the first time? **About 3 in.**
5. Did you overestimate or underestimate for Exercise 4? **Underestimate**
6. **Writing in Math** Explain how using compatible numbers is different than rounding. **Sample answer: Using compatible numbers, you can use any numbers that are close to the actual numbers and that are easy to compute. When you round, you find the nearest whole number.**

48 Use with Lesson 4-4.

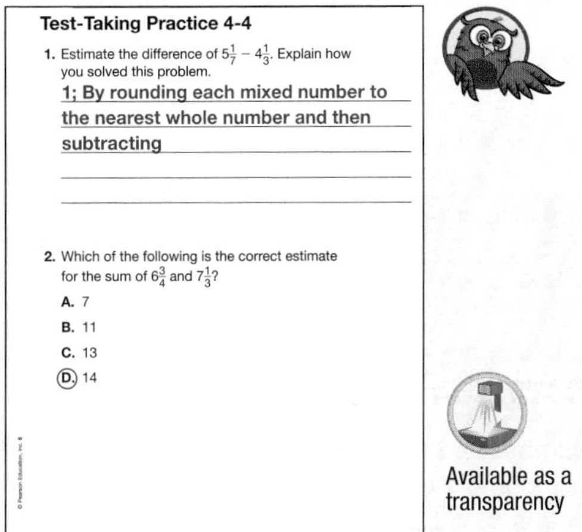

Test-Taking Practice 4-4

1. Estimate the difference of $5\frac{1}{7} - 4\frac{1}{3}$. Explain how you solved this problem. **1; By rounding each mixed number to the nearest whole number and then subtracting**
2. Which of the following is the correct estimate for the sum of $6\frac{3}{4}$ and $7\frac{1}{3}$?

A. 7
B. 11
C. 13
(D.) 14

Available as a transparency

4-5 Adding Mixed Numbers

Lesson Organizer

Quick Lesson Overview

Objective Find sums of mixed numbers with and without renaming.

Math Understanding Mixed numbers can be expressed as improper fractions, or they can be broken apart into their whole-number and fractional parts. This provides a basis for estimating and doing operations with two mixed numbers, with a mixed number and a whole number, and with a mixed number and a fraction.

Vocabulary Mixed number (p. 168)

Professional Development Note

Managing Instruction Customary measurements offer good opportunities for adding mixed numbers. Have students work with a family member to find perimeters of rooms in feet. Have them measure each length and express inches as fractions of feet *(2 inches = $\frac{1}{6}$ foot, 3 inches = $\frac{1}{4}$ foot, and so on)*, and then add to find the perimeter.

NCTM Standards

- Number and Operations

(For a complete correlation to the NCTM Standards and Grades 6–8 Expectations, see pages 202G–H.)

Getting Started

Spiral Review

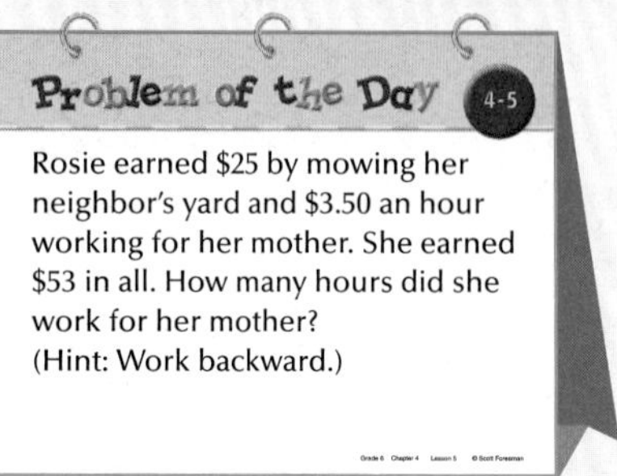

Problem of the Day 4-5

Rosie earned $25 by mowing her neighbor's yard and $3.50 an hour working for her mother. She earned $53 in all. How many hours did she work for her mother?
(Hint: Work backward.)

Topics Reviewed

- Subtracting whole numbers; dividing decimals
- Problem-Solving Strategy: Work Backward

Answer Rosie worked 8 hr for her mother.

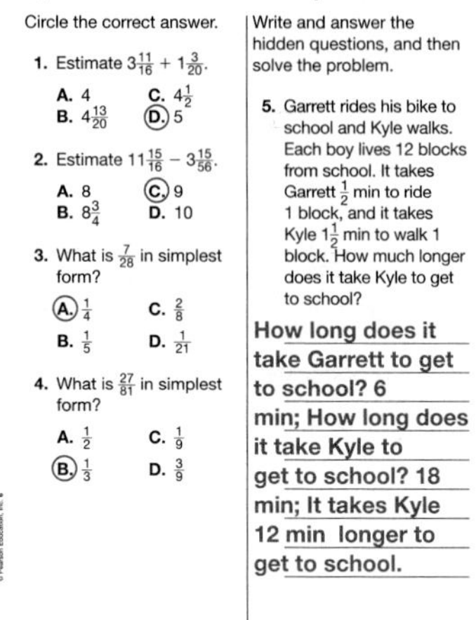

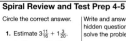

Spiral Review and Test Prep 4-5

Circle the correct answer.

1. Estimate $3\frac{11}{16} + 1\frac{3}{20}$.
   A. 4 B. $4\frac{13}{20}$ C. $4\frac{1}{2}$ (D.) 5
2. Estimate $11\frac{15}{16} - 3\frac{15}{56}$.
   A. 8 B. $8\frac{3}{4}$ (C.) 9 D. 10
3. What is $\frac{7}{28}$ in simplest form?
   (A.) $\frac{1}{4}$ B. $\frac{1}{5}$ C. $\frac{2}{8}$ D. $\frac{1}{21}$
4. What is $\frac{27}{81}$ in simplest form?
   A. $\frac{1}{2}$ (B.) $\frac{1}{3}$ C. $\frac{1}{9}$ D. $\frac{3}{9}$

Write and answer the hidden questions, and then solve the problem.

5. Garrett rides his bike to school and Kyle walks. Each boy lives 12 blocks from school. It takes Garrett $\frac{1}{2}$ min to ride 1 block, and it takes Kyle $1\frac{1}{2}$ min to walk 1 block. How much longer does it take Kyle to get to school?
   How long does it take Garrett to get to school? 6 min; How long does it take Kyle to get to school? 18 min; It takes Kyle 12 min longer to get to school.

Use with Lesson 4-5. 49

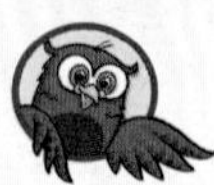

Available as a transparency and as a blackline master

Topics Reviewed

1. Estimating sums of fractions and mixed numbers; **2.** Estimating differences of fractions and mixed numbers; **3.–4.** Simplest form; **5.** Multiple-step problems

Investigating the Concept

Circle Models for Mixed-Number Addition

20–25 MIN **Visual/Spatial**

Materials *(per student)* Colored pencils

What to Do

- **Draw two 12-part circles and shade them to show $\frac{1}{3}$ and $\frac{3}{4}$. Now draw 4 circles to show $4\frac{1}{3}$ and 2 circles to show $2\frac{3}{4}$.**
- **How can you find the sum of the fractions?** *(Count the twelfths.)* **What is the sum?** *($\frac{13}{12}$)* **Rename $\frac{13}{12}$.** *($1\frac{1}{12}$)* **Add that to the whole number sum.** *($4 + 2 + 1\frac{1}{12} = 7\frac{1}{12}$)*

Ongoing Assessment

- **Number Sense How can you tell from the models that the sum is greater than 6?** *(The sum of just the whole numbers, without the fractions, is 6.)*
- **Use 12-part circles to show another mixed-number addition problem.**

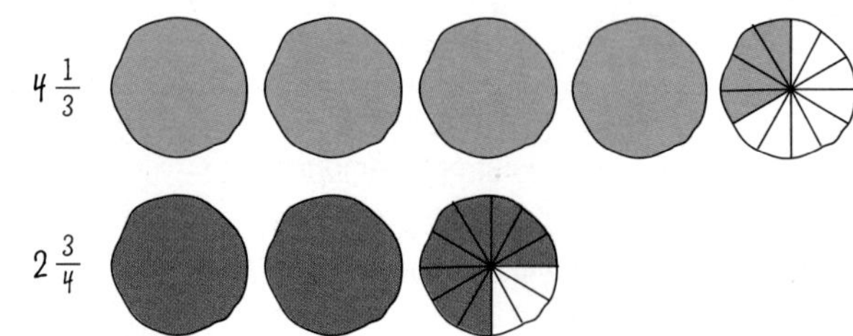

Reaching All Learners

Math Vocabulary

Using Terms in Context

15–20 MIN **Linguistic**

- Write these terms on the board: numerator, denominator, mixed number, whole number, improper fraction, proper fraction, simplify, simplest form, common factor, equivalent fractions, like denominators, unlike denominators, rename, common denominator
- Have students write sentences to illustrate that they know the meanings of the terms. Examples:

  I divided by the common factor 2 to find the simplest form of $\frac{4}{6}$.

  In the problem $3\frac{1}{2} + 5\frac{3}{4}$, the fraction parts have unlike denominators.
- Have volunteers share their sentences.

Activate Prior Knowledge/Build Background

English Language Learners

Creating Mixed Numbers

10–15 MIN **Visual/Spatial/Auditory**

Materials *(per pair)* Index cards with whole numbers 1–10 and fractions (on separate cards)

- Display a whole number with a fraction card. **Read the number. What do you call a number with a whole number and a fraction?** *(Mixed number)*
- Using fractions with like denominators, display a mixed-number addition problem. Have one partner add the fractions first, then the whole numbers. Have the other partner add the whole numbers first, then the fractions. Then have partners check to see if they got the same answer and retell how they worked through the problem.
- Repeat the activity using different number and fraction cards.

4	$\frac{1}{5}$	+	2	$\frac{3}{5}$

Reteaching

Taking Turns to Add

15–20 MIN **Social/Cooperative**

- Begin the problem shown, using boxes for the equivalent fractions.
- **What do we need to add the fractions?** *(A common denominator)* Have volunteers put 10 in the denominator boxes, find the equivalent fractions, add, and simplify the answer.
- Have each student create a mixed number with 2, 5, or 10 as the denominator. Have partners take turns doing the steps to add their two mixed numbers.

$$\begin{array}{rcr} 3\frac{1}{2} & = & 3\frac{\square}{\square} \\ +\,2\frac{4}{5} & = & +\,2\frac{\square}{\square} \\ \hline \end{array}$$

Advanced Learners

Mixed-Number Magic Squares

15–20 MIN **Logical/Mathematical**

- On the board, copy the magic square shown. **In a magic square, the sum of each row, column, and diagonal is the same. What is the magic sum?** *($4\frac{1}{2}$)*
- Have students create another magic square by adding $\frac{3}{4}$ to the number in each cell. **What is the new magic sum?** *($6\frac{3}{4}$)*
- Have students create a different magic square that uses mixed numbers.

$1\frac{3}{4}$	$1\frac{1}{6}$	$1\frac{7}{12}$
$1\frac{1}{3}$	$1\frac{1}{2}$	$1\frac{2}{3}$
$1\frac{5}{12}$	$1\frac{5}{6}$	$1\frac{1}{4}$

Objective Find sums of mixed numbers with and without renaming.

1 Warm Up

Activate Prior Knowledge Review writing improper fractions as mixed numbers.

2 Teach

LEARN In Example B, point out that both fraction parts are greater than $\frac{1}{2}$. So, the sum of the fractions will be greater than 1.

Ongoing Assessment

Talk About It: Question 1

If students are not certain whether it makes any difference whether they add the fractions or the whole numbers first,

then have them experiment with a few problems to see that it makes no difference. In each case, they add the whole numbers and the fractions separately and then combine the two sums.

CHECK

Error Intervention

If students forget to rename improper fractions in the sum,

then remind them that the numerator must be less than the denominator. Review the fact that a fraction equals 1 when the numerator and denominator are equal. *(Also see* Reteaching, *p. 218B.)*

Key Idea
To add mixed numbers, you can add the fraction parts to the whole number parts, and simplify.

Vocabulary
- mixed number (p. 168)

Think It Through
I should **estimate** the sum before working the problem.

Adding Mixed Numbers

WARM UP

Write as mixed numbers.

1. $\frac{38}{3}$ $12\frac{2}{3}$
2. $\frac{41}{9}$ $4\frac{5}{9}$
3. $\frac{50}{7}$ $7\frac{1}{7}$
4. $\frac{805}{8}$ $100\frac{5}{8}$

LEARN

How can you find the sum of mixed numbers?

Example A

Rossita measured the amount of precipitation over a 2-month period. It rained $2\frac{3}{10}$ inches in June and $2\frac{1}{2}$ inches in July. What was the total precipitation for June and July?

Find $2\frac{3}{10} + 2\frac{1}{2}$. Estimate: 2 + 3 = 5

Write equivalent fractions with the LCD.

$$2\frac{3}{10} = 2\frac{3}{10}$$
$$+\,2\frac{1}{2} = +\,2\frac{5}{10}$$

STEP 2

Add the whole numbers. Add the fractions. Simplify if possible.

$$2\frac{3}{10} = 2\frac{3}{10}$$
$$+\,2\frac{1}{2} = +\,2\frac{5}{10}$$
$$4\frac{8}{10} = 4\frac{4}{5}$$

Example B

Find $7\frac{9}{10} + 3\frac{3}{5}$. Estimate: 8 + 4 = 12

Write equivalent fractions with the LCD.

$$7\frac{9}{10} = 7\frac{9}{10}$$
$$+\,3\frac{3}{5} = +\,3\frac{6}{10}$$

STEP 2

Add the whole numbers. Add the fractions. Rename improper fractions as **mixed numbers.** Simplify.

$$7\frac{9}{10} = 7\frac{9}{10} = 7\frac{9}{10}$$
$$+\,3\frac{3}{5} = +\,3\frac{6}{10} = +\,3\frac{6}{10}$$
$$10\frac{15}{10} = 11\frac{1}{2}$$

$\frac{15}{10} = 1\frac{5}{10} = 1\frac{1}{2}$

Talk About It

1. Does it matter whether you add the fractions first or the whole numbers first? **No**

Reteaching — Below Level

Adding Mixed Numbers

R 4-5

To add mixed numbers, you can add the fractional parts to the whole number parts, and then simplify.

Find $2\frac{2}{4} + 3\frac{1}{4}$.

The fractions have a common denominator. Add the fractions. Then add the whole numbers.

$$2\frac{2}{4} + 3\frac{1}{4} = 5\frac{3}{4}$$

Find $3\frac{2}{3} + 4\frac{1}{9}$.

Write equivalent fractions with the LCD.

$$3\frac{2}{3} = 3\frac{6}{9}$$
$$+\,4\frac{1}{9} = 4\frac{1}{9}$$

Add the whole numbers. Add the fractions. Simplify if possible.

$$3\frac{6}{9} + 4\frac{1}{9} = 7\frac{7}{9}$$

Find $4 + 3\frac{3}{5}$.

Add the whole numbers; then add the fraction.

$$4 + 3\frac{3}{5} = 7\frac{3}{5}$$

Find each sum. Simplify your answer.

1. $2\frac{1}{5} + 2\frac{3}{5} =$ **$4\frac{4}{5}$**
2. $4\frac{2}{3} + 1\frac{1}{6} =$ **$5\frac{5}{6}$**
3. $5\frac{3}{5} + \frac{3}{10} =$ **$5\frac{9}{10}$**
4. $8\frac{5}{8} + 1\frac{5}{12} =$ **$10\frac{1}{24}$**
5. $6\frac{1}{4} + 11\frac{3}{8} =$ **$17\frac{5}{8}$**
6. $7 + 8\frac{1}{3} =$ **$15\frac{1}{3}$**
7. In 2001, the men's indoor pole vault record was $20\frac{1}{6}$ ft. The women's record for the indoor pole vault was $15\frac{5}{12}$ ft. What is the combined height of the two records? **$35\frac{7}{12}$ ft**
8. **Writing in Math** How high is a stack of library books if one book is $1\frac{3}{8}$ in. high, the second book is $1\frac{5}{6}$ in. high, and the third is $2\frac{1}{3}$ in. high? Explain how you solved this problem.
$5\frac{13}{24}$ in.; You need to find the LCD to solve this problem.

Use with Lesson 4-5. 49

Practice — On Level

Adding Mixed Numbers

P 4-5

Find each sum. Simplify your answer.

1. $5 + 3\frac{1}{6} =$ **$8\frac{1}{6}$**
2. $4\frac{4}{5} + 8\frac{1}{10} =$ **$12\frac{9}{10}$**
3. $1\frac{5}{8} + \frac{15}{16} =$ **$2\frac{9}{16}$**
4. $6\frac{2}{3} + \frac{5}{4} =$ **$7\frac{11}{12}$**
5. $2\frac{7}{8} + 4 =$ **$6\frac{7}{8}$**
6. $7\frac{6}{10} + 1\frac{9}{20} =$ **$9\frac{1}{20}$**
7. $\frac{7}{8} + 3\frac{3}{5} + 2 =$ **$6\frac{19}{40}$**
8. $9 + 3\frac{2}{3} + \frac{5}{6} =$ **$13\frac{1}{2}$**
9. **Number Sense** Give an example of two mixed numbers whose sum is a whole number.
Sample answer: Any two mixed numbers that include halves as fractional parts, such as $6\frac{1}{2} + 2\frac{5}{10}$
10. An ostrich egg is $6\frac{4}{5}$ in. long. A California condor's egg is $4\frac{3}{10}$ in. long, and an albatross egg is $5\frac{7}{10}$ in. long. If the three eggs are placed end to end, what is the total length in inches? **$16\frac{4}{5}$ in.**
11. Shanda can travel 10 mi on her electric scooter before she has to recharge the batteries. If it is $4\frac{5}{8}$ mi to the library and $5\frac{2}{5}$ mi to her friend's house, can she make both trips before she needs to recharge the batteries?
No; $4\frac{5}{8} + 5\frac{2}{5} = 10\frac{1}{40}$, which is greater than 10

Test Prep

12. Which is the fractional portion of the solution to $5\frac{3}{8} + 2\frac{3}{12}$?
A. $\frac{6}{12}$ **(B.)** $\frac{15}{24}$ C. $\frac{6}{8}$ D. $\frac{15}{8}$
13. **Writing in Math** Explain the steps to adding mixed numbers. What must you do first?
Sample answer: Find a common denominator, add the whole numbers, add the fractions, and simplify if possible.

Use with Lesson 4-5. 49

 EC NTL 12 11 10 9 8 7 6

CHECK

For another example, see Set 4-5 on p. 241.

Find each sum. Simplify your answer.

1. $4\frac{3}{8} + 5\frac{5}{12}$ **$9\frac{19}{24}$** **2.** $1\frac{1}{4} + 3\frac{3}{5}$ **$4\frac{17}{20}$** **3.** $3\frac{5}{6} + 7\frac{8}{9}$ **$11\frac{13}{18}$** **4.** $2\frac{3}{4} + 6\frac{7}{8}$ **$9\frac{5}{8}$**

5. Reasoning Before you add, how can you tell whether the fraction part of the sum will be an improper fraction? **If both fractions are greater than $\frac{1}{2}$ their sum will be an improper fraction.**

PRACTICE

For more practice, see Set 4-5 on p. 244.

A Skills and Understanding

Find each sum. Simplify your answer.

6. $8 + 7\frac{2}{5}$ **$15\frac{2}{5}$** **7.** $8\frac{2}{9} + 1\frac{7}{12}$ **$9\frac{29}{36}$** **8.** $4\frac{1}{12} + 3\frac{5}{12}$ **$7\frac{1}{2}$** **9.** $\frac{8}{15} + 2\frac{11}{15}$ **$3\frac{4}{15}$** **10.** $8\frac{1}{6} + \frac{10}{12}$ **9**

11. $12\frac{1}{2} + 9$ **$21\frac{1}{2}$** **12.** $3\frac{3}{4} + 8\frac{7}{8}$ **$12\frac{5}{8}$** **13.** $8\frac{9}{10} + 2\frac{3}{4}$ **$11\frac{13}{20}$** **14.** $2\frac{2}{5} + 8\frac{7}{10} + 4\frac{1}{6}$ **$15\frac{4}{15}$** **15.** $\frac{5}{6} + 3\frac{5}{12} + 9\frac{3}{4}$ **14**

16. Number Sense Is the sum of two mixed numbers always a mixed number? Explain. **No; If the sum of the fractions is a whole number, the answer will be a whole number.**

B Reasoning and Problem Solving

17. Find the annual average precipitation for Boise and Phoenix. **$11\frac{4}{5}$ in., $6\frac{9}{10}$ in.**

18. By how many inches do the two annual sums differ? **$4\frac{9}{10}$ in.**

19. Writing in Math Explain how to find $5\frac{7}{10} + 6\frac{11}{15}$. **Add the whole numbers. Then find the LCD and add the fractions, simplify, and add to the whole number.**

Data File

Average Annual Precipitation (in inches)

City	Jan. to March	April to June	July to Aug.	Sept. to Dec.
Boise, ID	$3\frac{7}{10}$	$3\frac{2}{5}$	$1\frac{3}{10}$	$3\frac{2}{5}$
Phoenix, AZ	$2\frac{1}{10}$	$\frac{3}{5}$	$2\frac{3}{10}$	$1\frac{9}{10}$

C Extensions

20. Mental Math Explain how you could find $5\frac{5}{8} + 3\frac{3}{4} + 2\frac{1}{4} + 8\frac{3}{8}$ mentally. **See above.**

20. Add the fractions that add to 1; $\frac{5}{8} + \frac{3}{8}$ and $\frac{3}{4} + \frac{1}{4}$; then add all the whole numbers.

21. Number Sense Without computing, tell which is greater, $2\frac{7}{8} + 3\frac{1}{4}$ or $2\frac{5}{6} + 3\frac{1}{4}$. **$2\frac{7}{8} + 3\frac{1}{4}$ because $2\frac{7}{8} > 2\frac{5}{6}$**

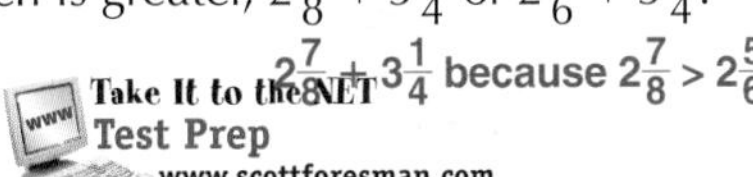

Estimate each sum or difference. **Sample answers are given.**

22. $11\frac{5}{16} - 7\frac{7}{8}$ **3** **23.** $5\frac{7}{8} + 3\frac{1}{3}$ **9** **24.** $12\frac{1}{10} - 10\frac{8}{9}$ **1** **25.** $3\frac{2}{3} + 5\frac{1}{5} + 9\frac{7}{10}$ **19**

26. Which property of numbers is illustrated by $15 + (5 \times 5) = (5 \times 5) + 15$?

A. Commutative Property of Multiplication
B. Distributive Property
C. Associative Property
(D.) Commutative Property of Addition

All text pages available online and on CD-ROM.

3 Practice

Exercise 18 Point out that the word *about* signals that an estimate is required.

Exercise 19 Suggest that students organize their explanations in steps. Help them begin by writing, "Step 1. Write the problem vertically."

Leveled Practice

Below Level Ex. 6–15, 17, 19, 22–26

On Level Ex. 8–19, 22–26

Above Level Ex. 10–26

Early Finishers Have students draw number lines showing sixteenths to model $1\frac{5}{16} + 1\frac{3}{4}$ and twelfths to model $2\frac{2}{3} + 1\frac{3}{4}$.

4 Assess

Journal Idea Have students explain why it is sometimes necessary to rename when adding mixed numbers.

Enrichment — Above Level

What Comes Next? E 4-5 PATTERNS

You have found patterns in number sequences before. You can also find patterns and rules for fraction sequences. Complete each pattern and write the rule.

1. $2\frac{1}{3}, 2\frac{2}{3}, 3, 3\frac{1}{3},$ **$3\frac{2}{3}$**, **4**, **$4\frac{1}{3}$**
   Rule: **Add $\frac{1}{3}$**
2. $\frac{1}{2}, 4, 7\frac{1}{2}, 11,$ **$14\frac{1}{2}$**, **18**, **$21\frac{1}{2}$**
   Rule: **Add $3\frac{1}{2}$**
3. $\frac{4}{7}, 2\frac{1}{7}, 3\frac{5}{7}, 5\frac{2}{7},$ **$6\frac{6}{7}$**, **$8\frac{3}{7}$**, **10**
   Rule: **Add $1\frac{4}{7}$**
4. $\frac{3}{4}, 1\frac{7}{12}, 2\frac{5}{12}, 3\frac{1}{4},$ **$4\frac{1}{12}$**, **$4\frac{11}{12}$**, **$5\frac{3}{4}$**
   Rule: **Add $\frac{5}{6}$**
5. $13\frac{4}{5}, 14\frac{9}{10}, 16, 17\frac{1}{10},$ **$18\frac{1}{5}$**, **$19\frac{3}{10}$**, **$20\frac{2}{5}$**
   Rule: **Add $1\frac{1}{10}$**
6. $6\frac{1}{16}, 10\frac{9}{16}, 15\frac{1}{16}, 19\frac{9}{16},$ **$24\frac{1}{16}$**, **$28\frac{9}{16}$**, **$33\frac{1}{16}$**
   Rule: **Add $4\frac{1}{2}$**

Draw the next three pictures for the pattern.

7. $\frac{1}{4}$ $\frac{3}{8}$ $\frac{1}{2}$ $\frac{5}{8}$ $\frac{3}{4}$ $\frac{7}{8}$

Use with Lesson 4-5. 49

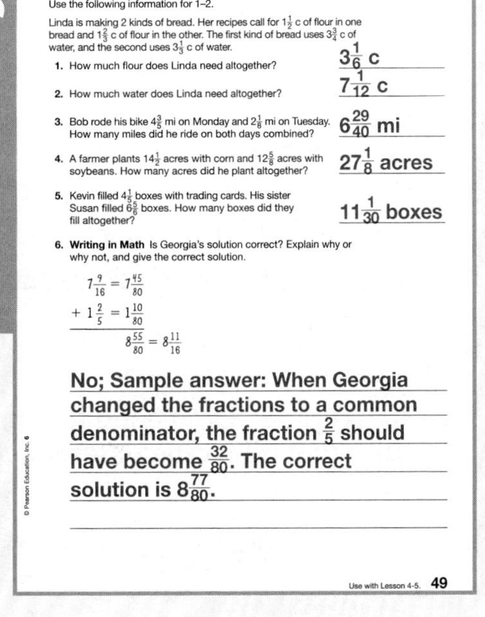

Problem Solving

Adding Mixed Numbers PS 4-5

Use the following information for 1–2.

Linda is making 2 kinds of bread. Her recipes call for $1\frac{1}{2}$ c of flour in one bread and $1\frac{2}{3}$ c of flour in the other. The first kind of bread uses $3\frac{3}{4}$ c of water, and the second uses $3\frac{1}{3}$ c of water.

1. How much flour does Linda need altogether? **$3\frac{1}{6}$ c**
2. How much water does Linda need altogether? **$7\frac{1}{12}$ c**
3. Bob rode his bike $4\frac{3}{5}$ mi on Monday and $2\frac{1}{8}$ mi on Tuesday. How many miles did he ride on both days combined? **$6\frac{29}{40}$ mi**
4. A farmer plants $14\frac{1}{2}$ acres with corn and $12\frac{5}{8}$ acres with soybeans. How many acres did he plant altogether? **$27\frac{1}{8}$ acres**
5. Kevin filled $4\frac{1}{5}$ boxes with trading cards. His sister Susan filled $6\frac{5}{6}$ boxes. How many boxes did they fill altogether? **$11\frac{1}{30}$ boxes**
6. **Writing in Math** Is Georgia's solution correct? Explain why or why not, and give the correct solution.

$$7\frac{9}{16} = 7\frac{45}{80}$$
$$+\ 1\frac{2}{5} = 1\frac{10}{80}$$
$$8\frac{55}{80} = 8\frac{11}{16}$$

No; Sample answer: When Georgia changed the fractions to a common denominator, the fraction $\frac{2}{5}$ should have become $\frac{32}{80}$. The correct solution is $8\frac{77}{80}$.

Use with Lesson 4-5. 49

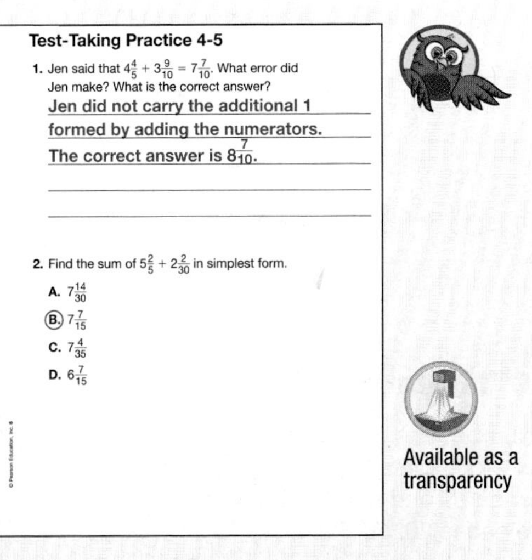

Test-Taking Practice 4-5

1. Jen said that $4\frac{4}{5} + 3\frac{9}{10} = 7\frac{7}{10}$. What error did Jen make? What is the correct answer?
   Jen did not carry the additional 1 formed by adding the numerators. The correct answer is $8\frac{7}{10}$.
2. Find the sum of $5\frac{2}{5} + 2\frac{2}{30}$ in simplest form.
   A. $7\frac{14}{30}$
   (B.) $7\frac{7}{15}$
   C. $7\frac{4}{35}$
   D. $6\frac{7}{15}$

Available as a transparency

Lesson Organizer

Quick Lesson Overview

Objective Find differences of mixed numbers with and without renaming.

Math Understanding Mixed numbers can be expressed as improper fractions, or they can be broken apart into their whole-number and fractional parts. This provides a basis for estimating and doing operations with two mixed numbers, with a mixed number and a whole number, and with a mixed number and a fraction.

Vocabulary Mixed number (p. 168)

Materials for Student Pages
Fraction Strips or Teaching Tool 9 or Fraction eTool

How Children Learn Math
Students may have become used to adding whole numbers first when adding mixed numbers. This is *not* a good idea when subtracting because fraction parts may need to be renamed.

NCTM Standards
- Number and Operations

(For a complete correlation to the NCTM Standards and Grades 6–8 Expectations, see pages 202G–H.)

Getting Started

Spiral Review

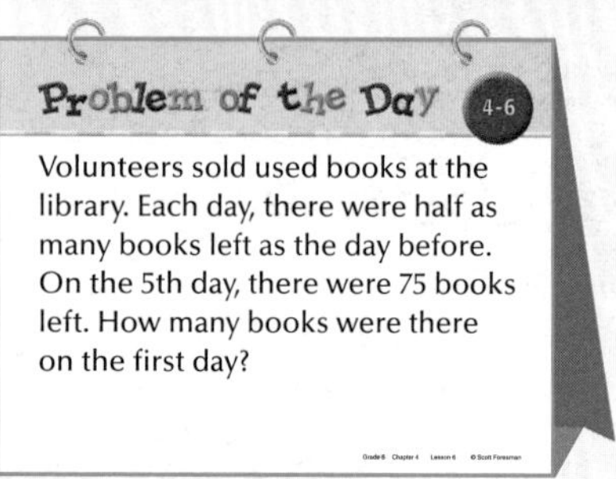
Problem of the Day 4-6

Volunteers sold used books at the library. Each day, there were half as many books left as the day before. On the 5th day, there were 75 books left. How many books were there on the first day?

Topics Reviewed
- Multiplying whole numbers
- Problem-Solving Strategy: Work Backward

Answer There were 1,200 books to sell on the first day.

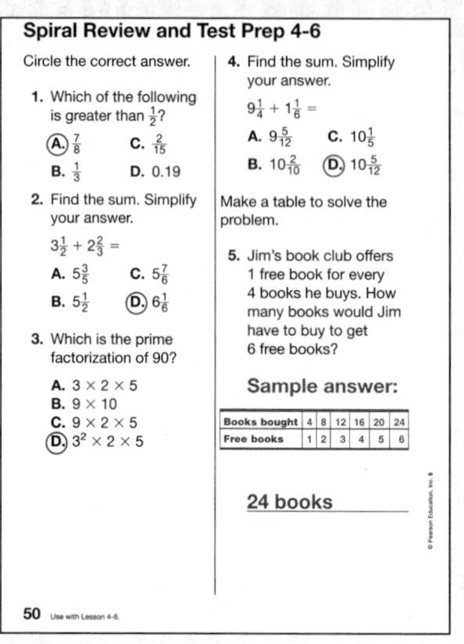
Spiral Review and Test Prep 4-6

Circle the correct answer.

1. Which of the following is greater than $\frac{1}{2}$?
   (A.) $\frac{7}{8}$ C. $\frac{2}{15}$
   B. $\frac{1}{3}$ D. 0.19
2. Find the sum. Simplify your answer.
   $3\frac{1}{2} + 2\frac{2}{3} =$
   A. $5\frac{3}{5}$ C. $5\frac{7}{6}$
   B. $5\frac{1}{2}$ (D.) $6\frac{1}{6}$
3. Which is the prime factorization of 90?
   A. $3 \times 2 \times 5$
   B. 9×10
   C. $9 \times 2 \times 5$
   (D.) $3^2 \times 2 \times 5$
4. Find the sum. Simplify your answer.
   $9\frac{1}{4} + 1\frac{1}{6} =$
   A. $9\frac{5}{12}$ C. $10\frac{1}{5}$
   B. $10\frac{2}{10}$ (D.) $10\frac{5}{12}$

Make a table to solve the problem.

5. Jim's book club offers 1 free book for every 4 books he buys. How many books would Jim have to buy to get 6 free books?

Sample answer:

Books bought	4	8	12	16	20	24
Free books	1	2	3	4	5	6

24 books

© Pearson Education, Inc. 6

50 Use with Lesson 4-6.

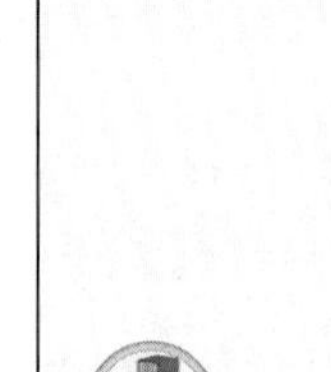

Available as a transparency and as a blackline master

Topics Reviewed
1. Comparing fractions; **2.** Adding mixed numbers; **3.** Prime factorization; **4.** Subtracting mixed numbers; **5.** Make a table

Investigating the Concept

Subtracting Mixed Numbers with Fraction Strips

20–25 MIN **Kinesthetic** PAIRS

Materials *(per pair)* Fraction Strips or Teaching Tool 15; colored pencils; scissors

What to Do
- Write $4\frac{1}{6} - 2\frac{5}{6}$ on the board. Have students cut out fraction strips to show $4\frac{1}{6}$.
- **Can you subtract $\frac{5}{6}$ from $\frac{1}{6}$?** *(No)* **Rename $4\frac{1}{6}$ to show more sixths. How can you do this?** *(Change a 1 strip to 6 sixths.)*
- **Cross out $2\frac{5}{6}$. How much is left?** *($1\frac{2}{6}$)* **What is the simplest form?** *($1\frac{1}{3}$)*

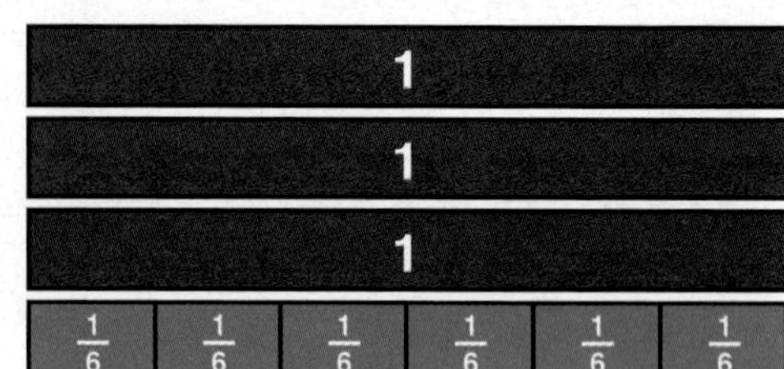

Ongoing Assessment
- **Reasoning If you need to rename when subtracting mixed numbers, how does that affect the difference of the whole numbers?** *(The whole-number difference is 1 less.)*

Reaching All Learners

Writing in Math

Write a Newspaper Story

 15–20 MIN **Linguistic** 

- Write on the board:

Miles Walked for Charity

Bob	Jan	Kim	Poe	Vic
$2\frac{1}{8}$	$1\frac{3}{4}$	$2\frac{5}{8}$	$3\frac{1}{2}$	$1\frac{7}{8}$

- **These five students raised money for a charity. Write a newspaper report about their walk.** Encourage students to make up the kind of charity and tell one or two adventures that occurred on the charity walk.
- **Somewhere in your report, subtract to compare two students' distances. Include the total distance walked by all five students.**

Extend Language

English Language Learners

Renaming Mixed Numbers

 10–15 MIN **Linguistic** 

- Write *rename* on the board. Circle *re*. **What does the prefix *re* in *rename* mean?** *(Again)* **What other words begin with *re* meaning "again"?** *(Redo, remake, rewrite)*
- **What does *rename* mean in math?** *(To show a number in a different way)* **Why do you rename a number?** *(To make an operation easier)* **How is the value of a number changed when it's renamed?** *(It remains the same.)*
- Display $2\frac{3}{8} = \frac{19}{8}$. Have students in the group explain this example of renaming.

Reteaching

Modeling Subtraction of Mixed Numbers

 10–15 MIN **Visual/Spatial** 

Materials *(per student)* Markers

- **Draw 4 circles and divide them into eighths.**
- **Model $3\frac{1}{4}$. Subtract $1\frac{7}{8}$ by crossing out that amount. How much is left?** *($1\frac{3}{8}$)*
- Have each student in the group draw a different mixed number between 3 and 4. Have students cross out circle parts to subtract another mixed number and write the equation for the model.

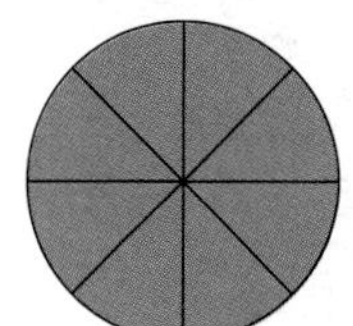 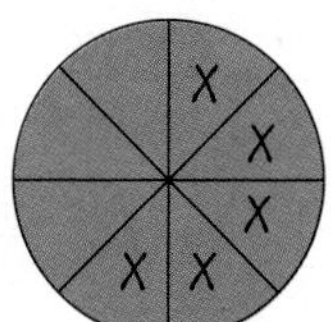 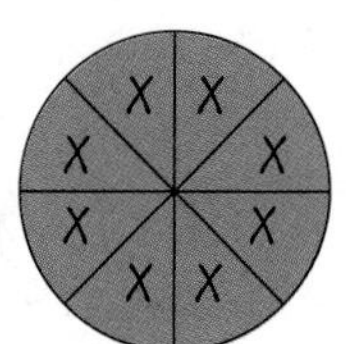 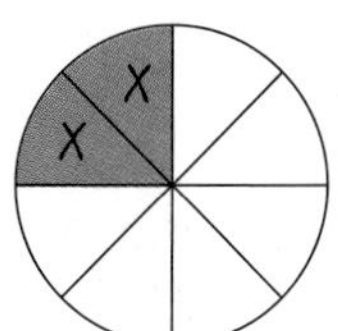

Math and Social Studies

Eighths of a Dollar

 15–20 MIN **Auditory** 

- **The first United States silver dollars were called "pieces of eight" because they could be cut into eight pie-shaped "bits" to make change. Thus, 1 bit = $12\frac{1}{2}$ cents and 2 bits = 25 cents. Stock prices used eighths until 2000, when stock prices began to be listed in decimal form.**
- **Over 5 days, the prices of a stock were $8\frac{1}{4}$, $7\frac{1}{8}$, $7\frac{3}{4}$, $6\frac{7}{8}$, and $7\frac{1}{4}$.** Write the numbers on the board. **What was the change in the prices each day?** *($1\frac{1}{8}$ down, $\frac{5}{8}$ up, $\frac{7}{8}$ down, $\frac{3}{8}$ up)*

Objective Find differences of mixed numbers with and without renaming.

1 Warm Up

Activate Prior Knowledge Review how to subtract fractions with unlike denominators.

2 Teach

LEARN Begin by having students "read" the pictures for the three steps: $2\frac{3}{8}$, $1\frac{11}{8}$, and $\frac{4}{8}$. Then have them model the activity using fraction strips.

Example B A common error is to subtract $6 - 2\frac{3}{4}$ and write $4\frac{3}{4}$ as the answer. Contrast $6 - 2\frac{3}{4}$ with $6\frac{3}{4} - 2$. In the first exercise, you need to rename; in the second, you don't.

Example C When one denominator is a multiple of the other, the greater denominator is the LCD. Illustrate with other fraction pairs such as $\frac{2}{3}$ and $\frac{5}{6}$, $\frac{7}{10}$ and $\frac{1}{5}$, and $\frac{5}{6}$ and $\frac{11}{12}$.

Ongoing Assessment

Talk About It: Question 1

If students cannot explain why 6 was renamed as $5 + \frac{4}{4}$,

then remind them that the goal of the renaming is to obtain (or have) a fraction with the same denominator and a greater numerator than the fraction being subtracted.

Lesson 4-6

Key Idea
To subtract mixed numbers, you subtract the fractional parts and the whole number parts, then simplify

Vocabulary
- mixed number (p. 168)

Materials
- fraction strips or e tools

Think It Through
I can **use a model** to solve the problem.

Subtracting Mixed Numbers

WARM UP

Simplify. See below.

1. $2\frac{3}{4} + \frac{5}{6}$
2. $\frac{11}{12} - \frac{3}{4}$
3. $\frac{12}{10} - \frac{7}{10}$
4. $7\frac{3}{5} + 2\frac{1}{2}$

1. $3\frac{7}{12}$
2. $\frac{1}{6}$
3. $\frac{1}{2}$
4. $10\frac{1}{10}$

LEARN

How can you model the difference of mixed numbers?

Activity

Find $2\frac{3}{8} - 1\frac{7}{8}$.

Step 1 Use fraction strips to show $2\frac{3}{8}$.

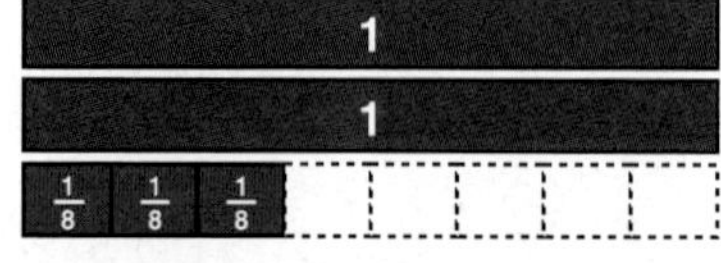

Step 2 Rename $2\frac{3}{8}$ to show more eighths by exchanging a 1 strip for eight $\frac{1}{8}$-strips.

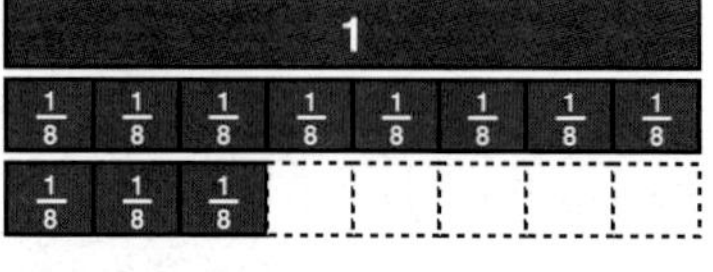

Step 3 Remove $1\frac{7}{8}$. Write the difference. Simplify if necessary.

$2\frac{3}{8} - 1\frac{7}{8} = \frac{4}{8} = \frac{1}{2}$

Use fraction strips to find each difference.

a. $5\frac{1}{4} - 3\frac{3}{4}$ $1\frac{1}{2}$ **b.** $19\frac{1}{7} - 15\frac{5}{7}$ $3\frac{3}{7}$ **c.** $10\frac{3}{8} - 7\frac{7}{8}$ $2\frac{1}{2}$ **d.** $6\frac{1}{5} - 4\frac{4}{5}$ $1\frac{2}{5}$

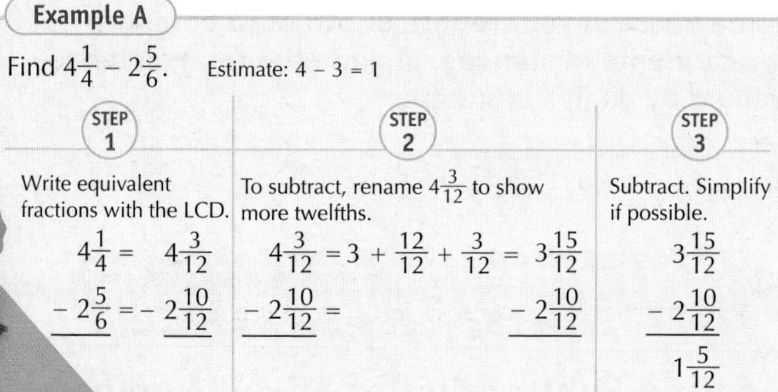

How can you find the difference of mixed numbers?

Example A

Find $4\frac{1}{4} - 2\frac{5}{6}$. Estimate: 4 − 3 = 1

STEP 1	STEP 2	STEP 3
Write equivalent fractions with the LCD.	To subtract, rename $4\frac{3}{12}$ to show more twelfths.	Subtract. Simplify if possible.
$4\frac{1}{4} = 4\frac{3}{12}$	$4\frac{3}{12} = 3 + \frac{12}{12} + \frac{3}{12} = 3\frac{15}{12}$	$3\frac{15}{12}$
$-2\frac{5}{6} = -2\frac{10}{12}$	$-2\frac{10}{12} = \quad -2\frac{10}{12}$	$-2\frac{10}{12}$
		$1\frac{5}{12}$

Below Level — Reteaching

Subtracting Mixed Numbers — R 4-6

To subtract mixed numbers, the fractional parts must have the same denominator.

	Step 1	Step 2	Step 3
Find $9\frac{1}{12} - 4\frac{5}{8}$.	Estimate. 9 − 4 = 5 Write equivalent fractions for the LCD. $9\frac{1}{12} = 9\frac{2}{24}$; $-4\frac{5}{8} = -4\frac{15}{24}$	Before you can subtract, rename $9\frac{2}{24}$ to show more twenty-fourths. $9\frac{2}{24} = 8 + \frac{24}{24} + \frac{2}{24} = 8\frac{26}{24}$; $-4\frac{15}{24}$ $-4\frac{15}{24}$	Subtract and simplify if possible. $8\frac{26}{24} - 4\frac{15}{24} = 4\frac{11}{24}$
Find $10 - 4\frac{2}{5}$.	There is no fraction from which to subtract $\frac{2}{5}$.	Rename 10 to show fifths. $10 = 9 + \frac{5}{5} = 9\frac{5}{5}$	Subtract. Simplify if possible. $9\frac{5}{5} - 4\frac{2}{5} = 5\frac{3}{5}$

Find each difference. Simplify if possible.

1. $5\frac{9}{10} - 2\frac{3}{5} =$ $3\frac{3}{10}$
2. $11\frac{7}{16} - 8\frac{3}{8} =$ $3\frac{1}{16}$
3. $9\frac{2}{3} - 9\frac{1}{6} =$ $\frac{1}{2}$
4. $4\frac{2}{3} - 2 =$ $2\frac{2}{3}$
5. $4\frac{1}{4} - \frac{7}{12} =$ $3\frac{2}{3}$
6. $5\frac{6}{7} - 2\frac{13}{14} =$ $2\frac{13}{14}$
7. **Number Sense** How do you know if you need to rename the first number in a subtraction problem involving mixed numbers?
If, after finding a common denominator, there are not enough fractional parts to subtract the second fraction from the first fraction, the first number will need to be renamed.

50 Use with Lesson 4-6.

On Level — Practice

Subtracting Mixed Numbers — P 4-6

Find each difference. Simplify if possible.

1. $2\frac{3}{5} - 1\frac{1}{5} =$ $1\frac{2}{5}$
2. $1\frac{4}{9} - \frac{8}{9} =$ $\frac{5}{9}$
3. $5\frac{5}{8} - 1\frac{9}{16} =$ $4\frac{1}{16}$
4. $12 - 4\frac{5}{6} =$ $7\frac{1}{6}$
5. $6\frac{15}{16} - 4 =$ $2\frac{15}{16}$
6. $3\frac{7}{12} - 2\frac{3}{4} =$ $\frac{5}{6}$
7. $9 - 7\frac{5}{8} =$ $1\frac{3}{8}$
8. $15\frac{1}{6} - 8\frac{2}{3} =$ $6\frac{1}{2}$
9. $6\frac{8}{9} - 1\frac{2}{3} =$ $5\frac{2}{9}$
10. $2\frac{3}{7} - 1\frac{5}{14} =$ $1\frac{1}{14}$
11. In which of the exercises above do you have to rename the first mixed number to show more fractional parts before subtracting?
Exercises 2, 4, 6, 7, and 8

The table at the right shows the lengths of various carpentry nails.

Carpentry Nails

Size	Length (inches)
5d	$1\frac{3}{4}$
9d	$2\frac{3}{4}$
12d	$3\frac{1}{4}$
30d	$4\frac{1}{2}$

12. How much longer is a 30d nail than a 5d nail?
$2\frac{3}{4}$ in. longer
13. How much longer is a 12d nail than a 9d nail?
$\frac{1}{2}$ in. longer

Test Prep

14. To subtract $4\frac{5}{6}$ from $10\frac{1}{3}$, which of the following must the mixed number $10\frac{1}{3}$ first be renamed as?
A. $9\frac{2}{3}$ B. $9\frac{4}{6}$ (C.) $9\frac{8}{6}$ D. $10\frac{2}{6}$
15. **Writing in Math** Jack says that once you have a common denominator you are ready to subtract two mixed numbers. What other step might be necessary before you can subtract? Give an example.
Sample answer: The larger number may need to be renamed. For example, $3\frac{1}{4} - 1\frac{1}{2} = 3\frac{1}{4} - 1\frac{2}{4} = 2\frac{5}{4} - 1\frac{2}{4}$.

50 Use with Lesson 4-6.

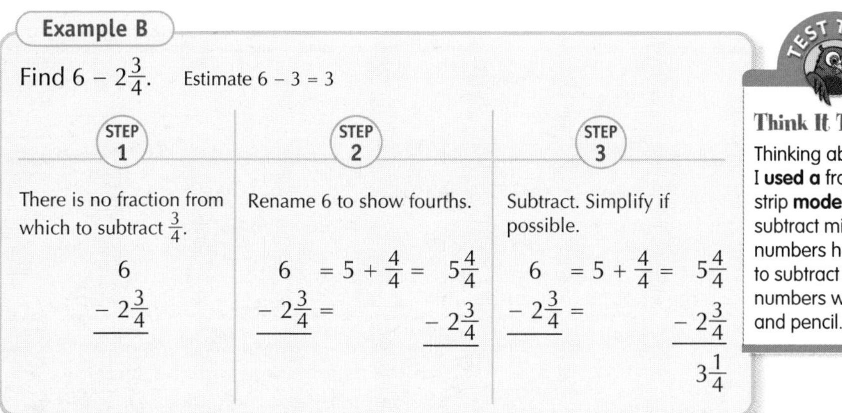

Example B

Find $6 - 2\frac{3}{4}$. Estimate $6 - 3 = 3$

STEP 1 There is no fraction from which to subtract $\frac{3}{4}$.

$$\begin{array}{r} 6 \\ -\ 2\frac{3}{4} \\ \hline \end{array}$$

STEP 2 Rename 6 to show fourths.

$$\begin{array}{rl} 6 & = 5 + \frac{4}{4} = 5\frac{4}{4} \\ -\ 2\frac{3}{4} & = \quad -\ 2\frac{3}{4} \\ \hline \end{array}$$

STEP 3 Subtract. Simplify if possible.

$$\begin{array}{rl} 6 & = 5 + \frac{4}{4} = 5\frac{4}{4} \\ -\ 2\frac{3}{4} & = \quad -\ 2\frac{3}{4} \\ \hline & \quad 3\frac{1}{4} \end{array}$$

TEST TALK

Think It Through

Thinking about how I **used a** fraction-strip **model** to subtract mixed numbers helps me to subtract mixed numbers with paper and pencil.

Talk About It

1. In Example B, explain why 6 was renamed $5 + \frac{4}{4}$.
   A fraction is needed from which to subtract $\frac{3}{4}$.
2. **Number Sense** How is subtracting $2\frac{3}{4}$ from 6 like subtracting 3.9 from 5?
   The 5 must be renamed 4 and 10 tenths in order to subtract.

Do you always have to rename both mixed numbers before subtracting?

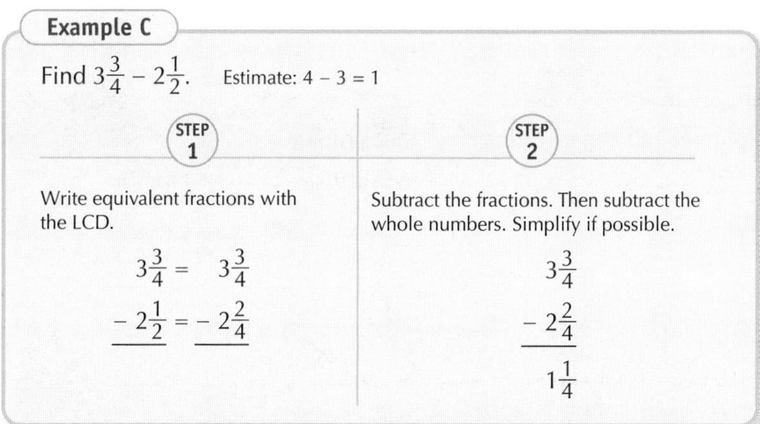

Example C

Find $3\frac{3}{4} - 2\frac{1}{2}$. Estimate: $4 - 3 = 1$

STEP 1 Write equivalent fractions with the LCD.

$$\begin{array}{rl} 3\frac{3}{4} & = \quad 3\frac{3}{4} \\ -\ 2\frac{1}{2} & = -\ 2\frac{2}{4} \\ \hline \end{array}$$

STEP 2 Subtract the fractions. Then subtract the whole numbers. Simplify if possible.

$$\begin{array}{r} 3\frac{3}{4} \\ -\ 2\frac{2}{4} \\ \hline 1\frac{1}{4} \end{array}$$

Talk About It

4. No; If the fractions are the same, the answer will be a whole number. If the answer is less than 1, it will be a proper fraction.

3. In Example C, why was $2\frac{1}{2}$ renamed as $2\frac{2}{4}$? **So that there was a common denominator for subtraction.**
4. **Number Sense** Is the difference of two mixed numbers always a mixed number? Explain.
   See above.

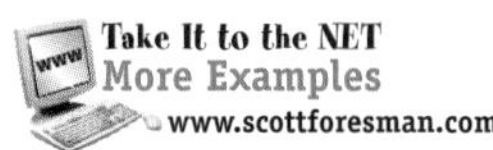

Take It to the NET
More Examples
www.scottforesman.com

CHECK

Error Intervention

If students make the mistake of using the idea of place value when renaming a fraction by renaming with a group of 10,

then have them use a fraction model to review changing a whole into equivalent fractional parts. *(Also see* Reteaching, *p. 220B.)*

3 Practice

Exercises 7–21 Have students scan the exercises and name an exercise that will require renaming. Have them explain why. *(Sample answer: Exercise 10, because there are no thirds to subtract from)*

Exercise 23 Remind students that a *terminating decimal* does not repeat.

TEST TALK **Exercise 28** Students may include drawings of fraction models to support their explanations.

Exercises 29–30 Students should subtract consecutive terms to determine the pattern in each exercise.

Enrichment — **Above Level**

Box Mixes

E 4-6
NUMBER SENSE

Fill in the boxes with missing fractions to make each subtraction sentence true, both going across and down. Then write the final difference for each exercise in the circle in the lower right-hand corner. Write all fractions in simplest form.

1.

$7\frac{1}{4}$	−	$5\frac{1}{2}$	=	$1\frac{3}{4}$
−		−		−
$3\frac{1}{12}$	−	$2\frac{3}{4}$	=	$\frac{1}{3}$
=		=		=
$4\frac{1}{6}$	−	$2\frac{3}{4}$	=	($1\frac{5}{12}$)

2.

$12\frac{5}{8}$	−	$7\frac{3}{8}$	=	$5\frac{1}{4}$
−		−		−
$4\frac{5}{12}$	−	$1\frac{47}{48}$	=	$2\frac{7}{16}$
=		=		=
$8\frac{5}{24}$	−	$5\frac{19}{48}$	=	($2\frac{13}{16}$)

3.

$6\frac{1}{3}$	−	$2\frac{1}{6}$	=	$4\frac{1}{6}$
−		−		−
$3\frac{5}{9}$	−	$2\frac{1}{9}$	=	$1\frac{4}{9}$
=		=		=
$2\frac{7}{9}$	−	$\frac{1}{18}$	=	($2\frac{13}{18}$)

4.

$5\frac{3}{5}$	−	$4\frac{1}{10}$	=	$1\frac{1}{2}$
−		−		−
$2\frac{1}{3}$	−	$2\frac{2}{15}$	=	$\frac{1}{5}$
=		=		=
$3\frac{4}{15}$	−	$1\frac{29}{30}$	=	($1\frac{3}{10}$)

Problem Solving

Subtracting Mixed Numbers

PS 4-6

Annual Snowfall Buffalo, New York, has one of the greatest average snowfalls in the United States. Use the table at the right for 1–2.

Annual Snowfall in Buffalo

Year	Snowfall (in inches)
1900–01	$96\frac{3}{5}$
1925–26	$79\frac{3}{5}$
1950–51	$71\frac{2}{5}$
1975–76	$82\frac{1}{2}$
2000–01	$158\frac{7}{10}$

1. How much more snowfall was there in Buffalo in 2000–2001 than in 1900–1901?
   $62\frac{1}{10}$ in.
2. What is the difference in snowfall for 1975–1976 and 1925–1926?
   $2\frac{9}{10}$ in. difference
3. A one-year-old maple tree is $7\frac{1}{16}$ in. tall. A two-year-old maple tree is $19\frac{1}{6}$ in. tall. How much taller is the two-year-old tree?
   $12\frac{5}{48}$ in. taller
4. A bag of onions weighs $43\frac{7}{32}$ lb. A bag of apples weighs $19\frac{1}{8}$ lb. How much more do the onions weigh than the apples?
   $24\frac{3}{32}$ lb more
5. Cindy drove $3\frac{3}{4}$ mi to get to a concert. She then walked from the car to the arena. Cindy traveled a total of $4\frac{3}{5}$ mi. How far did she walk? **$\frac{17}{20}$ mi**
6. **Writing in Math** Explain how to find $8\frac{1}{5} - 2\frac{5}{6}$.
   Sample answer: First, find the LCD. Find equivalent fractions using the LCD and subtract the lesser one from the greater one. Then subtract the whole numbers: $8\frac{1}{5} - 2\frac{5}{6} = 7\frac{36}{30} - 2\frac{25}{30} = 5\frac{11}{30}$.

Reading Assist Compare and Contrast The term *rename* is used for two different purposes in this lesson. Ask students to describe each and give an example. One is to rename the fraction part so the two mixed numbers will have a common denominator. The other is to rename the mixed number you are subtracting from so that the fraction of the minuend is greater than the fraction of the subtrahend.

Leveled Practice

Below Level Ex. 7–11, 12–28 even, 31–38

On Level Ex. 7–16, 23–25, 28, 31–38

Above Level Ex. 11–21 odd, 22, 24–38

CHECK

For another example, see Set 4-6 on p. 241.

Find each difference. Simplify if possible.

1. $8\frac{5}{6} - 3\frac{8}{9}$ **$4\frac{17}{18}$** **2.** $5\frac{1}{4} - 2\frac{7}{10}$ **$2\frac{11}{20}$** **3.** $11\frac{1}{2} - \frac{3}{4}$ **$10\frac{3}{4}$** **4.** $3 - \frac{5}{8}$ **$2\frac{3}{8}$** **5.** $8\frac{9}{10} - 7\frac{3}{10}$ **$1\frac{3}{5}$**

6. Number Sense If you rewrite the numbers in Exercise 2 as decimals, will you need to do any renaming before subtracting? Explain. **See below.**

6. Yes; the 2 in the tenths place of 5.25 is not large enough to subtract the 7 in 2.7.

PRACTICE

For more practice, see Set 4-6 on p. 244.

A Skills and Understanding

28. No. When renaming, the 1 must be written as a fraction with the same denominator and then added; $\frac{6}{6} + \frac{1}{6} = \frac{7}{6}$.

Find each difference. Simplify if possible.

7. $3\frac{5}{16} - 2\frac{1}{8}$ **$1\frac{3}{16}$** **8.** $8\frac{7}{12} - 4\frac{5}{6}$ **$3\frac{3}{4}$** **9.** $2\frac{5}{6} - \frac{3}{8}$ **$2\frac{11}{24}$** **10.** $7 - 3\frac{2}{3}$ **$3\frac{1}{3}$** **11.** $10\frac{3}{4} - 10\frac{1}{8}$ **$\frac{5}{8}$**

12. $4\frac{1}{6} - 3\frac{8}{9}$ **$\frac{5}{18}$** **13.** $3\frac{7}{8} - 2\frac{3}{8}$ **$1\frac{1}{2}$** **14.** $15\frac{9}{10} - 8\frac{1}{6}$ **$7\frac{11}{15}$** **15.** $4\frac{1}{5} - 3\frac{3}{5}$ **$\frac{3}{5}$** **16.** $4\frac{2}{3} - 3$ **$1\frac{2}{3}$**

17. $8\frac{2}{5} - 8$ **$\frac{2}{5}$** **18.** $6 - 5\frac{3}{4}$ **$\frac{1}{4}$** **19.** $2\frac{2}{5} - \frac{9}{10}$ **$1\frac{1}{2}$** **20.** $2\frac{1}{3} - 1\frac{3}{4}$ **$\frac{7}{12}$** **21.** $1\frac{5}{12} - \frac{9}{16}$ **$\frac{41}{48}$**

22. Which of the exercises above could you compute mentally? **Sample answer: 13, 16, and 17. No simplifying or renaming of fractions was needed.**

23. Number Sense Which of the numbers in Exercises 7–16 can be written as terminating decimals? **7, 8, 11, 13, and 15**

B Reasoning and Problem Solving

Math and Science

Use the data file to find the difference in length for each pair of beetles.

24. Goliath and water scavenger **$4\frac{1}{5}$ in.**

25. Stag and unicorn **$\frac{37}{40}$ in.**

26. Rhinoceros and ladybug **$\frac{7}{10}$ in.**

27. Ladybug and golden tortoise **$\frac{1}{20}$ in.**

28. Writing in Math Keanu's explanation for renaming mixed numbers is shown below. Is his method correct? Why or why not? **See above right.**

$$9\frac{1}{6} = 8\frac{11}{6}$$
$$-2\frac{5}{6} = 2\frac{5}{6}$$
$$6\frac{6}{6} = 7$$

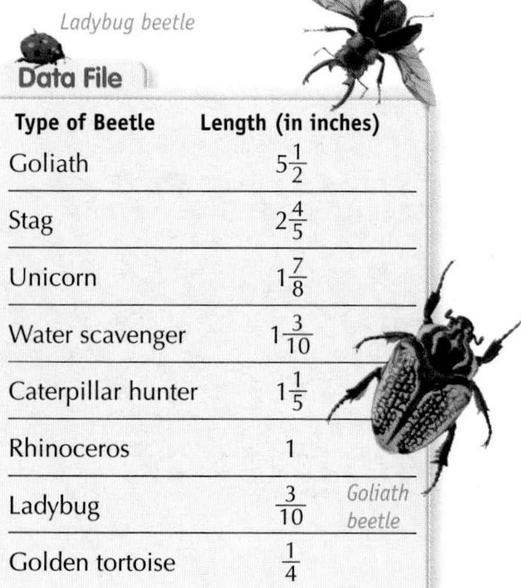

Data File

Type of Beetle	Length (in inches)
Goliath	$5\frac{1}{2}$
Stag	$2\frac{4}{5}$
Unicorn	$1\frac{7}{8}$
Water scavenger	$1\frac{3}{10}$
Caterpillar hunter	$1\frac{1}{5}$
Rhinoceros	1
Ladybug	$\frac{3}{10}$
Golden tortoise	$\frac{1}{4}$

222

Test-Taking Practice

Test-Taking Practice, Item 1, p. 223 There are two parts to the problem; the pair of numbers and the explanation are each worth two points. Remind students that they should answer as much as they can since partial credit is given for this type of problem.

Discuss the sample responses shown and compare them to papers produced by your students.

4-point answer Correct answer and explanation; shows knowledge of subtracting mixed numbers.

$5\frac{3}{5} - 4\frac{2}{5} = 1\frac{1}{5}$

Add $1\frac{1}{5}$ to a mixed number. Those two numbers have a difference of $1\frac{1}{5}$.

PRACTICE

C Extensions

Patterns Write the next three numbers in each pattern. Then give the rule.

29. $15\frac{1}{8}, 13\frac{3}{4}, 12\frac{3}{8}, \ldots$ **$11, 9\frac{5}{8}, 8\frac{1}{4}$; subtract $1\frac{3}{8}$**

30. $4\frac{4}{5}, 5\frac{1}{2}, 6\frac{1}{5}, \ldots$ **$6\frac{9}{10}, 7\frac{3}{5}, 8\frac{3}{10}$; add $\frac{7}{10}$**

Mixed Review and Test Prep

Estimate each sum or difference. **Sample answers are given.**

31. $\frac{5}{6} + \frac{3}{5}$ **2**

32. $4\frac{1}{3} - 2\frac{7}{8}$ **1**

33. $6\frac{3}{4} + 6\frac{1}{8} + 10\frac{3}{10}$ **23**

Find each sum. Simplify if possible.

34. $3\frac{4}{5} + 8\frac{3}{4}$ **$12\frac{11}{20}$**

35. $5\frac{5}{6} + \frac{7}{12}$ **$6\frac{5}{12}$**

36. $\frac{7}{12} + 4\frac{1}{6} + 2\frac{1}{4}$ **7**

37. Algebra Evaluate the expression $4 \times 4 \div 2^2 - (2 + 2)$.

A. 64 **C.** 4

B. 8 **(D.)** 0

38. Algebra Evaluate the expression $30 \div (5 \times 3) + 4 \times 2$.

A. 32 **C.** 14

B. 20 **(D.)** 10

Discover Math in Your World

SCHOOL

A Braking Event

Perception time $\approx \frac{3}{4}$ second

Perception time is the average amount of time it takes a driver to perceive a braking event.

Reaction time $\approx \frac{3}{4}$ second

Reaction time is the time it takes the driver to move his or her foot from the gas pedal to the brake pedal.

1. What is the total time for perception and reaction? **About $1\frac{1}{2}$ seconds**
2. A car going 60 mph covers 88 feet per second. How many feet would the car travel during the total time for perception and reaction? **About 132 feet**

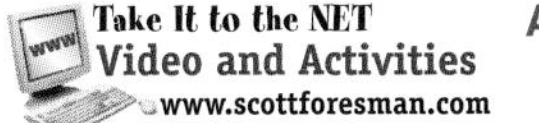

3-point answer Incorrect answer; correct explanation; knowledge of subtracting mixed numbers.

$5\frac{3}{5} - 4\frac{2}{5} = 1\frac{3}{10}$

Add $1\frac{1}{5}$ to a mixed number.

Those two numbers have a difference of $1\frac{1}{5}$.

3-point answer Correct answer; incomplete explanation; knowledge of subtracting mixed numbers.

$5\frac{3}{5} - 4\frac{2}{5} = 1\frac{1}{5}$

Subtract $1\frac{1}{5}$ from another number.

Early Finishers Ask students to find the denominators in the following equations:

$\frac{3}{4} + \frac{3}{?} = 1$ *(12)* $\frac{4}{5} + \frac{4}{?} = 1$ *(20)*

$\frac{5}{6} + \frac{5}{?} = 1$ *(30)* $\frac{6}{7} + \frac{6}{?} = 1$ *(42)*

Discover Math in Your World Students will need to multiply 88 by $1\frac{1}{2}$. Remind them that the Distributive Property allows them to write $88(1 + \frac{1}{2}) = (88 \times 1) + (88 \times \frac{1}{2})$. Students may be interested in stopping distances for other speeds. Speeds in miles per hour can be converted to feet per second by multiplying by $\frac{22}{15}$.

mph	20	30	40	55
ft/s	$29\frac{1}{3}$	44	$58\frac{2}{3}$	$80\frac{2}{3}$

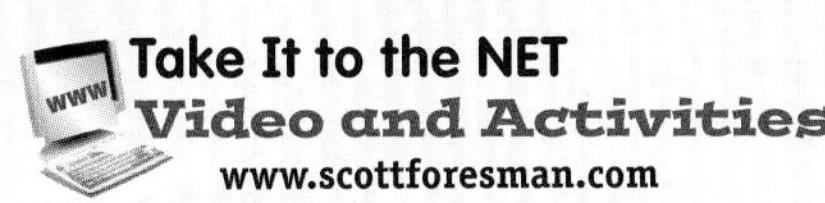

The video includes pre-viewing and post-viewing questions. A Discovery Channel Blackline Master is also provided.

Assess

Journal Idea Have students explain how to subtract $1\frac{3}{4}$ from $5\frac{3}{8}$, and include a diagram with their explanation.

Test-Taking Practice 4-6

1. What are two mixed numbers whose difference is $1\frac{1}{5}$? Explain how you solved this problem.
Sample answer: $5\frac{3}{5} - 4\frac{2}{5} = 1\frac{1}{5}$; Add $1\frac{1}{5}$ to a mixed number and those two mixed numbers have a difference of $1\frac{1}{5}$.

2. Which is the difference of $12\frac{5}{6} - 11\frac{2}{24}$ in simplest form?

A. $1\frac{16}{24}$

B. $1\frac{8}{12}$

C. $1\frac{4}{6}$

(D.) $1\frac{3}{4}$

Available as a transparency

4-7 Choose a Computation Method

Lesson Organizer

Quick Lesson Overview

Objective For a variety of problems, state the computation method to be used and add or subtract using that method.

Math Understanding The kinds of numbers in a calculation, and the ease with which one can apply different calculation methods, together determine an appropriate computation method.

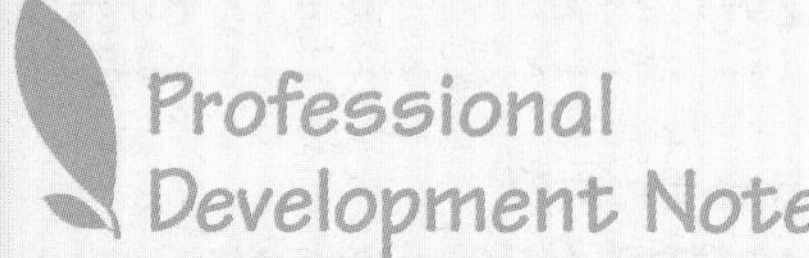

Managing Instruction If you do not have a classroom set of calculators, have students work on this lesson in small groups. Group members can take turns using the calculator.

NCTM Standards

- Number and Operations

(For a complete correlation to the NCTM Standards and Grades 6–8 Expectations, see pages 202G-H.)

Getting Started

Spiral Review

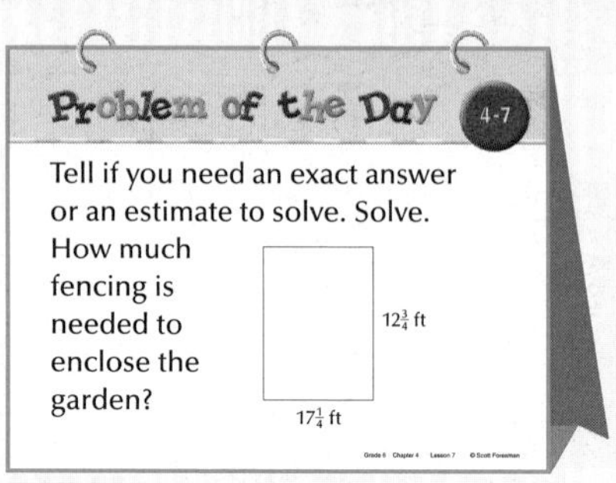

Problem of the Day 4-7

Tell if you need an exact answer or an estimate to solve. Solve.

How much fencing is needed to enclose the garden?

$12\frac{3}{4}$ ft

$17\frac{1}{4}$ ft

Grade 6 Chapter 4 Lesson 7 © Scott Foresman

Topics Reviewed

- Perimeter; adding fractions
- Problem-Solving Skill: Exact Answer

Answer Exact answer; The amount of fencing needed is 2 x 30 or 60 ft.

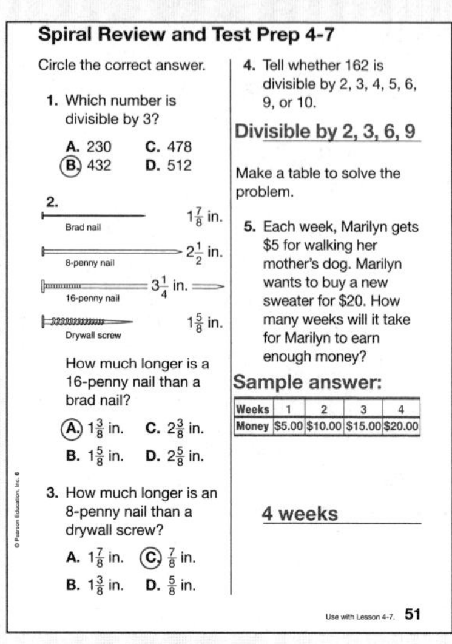

Spiral Review and Test Prep 4-7

Circle the correct answer.

1. Which number is divisible by 3?

   A. 230 (B.) 432 C. 478 D. 512

2. Brad nail $1\frac{7}{8}$ in.; 8-penny nail $2\frac{1}{2}$ in.; 16-penny nail $3\frac{1}{4}$ in.; Drywall screw $1\frac{5}{8}$ in.

   How much longer is a 16-penny nail than a brad nail?

   (A.) $1\frac{3}{8}$ in. B. $1\frac{5}{8}$ in. C. $2\frac{3}{8}$ in. D. $2\frac{5}{8}$ in.

3. How much longer is an 8-penny nail than a drywall screw?

   A. $1\frac{7}{8}$ in. B. $1\frac{3}{8}$ in. (C.) $\frac{7}{8}$ in. D. $\frac{5}{8}$ in.

4. Tell whether 162 is divisible by 2, 3, 4, 5, 6, 9, or 10.

   Divisible by 2, 3, 6, 9

Make a table to solve the problem.

5. Each week, Marilyn gets $5 for walking her mother's dog. Marilyn wants to buy a new sweater for $20. How many weeks will it take for Marilyn to earn enough money?

   Sample answer:

Weeks	1	2	3	4
Money	$5.00	$10.00	$15.00	$20.00

   4 weeks

© Pearson Education, Inc. 6

Use with Lesson 4-7. 51

Available as a transparency and as a blackline master

Topics Reviewed

1., 4. Factors, multiples, and divisibility; **2.–3.** Subtracting mixed numbers; **5.** Make a table

Investigating the Concept

Computation Methods for Mixed Numbers

15–20 MIN **Logical/Mathematical**

Materials *(per student)* Calculator

What to Do

- **When should you use a calculator to compute with whole numbers?** *(When there are many numbers, large numbers, or a lot of regrouping.)*
- Write $3\frac{11}{18} + 5\frac{19}{30}$ on the board. **Would you use a calculator? Why?** *(Yes; Denominators are different, one denominator is not a multiple of the other, the fraction sum is greater than 1.)*
- Compare mental math with whole numbers and fractions. Use 125 + 275 and $5\frac{1}{6} + 2\frac{5}{6}$ as an example. In both cases, the numbers are compatible.

Ongoing Assessment

- **What are three computation methods for mixed numbers?** *(Mental math, paper and pencil, and calculator)*
- **Reasoning What part(s) of a mixed-number computation helps you choose a computation method?** *(Denominators)*

Mental Math

$8\frac{7}{12} - 4\frac{5}{12}$

Paper and Pencil

$4\frac{5}{6} + 3\frac{2}{3}$

Calculator

$5\frac{5}{18} - 3\frac{11}{12}$

Reaching All Learners

Writing in Math

Describing Mental Math Problems

 15–20 MIN **Auditory** SMALL GROUP

- Discuss why mental math is a good method for each exercise. $4\frac{2}{3} + 5$ *(Second number has no fraction.)* $3\frac{1}{4} + 7\frac{3}{4}$ *(Fractions add to 1.)* $1\frac{3}{8} + 6\frac{1}{8}$ *and* $8\frac{6}{7} - 1\frac{1}{7}$ *(Denominators are the same, and no regrouping is needed.)*
- Have groups create a chart comparing addition and subtraction problems appropriate for mental math.

Adding	Subtracting
Like denominators	Like denominators
No regrouping	No regrouping
Fraction sum less than 1	First fraction greater than second
One number a whole number	Second number a whole number

Activate Prior Knowledge/Build Background

English Language Learners

Commuting and Computing

 10–15 MIN **Logical/Mathematical** SMALL GROUP

- Lead students in a discussion about methods and choices such as this: **What method of transportation do you use to travel to school—walking, bicycling, riding in a car, or taking a bus? Why?**
- Display: $\frac{3}{5} + \frac{1}{5}$; $\frac{5}{12} + \frac{2}{3}$; $\frac{4}{20} + \frac{3}{5} + \frac{2}{4} + \frac{2}{9}$. Have students discuss: **What computation method would you use to solve each of these problems—mental math, paper and pencil, or a calculator? Why?**

Reteaching

Mind Against Machine

 15–20 MIN **Social/Cooperative** PAIRS

Materials *(per pair)* Calculator

- Write $6\frac{1}{9} + 2\frac{4}{9}$ on the board. Have one partner use mental math and the other use a calculator. Mental math will probably be faster.
- Change $2\frac{4}{9}$ to $2\frac{5}{9}$ and repeat. **What was different?** *(The fraction sum needed to be simplified.)*
- Continue making the problem more difficult as shown with the circled numbers. Discuss when the calculator becomes the more efficient computation method.

$$6\frac{1}{9} + 2\frac{4}{9} \rightarrow 6\frac{1}{9} + 2\frac{(5)}{9} \rightarrow 6\frac{1}{(3)} + 2\frac{5}{9} \rightarrow 6\frac{(2)}{3} + 2\frac{5}{9} \rightarrow 6\frac{2}{3} + 2\frac{5}{(8)}$$

Math and Technology

Don't Pass Ten

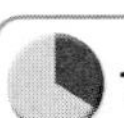 15–20 MIN **Logical/Mathematical**

Materials *(per pair)* Calculator

- **In this game, you'll use mental math to add mixed numbers. The goal is to make your opponent get a sum greater than ten.**
- Have students take turns with the calculator. Each student should add a mixed number that is between 2 and 3.
- The first student to get a sum greater than 10 loses that round. The other student earns 1 point.
- Play continues until one student has earned 10 points.

Objective For a variety of problems, state the computation method to be used and add or subtract using that method.

1 Warm Up

Activate Prior Knowledge Review using mental math to add and subtract fractions with like denominators. Also, review using a calculator.

2 Teach

LEARN Point out that using mental math refers to finding an exact value, which is not the same as estimating.

Ongoing Assessment

Talk About It: Question 1

If students have difficulty identifying good combinations for mental math,

then have them look for pairs with fraction parts that add to 1, for example, $7\frac{3}{4}$ and $2\frac{1}{4}$.

CHECK

Error Intervention

If students make frequent errors using mental math,

then make sure they are first checking to see if the denominators are the same. Provide examples of fraction parts with a sum of 1. Suggest that they check their mental math solutions with another method until they feel confident using mental math. *(Also see* Reteaching, *p. 224B.)*

Lesson 4-7

Key Idea
When computing, you can use mental math, paper and pencil, or a calculator, depending on the numbers involved.

Materials
• calculator

Choose a Computation Method

WARM UP

Use mental math if possible.

1. $3\frac{3}{8} - \frac{1}{8}$ $3\frac{1}{4}$
2. $4\frac{5}{12} + 3\frac{1}{4}$ $7\frac{2}{3}$
3. $2\frac{7}{10} + 11\frac{3}{10}$ 14
4. $8\frac{5}{6} - 3\frac{1}{2}$ $5\frac{1}{3}$

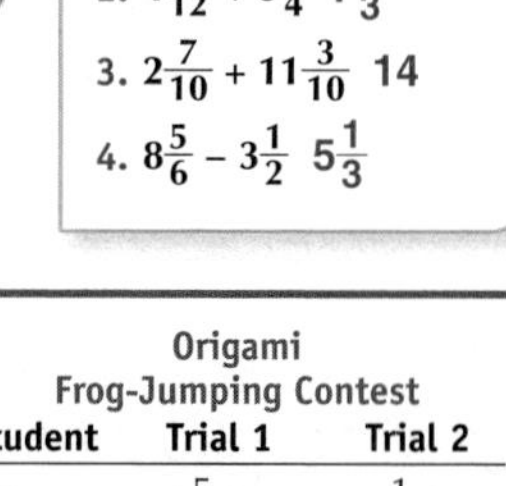

LEARN

What computation method should you use?

Mr. Womack's class made origami frogs and had a frog-jumping contest. Results appear in the table at the right.

Origami Frog-Jumping Contest

Student	Trial 1	Trial 2
Ali	$4\frac{5}{8}$ in.	$9\frac{1}{4}$ in.
Rosa	$7\frac{3}{4}$ in.	$2\frac{1}{4}$ in.
Kenji	$7\frac{5}{16}$ in.	$11\frac{1}{16}$ in.
Darrell	$4\frac{3}{4}$ in.	8 in.

Example A

Find the total distance Rosa's frog jumped.

Find $7\frac{3}{4} + 2\frac{1}{4}$.

This is easy to do using **mental math.**

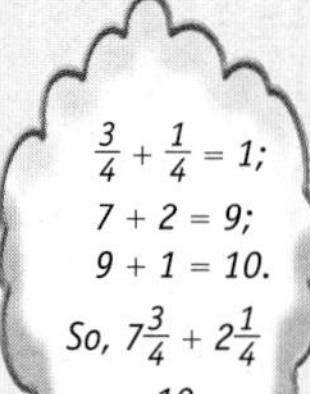

Example B

For Trial 1, how much farther did Kenji's frog jump than Darrell's frog?

Find $7\frac{5}{16} - 4\frac{3}{4}$.

There are two fractions, and it's easy to find a common denominator, so I'll use **paper and pencil.**

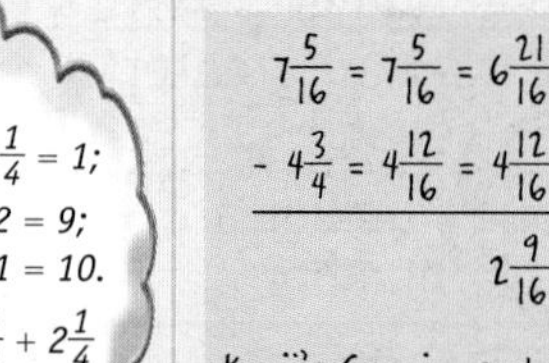

$7\frac{5}{16} = 7\frac{5}{16} = 6\frac{21}{16}$
$-\ 4\frac{3}{4} = 4\frac{12}{16} = 4\frac{12}{16}$
$2\frac{9}{16}$
Kenji's frog jumped $2\frac{9}{16}$ inches farther than Darrell's frog.

Example C

Find the average length of the jumps in Trial 1.

Find $(4\frac{5}{8} + 7\frac{3}{4} + 7\frac{5}{16} + 4\frac{3}{4}) \div 4$.

There are 4 fractions to add and they have different denominators. The sum needs to be divided by 4. I'll use a **calculator.**

Press:

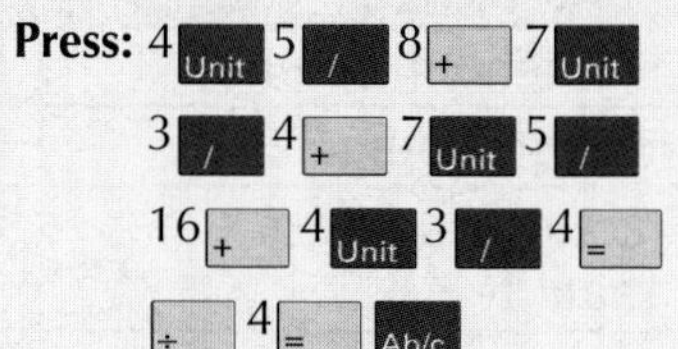

Display: 6u 7/64

Think It Through
Sometimes using **mental math** or **paper and pencil** is faster than using a **calculator.**

Talk About It Sample answer: $7\frac{5}{16} + 11\frac{1}{16}$, $4\frac{3}{4} + 8$, $4\frac{3}{4} + 2\frac{1}{4}$

1. **Number Sense** Name some other numbers from the data table above that can easily be added using mental math.

224

Reteaching Below Level

Choose a Computation Method R 4-7

Depending on the type of problem, you can use different methods to find the solution. Your goal should be to use the most accurate and efficient method. The different choices are:

Mental Math Think: Are the numbers easy to work with? If there are fractions, is there already a common denominator? Will an estimate solve the problem?

Example: Find $4\frac{1}{5} + 2\frac{2}{5}$.

Paper and Pencil Think: Can I easily convert the fractions to a common denominator? Are the calculations fairly straightforward?

Example: Find $6\frac{1}{4} - 2\frac{1}{2}$.

Calculator Think: Are there many steps needed to find the solution? Would using pencil and paper take too long? Would the numbers be too cumbersome?

Example: Find $3\frac{2}{12} + 4\frac{1}{3} + 9\frac{3}{4} + 7\frac{2}{6}$.

Find each sum or difference. Tell which computation method you used.

1. $8\frac{4}{5} - 1\frac{2}{5} =$ $7\frac{2}{5}$; mental math
2. $\frac{11}{16} + 4\frac{15}{32} =$ $5\frac{5}{32}$; pencil and paper
3. $14 - 12\frac{5}{9} + \frac{2}{3} =$ $2\frac{1}{9}$; pencil and paper
4. $3\frac{9}{16} - 2 =$ $1\frac{9}{16}$; mental math
5. $7\frac{1}{3} + 7\frac{8}{14} =$ $14\frac{19}{21}$; calculator
6. $2\frac{1}{9} + 2\frac{1}{9} =$ $4\frac{2}{9}$; mental math
7. A dog had three puppies. One puppy weighed $2\frac{1}{8}$ lb, one weighed $2\frac{3}{4}$ lb, and the third weighed 3 lb. What is the combined weight of the puppies? What method did you use? $7\frac{7}{8}$ lb; calculator
8. **Writing in Math** Why would it be faster to use mental math rather than a calculator to find $4\frac{1}{14} + 2\frac{2}{7}$? Explain. It is easy to find the LCD of $\frac{1}{14}$ and $\frac{2}{7}$ using mental math.

Use with Lesson 4-7. 51

Practice On Level

Choose a Computation Method P 4-7

Find each sum or difference. Tell what computation method you used.

1. $2\frac{1}{5} + 4\frac{3}{5} =$ $6\frac{4}{5}$ mental math
2. $12 - 7\frac{5}{6} =$ $4\frac{1}{6}$ pencil and paper
3. $6\frac{3}{8} + 2\frac{1}{4} =$ $8\frac{5}{8}$ pencil and paper
4. $15\frac{1}{2} - 9 =$ $6\frac{1}{2}$ mental math
5. $4\frac{4}{9} - 2\frac{8}{9} =$ $1\frac{5}{9}$ pencil and paper
6. $6\frac{1}{7} + 6\frac{4}{7} =$ $12\frac{5}{7}$ mental math
7. $8\frac{3}{4} + 1\frac{5}{16} =$ $10\frac{1}{16}$ pencil and paper
8. $3\frac{4}{5} - 2\frac{8}{15} =$ $1\frac{4}{15}$ pencil and paper
9. $\frac{11}{12} + 4\frac{4}{15} =$ $5\frac{11}{60}$ calculator
10. $\frac{5}{6} + \frac{2}{3} - \frac{1}{15} =$ $1\frac{13}{30}$ calculator
11. Jon's dog weighs $49\frac{1}{4}$ lb and his cat weighs $11\frac{15}{16}$ lb. Find the combined weight of the two pets. $61\frac{3}{16}$ lb
12. A croquet ball has a diameter of $3\frac{5}{8}$ in. If the wicket the ball passes through is 4 in. wide, how much room is there to spare? Use mental math to find the answer. $\frac{3}{8}$ in.

Test Prep

13. For which of the following sums or differences would mental math be most efficient?
    A. $4\frac{1}{3} + 5\frac{2}{5}$ (B.) $6\frac{7}{8} - 3\frac{5}{8}$ C. $4\frac{1}{6} - 2\frac{5}{6}$ D. $\frac{5}{7} + \frac{1}{14} + \frac{1}{2}$
14. **Writing in Math** Describe a problem that could be easily solved using mental math. Explain why this method works best. Sample answer: Measuring lengths of fabric using eighths. The denominators are the same.

Use with Lesson 4-7. 51

CHECK

For another example, see Set 4-7 on p. 242.

Find each sum or difference. Tell what computation method you used.

1. $9\frac{1}{4} + 8$ **$17\frac{1}{4}$; mental math**
2. $3\frac{1}{6} - \frac{2}{3}$ **$2\frac{1}{2}$; paper and pencil**
3. $4\frac{3}{4} + 5\frac{5}{6}$ **$10\frac{7}{12}$; paper and pencil**
4. $2\frac{5}{8} + 4\frac{5}{12} + 1\frac{17}{18}$ **$8\frac{71}{72}$; calculator**
5. **Number Sense** Evan used paper and pencil to find $2\frac{1}{2} + \frac{3}{4}$. Could he have found the answer more quickly by using mental math? Explain. **See below.**

PRACTICE

For more practice, see Set 4-7 on p. 245.

A Skills and Understanding

5. Yes; If he thought of $\frac{3}{4}$ as $\frac{1}{2} + \frac{1}{4}$ he could have added the $\frac{1}{2}$ mentally to make 3, then added the $\frac{1}{4}$.

Find each sum or difference. Tell what computation method you used.

6. $11\frac{5}{6} - 4\frac{3}{8}$ **$7\frac{11}{24}$; paper and pencil**
7. $7\frac{7}{9} + 4\frac{2}{9}$ **12; mental math**
8. $12\frac{1}{4} + 20\frac{3}{4}$ **33; mental math**
9. $4\frac{5}{16} - 3\frac{11}{12}$ **$\frac{19}{48}$; calculator**
10. $12 - 4\frac{5}{7}$ **$7\frac{2}{7}$; mental math**
11. $14\frac{7}{8} + 5\frac{2}{15}$ **$20\frac{1}{120}$; calculator**
12. $5\frac{3}{4} - 4\frac{5}{6}$ **$\frac{11}{12}$; paper and pencil**
13. $8\frac{1}{5} + 3\frac{2}{5}$ **$11\frac{3}{5}$; mental math**
14. $8\frac{1}{4} - 2\frac{2}{3}$ **$5\frac{7}{12}$; paper and pencil**
15. $23 + 17\frac{2}{3}$ **$40\frac{2}{3}$; mental math**
16. $18\frac{9}{10} - 9\frac{3}{10}$
17. $6\frac{5}{8} - 2\frac{7}{10}$
18. $7\frac{1}{12} + 2\frac{1}{3}$
19. $5\frac{5}{6} - 5\frac{5}{8}$
20. $7\frac{3}{5} + 8\frac{1}{6}$

16–20. See margin.

21. **Number Sense** Why is using a calculator NOT an efficient method for finding $3\frac{1}{4} + \frac{5}{8}$?
$\frac{1}{4}$ can be simplified to $\frac{2}{8}$ and added mentally.

B Reasoning and Problem Solving

22. How much higher was Blake's pole vault than his high jump? **$10\frac{5}{6}$ ft**
23. Blake's triple jump was $29\frac{1}{4}$ feet more than his long jump. How long was his triple jump? **$57\frac{3}{4}$ ft**
24. **Writing in Math** Would it make more sense to use mental math to find $13\frac{5}{6} + 8\frac{1}{2}$ or to find $5\frac{3}{4} + 2\frac{3}{8}$? Explain your reasoning. **See margin.**

Blake's Jumps
High jump: $7\frac{2}{3}$ ft
Pole vault: $18\frac{1}{2}$ ft
Long jump: $28\frac{1}{2}$ ft

Mixed Review and Test Prep

Take It to the NET
Test Prep
www.scottforesman.com

Find each difference. Estimate first.

25. $7\frac{3}{8} - 2\frac{5}{6}$ **$4\frac{13}{24}$**
26. $10 - 4\frac{4}{15}$ **$5\frac{11}{15}$**
27. $8\frac{1}{10} - 7\frac{6}{10}$ **$\frac{1}{2}$**
28. $5\frac{1}{3} - \frac{11}{12}$ **$4\frac{5}{12}$**

Algebra Solve each equation.

29. $\frac{n}{0.3} = 6.6$ **$n = 1.98$**
30. $36 = 3y$ **$y = 12$**
31. $3.9 + m = 7.2$ **$m = 3.3$**
32. $x - 15 = 15$ **$x = 30$**
33. Which of the following is NOT a solution of $d + 3\frac{2}{3} = 5\frac{1}{6}$?

A. $\frac{3}{2}$ B. $\frac{9}{6}$ C. $1\frac{1}{2}$ **(D.)** $1\frac{2}{3}$

 All text pages available online and on CD-ROM.

3 Practice

Exercise 21 Point out that $\frac{1}{4} = \frac{2}{8}$, so simplifying is not needed. The numbers can be added using mental math.

TEST TALK **Exercise 24** Encourage students to name another computation method, if it applies. Reasons why another method is better should be given in the explanation.

Leveled Practice

Below Level	Ex. 6–20 even, 22–33
On Level	Ex. 6–20 even, 22–33
Above Level	Ex. 7–21 odd, 22–33

Early Finishers Have students make up an addition and a subtraction problem for each of the computation methods. Have them exchange problems with a partner to solve.

4 Assess

Journal Idea Have students explain one advantage of each computation method: mental math, paper and pencil, scientific calculator.

For Additional Answers, see pages C1–C4.

Enrichment — Above Level

Find the Letter

E 4-7 ALGEBRA

Solve each equation. It may help to rewrite each equation with a common denominator first. An example is shown below.

Solve $\frac{x}{4} + \frac{2}{3} = \frac{11}{12}$.

Let ? represent $\frac{x}{4}$.	$? + \frac{2}{3} = \frac{11}{12}$
Rewrite with a common denominator.	$? + \frac{8}{12} = \frac{11}{12}$
Solve the equation.	$? = \frac{3}{12}$
Substitute the original value for "?".	$\frac{x}{4} = \frac{3}{12}$
Solve for x.	$x = 1$
Check your equation.	$\frac{x}{4} + \frac{2}{3} = \frac{11}{12}$ $\frac{1}{4} + \frac{2}{3} = \frac{11}{12}$ $\frac{3}{12} + \frac{8}{12} = \frac{11}{12}$

Solve. Then check your equation.

1. $\frac{1}{5} + \frac{t}{4} = \frac{19}{20}$ $t =$ **3** **$\frac{1}{5} + \frac{3}{4} = \frac{19}{20}$**
2. $\frac{p}{7} + \frac{1}{2} = \frac{9}{14}$ $p =$ **1** **$\frac{1}{7} + \frac{1}{2} = \frac{9}{14}$**
3. $\frac{1}{2} + \frac{3}{r} = \frac{13}{14}$ $r =$ **7** **$\frac{1}{2} + \frac{3}{7} = \frac{13}{14}$**
4. $\frac{7}{f} - \frac{1}{3} = \frac{4}{9}$ $f =$ **9** **$\frac{7}{9} - \frac{1}{3} = \frac{4}{9}$**
5. $\frac{a}{6} + \frac{5}{12} = 1\frac{1}{4}$ $a =$ **5** **$\frac{5}{6} + \frac{5}{12} = 1\frac{1}{4}$**
6. $\frac{k}{4} + \frac{21}{24} = 1\frac{5}{8}$ $k =$ **3** **$\frac{3}{4} + \frac{21}{24} = 1\frac{5}{8}$**

Use with Lesson 4-7. 51

Problem Solving

Choose a Computation Method

PS 4-7

Running Three runners are keeping a log of how many miles they have run over two weeks.

Distances Run (in miles)

Runner	Week 1	Week 2
Kyle	$15\frac{5}{12}$	$12\frac{23}{36}$
Deborah	$9\frac{5}{6}$	$10\frac{7}{8}$
Steve	$10\frac{1}{4}$	$8\frac{1}{6}$

1. How many miles did Steve run in two weeks? **$18\frac{5}{12}$ mi**
2. How many more miles did Kyle run in Week 1 than in Week 2? **$2\frac{7}{9}$ mi**
3. How many more miles did Deborah run in Week 2 than in Week 1? **$1\frac{1}{24}$ mi**
4. Which of the runners ran the farthest? What was the total? **Kyle; $28\frac{1}{18}$ mi**
5. **Writing in Math** Find the total mileage for all three runners. Explain how you found the LCD. **$67\frac{13}{72}$ mi; Kyle's total was $28\frac{1}{18}$ mi, Deborah's was $20\frac{17}{24}$ mi, and Steve's was $18\frac{5}{12}$ mi.; Sample answer: The LCD for each is 72 because 18, 24, and 12 are all factors of 72.**

Use with Lesson 4-7. 51

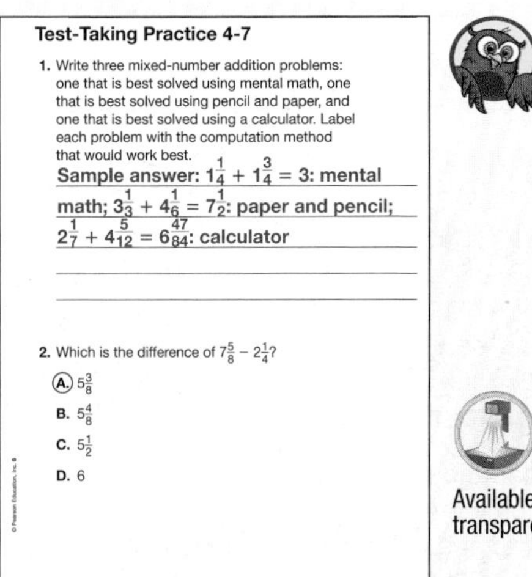

Test-Taking Practice 4-7

1. Write three mixed-number addition problems: one that is best solved using mental math, one that is best solved using pencil and paper, and one that is best solved using a calculator. Label each problem with the computation method that would work best.
Sample answer: $1\frac{1}{4} + 1\frac{3}{4} = 3$: mental math; $3\frac{1}{3} + 4\frac{1}{6} = 7\frac{1}{2}$: paper and pencil; $2\frac{1}{7} + 4\frac{5}{12} = 6\frac{47}{84}$: calculator
2. Which is the difference of $7\frac{5}{8} - 2\frac{1}{4}$?

(A.) $5\frac{3}{8}$
B. $5\frac{4}{8}$
C. $5\frac{1}{2}$
D. 6

Available as a transparency

Exact Answer or Estimate?

Lesson Organizer

Quick Lesson Overview

Objective Obtain exact or estimated results to solve problems in real-world contexts.

Math Understanding Some problems require exact answers, while others need only an estimate.

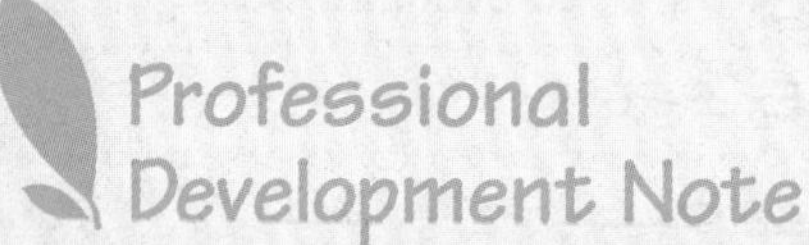

Managing Instruction Have students work on problems in pairs. Have one partner estimate values and one calculate exact values. Have them reread the problem to see which type of answer was needed.

NCTM Standards

- Number and Operations

(For a complete correlation to the NCTM Standards and Grades 6–8 Expectations, see pages 202G–H.)

Getting Started

Spiral Review

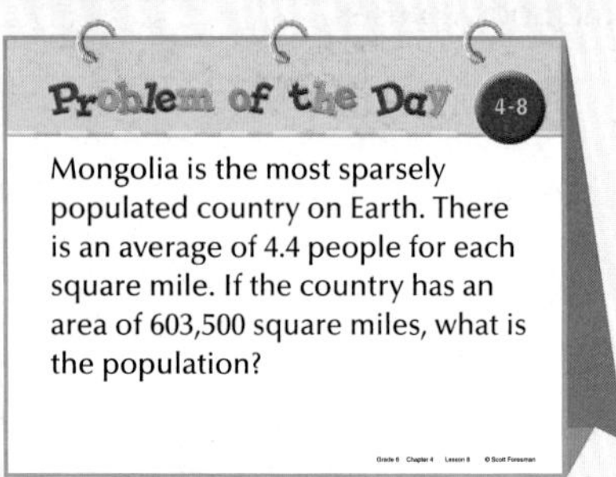

Problem of the Day 4-8

Mongolia is the most sparsely populated country on Earth. There is an average of 4.4 people for each square mile. If the country has an area of 603,500 square miles, what is the population?

Topics Reviewed

- Multiplying whole numbers and decimals
- Problem-Solving Skill: One-Step Problem

Answer The population of Mongolia is 2,655,400.

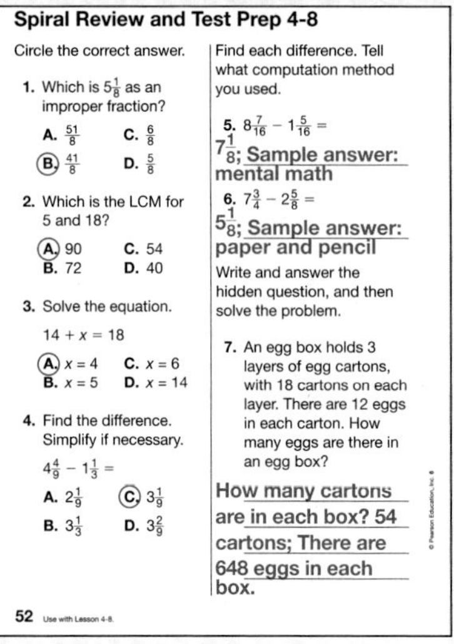

Spiral Review and Test Prep 4-8

Circle the correct answer.

1. Which is $5\frac{1}{8}$ as an improper fraction?
   A. $\frac{51}{8}$ (B.) $\frac{41}{8}$ C. $\frac{6}{8}$ D. $\frac{5}{8}$
2. Which is the LCM for 5 and 18?
   (A.) 90 B. 72 C. 54 D. 40
3. Solve the equation.
   $14 + x = 18$
   (A.) $x = 4$ B. $x = 5$ C. $x = 6$ D. $x = 14$
4. Find the difference. Simplify if necessary.
   $4\frac{4}{9} - 1\frac{1}{3} =$
   A. $2\frac{1}{9}$ B. $3\frac{1}{3}$ (C.) $3\frac{1}{9}$ D. $3\frac{2}{9}$

Find each difference. Tell what computation method you used.

5. $8\frac{7}{16} - 1\frac{5}{16} =$
   $7\frac{1}{8}$; Sample answer: mental math
6. $7\frac{3}{4} - 2\frac{5}{8} =$
   $5\frac{1}{8}$; Sample answer: paper and pencil

Write and answer the hidden question, and then solve the problem.

7. An egg box holds 3 layers of egg cartons, with 18 cartons on each layer. There are 12 eggs in each carton. How many eggs are there in an egg box?
   How many cartons are in each box? 54 cartons; There are 648 eggs in each box.

52 Use with Lesson 4-8.

Available as a transparency and as a blackline master

Topics Reviewed

1. Improper fractions and mixed numbers; **2.** Least common multiple; **3.** Solving equations with whole numbers; **4.** Subtracting mixed numbers; **5.–6.** Choose a computation method; **7.** Multiple-step problems

Investigating the Concept

Exact Answers and Estimates

20–25 MIN **Visual/Spatial**

What to Do

- Sketch the map shown below on the board. Use the locations shown, or have students suggest city or place names. Write on the board: How far is it from the lake to the zoo? Is it more than 2 miles from the lake to the zoo?
- **One question needs an exact answer. The other needs an estimate. Which is which?** *("How far" needs an exact answer. "Is it more" needs an estimate.)*
- Have students take turns creating questions related to the map. They should alternate exact-answer questions with estimate questions.

Ongoing Assessment

- **Number Sense Plan a walk that is exactly 6 miles long.** *(Lake—Museum—Zoo—Museum—Lake)* **Plan a walk that is about 3 miles.** *(Possible answers: Museum—Park—Zoo)*

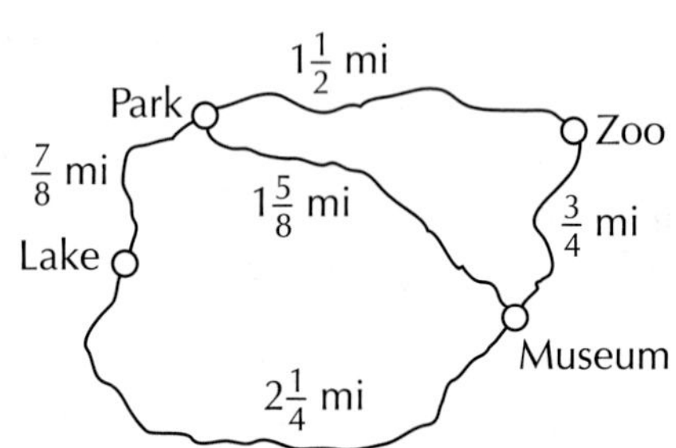

Reaching All Learners

Reading in Math

Scan for Estimation Clues

 10–15 MIN **Auditory** 

- Write the two estimation clues on the board.
- **These clues tell whether you need an exact or estimated answer. Where in a word problem are you likely to find clues like these?** *(In the last sentence)*
- Have students scan the lesson problems for clues of this type. Point out that they may need to read only the last sentence of a problem.

Estimation Clues
What was the total of ____?
Was the total more or less than ____?

Access Content

English Language Learners

Totally About the Answer

 10–15 MIN **Linguistic/Kinesthetic** SMALL GROUP

- Have volunteers read the lesson question, the first paragraph, and Examples A and B on page 226.
- Have group members discuss: **What words in the Example A question suggest that an exact answer is needed?** Ask students to change the question to suggest that an estimate is needed.
- **What words in the Example B question suggest that an estimate is needed?** Ask students to change the question to suggest that an exact answer is needed.
- Write the new questions on the board. Have volunteers circle the key words.

Reteaching

Estimation Decisions

 15–20 MIN **Visual/Spatial** 

- On the board, begin drawing the flow chart. **The problem may ask for a word answer such as "Joe has more." In these, you probably can estimate.**
- Continue the discussion until the flow chart is complete. Use problems from the lesson to illustrate how the flow chart works.

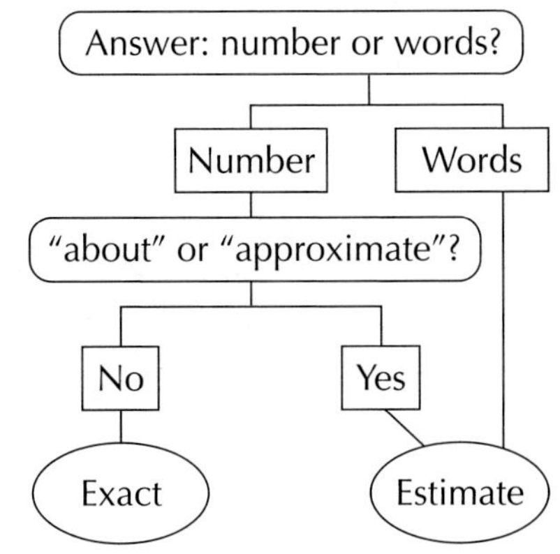

Advanced Learners

Overestimates and Underestimates

 15–20 MIN **Linguistic** 

Materials *(per group)* Newspapers

- **Would you overestimate or underestimate? Why?**
- **How much sugar should you put in a pitcher of lemonade?** *(Underestimate; you can add more.)*
- **What is the most you will spend for shoes and socks?** *(Overestimate; you need to have enough money.)*
- **How much time is needed for homework?** *(Overestimate; you don't want to run out of time.)*
- Have pairs look for examples of overestimates and underestimates in newspaper stories.

Objective Obtain exact or estimated results to solve problems in real-world contexts.

1 Warm Up

Activate Prior Knowledge Review how to identify what a word problem is asking students to find. Have students describe the form of the answer–a number, a word or phrase, or a drawing or graph.

2 Teach

LEARN In Example B, students can multiply 25 teams of 20 players to get 500. Since both 28 and 21 were rounded down, the actual number must be greater than 500.

Ongoing Assessment

Talk About It: Question 3

If students cannot tell whether an exact answer or an estimate is needed,

then point out that a numerical answer is asked for in Example A, while Example B asks them to merely tell more or less.

CHECK

Error Intervention

If students have difficulty deciding whether to estimate,

then show them how to translate the problems into simpler forms. For example, Exercise 2 can be simplified to "Is $54 \times 2 \times 36$ more than or less than 5,000?" *(Also see Reteaching, p. 226B.)*

Lesson 4-8

Problem-Solving Skill

Reading Helps!

Making judgments can help you with... identifying whether you need an exact answer or estimate.

Key Idea
Sometimes you need an exact answer to solve a problem, and sometimes an estimate is enough.

Exact Answer or Estimate

LEARN

Do you always need an exact answer to a word problem?

Look for phrases in the problem that suggest whether an exact answer or estimate is needed. If an estimate is all that's needed, you can often estimate using mental math.

Example A

On a map, Kim used a ruler to measure three line segments between cities. She measured $3\frac{1}{8}$, $2\frac{1}{2}$, and $2\frac{3}{16}$ inches. What was the total distance Kim measured?

Read and Understand

Step 1: What do you know?

The three distances are $3\frac{1}{8}$, $2\frac{1}{2}$ and $2\frac{3}{16}$.

Step 2: What are you trying to find?

The problem asks for the total distance. An exact answer is needed.

Example B

In 2002, each of 28 soccer teams had 21 players. Was this more or less than the 500 players who played in 2001?

Read and Understand

Step 1: What do you know?

In 2002, there were 28 teams with 21 players each.

In 2001, there were 500 players.

Step 2: What are you trying to find?

You need to know if the total is "more or less than 500," so an estimate is all that is needed.

Talk About It 3. Example A asked for a total distance while Example B only asked for more or less then 500.

1. Would you use mental math or paper and pencil to solve Example A? Example B? **Paper and pencil; mental math**
2. What is the answer to Example A? Example B? **$7\frac{13}{16}$; about 100 more**
3. Why was an exact answer needed in Example A, and an estimate needed in Example B? **See above.**

226

Reteaching — Below Level

PROBLEM-SOLVING SKILL R 4-8

Exact Answer or Estimate?

Estimates	Exact Answers
Phrases such as "will there be enough" and "more or less than" mean that an estimate will give you enough information to answer the problem.	If the problem asks "what is the total" or "how many" or "how much," calculate the exact amount.
Ted biked 14 mi on Monday, 11 mi on Tuesday, and 15 mi on Wednesday. Tom averaged 12 mi per day over the same three days. Did Tom bike a longer or shorter distance than Ted?	A room is $12\frac{1}{2}$ ft wide and $14\frac{1}{3}$ ft long. What is the area of the room in square feet?
Read and Understand	**Read and Understand**
Step 1: What do you know?	**Step 1:** What do you know?
The four distances are 14, 11, 15, and 12.	A room is $12\frac{1}{2}$ ft wide and $14\frac{1}{3}$ ft long.
Step 2: What are you trying to find?	**Step 2:** What are you trying to find?
The problem asks who biked the longer distance. You don't have to add Ted's miles to see that he biked a longer distance. An estimate is all that is needed.	The problem asks for the area of the room. You need an exact answer.

Tell whether an exact answer or an estimate is needed. Then solve.

1. Shelly's class made a quilt. The materials cost $65.75. They sold raffle tickets for the quilt and collected $128.00. How much profit did they make after they paid for the materials? **Exact answer; $62.25**
2. The school garden is divided into 4 different sections. $\frac{1}{6}$ of the garden is roses, $\frac{1}{4}$ of the garden is tomatoes, $\frac{1}{12}$ of the garden is lilies, and $\frac{1}{2}$ of the garden is peas. Are there more flowers or vegetables in the garden? **Estimate; more vegetables**
3. **Reasonableness** Maura has to contribute 10 hr to a service project to receive a special award. She has already put in 4 hr. She claims that if she can work on the project for $\frac{3}{4}$ hr each week she will meet her goal in 7 weeks. Is she correct? **Estimate; No, she will not meet her goal.**

52 Use with Lesson 4-8.

Practice — On Level

PROBLEM-SOLVING SKILL P 4-8

Exact Answer or Estimate?

Tell whether an exact answer or an estimate is needed. Then solve.

1. The maximum weight allowed on an elevator is 1,800 lb. If there are 9 people on the elevator and the average weight of each person is 175 lb, is the total weight over or under the limit? **Estimate; The total weight is under the limit.**
2. In 1970, the U.S. dollar was worth $3\frac{3}{5}$ German marks. In 2000, the dollar was worth only 2 German marks. How much did the value of the dollar decline? **Exact; The value decreased by $1\frac{3}{5}$ marks.**
3. A cell phone company is giving away 500 free minutes per month with each new phone. If the average person talks 15 min per day on their cell phone, will they have to pay for any calls during the month of June? (Remember: There are 30 days in June.) **Estimate; The cell phone user will not have to pay for any calls.**

Katya has a lemonade stand. She sells lemonade for $0.15 per glass. Her pitcher holds 8 servings.

4. After one hour the pitcher is $\frac{1}{4}$ full. How much money has she made? **Exact; Katya has made $0.90.**
5. **Reasonableness** Katya says that if she can sell 4 pitchers of lemonade she will earn more than $5.00. Is she correct? How do you know? **Estimate; Katya will not earn more than $5.00. One pitcher of lemonade is $\$0.15 \times 8 = \$1.20$. $\$1.20 \times 4 = \$4.80$.**

52 Use with Lesson 4-8.

CHECK

For another example, see Set 4-8 on p. 242.

Tell whether an exact answer or an estimate is needed. Then solve.

1. An advertisement is to have 8 lines of printing. The letters are to be $1\frac{1}{2}$ inches high with $\frac{1}{4}$ inch between lines. How much vertical space is needed for the printing? **Exact answer; $13\frac{3}{4}$ inches**
2. Flight 719 carries 54 passengers, each with 2 suitcases. Each suitcase has an average weight of 36 pounds. If the airplane was built to carry 5,000 pounds of luggage, is the flight over or under its limit? **Estimate; under**

PRACTICE

For more practice, see Set 4-8 on p. 245.

Tell whether an exact answer or an estimate is needed. Then solve.

3. Jess is making 3 recipes that each require flour. One recipe calls for $\frac{2}{3}$ cup flour, another calls for $\frac{7}{8}$ cup, and the third requires $\frac{3}{4}$ cup. How much flour will Jess need? **Exact answer; $2\frac{7}{24}$ cups**
4. To get the most for her money, should Alissha's grandmother buy 60 vitamins for $8.82 or 90 of the same vitamins for $10.85? **Exact answer; She should buy 90 vitamins.**
5. It is recommended that you tip a good waiter about $0.20 for each dollar of the meal's total cost. If your bill is $14.80, how much of a tip should you leave? **Estimate; about $3.00**

7. Estimate; no; she will have $\frac{1}{10}$ mile to go.

The map of Yolanda's neighborhood park is pictured at the right.

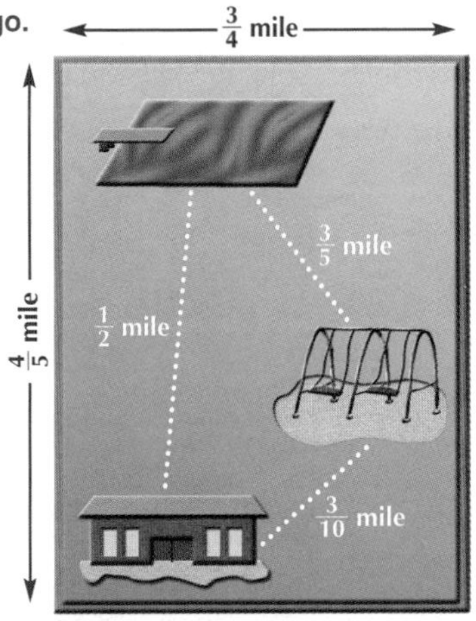

$\frac{3}{4}$ mile

$\frac{3}{5}$ mile

$\frac{1}{2}$ mile

$\frac{4}{5}$ mile

$\frac{3}{10}$ mile

6. How much greater is the length of the park than the width? **Exact answer; $\frac{1}{20}$ mile**
7. When she walks, Yolanda covers $\frac{1}{10}$ mile every 2 minutes. Can she walk from the clubhouse to the pool in 8 minutes? **See above right.**
8. **Reasonableness** Yolanda has a goal to walk 3 miles each day. She decides that everyday she will walk the perimeter of the park twice. Will she meet or exceed her goal? Explain. **See below right.**
9. Using the map of the park above, describe an alternate walking route that Yolanda could take to reach her 3-mile-a-day goal. **Sample answer: walk around the perimeter of the swings, clubhouse and pool two times**
10. The coach of a baseball team has $500 with which to buy equipment. Including tax, a shirt costs $18.95, a cap costs $14.95, and a bat costs $28.95. Can the coach buy a shirt and a cap for each of the 15 players? **Exact answer; no; the total cost is $508.50.**

8. Estimate; exceed; once around the park is about 3 miles, so twice would easily exceed her goal.

All text pages available online and on CD-ROM.

3 Practice

Exercise 4 Students can compare estimated unit prices: ($8.82 ÷ 60) and ($10.85 ÷ 90). In the larger size, the pills are about 12¢ each. In the smaller size, they are nearly 15¢ each.

Exercise 10 Students can include drawings of the map in their description of an alternate route Yolanda could take.

Leveled Practice

Below Level Ex. 3–10

On Level Ex. 3–10

Above Level Ex. 3–10

Early Finishers Write these two questions on the board: How much more does Julie have? Does Julie have more?

Have students create two problems using the questions and explain why one requires an exact value and the other needs only an estimate.

4 Assess

Journal Idea Tell students to imagine that they are buying 8 things at a grocery store. Have them explain when an estimate is useful and when an exact value is needed.

Enrichment — Above Level

Class of 2008 E 4-8 REASONABLENESS

Circle the letter that describes the best answer choice.

1. Miss Hancock teaches sixth grade. In September there were 9 girls and 15 boys in her class. In October one of the girls moved away. In January two boys joined the class. How many boys are there in Miss Hancock's class now?
   A. There are more boys than girls in the class.
   B. There are more boys now than there were in September.
   (C.) There are 17 boys in Miss Hancock's class now.
2. In the entire sixth grade, there are 51 girls and 46 boys. About $\frac{3}{4}$ of the students are right-handed. Are there more than or less than 70 students who are right-handed?
   A. Between 72 and 73 students are right-handed.
   (B.) More than 70 students are right-handed.
   C. About $\frac{1}{4}$ of the students are left-handed.
3. About $\frac{5}{6}$ of the students in the sixth-grade accelerated math program go on to earn a college degree. There are 36 sixth graders in the accelerated math program. How many students will probably earn a college degree?
   (A.) Thirty sixth graders will probably earn a college degree.
   B. Less than 36 sixth graders will probably earn a college degree.
   C. About 10 sixth graders will not earn a college degree.
4. The table shows the number of boys and girls in the sixth grade for the past four years. How many more boys than girls were in the sixth grade in 2000?
   A. There were more boys than girls in the sixth grade in 2000.
   (B.) There were 5 more boys than girls in the sixth grade in 2000.
   C. There were more girls than boys in 2003.

Sixth Graders

Year	Boys	Girls
2000	44	39
2001	43	48
2002	40	56
2003	46	51

52 Use with Lesson 4-8.

Problem Solving

PROBLEM-SOLVING SKILL PS 4-8

Exact Answer or Estimate?

The number of people using personal computers is becoming greater every year. The table shows the fraction of people using personal computers in two countries. Has personal computer use increased by a greater fraction in the United States or in Australia?

Country	1990	2000
Australia	$\frac{3}{20}$	$\frac{9}{20}$
United States	$\frac{1}{5}$	$\frac{3}{5}$

Read and Understand

1. What are you trying to find?
   Which country had a greater increase

Plan and Solve

2. Is an exact answer or an estimate needed? Explain.
   Estimate; Sample answer: An estimate should be enough to tell which country had computer use increase by a greater fraction.
3. Write the answer in a complete sentence.
   Personal computer use increased by a greater fraction in the United States than in Australia.

Look Back and Check

4. Explain how you can check your answer.
   Sample answer: By converting $\frac{2}{5}$ and $\frac{6}{20}$ to have the same denominator ($\frac{2}{5} = \frac{4}{10}$ and $\frac{6}{20} = \frac{3}{10}$) to find that $\frac{2}{5}$ is greater than $\frac{6}{20}$.

52 Use with Lesson 4-8.

Test-Taking Practice 4-8

1. Tell whether an exact answer or an estimate is needed. Then solve.
   Penelope needs to buy 17 notebooks for a class project. Each notebook costs $1.19. Penelope has $20.00. Does she have enough money? Explain how you found your answer.
   Exact answer; No; Sample answer: 17 × $1.19 = $20.23, which is greater than $20.00.
2. The route for the student race is $1\frac{3}{5}$ mi. The route for the adult race is $5\frac{9}{10}$ mi. Lee needs to use ribbons to mark two race routes. How much ribbon does he need?
   Which of the following correctly shows the kind of answer needed and the solution?
   A. Estimate, 6 mi
   B. Estimate, 7 mi
   (C.) Exact answer, $7\frac{1}{2}$ mi
   D. Exact answer, $6\frac{9}{10}$ mi

Available as a transparency

Hovercraft

Lesson Organizer

Quick Lesson Overview

Objective Review and apply key concepts, skills, and strategies learned in this and previous chapters.

Math Understanding Some real-world problems can be solved using known concepts, skills, and strategies.

Math Background Fractions can be found in the earliest written mathematical records. The ancient Egyptians developed a system to do arithmetic with fractions.

NCTM Standards

- Number and Operations
- Algebra

(For a complete correlation to the NCTM Standards and Grades 6–8 Expectations, see page 202G–H.)

Getting Started

Spiral Review

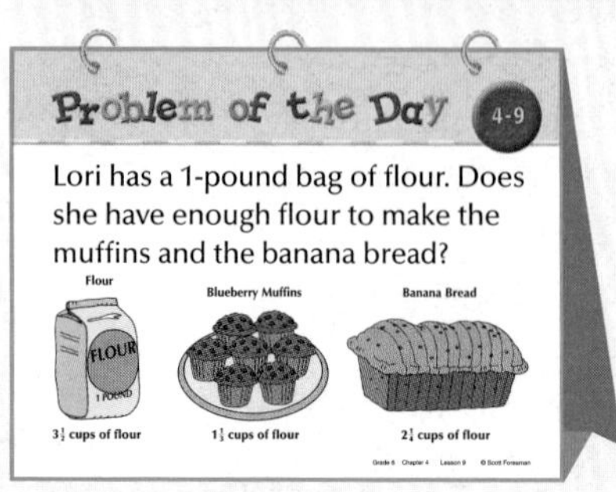

Problem of the Day
4-9
Lori has a 1-pound bag of flour. Does she have enough flour to make the muffins and the banana bread?
Flour
Blueberry Muffins
Banana Bread
FLOUR
1 POUND
$3\frac{1}{2}$ cups of flour
$1\frac{1}{3}$ cups of flour
$2\frac{1}{4}$ cups of flour

Topics Reviewed

- Adding and comparing mixed numbers
- Problem-Solving Skill: Multiple-Step Problem

Answer Lori does not have enough flour.

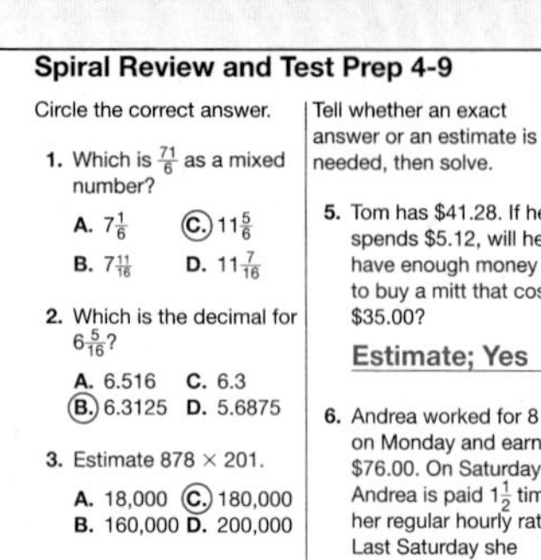

Spiral Review and Test Prep 4-9

Circle the correct answer.

1. Which is $\frac{71}{6}$ as a mixed number?
   A. $7\frac{1}{6}$ (C.) $11\frac{5}{6}$
   B. $7\frac{11}{16}$ D. $11\frac{7}{16}$

2. Which is the decimal for $6\frac{5}{16}$?
   A. 6.516 C. 6.3
   (B.) 6.3125 D. 5.6875

3. Estimate 878×201.
   A. 18,000 (C.) 180,000
   B. 160,000 D. 200,000

4. For which of the following problems would you most likely use mental math?
   A. $7\frac{1}{8} + 2\frac{14}{17}$
   B. $7\frac{1}{13} + 2\frac{1}{8}$
   C. $7\frac{1}{9} + 2\frac{3}{13}$
   (D.) $7\frac{1}{8} + 2\frac{1}{8}$

Tell whether an exact answer or an estimate is needed, then solve.

5. Tom has $41.28. If he spends $5.12, will he have enough money left to buy a mitt that costs $35.00?
   Estimate; Yes

6. Andrea worked for 8 hr on Monday and earned $76.00. On Saturdays, Andrea is paid $1\frac{1}{2}$ times her regular hourly rate. Last Saturday she worked for 6 hr. How much did she earn?
   She earned $85.50.

© Pearson Education, Inc. 6

Use with Lesson 4-9. 53

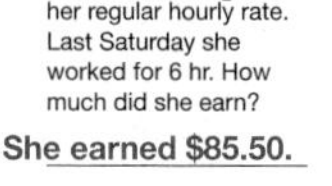

Available as a transparency and as a blackline master

Topics Reviewed

1. Improper fractions and mixed numbers; **2.** Connecting fractions and decimals; **3.** Estimating products; **4.** Mental math; **5.** Exact answer or estimate?; **6.** Multiple-step problem

Investigating the Concept

Fractional Parts of a Whole

10-15 MIN **Kinesthetic/Social/Cooperative**

Materials *(per pair)* Counters or Teaching Tool 9

What to Do

- Use this activity for students to practice identifying fractional parts of a set. Have Partner 1 choose a set of counters so some are red and some are yellow and the fraction of the set that is each color can be reduced.
- Tell Partner 2 to write the fraction of the set that is each color and then rewrite each fraction in simplest form. *(Sample answer: $\frac{5}{15} = \frac{1}{3}$, red; $\frac{10}{15} = \frac{2}{3}$, yellow)*
- Repeat several times, with students switching roles each time.

Ongoing Assessment

- **Number Sense If you used 16 counters, how many could you make red, so the fraction that is red could be reduced?** *(You could make 2, 4, 6, 8, 10, 12, or 14 red.)*

Reaching All Learners

Reading in Math

Using Key Facts and Summarizing

 10–15 MIN **Social/Cooperative** 

- Have one student read Exercise 5 on page 229 aloud and tell how to find out how many cars can be transported on the car deck when it is filled. *(Use the Key Facts box on page 228.)*
- Have the other student tell what he or she knows and what he or she needs to find. *(We know that the hovercraft can transport 30 vehicles. We need to find the faction of the deck that is filled when 24 cars are transported and the fraction of the deck that is empty.)*
- Tell students to change roles and do Exercise 3 on page 228, similarly.

Access Content

English Language Learners

Questions About Key Facts

 15–20 MIN **Social/Cooperative/Linguistic** 

- Have volunteers read each *Key Fact* on page 228. Discuss any unfamiliar terms such as *knots, cruising,* and *propeller.*
- Read Exercise 3 on page 228.
- **Using Exercise 3 as a model, create questions using each of the *Key Facts.***
- Have partners exchange questions and think aloud as they answer each other's questions.

If the hovercraft is only loaded to $\frac{1}{8}$ of its capacity, how much does it weigh?

Reteaching

Multiplying Decimals

 15–20 MIN **Visual/Spatial/Kinesthetic** 

Materials Place-Value Blocks or Teaching Tool 7, Four index cards with the following decimal numbers: 2.12, 2.57, 1.92, and 1.17

What to Do

- Place the cards face down. Have one student draw a card and each student show the number with place-value blocks.
- Have one student use the place-value blocks to find two times the number drawn, regrouping as needed. Have the other student find the product with the algorithm. *(Sample answer: $2 \times 1.17 = 2.34$)*
- Have students repeat until all the cards are used, switching roles each time. *($2 \times 2.12 = 4.24$; $2 \times 2.57 = 5.14$; $2 \times 1.92 = 3.84$)*

Advanced Learners

Identifying Fractional Parts

 10–15 MIN **Logical/Mathematical** 

Materials Tangram Pieces (Teaching Tool 45), Scissors

- Give each student a copy of the tangram square.
- Have students determine the fractional part of the square that each piece represents and record it on paper. Students may need to cut out the pieces to determine relative sizes. *(A and B are $\frac{1}{4}$; C, E, and. G are $\frac{1}{8}$; D and F are $\frac{1}{16}$.)*
- Have students then add the fractional parts to see if they have a sum of one. *($\frac{1}{4} + \frac{1}{4} + \frac{1}{8} + \frac{1}{16} + \frac{1}{8} + \frac{1}{16} + \frac{1}{8} = 1$)*

Objective Review and apply key concepts, skills, and strategies learned in this and previous chapters.

Activate Prior Knowledge Ask students to simplify the fraction $\frac{40}{75}$. $(\frac{8}{15})$

2 Teach

Explain to the students that they will use what they already know.

Ongoing Assessment

Talk About It: Exercise 1

- **What are we trying to find out?** *(What fractions of the passenger cabin are filled and empty)*
- **What do we know?** *(80 of 424 possible passengers were on the hovercrafts.)*
- **What strategy would you use?** *(Write fractions with a denominator of 424 and then simplify.)*

Error Intervention

If students are having difficulty deciding which fact to use from the *Key Facts* table to solve a problem,

then have them match words used in the problem with words used in the table.

Lesson 4-9

Problem-Solving Applications

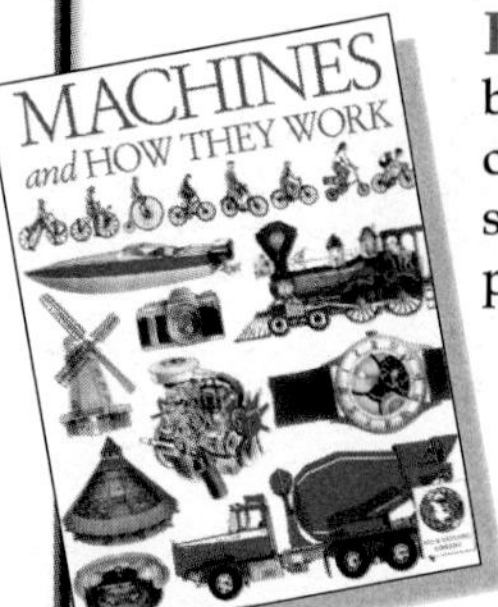

Hovercraft A hovercraft can move faster than conventional boats because it floats above the water on a cushion of air. This cushion is created by large fans and it is contained by an inflatable skirt running around the bottom of the boat. Usually, large propellers are used to move the craft forward.

Trivia To make his first working model, the inventor of the hovercraft placed an empty cat food can inside an empty coffee can.

1 Two of the *Swift's* sister ships were stretched so that they could carry up to 424 passengers. If only 80 passengers traveled on these stretched hovercrafts, what fraction of the passenger cabin was filled? What fraction was empty? $\frac{10}{53}$, $\frac{43}{53}$

2 It takes a conventional ferryboat more than 1 hour and 15 minutes to cross the English Channel. The *Swift* could cross the English channel in about 25 minutes. What fraction of a conventional ferryboat's time is this? $\frac{1}{3}$

Using Key Facts

3 The length of the passenger cabin was about 0.63 times the total length of the *Swift*. What was the length of the passenger cabin? **25.2 m**

4 During initial sea-trials, the *Swift* reached a record-breaking speed that was about 1.66 times faster than its cruising speed. How fast could this hovercraft travel? Write an equation that would help you solve this question. **99.6 knots; F = 1.66 *t* where F is fastest speed and *t* is the cruising speed**

Key Facts
***Swift* Hovercraft**
- Weight when fully loaded = 200 tons
- Cruising speed = 60 knots
- Length = 40 meters
- Width = 23 meters
- Propeller diameter = 21 feet
- Maximum number of passengers = 254
- Maximum number of vehicles = 30

Below Level — Reteaching

PROBLEM-SOLVING APPLICATIONS R 4-9

Building Square

Peter is building two shelves. One shelf needs to be $2\frac{1}{2}$ ft long. The other shelf needs to be $3\frac{2}{5}$ ft long. How much wood will Peter need for these shelves?

Use the LCM to find a common denominator. The LCM of 2 and 5 is 10.

$$\begin{array}{r} 2\frac{1}{2} = 2\frac{5}{10} \\ +3\frac{2}{5} = 3\frac{4}{10} \\ \hline 5\frac{9}{10} \end{array}$$

So, Peter will need $5\frac{9}{10}$ ft of wood.

Use the data file to answer the following questions.

Data File

Board	Length (in feet)
A	$1\frac{3}{4}$
B	$3\frac{5}{8}$
C	$10\frac{1}{2}$
D	$8\frac{2}{3}$

1. Peter needs four of Board A to make a picture frame. How many total feet of wood is that? **7 ft**
2. What is the difference in lengths of Board B and Board C? **$6\frac{7}{8}$ ft**
3. Peter wants to place a shelf all the way across the wall of his kitchen. The wall is 23 ft long. If Peter uses two of Board C, will he have enough wood to go across the wall? Would you use mental math or paper and pencil to find this answer? **No, he will only have 21 ft of wood; mental math**
4. How long would Board B be if Peter cut $2\frac{1}{2}$ ft. from it? **$1\frac{1}{8}$ ft**
5. **Estimation** Peter has five of Board D. About how many feet of wood is that in total? **About 45 ft**

Use with Lesson 4-9. 53

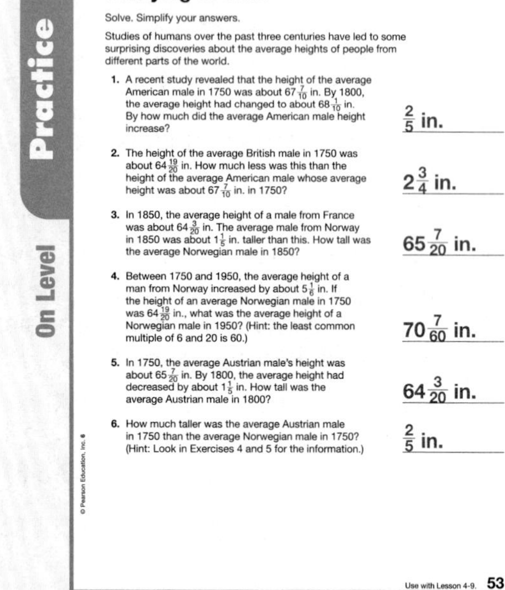

On Level — Practice

PROBLEM-SOLVING APPLICATIONS P 4-9

Studying Growth

Solve. Simplify your answers.

Studies of humans over the past three centuries have led to some surprising discoveries about the average heights of people from different parts of the world.

1. A recent study revealed that the height of the average American male in 1750 was about $67\frac{7}{10}$ in. By 1800, the average height had changed to about $68\frac{1}{10}$ in. By how much did the average American male height increase? **$\frac{2}{5}$ in.**
2. The height of the average British male in 1750 was about $64\frac{19}{20}$ in. How much less was this than the height of the average American male whose average height was about $67\frac{7}{10}$ in. in 1750? **$2\frac{3}{4}$ in.**
3. In 1850, the average height of a male from France was about $64\frac{3}{20}$ in. The average male from Norway in 1850 was about $1\frac{1}{5}$ in. taller than this. How tall was the average Norwegian male in 1850? **$65\frac{7}{20}$ in.**
4. Between 1750 and 1950, the average height of a man from Norway increased by about $5\frac{1}{6}$ in. If the height of an average Norwegian male in 1750 was $64\frac{19}{20}$ in., what was the average height of a Norwegian male in 1950? (Hint: the least common multiple of 6 and 20 is 60.) **$70\frac{7}{60}$ in.**
5. In 1750, the average Austrian male's height was about $65\frac{7}{20}$ in. By 1800, the average height had decreased by about $1\frac{1}{5}$ in. How tall was the average Austrian male in 1800? **$64\frac{3}{20}$ in.**
6. How much taller was the average Austrian male in 1750 than the average Norwegian male in 1750? (Hint: Look in Exercises 4 and 5 for the information.) **$\frac{2}{5}$ in.**

Use with Lesson 4-9. 53

5 If only 24 cars were transported on a trip, what fraction of the car deck was filled? What fraction was empty? $\frac{4}{5}$, $\frac{1}{5}$

6 **Writing in Math** Write your own fraction problem using any of the facts mentioned on these pages. Write the answer in a complete sentence. **Sample answer: If the Swift had 15 cars, what fraction of the deck would be filled? It would be half filled.**

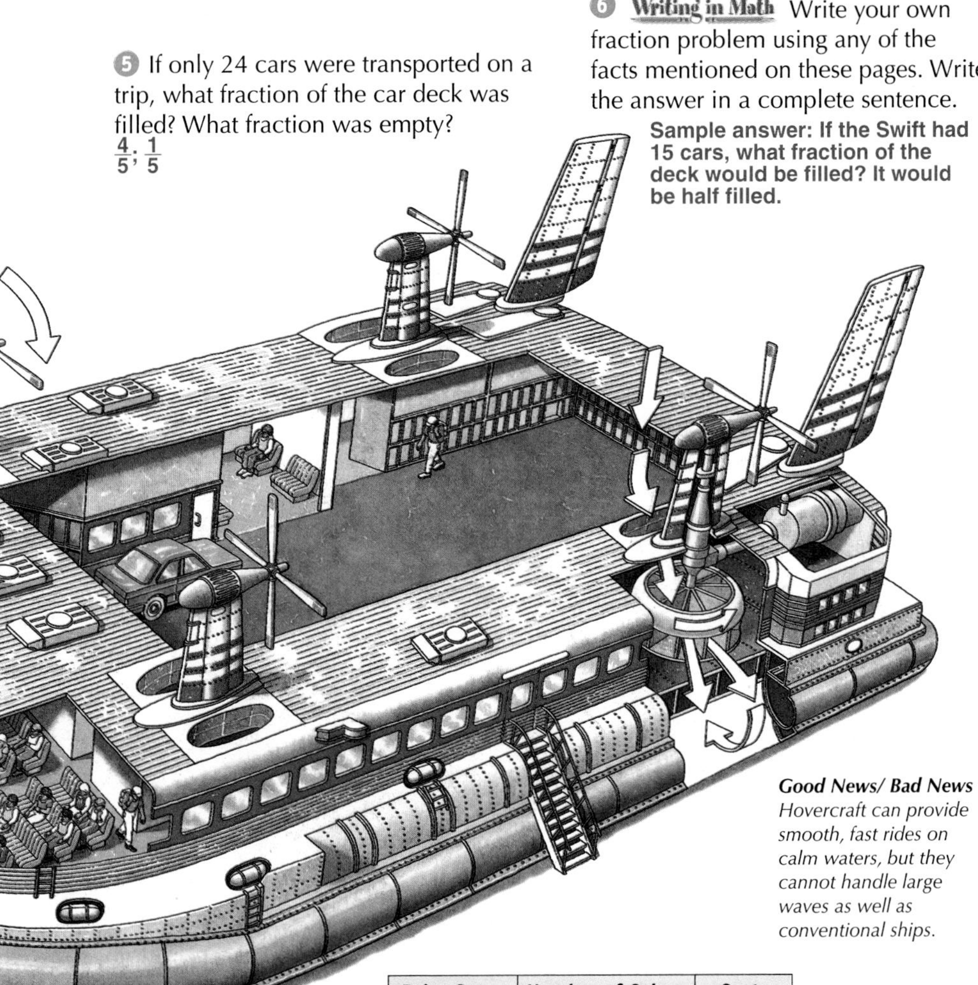

Good News/ Bad News
Hovercraft can provide smooth, fast rides on calm waters, but they cannot handle large waves as well as conventional ships.

Paint Set	Number of Colors	Cost
Metallic	4	$3.80
Fluorescent	6	$5.46
Glossy	3	$2.58

7 **Decision Making** Racing radio-controlled model hovercrafts is a popular hobby in some areas. Suppose you needed to purchase one paint set for a small model. Which set of paints from the table above would you buy? How much would that paint cost per color? Is your choice of paint the most economical? **Sample answer: glossy; $0.86 per bottle; yes**

3 Practice

TEST TALK **Exercise 6** Remind students to read all the information on these two pages before using any facts to write and solve their word problems.

Exercise 7 Point out that there are three questions to be answered in this exercise. Although students may choose any set of paints, they must tell whether their choice is most economical.

Leveled Practice

Below Level Work alone on Ex. 1–3. Work on Ex. 4–7 with a partner.

On Level Work alone on Ex. 1–5. Work on Ex. 6 and 7 with a partner.

Above Level Work alone on Ex. 1–6. Work on Ex. 7 with a partner.

Early Finishers Have students find the cost per color for each paint set listed in the chart above Exercise 7.

4 Assess

Journal Idea Have students explain how they found the answer for Exercise 2.

Enrichment — Above Level

The Fraction Game

E 4-9
NUMBER SENSE

Three friends are playing a fraction game. Each player picks two fraction cards. On odd hands, players find the sum of the two cards. On even hands, players find the difference of the two cards. The player with the greatest answer wins the hand.

The first three hands of the game are shown below. Rewrite each fraction, using the least common denominator. Then write the sum or difference in simplest form. Find which player won each hand and write the letter in the box.

1. Player A: $1\frac{1}{3}$, $2\frac{1}{6}$ — Player B: $3\frac{1}{4}$, $\frac{1}{8}$ — Player C: $2\frac{1}{2}$, $\frac{5}{6}$ — Winner? **A**

$1\frac{2}{6} + 2\frac{1}{6} = 3\frac{1}{2}$ $3\frac{2}{8} + \frac{1}{8} = 3\frac{3}{8}$ $2\frac{3}{6} + \frac{5}{6} = 3\frac{1}{3}$

2. Player A: $7\frac{1}{10}$, $4\frac{1}{2}$ — Player B: $6\frac{7}{8}$, $2\frac{1}{3}$ — Player C: $5\frac{4}{7}$, $1\frac{1}{4}$ — Winner? **B**

$7\frac{1}{10} - 4\frac{5}{10} = 2\frac{3}{5}$ $6\frac{21}{24} - 2\frac{8}{24} = 4\frac{13}{24}$ $5\frac{16}{28} - 1\frac{7}{28} = 4\frac{9}{28}$

3. Player A: $\frac{7}{10}$, $4\frac{1}{4}$ — Player B: $3\frac{5}{8}$, $1\frac{1}{6}$ — Player C: $2\frac{4}{13}$, $2\frac{19}{26}$ — Winner? **C**

$\frac{14}{20} + 4\frac{5}{20} = 4\frac{19}{20}$ $3\frac{15}{24} + 1\frac{4}{24} = 4\frac{19}{24}$ $2\frac{8}{26} + 2\frac{19}{26} = 5\frac{1}{26}$

Use with Lesson 4-9. 53

Problem Solving

PROBLEM-SOLVING APPLICATION PS 4-9

Plug It In

Maurice just got a new computer. He needs to run a modem cord from the phone line in the wall to his computer. He needs $72\frac{1}{2}$ in. of cord to reach from the wall to the desk. He also needs $27\frac{1}{3}$ in. of cord to reach from the desk to the back of the computer. How long does Maurice's modem cord need to be?

Read and Understand

1. How much cord does Maurice need to reach from the wall to the desk? **$72\frac{1}{2}$ in.**
2. How much cord does Maurice need to reach from the desk to the computer? **$27\frac{1}{3}$ in.**
3. What are you trying to find? **How much modem cord Maurice needs**

Plan and Solve

4. What strategy or strategies can you use to solve the problem? **Write a number sentence**
5. Write the answer in a complete sentence. **Maurice needs a modem cord that is at least $99\frac{5}{6}$ in.**
6. Explain how you found your answer. **Sample answer: By adding the two lengths to find the total: $72\frac{1}{2} + 27\frac{1}{3} = 72\frac{3}{6} + 27\frac{2}{6} = 99\frac{5}{6}$ in.**

Look Back and Check

7. Explain how you can check your answer. **$99\frac{5}{6} - 72\frac{1}{2} = 99\frac{5}{6} - 72\frac{3}{6} = 27\frac{2}{6} = 27\frac{1}{3}$**

Use with Lesson 4-9. 53

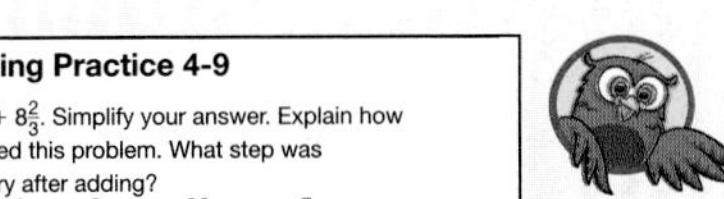

Test-Taking Practice 4-9

1. Add $5\frac{4}{7} + 8\frac{2}{3}$. Simplify your answer. Explain how you solved this problem. What step was necessary after adding?
$14\frac{5}{21}$; $5\frac{4}{7} + 8\frac{2}{3} = 13\frac{26}{21} = 14\frac{5}{21}$; Convert the improper fraction $13\frac{26}{21}$ into the mixed number $14\frac{5}{21}$ to simplify the answer.

2. Which shows the difference of $4\frac{7}{12} - 1\frac{5}{8}$ in simplest form?
A. $2\frac{7}{24}$
(B) $2\frac{23}{24}$
C. $2\frac{7}{8}$
D. $2\frac{13}{14}$

Available as a transparency

Review

Purpose Help students review content learned in Section B.

Using Student Pages 230–231

Do You Know How? exercises are appropriate for written work.

Do You Understand? questions are designed for whole-class discussion or small-group discussion followed by a report to the whole class.

Vocabulary Review

You may wish to review these terms before assigning the page.

round *(p. 14)*

mixed number *(p. 168)*

Section B: Lessons 4-4 through 4-9

Review

Do You Know How? | **Do You Understand?**

Estimating Sums and Differences of Fractions and Mixed Numbers (4-4)

Estimate each sum or difference. **Sample answers are given.**

1. $2\frac{4}{5} + 9\frac{3}{8}$ **12**
2. $1\frac{9}{10} - \frac{5}{6}$ **1**
3. $1\frac{7}{8} + 3\frac{1}{4}$ **5**
4. $4\frac{1}{3} - 2\frac{7}{9}$ **1**

Sample answers are given.

A Explain how you estimated each sum or difference. **I rounded to the nearest whole number.**

B For which exercises could you give a mixed number estimate? Explain how you could give an estimate that is a mixed number. **See below.**

Adding Mixed Numbers (4-5); Subtracting Mixed Numbers (4-6)

Find each sum or difference. Simplify if possible.

5. $5\frac{3}{10} + 2\frac{9}{10}$ **$8\frac{1}{5}$**
6. $4\frac{5}{6} - 2\frac{1}{6}$ **$2\frac{2}{3}$**
7. $8 + 3\frac{4}{5}$ **$11\frac{4}{5}$**
8. $5\frac{7}{8} - 3\frac{1}{3}$ **$2\frac{13}{24}$**
9. $12\frac{8}{9} - 4$ **$8\frac{8}{9}$**
10. $7\frac{3}{10} + 2\frac{3}{5}$ **$9\frac{9}{10}$**
11. $4\frac{5}{8} + 2\frac{7}{12}$ **$7\frac{5}{24}$**
12. $7 - 3\frac{3}{4}$ **$3\frac{1}{4}$**

C. I added or subtracted the whole numbers, then the fractions.

C Explain how you found the sum or difference in Exercises 7 and 9. **See above.**

D Tell how you would round each addend in Exercise 11. **See below.**

E Which exercises would be easiest to rewrite using decimals? Explain why. **#5, #7, #10, #12. The decimal equivalents for the fractions in these exercises are terminating.**

D. $4\frac{5}{8}$ is greater than $4\frac{1}{2}$, so round to 5; $2\frac{7}{12}$ is closest to 3.

Choose a Computation Method (4-7)

Find each answer. Tell what computation method you used.

13. $9\frac{1}{3} - 5\frac{7}{8}$ **$3\frac{11}{24}$; paper and pencil**
14. $2\frac{3}{4} + 15$ **$17\frac{3}{4}$; mental math**
15. $11 - 5\frac{3}{5}$ **$5\frac{2}{5}$; paper and pencil**
16. $4\frac{1}{5} + 6\frac{4}{5}$ **11; mental math**

F Explain why you chose the method you used in Exercise 16. **I used mental math because $\frac{1}{5} + \frac{4}{5} = 1$ and $4 + 6 + 1 = 11$.**

B. 1 and 3; round $2\frac{4}{5}$ to 3 and $9\frac{3}{8}$ to $9\frac{1}{2}$; $3 + 9\frac{1}{2} = 12\frac{1}{2}$; round $1\frac{7}{8}$ to 2 and leave $3\frac{1}{4}$ as is; $2 + 3\frac{1}{4} = 5\frac{1}{4}$.

Problem-Solving Skill: Exact Answer or Estimate? (4-8)

17. Janelle has \$21. She estimates that 5 raffle tickets will cost \$20. Can Janelle buy the tickets if each ticket costs \$4.40? Explain. **No. $5 \times 4 = 20$ and $0.4 \times 5 = 2$; $20 + 2 = 22$.**

G Tell how you decided whether to find an estimate or exact answer for Exercise 17. **The estimate and the amount of money are close enough that an exact answer needed to be found.**

230 Chapter 4 Section B Review

Item Analysis for Diagnosis and Intervention

Objective	Review Items	Diagnostic Checkpoint Items	Student Book Pages*	Intervention System
Estimate sums and differences of fractions and mixed numbers.	1–4	3–6	216–217	H33
Add mixed numbers.	5, 7, 10–11	2, 7, 9, 12–13, 17	218–219	H34
Subtract mixed numbers.	6, 8–9, 12	1, 8, 10–11, 14, 18	220–223	H35
Choose a computation method.	13–16	19	224–225	H36
Determine whether an exact answer or an estimate can answer a question.	17	15–16	226–227	M8

*For each lesson, there is a *Reteaching* activity in *Reaching All Learners* and a *Reteaching* master.

Chapter 4 Section B

Diagnostic Checkpoint

MULTIPLE CHOICE

Think It Through For multiple-choice items, first **eliminate any unreasonable answers.**

1. Find $9\frac{1}{3} - 2\frac{3}{4}$. (4-6)

   A. $7\frac{4}{7}$ B. $7\frac{7}{12}$ C. $7\frac{1}{12}$ (D.) $6\frac{7}{12}$

2. Mrs. Anderson made $3\frac{1}{2}$ dozen apple muffins and $2\frac{1}{4}$ dozen bran muffins. How many muffins did she make altogether? (4-5)

   (A.) $5\frac{3}{4}$ dozen B. $5\frac{1}{4}$ dozen C. $5\frac{1}{6}$ dozen D. $1\frac{1}{4}$ dozen

FREE RESPONSE

Estimate each sum or difference. (4-4) **Sample answers are given.**

3. $\frac{3}{8} + \frac{7}{12}$ **1** 4. $\frac{11}{12} - \frac{1}{8}$ **1** 5. $6\frac{2}{5} + 3\frac{9}{10}$ **10** 6. $1\frac{1}{4} - \frac{7}{8}$ **$\frac{1}{2}$**

Find each sum or difference. Simplify if possible. (4-5, 4-6, 4-9)

7. $8\frac{5}{6} + 3\frac{5}{6}$ **$12\frac{2}{3}$** 8. $3\frac{9}{16} - \frac{5}{16}$ **$3\frac{1}{4}$** 9. $12\frac{7}{8} + 13$ **$25\frac{7}{8}$** 10. $7\frac{2}{9} - 5$ **$2\frac{2}{9}$**

11. $9 - 8\frac{3}{4}$ **$\frac{1}{4}$** 12. $2\frac{3}{8} + 6\frac{3}{5}$ **$8\frac{39}{40}$** 13. $5\frac{5}{12} + 6\frac{7}{8}$ **$12\frac{7}{24}$** 14. $4\frac{1}{3} - 2\frac{5}{12}$ **$1\frac{11}{12}$**

Grandma Siegel is 65 years old. Her grandson Ian is 9 years old, and her granddaughter Caitlyn is 14 years old. Use the table at the right. (4-8, 4-9).

Botanic Garden Fees

General Admission		Garden Trains Exhibit	
Adults	$6	Adults	$4.25
Under 12	$4	Under 12	$3.75
Seniors (62+)	$5	Seniors (62+)	$3.75

15. Grandma Siegel has $27. Does she have enough money to cover the general admission and trains exhibit for herself and her grandchildren? Tell whether an exact answer or estimate is needed. **Yes; exact answer**

16. Close Knit Outlet is having a sweater sale. The pre-tax sale price for any sweater is $17.95. About how much money should Ana bring to the outlet if she plans to buy 3 sweaters? (4-8, 4-9) **About $60**

Writing in Math

17. When you are adding a mixed number in simplest form to a whole number, can you have a whole number solution? Why or why not? (4-5) **No; the fraction part of the mixed number requires another fraction to be combined into a whole number.**

18. Give an example of when you need to rename a mixed number before subtracting. (4-6) **Sample answer: $1\frac{1}{8} - \frac{5}{6}$**

19. Which computation method would you use to find $5\frac{8}{15} + 2\frac{11}{12}$? Explain why. (4-7) **Paper and pencil; I would need to use paper and pencil to find an LCD and equivalent fractions.**

Sample student work for Exercise 17

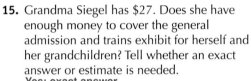

No, if you add a mixed number to a whole number, you get a mixed number.

The rubric below is a scoring guide that shows how many points to give an answer to Exercise 17. Many teachers would assign a score of 1 point to this explanation. Discuss the sample response shown and compare it to papers produced by students.

Scoring Rubric

4 Full credit: 4 points
The answer is correct; knows how to add mixed numbers and whole numbers; explanation is complete.

3 Partial credit: 3 points
The answer is correct; knows how to add mixed numbers and whole numbers; explanation is incomplete.

2 Partial credit: 2 points
The answer is incorrect; explanation shows understanding.

1 Partial credit: 1 point
The answer is correct; gives no explanation.

0 No credit
The answer is incorrect; shows no understanding.

Test Talk

Purpose Promote focused instruction on test-taking strategies.

Using Student Pages 232–233

The purpose of these pages is to help students make smart answer choices on multiple-choice test items. Students work through two problems, learning strategies to eliminate incorrect answer choices and then noting ways to check their final choice to make sure it is reasonable.

Have students look at Exercise 1; then have them read through the first three strategies to understand that this problem requires looking for a pattern. Next, direct students to the *Make Smart Choices* strategy. Have a volunteer explain why answer choices B and A can be eliminated. Discuss why either C or D might be a reasonable answer and how the final answer was arrived at. For Exercise 2, have students read the problem and *Think It Through*. Help students see why choices A and C were eliminated and how working backward made it possible to eliminate choice B.

Assign Exercises 3 and 4 for students to do independently. Point out that Exercise 3 is solved similarly to Exercise 2; Exercise 4 is solved similarly to Exercise 1. Accept reasonable variations in students' explanations of how they arrived at answers.

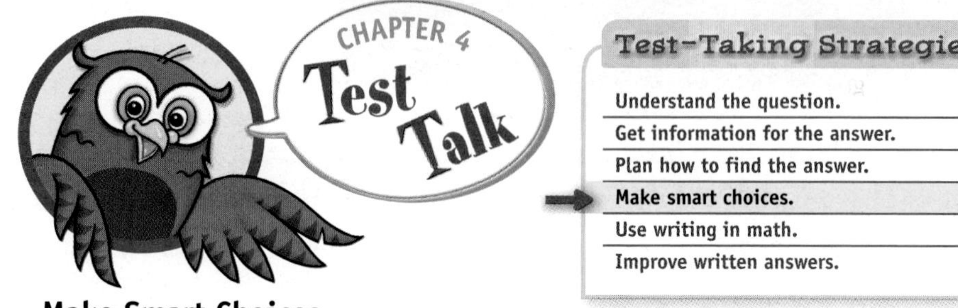

CHAPTER 4
Test Talk
Test-Taking Strategies
Understand the question.
Get information for the answer.
Plan how to find the answer.
Make smart choices.
Use writing in math.
Improve written answers.

Make Smart Choices

To answer a multiple-choice test question, you need to choose an answer from answer choices. The steps below will help you make a smart choice.

1. The following figures below are made with square tiles.

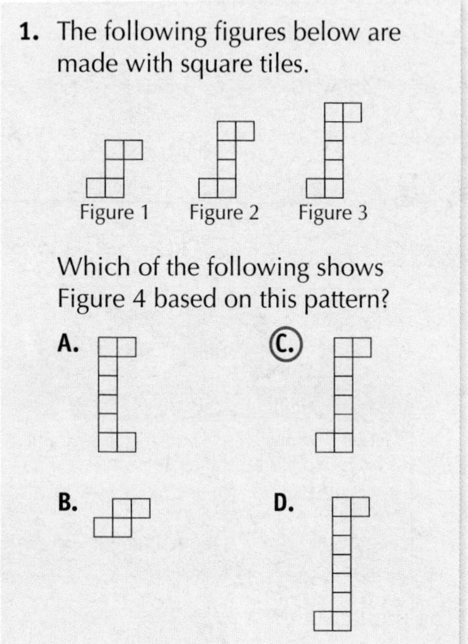

Understand the question.

- Look for important words. Finish the statement "I need to find ... ."

__I need to find__ the next figure in the pattern.

Get information for the answer.

The __picture__ shows the first three figures of the pattern.

Plan how to find the answer.

I need to __look for a pattern__ and use that pattern to choose the next figure. First I should look at the choices and eliminate those that do not make sense.

Make Smart Choices.

- Eliminate wrong answers.

The number of tiles is increasing, so answer choice B is wrong.

Each figure shows a column of tiles with an extra tile at the top and bottom, one on the left side and one on the right. Answer choice A has both extra tiles on the right side, so answer choice A is wrong.

- Try working backward from an answer.
- Check answers for reasonableness; estimate.

The correct answer is either C or D. Both are reasonable because they both show the correct arrangement of tiles and both have more tiles than Figure 3.

I'll use the pattern of the number of tiles to __make a smart choice.__ The pattern is 5 tiles, 6 tiles, 7 tiles. So the next figure has to have 8 tiles.

The correct answer is C.

232

2. The table below shows the number of marigolds planted in flats, or trays.

Number of flats	1	2	3	4	5
Number of marigolds	36	72	108	144	180

If f is the number of flats, which expression could be used to find the number of marigolds in f flats?

A. $180 \div f$

B. $36 + f$

C. $f - 36$

(D.) $36f$

Think It Through

*I need to find an expression that shows how many marigolds are in f flats. I should look for a pattern. The number of marigolds goes up 36 with each flat. Addition or multiplication might work. So I can **eliminate answer choices** A and C. Now I'll **work backward** and test answer choice B, 36 + f. If f = 1, then there are 36 + 1, or 37, marigolds. That's not right. So answer choice D must be correct. Just to be sure, I'll check if 36f works for f = 1, f = 2, f = 3, f = 4, and f = 5.*

Test-Taking Strategies

Understand the Question

- Look for important words.
- Turn the question into a statement: "I need to find out . . ."

Get Information for the Answer

- Get information from text.
- Get information from pictures, maps, diagrams, tables, graphs.

Plan How to Find the Answer

- Think about problem-solving skills and strategies.
- Choose computation methods.

Make Smart Choices

- Eliminate wrong answers.
- Try working backward from an answer.
- Check answers for reasonableness; estimate.

Use Writing in Math

- Make your answer brief but complete.
- Use words from the problem and use math terms accurately.
- Describe steps in order.
- Draw pictures if they help you explain your thinking.

Improve Written Answers

- Check if your answer is complete.
- Check if your answer is clear and easy to follow.
- Check if your answer makes sense.

Now it's your turn.

For each problem, give the answer and explain how you made your choice.

3. The table below shows the ages of Dominic and his mother at various times in their lives.

Age in years of Dominic's mother	35	40	45	50	55
Age in years of Dominic	6	11	16	21	26

If Dominic's mother is m years old, which expression could be used to find Dominic's age?

A. $m \div 5$

(B.) $m - 29$

C. $35m$

D. $m + 29$

Sample explanation: Check answers for reasonableness and work backward.

4. Molly is making designs with rectangular tiles.

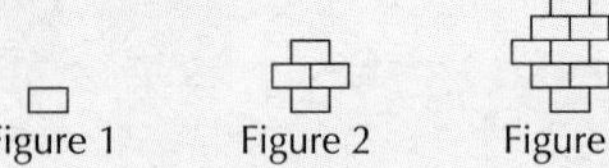

Figure 1 Figure 2 Figure 3

Which of the following shows Figure 4 based on this pattern?

(A.) 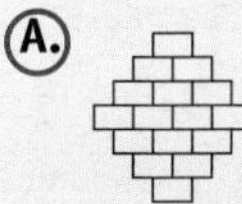

C. 

B. 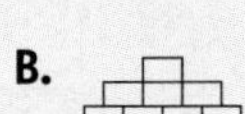

D. 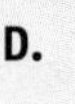

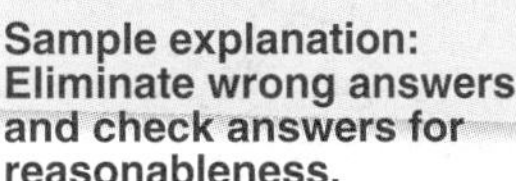

Sample explanation: Eliminate wrong answers and check answers for reasonableness.

Key Vocabulary and Concept Review

Using Student Pages 234–235

Purpose Provide students with a review of vocabulary and concepts in Chapter 4 through worked-out examples, vocabulary tips, and self-checking exercises.

Key Vocabulary and Concept Review focuses on the vocabulary of the chapter. It provides real-life connections to strengthen students' understanding of mathematical terms.

In addition, it reviews the concepts studied in the chapter. Exercises allow students to show they understand the meanings of words and they can apply the concepts.

Answers are printed upside down in red, so students can check their own work. Lesson references are given, so students can look back at any time.

MindPoint Quiz Show CD-ROM
Use *MindPoint Quiz Show* for additional practice on Chapter 4.

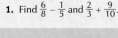

Chapter 4

Key Vocabulary and Concept Review

Self Check

We have hair color in common, because we both have brown hair.

Use **renaming** to add or subtract fractions. (Lessons 4-1, 4-2)

Find $\frac{5}{6} + \frac{5}{8}$.

1. Find the **lowest common denominator (LCD).** It is the **lowest common multiple (LCM)** of the two denominators.

6: 6, 12, 18, **24**, 30, 36, 42, 48
8: 8, 16, 24, 32, 40

2. Rename the fractions as equivalent fractions with the same denominator.

$\frac{5}{6} = \frac{5 \times 4}{6 \times 4} = \frac{20}{24}$ $\frac{5}{8} = \frac{5 \times 3}{8 \times 3} = \frac{15}{24}$

3. Add. Then write improper fractions as mixed numbers in simplest form.

$\frac{20}{24} + \frac{15}{24} = \frac{35}{24} = 1\frac{11}{24}$

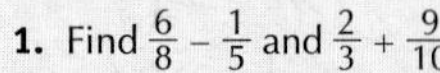

1. Find $\frac{6}{8} - \frac{1}{5}$ and $\frac{2}{3} + \frac{9}{10}$.

They are alike in that they have the same color hair.
Like denominators are denominators that have the same value. (p. 204)

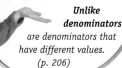

They were unlike in that they are wearing different color shirts.
Unlike denominators are denominators that have different values. (p. 206)

Self Check

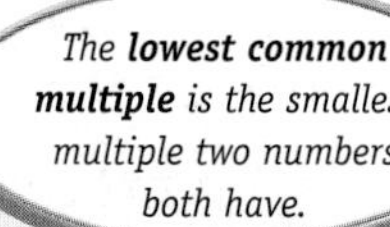

The **lowest common multiple** is the smallest multiple two numbers both have.

Look at the relationships between the numbers to discover the **pattern.** (Lesson 4-3)

Find the next three numbers in the pattern. Name the pattern.

$$12, 11\frac{1}{2}, 10\frac{1}{2}, 9, \_\_, \_\_, \_\_$$

$12 - \mathbf{\frac{1}{2}} = 11\frac{1}{2}$; $11\frac{1}{2} - \mathbf{1} = 10\frac{1}{2}$; $10\frac{1}{2} - \mathbf{1\frac{1}{2}} = 9$;

The pattern involves subtracting. Each number is subtracted by $\frac{1}{2}$ more.

$9 - 2 = 7$; $7 - 2\frac{1}{2} = 4\frac{1}{2}$; $4\frac{1}{2} - 3 - 1\frac{1}{2}$. The next three numbers are 7, $4\frac{1}{2}$, and $1\frac{1}{2}$.

2. Find the next three numbers in the pattern: $\frac{3}{4}, \frac{6}{8}, \frac{9}{12}, \frac{12}{16}, \_\_, \_\_, \_\_$.

 EC NTL 12 11 10 9 8 7 6

The restaurant where my aunt works was renamed from "Large Taco" to "Taco Biggie." When fractions are ***renamed*** *they have a new denominator but the same value.*

Use **renaming** to add or subtract mixed numbers. (Lesson 4-4, 4-5, 4-6, 4-7)

Find $4\frac{8}{9} - 1\frac{5}{6}$.

1. Rewrite the fractions using the LCD.

9: 9, **18,** 27
6: 6, 12, **18,** 24

$4\frac{8}{9} = 4\frac{8 \times 2}{9 \times 2} = 4\frac{16}{18}$ $\quad 1\frac{5}{6} = 1\frac{5 \times 3}{6 \times 3} = 1\frac{15}{18}$

2. Subtract the fractions, then the whole numbers. Make sure the answer is in simplest form.

$4\frac{16}{18} - 1\frac{15}{18} = \mathbf{3\frac{1}{18}}$

3. Find $6\frac{5}{8} - 3\frac{1}{6}$ and $2\frac{2}{4} + 10\frac{2}{5}$.

Decide whether you need an estimate or an exact answer when **solving problems.** (Lesson 4-8)

Decide whether an estimate or an exact answer is needed. Then solve.

Jillian walked $1\frac{1}{2}$ miles on Monday, $2\frac{1}{4}$ miles on Tuesday, and $1\frac{2}{5}$ miles on Wednesday. How far did she walk during the three days?

The question asks for the total, so an exact answer is needed. Find the total.

Find the total for Monday and Tuesday. $1\frac{1}{2} + 2\frac{1}{4} = 1\frac{2}{4} + 2\frac{1}{4} = 3\frac{3}{4}$.

Add Wednesday to the total. $3\frac{3}{4} + 1\frac{2}{5} = 3\frac{15}{20} + 1\frac{8}{20} = 4\frac{23}{20} = 5\frac{3}{20}$

Jillian walked $5\frac{3}{20}$ miles during the three days.

4. The student acting club sold 149 tickets to their spring play. They hope to donate at least $500 to charity from the money raised through ticket sales. If each ticket was sold for $3.75, will they be able to meet their goal?

1. $\frac{11}{20}$ and $1\frac{17}{30}$; 2. $\frac{15}{20}$, $\frac{18}{24}$, $\frac{21}{28}$; 3. $3\frac{11}{24}$ and $12\frac{9}{10}$; 4. yes, the estimate for the total money raised is $4 × 150 = $600

Chapter Test

Using Student Pages 236–237

Purpose Assess students' progress by checking their understanding of the concepts and skills in Chapter 4. Use as a review, practice test, or chapter test.

Sample student work for Exercise 22

I found a pattern. From the first shape to the second, there are 3 triangles added, then 5 triangles are added to make the third. So 7 would be added to make the fourth, then 9 for the fifth. That's 25 triangles.

The score for this paper is 4. The student's answer is correct and demonstrates an understanding of how to find a pattern.

Scoring Rubric

4 Full credit: 4 points
The answer is correct; indicates an appropriate strategy; complete explanation.

3 Partial credit: 3 points
The answer is correct; indicates an appropriate strategy; explanation is incomplete.

2 Partial credit: 2 points
The answer is incorrect; indicates an appropriate strategy; good explanation.

1 Partial credit: 1 point
The answer is correct; no explanation.

0 No credit
The answer is incorrect; no strategy indicated; no explanation.

CHAPTER 4

Chapter Test

MULTIPLE CHOICE

Choose the correct letter for each answer.

1. Find $\frac{7}{8} + \frac{7}{8}$.

A. $\frac{7}{16}$ **B.** $\frac{7}{8}$ **C.** $1\frac{1}{2}$ **(D.)** $1\frac{3}{4}$

2. Find $\frac{11}{12} - \frac{2}{3}$.

(A.) $\frac{1}{4}$ **B.** $\frac{3}{5}$ **C.** $\frac{3}{4}$ **D.** 1

3. Choose the best estimate for $6\frac{1}{4} + 3\frac{3}{8}$.

A. 8 **(B.)** 9 **C.** 11 **D.** 12

4. Choose the best estimate for $5\frac{8}{9} - 3\frac{1}{8}$.

A. 5 **B.** 4 **(C.)** 3 **D.** 2

5. Find $7\frac{9}{10} + 2\frac{3}{10}$.

A. $5\frac{3}{5}$
B. $9\frac{1}{5}$
C. $9\frac{3}{5}$
(D.) $10\frac{1}{5}$

6. Find the sum of $3\frac{5}{6}$ and $2\frac{1}{4}$.

A. $1\frac{7}{12}$ **B.** $5\frac{3}{5}$ **(C.)** $6\frac{1}{12}$ **D.** $6\frac{1}{6}$

7. Find the difference between $3\frac{7}{10}$ and $\frac{2}{5}$.

A. $2\frac{3}{10}$ **(B.)** $3\frac{3}{10}$ **C.** $3\frac{1}{2}$ **D.** $4\frac{1}{10}$

8. Find $12\frac{3}{8} - 4\frac{7}{8}$.

A. $9\frac{1}{4}$ **B.** $8\frac{1}{2}$ **(C.)** $7\frac{1}{2}$ **D.** $7\frac{1}{4}$

9. Find the difference $8 - 7\frac{9}{10}$.

A. $17\frac{9}{10}$ **B.** $17\frac{1}{10}$ **C.** $1\frac{1}{10}$ **(D.)** $\frac{1}{10}$

10. Which number is NOT a common denominator for $\frac{3}{4}$, $\frac{5}{6}$, and $\frac{7}{8}$?

A. 72
B. 48
C. 24
(D.) 12

TEST TALK
Think It Through
I should **watch for words like NOT.**

11. Name the next 3 numbers in the pattern 2, 4, 8, 16, 32, ■, ■, ■.

A. 34, 36, 38
B. 48, 80, 128
(C.) 64, 128, 256
D. 42, 54, 68

236

Item Analysis for Diagnosis and Intervention

Objective	Items	Student Book Pages*	Intervention System
Add and subtract fractions with like denominators.	1, 18	204–205	H29
Add and subtract fractions with unlike denominators.	2, 10, 17	206–209	H31
Look for patterns to solve problems.	11, 22	212–213	M36
Estimate sums and differences of fractions and mixed numbers.	3–4, 15–16	216–217	H33

*For each lesson, there is a *Reteaching* activity in *Reaching All Learners* and a *Reteaching* master.

For 12–14, refer to the table below.

School Play Ticket Information Adults:$6.50 Children: $3.50		
Day	Tickets Sold Adult	Tickets Sold Children
1	126	89
2	97	106
3	145	138
4	194	176

12. What was the total of the ticket sales for Day 3? Is an exact answer or estimate needed?

(A.) $1,425.50; exact

B. $1,000.50; exact

C. $1,400; estimate

D. $1,800; estimate

13. For all four days, were more children or adult tickets sold? About how many more? Is an exact answer or an estimate needed?

A. adult; 37; exact

(B.) adult; 70; estimate

C. children; 80; estimate

D. children; 37; exact

14. What would it cost for 1 grandparent, 1 parent, and 3 children to see the play? Is an exact answer or estimate needed?

(A.) $23.50; exact

B. $26.50; exact

C. $23.00; estimate

D. $27.00; estimate

FREE RESPONSE

Estimate each answer. **Sample answers are given.**

15. $2\frac{4}{5} + 1\frac{1}{3}$ **4** **16.** $11\frac{1}{6} - 4\frac{7}{9}$ **6**

Find each answer. Simplify if possible.

17. $\frac{3}{4} + \frac{9}{16}$ $1\frac{5}{16}$ **18.** $\frac{8}{9} - \frac{5}{9}$ $\frac{1}{3}$

19. $2\frac{7}{8} + 3\frac{1}{3}$ $6\frac{5}{24}$ **20.** $5\frac{3}{4} - \frac{1}{6}$ $5\frac{7}{12}$

21. Tell what computation method you would use to find $8 - 1\frac{2}{3}$. **Mental math**

Writing in Math

22. In the pattern below, how many triangles are needed to build the 5th shape? Explain the strategy you used. **See below.**

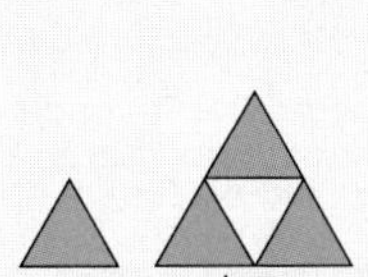
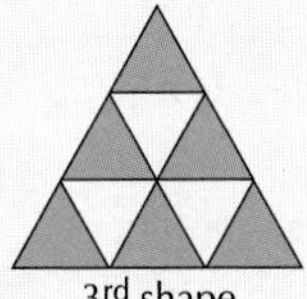

1st shape 2nd shape 3rd shape

23. Explain how to subtract $3\frac{5}{8}$ from $4\frac{1}{4}$. **See below.**

24. Explain how you could use mental math to find $5\frac{3}{10} + 7\frac{3}{8} + 2\frac{1}{5} + 4\frac{5}{8}$. **See below.**

22. 25 triangles; Sample answer: I compared shapes and saw a pattern of adding 3, then 5, then 7, and then 9.

23. Rewrite fractions with a common denominator, $4\frac{2}{8} - 3\frac{5}{8}$. Rename $4\frac{2}{8}$ as $3 + \frac{8}{8} + \frac{2}{8} = 3\frac{10}{8}$. Subtract whole numbers and fractions.

24. I would regroup the addends by the denominators of the fractions to get $\left(7\frac{3}{8} + 4\frac{5}{8}\right) + \left(5\frac{3}{10} + 2\frac{2}{10}\right) = \left(11 + \frac{8}{8}\right) + \left(7 + \frac{1}{2}\right) = \left(12 + 7\frac{1}{2}\right) = 19\frac{1}{2}$.

Assessment Sourcebook

Additional assessment options may be found in the *Assessment Sourcebook.*

- Chapter 4 Test (Forms A and B)
- Chapter 4 Performance Assessment
- Chapters 1–6 Cumulative Test (Use after Chapter 6.)

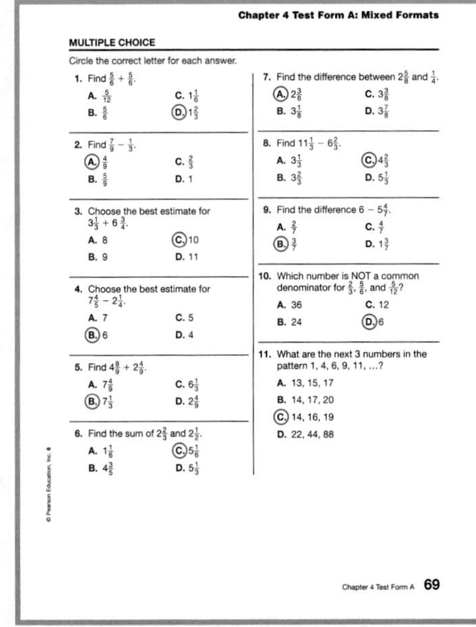

Chapter 4 Test Form A: Mixed Formats

MULTIPLE CHOICE

Circle the correct letter for each answer.

1. Find $\frac{5}{6} + \frac{5}{6}$.
A. $\frac{5}{12}$ B. $\frac{5}{6}$ C. $1\frac{1}{6}$ (D.) $1\frac{2}{3}$

2. Find $\frac{7}{9} - \frac{1}{3}$.
(A.) $\frac{4}{9}$ B. $\frac{5}{9}$ C. $\frac{2}{3}$ D. 1

3. Choose the best estimate for $3\frac{1}{3} + 6\frac{3}{4}$.
A. 8 B. 9 (C.) 10 D. 11

4. Choose the best estimate for $7\frac{4}{5} - 2\frac{1}{4}$.
A. 7 (B.) 6 C. 5 D. 4

5. Find $4\frac{8}{9} + 2\frac{4}{9}$.
A. $7\frac{4}{9}$ (B.) $7\frac{1}{3}$ C. $6\frac{1}{3}$ D. $2\frac{4}{9}$

6. Find the sum of $2\frac{2}{3}$ and $2\frac{1}{2}$.
A. $1\frac{1}{6}$ B. $4\frac{3}{5}$ (C.) $5\frac{1}{6}$ D. $5\frac{1}{3}$

7. Find the difference between $2\frac{5}{8}$ and $\frac{1}{4}$.
(A.) $2\frac{3}{8}$ B. $3\frac{1}{8}$ C. $3\frac{3}{8}$ D. $3\frac{7}{8}$

8. Find $11\frac{1}{3} - 6\frac{2}{3}$.
A. $3\frac{1}{3}$ B. $3\frac{2}{3}$ (C.) $4\frac{2}{3}$ D. $5\frac{1}{3}$

9. Find the difference $6 - 5\frac{4}{7}$.
A. $\frac{2}{7}$ (B.) $\frac{3}{7}$ C. $\frac{4}{7}$ D. $1\frac{3}{7}$

10. Which number is NOT a common denominator for $\frac{2}{3}$, $\frac{5}{6}$, and $\frac{5}{12}$?
A. 36 B. 24 C. 12 (D.) 6

11. What are the next 3 numbers in the pattern 1, 4, 6, 9, 11, ...?
A. 13, 15, 17 B. 14, 17, 20 (C.) 14, 16, 19 D. 22, 44, 88

Chapter 4 Test Form A 69

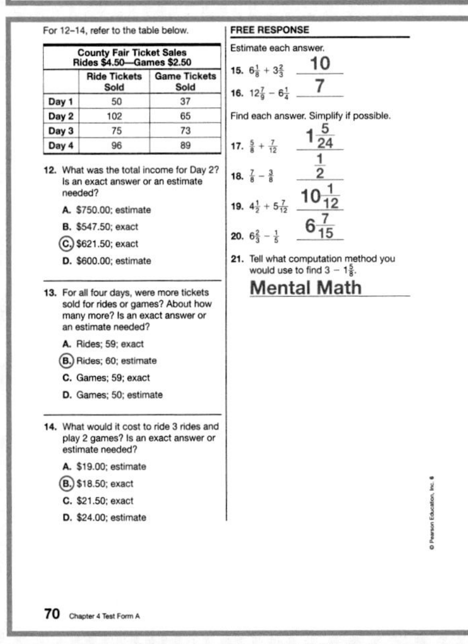

For 12–14, refer to the table below.

County Fair Ticket Sales Rides $4.50—Games $2.50		
	Ride Tickets Sold	Game Tickets Sold
Day 1	50	37
Day 2	102	65
Day 3	75	73
Day 4	96	89

12. What was the total income for Day 2? Is an exact answer or an estimate needed?
A. $750.00; estimate B. $547.50; exact (C.) $621.50; exact D. $600.00; estimate

13. For all four days, were more tickets sold for rides or games? About how many more? Is an exact answer or an estimate needed?
A. Rides; 59; exact (B.) Rides; 60; estimate C. Games; 59; exact D. Games; 50; estimate

14. What would it cost to ride 3 rides and play 2 games? Is an exact answer or estimate needed?
A. $19.00; estimate (B.) $18.50; exact C. $21.50; exact D. $24.00; estimate

FREE RESPONSE

Estimate each answer.

15. $6\frac{1}{8} + 3\frac{2}{3}$ 10

16. $12\frac{7}{9} - 6\frac{1}{4}$ 7

Find each answer. Simplify if possible.

17. $\frac{5}{8} + \frac{7}{12}$ $1\frac{5}{24}$

18. $\frac{7}{8} - \frac{3}{8}$ $\frac{1}{2}$

19. $4\frac{1}{2} + 5\frac{7}{12}$ $10\frac{1}{12}$

20. $6\frac{2}{3} - \frac{1}{5}$ $6\frac{7}{15}$

21. Tell what computation method you would use to find $3 - 1\frac{5}{8}$.
Mental Math

70 Chapter 4 Test Form A

WRITING IN MATH

22. In the pattern below, how many squares are formed at the 5th stage? Explain the strategy you used.

Stage 1 Stage 2 Stage 3

256 squares; Sample answer: The numbers of squares are 1, 4, and 16 = 4×4 or 4^2. So, in Stage 4, there should be 4^3 squares and in Stage 5, 4^4 squares.

23. Explain how to subtract $6\frac{1}{3}$ from $8\frac{1}{6}$.
Rewrite the fractions with a common denominator, $8\frac{1}{6} - 6\frac{2}{6}$. Rename $8\frac{1}{6}$ as $7 + \frac{6}{6} + \frac{1}{6} = 7\frac{7}{6}$. Subtract whole numbers and fractions.

24. Explain how you could use mental math to add $6\frac{2}{7} + 3\frac{5}{7}$.
Find the sum of the fractions, $\frac{2}{7} + \frac{5}{7} = \frac{7}{7} = 1$. Add the whole numbers together, $6 + 3 = 9$. Combine the two sums, $9 + 1 = 10$

Chapter 4 Test Form A 71

Item Analysis for Diagnosis and Intervention

Objective	Items	Student Book Pages*	Intervention System
Add mixed numbers.	5–6, 19, 24	218–219	H34
Subtract mixed numbers.	7–9, 20, 23	220–223	H35
Choose a computation method.	21	224–225	H36
Determine whether an exact answer or an estimate can answer a question.	12–14	226–227	M8

*For each lesson, there is a *Reteaching* activity in *Reaching All Learners* and a *Reteaching* master.

Cumulative Review and Test Prep

Using Student Pages 238–239

Purpose Provide students with a review of math concepts from Chapters 1–4 and previous grades.

For intervention, use the resources listed below.

Chapters 1–4

Cumulative Review and Test Prep

Number and Operation

MULTIPLE CHOICE

1. In 1994, Leroy Burrell ran 100 meters in 9.85 seconds. Round his time to the nearest second.

A. 9 seconds

B. 9.8 seconds

C. 9.9 seconds

(D.) 10 seconds

2. Give the best estimate for the product 43 × 25.

A. 800

(B.) 1,000

C. 1,500

D. 2,000

FREE RESPONSE

3. Tamika made a fruit salad with $2\frac{1}{2}$ cups raspberries, $3\frac{3}{4}$ cups strawberries, and 4 cups sliced peaches. How many more cups of berries did she use than peaches? **$2\frac{1}{4}$ cups**

4. One week, the prices for JGA stocks were 25.5, 24.75, 25.25, 29, and 30.5 points. What was the average for the 5 days? **27 points**

5. Carnie answered $\frac{7}{8}$ of the test questions correctly. Write this fraction as a decimal. **0.875**

Writing in Math

6. Explain how you would write 34.607 in expanded notation. **See above.**

6. I would write each place value separately: 30 + 4 + 0.6 + 0.007

7. Explain how you would compare 3.57 and $3\frac{3}{5}$. **I would write $3\frac{3}{5}$ as the decimal, 3.60, then compare.**

238

Geometry and Measurement

MULTIPLE CHOICE

8. An angle that measures 90° is

A. a straight angle.

(B.) a right angle.

C. an obtuse angle.

D. an acute angle.

9. Betsy's biology lab starts at 11:30 A.M. The lab lasts 1 hour 45 minutes. At what time does Betsy's lab end?

A. 12:15 A.M. **C.** 12:15 P.M.

B. 1:15 A.M. **(D.)** 1:15 P.M.

FREE RESPONSE

10. A pattern for a woven wall hanging calls for different colored ribbon. How many meters of ribbon are called for altogether?

Color	Length (cm)
Green	150
Yellow	120
Blue	150
Pink	120

5 meters 40 centimeters or 5.4 meters

11. Give all the names that apply to the figure. **See below.**

Writing in Math

12. Explain the difference between the perimeter and area of a rectangle. **See above.**

12. Perimeter is the distance around and area is the number of square units needed to fill the rectangle.

13. Name two things you would measure in feet. Explain your choices. **Sample answer: length of my family's car, perimeter of my yard; both items should be too large to be measured in inches and too small to be measured in miles.**

11. Parallelogram, quadrilateral, polygon

Item Analysis for Diagnosis and Intervention

Objective	Items	Student Book Pages*	Intervention System
Round decimals.	1	80–81	I10
Estimate products of whole numbers.	2	18–19	G56
Add and subtract mixed numbers.	3	218–223	H34
Add, subtract, and divide decimals.	4, 23	86–89, 94–97	I15, I16, I27
Write fractions as decimals.	5	172–175	H21
Understand decimals through hundred-thousandths.	6	76–77	I5
Compare and order fractions and decimals.	7	176–179	H26
Identify types of angles.	8	Grade 5	K49
Find elapsed time.	9	Grade 5	K16
Convert between metric units of length.	10	Grade 5	K10
Identify and analyze attributes of two-dimensional shapes.	11	Grade 5	K51

*For each lesson, there is a *Reteaching* activity in *Reaching All Learners* and a *Reteaching* master.

Data Analysis and Probability

MULTIPLE CHOICE

14. How many different coin and color possibilities are there if you toss a coin and spin the spinner?

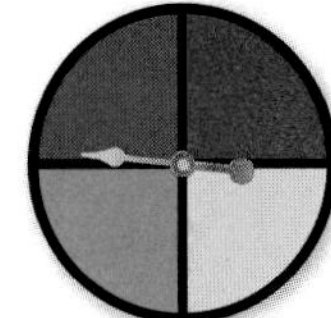

A. 4 **C.** 8

B. 6 **(D.)** 16

15. What type of graph would NOT be best for showing the ethnic makeup of a school's population?

A. circle graph **C.** line graph

B. bar graph **(D.)** pictograph

FREE RESPONSE

In 16–17, use the line graph.

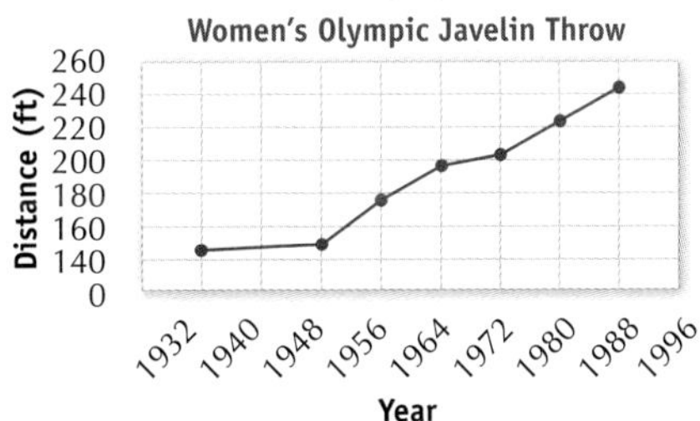

16. Which was the first year to have a distance greater than 200 feet? **1972**

17. What distance might you predict for 1996? **Sample answer: 260 feet**

Writing in Math

18. There are 12 red counters and 6 blue counters in a bag. Explain how you would determine the probability of choosing a blue counter. **Find the total number of counters; $12 + 6 = 18$. The number of blue counters to the total number of counters is $\frac{6}{18}$ or $\frac{1}{3}$.**

Algebra

MULTIPLE CHOICE

19. Which equation has the solution $x = 4.5$?

A. $x - 2 = 6.5$

B. $\frac{x}{3} = 13.5$

(C.) $2x = 9$

D. $x + 2 = 2.5$

20. Calculate the value of $2 \times 3.5 + 8 \div 0.5 + 1.5$.

A. 11 **C.** 31.5

(B.) 24.5 **D.** 47.5

21. Solve $\frac{n}{1.2} = 6$.

A. $n = 0.2$ **(C.)** $n = 7.2$

B. $n = 5$ **D.** $n = 72$

22. 21, 34, 55; each number in the series is the sum of the two numbers before it.

FREE RESPONSE

22. Find the next 3 numbers in this pattern. Then give the rule.
1, 1, 2, 3, 5, 8, 13, ▪, ▪, ▪
See above.

23. Gary's best time for the 100-meter dash is 11.6 seconds. This time is 1.68 seconds more than the record time set by Carl Lewis in 1988. What was Lewis's time? **9.92 seconds**

24. An orange has 62 calories. It has x fewer calories than a nectarine. Write an expression for the number of calories a nectarine has. **$62 + x$**

Writing in Math

25. Explain how you would find 8×52 mentally. **I would multiply 8×50 and 8×2 and add the products to get 416.**

26. Explain how you would solve and check $\frac{n}{6} = 3.6$. **I would multiply 6×3.6; $n = 21.6$. To check, I would substitute 21.6 for n.**

Item Analysis for Diagnosis and Intervention

Objective	Items	Student Book Pages*	Intervention System
Understand difference between perimeter and area.	12	Grade 5	K26, K28
Use appropriate units of measure.	13	Grade 5	K2
Find all the outcomes.	14	Grade 5	L17
Use the appropriate graph to show data.	15	Grade 5	L6
Interpret line graphs to solve problems.	16–17	Grade 5	L5
Determine the probability of an event.	18	Grade 5	L18
Solve equations with decimals.	19, 21	112–113	J32
Use order of operations to evaluate numerical expressions.	20	24–27	J29
Look for patterns to solve problems.	22	212–213	M36
Write an algebraic expression.	24	40–43	J30
Use properties of whole numbers to find products mentally.	25	32–35	G68
Use Properties of Equality to isolate the variable in an equation.	26	44–47	J24

*For each lesson, there is a *Reteaching* activity in *Reaching All Learners* and a *Reteaching* master.

Reteaching

Using Student Pages 240–242

Purpose Provide students with more examples and practice for each lesson in the chapter.

- Use *Reteaching* pages for students having difficulty with *Check* exercises.
- For additional practice, use *More Practice* exercises starting on page 243.
- For intervention, use the resources listed below.

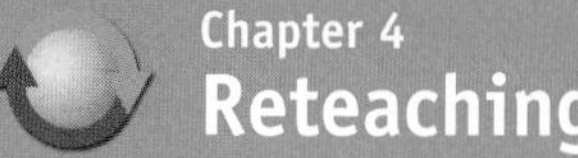

Chapter 4

Reteaching

Set 4-1 (pages 204–205)

Find $\frac{11}{15} + \frac{8}{15}$.

$\frac{11}{15} + \frac{8}{15} = \frac{19}{15}$ The denominators are the same, so just add the numerators.

$= 1\frac{4}{15}$ Since 19 is greater than 15, write the answer as a mixed number.

Find $\frac{7}{8} - \frac{3}{8}$.

$\frac{7}{8} - \frac{3}{8} = \frac{4}{8}$ The denominators are the same, so just subtract the numerators.

$= \frac{1}{2}$ Simplify.

Remember when the numerator is greater than the denominator, your answer will be a mixed number.

1. $\frac{5}{7} + \frac{3}{7}$ **$1\frac{1}{7}$**
2. $\frac{8}{9} - \frac{2}{9}$ **$\frac{2}{3}$**
3. $\frac{12}{13} - \frac{10}{13}$ **$\frac{2}{13}$**
4. $\frac{7}{8} + \frac{3}{8}$ **$1\frac{1}{4}$**
5. $\frac{7}{10} - \frac{3}{10}$ **$\frac{2}{5}$**
6. $\frac{4}{15} + \frac{13}{15}$ **$1\frac{2}{15}$**

Set 4-2 (pages 206–209)

Find $\frac{3}{4} + \frac{5}{6}$.

The LCD of 4 and 6 is 12.	Add the fractions.	Simplify if possible.
$\frac{3}{4} = \frac{9}{12}$ $+\frac{5}{6} = +\frac{10}{12}$	$\frac{9}{12}$ $+\frac{10}{12}$ $\frac{19}{12}$	$\frac{19}{12} = 1\frac{7}{12}$

Find $\frac{4}{5} - \frac{3}{10}$.

The LCD of 5 and 10 is 10.	Subtract the fractions.	Simplify if possible.
$\frac{4}{5} = \frac{8}{10}$ $-\frac{3}{10} = -\frac{3}{10}$	$\frac{8}{10}$ $-\frac{3}{10}$ $\frac{5}{10}$	$\frac{5}{10} = \frac{1}{2}$

Remember that the least common denominator (LCD) is the least common multiple (LCM) of the denominators.

1. $\frac{2}{5} + \frac{1}{4}$ **$\frac{13}{20}$**
2. $\frac{6}{7} - \frac{1}{2}$ **$\frac{5}{14}$**
3. $\frac{2}{3} + \frac{1}{4}$ **$\frac{11}{12}$**
4. $\frac{7}{9} - \frac{2}{3}$ **$\frac{1}{9}$**
5. $\frac{5}{8} - \frac{1}{6}$ **$\frac{11}{24}$**
6. $\frac{3}{10} + \frac{1}{8}$ **$\frac{17}{40}$**
7. $\frac{3}{8} + \frac{1}{3}$ **$\frac{17}{24}$**
8. $\frac{9}{10} - \frac{3}{5}$ **$\frac{3}{10}$**
9. $\frac{15}{16} - \frac{5}{8}$ **$\frac{5}{16}$**
10. $\frac{3}{8} + \frac{5}{12}$ **$\frac{19}{24}$**

Set 4-3 (pages 212–213)

Find the next 3 numbers.

$\frac{1}{3}, 1, 1\frac{2}{3}, 2\frac{1}{3}, 3$, ■, ■, ■

The pattern is "add $\frac{2}{3}$."

$3 + \frac{2}{3} = 3\frac{2}{3}$; $3\frac{2}{3} + \frac{2}{3} = 4\frac{1}{3}$; $4\frac{1}{3} + \frac{2}{3} = 5$

The next three numbers are $3\frac{2}{3}, 4\frac{1}{3}, 5$.

Remember you can subtract the numbers to discover a pattern.

1. 10, $9\frac{1}{4}, 8\frac{1}{2}, 7\frac{3}{4}$, ■, ■, ■ **7, $6\frac{1}{4}$, $5\frac{1}{2}$; subtract $\frac{3}{4}$**
2. 3, $3\frac{1}{10}, 3\frac{1}{5}, 3\frac{3}{10}, 3\frac{2}{5}$, ■, ■, ■ **$3\frac{1}{2}$, $3\frac{3}{5}$, $3\frac{7}{10}$; add $\frac{1}{10}$**

240

Item Analysis for Diagnosis and Intervention

Objective	Review Items	Student Book Pages*	Intervention System
Add and subtract fractions with like denominators.	Set 4–1	204–205	H29
Add and subtract fractions with unlike denominators.	Set 4–2	206–209	H31
Look for patterns to solve problems.	Set 4–3	212–213	M36
Estimate sums and differences of fractions and mixed numbers.	Set 4–4	216–217	H33
Add mixed numbers.	Set 4–5	218–219	H34
Subtract mixed numbers.	Set 4–6	220–223	H35
Choose a computation method.	Set 4–7	224–225	H36
Determine whether an exact answer or an estimate can answer a question.	Set 4–8	226–227	M8

*For each lesson, there is a *Reteaching* activity in *Reaching All Learners* and a *Reteaching* master.

Set 4-4 (pages 216–217)

Estimate $1\frac{5}{6} + 2\frac{1}{4}$.

$1\frac{5}{6} + 2\frac{1}{4}$

$\downarrow \quad \downarrow$ Round to the nearest whole number.

$2 + 2 = 4$

$1\frac{5}{6} + 2\frac{1}{4} \approx 4$

Estimate $5\frac{5}{8} - 3\frac{1}{6}$.

$5\frac{5}{8} - 3\frac{1}{6}$

$\downarrow \quad \downarrow$ Round to the nearest whole number.

$6 - 3 = 3$

$5\frac{5}{8} - 3\frac{1}{6} \approx 3$

Remember you can think of the numbers on a number line to help you estimate.

Sample answers are given.

1. $2\frac{1}{8} + 3\frac{4}{5}$ **6** **2.** $2\frac{7}{8} - \frac{1}{3}$ **3**

3. $4\frac{2}{5} + 9\frac{3}{4}$ **14** **4.** $12\frac{3}{8} - 9\frac{5}{7}$ **2**

5. $2\frac{1}{3} + 5\frac{4}{9}$ **7** **6.** $\frac{8}{11} + \frac{4}{5}$ **2**

7. $11\frac{1}{4} - \frac{3}{10}$ **11** **8.** $7\frac{1}{2} - 3\frac{7}{10}$ **4**

9. $2\frac{11}{12} + 8\frac{1}{16}$ **11** **10.** $9\frac{1}{9} - 8\frac{7}{8}$ **0**

Set 4-5 (pages 218–219)

Find $8\frac{4}{5} + 6\frac{3}{4}$.

The LCD of 5 and 4 is 20.	Add.	Simplify if possible.
$\frac{4}{5} = \frac{16}{20}$	$8\frac{16}{20}$	$14\frac{31}{20} =$
$\frac{3}{4} = \frac{15}{20}$	$+ 6\frac{15}{20}$	$14 + \frac{20}{20} + \frac{11}{20}$
	$14\frac{31}{20}$	$= 15\frac{11}{20}$

Remember to write equivalent fractions with the least common denominator.

1. $13\frac{1}{6} + 9\frac{5}{12}$ **$22\frac{7}{12}$** **2.** $8\frac{7}{8} + 3\frac{1}{4}$ **$12\frac{1}{8}$**

3. $6\frac{2}{9} + 3\frac{5}{6}$ **$10\frac{1}{18}$** **4.** $5\frac{4}{5} + 3\frac{1}{3}$ **$9\frac{2}{15}$**

5. $4\frac{7}{10} + 8\frac{1}{4}$ **$12\frac{19}{20}$** **6.** $3\frac{5}{8} + 1\frac{3}{8}$ **5**

7. $15\frac{3}{4} + 7\frac{7}{10}$ **$23\frac{9}{20}$** **8.** $23\frac{9}{16} + 19\frac{3}{4}$ **$43\frac{5}{16}$**

Set 4-6 (pages 220–223)

Find $13\frac{1}{6} - 7\frac{5}{6}$. Estimate: 13 − 8 = 5

$$\begin{array}{r} 13\frac{1}{6} = 12 + \frac{6}{6} + \frac{1}{6} = 12\frac{7}{6} \\ -\ 7\frac{5}{6} \\ \hline \end{array}$$

Since $\frac{5}{6} > \frac{1}{6}$, rename $13\frac{1}{6}$ to show more sixths.

$$\begin{array}{r} 12\frac{7}{6} \\ -\ 7\frac{5}{6} \\ \hline 5\frac{2}{6} = 5\frac{1}{3} \end{array}$$

Remember that you can rename a whole number as a mixed number.

1. $23 - 18\frac{1}{3}$ **$4\frac{2}{3}$** **2.** $4\frac{7}{8} - 2\frac{5}{8}$ **$2\frac{1}{4}$**

3. $12\frac{1}{4} - 3\frac{1}{2}$ **$8\frac{3}{4}$** **4.** $18 - 9\frac{3}{5}$ **$8\frac{2}{5}$**

5. $14\frac{1}{3} - 5\frac{2}{3}$ **$8\frac{2}{3}$** **6.** $12\frac{1}{4} - 7\frac{5}{6}$ **$4\frac{5}{12}$**

7. $15\frac{3}{8} - 9\frac{5}{6}$ **$5\frac{13}{24}$** **8.** $14\frac{4}{9} - 6\frac{5}{6}$ **$7\frac{11}{18}$**

Chapter 4

Reteaching (continued)

Set 4-7 (pages 224–225)

Find $4\frac{3}{4} + 7\frac{1}{4}$.

Since the fractions are easy to add, use mental math.

$4\frac{3}{4} + 7\frac{1}{4} = 12$

$\frac{3}{4} + \frac{1}{4} = 1;\ 4 + 7 + 1 = 12$

Find $2\frac{3}{7} + 4\frac{1}{4}$.

Since the fractions need to be renamed, use paper and pencil.

$$\begin{array}{rcr} 2\frac{3}{7} & = & 2\frac{12}{28} \\ +\ 4\frac{1}{4} & = & +\ 4\frac{7}{28} \\ \hline & & 6\frac{19}{28} \end{array}$$

Find $5\frac{3}{20} + 9\frac{13}{16}$.

The fractions are not easy to add. So, use a calculator.

Press: 5 [Unit] 3 [/] 20 + 9 [Unit] 13 [/] 16 [=]

Display: 14u 77/80

Remember to decide which computation method would be the best for a given problem.

Find each answer. Tell what computation method you used. **Sample computation methods are given.**

1. $3\frac{1}{3} + 2\frac{1}{2} + 5\frac{2}{3}$ **$11\frac{1}{2}$; mental math**
2. $9\frac{3}{8} - 4\frac{1}{25}$ **$5\frac{67}{200}$; calculator**
3. $6\frac{1}{4} + 5\frac{2}{5}$ **$11\frac{13}{20}$; paper and pencil**
4. $18\frac{5}{12} - 16\frac{7}{8}$ **$1\frac{13}{24}$; paper and pencil**
5. $3\frac{1}{6} - 2\frac{3}{4}$ **$\frac{5}{12}$; paper and pencil**
6. $8\frac{9}{10} + 3\frac{1}{2}$ **$12\frac{2}{5}$; mental math**
7. $7\frac{7}{8} + 3\frac{1}{2} + 1\frac{1}{4} + \frac{1}{4} + 2\frac{1}{8}$
   15; mental math
8. $5\frac{3}{10} + 8\frac{1}{6} + 3\frac{3}{4} + 2\frac{7}{8} + 1\frac{1}{2}$
   $21\frac{71}{120}$; calculator

Set 4-8 (pages 226–227)

The length of Maria's desk is $60\frac{3}{4}$ inches and the width is $34\frac{1}{4}$ inches. How much longer is the length than the width? Tell whether an exact answer or estimate is needed.

Finding the difference in measurements requires an exact answer.

$$\begin{array}{r} 60\frac{3}{4} \\ -\ 34\frac{1}{4} \\ \hline 26\frac{2}{4} = 26\frac{1}{2} \end{array}$$

Her desk is $26\frac{1}{2}$ inches longer than it is wide.

Remember to look for key words that will help you determine whether to find an estimate or exact answer.

Lisa ran $1\frac{1}{2}$ mi on Monday, $2\frac{3}{4}$ mi on Wednesday, and $1\frac{7}{8}$ mi. on Friday.

1. What was Lisa's total distance for the three days? **$6\frac{1}{8}$ miles**
2. How much farther did Lisa run on Wednesday than on Monday? **$1\frac{1}{4}$ miles**
3. About how much farther did Lisa run on Wednesday than on Friday? **About 1 mile**

242

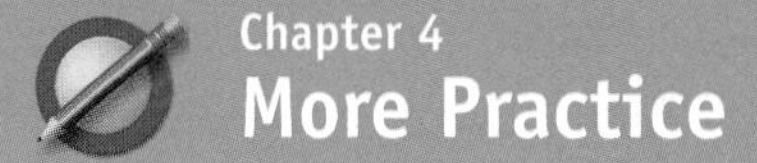

Chapter 4
More Practice

Set 4-1 (pages 204–205)

Find each sum or difference. Simplify if possible.

1. $\frac{5}{6} - \frac{1}{6}$ $\frac{2}{3}$	**2.** $\frac{1}{8} + \frac{3}{8}$ $\frac{1}{2}$	**3.** $\frac{5}{16} - \frac{3}{16}$ $\frac{1}{8}$	**4.** $\frac{7}{9} - \frac{4}{9}$ $\frac{1}{3}$
5. $\frac{4}{9} + \frac{8}{9}$ $1\frac{1}{3}$	**6.** $\frac{3}{4} + \frac{3}{4}$ $1\frac{1}{2}$	**7.** $\frac{8}{15} - \frac{2}{15}$ $\frac{2}{5}$	**8.** $\frac{8}{11} - \frac{2}{11}$ $\frac{6}{11}$
9. $\frac{5}{6} + \frac{5}{6}$ $1\frac{2}{3}$	**10.** $\frac{7}{10} + \frac{6}{10}$ $1\frac{3}{10}$	**11.** $\frac{11}{8} - \frac{3}{8}$ 1	**12.** $\frac{3}{7} + \frac{5}{7}$ $1\frac{1}{7}$
13. $\frac{9}{20} - \frac{3}{20}$ $\frac{3}{10}$	**14.** $\frac{3}{16} + \frac{13}{16}$ 1	**15.** $\frac{7}{12} + \frac{11}{12}$ $1\frac{1}{2}$	**16.** $\frac{11}{18} - \frac{5}{18}$ $\frac{1}{3}$

17. Marcus had $\frac{3}{4}$ cup of milk in a bowl. He added $\frac{1}{2}$ cup of milk. How much did he have in all?
$1\frac{1}{4}$ cups

Set 4-2 (pages 206–209)

Find each sum or difference. Simplify if possible.

1. $\frac{7}{10} - \frac{5}{8}$ $\frac{3}{40}$	**2.** $\frac{7}{8} + \frac{1}{12}$ $\frac{23}{24}$	**3.** $\frac{15}{16} - \frac{3}{8}$ $\frac{9}{16}$	**4.** $\frac{9}{10} - \frac{1}{5}$ $\frac{7}{10}$
5. $\frac{1}{8} + \frac{5}{6}$ $\frac{23}{24}$	**6.** $\frac{2}{3} + \frac{4}{5}$ $1\frac{7}{15}$	**7.** $\frac{5}{8} - \frac{7}{16}$ $\frac{3}{16}$	**8.** $\frac{3}{4} + \frac{7}{12}$ $1\frac{1}{3}$
9. $\frac{7}{9} - \frac{2}{3}$ $\frac{1}{9}$	**10.** $\frac{1}{5} + \frac{1}{6}$ $\frac{11}{30}$	**11.** $\frac{3}{4} - \frac{1}{5}$ $\frac{11}{20}$	**12.** $\frac{8}{9} + \frac{1}{6}$ $1\frac{1}{18}$
13. $\frac{7}{8} + \frac{1}{3}$ $1\frac{5}{24}$	**14.** $\frac{3}{4} - \frac{1}{10}$ $\frac{13}{20}$	**15.** $\frac{3}{5} + \frac{1}{3}$ $\frac{14}{15}$	**16.** $\frac{11}{12} - \frac{1}{4}$ $\frac{2}{3}$

17. Tom and Leona measured the rainfall in their neighborhoods. Tom measured $\frac{5}{8}$ inch and Leona measured $\frac{3}{4}$ inch How much more rain fell in Leona's neighborhood?
$\frac{1}{8}$ in. more

Set 4-3 (pages 212–213)

Find the missing numbers, or draw the next 3 figures.

1. 3, $3\frac{4}{5}$, $4\frac{3}{5}$, $5\frac{2}{5}$, ▒, ▒, ▒
$6\frac{1}{5}$, 7, $7\frac{4}{5}$

2.

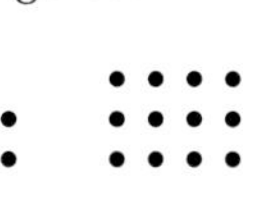

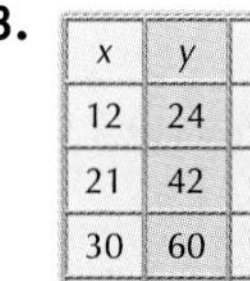

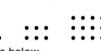

See below.

3.

x	y	z
12	24	36
21	42	63
30	60	90
?	?	117
?	96	?

39; 78
48; 144

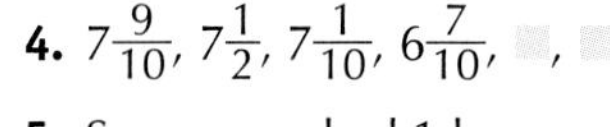

4. $7\frac{9}{10}$, $7\frac{1}{2}$, $7\frac{1}{10}$, $6\frac{7}{10}$, ▒, ▒, ▒ **$6\frac{3}{10}$, $5\frac{9}{10}$, $5\frac{1}{2}$**

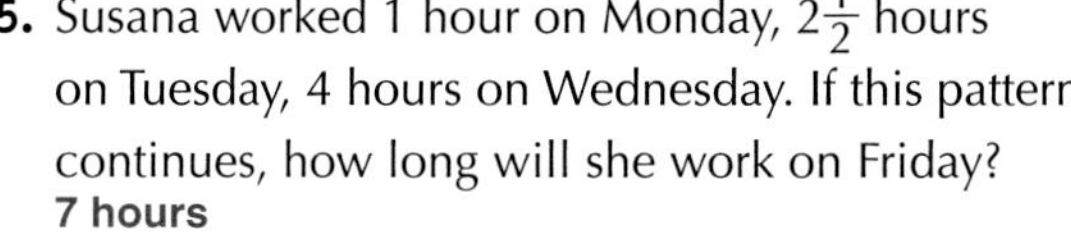

5. Susana worked 1 hour on Monday, $2\frac{1}{2}$ hours on Tuesday, 4 hours on Wednesday. If this pattern continues, how long will she work on Friday?
7 hours

2.

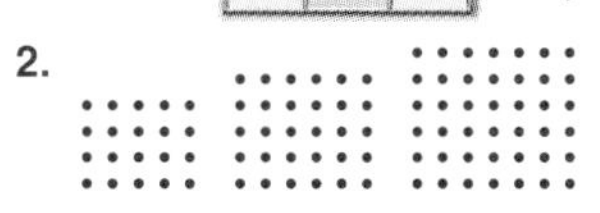

More Practice

Using Student Pages 243–245

Purpose Provide students with additional practice for each lesson in the chapter.

- Use *More Practice* pages during each lesson or after the chapter as a review.
- For intervention, use the resources listed below.

Item Analysis for Diagnosis and Intervention

Objective	Review Items	Student Book Pages*	Intervention System
Add and subtract fractions with like denominators.	Set 4–1	204–205	H29
Add and subtract fractions with unlike denominators.	Set 4–2	206–209	H31
Look for patterns to solve problems.	Set 4–3	212–213	M36
Estimate sums and differences of fractions and mixed numbers.	Set 4–4	216–217	H33
Add mixed numbers.	Set 4–5	218–219	H34
Subtract mixed numbers.	Set 4–6	220–223	H35
Choose a computation method.	Set 4–7	224–225	H36
Determine whether an exact answer or an estimate can answer a question.	Set 4–8	226–227	M8

*For each lesson, there is a *Reteaching* activity in *Reaching All Learners* and a *Reteaching* master.

Chapter 4

More Practice (continued)

Set 4-4 (pages 216–217)

Estimate each sum or difference.
Sample answers are given.

1. $2\frac{2}{3} + 1\frac{1}{5}$ **4** **2.** $7\frac{3}{8} + 3\frac{7}{12}$ **11** **3.** $2\frac{3}{4} - 1\frac{2}{9}$ **2** **4.** $2\frac{5}{6} - 1\frac{1}{7}$ **2**

5. $9\frac{1}{3} + 5\frac{4}{5}$ **15** **6.** $9\frac{7}{8} - 3\frac{3}{4}$ **6** **7.** $12\frac{1}{15} + 7\frac{5}{16}$ **19** **8.** $6\frac{3}{7} - 2\frac{3}{5}$ **3**

9. $4\frac{5}{8} + 2\frac{2}{3}$ **8** **10.** $3\frac{9}{10} - 3\frac{1}{3}$ **1** **11.** $9\frac{1}{3} + 3\frac{4}{5}$ **13** **12.** $16\frac{1}{5} - 10\frac{3}{4}$ **5**

13. Lorissa worked $7\frac{3}{4}$ hours on Saturday and $5\frac{1}{3}$ hours on Sunday. Estimate her total weekend hours.
13 hours

Set 4-5 (pages 218–219)

Find each sum. Simplify if possible.

1. $7\frac{5}{6} + 3\frac{1}{4}$ **$11\frac{1}{12}$** **2.** $9\frac{2}{3} + 2\frac{1}{2}$ **$12\frac{1}{6}$** **3.** $6\frac{3}{5} + 1\frac{3}{4}$ **$8\frac{7}{20}$** **4.** $8\frac{7}{9} + 3\frac{2}{3}$ **$12\frac{4}{9}$**

5. $18\frac{3}{8} + 2\frac{1}{6}$ **$20\frac{13}{24}$** **6.** $12\frac{1}{2} + 6\frac{7}{8}$ **$19\frac{3}{8}$** **7.** $1\frac{2}{5} + 3\frac{1}{3}$ **$4\frac{11}{15}$** **8.** $10\frac{7}{10} + 3\frac{2}{5}$ **$14\frac{1}{10}$**

9. $2\frac{1}{5} + 2\frac{3}{10}$ **$4\frac{1}{2}$** **10.** $5\frac{3}{5} + 4\frac{1}{4}$ **$9\frac{17}{20}$** **11.** $11\frac{7}{10} + 2\frac{3}{4}$ **$14\frac{9}{20}$** **12.** $9\frac{1}{2} + 6\frac{1}{4}$ **$15\frac{3}{4}$**

13. Sonia has $1\frac{3}{4}$ cups of apples and $2\frac{1}{3}$ cups of grapes. How many cups of fruit does she have?
$4\frac{1}{12}$ cups

Set 4-6 (pages 220–223)

Find each difference. Simplify if possible.

1. $8 - 3\frac{2}{3}$ **$4\frac{1}{3}$** **2.** $7\frac{1}{6} - 2\frac{3}{4}$ **$4\frac{5}{12}$** **3.** $18\frac{1}{2} - 12\frac{7}{8}$ **$5\frac{5}{8}$** **4.** $5\frac{1}{4} - 2\frac{9}{10}$ **$2\frac{7}{20}$**

5. $9\frac{2}{5} - 4\frac{5}{6}$ **$4\frac{17}{30}$** **6.** $3\frac{3}{4} - 1\frac{1}{4}$ **$2\frac{1}{2}$** **7.** $8\frac{1}{3} - 2\frac{7}{8}$ **$5\frac{11}{24}$** **8.** $6 - 5\frac{3}{4}$ **$\frac{1}{4}$**

9. $8\frac{1}{4} - 7\frac{5}{8}$ **$\frac{5}{8}$** **10.** $4\frac{1}{3} - 3\frac{8}{9}$ **$\frac{4}{9}$** **11.** $7\frac{3}{8} - 1\frac{7}{8}$ **$5\frac{1}{2}$** **12.** $3\frac{2}{5} - 1\frac{7}{10}$ **$1\frac{7}{10}$**

13. Last week Joe ran $5\frac{7}{8}$ miles and Jocelyn ran $6\frac{1}{2}$ miles. How much farther did Jocelyn run? **$\frac{5}{8}$ mile**

14. In San Diego, California, the shortest day of the year has 10 hours of daylight. In Bangor, Maine, the shortest day of the year has $8\frac{14}{15}$ hours of daylight. How much more daylight does San Diego have on the shortest day than Bangor? **$1\frac{1}{15}$ hours**

Take It to the NET
More Practice
www.scottforesman.com

Set 4-7 (pages 224–225)

Find each sum or difference. Tell what computation method you used. **Sample computation methods are given.**

1. $3\frac{1}{4} + 5\frac{5}{6}$ **$9\frac{1}{12}$; paper and pencil**
2. $2\frac{3}{10} + 9\frac{2}{5}$ **$11\frac{7}{10}$; paper and pencil**
3. $7\frac{13}{28} - 4\frac{11}{21}$ **$2\frac{79}{84}$; calculator**
4. $7 + 2\frac{1}{2}$ **$9\frac{1}{2}$; mental math**
5. $8\frac{4}{7} - 3\frac{4}{5}$ **$4\frac{27}{35}$; calculator**
6. $5\frac{3}{8} - 2\frac{3}{16}$ **$3\frac{3}{16}$; mental math**
7. $6 - 3\frac{2}{3}$ **$2\frac{1}{3}$; mental math**
8. $3\frac{1}{4} + 8\frac{3}{4}$ **12; mental math**
9. $7\frac{1}{6} - 3\frac{2}{5}$ **$3\frac{23}{30}$; paper and pencil**
10. $11\frac{3}{4} - 8\frac{1}{8}$ **$3\frac{5}{8}$; mental math**
11. $9\frac{14}{25} + 6\frac{11}{20}$ **$16\frac{11}{100}$; paper and pencil**
12. $9\frac{1}{2} - 4 + 2\frac{1}{2}$ **8; mental math**

Set 4-8 (pages 226–227)

For Exercises 1–3, use the table at the right. Tell whether an exact answer or an estimate is needed. Then solve.

Julian's Work Schedule	
Day	**Hours Worked**
Monday	$7\frac{3}{4}$
Tuesday	$4\frac{1}{4}$
Wednesday	$8\frac{1}{2}$
Thursday	$5\frac{1}{12}$
Friday	$6\frac{11}{12}$

1. How many more hours did Julian work on Monday than Tuesday? **exact answer; $3\frac{1}{2}$ hours**
2. About how many hours did Julian work in that week? **estimate; about 33 hours**
3. What was the total number of hours Julian worked on Monday and Tuesday? **exact answer; 12 hours**

Tell whether an exact answer or an estimate is needed. Then solve.

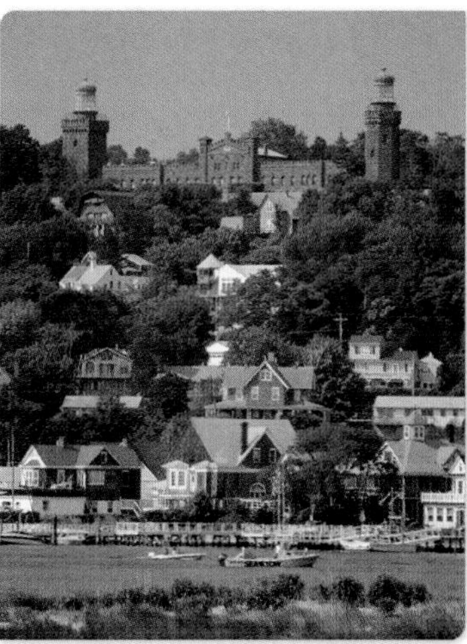

4. Calista wants to plant tomato seeds in her garden. Packets of seeds cost $0.89 each. How much money should Calista take to the store to buy six packets? **estimate; $6**
5. Satisfied customers often will acknowledge good service by leaving a tip of about $0.20 for each dollar spent. If a bill is $50.23, how much tip should a satisfied customer leave? **estimate; $10**
6. Dimitri lives near a river that floods. He should evacuate his home when the river reaches 28 feet. The river is now $21\frac{7}{10}$ feet and is predicted to rise another $6\frac{1}{2}$ feet this evening. Will Dimitri need to evacuate? **exact; yes**

CHAPTER 5

Lesson Planner

Multiplying and Dividing Fractions

Suggested Pacing: 12 to 13 days

Section A Multiplying Fractions

5-1 pp. 248–251	5-2 pp. 252–255	5-3 pp. 256–257	5-4 pp. 258–259
Multiplying a Fraction and a Whole Number **Objective** Multiply a fraction times a whole number. **Math Understanding** Multiplying a whole number by a fraction involves division as well as multiplication. The product is a fraction of the whole number. **Focus Questions** • What does it mean to multiply a fraction and a whole number? • What are some ways to multiply a fraction and a whole number? **Enrichment: Writing Repeating Decimals as Fractions, p. 251**	**Multiplying Fractions** **Objective** Give the product of two fractions. **Math Understanding** When you multiply two fractions that are both less than 1, the product is smaller than either fraction. **Focus Questions** • How do you find products of fractions? • How can you simplify before you multiply? **Vocabulary** Greatest common factor (GCF) (p. 150) **Practice Game: GCF Spin, p. 255** **Learning with Technology: Multiplication with the Fraction eTool, p. 255**	**Estimating with Fractions and Mixed Numbers** **Objective** Estimate the product or quotient of two fractions. **Math Understanding** Mixed numbers can be expressed as improper fractions, or they can be broken apart into their whole-number and fractional parts. This provides a basis for estimating and doing operations with two mixed numbers, with a mixed number and a whole number, and with a mixed number and a fraction. **Focus Question** • What are some ways to estimate? **Vocabulary** Compatible numbers (p. 18), round (p. 14)	**Multiplying Mixed Numbers** **Objective** Multiply mixed numbers. **Math Understanding** Mixed numbers can be expressed as improper fractions, or they can be broken apart into their whole-number and fractional parts. This provides a basis for estimating and doing operations with two mixed numbers, with a mixed number and a whole number, and with a mixed number and a fraction. **Focus Question** • How can you find the product of mixed numbers? **Section A Review, p. 260** **Section A Diagnostic Checkpoint, p. 261** Reading For Math Success pp. 262–263

Diagnosing Readiness, pp. 246–247

Resources in the Student Book

Ongoing Assessment and Test Prep *Also see pp. 246G–246H.*

Instant Check System™
- **Diagnosing Readiness** start of chapter
- **Warm Up** start of lessons
- **Talk About It** after examples
- **Check** before Practice
- **Diagnostic Checkpoint** end of sections

Test Prep
- **Test Talk: Think It Through** in lessons
- **Mixed Review and Test Prep** in lessons
- **Test Talk** end of chapter
- **Cumulative Review and Test Prep** end of chapter

Daily Real-World Problem Solving plus ...

Problem-Solving Applications lesson on pp. 280–281 uses data from Dorling Kindersley literature.

Discover Math in Your World on p. 269 uses data from a topic in the Discovery Channel School Video Library, Segment 5.

Section B Dividing Fractions

5-5 pp. 264–265	5-6 pp. 266–269	5-7 pp. 270–271
Problem-Solving Strategy **Make an Organized List** **Objective** Solve word problems by making organized lists. **Math Understanding** Making an organized list can help to represent what you know in solving a problem. **Focus Question** • How can you make an organized list to solve problems?	**Dividing Fractions** **Objective** Divide fractions. **Math Understanding** When we divide by a fraction that is less than 1, the quotient is greater than the number being divided (the dividend). **Focus Questions** • How can you model division of fractions? •  Activity How can you divide fractions? **Vocabulary** Reciprocal, multiplicative inverse  Discovery Channel School **Discover Math in Your World: Not-So-Sweet Honeybee, p. 269**	**Dividing Mixed Numbers** **Objective** Find the quotients of divisions with mixed numbers. **Math Understanding** Mixed numbers can be expressed as improper fractions, or they can be broken apart into their whole-number and fractional parts. This provides a basis for estimating and doing operations with two mixed numbers, with a mixed number and a whole number, and with a mixed number and a fraction. **Focus Question** • How can you find the quotient of mixed numbers? **Section B Review, p. 272** **Section B Diagnostic Checkpoint, p. 273**

Reading and Writing in Math *Throughout*

This feature shows how reading skills and strategies can help with problem-solving skills and strategies in math. Also, **Reading Assists** are in the Teacher's Edition.

All lessons include **Writing in Math** exercises. Also, daily **Journal Ideas** are in the Teacher's Edition.

Technology Resources for Students *Also see p. T20.*

More examples, more practice, test prep, Discovery Channel School Video Library, and Math eTools

e tools

Math eTools: electronic manipulatives online, on CD-ROM, and in the Online Student's Edition

All text pages are available online and on CD-ROM. The Online Student's Edition includes Math eTools plus glossary links for vocabulary.

CHAPTER 5

Lesson Planner

Multiplying and Dividing Fractions (continued)

Section C Algebra: Using Fractions

5-8 pp. 274–275	5-9 pp. 276–277	5-10 pp. 278–279	5-11 pp. 280–281
Algebra Expressions with Fractions **Objective** Write word phrases as, and evaluate, algebraic expressions with fractions. **Math Understanding** Word phrases that express mathematical situations can be translated into specific expressions using numbers and operations, and expressions can be evaluated by substituting given values for the variable. **Focus Questions** • How can you write algebraic expressions with fractions? • How can you evaluate algebraic expressions with fractions?	**Algebra** Solving Equations with Fractions **Objective** Solve one-step equations in one variable with fractions. **Math Understanding** Using inverse operations and properties of equality can help you solve for the variable in an equation. **Focus Question** • How can you solve equations involving fractions and mixed numbers?	Problem-Solving Skill Writing to Explain **Objective** Explain solutions to word problems. **Math Understanding** An explanation of the solution to a problem includes information that is known and how you have used this information. **Focus Question** • How do you write a good explanation?	DK Problem-Solving Applications Honeybees **Objective** Review and apply key concepts, skills, and strategies learned in this and previous chapters. **Math Understanding** Some real-world problems can be solved using known concepts, skills, and strategies. **Section C Review, p. 282** **Section C Diagnostic Checkpoint, p. 283**

Wrap Up

pp. 284–297

Test Talk: Use Writing in Math, pp. 284–285

Key Vocabulary and Concept Review, pp. 286–287

Chapter 5 Test, pp. 288–289

Cumulative Review and Test Prep, pp. 290–291

Reteaching, pp. 292–294

More Practice, pp. 295–297

Additional Resources for...

Reaching All Learners

- **Practice** Masters/Workbook, every lesson
- **Reteaching** Masters/Workbook, every lesson
- **Enrichment** Masters/Workbook, every lesson
- **Every Student Learns** A teacher resource with daily suggestions for helping students overcome language barriers to learning math
- **Spiral Review and Test Prep** Transparencies and Masters/Workbook, every lesson
- **Math Games** Use *Tropical Fish* anytime after Lesson 5-4.
- **Investigation** See pp. 246I–246J.

Problem Solving

- **Problem Solving** Masters/Workbook, every lesson
- **Problem of the Day** Flipchart/Transparencies, every lesson
- **Discovery Channel** Masters, follow-up to Segment 5 in the Discovery Channel School Video Library

Notes

Reading in Math

- **Vocabulary Kit** Word Cards plus transparencies and activities for instructional word walls and for small groups
- **Dorling Kindersley Literature Library** Books with interesting data

Assessment, Intervention, and Test Prep

- **Assessment Sourcebook** See pp. 246G–246H.
- **Math Diagnosis and Intervention System** See pp. 246G–246H.
- **Test-Taking Practice** Transparencies, every lesson
- **SAT 9, SAT 10, TerraNova, ITBS Practice and Test Prep** Includes practice tests, correlations, and more.
- **Benchmark Tests** Multiple-choice tests on content in Chapters 1–2, 3–4, 5–6, 7–8, 9–10 and in the National Assessment of Educational Progress.

Teacher Support

- **Teaching Tools** Masters: paper manipulatives and more
- **Home-School Connection** Masters, use Chapter 5 Family Letter at the start of the chapter. Use Study Buddies 9 and 10 after Lessons 5-4 and 5-6.
- **Professional Development Resources** See p. T18.
- **Technology Resources** TE and more; see p. T20.

CHAPTER 5 Professional Development

Skills Trace - Multiplying and Dividing Fractions

BEFORE Chapter 5	DURING Chapter 5	AFTER Chapter 5
Grade 5 introduced multiplication of fractions and mixed numbers and division of fractions. **Chapter 3 in Grade 6** reviewed fraction concepts that are needed for operating with fractions. **Chapter 4 in Grade 6** focused on estimating and finding sums and differences of fractions and mixed numbers.	**Chapter 5** focuses on estimating and finding products and quotients of fractions and mixed numbers and applying these skills in solving equations.	**Chapter 7 in Grade 6** applies multiplying and dividing fractions and mixed numbers in solving percent problems. Grade 7 applies multiplying and dividing fractions in solving percent problems and writing and solving equations.

Math Background and Teaching Tips

Section A

Multiplying Fractions
pp. 248–261

Students may have developed the incorrect notion that multiplication always results in a greater number. When one factor is a whole number greater than 1, and the other number is a fraction less than 1, the product will be greater than the fraction but less than the whole number. When both factors are fractions less than one, the product will be less than either factor.

TIP! Reading Mathematics *Emphasize to students that × means "of." For example, $\frac{3}{5} \times \frac{3}{4}$ means $\frac{3}{5}$ of $\frac{3}{4}$. This will help students understand the area model for multiplying fractions.*

The area model, in which a square is used to represent the whole, is an effective method for developing the algorithm for multiplying fractions.

$\frac{a}{b} \times \frac{c}{d} = \frac{ac}{bd}$.

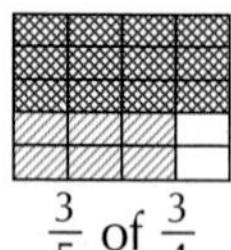

$\frac{3}{5}$ of $\frac{3}{4}$

Find $\frac{3}{5}$ of $\frac{3}{4}$.

$\frac{3}{5}$ of $\frac{3}{4}$ means $\frac{3}{5} \times \frac{3}{4}$.

The shaded region shows the product of $\frac{3}{5} \times \frac{3}{4}$. The square is divided into 20 equal parts of which 9 are in the region with overlapping colors representing the product.

So, $\frac{3}{5} \times \frac{3}{4} = \frac{9}{20}$.

Math Understandings

- Multiplying a whole number by a fraction involves division as well as multiplication. The product is a fraction of the whole number.
- When we multiply two fractions that are both less than 1, the product is less than either fraction.
- Mixed numbers can be expressed as improper fractions, or they can be broken apart into their whole-number and fractional parts.

TIP! Use Representations *A number line is a good model for showing the product of a whole number and a fraction as repeated addition.*

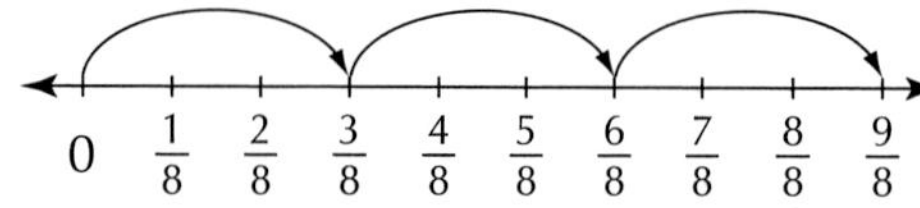

$3 \times \frac{3}{8} = \frac{3}{1} \times \frac{3}{8} = \frac{9}{8} = 1\frac{1}{8}$

In the traditional algorithm for multiplying a mixed number by a whole number, both are converted into improper fractions and then multiplied.

$$6 \times 2\frac{1}{3}$$
$$\downarrow \quad \downarrow$$
$$\frac{6}{1} \times \frac{7}{3} = \frac{42}{3} = 14$$

An alternative method is to break apart the mixed number and distribute the whole number factor.

$$6 \times 2\frac{1}{3} = (6 \times 2) + (6 \times \frac{1}{3})$$
$$= 12 + 2$$
$$= 14$$

Section B

Dividing Fractions pp. 264–273

The traditional algorithm for division with a fraction is to invert the divisor and multiply. This is commonly known as the reciprocal method and is expressed in general as:

$$\frac{a}{b} \div \frac{c}{d} = \frac{a}{b} \times \frac{d}{c}$$
$$\frac{3}{4} \div \frac{1}{2} = \frac{3}{4} \times \frac{2}{1}$$
$$= \frac{6}{4}$$
$$= 1\frac{2}{4} = 1\frac{1}{2}$$

The reason this works is that we can multiply the divisor and the dividend by the same nonzero number and not change the quotient.

Let *a*, *b*, *c*, and *d* be counting numbers.

$\frac{a}{b} \div \frac{c}{d} = \left(\frac{a}{b} x \frac{d}{c}\right) \div \left(\frac{c}{d} x \frac{d}{c}\right)$ Multiply the divisor and dividend by $\frac{d}{c}$.

$= \left(\frac{a}{b} \times \frac{d}{c}\right) \div (1)$ $\quad \frac{c}{d} \times \frac{d}{c} = 1$

$= \frac{a}{b} \times \frac{d}{c}$ Dividing by 1

Understanding what the quotient means when dividing fractions is important. For $\frac{3}{4} \div \frac{1}{2} = 1\frac{1}{2}$, the $1\frac{1}{2}$ means that there are "one and one-half one-halves in three-fourths." The quotient does not represent one whole and one-half of another whole.

Another method for dividing fractions is the common denominator algorithm that relies on the measurement, or repeated subtraction, concept of division.

Math Understandings

- Making an organized list can help to represent what you know in solving a problem.
- When we divide by a fraction that is less than 1, the quotient is greater than the number being divided (the dividend).
- Mixed numbers can be expressed as improper fractions, or they can be broken apart into their whole-number and fractional parts.

Find $2\frac{1}{4} \div \frac{3}{8}$.

Think: How many sets of $\frac{3}{8}$ can be made from $2\frac{1}{4}$?

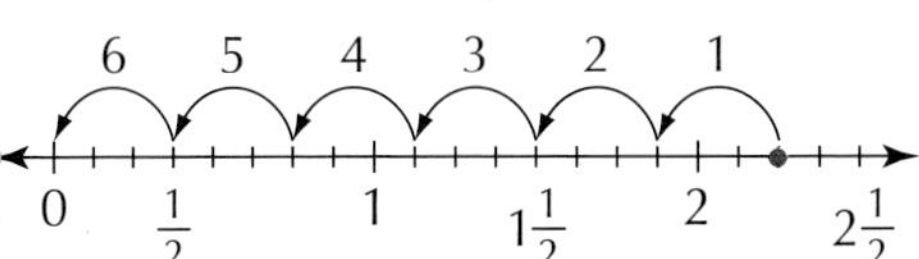

Once each number is expressed in terms of the same fractional part (common denominator), the answer can be found by dividing the numerators.

$2\frac{1}{4} \div \frac{3}{8}$ Convert all whole numbers and mixed numbers to improper fractions.

↓

$\frac{9}{4} \div \frac{3}{8}$ Express the fractions using a common denominator.

↓

$\frac{18}{8} \div \frac{3}{8}$ Divide the numerators: $18 \div 3 = 6$

So, $2\frac{1}{4} \div \frac{3}{8} = 6$.

The answer is the same as inverting and multiplying.

$\frac{9}{4} \div \frac{3}{8} = \frac{9}{4} \times \frac{8}{3} = \frac{72}{12} = 6$

Section C

Algebra: Using Fractions

pp. 274–283

Students have already been introduced to evaluating expressions and solving equations with whole numbers. The same principles can be applied when evaluating expressions and solving equations with fractions.

Recall that solving equations involves the use of two important ideas, inverse operations and the two properties of equality—the Addition Property of Equality and the Multiplication Property of Equality.

Addition Property of Equality

If $a = b$, then $a + c = b + c$.

Multiplication Property of Equality

If $a = b$, then $ac = bc$

Since subtraction is defined in terms of addition and division is defined in terms of multiplication, properties that involve subtracting the same number from both sides or dividing both sides by the same number are sometimes referred to as the subtraction and division properties of equality.

TIP! Reinforce Big Ideas *Make sure students understand that after substituting numbers for the variables in an algebraic expression, the resulting numerical expression can be simplified by applying the order of operations. Remind students about the order of operations: operations in parentheses first, multiplications, divisions, additions, subtractions.*

Math Understandings

- Word phrases that express mathematical situations can be translated into specific expressions using numbers and operations, and expressions can be evaluated by substituting given values for the variable.
- Using inverse operations and properties of equality can help you solve for the variable in an equation.
- An explanation of the solution to a problem includes information that is known and how you have used this information.

Evaluate $8 + \frac{1}{2}(n - 3)$ for $n = 5$.

$8 + \frac{1}{2}(5 - 3)$ Operate within parentheses.

$8 + \frac{1}{2}(2)$ Multiply.

$8 + 1 = 9$ Add.

When estimating, knowing if a fraction is closer to 0, $\frac{1}{2}$, or 1 is useful. Fractions can be replaced with the nearest whole number or the nearest half to estimate.

Add: $\frac{8}{9} + \frac{7}{16} + \frac{3}{26}$

$\frac{8}{9}$ is close to 1. $\frac{7}{16}$ is close to $\frac{1}{2}$. $\frac{3}{26}$ is close to 0.

$1 + \frac{1}{2} + 0 = 1\frac{1}{2}$

So, $\frac{8}{9} + \frac{7}{16} + \frac{3}{26}$ is about $1\frac{1}{2}$.

CHAPTER 5

Assessment, Intervention, Test Prep

Assessment Resources

DIAGNOSING READINESS

Start of Year Diagnosing Readiness for Grade 6, Assessment Sourcebook, pp. 43–46 and in Online Intervention

✓ **Start of Chapter** Diagnosing Readiness for Chapter 5, Student Book pp. 246–247 and in Online Intervention

✓ **Start of Lesson** Warm Up, Student Book pp. 248, 252, 256, 258, 266, 270, 274, 276

✓ Instant Check System™

ONGOING ASSESSMENT

✓ **During Instruction** Talk About It, Student Book, every lesson

✓ **Before Independent Practice** Check, Student Book, every lesson

✓ **After a Section** Diagnostic Checkpoint, pp. 261, 273, 283 and in Online Intervention

Basic-Facts Timed Test 5 Assessment Sourcebook, p. 31

FORMAL EVALUATION

Chapter Tests Chapter 5 Test, Student Book pp. 288–289; Assessment Sourcebook Forms A and B pp. 75–80, Form C Performance Assessment p. 9; Multiple-Choice Chapter Test in Online Intervention

Cumulative Tests Chapters 1–3, 1–6, 1–9, 1–12; Assessment Sourcebook, pp. 65–68, 87–90, 109–112, 131–134; Online Intervention

Test Generator Computer-generated tests; can be customized

Correlation to Assessments, Intervention, and Standardized Tests

		Assessments		Intervention	Standardized Tests				
	Lessons	Diagnostic Checkpoint	Chapter Test	Math Diagnosis and Intervention System	SAT 9/10	ITBS	CTBS	CAT	MAT
5-1	Multiplying a Fraction and a Whole Number	p. 261: Ex. 1, 3–6	Ex. 1, 14	Booklet H: H37	•/•	•	•	•	•
5-2	Multiplying Fractions	p. 261: Ex. 2, 7–12	Ex. 2, 12	Booklet H: H39	•/•	•	•	•	•
5-3	Estimating with Fractions and Mixed Numbers	p. 261: Ex. 13–16, 25	Ex. 3, 17, 18	Booklet H: H38	/•		•		•
5-4	Multiplying Mixed Numbers	p. 261: Ex. 17–24, 26	Ex. 4, 5, 11, 13, 14	Booklet H: H40	•/•	•	•	•	•
5-5	Problem-Solving Strategy: Make an Organized List	p. 273: Ex. 3	Ex. 26	Booklet M: M28	•/•	•	•		•
5-6	Dividing Fractions	p. 273: Ex. 1, 4–15, 27–28	Ex. 8, 15, 16, 21, 24	Booklet H: H42	•/•		•	•	
5-7	Dividing Mixed Numbers	p. 273: Ex. 16–26	Ex. 6, 7, 23	Booklet H: H43	•/		•	•	
5-8	Expressions with Fractions	p. 283: Ex. 3–8	Ex. 9, 21, 22	Booklet J: J33	/•	•	•	•	•
5-9	Solving Equations with Fractions	p. 283: Ex. 1, 2, 9–20, 22, 23	Ex. 8, 10, 23, 24, 27	Booklet J: J33	•/•	•	•	•	•
5-10	Problem-Solving Skill: Writing to Explain	p. 283: Ex. 21–23	Ex. 25, 27	Booklet M: M18	/•	•	•	•	•

KEY: **SAT 9** Stanford Achievement Test; **SAT 10** Stanford Achievement Test; **ITBS** Iowa Test of Basic Skills; **CAT** California Achievement Test; **CTBS** Comprehensive Test of Basic Skills (TerraNova); **MAT** Metropolitan Achievement Test

Intervention and Test Prep Resources

INTERVENTION

During Instruction Helpful "If... Then..." suggestions in the Teacher's Edition in Ongoing Assessment and Error Intervention.

During Practice "Reteaching" and "More Practice" sets at the back of the chapter, referenced under "Check" and "Practice" in the lessons.

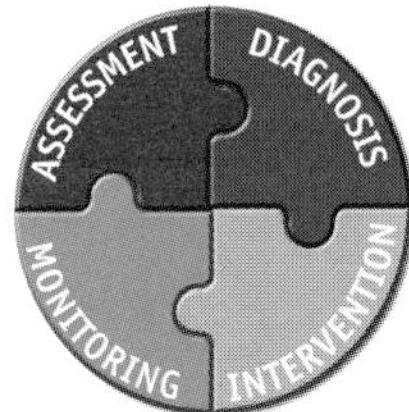

Math Diagnosis and Intervention System Diagnostic tests, individual and class record forms, two-page Intervention Lessons (example, practice, test prep), and one-page Intervention Practice (multiple choice), all in cross-grade strand booklets (Booklets A-E for Grades 1–3, Booklets F-M for Grades 4–6).

Online Intervention Diagnostic tests; individual, class, school, and district reports; remediation including tutorials, video, games, practice exercises.

 TEST PREP

Test Talk: Think It Through within lessons and tests

Mixed Review and Test Prep end of lessons

Test Talk before the chapter test, pp. 284–285

Cumulative Review and Test Prep after each chapter, pp. 290–291

Test-Taking Strategies, pp. xv–xix before Chapter 1

Pacing for Test Success, pp. T36–T47

Test-Taking Practice Transparencies for every lesson

Spiral Review and Test Prep for every lesson

SAT 9, SAT 10, ITBS, TerraNova Practice and Test Prep section quizzes, practice tests

Take It to the Net: Test Prep www.scottforesman.com, referenced in lessons

Correlation to NCTM Standards and Grades 6–8 Expectations

Number and Operations

Understand meanings of operations and how they relate to one another.

Grades 6–8 Expectations

- Understand the meaning and effects of arithmetic operations with fractions, decimals, and integers. *Lessons 5-1, 5-2, 5-4, 5-6, 5-7, 5-10, 5-11*
- Use the associative and commutative properties of addition and multiplication and the distributive property of multiplication over addition to simplify computations with integers, fractions, and decimals. *Lesson 5-4*
- Understand and use the inverse relationships of addition and subtraction, multiplication and division, and squaring and finding square roots to simplify computations and solve problems. *Lesson 5-9*

Compute fluently and make reasonable estimates.

Grades 6–8 Expectations

- Develop and analyze algorithms for computing with fractions, decimals, and integers and develop fluency in their use. *Lessons 5-1, 5-2, 5-4, 5-6, 5-7*
- Develop and use strategies to estimate the results of rational-number computations and judge the reasonableness of the results. *Lessons 5-3, 5-4*

Algebra

Represent and analyze mathematical situations and structures using algebraic symbols.

Grades 6–8 Expectations

- Use symbolic algebra to represent situations and to solve problems, especially those that involve linear relationships. *Lessons 5-8, 5-9*
- Recognize and generate equivalent forms for simple algebraic expressions and solve linear equations. *Lesson 5-9*

Use mathematical models to represent and understand quantitative relationships.

Grades 6–8 Expectations

- Model and solve contextualized problems using various representations, such as graphs, tables, and equations. *Lessons 5-8, 5-9*

Data Analysis and Probability

Understand and apply basic concepts of probability.

Grades 6–8 Expectations

- Compute probabilities for simple compound events, using such methods as organized lists, tree diagrams, and area models. *Lesson 5-5*

The NCTM 2000 Pre-K through Grade 12 Content Standards are Number and Operations, Algebra, Geometry, Measurement, and Data Analysis and Probability. The Process Standards (Problem Solving, Reasoning and Proof, Communication, Connections, and Representation) are incorporated throughout lessons.

Investigation

Multiplying and Dividing Fractions

Activity 1

Use in place of the Investigating the Concept activity before Lesson 5-2.

Multiplying Fractions

Overview Students create and explain ways to use fraction strips to multiply fractions before learning the traditional algorithm used to multiply fractions in Lesson 5-2.

Materials (per small group) Fraction Strips (Teaching Tool 15); scissors

The Task

- Write $\frac{1}{2}$ of $\frac{1}{3}$, $\frac{3}{4}$ of $\frac{1}{2}$, and $\frac{2}{3}$ of $\frac{2}{3}$ on the chalkboard.
- **How could you use fraction strips to find these products? Draw pictures or write to explain how you found each product.**
- **Look for patterns between the numerators in each problem and the numerators in the product. Look for patterns between the denominators. Write about the patterns you notice.**

Observing and Questioning

- Observe how students approach this task. If needed, ask the following questions to spur thinking.
- **What does it mean to say that you have eaten $\frac{1}{2}$ of a sandwich? How can this help you decide what fraction strip to start with to find $\frac{1}{2}$ of $\frac{1}{3}$?**
- **How can you show a fraction strip divided into equal parts?**
- **How can you find out what fraction describes a part of a fraction strip?**

Sharing and Summarizing

- As students share their methods for finding products of fractions, ask, **What part of your fraction-strip models represents the denominator of each product? the numerator?**
- **Key Idea** Summarize strategies that students used. Students should recognize that to multiply fractions they multiply the numerators, then multiply the denominators.
- Point out to students that when multiplying a fraction by a fraction, the product is less than either factor. Look at a few examples together to see that this is true.

Follow-Up

- Have students use their patterns to predict $\frac{1}{4}$ of $\frac{1}{2}$. Then have them use fraction strips to verify their prediction.
- **Extension** Have students use fraction strips to find $\frac{2}{5}$ of $\frac{5}{8}$ and explain whether it follows the patterns.

Brooke

$\frac{1}{2}$ of $\frac{1}{3}$

Two $\frac{1}{6}$s are as long as $\frac{1}{3}$.

Each $\frac{1}{6}$ is half of $\frac{1}{3}$.

So, $\frac{1}{2}$ of $\frac{1}{3} = \frac{1}{6}$.

Josh

$\frac{3}{4}$ of $\frac{1}{2}$

I folded a $\frac{1}{2}$ strip into 4 equal parts. A $\frac{1}{8}$ strip covers one of those parts. So, three $\frac{1}{8}$ strips cover $\frac{3}{4}$ of the $\frac{1}{2}$ strip.

$\frac{3}{4}$ of $\frac{1}{2} = \frac{3}{8}$

Liz

$\frac{2}{3}$ of $\frac{2}{3} = \frac{4}{9}$

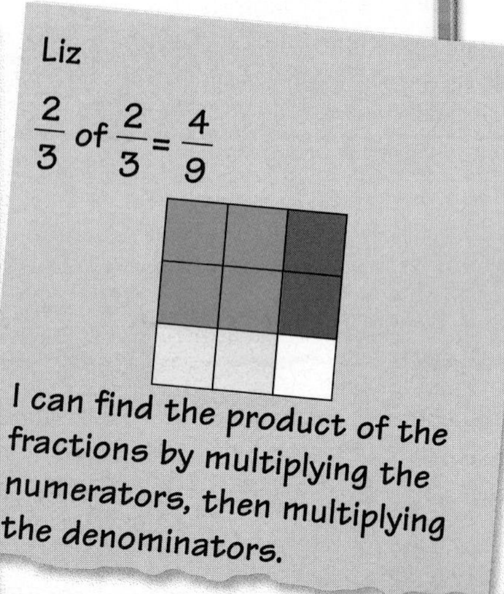

I can find the product of the fractions by multiplying the numerators, then multiplying the denominators.

Activity 2

Use in place of the Investigating the Concept activity before Lesson 5-6.

Making Wholes with Fraction Strips

Overview Students use fraction strips to explore the meaning of division involving whole numbers and fractions before learning the traditional algorithm used to divide fractions in Lesson 5-6.

Materials (per small group) Fraction Strips (Teaching Tool 15); scissors

The Task

- **Cut out several unit strips (whole strips) and several strips for $\frac{2}{5}$. Determine how many of the $\frac{2}{5}$- strips you need to make a whole number of unit strips. Make a sketch of your fraction-strip model. Then write one multiplication sentence and one division sentence for your model.**
- **When you have finished, try this again using fraction strips for $\frac{3}{4}$.**

Observing and Questioning

- Observe how students write multiplication and division sentences. To help them, ask the following questions.
- **How can you use multiplication to describe the relationship of the fraction strips to the unit strips?**
- **How can you use division?**
- **Can thinking about multiplication help you write division sentences? How?**

Sharing and Summarizing

- After students share their work, summarize the methods used. For example, Jason thought about the meaning of division, and Molly used inverse operations.
- **How can you use multiplication to help you write a division sentence?**
- **Key Idea** Discuss that whole numbers can be divided by fractions and multiplication can help you divide fractions.

Follow-Up

- Have students choose one of the sets of multiplication and division sentences they wrote and write a word problem to go with each sentence.

How many $\frac{2}{5}$s are in 2?

That's $2 \div \frac{2}{5}$, or 5.

Molly

$\frac{3}{4} \times 4 = 3$ $\quad 3 \div \frac{3}{4} = 4$

1 whole		1 whole		1 whole
$\frac{3}{4}$	$\frac{3}{4}$		$\frac{3}{4}$	$\frac{3}{4}$

Jason

$\frac{2}{5} \times 5 = 2$ $\quad 2 \div \frac{2}{5} = 5$

$\frac{2}{5}$	$\frac{2}{5}$	$\frac{2}{5}$	$\frac{2}{5}$	$\frac{2}{5}$
1 whole			1 whole	

CHAPTER 5

Multiplying and Dividing Fractions

The focus of Chapter 5 is multiplying and dividing fractions and mixed numbers. Writing and evaluating expressions and solving equations with fractions and mixed numbers are also contained in this chapter.

Vocabulary

Also, see Glossary, *pp. 742–748.*

greatest common factor (GCF) *(p. 150)*

compatible numbers *(p. 18)*

round *(p. 14)*

reciprocal *(p. 267)*

multiplicative inverse *(p. 267)*

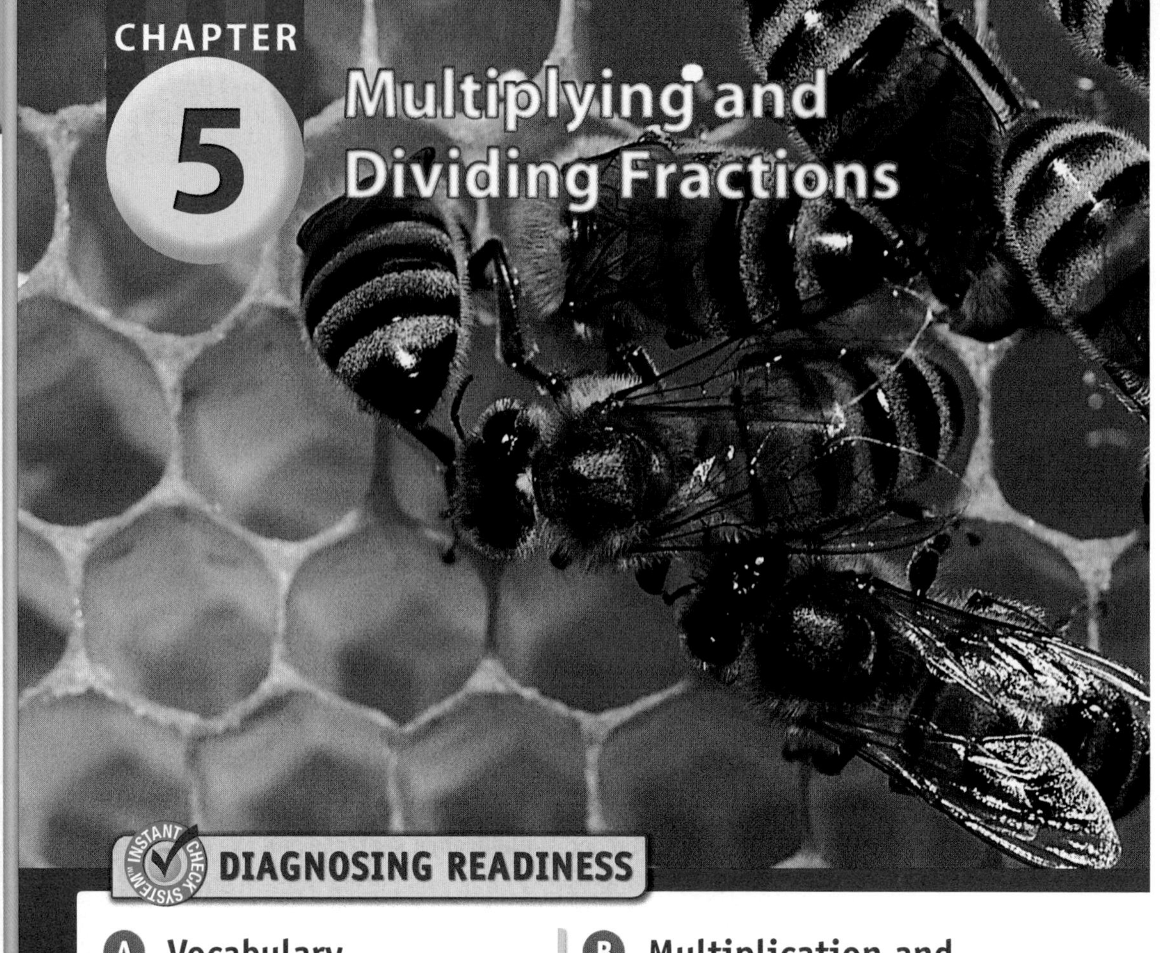

INSTANT CHECK SYSTEM DIAGNOSING READINESS

A Vocabulary
(pages 40, 44, 160, 168)

Choose the best term from the box.

1. A quantity that can change or vary is called a ?. **variable**
2. A ? combines a whole number and a fraction. **mixed number**
3. Multiplication and division are ?. **inverse operations**
4. The ? of a proper fraction is less than its ?. **numerator; denominator**

Vocabulary

- **mixed number** *(p. 168)*
- **denominator** *(p. 160)*
- **improper fraction** *(p. 168)*
- **variable** *(p. 40)*
- **inverse operations** *(p. 44)*
- **numerator** *(p. 160)*

246

B Multiplication and Division *(pages 24–27)*

Multiply or divide.

5. 3×8 **24**
6. $45 \div 9$ **5**
7. $(5 \times 6) \div 3$ **10**
8. $60 \div (4 \times 3)$ **5**
9. $72 \div (3 \times 3)$ **8**
10. $(88 \div 4) \times 5$ **110**
11. $(36 \div 9) \times 7$ **28**
12. $(12 \times 9) \div 4$ **27**
13. Mr. Bruckner bought 7 packs of pencils. There are 12 pencils in each pack. If he wants to divide the pencils evenly among 18 students, how many pencils will each student get? Will there be any pencils left over? If so, how many? **4; yes; 12**

Math Vocabulary Kit

Every vocabulary word is written on a card with the definition of the word printed on the back. Vocabulary activities are provided in the *Math Vocabulary Kit Teacher's Guide.*

Add the words from the *Vocabulary* list at the left to your Math Word Wall.

multiplicative inverse

greatest common factor (GCF)

reciprocal

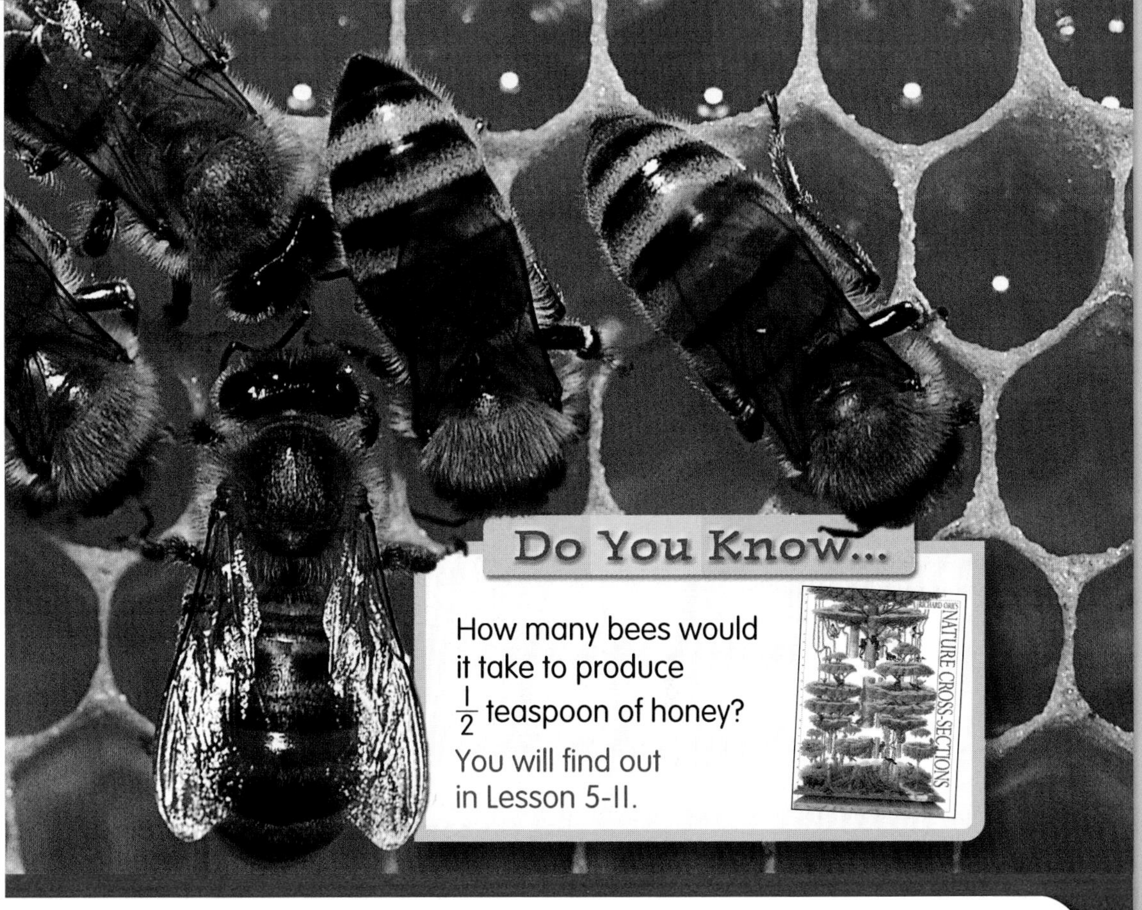

Do You Know...
How many bees would it take to produce $\frac{1}{2}$ teaspoon of honey?
You will find out in Lesson 5-11.
NATURE CROSS-SECTIONS

C Fractions and Mixed Numbers

(pages 160–163, 168–169, 216–217)

Write the shaded part as a fraction.

14. 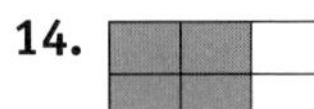 $\frac{2}{3}$ **15.** 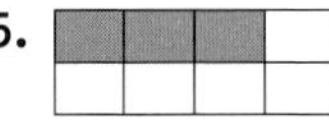 $\frac{3}{8}$

Round to the nearest whole number.

16. $3\frac{3}{4}$ **4** **17.** $5\frac{5}{6}$ **6** **18.** $\frac{3}{5}$ **1**

19. $9\frac{1}{5}$ **9** **20.** $7\frac{3}{8}$ **7** **21.** $\frac{2}{11}$ **0**

Write each mixed number as an improper fraction.

22. $3\frac{3}{8}$ $\frac{27}{8}$ **23.** $1\frac{4}{5}$ $\frac{9}{5}$ **24.** $2\frac{1}{3}$ $\frac{7}{3}$

D Solving Equations

(pages 48–51, 112–113)

Solve.

25. $7a = 28$ **$a = 4$** **26.** $g \div 9 = 6$ **$g = 54$**
27. $55 = h + 13$ **$h = 42$** **28.** $36 = 3.6t$ **$t = 10$**
29. $1.5y = 1.5$ **$y = 1$** **30.** $352 = 8m$ **$m = 44$**
31. $71 = k - 583$ **$k = 654$** **32.** $n \div 43 = 2$ **$n = 86$**

33. Jen takes pictures for the yearbook. Each roll of Jen's film allows her to take 36 photographs. Write and solve an equation to find the number of rolls of film Jen needs to take 1,260 photographs. **$36r = 1{,}260$; $r = 35$**

247

DIAGNOSING READINESS

Purpose Diagnose students' readiness by assessing prerequisite content.

- Assign each set of exercises and go over the answers.
- Check to see which students did not get at least 66% of the exercises correct in a section.

  Section A: 3 out of 4
  Section B: 6 out of 9
  Section C: 7 out of 11
  Section D: 6 out of 9
- For intervention, use the resources listed at the right.

Item Analysis for Diagnosis and Intervention

Objective	Items	Student Book Pages*	Intervention System
Recall the definitions of mixed number, denominator, improper fraction, variable, inverse operations, and numerator.	1–4	40, 44, 160, 168	J30, J24 H12, H14, H15
Evaluate algebraic expressions.	5–13	24–27	J29
Understand fractions, round fractions and mixed numbers, and write mixed numbers as improper fractions.	14–23	160–163, 168–169, 216–217	H12, H14, H15
Solve algebraic equations.	25–33	48–51	J31

*For each lesson, there is a *Reteaching* activity in *Reaching All Learners* and a *Reteaching* master.

Literature: Dorling Kindersley and Other Sources

Factastic Millennium Facts
Russell Ash. New York: Dorling Kindersley Publishing, Inc., 1999.

Use with Lesson 5-2 Packed with intriguing information and entertaining anecdotes, this book filled with facts from the last 1,000 years provides many opportunities for work with fractions.

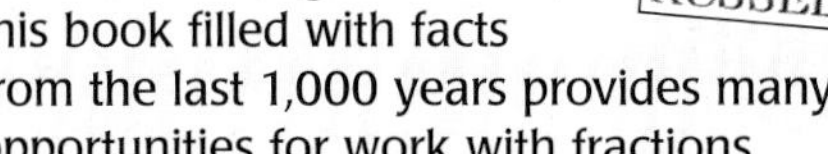

Available in the Scott Foresman Dorling Kindersley Literature Library.

Fractions
David Stienecker. Tarrytown, NY: Benchmark Books, 1996.

Use with Lesson 5-2 Includes an assortment of activities and illustrations to explain the concepts of fractions and presents activities and games to multiply and divide with fractions.

Fabulous Fractions
Lynette Long. New York: John Wiley & Sons, Inc., 2001.

Use with Lesson 5-6 Includes activities to understand fractions and all four operations with fractions, including "Brain Stretchers."

Math Leveled Literature Library
Anno's Mysterious Multiplying Jar
(Challenging)
Masaichiro and Mitsumasa Anno. New York: Penguin Putnam, 1983.

Simple text and pictures introduce the mathematical concept of factorials.

5-1 Multiplying a Fraction and a Whole Number

Lesson Organizer

Quick Lesson Overview

Objective Multiply a fraction times a whole number.

Math Understanding Multiplying a whole number by a fraction involves division as well as multiplication. The product is a fraction of the whole number.

Professional Development Note

Managing Instruction If possible, provide students with calculators that multiply fractions. To keep track of the calculators, write an ID number on each calculator and check them out to students by number.

Getting Started

Spiral Review

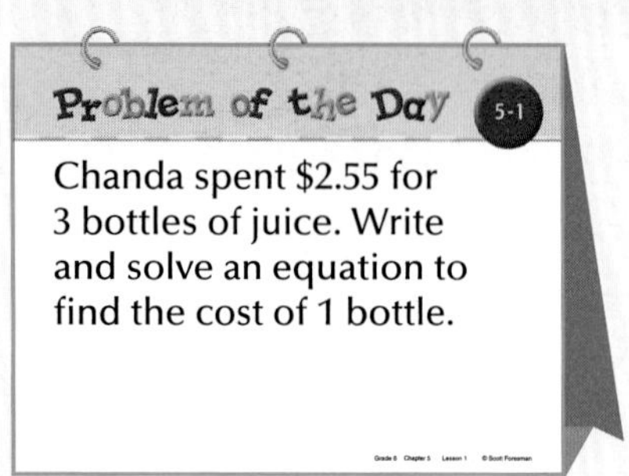

Problem of the Day 5-1

Chanda spent $2.55 for 3 bottles of juice. Write and solve an equation to find the cost of 1 bottle.

Topics Reviewed

- Solving equations; dividing decimals by whole numbers
- Problem-Solving Strategy: Write an Equation

Answer Each bottle of juice costs $0.85.

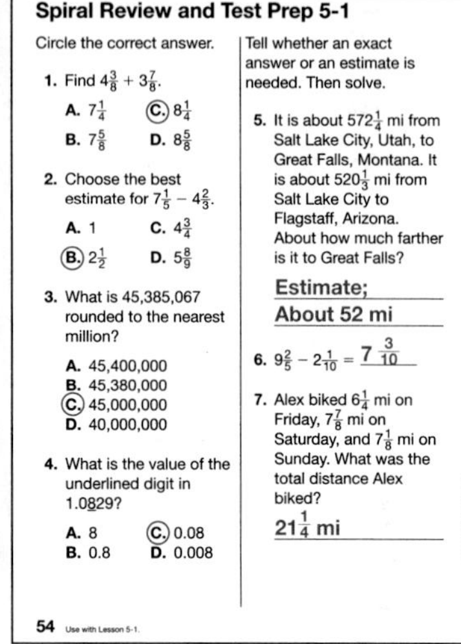

Spiral Review and Test Prep 5-1

Circle the correct answer.

1. Find $4\frac{3}{8} + 3\frac{7}{8}$.
   A. $7\frac{1}{4}$ (C.) $8\frac{1}{4}$
   B. $7\frac{5}{8}$ D. $8\frac{5}{8}$
2. Choose the best estimate for $7\frac{1}{5} - 4\frac{2}{3}$.
   A. 1 C. $4\frac{3}{4}$
   (B.) $2\frac{1}{2}$ D. $5\frac{8}{9}$
3. What is 45,385,067 rounded to the nearest million?
   A. 45,400,000
   B. 45,380,000
   (C.) 45,000,000
   D. 40,000,000
4. What is the value of the underlined digit in 1.0<u>8</u>29?
   A. 8 (C.) 0.08
   B. 0.8 D. 0.008

Tell whether an exact answer or an estimate is needed. Then solve.

5. It is about $572\frac{1}{4}$ mi from Salt Lake City, Utah, to Great Falls, Montana. It is about $520\frac{1}{3}$ mi from Salt Lake City to Flagstaff, Arizona. About how much farther is it to Great Falls?
   Estimate; About 52 mi
6. $9\frac{2}{5} - 2\frac{1}{10} = 7\frac{3}{10}$
7. Alex biked $6\frac{1}{4}$ mi on Friday, $7\frac{7}{8}$ mi on Saturday, and $7\frac{1}{8}$ mi on Sunday. What was the total distance Alex biked?
   $21\frac{1}{4}$ mi

54 Use with Lesson 5-1.

Available as a transparency and as a blackline master

Topics Reviewed

1. Adding mixed numbers; **2.** Estimating sums and differences of fractions and mixed numbers; **3.** Rounding; **4.** Place value; **5.** Exact or estimate; **6.–7.** Subtracting and adding mixed numbers

Investigating the Concept

Using Counters to Multiply

5–10 MIN **Visual/Spatial/Kinesthetic**

Materials *(per pair)* Counters or Teaching Tool 9

What to Do

- Ask pairs to model the whole number 20 using counters. **Suppose we want to find $\frac{3}{5}$ of 20. Start by dividing the counters into five equal groups. How many counters are there in each group?** *(4 counters)*
- **Now consider three of the five groups. How many counters in the three groups?** *(12 counters)*
- **What is $\frac{3}{5} \times 20$?** *(12)* **How did you use the counters to answer the question?** *(Sample answer: We formed five equal groups. Then we separated out three groups. Each group has four counters, so there are 12 counters in $\frac{3}{5} \times 20$.)*

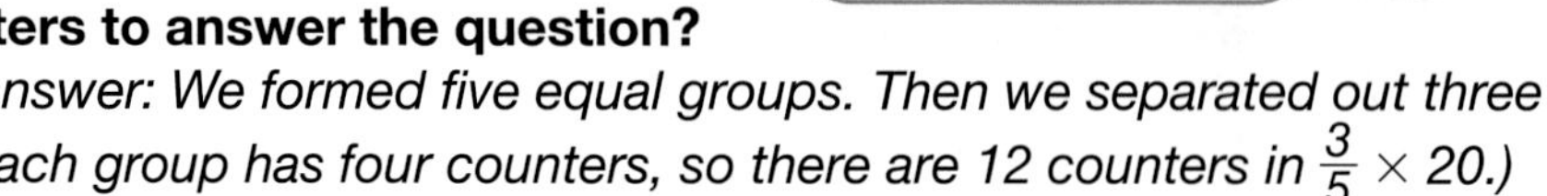

Ongoing Assessment

- **Reasoning Use the counters to find $\frac{2}{5}$ of 20.** *(8)* **Use counters to help you find $\frac{2}{3}$ of 6.** *(4)*

NCTM Standards

- Numbers and Operations

(For a complete correlation to the NCTM Standards and Grades 6–8 Expectations, see pages 246G–H.)

 EC NTL 12 11 10 9 8 7 6 5 4 3 2

Reaching All Learners

Math and Literature

Fanny at Chez Panisse

 15–20 MIN **Auditory** 

Materials *Fanny at Chez Panisse* by Alice Waters *et al* (HarperCollins, 1997)

- In this book, Fanny describes her experiences at her mother's well-known restaurant in Berkeley, California. Choose some parts of the book to read aloud.
- Write the recipe for 1-2-3-4 cake on the board. **If we want to make half a recipe, how much sugar do we need?** *(1 cup)* **If we want to make 4 recipes for a party, how much salt do we need?** *(2 tsp)*

Activate Prior Knowledge/Build Background

English Language Learners

Multiplying Fractions

 10–15 MIN **Auditory/Visual/Spatial** 

Materials Counters or Teaching Tool 9

- Display 7 red counters and 5 yellow counters. Model asking questions about fractions. **What is the total number of counters?** *(12 counters)* **How many counters are red?** *(7 counters)* **What fraction of the total number are red?** *($\frac{7}{12}$)* **How would you express 3 times this fraction?** *($3 \times \frac{7}{12}$)*
- Have partners arrange the counters into representations of fractions. Ask them to take turns asking and answering the above questions in their own words.

Reteaching

Using Picture Clues

 5–10 MIN **Visual/Spatial** 

- Draw this diagram on the board.

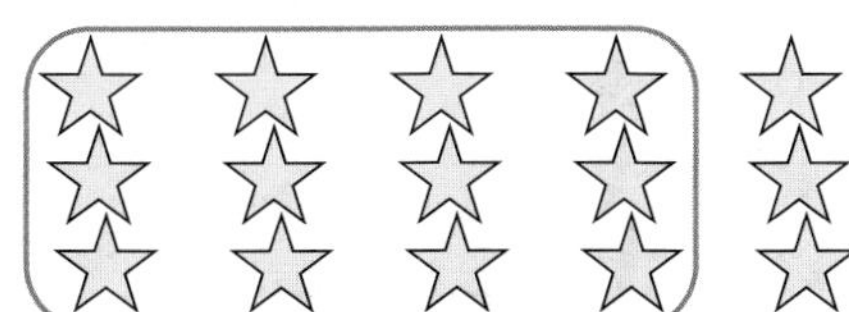

- **How many stars are there?** *(15 stars)*
- **How many groups are there?** *(5 groups)* **How many of the groups are circled?** *(4 groups)* **What is the fraction of stars chosen?** *($\frac{4}{5}$)*
- **What problem is shown here?** *($\frac{4}{5} \times 15$)* **What is $\frac{4}{5} \times 15$?** *(12)*
- Repeat with similar drawings.

Math and Music

Play Those Notes

 5–10 MIN **Logical/Mathematical** 

- Show students the musical notes shown below.
- **In $\frac{4}{4}$ time, a whole note lasts four beats and a half note 2 beats. For how long is a quarter note held?** *(1 beat)* **A sixteenth note?** *($\frac{1}{4}$ beat)*
- **Suppose I start a four-beat measure with a half note and a quarter note and finish with all sixteenth notes. How many sixteenth notes would I need?** *(4 sixteenth notes)*

whole note	half note	quarter note	eighth note	sixteenth note	thirty-second note

1	$\frac{1}{2}$	$\frac{1}{4}$	$\frac{1}{8}$	$\frac{1}{16}$	$\frac{1}{32}$

Objective Multiply a fraction times a whole number.

1 Warm Up

Activate Prior Knowledge Review repeated addition of fractions and review dividing whole numbers.

2 Teach

LEARN In Example A, discuss whether the answer will be greater or less than 8. Students should realize that the product will be less than 8 because they are multiplying 8 by a fraction that is less than 1.

Example B Before you discuss this example, have students predict whether the product $\frac{3}{4} \times 8$ will be different from or the same as $8 \times \frac{3}{4}$. Ask them to tell the property that can justify their prediction. *(Commutative Property of Multiplication)*

Lesson 5-1

Key Idea
There are different methods you can use to multiply whole numbers by fractions.

Think It Through
- I can **draw a picture** to show the main idea.
- I can **use what I know** about adding fractions to multiply with fractions.

Multiplying a Fraction and a Whole Number

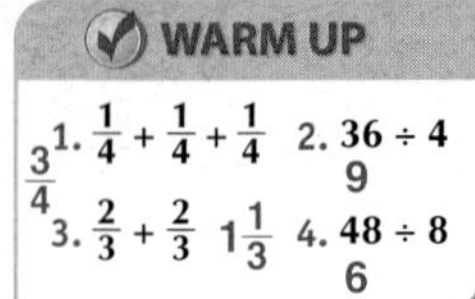

1. $\frac{1}{4}+\frac{1}{4}+\frac{1}{4}$ $\frac{3}{4}$
2. $36 \div 4$ 9
3. $\frac{2}{3}+\frac{2}{3}$ $1\frac{1}{3}$
4. $48 \div 8$ 6

LEARN

What does it mean to multiply a fraction and a whole number?

Example A

One batch of an oatmeal muffin recipe uses $\frac{3}{4}$ cup of rolled oats. How many cups of rolled oats are needed to make 8 batches?

Find $8 \times \frac{3}{4}$.

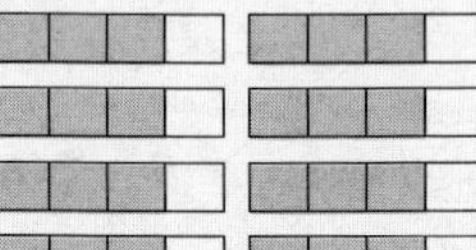

The model shows 8 groups of $\frac{3}{4}$.

$$8 \times \frac{3}{4} = \frac{3}{4}+\frac{3}{4}+\frac{3}{4}+\frac{3}{4}+\frac{3}{4}+\frac{3}{4}+\frac{3}{4}+\frac{3}{4} = \frac{24}{4} = 6.$$

Six cups are needed for 8 batches.

Example B

Seline read 8 books. Three fourths of them were mysteries. How many mystery books did Seline read?

Find $\frac{3}{4}$ of 8, or $\frac{3}{4} \times 8$.

The model shows $\frac{3}{4}$ of 8 wholes.

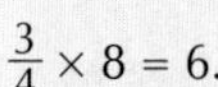

$\frac{3}{4} \times 8 = 6.$

Seline read 6 mystery books.

Talk About It

Both products are 6; $8 \times \frac{3}{4}$ represents 8 groups of $\frac{3}{4}$, and $\frac{3}{4}$ of 8 represents $\frac{3}{4}$ of 8 wholes.

1. How are the products $8 \times \frac{3}{4}$ and $\frac{3}{4}$ of 8 the same? How are they represented differently? See above.
2. Draw a number line to find $6 \times \frac{1}{6}$.

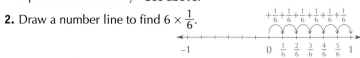

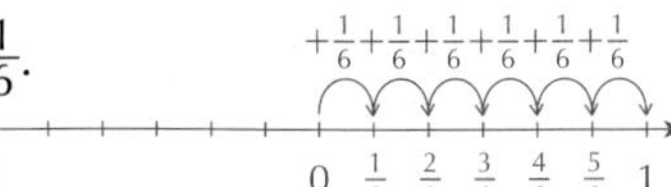

248

Reteaching — Below Level

Multiplying a Fraction and a Whole Number

R 5-1

Find $12 \times \frac{1}{4}$.

$12 \times \frac{1}{4}$ is the same as dividing 12 by 4.

$12 \div 4 = 3$

$12 \times \frac{1}{4} = 3$

Find $\frac{3}{5}$ of 15, or $\frac{3}{5} \times 15$.

$15 \div 5 = 3$, so $\frac{1}{5} \times 15 = 3$.

Since $\frac{3}{5}$ is 3 times $\frac{1}{5}$,

$\frac{3}{5} \times 15 = 3 \times \left(\frac{1}{5} \times 15\right) = 3 \times 3 = 9.$

$\frac{3}{5} \times 15 = 9$

Find each product.

1. $\frac{4}{5} \times 20 =$ 16
2. $\frac{6}{7}$ of 14 = 12
3. $24 \times \frac{3}{4} =$ 18
4. $\frac{2}{5}$ of 15 = 6
5. $400 \times \frac{3}{8} =$ 150
6. $\frac{7}{10}$ of 80 = 56
7. **Reasoning** Can you use division and mental math to find $\frac{2}{3}$ of 24? Why or why not?
   Yes, because 3 is the greatest common factor of 3 and 24.

The chart shows the average high temperatures for different months in Phoenix, Arizona.

Phoenix Weather

Month	Average High
February	70°F
May	93°F
July	105°F

8. What is $\frac{4}{5}$ the average temperature in July? 84°F
9. What is $\frac{1}{2}$ the average temperature in February? 35°F
10. What is $\frac{2}{3}$ the average temperature in May? 62°F

54 Use with Lesson 5-1.

Practice — On Level

Multiplying a Fraction and a Whole Number

P 5-1

Find each product.

1. $\frac{3}{4} \times 16 =$ 12
2. $\frac{5}{6} \times 30 =$ 25
3. $42 \times \frac{5}{6} =$ 35
4. $\frac{1}{8}$ of 72 = 9
5. $900 \times \frac{2}{3} =$ 600
6. $\frac{13}{20}$ of 100 = 65
7. **Reasoning** Without multiplying, tell which is greater, $\frac{5}{6}$ of 81 or $\frac{9}{10}$ of 81. Explain.
   Sample answer: $\frac{9}{10}$ of 81 because $\frac{9}{10}$ is greater than $\frac{5}{6}$

Driving Distances

Departure City	Destination City	Distance
Pittsfield, Massachusetts	Providence, Rhode Island	132 mi
Reno, Nevada	Wendover, Utah	400 mi

8. Mike drove $\frac{1}{3}$ of the distance between Pittsfield, Massachusetts, and Providence, Rhode Island. How far did he drive? 44 mi
9. Bimal drove $\frac{3}{5}$ of the distance between Reno, Nevada, and Wendover, Utah. How far did he drive? 240 mi
10. **Estimation** How many more miles does Bimal have to drive to get to Wendover, Utah? 160 mi

Test Prep

11. There are 25 students in Mr. Fitch's sixth-grade class. If $\frac{3}{5}$ of the students are girls, how many girls are in Mr. Fitch's class?
    A. 5 girls B. 10 girls (C.) 15 girls D. 20 girls
12. **Writing in Math** Explain how you would find the product of 36 and $\frac{2}{3}$.
    Write the problem as $36 \times \frac{2}{3}$.
    $36 \div 3 = 12$, so $\frac{1}{3} \times 36 = 12$.
    $\frac{2}{3} \times 36 = 2 \times (\frac{1}{3} \times 36) = 2 \times 12 = 24.$

54 Use with Lesson 5-1.

What are some ways to multiply a fraction and a whole number?

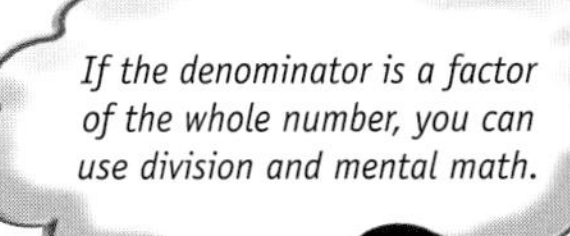

If the denominator is a factor of the whole number, you can use division and mental math.

Example C

Find $25 \times \frac{1}{5}$.

$25 \times \frac{1}{5}$ is the same as dividing 25 by 5.

$25 \div 5 = 5$

$25 \times \frac{1}{5} = 5$

Example D

Find $\frac{5}{6} \times 18$.

$18 \div 6 = 3$, so $\frac{1}{6} \times 18 = 3$.

Since $\frac{5}{6}$ is 5 times $\frac{1}{6}$,

$\frac{5}{6} \times 18 = 5 \times (\frac{1}{6} \times 18) = 5 \times 3 = 15.$

$\frac{5}{6} \times 18 = 15$

Talk About It

3. Use mental math to find the number of cups of rolled oats needed for 20 batches in Example A. **15 cups**
4. Could you use division and mental math to find $\frac{3}{4}$ of 18? Explain. **No; 4 is not a factor of 18.**
5. **Number Sense** Explain how to find $\frac{7}{10}$ of 100. **Find $\frac{1}{10} \times 100$ and multiply by 7 to get 70.**

CHECK

For another example, see Set 5-1 on p. 292.

Find each product.

1. $12 \times \frac{1}{3}$ **4**
2. $\frac{5}{6} \times 24$ **20**
3. $\frac{2}{3}$ of 27 **18**
4. $\frac{7}{8}$ of 80 **70**
5. $45 \times \frac{3}{5}$ **27**
6. $\frac{1}{9} \times 36$ **4**
7. $\frac{4}{7}$ of 28 **16**
8. $\frac{11}{13} \times 39$ **33**
9. **Reasoning** Without multiplying, tell whether $18 \times \frac{8}{9}$ is greater than or less than 18. How do you know? **Less than 18; I know that $18 \times 1 = 18$, and since $\frac{8}{9} < 1$, the product $18 \times \frac{8}{9}$ must be less than 18.**

Examples C and D Have students also model these two examples using fraction strips or counters.

Ongoing Assessment

Talk About It: Question 1

If students need help with the comparison,

then explain that the word "of" before a number usually means *multiply*. Suggest that they look at the pictures to see differences.

CHECK

Error Intervention

If students have difficulty using mental math to find the answers,

then suggest they first model the problems using fraction strips or counters. *(Also see* Reteaching, *p. 248B.)*

Enrichment — Above Level

Presidential Multiplication

E 5-1 NUMBER SENSE

Find each product. Then cross out your answers in the box to solve the riddle.

1. $\frac{3}{4}$ of 80 = **60**
2. $25 \times \frac{1}{5}$ = **5**
3. $\frac{1}{3}$ of 33 = **11**
4. $\frac{5}{6} \times 54$ = **45**
5. $\frac{3}{8} \times 64$ = **24**
6. $\frac{3}{10}$ of 600 = **180**
7. $90 \times \frac{8}{9}$ = **80**
8. $\frac{7}{16}$ of 32 = **14**
9. $\frac{11}{12}$ of 144 = **132**
10. $\frac{19}{20} \times 1{,}000$ = **950**
11. $280 \times \frac{3}{7}$ = **120**
12. $\frac{1}{2}$ of 878 = **439**
13. $\frac{2}{9} \times 36$ = **8**
14. $160 \times \frac{5}{8}$ = **100**
15. $\frac{1}{7}$ of 63 = **9**
16. $\frac{4}{15} \times 75$ = **20**
17. $500 \times \frac{21}{25}$ = **420**
18. $\frac{7}{12}$ of 108 = **63**
19. $\frac{9}{11} \times 99$ = **81**
20. $\frac{199}{200}$ of 1,000 = **995**
21. $400 \times \frac{1}{10}$ = **40**
22. $\frac{7}{8} \times 176$ = **154**

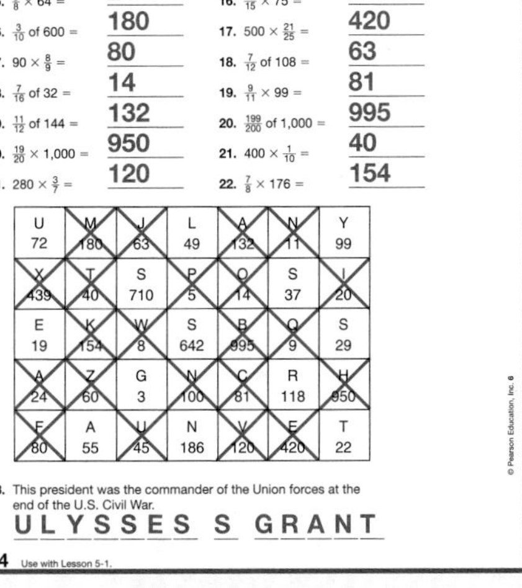

U 72	M 180	J 63	L 49	A 132	N 11	Y 99
X 439	T 40	S 710	P 5	O 14	S 37	I 20
E 19	K 154	W 8	S 642	B 995	Q 9	S 29
A 24	Z 60	G 3	N 100	C 81	R 118	H 950
F 80	A 55	U 45	N 186	V 120	E 420	T 22

23. This president was the commander of the Union forces at the end of the U.S. Civil War. **U L Y S S E S S G R A N T**

Problem Solving

Multiplying a Fraction and a Whole Number

PS 5-1

Field Trip At Kennedy Elementary School, 130 students went on field trips. One-half of them traveled to the science museum. Of the remaining students, $\frac{3}{5}$ visited the ice cream factory. The rest of the students went to an art museum.

1. How many students went to the science museum? **65 students**
2. How many students visited the ice cream factory? **39 students**
3. How many students went to the art museum? **26 students**

School Lunches The school cafeteria offers three lunch choices each day. Students also have a choice of bringing a packed lunch from home. The graph shows the fraction of students who chose each lunch option on Tuesday.

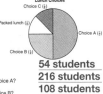

Lunch Choices

Choice C ($\frac{1}{8}$)
Packed lunch ($\frac{1}{8}$)
Choice A ($\frac{1}{2}$)
Choice B ($\frac{1}{4}$)

4. On Tuesday, 432 students attended school. How many students brought packed lunches? **54 students**
5. How many students bought lunch Choice A? **216 students**
6. How many students chose lunch Choice B? **108 students**
7. **Writing in Math** Is 45 a reasonable answer for $9 \times \frac{1}{5}$? Write a complete sentence to explain why or why not. **Sample answer: No, it is not a reasonable answer because when you multiply a number by a fraction less than 1, the answer should be less than the number you started with.**

3 Practice

Exercises 24–27 In these exercises, students must first use the graph to identify a fraction. Then they multiply that fraction by 60 to find the answer. You may wish to discuss the feasibility of modeling to find these answers.

TEST TALK **Exercise 30** If students need help, suggest that they first draw a picture to model the problem.

Reading Assist Summarize Have students summarize the process illustrated in Example D for multiplying a fraction by a whole number. *(Sample answer: Divide the whole number by the denominator of the fraction. Then multiply the result by the numerator.)*

PRACTICE *For more practice, see Set 5-1 on p. 295.*

A Skills and Understanding

Find each product.

10. $\frac{2}{3} \times 12$ **8** **11.** $15 \times \frac{4}{5}$ **12** **12.** $\frac{3}{10} \times 90$ **27** **13.** $45 \times \frac{8}{9}$ **40**

14. $\frac{2}{5}$ of 35 **14** **15.** $\frac{5}{16}$ of 48 **15** **16.** $\frac{7}{10}$ of 800 **560** **17.** $\frac{1}{9}$ of 54 **6**

18. $\frac{5}{7} \times 28$ **20** **19.** $72 \times \frac{5}{6}$ **60** **20.** $\frac{9}{10}$ of 50 **45** **21.** $\frac{24}{25}$ of 100 **96**

22. While 10 is not a factor of 15, you can find $\frac{1}{10}$ of 15 by dividing 15 by 10; 15 ÷ 10 = 1.5 and 1.5 × 3 = 4.5

22. Reasoning Can you use division and mental math to find $15 \times \frac{3}{10}$? Explain. **See above.**

23. Number Sense Find $30 \times \frac{3}{5}$. Change the numbers to decimals and multiply. Are the products the same? Explain.
18; 30 × 0.6 = 18; Yes. $\frac{3}{5}$ is equal to 0.6, so the product will remain the same.

B Reasoning and Problem Solving

Math and Music

The graph at the right shows the fraction of students that make up each section of a 60-member orchestra. Find the number of students in each section.

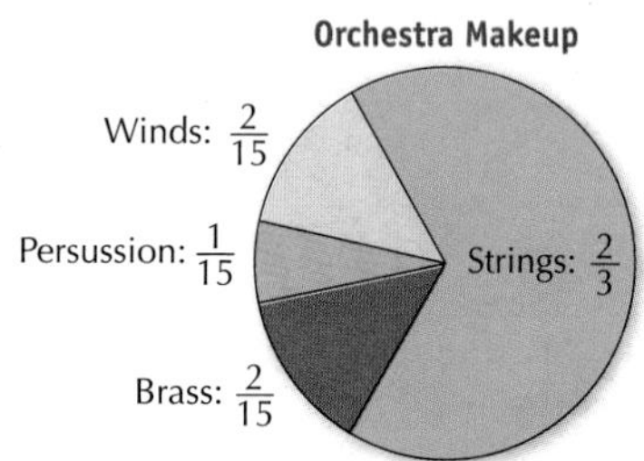

24. Strings **40 students** **25.** Brass **8 students**

26. Percussion **4 students** **27.** Winds **8 students**

28. What fraction of the orchestra is shown by the brass and percussion sections combined? $\frac{1}{5}$

29. The two dozen roses that Tamika ordered to distribute at the final curtain call are shown at the right. She gives half of them to the conductor. She gives half of the remaining roses to the pianist and the other half to the vocalist. How many roses does the vocalist get? **6 roses**

30. Writing in Math Is the explanation below correct? If not, tell why and write a correct response.

> Find $42 \times \frac{6}{7}$.
>
> $42 \times \frac{6}{7} = 42 \times \frac{1}{6} = 7$ and $7 \times 6 = 42$.

No. The student should have multiplied 42 by $\frac{1}{7}$, not $\frac{1}{6}$. $42 \times \frac{6}{7} = 42 \times \frac{1}{7} \times 6 = 6 \times 6 = 36$.

250

Test-Taking Practice

Test-Taking Practice, Item 1, p. 251 There are two parts to the question; the answer and explanation are each worth two points. Remind students that they should answer as much as they can since partial credit is given for this type of problem.

Discuss the sample responses shown and compare them to papers produced by your students.

4-point answer Answer is correct; explanation shows complete understanding of multiplying fractions.

> Mr. Lorenzini will need 4c of flour.
> I multiplied $\frac{2}{3}$ by 6 and got 4.

PRACTICE

C Extensions

31. **Algebra** Simplify the expression $20 - \frac{1}{6}(55 + 35)$. **5**

32. **Reasoning** Two thirds of a number is 18. Find the number. **27**

Mixed Review and Test Prep

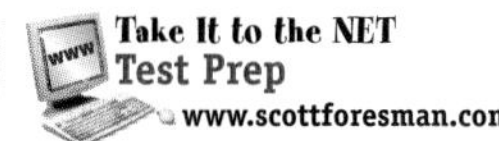

Tell whether an exact answer or estimate is needed. Then solve.

33. It costs $450 per day to maintain and run the arboretum. Admission to the arboretum is $2.50. Will the arboretum make a profit if at least 200 people pay admission each day? Explain. **Estimate; yes; I can estimate using mental math; $2.50 × 200 = $500, which is $50 more than $450.**

Find each sum or difference. Tell what computation method you used. **Computation methods may vary.**

34. $10\frac{1}{5} - 5\frac{3}{4}$ **$4\frac{9}{20}$ pencil and paper**

35. $\frac{4}{7} + \frac{8}{9}$ **$1\frac{29}{63}$ pencil and paper**

36. $6 - 3\frac{2}{5}$ **$2\frac{3}{5}$ mental math**

37. **Algebra** Find $4 + 2 \times 3 - 4 \div 2$.

A. 3 B. 7 **(C.) 8** D. 16

Enrichment

Writing Repeating Decimals as Fractions

A short way of writing the repeating decimal 0.323232... is $0.\overline{32}$. You can write this repeating decimal as a fraction.

Write $1n = 0.323232...$ Since two digits repeat, multiply both sides by 100 to get $100n = 32.323232...$

Subtract and solve for n.

$$\begin{aligned} 100n &= 32.323232... \\ -\ 1n &= 0.323232... \\ \hline 99n &= 32 \\ n &= \frac{32}{99} \end{aligned}$$

To write $0.1\overline{643}$ as a fraction, write $1n = 0.1643643...$

Three digits repeat, so multiply both sides by 1,000 to get $1{,}000n = 164.3643643...$

Subtract and solve for n. Simplify.

$$\begin{aligned} 1{,}000n &= 164.3643643... \\ -\ 1n &= 0.1643643... \\ \hline 999n &= 164.2 \\ n &= \frac{164.2}{999} = \frac{1{,}642}{9{,}990} = \frac{821}{4{,}995} \end{aligned}$$

For 1–4, write each decimal as a fraction with whole numbers in the numerator and denominator.

1. $0.\overline{4}$ **$\frac{4}{9}$**
2. $0.\overline{25}$ **$\frac{25}{99}$**
3. $0.\overline{153}$ **$\frac{17}{111}$**
4. $0.2\overline{73}$ **$\frac{271}{990}$**

3-point answer Answer is partially correct; explanation shows understanding of multiplying fractions.

Mr. Lorenzini will need $\frac{12}{3}$ c.
Multiply $\frac{2}{3}$ by 6.

2-point answer Answer is correct; explanation shows little understanding of multiplying fractions.

Mr. Lorenzini needs 4 c. of flour.
Just multiply.

Leveled Practice

Below Level Ex. 10–19, 22–26, 29, 30, 33–37

On Level Ex. 10–18 even, 19–30, 33–37

Above Level Ex. 11–21 odd, 22–37

Early Finishers Have students work with partners to create a 3-by-3 grid containing problems like those in this lesson. Then have them play tic-tac-toe. Students select a square, but must give the correct product to place an X or an O.

Enrichment The key feature of this technique is to identify the number of digits in the repeating pattern and to then multiply the decimal by 10 to that power. In Exercise 1, students need to multiply by 10^1 or 10; in Exercise 2, they multiply by 10^2 or 100.

4 Assess

Journal Idea Have students explain how to use a model to find the product $\frac{5}{6} \times 12$.

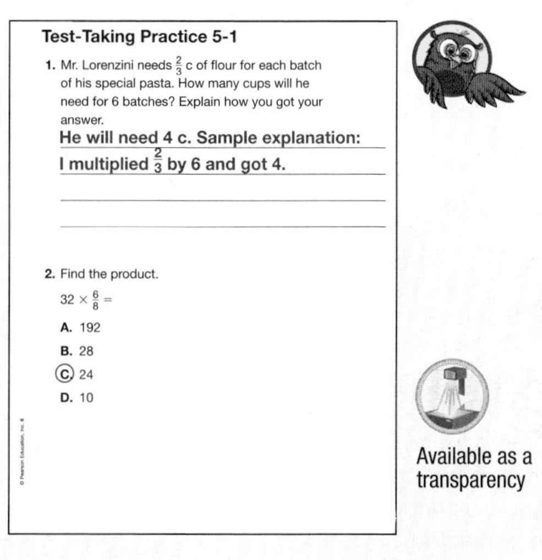

Test-Taking Practice 5-1

1. Mr. Lorenzini needs $\frac{2}{3}$ c of flour for each batch of his special pasta. How many cups will he need for 6 batches? Explain how you got your answer.
He will need 4 c. Sample explanation: I multiplied $\frac{2}{3}$ by 6 and got 4.

2. Find the product.
$32 \times \frac{6}{8} =$
A. 192
B. 28
(C) 24
D. 10

Available as a transparency

Lesson Organizer

Quick Lesson Overview

Objective Give the product of two fractions.

Math Understanding When we multiply two fractions that are both less than 1, the product is smaller than either fraction.

Vocabulary Greatest common factor (GCF) (p. 150)

Professional Development Note

Research Base

Susan Lamon, a leading figure in the research on fractions, recommends an area model-operator approach for multiplication of fractions (Lamon, 1999). That is, a rectangle is used to show one fraction and then the other fraction is used as an operator to obtain a fractional part of this region. This is the approach used in this lesson.

NCTM Standards

- Numbers and Operations

(For a complete correlation to the NCTM Standards and Grades 6–8 Expectations, see pages 246G–H.)

Getting Started

Spiral Review

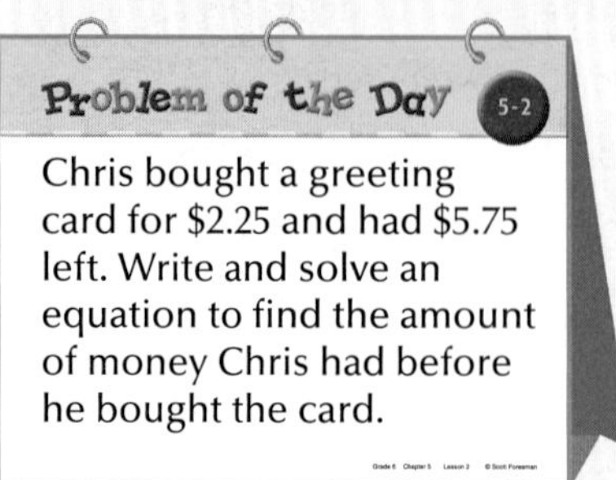
Problem of the Day 5-2

Chris bought a greeting card for $2.25 and had $5.75 left. Write and solve an equation to find the amount of money Chris had before he bought the card.

Topics Reviewed

- Solving equations; adding decimals
- Problem-Solving Strategy: Write an Equation

Answer Chris started with $8.00.

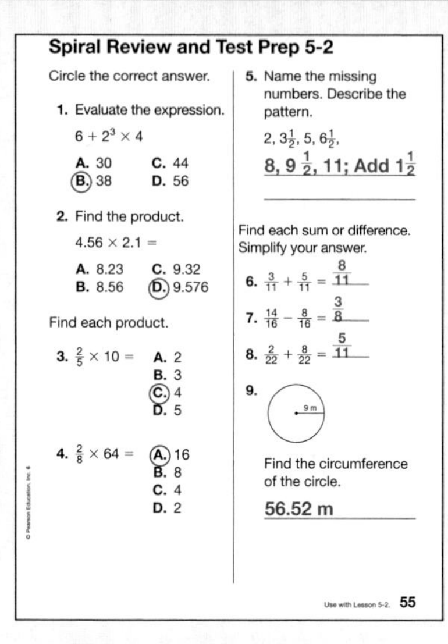
Spiral Review and Test Prep 5-2

Circle the correct answer.

1. Evaluate the expression. $6 + 2^3 \times 4$
   A. 30 (B.) 38 C. 44 D. 56
2. Find the product. $4.56 \times 2.1 =$
   A. 8.23 B. 8.56 C. 9.32 (D.) 9.576

Find each product.

3. $\frac{2}{5} \times 10 =$ A. 2 B. 3 (C.) 4 D. 5
4. $\frac{2}{8} \times 64 =$ (A.) 16 B. 8 C. 4 D. 2
5. Name the missing numbers. Describe the pattern. $2, 3\frac{1}{2}, 5, 6\frac{1}{2},$ $8, 9\frac{1}{2}, 11$; Add $1\frac{1}{2}$

Find each sum or difference. Simplify your answer.

6. $\frac{3}{11} + \frac{5}{11} = \frac{8}{11}$
7. $\frac{14}{16} - \frac{8}{16} = \frac{3}{8}$
8. $\frac{2}{22} + \frac{8}{22} = \frac{5}{11}$
9. Find the circumference of the circle. 56.52 m

Use with Lesson 5-2. 55

Available as a transparency and as a blackline master

Topics Reviewed

1. Order of operations; **2.** Multiplying decimals; **3.–4.** Multiplying a fraction and a whole number; **5.** Look for a pattern; **6.–8.** Adding and subtracting fractions with like denominators; **9.** Finding circumference

Investigating the Concept

Paper Folding

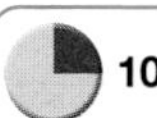
10–15 MIN **Social/Cooperative/Kinesthetic**

Materials *(per pair)* sheet of paper; 2 markers or colored pencils

What to Do

- Direct each pair to start with a sheet of paper and two markers or colored pencils. Have Partner 1 fold the paper vertically into eight equal parts and shade $\frac{5}{8}$. Then have Partner 2 fold the paper horizontally into four equal parts and, with a different color, shade $\frac{3}{4}$.
- **Into how many equal parts is the paper divided?** *(32 parts)* **How many are shaded twice?** *(15 parts)* **Write the problem shown by the folds.** $(\frac{5}{8} \times \frac{3}{4} = \frac{15}{32})$
- Write $\frac{5}{8} \times \frac{3}{4} = \frac{15}{32}$ on the board. Show students how they could multiply the numerators and denominators to find the product.

Ongoing Assessment

- **Number Sense Compare the product of the two fractions $\frac{5}{8}$ and $\frac{3}{4}$ to the two fractions.** *(The product will be less than the smaller fraction because you are finding a part of that smaller fraction.)*

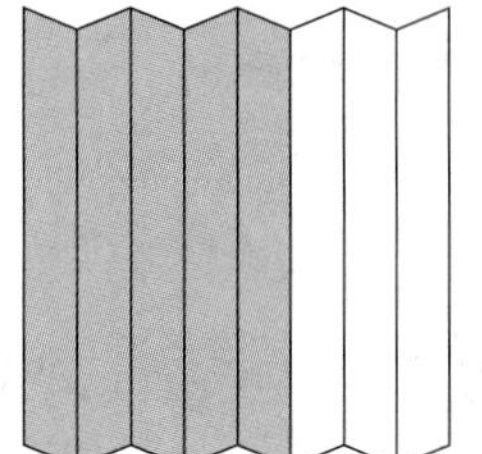

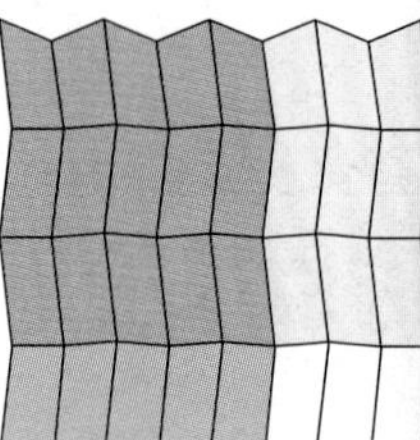

Reaching All Learners

Writing in Math

Developing a Story

 10–15 MIN **Linguistic** 

- Give each group a multiplication exercise, such as $\frac{2}{3} \times \frac{5}{6}$.
- **Each group member is to write one line of a story which can be represented by $\frac{2}{3} \times \frac{5}{6}$. The group will then read the story to the class.**
- **What is the solution to your problem?** *($\frac{5}{9}$)*
- Repeat the activity. Have a different student in each group start the story.

> Student 1: I found $\frac{2}{3}$ of a pizza in the refrigerator.
> Student 2: I decided to eat $\frac{5}{6}$ of the pizza.
> Student 3: What part of the pizza did I eat?

Access Content

English Language Learners

Finding Fractions of Fractions

 10–15 MIN **Auditory/Visual/Spatial** 

- Have a volunteer read the word problem on page 252. Have groups discuss the questions below.
- **What do you know?** *($\frac{4}{5}$ of the seating is reserved. Faculty members occupy $\frac{1}{6}$ of the reserved seats.)* **What do you need to find out?** *(What fraction of the total number of seats is for faculty?)* **Express what you need to find out as a math problem.** *($\frac{1}{6} \times \frac{4}{5}$)*
- Have students talk through showing the information in a chart.

Already Know	Need to Find Out	Math Problem
$\frac{4}{5}$ seats reserved	fraction of total seats for faculty	$\frac{1}{6} \times \frac{4}{5}$
$\frac{1}{6}$ of reserved seats for faculty		

Reteaching

Count It Out

 10–15 MIN **Kinesthetic/Visual/Spatial** 

Materials *(per pair)* Red, yellow, and blue tiles or Teaching Tool 9: 15 of each color

- Have Partner 1 model 15 with 15 red tiles.
- **How many tiles are $\frac{2}{3}$ of the tiles?** *(10 tiles)* Have Partner 2 replace 10 red tiles with 10 yellow tiles.
- **How many tiles are $\frac{1}{2}$ of the yellow tiles?** *(5 tiles)* Have Partner 1 replace 5 yellow tiles with 5 blue tiles.
- **What fraction of the whole set do the blue tiles represent?** *($\frac{1}{3}$)* **What is $\frac{1}{2} \times \frac{2}{3}$?** *($\frac{1}{3}$)*

Math and Technology

Finding Products

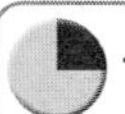 10–15 MIN **Visual** 

Materials *(per pair)* Calculator

- Have students enter a fraction into their calculator.
- Have them multiply the fraction by whole numbers and proper fractions and then simplify and record each product.
- Ask students to explain whether the products increased or decreased as they multiplied their fractions by a whole number or fraction.

Objective Give the product of two fractions.

1 Warm Up

Activate Prior Knowledge Review simplifying fractions by dividing the numerator and denominator by the *greatest common factor* (GCF).

2 Teach

LEARN Before studying the details of Example A, ask students if they think the answer will be more or less than $\frac{1}{6}$.

Example B After discussing the example, you might ask students to discuss whether they think simplifying before multiplying makes the solution easier.

Lesson 5-2

Key Idea
You can use common factors to help you multiply fractions.

Vocabulary
- greatest common factor (GCF) (p. 150)

Multiplying Fractions

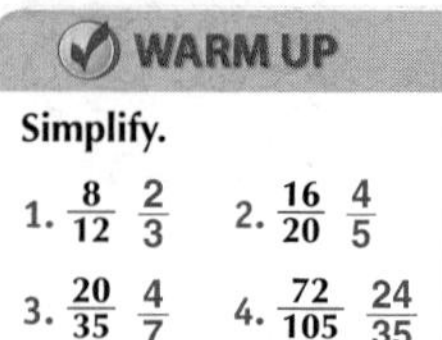

WARM UP

Simplify.

1. $\frac{8}{12}$ $\frac{2}{3}$
2. $\frac{16}{20}$ $\frac{4}{5}$
3. $\frac{20}{35}$ $\frac{4}{7}$
4. $\frac{72}{105}$ $\frac{24}{35}$

LEARN

How do you find products of fractions?

For Newton School's award ceremony, $\frac{4}{5}$ of the auditorium seating is reserved. Faculty members occupy $\frac{1}{6}$ of that space. What part of the reserved space is occupied by faculty?

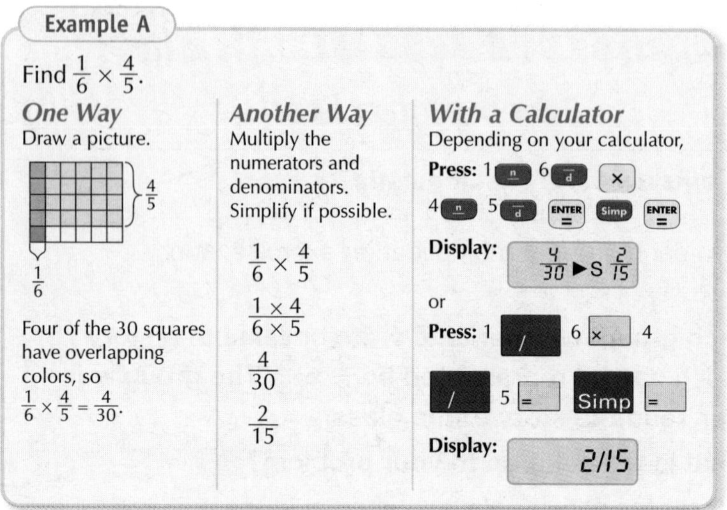

Example A

Find $\frac{1}{6} \times \frac{4}{5}$.

One Way
Draw a picture.

Four of the 30 squares have overlapping colors, so $\frac{1}{6} \times \frac{4}{5} = \frac{4}{30}$.

Another Way
Multiply the numerators and denominators. Simplify if possible.

$\frac{1}{6} \times \frac{4}{5}$

$\frac{1 \times 4}{6 \times 5}$

$\frac{4}{30}$

$\frac{2}{15}$

With a Calculator
Depending on your calculator,

Press: 1 n 6 d × 4 n 5 d ENTER Simp ENTER

Display: 4/30 ▶S 2/15

or

Press: 1 / 6 × 4 / 5 = Simp =

Display: 2/15

Two fifteenths of the reserved space is for faculty.

How can you simplify before you multiply?

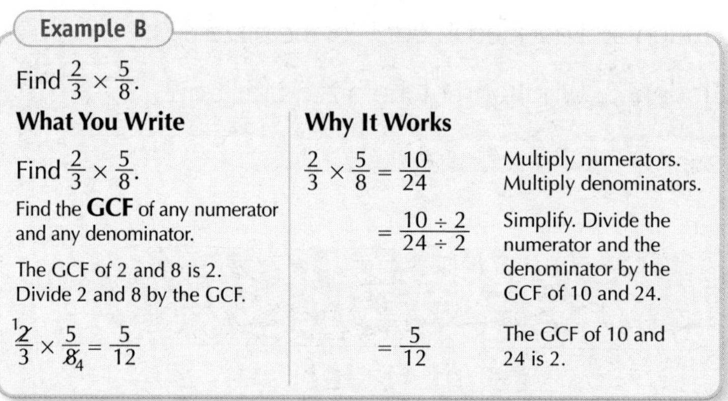

Example B

Find $\frac{2}{3} \times \frac{5}{8}$.

What You Write

Find $\frac{2}{3} \times \frac{5}{8}$.

Find the **GCF** of any numerator and any denominator.

The GCF of 2 and 8 is 2. Divide 2 and 8 by the GCF.

$\frac{{}^{1}\not{2}}{3} \times \frac{5}{\not{8}_{4}} = \frac{5}{12}$

Why It Works

$\frac{2}{3} \times \frac{5}{8} = \frac{10}{24}$ Multiply numerators. Multiply denominators.

$= \frac{10 \div 2}{24 \div 2}$ Simplify. Divide the numerator and the denominator by the GCF of 10 and 24.

$= \frac{5}{12}$ The GCF of 10 and 24 is 2.

TEST TALK

Think It Through
I can **use the greatest common factor** to simplify the fractions before multiplying.

252

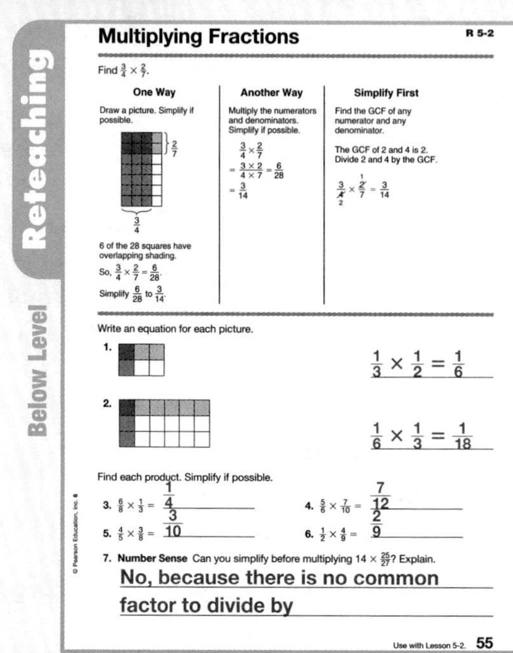

Below Level — Reteaching

Multiplying Fractions R 5-2

Find $\frac{3}{4} \times \frac{2}{7}$.

One Way: Draw a picture. Simplify if possible. 6 of the 28 squares have overlapping shading. So, $\frac{3}{4} \times \frac{2}{7} = \frac{6}{28}$. Simplify $\frac{6}{28}$ to $\frac{3}{14}$.

Another Way: Multiply the numerators and denominators. Simplify if possible. $\frac{3}{4} \times \frac{2}{7} = \frac{3 \times 2}{4 \times 7} = \frac{6}{28} = \frac{3}{14}$

Simplify First: Find the GCF of any numerator and any denominator. The GCF of 2 and 4 is 2. Divide 2 and 4 by the GCF. $\frac{3}{4} \times \frac{2}{7} = \frac{3}{14}$

Write an equation for each picture.

1. $\frac{1}{3} \times \frac{1}{2} = \frac{1}{6}$
2. $\frac{1}{6} \times \frac{1}{3} = \frac{1}{18}$

Find each product. Simplify if possible.

3. $\frac{6}{8} \times \frac{1}{3} =$ $\frac{1}{4}$
4. $\frac{5}{6} \times \frac{7}{10} =$ $\frac{7}{12}$
5. $\frac{4}{5} \times \frac{3}{8} =$ $\frac{3}{10}$
6. $\frac{1}{2} \times \frac{4}{9} =$ $\frac{2}{9}$
7. Number Sense Can you simplify before multiplying $14 \times \frac{25}{37}$? Explain. No, because there is no common factor to divide by

Use with Lesson 5-2. 55

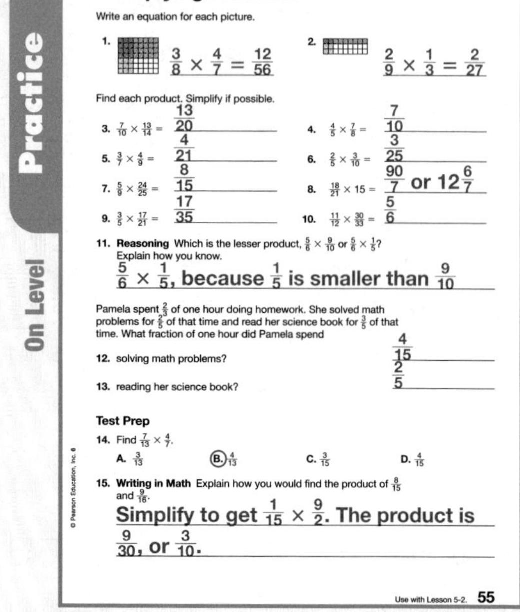

On Level — Practice

Multiplying Fractions P 5-2

Write an equation for each picture.

1. $\frac{3}{8} \times \frac{4}{7} = \frac{12}{56}$
2. $\frac{2}{9} \times \frac{1}{3} = \frac{2}{27}$

Find each product. Simplify if possible.

3. $\frac{7}{10} \times \frac{13}{14} =$ $\frac{13}{20}$
4. $\frac{4}{5} \times \frac{7}{8} =$ $\frac{7}{10}$
5. $\frac{3}{7} \times \frac{4}{9} =$ $\frac{4}{21}$
6. $\frac{2}{5} \times \frac{3}{10} =$ $\frac{3}{25}$
7. $\frac{5}{6} \times \frac{24}{25} =$ $\frac{8}{15}$
8. $\frac{18}{21} \times 15 =$ $\frac{90}{7}$ or $12\frac{6}{7}$
9. $\frac{3}{5} \times \frac{17}{21} =$ $\frac{17}{35}$
10. $\frac{11}{12} \times \frac{30}{33} =$ $\frac{5}{6}$
11. Reasoning Which is the lesser product, $\frac{5}{6} \times \frac{9}{10}$ or $\frac{5}{6} \times \frac{1}{5}$? Explain how you know. $\frac{5}{6} \times \frac{1}{5}$, because $\frac{1}{5}$ is smaller than $\frac{9}{10}$

Pamela spent $\frac{2}{3}$ of one hour doing homework. She solved math problems for $\frac{2}{5}$ of that time and read her science book for $\frac{3}{5}$ of that time. What fraction of one hour did Pamela spend

12. solving math problems? $\frac{4}{15}$
13. reading her science book? $\frac{2}{5}$

Test Prep

14. Find $\frac{7}{13} \times \frac{4}{7}$.
A. $\frac{3}{13}$ (B.) $\frac{4}{13}$ C. $\frac{3}{15}$ D. $\frac{4}{15}$

15. Writing in Math Explain how you would find the product of $\frac{6}{15}$ and $\frac{9}{16}$. Simplify to get $\frac{1}{15} \times \frac{9}{2}$. The product is $\frac{9}{30}$, or $\frac{3}{10}$.

Use with Lesson 5-2. 55

Example C

Find $\frac{3}{4} \times \frac{8}{9}$.

What You Write

Find $\frac{3}{4} \times \frac{8}{9}$. The GCF of 3 and 9 is 3. The GCF of 4 and 8 is 4.

$\frac{{}^{1}\cancel{3}}{{}_{1}\cancel{4}} \times \frac{\cancel{8}^{2}}{\cancel{9}_{3}} = \frac{2}{3}$ Divide the numerators and denominators by the GCFs.

Why It Works

$\frac{3}{4} \times \frac{8}{9} = \frac{24}{36}$ Multiply numerators. Multiply denominators.

$= \frac{24 \div 12}{36 \div 12}$ Simplify. Divide the numerator and the denominator by the GCF of 24 and 36. The GCF of 24 and 36 is 12.

$= \frac{2}{3}$

Sometimes you can't find a fraction of a whole number mentally.

Example D

Find $75 \times \frac{11}{30}$.

$75 \times \frac{11}{30} = \frac{75}{1} \times \frac{11}{30}$ Since 75 is a rational number, you can write it as $\frac{75}{1}$.

$= \frac{{}^{5}\cancel{75}}{1} \times \frac{11}{\cancel{30}_{2}}$ Divide the numerator and denominator by the GCF.

$= \frac{55}{2} = 27\frac{1}{2}$ Multiply. Write the product as a mixed number.

Talk About It

1. The answer would be $\frac{12}{18}$, which is not in simplest form.

1. Suppose in Example C, 4 and 8 were divided by 2 instead of the GCF. How would the answer be different? **See above**

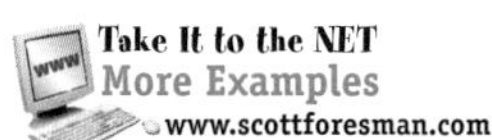

2. Would writing 75 as $\frac{300}{4}$ change the answer in Example D? Explain.
No. After simplification the answer would be the same.

CHECK

For another example, see Set 5-2 on p. 292.

Write an equation for each picture.

1. $\frac{2}{3} \times \frac{1}{4} = \frac{2}{12}$

2. 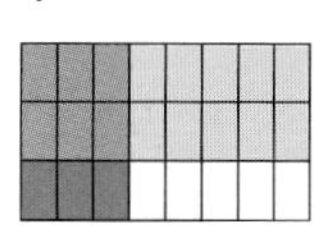 $\frac{2}{3} \times \frac{3}{8} = \frac{6}{24}$

3. 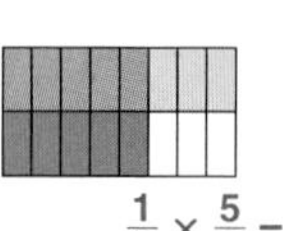 $\frac{1}{2} \times \frac{5}{8} = \frac{5}{16}$

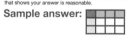

4. 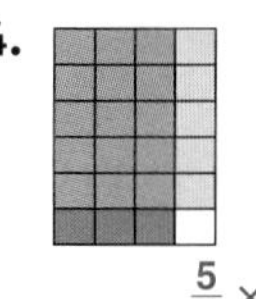 $\frac{5}{6} \times \frac{3}{4} = \frac{15}{24}$

Find each product. Simplify if possible.

5. $\frac{6}{11} \times \frac{4}{9}$ **$\frac{8}{33}$**
6. $\frac{2}{3} \times \frac{9}{10}$ **$\frac{3}{5}$**
7. $\frac{8}{15} \times \frac{5}{12}$ **$\frac{2}{9}$**
8. $\frac{14}{25} \times \frac{15}{21}$ **$\frac{2}{5}$**
9. $\frac{3}{4} \times 10$ **$7\frac{1}{2}$**
10. $\frac{5}{8} \times \frac{3}{10}$ **$\frac{3}{16}$**
11. $\frac{10}{12} \times \frac{3}{5}$ **$\frac{1}{2}$**
12. $18 \times \frac{3}{4}$ **$13\frac{1}{2}$**

13. **Number Sense** Find $\frac{1}{2} \times \frac{4}{5}$. Write the fractions as decimals and multiply. Are the products the same? Explain. **$\frac{2}{5}$; 0.5 × 0.8 = 0.4; Yes. $\frac{2}{5}$ = 0.4, so the products are the same.**

Example C Before studying this example, ask students to identify any common factors they see in the numerators and denominators of the multiplication problem $\frac{3}{4} \times \frac{8}{9}$.

Ongoing Assessment

Talk About It: Question 2

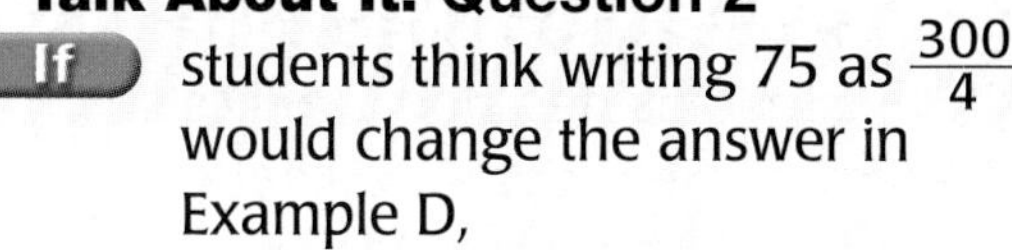

If students think writing 75 as $\frac{300}{4}$ would change the answer in Example D,

then ask them to compare 75 and $\frac{300}{4}$. If they do not see that these numbers are equal, ask them to simplify $\frac{300}{4}$.

CHECK

Error Intervention

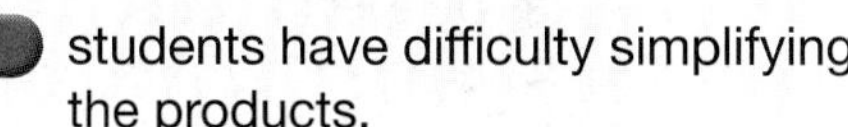

If students have difficulty simplifying the products,

then encourage them to simplify the fractions before multiplying, as it is often easier to find the GCF for the smaller numbers making up the fractions before they are multiplied. *(Also see* Reteaching, *p. 252B.)*

Enrichment — Above Level

What's the Fraction Pattern?

E 5-2 PATTERNS

The fractions in the chart form a pattern.

1. Complete the chart.

$\frac{1}{2}$	$\frac{1}{3}$	$\frac{1}{4}$	$\frac{1}{5}$	$\frac{1}{6}$	$\frac{1}{7}$	$\frac{1}{8}$	$\frac{1}{9}$
1	$\frac{2}{3}$	$\frac{1}{2}$	$\frac{2}{5}$	$\frac{1}{3}$	$\frac{2}{7}$	$\frac{1}{4}$	$\frac{2}{9}$
$1\frac{1}{2}$	1	$\frac{3}{4}$	$\frac{3}{5}$	$\frac{1}{2}$	$\frac{3}{7}$	$\frac{3}{8}$	$\frac{1}{3}$
2	$1\frac{1}{3}$	1	$\frac{4}{5}$	$\frac{2}{3}$	$\frac{4}{7}$	$\frac{1}{2}$	$\frac{4}{9}$
$2\frac{1}{2}$	$1\frac{2}{3}$	$1\frac{1}{4}$	1	$\frac{5}{6}$	$\frac{5}{7}$	$\frac{5}{8}$	$\frac{5}{9}$

2. Describe the pattern.
Fractions in the 1st row are multiplied by 2 to get the numbers in the 2nd row, by 3 to get the numbers in the 3rd row, by 4 to get the numbers in the 4th row, and by 5 to get the numbers in the 5th row.

3. How would you find the numbers in the 100th row of this pattern?
Multiply each fraction in the first row by 100.

Problem Solving

Multiplying Fractions

PS 5-2

Pizza The students at Franklin School sold pizzas for a fund-raising project. Sixth graders sold $\frac{1}{3}$ of all the pizzas.

1. Students in Ms. Johnson's class sold $\frac{1}{4}$ of all the pizzas sold by the sixth grade. Ms. Johnson's class represents what fraction of the total number of pizzas sold? Draw a picture that shows your answer is reasonable. **$\frac{1}{12}$**
Sample answer:

2. If 408 pizzas were sold, how many did Ms. Johnson's class sell? **34 pizzas**

3. Fourth graders sold $\frac{1}{2}$ of all the pizzas that were not sold by sixth graders. What fraction of the total pizzas did the fourth graders sell?
$\frac{1}{3}$ of the total pizzas

Low on Fuel? The fuel gauge at the right shows how much gas was in the tank when the Miller family left for their vacation. Use the fuel gauge for 4–6.

Fuel Gauge

4. After the Millers had used $\frac{1}{2}$ of the gas they started with, what fraction of the full tank was left?
$\frac{3}{8}$ of a full tank was left

5. The Millers bought more gasoline after they used $\frac{2}{3}$ of the gas they started with. What fraction of the tank of gas did they need to buy in order to have a full tank?
$\frac{3}{4}$ of a tank

6. **Writing in Math** Write a sentence that explains your answer to Exercise 5.
Sample answer: $\frac{2}{3} \times \frac{3}{4} = \frac{1}{2}$; $\frac{3}{4} - \frac{1}{2} = \frac{1}{4}$; The Millers needed $\frac{3}{4}$ of a tank more to fill it.

3 Practice

Exercises 18–25 It may help some students to continue to draw diagrams as models to help them represent and solve the problems.

Exercise 30 Suggest that students describe Candice's steps in order. As a check that the product is correct, students may multiply the fractions first and then simplify the result.

Reading Assist Summarize Ask students to summarize the procedure illustrated in Example C for finding the product of two fractions. *(Look for greatest common factors of the numerators and denominators. Divide the numerators and denominators by their greatest common factors. Then find the product of the simplified numerators and the product of the simplified denominators.)*

PRACTICE

For more practice, see Set 5-2 on p. 295.

A Skills and Understanding

Write an equation for each picture.

14. 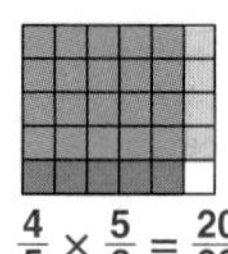 $\frac{4}{5} \times \frac{5}{6} = \frac{20}{30}$

15. 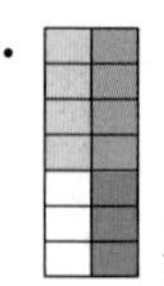 $\frac{1}{2} \times \frac{4}{7} = \frac{4}{14}$

16. 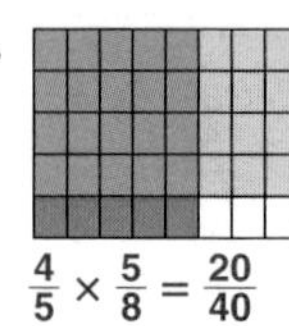 $\frac{4}{5} \times \frac{5}{8} = \frac{20}{40}$

17. 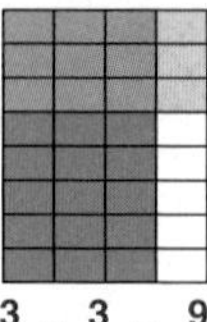 $\frac{3}{8} \times \frac{3}{4} = \frac{9}{32}$

Find each product. Simplify if possible.

18. $\frac{9}{14} \times \frac{28}{29}$ $\frac{18}{29}$
19. $\frac{4}{9} \times \frac{3}{10}$ $\frac{2}{15}$
20. $\frac{11}{18} \times \frac{27}{50}$ $\frac{33}{100}$
21. $\frac{10}{12} \times \frac{6}{8}$ $\frac{5}{8}$
22. $\frac{3}{11} \times \frac{22}{27}$ $\frac{2}{9}$
23. $\frac{5}{6} \times 32$ $26\frac{2}{3}$
24. $\frac{7}{8} \times \frac{1}{7}$ $\frac{1}{8}$
25. $28 \times \frac{5}{12}$ $11\frac{2}{3}$
26. **Reasoning** Which is greater, $\frac{4}{5} \times \frac{1}{2}$ or $\frac{4}{5} \times \frac{1}{4}$? Explain how you know.
$\frac{4}{5} \times \frac{1}{2}$, $\frac{1}{2}$ of any number will always be greater than $\frac{1}{4}$ of the same number.

B Reasoning and Problem Solving

30. Yes. She divided the numerator and denominator by the GCF to simplify each fraction. Then she multiplied correctly.

Math and Everyday Life

Millie plants $\frac{2}{3}$ of her garden with vegetables and $\frac{1}{3}$ of it with flowers. Three fourths of the flower section is red geraniums; the rest of the flower section is daisies. What fraction of the entire garden is planted in

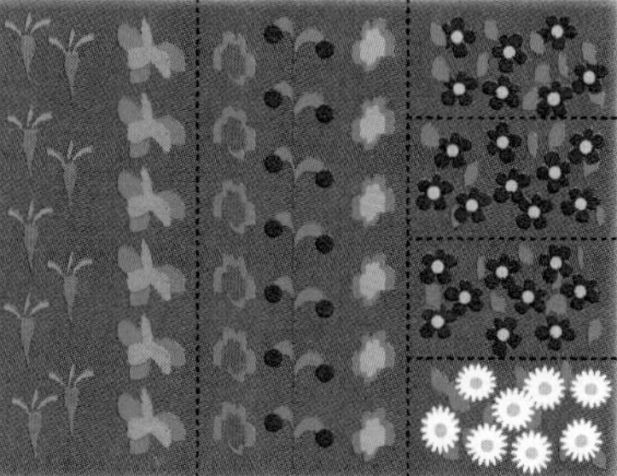

Area of Millie's garden: 2 acres

27. geraniums? $\frac{1}{4}$
28. daisies? $\frac{1}{12}$
29. How many acres will be planted in vegetables? $1\frac{1}{3}$ acres
30. **Writing in Math** Has Candice simplified and multiplied the fractions correctly? Explain.
See above.

Find $\frac{4}{10} \times \frac{3}{9}$.

$\frac{\cancel{4}^{2}}{_{5}\cancel{10}} \times \frac{\cancel{3}^{1}}{\cancel{9}_{3}} = \frac{2}{15}$.

C Extensions

31. Use mental math to find $\frac{4}{5} \times \left(\frac{1}{4} \times 5\right)$.
1

Algebra Use the Distributive Property to find each product mentally.

32. $\frac{1}{2} \times 2\frac{1}{2}$ See below.
33. $8 \times 4\frac{3}{4}$ $8\left(4 + \frac{3}{4}\right) = 32 + 6 = 38$
34. $3\frac{2}{3} \times 9$ $9\left(3 + \frac{2}{3}\right) = 27 + 6 = 33$
35. **Algebra** Simplify $\frac{7}{12}\left(\frac{5}{6} - \frac{1}{2}\right)$.
$\frac{7}{36}$

32. $\frac{1}{2}\left(2 + \frac{1}{2}\right) = 1 + \frac{1}{4} = 1\frac{1}{4}$

254

Test-Taking Practice

Test-Taking Practice, Item 1, p. 255
There are two parts to the question; the equation and simplification are each worth two points. Remind students that they should answer as much as they can since partial credit is given for this type of problem.

Discuss the sample responses shown and compare them to papers produced by your students.

4-point answer Equation and simplification are correct; complete understanding of multiplying fractions.

$\frac{3}{5} \times \frac{2}{6} = \frac{6}{30} = \frac{1}{5}$

PRACTICE

Mixed Review and Test Prep

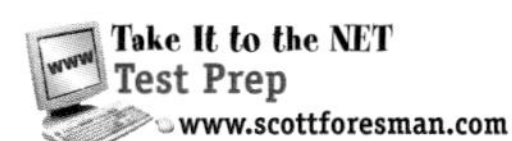

36. Find $\frac{1}{3} \times 5$. Simplify if possible. $1\frac{2}{3}$

37. Which is the GCF of 36 and 117?

A. 1 B. 3 C. 4 (D.) 9

Practice Game

GCF Spin

Players: 2 **Materials:** Spinner (labeled 0–9)

1. Each player spins the spinner 4 times to build two numbers. Numbers may have 1, 2, or 3 digits in any combination.
2. Players find the GCF of the two numbers and record the GCF as a point value.
3. The player with the most points after 5 rounds is the winner.

Learning with Technology

Multiplication with the Fraction eTool

2. 4; The product is 4 parts of 15, or $\frac{4}{15}$.

You can use the array feature to multiply fractions. To multiply $\frac{1}{3}$ and $\frac{4}{5}$, enter 3 for the horizontal axis and 5 for the vertical axis. Use the slider to shade the numerators, 1 column along the horizontal axis and 4 rows along the vertical axis.

1. 15; The product will be expressed in parts of 15.

1. How many rectangles are created when 3 and 5 are selected as denominators? What does this tell you about the product? **See above.**
2. How many rectangles are included in the highlighting for both sliders? What does this tell you about the product? **See above.**

Use the Fraction eTool to find each product.

3. $\frac{2}{3} \times \frac{3}{8}$ $\frac{1}{4}$ 4. $\frac{1}{4} \times \frac{2}{3}$ $\frac{1}{6}$

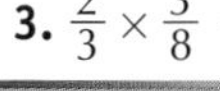

Leveled Practice

Below Level Ex. 14–25, 29, 30, 36, 37

On Level Ex. 15–21 odd, 22–31, 36, 37

Above Level Ex. 22–37

Early Finishers Have each student write a fraction between 0 and 1. Then pair students and have them find the product of their two fractions.

Practice Game Students need a spinner or Teaching Tool 4, labeled 0–9. Have students divide the spinner with five equal sections into a spinner with ten equal sections.

Students gain practice in identifying factors of numbers and then the greatest common factor of two numbers.

Learning with Technology Have students compare and contrast the use of the Fraction eTool with the use of a paper-and-pencil drawing to find the product of two fractions.

4 Assess

Journal Idea Have students explain the steps in finding the product $\frac{3}{8} \times \frac{20}{27}$.

3-point answer Equation is correct; simplification is incomplete; shows understanding of multiplying fractions.

$\frac{3}{5} \times \frac{2}{6} = \frac{6}{30}$

2-point answer Equation is correct; simplification is incorrect; shows little understanding of multiplying fractions.

$\frac{3}{5} \times \frac{2}{6} = \frac{6}{30} = \frac{1}{6}$

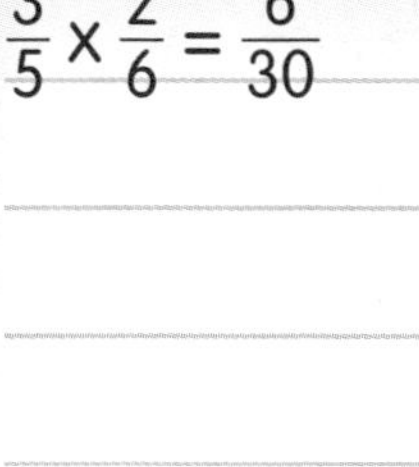

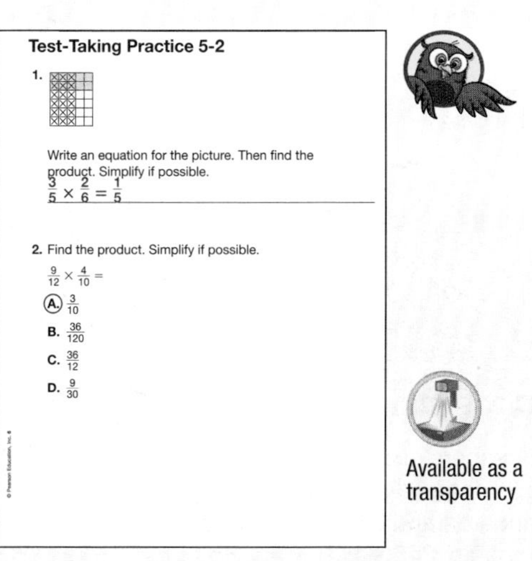
Test-Taking Practice 5-2

1. Write an equation for the picture. Then find the product. Simplify if possible.

$\frac{3}{5} \times \frac{2}{6} = \frac{1}{5}$

2. Find the product. Simplify if possible.

$\frac{9}{12} \times \frac{4}{10} =$

(A.) $\frac{3}{10}$

B. $\frac{36}{120}$

C. $\frac{36}{12}$

D. $\frac{9}{30}$

Available as a transparency

Estimating with Fractions and Mixed Numbers

Lesson Organizer

Quick Lesson Overview 

Objective Estimate the product or quotient of two fractions.

Math Understanding Mixed numbers can be expressed as improper fractions, or they can be broken apart into their whole-number and fractional parts. This provides a basis for estimating and doing operations with two mixed numbers, with a mixed number and a whole number, and with a mixed number and a fraction.

Vocabulary Compatible numbers (p. 18), round (p. 14)

Math Background Good "number sense" is important for students to monitor their work as they multiply and divide mixed numbers and fractions. Practicing estimating, using compatible numbers and rounding, can help students develop that number sense.

NCTM Standards

- Numbers and Operations

(For a complete correlation to the NCTM Standards and Grades 6–8 Expectations, see pages 246G–H.)

Getting Started

Spiral Review

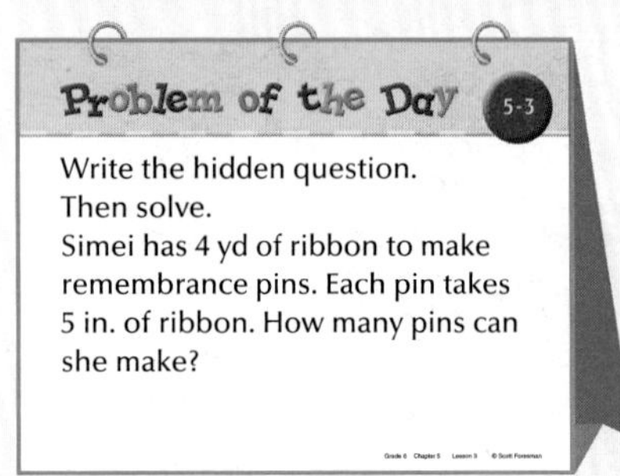

Problem of the Day 5-3

Write the hidden question.
Then solve.
Simei has 4 yd of ribbon to make remembrance pins. Each pin takes 5 in. of ribbon. How many pins can she make?

Topics Reviewed

- Multiplying and dividing whole numbers; converting measurement units
- Problem-Solving Skill: Multiple-Step Problem

Answer Hidden Question 1: How many inches of ribbon does Simei have? Simei can make 28 pins, and have 4 in. of ribbon left over.

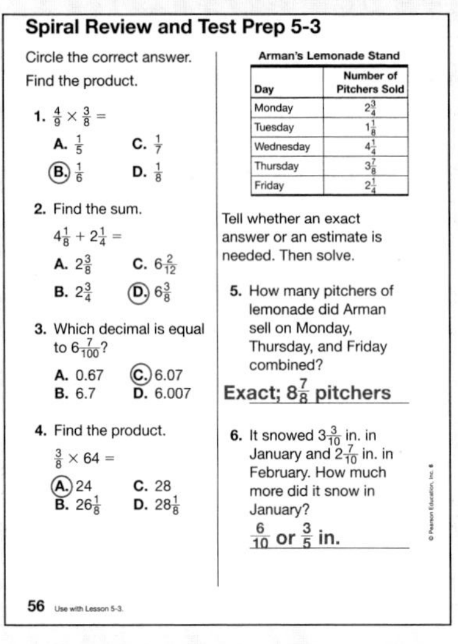

Spiral Review and Test Prep 5-3

Circle the correct answer.

Find the product.

1. $\frac{4}{9} \times \frac{3}{8} =$
   A. $\frac{1}{5}$ C. $\frac{1}{7}$
   (B.) $\frac{1}{6}$ D. $\frac{1}{8}$

2. Find the sum.
   $4\frac{1}{8} + 2\frac{1}{4} =$
   A. $2\frac{3}{8}$ C. $6\frac{2}{12}$
   B. $2\frac{3}{4}$ (D.) $6\frac{3}{8}$

3. Which decimal is equal to $6\frac{7}{100}$?
   A. 0.67 (C.) 6.07
   B. 6.7 D. 6.007

4. Find the product.
   $\frac{3}{8} \times 64 =$
   (A.) 24 C. 28
   B. $26\frac{1}{8}$ D. $28\frac{1}{8}$

Arman's Lemonade Stand

Day	Number of Pitchers Sold
Monday	$2\frac{3}{4}$
Tuesday	$1\frac{1}{8}$
Wednesday	$4\frac{1}{4}$
Thursday	$3\frac{7}{8}$
Friday	$2\frac{1}{4}$

Tell whether an exact answer or an estimate is needed. Then solve.

5. How many pitchers of lemonade did Arman sell on Monday, Thursday, and Friday combined?
   Exact; $8\frac{7}{8}$ pitchers

6. It snowed $3\frac{3}{10}$ in. in January and $2\frac{7}{10}$ in. in February. How much more did it snow in January?
   $\frac{6}{10}$ or $\frac{3}{5}$ in.

56 Use with Lesson 5-3.

Available as a transparency and as a blackline master

Topics Reviewed

1. Multiplying fractions; **2.** Adding mixed numbers; **3.** Connecting fractions to decimals; **4.** Multiplying fractions; **5.** Exact or estimate; **6.** Subtracting mixed numbers

Investigating the Concept

Estimate on the Line

 10–15 MIN **Kinesthetic** 

Materials Masking tape and markers

What to Do

- Make a number line on the floor. Show numbers from 0 to 6 and divide each unit into 8 equal parts.
- Write $5\frac{3}{4} \div 2\frac{7}{8}$ on the board. Have volunteers stand at $5\frac{3}{4}$ and $2\frac{7}{8}$. **Which whole number is closest to $5\frac{3}{4}$?** *(6)* **Which whole number is closest to $2\frac{7}{8}$?** *(3)* Write 6 and 3 on cards and place them below $5\frac{3}{4}$ and $2\frac{7}{8}$. **6 and 3 can be used to estimate $5\frac{3}{4}$ and $2\frac{7}{8}$. What is a reasonable estimate of $5\frac{3}{4} \div 2\frac{7}{8}$?** *(2)*
- **Estimate $\frac{3}{4} \times 38$. Are 4 and 38 compatible numbers?** *(No)* **What other number might you use that would be compatible with the denominator 4?** *(Sample answer: 40)* **What is $\frac{3}{4} \times 40$?** *(30)* **What is a reasonable estimate of $\frac{3}{4} \times 38$?** *(30)*

Ongoing Assessment

- **Number Sense** **Estimate $23\frac{1}{3} \div 6\frac{1}{5}$.** *(Sample answer: 4)*

0 1 2 3 4 5 6

Reaching All Learners

Reading in Math

Using Story Clues

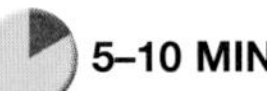

5–10 MIN **Linguistic**

- On the board, write the two stories shown below.
- **Read the stories. Would you over- or under-estimate to solve each problem? Explain.** *(I would overestimate in the first problem to be sure I had enough money; I would underestimate in the second problem because I want to be sure I have enough.)*

- I want to purchase $15\frac{1}{2}$ pounds of meat at $3 per pound. How much money do I need?
- I want to buy potatoes that come in $2\frac{1}{2}$-pound bags. If I buy 6 bags, do I have at least $15\frac{1}{2}$ pounds?

Extend Language

English Language Learners

Working Together

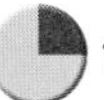

10–15 MIN **Verbal/Social/Cooperative**

- On the board, write *Estimate* $\frac{3}{4} \times 15$. Have small groups discuss whether it's better to use compatible numbers or rounding to estimate.
- After they've come to an agreement, have members of the group work together to form an explanation of the process they chose.
- Have a member write the process down and read it to the class. Class members can confirm the process or make suggestions.

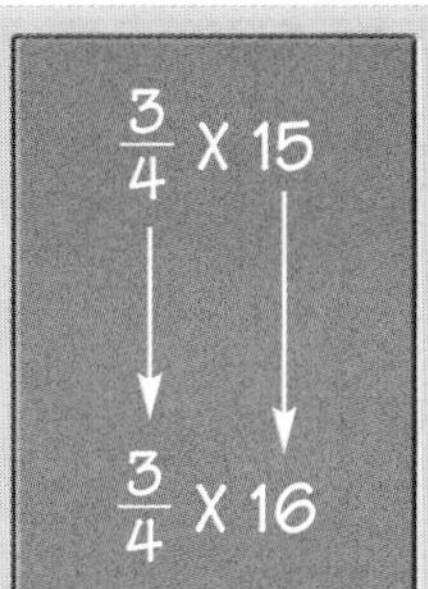

Reteaching

Am I Compatible?

5–10 MIN **Social/Cooperative**

- Write $\frac{5}{6} \times 28\frac{5}{7}$ on the board.
- Have Partner 1 round the mixed number to the nearest whole number. *(29)* **With which number should your rounded number be compatible?** *(The denominator, 6)* Have Partner 2 circle the denominator and suggest a compatible number for it. *(30)*
- Have the partners work together to determine a reasonable estimate. *(Sample answer: 25)*
- Have partners change roles and do the same steps for $22\frac{3}{5} \div \frac{2}{3}$.

$\frac{5}{6} \times 29$ 30 and 6 are compatible because 30 is divisible by 6.

Students with Special Needs

Using Reminders

5–10 MIN **Visual/Spatial**

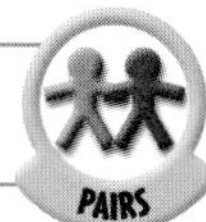

Materials *(per pair)* Index card on which you have written the steps: 1. Round each mixed number. 2. Are the numbers compatible? If not find compatible numbers. 3. Complete the estimate.

- Write $18\frac{3}{4} \times 3\frac{1}{3}$ on the board.
- Have students work with partners to answer the questions. **How did you round?** *(Sample answer: 19×3)* **Are the numbers compatible, or easy to multiply?** *(No)* **What are compatible numbers for this product?** *(Sample answer: 20 and 3)* **What is an estimate of the product?** *(Sample answer: $20 \times 3 = 60$)*

Objective Estimate the product or quotient of two fractions.

1 Warm Up

Activate Prior Knowledge Review how to find the product of two fractions or of a fraction and a whole number.

2 Teach

LEARN When the numbers involved are mixed numbers, it is often easier for students to use a two-step process: first round each mixed number to the nearest whole number, and then change the whole numbers to compatible numbers.

Ongoing Assessment

Talk About It: Question 1

If students do not know how to answer this question,

then ask them if the compatible number 24 is greater or less than the actual number of banners. Once they realize that the compatible number 24 is less than the actual number of banners, they should be able to decide if 21 yards is enough.

Lesson 5-3

Key Idea
There are several ways to estimate products and quotients of fractions and mixed numbers.

Vocabulary
- compatible numbers (p. 18)
- rounding (p. 14)

Estimating with Fractions and Mixed Numbers

WARM UP

1. $\frac{1}{3} \times 12$ 4
2. $\frac{1}{2} \times \frac{3}{4}$ $\frac{3}{8}$
3. $\frac{2}{3} \times 3$ 2
4. $\frac{3}{5} \times 50$ 30

LEARN

What are some ways to estimate?

LaToya is making school banners for the tournament parade. It takes $\frac{7}{8}$ yard of felt to make each banner. Estimate the amount of felt needed for 25 banners.

Example A

One Way

Estimate $\frac{7}{8} \times 25$ using **compatible numbers.**

$\frac{7}{8} \times 25$ → $\frac{7}{8} \times 24$ Change the whole number to the nearest number compatible with the denominator of the fraction.

Since 24 is divisible by 8, and $\frac{1}{8} \times 24 = 3$, then $\frac{7}{8} = 3 \times 7 = 21$.

LaToya needs about 21 yards of felt.

Another Way

Estimate $\frac{7}{8} \times 25$ using **rounding.**

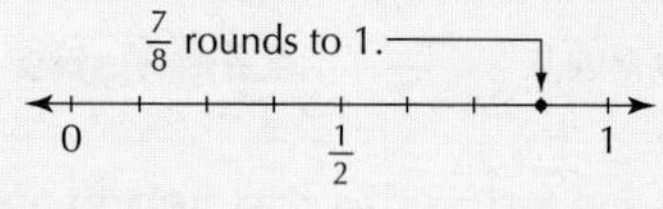

Since $\frac{7}{8}$ is greater than $\frac{1}{2}$, $\frac{7}{8}$ rounds to 1.
So, $\frac{7}{8} \times 25 \approx 1 \times 25$, or 25.

LaToya needs about 25 yards of felt.

Example B

Estimate $4\frac{5}{6} \times 19\frac{3}{4}$ using rounding.

$4\frac{5}{6} \times 19\frac{3}{4}$ → $5 \times 20 = 100$ Round each mixed number to the nearest whole number.

$4\frac{5}{6} \times 19\frac{3}{4} \approx 100$

Example C

Estimate $11\frac{1}{3} \div 2\frac{4}{5}$ using rounding and compatible numbers.

$11\frac{1}{3} \div 2\frac{4}{5}$ → $11 \div 3$ Round each mixed number to the nearest whole number.

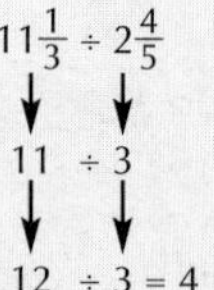

$11 \div 3$ → $12 \div 3 = 4$ Use compatible numbers to divide.

$11\frac{1}{3} \div 2\frac{4}{5} \approx 4$

Talk About It

1. In Example A, is 21 yards of felt enough? Without computing, explain how you know.

1. No. The number of banners was rounded down to a compatible number, so the actual amount needed is more than the estimate.

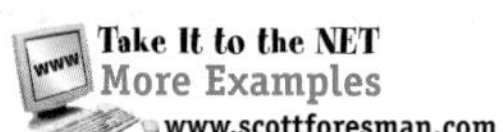

256

Reteaching — Below Level

Estimating with Fractions and Mixed Numbers R 5-3

Estimate $5\frac{1}{8} \times 23\frac{5}{6}$ using rounding and compatible numbers.

$5\frac{1}{8} \times 23\frac{5}{6}$ → 5×24 Round each mixed number to the nearest whole number.

5×24 → $4 \times 25 = 100$ 4 × 25 is easier to multiply than 5 × 24.

$5\frac{1}{8} \times 23\frac{5}{6} \approx 100$

Estimate $17\frac{1}{7} \div 3\frac{8}{9}$ using rounding and compatible numbers.

$17\frac{1}{7} \div 3\frac{8}{9}$ → $17 \div 4$ Round each mixed number to the nearest whole number.

$17 \div 4$ → $16 \div 4 = 4$ Use compatible numbers to divide.

$17\frac{1}{8} \div 3\frac{8}{9} \approx 4$

Sample answers are given. Students' estimations may vary.

Estimate each product or quotient.

1. $\frac{6}{7} \times 12$ About 12
2. $25 \div 4\frac{2}{3}$ About 5
3. $3\frac{8}{9} \times 7\frac{3}{4}$ About 32
4. $19\frac{12}{15} \div 5\frac{1}{4}$ About 4
5. $2\frac{1}{5} \times 36$ About 72
6. $39 \div 7\frac{2}{3}$ About 5
7. $12\frac{1}{8} \times 2\frac{9}{10}$ About 36
8. $35\frac{4}{5} \div 5\frac{7}{8}$ About 6
9. $\frac{15}{16} \times 62$ About 62
10. $48\frac{7}{9} \div 9\frac{2}{3}$ About 5

11. **Writing in Math** Explain how you would estimate $3\frac{5}{6} \times 29\frac{4}{5}$ using compatible numbers.
Sample answer: Multiply 4 by 30 to get 120

56 Use with Lesson 5-3.

Practice — On Level

Estimating with Fractions and Mixed Numbers P 5-3

Sample answers. Students' estimations may vary.

Estimate each product or quotient.

1. $\frac{4}{5} \times 21$ 21
2. $2\frac{7}{8} \times 9\frac{1}{4}$ 27
3. $\frac{12}{13} \times 82$ 82
4. $18\frac{7}{8} \times 6\frac{1}{16}$ 120
5. $30 \div 6\frac{3}{4}$ 5
6. $24\frac{3}{16} \div 7\frac{2}{3}$ 3
7. $37 \div 5\frac{2}{3}$ 6
8. $27\frac{4}{9} \div 8\frac{3}{4}$ 3
9. $16\frac{11}{12} \times 3\frac{4}{5}$ 68
10. $90\frac{1}{10} \div 9\frac{9}{10}$ 9
11. $11\frac{3}{8} \times \frac{18}{19}$ 11
12. $12\frac{1}{4} \div 4\frac{3}{10}$ 3

About how much flour is needed to make

Recipe	Cups of Flour
Zucchini bread (1 loaf)	$2\frac{1}{2}$
Bran muffins ($\frac{1}{2}$ dozen)	$1\frac{1}{3}$
Wheat rolls (2 batches)	$2\frac{1}{4}$

13. 2 loaves of zucchini bread? 5 c
14. 2 dozen bran muffins? $5\frac{1}{3}$ c
15. 8 batches of wheat rolls? 9 c

16. **Number Sense** What benchmark fraction could you use to estimate the product of 54 and $\frac{7}{16}$? $\frac{1}{2}$

Test Prep

17. Estimate $31\frac{1}{8} \times 5\frac{1}{4}$.
(A) 150 B. 170 C. 180 D. 190

18. **Writing in Math** Explain how you would estimate $16\frac{5}{9} \div 3\frac{7}{8}$.
Round $16\frac{5}{9}$ to 17. Round $3\frac{7}{8}$ to 4. Use compatible numbers and divide 16 by 4. The quotient is approximately 4.

56 Use with Lesson 5-3.

CHECK

For another example, see Set 5-3 on p. 292.

Estimate each product or quotient. **Sample answers are given.**

1. $\frac{3}{5} \times 16$ **9**
2. $20 \times \frac{4}{9}$ **8**
3. $12\frac{5}{8} \times 3\frac{1}{3}$ **39**
4. $29\frac{11}{12} \div 4\frac{4}{5}$ **6**
5. **Number Sense** Estimate $\frac{6}{7} \times 27$ using compatible numbers. Then estimate using rounding. Which estimate is closest to the actual product? Why? **See below.**

PRACTICE

For more practice, see Set 5-3 on p. 295.

5. 24; 27; compatible numbers; The first estimate $\left(\frac{6}{7} \times 28\right)$ is only $\frac{6}{7}$ too much. The second estimate (1×27) is $1\frac{6}{7}$ too much.

A Skills and Understanding

Estimate each product or quotient. **Sample answers are given.**

6. $\frac{1}{3} \times 35$ **12**
7. $58 \times \frac{7}{8}$ **49**
8. $\frac{5}{7} \times 20$ **15**
9. $4\frac{2}{5} \times 5\frac{7}{8}$ **24**
10. $30\frac{1}{9} \div 19\frac{1}{2}$ **$1\frac{1}{2}$**
11. $17\frac{7}{8} \times 2\frac{5}{6}$ **54**
12. $24 \div 5\frac{3}{8}$ **5**
13. $9\frac{5}{8} \div 2\frac{4}{7}$ **5**
14. **Number Sense** What benchmark fraction could you use to estimate the product in Exercise 8? **$\frac{3}{4}$**

TEST TALK
Think It Through
Sometimes I can use benchmark fractions to estimate a product or quotient.

B Reasoning and Problem Solving

Ms. Candar's woodworking class is making wooden letters and signs for the parade floats. The amount of lumber needed to make each item appears in the table.

Items	Length in feet
Lowercase wooden letter	$\frac{7}{12}$
Capital wooden letter	$\frac{3}{4}$
Small sign	$\frac{11}{12}$
Large sign	$1\frac{1}{3}$

15. Estimate the amount of lumber needed to make the capital vowels *a, e, i, o,* and *u.* **Sample answer: about 4 feet**
16. Estimate the number of large signs that can be made from an 8-foot piece of lumber. Is your estimate an overestimate or underestimate? **Sample answer: about 8 signs; overestimate**
17. **Writing in Math** Explain how you would estimate $\frac{5}{11} \times \frac{2}{9}$ using one or two benchmark fractions. **$\frac{5}{11}$ is almost $\frac{1}{2}$, and $\frac{2}{9}$ is almost $\frac{1}{3}$; $\frac{1}{2} \times \frac{1}{3} = \frac{1}{6}$.**

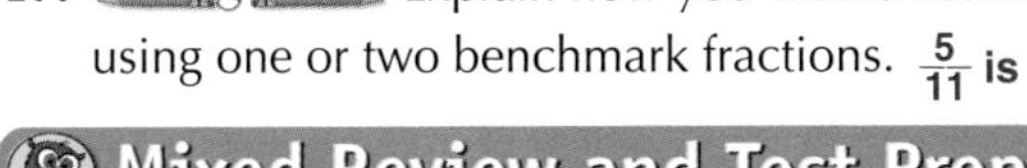

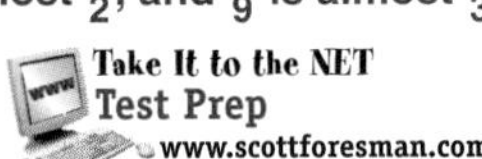

Find each product. Simplify if possible.

18. $18 \times \frac{7}{9}$ **14**
19. $\frac{2}{5} \times \frac{15}{22}$ **$\frac{3}{11}$**
20. $\frac{5}{8} \times \frac{4}{25}$ **$\frac{1}{10}$**
21. Which fraction is NOT equivalent to $\frac{8}{24}$?

A. $\frac{10}{30}$ B. $\frac{15}{45}$ C. $\frac{18}{54}$ **(D.)** $\frac{24}{75}$

All text pages available online and on CD-ROM.

Error Intervention

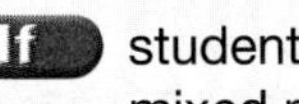

students have difficulty rounding mixed numbers,

then have students show each mixed number on a number line. Then they can use the number line to find the closest whole number. *(Also see* Reteaching, *p. 256B.)*

3 Practice

TEST TALK **Exercise 17** It may be helpful to review benchmark fractions: $\frac{1}{4}, \frac{1}{3}, \frac{1}{2}, \frac{2}{3}, \frac{3}{4}$. Students should be able to locate each of the benchmark fractions on a number line.

Leveled Practice

Below Level Ex. 6–21

On Level Ex. 6–21

Above Level Ex. 6–21

Early Finishers Have students look at Exercises 9–13 and replace the fraction part of each mixed number with a different fraction. Then have them estimate each product or quotient using the "new" mixed numbers.

4 Assess

Journal Idea Have students explain how to use a combination of rounding and compatible numbers to estimate $43\frac{3}{4} \div 5\frac{1}{2}$.

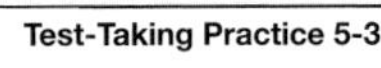

Test-Taking Practice 5-3

1. Use either compatible numbers or rounding to estimate $\frac{9}{10} \times 47$. Tell which method you used and explain how you got your answer. **Sample answer: Rounding: Round $\frac{9}{10}$ to 1; $1 \times 47 = 47$. Compatible numbers: Substitute 50 for 47, because 50 is compatible with the denominator 10. Since $\frac{1}{10} \times 50 = 5$, then $\frac{9}{10} \times 50 = 45$.**
2. Estimate the quotient.

$63\frac{2}{3} \div 7\frac{1}{2}$

(A.) About 8
B. About 6
C. About 5
D. About 4

Available as a transparency

Above Level **Enrichment**

Canine County E 5-3 ESTIMATION

Look at the map of Canine County below. The road from Dachshund to Labrador is 15 km. Use this information and the map to answer the questions.

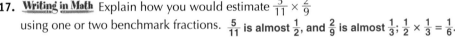

Dachshund, 15 km, Labrador, Poodle, Bulldog, Spaniel, Retriever, Husky, Beagle, St. Bernard, Great Dane

Sample answers are given.

1. The road that connects Dachshund and Labrador is about the same length as the road between which two towns? **Retriever and Beagle**
2. Which two towns are about 32 km apart? **Spaniel and Great Dane**
3. About how many times as long as the road from Dachshund to Labrador is the road between Labrador and Poodle? **About $2\frac{1}{3}$ times**
4. Which two towns are about four times as far apart as Husky and St. Bernard? **Bulldog and Poodle**
5. Between which two towns is the road about $2\frac{1}{2}$ times as long as the road from Dachshund to Spaniel? **Great Dane and Husky**
6. The bicycle warehouse is about $\frac{1}{4}$ of the way from Bulldog to Beagle. About how many kilometers would a truck drive to bring a load of bicycles to a store in Husky? **About 80 km**

56 Use with Lesson 5-3.

Problem Solving

Estimating with Fractions and Mixed Numbers PS 5-3

A New Playground McKinley Elementary School is planning to build a new playground.

1. Each of the 5 pieces of playground equipment requires $\frac{2}{9}$ of an acre of land. Estimate the minimum space needed for all 5 pieces using a compatible number. **Sample answer: 1 acre, $\frac{2}{9}$ is close to $\frac{2}{10} = \frac{1}{5} \times 5 = 1$.**
2. Is your answer to Exercise 1 an overestimate or an underestimate? Explain. **Sample answer: Underestimate, $\frac{2}{10}$ is less than $\frac{2}{9}$.**

Lots of Lettuce Manatees are large marine mammals that live in warm waters. In zoos, they eat romaine lettuce as a part of their diet. A single manatee will usually eat $2\frac{1}{2}$ cases of lettuce per day.

3. January has 31 days. Using rounding, estimate how many cases of lettuce should be ordered to feed one manatee in January. **Sample answer: 75 cases, round 31 to 30, $2 \times 30 = 60$, $60 + 15 = 75$; actual number of cases needed $= 77\frac{1}{2}$**
4. Estimate the number of cases of lettuce the zookeeper should order to feed 3 manatees for 65 days. **Sample answer: 540 cases, round $2\frac{1}{2}$ cases to 3, $3 \times 3 = 9$, round 65 days to 60, $9 \times 60 = 540$; actual is $487\frac{1}{2}$**
5. **Writing in Math** Would you use rounding, compatible numbers, or both to estimate the product of $\frac{4}{5} \times 24$? Write your answer in a complete sentence. **Sample answer: I would round 24 to 25, which is compatible with $\frac{4}{5}$, to simplify to $4 \times 5 = 20$; actual answer is $19\frac{1}{5}$.**

56 Use with Lesson 5-3.

5-4 Multiplying Mixed Numbers

Lesson Organizer

Quick Lesson Overview

Objective Multiply mixed numbers.

Math Understanding Mixed numbers can be expressed as improper fractions, or they can be broken apart into their whole-number and fractional parts. This provides a basis for estimating and doing operations with two mixed numbers, with a mixed number and a whole number, and with a mixed number and a fraction.

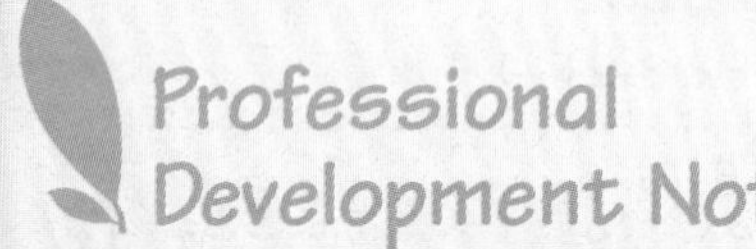

Managing Instruction Encourage students to talk to a family member about favorite recipes, especially ones that involve ingredients measured in fractions. Then have the student and family members decide how much of various ingredients would be needed to change the recipe by doubling or tripling it.

NCTM Standards

- Numbers and Operations

(For a complete correlation to the NCTM Standards and Grades 6–8 Expectations, see pages 246G–H.)

Getting Started

Spiral Review

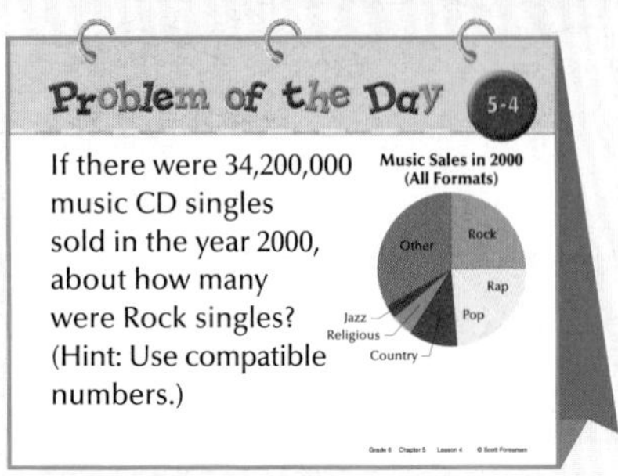

Problem of the Day 5-4

If there were 34,200,000 music CD singles sold in the year 2000, about how many were Rock singles? (Hint: Use compatible numbers.)

Topics Reviewed

- Reading circle graphs; multiplying whole numbers and fractions
- Problem-Solving Skill: One-Step Problem

Answer Sample: There were about 9,000,000 Rock singles sold in the year 2000.

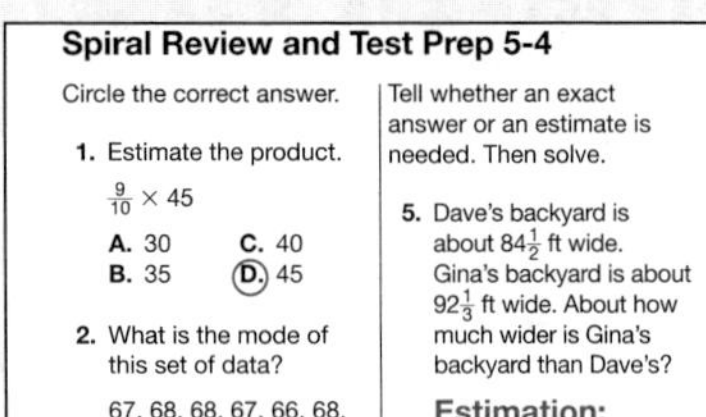

Spiral Review and Test Prep 5-4

Circle the correct answer.

1. Estimate the product.
$\frac{9}{10} \times 45$
A. 30 C. 40
B. 35 (D.) 45

2. What is the mode of this set of data?
67, 68, 68, 67, 66, 68, 66, 67, 64, 68
A. 64 C. 67
B. 66 (D.) 68

3. What is the GCF of 24 and 36?
A. 6 C. 10
B. 9 (D.) 12

4. Find the sum.
$\frac{3}{8} + \frac{1}{4} =$
(A.) $\frac{5}{8}$ C. $\frac{7}{8}$
B. $\frac{3}{4}$ D. $1\frac{1}{4}$

Tell whether an exact answer or an estimate is needed. Then solve.

5. Dave's backyard is about $84\frac{1}{2}$ ft wide. Gina's backyard is about $92\frac{1}{3}$ ft wide. About how much wider is Gina's backyard than Dave's?
Estimation; About 7 ft

6. Mark has $24\frac{1}{2}$ ft of rope. He is cutting the rope into pieces that are $5\frac{3}{4}$ ft long. About how many pieces of rope can he cut?
About 4 pieces

7. Rodney is $5\frac{1}{2}$ ft tall. Gale is $4\frac{1}{2}$ ft tall. What is their combined height?
10 ft

Use with Lesson 5-4. 57

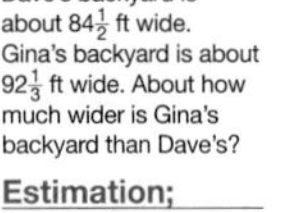

Available as a transparency and as a blackline master

Topics Reviewed

1., 6. Estimating with fractions and mixed numbers; **2.** Mean, median, and mode; **3.** Greatest common factor; **4.** Adding fractions with unlike denominators; **5.** Exact or estimate; **7.** Adding mixed numbers

Investigating the Concept

Model the Product

5–10 MIN **Kinesthetic**

Materials *(per pair)* Colored pencils or markers

What to Do

- **Give an estimate for $2\frac{1}{3} \times 1\frac{1}{2}$** *(Sample: $2 \times 2 = 4$)*
- **Partner 1, draw a model of $1\frac{1}{2}$ using one color.**
- **What is $2\frac{1}{3}$ as an improper fraction?** *($\frac{7}{3}$)* **Partner 2, use another color to show $\frac{1}{3}$ of $1\frac{1}{2}$ on your partner's drawing.**
- **What is $\frac{1}{3}$ of $1\frac{1}{2}$?** *($\frac{3}{6}$, or $\frac{1}{2}$)* **So, what is $\frac{7}{3}$ of $1\frac{1}{2}$?** *($7 \times \frac{1}{2} = \frac{7}{2}$, or $3\frac{1}{2}$)*

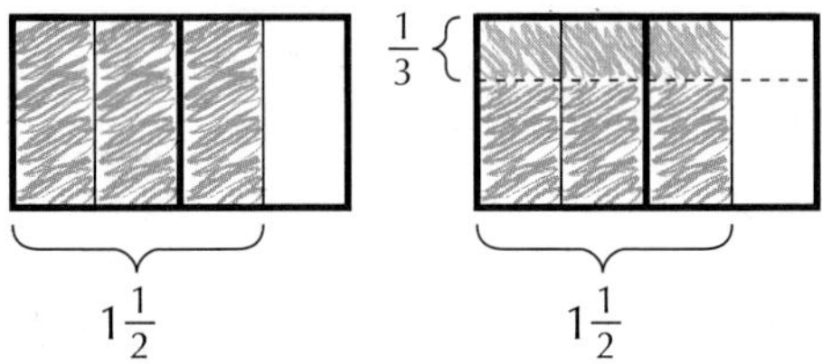

Ongoing Assessment

- **Number Sense Is the product of $3\frac{1}{3} \times 4\frac{1}{5}$ greater than or less than either factor? Explain.** *(Greater; each factor is greater than 1.)*

Reaching All Learners

Math Vocabulary

Using Story Clues

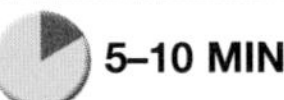 5–10 MIN **Auditory** 

- Write the following vocabulary on the board: Distributive Property, improper fraction, simplest form, greatest common factor.
- Read each sentence and have students choose the correct word.

$\frac{12}{7}$ is the _____ for $1\frac{5}{7}$. *(Improper fraction)*

To write $\frac{8}{12}$ in _____, you divide 8 and 12 by the _____ for 8 and 12. *(Simplest form, greatest common factor)*

When you write $3 \times 1\frac{1}{2}$ as $(3 \times 1) + (3 \times \frac{1}{2})$, you use the _____. *(Distributive Property)*

Extend Language

English Language Learners

Words and Numbers

 10–15 MIN **Linguistic/Verbal** 

- Revisit Problem 17 on page 259 with students.
- Have students review how they used math words to describe setting up the problem to solve it. *(Ten and one half times one and one third equals what?)*
- Ask a volunteer to write the problem as numbers on the board. *($10\frac{1}{2} \times 1\frac{1}{3}$)*
- Ask partners to write a similar word problem. Then have them exchange word problems. **Read the problem and describe setting it up to solve it.**

Reteaching

Finding Improper Fractions

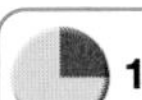 10–15 MIN **Visual/Spatial** 

Materials *(per pair)* Fraction Strips or Teaching Tool 15

- **Use your fraction strips to model $2\frac{1}{2}$. Replace each whole with two halves. How many halves are there?** *(5 halves)* **What is the improper fraction?** *($\frac{5}{2}$)*
- **Model $2\frac{2}{3}$. What is the improper fraction?** *($\frac{8}{3}$)*
- **Work together to find the product $\frac{5}{2} \times \frac{8}{3}$.** *($\frac{20}{3}$, or $6\frac{2}{3}$)*
- Write the solution on the board:

$\frac{1}{2}$	$\frac{1}{2}$	$\frac{1}{2}$	$\frac{1}{2}$	$\frac{1}{2}$

$2\frac{1}{2} = \frac{5}{2}$

Advanced Learners

Using the Distributive Property

 10–15 MIN **Logical/Mathematical** 

- Write $5\frac{5}{6} \times 2\frac{4}{7}$ on the board.
- **Write each mixed number as a sum. Then use the sums and the Distributive Property to find the product.** After students have worked together to find the answer, have them put the solution on the board.

$$\begin{aligned}(5 + \tfrac{5}{6})(2 + \tfrac{4}{7}) &= 5(2 + \tfrac{4}{7}) + \tfrac{5}{6}(2 + \tfrac{4}{7}) \\ &= 5(2) + 5(\tfrac{4}{7}) + (\tfrac{5}{6})2 + (\tfrac{5}{6})(\tfrac{4}{7}) \\ &= 10 + \tfrac{20}{7} + \tfrac{5}{3} + \tfrac{10}{21} \\ &= 10 + \tfrac{60}{21} + \tfrac{35}{21} + \tfrac{10}{21} \\ &= 10 + \tfrac{105}{21} = 10 + 5 = 15\end{aligned}$$

- **Check the product using the method you have learned.**

Objective Multiply mixed numbers.

1 Warm Up

Activate Prior Knowledge Review multiplication of fractions.

2 Teach

LEARN Encourage student suggestions about how to find the product of mixed numbers. Emphasize that students should estimate the product before completing each example.

Ongoing Assessment

Talk About It: Question 1

If students have difficulty deciding which of the methods from Example B to use,

then have them work with a partner to solve the problem using each of the three methods.

CHECK

Error Intervention

If students make errors in writing mixed numbers as improper fractions,

then have them model the mixed number using grid paper. **What does the denominator of the fraction tell you?** *(It is the number of smaller rectangles for each unit.)* Then students can divide each unit into that many rectangles and write the mixed number as an improper fraction. *(Also see* Reteaching, *p. 258B.)*

Lesson 5-4

Key Idea
You can use what you know about multiplying fractions to multiply mixed numbers.

Multiplying Mixed Numbers

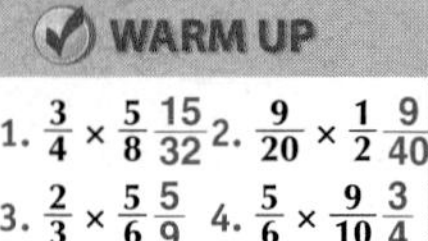

WARM UP
1. $\frac{3}{4} \times \frac{5}{8}$ $\frac{15}{32}$
2. $\frac{9}{20} \times \frac{1}{2}$ $\frac{9}{40}$
3. $\frac{2}{3} \times \frac{5}{6}$ $\frac{5}{9}$
4. $\frac{5}{6} \times \frac{9}{10}$ $\frac{3}{4}$

LEARN

How can you find the product of mixed numbers?

TEST TALK

Think It Through
I should **estimate** the product before working the problem.

Example A

Find $5\frac{1}{2} \times 2\frac{2}{3}$. Estimate: $6 \times 3 = 18$

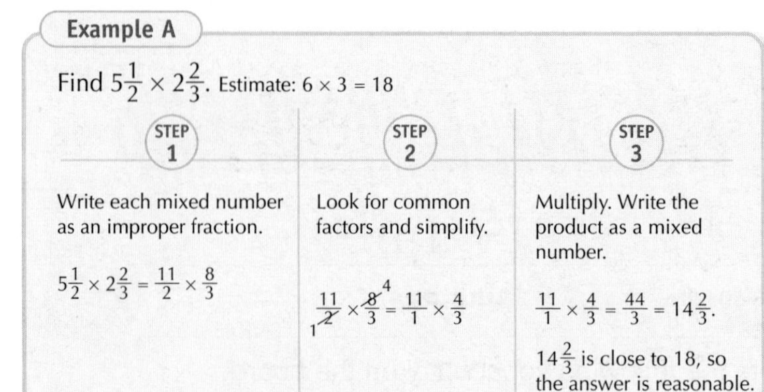

Example B

Franco has two dogs. His toy terrier is $9\frac{3}{16}$ inches tall. His Great Dane puppy is 3 times as tall as the terrier. How tall is his Great Dane?

Find $3 \times 9\frac{3}{16}$. Estimate: $3 \times 9 = 27$

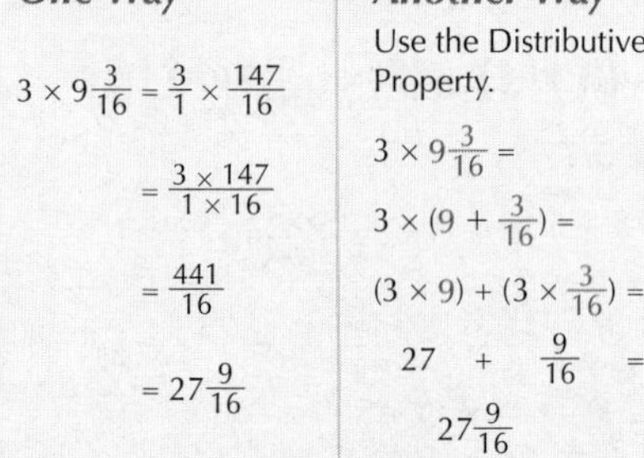

One Way
$3 \times 9\frac{3}{16} = \frac{3}{1} \times \frac{147}{16}$
$= \frac{3 \times 147}{1 \times 16}$
$= \frac{441}{16}$
$= 27\frac{9}{16}$
Another Way
Use the Distributive Property.
$3 \times 9\frac{3}{16} =$
$3 \times (9 + \frac{3}{16}) =$
$(3 \times 9) + (3 \times \frac{3}{16}) =$
$27 + \frac{9}{16} =$
$27\frac{9}{16}$

With a Calculator

Press: 3 [×] 9 [Unit] 3 [/] 16

Display: 441/16

Press: [Ab/c] [=]

Display: 27u9/16

The Great Dane is $27\frac{9}{16}$ inches tall.

Talk About It

1. Which way in Example B would you use to find $8 \times 3\frac{3}{4}$? Why? **See above.**

1. Sample answer: I would use the first method because the GCF of 8 and 4 is 4; $\frac{8}{1} \times \frac{15}{4} = 2 \times 15 = 30$.

258

Below Level — Reteaching

Multiplying Mixed Numbers — R 5-4

How to find the product of two mixed numbers:

Find $3\frac{2}{3} \times 4\frac{1}{2}$.

Step 1
Estimate by rounding.
$3\frac{2}{3} \times 4\frac{1}{2} \rightarrow 4 \times 5 = 20$
Then write each mixed number as an improper fraction.
$3\frac{2}{3} \times 4\frac{1}{2} \rightarrow \frac{11}{3} \times \frac{9}{2}$

Step 2
Look for common factors and simplify.
$\frac{11}{\not{3}_1} \times \frac{\not{9}^3}{2} = \frac{11}{1} \times \frac{3}{2}$

Step 3
Multiply. Write the product as a mixed number.
$\frac{11}{1} \times \frac{3}{2} = \frac{33}{2} = 16\frac{1}{2}$
$16\frac{1}{2}$ is close to 20, so the answer is reasonable.

Find each product. Simplify if possible.

1. $2\frac{3}{4} \times 3\frac{1}{2} =$ **$9\frac{5}{8}$**
2. $2\frac{1}{5} \times 2\frac{2}{3} =$ **$5\frac{13}{15}$**
3. $6 \times 3\frac{1}{4} =$ **$19\frac{1}{2}$**
4. $1\frac{2}{5} \times 3\frac{1}{4} =$ **$4\frac{11}{20}$**
5. $4\frac{1}{2} \times 16 =$ **72**
6. $1\frac{3}{8} \times 2\frac{1}{2} =$ **$3\frac{7}{16}$**
7. **Number Sense** Is $2 \times 17\frac{5}{6}$ greater than or less than 36? Explain.
Less, because $2 \times 18 = 36$. $17\frac{5}{6}$ is less than 18, so the product is less than 36.

Use with Lesson 5-4. 57

On Level — Practice

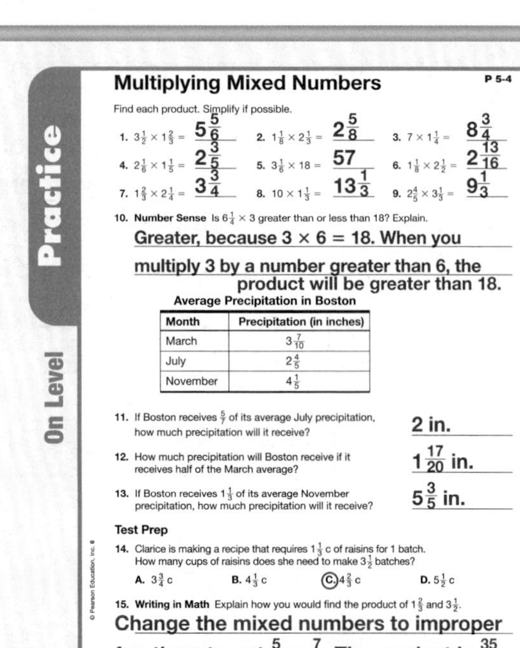

Multiplying Mixed Numbers — P 5-4

Find each product. Simplify if possible.

1. $3\frac{1}{2} \times 1\frac{2}{3} =$ **$5\frac{5}{6}$**
2. $1\frac{1}{8} \times 2\frac{1}{3} =$ **$2\frac{5}{8}$**
3. $7 \times 1\frac{1}{4} =$ **$8\frac{3}{4}$**
4. $2\frac{1}{6} \times 1\frac{1}{5} =$ **$2\frac{3}{5}$**
5. $3\frac{1}{6} \times 18 =$ **57**
6. $1\frac{1}{8} \times 2\frac{1}{2} =$ **$2\frac{13}{16}$**
7. $1\frac{2}{3} \times 2\frac{1}{4} =$ **$3\frac{3}{4}$**
8. $10 \times 1\frac{1}{3} =$ **$13\frac{1}{3}$**
9. $2\frac{4}{5} \times 3\frac{1}{3} =$ **$9\frac{1}{3}$**
10. **Number Sense** Is $6\frac{1}{4} \times 3$ greater than or less than 18? Explain.
Greater, because $3 \times 6 = 18$. When you multiply 3 by a number greater than 6, the product will be greater than 18.

Average Precipitation in Boston

Month	Precipitation (in inches)
March	$3\frac{7}{10}$
July	$2\frac{4}{5}$
November	$4\frac{1}{5}$

11. If Boston receives $\frac{5}{7}$ of its average July precipitation, how much precipitation will it receive? **2 in.**
12. How much precipitation will Boston receive if it receives half of the March average? **$1\frac{17}{20}$ in.**
13. If Boston receives $1\frac{1}{3}$ of its average November precipitation, how much precipitation will it receive? **$5\frac{3}{5}$ in.**

Test Prep

14. Clarice is making a recipe that requires $1\frac{1}{3}$ c of raisins for 1 batch. How many cups of raisins does she need to make $3\frac{1}{2}$ batches?
A. $3\frac{3}{4}$ c B. $4\frac{1}{3}$ c (C.) $4\frac{2}{3}$ c D. $5\frac{1}{2}$ c
15. **Writing in Math** Explain how you would find the product of $1\frac{2}{3}$ and $3\frac{1}{2}$.
Change the mixed numbers to improper fractions to get $\frac{5}{3} \times \frac{7}{2}$. The product is $\frac{35}{6}$, or $5\frac{5}{6}$.

Use with Lesson 5-4. 57

CHECK

For another example, see Set 5-4 on p. 293.

Find each product. Simplify if possible.

1. $2\frac{3}{4} \times 4\frac{2}{3}$ **$12\frac{5}{6}$** **2.** $5\frac{1}{2} \times 1\frac{1}{6}$ **$6\frac{5}{12}$** **3.** $\frac{5}{8} \times 7\frac{1}{3}$ **$4\frac{7}{12}$** **4.** $12 \times 1\frac{1}{2}$ **18**

5. Number Sense Is $2\frac{1}{2} \times 4\frac{3}{4}$ greater than or less than 15? Explain. **See below.**

PRACTICE

For more practice, see Set 5-4 on p. 296.

A Skills and Understanding

5. Less than 15; since both factors are rounded up to get 3 × 5 = 15, the estimated product is an overestimate.

Find each product. Simplify if possible.

6. $1\frac{1}{3} \times 2\frac{4}{5}$ **$3\frac{11}{15}$** **7.** $2\frac{3}{5} \times 4\frac{1}{6}$ **$10\frac{5}{6}$** **8.** $5\frac{1}{9} \times 13\frac{2}{3}$ **$69\frac{23}{27}$** **9.** $5 \times 2\frac{1}{2}$ **$12\frac{1}{2}$**

10. $3\frac{1}{3} \times 1\frac{1}{5}$ **4** **11.** $4\frac{1}{2} \times 1\frac{2}{3}$ **$7\frac{1}{2}$** **12.** $5\frac{1}{5} \times 1\frac{1}{2}$ **$7\frac{4}{5}$** **13.** $5\frac{1}{8} \times 16$ **82**

14. Number Sense Is $5\frac{2}{3} \times 2$ greater than or less than 11? Explain. **Greater than 11; Using the Distributive Property, 5 × 2 = 10, and $\frac{2}{3} \times 2 > 1$.**

B Reasoning and Problem Solving

17. 14 pounds. Sample answer: I changed the mixed numbers to improper fractions. $\frac{21}{2} \times \frac{4}{3} = \frac{84}{6} = 14$.

There are 3 types of poodle that differ mainly by height—standard, miniature, and toy. Mara's grandmother has one of each type.

15. Tartan, her standard poodle, is $20\frac{5}{8}$ inches tall. Tiki, her miniature, is $\frac{2}{3}$ Tartan's height. How tall is Tiki? **$13\frac{3}{4}$ inches tall**

16. Mr. Samara's beagle is $1\frac{1}{2}$ times as tall as Gigi, her $8\frac{1}{4}$-inch tall toy poodle. How tall is Mr. Samara's beagle? **$12\frac{3}{8}$ inches tall**

17. Writing in Math In *Duncan's Way*, the family loaded supplies on the baking boat. The amount of flour they loaded was $1\frac{1}{3}$ times the amount of sugar. If they loaded $10\frac{1}{2}$ pounds of sugar, how much flour did they load? Explain how you found your answer. **See above.**

Mixed Review and Test Prep

Take It to the NET
Test Prep
www.scottforesman.com

Estimate each answer. **Sample answers are given.**

18. $\frac{5}{6} \times 17$ **15** **19.** $15\frac{1}{5} \times 2\frac{4}{9}$ **$37\frac{1}{2}$** **20.** $15\frac{1}{2} \div 2\frac{7}{8}$ **5**

21. $\frac{2}{9} \times 64$ **14** **22.** $32\frac{3}{5} \div 2\frac{5}{9}$ **11** **23.** $57 \times 1\frac{1}{4}$ **72**

24. Which is the least common multiple of 12 and 18?

A. 4 **B.** 12 **C.** 24 **(D.)** 36

All text pages available online and on CD-ROM.

3 Practice

Exercise 17 Encourage students to include an estimate or diagrams in their explanation.

Leveled Practice

Below Level Ex. 6–15, 17–24

On Level Ex. 7–24

Above Level Ex. 7–24

Early Finishers Have pairs make a magic square with Row 1: $1\frac{5}{8}, \frac{3}{4}, 1\frac{3}{8}$; Row 2: 1, $1\frac{1}{4}$, $1\frac{1}{2}$; Row 3: $1\frac{1}{8}, 1\frac{3}{4}, \frac{7}{8}$. Remind students that a magic square contains rows, columns, and diagonals having the same sums.Then have them multiply each number by $2\frac{2}{3}$ and see if the resulting numbers still form a magic square.

4 Assess

Journal Idea Have students list the steps they use to find the product of two mixed numbers.

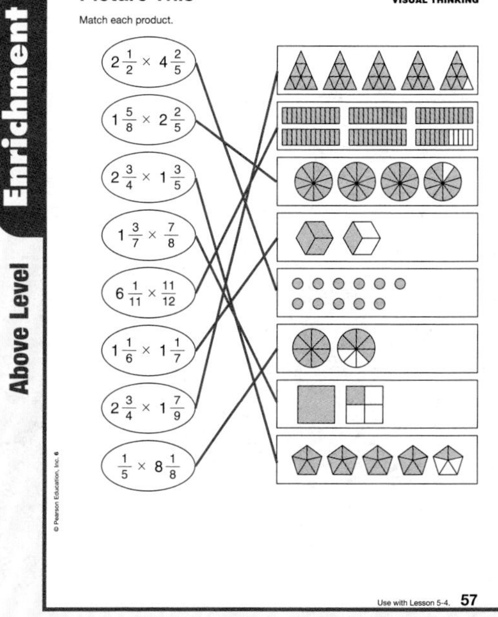

Enrichment — Above Level

Picture This E 5-4 VISUAL THINKING

Match each product.

$2\frac{1}{2} \times 4\frac{2}{5}$

$1\frac{5}{8} \times 2\frac{2}{5}$

$2\frac{3}{4} \times 1\frac{3}{5}$

$1\frac{3}{7} \times \frac{7}{8}$

$6\frac{1}{11} \times \frac{11}{12}$

$1\frac{1}{6} \times 1\frac{1}{7}$

$2\frac{3}{4} \times 1\frac{7}{9}$

$\frac{1}{5} \times 8\frac{1}{8}$

Use with Lesson 5-4. 57

Problem Solving

Multiplying Mixed Numbers PS 5-4

Football Practice The measurements of a football field are shown in the chart. Use the data to solve the exercises about football practice.

Football Field Measurements	
Length	120 yd
Width	$53\frac{1}{3}$ yd
Height of goal posts	$6\frac{2}{3}$ yd

1. The coach asked the team to run the width of the field $4\frac{1}{2}$ times. How many total yards is this? **240 yd**

2. At the next practice, the coach asked the team to run the length of the field $3\frac{3}{4}$ times. How many total yards is this? **450 yd**

3. At each practice of the season, the coach brought bottled water in $1\frac{1}{2}$ gal containers. The running squad drank $5\frac{5}{6}$ containers on one hot day. How many gallons of water did they drink? **$8\frac{3}{4}$ gal**

Frog Jumping A frog-jumping contest was held at the spring fun fair. Eduardo's frog jumped $1\frac{1}{3}$ ft.

4. Miguel's frog jumped $1\frac{3}{4}$ times as far as Eduardo's frog. How far did Miguel's frog jump? **$2\frac{1}{3}$ ft**

5. Margaret's frog jumped $\frac{5}{6}$ times as far as Eduardo's frog. How far did Margaret's frog jump? **$1\frac{1}{9}$ ft**

6. Thomas's frog jumped $1\frac{1}{2}$ times as far as Eduardo's frog. Ben's frog jumped $1\frac{3}{8}$ times as far as Thomas's frog. How far did Ben's frog jump? **$2\frac{3}{4}$ ft**

7. **Writing in Math** The winning frog jumped 6 times as far as Eduardo's frog. Use the Distributive Property to find out how far the champion frog jumped. Explain why this is a good method to use for this problem. **Sample answer: 8 ft; $6 \times 1\frac{1}{3}$ $(6 \times 1) + (6 \times \frac{1}{3}) = 6 + 2 = 8$; The Distributive Property is a good method because it simplifies the numbers. It is easy to see that $\frac{1}{3} \times 6 = 2$, which is added to 6.**

Use with Lesson 5-4. 57

Test-Taking Practice 5-4

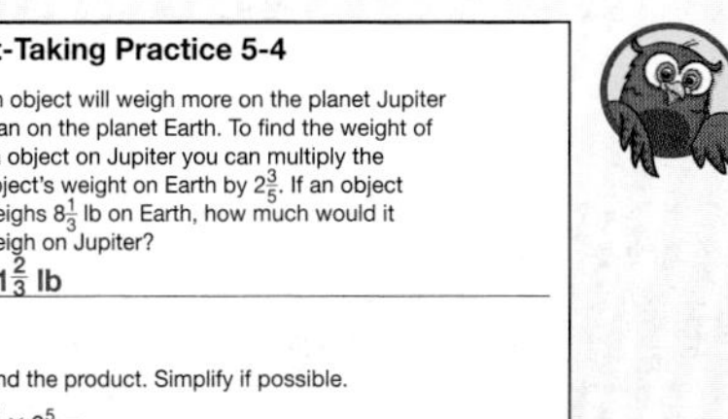

1. An object will weigh more on the planet Jupiter than on the planet Earth. To find the weight of an object on Jupiter you can multiply the object's weight on Earth by $2\frac{3}{5}$. If an object weighs $8\frac{1}{3}$ lb on Earth, how much would it weigh on Jupiter? **$21\frac{2}{3}$ lb**

2. Find the product. Simplify if possible.

$2\frac{2}{3} \times 2\frac{5}{8} =$

A. $5\frac{5}{24}$

B. $\frac{169}{24}$

C. $6\frac{1}{3}$

(D.) 7

Available as a transparency

Review

Purpose Help students review content learned in Section A.

Using Student Pages 260–261

Do You Know How? exercises are appropriate for written work.

Do You Understand? questions are designed for whole-class discussion or small-group discussion followed by a report to the whole class.

Vocabulary Review

You may wish to review these terms before assigning the page.

greatest common factor (GCF) *(p. 150)*

compatible numbers *(p. 18)*

round *(p. 14)*

Section A: Lessons 5-1 through 5-4

Review

Do You Know How?

Do You Understand?

Multiplying a Fraction and a Whole Number (5-1)

Find each product.

1. $\frac{1}{3} \times 6$ **2**
2. $\frac{1}{5} \times 10$ **2**
3. $\frac{4}{7} \times 21$ **12**
4. $36 \times \frac{3}{4}$ **27**
5. $56 \times \frac{5}{8}$ **35**
6. $30 \times \frac{3}{10}$ **9**

A Draw a picture to show Exercise 1. **See above.**

B Tell how you found the product in Exercise 5. **Sample answer: I simplified by finding the GCF of 56 and 8. Then I multiplied 7 × 5 to get 35.**

Multiplying Fractions (5-2)

Find each product. Simplify if possible.

7. $\frac{2}{3} \times \frac{9}{16}$ **$\frac{3}{8}$**
8. $\frac{4}{5} \times \frac{3}{8}$ **$\frac{3}{10}$**
9. $\frac{1}{2} \times \frac{4}{7}$ **$\frac{2}{7}$**
10. $\frac{5}{8} \times \frac{7}{10}$ **$\frac{7}{16}$**
11. $\frac{3}{4} \times \frac{5}{12}$ **$\frac{5}{16}$**
12. $\frac{7}{11} \times \frac{22}{35}$ **$\frac{2}{5}$**

I can divide 3 and 12 by the GCF, 3.

C Explain how you can simplify before multiplying in Exercise 11. **See above.**

D Draw a picture for $\frac{3}{4} \times \frac{2}{3}$.

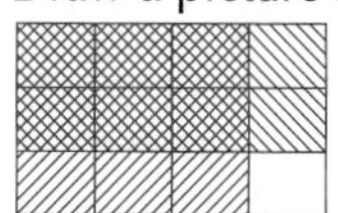

Estimating with Fractions and Mixed Numbers (5-3)
Sample answers given.

Estimate each product or quotient.

13. $\frac{4}{5} \times 16$ **12**
14. $3\frac{1}{5} \times 31$ **93**
15. $5\frac{5}{7} \times 5\frac{8}{9}$ **36**
16. $9\frac{2}{9} \times 3\frac{4}{9}$ **27**
17. $2\frac{3}{5} \times 4\frac{1}{6}$ **12**
18. $12\frac{4}{5} \div 3\frac{2}{3}$ **4**
19. $22\frac{1}{2} \div 10\frac{3}{8}$ **2**
20. $34\frac{3}{5} \div 7\frac{7}{12}$ **5**

Sample answers: Rounding: 3 × 4 = 12; benchmark fraction: $2\frac{1}{2} \times 4 = 10$

E Describe two ways to estimate Exercise 17. **See above.**

F What benchmark fraction could you use to estimate $\frac{7}{9} \times 48$?
Sample answer: $\frac{2}{3}$

Multiplying Mixed Numbers (5-4)

Find each product. Simplify if possible.

21. $2\frac{1}{3} \times 1\frac{2}{7}$ **3**
22. $1\frac{1}{2} \times 4$ **6**
23. $5\frac{5}{7} \times 7$ **40**
24. $9\frac{2}{9} \times 3\frac{4}{9}$ **$31\frac{62}{81}$**
25. $2\frac{3}{5} \times 4\frac{1}{6}$ **$10\frac{5}{6}$**
26. $1\frac{4}{5} \times 1\frac{2}{3}$ **3**
27. $4\frac{1}{2} \times 1\frac{2}{3}$ **$7\frac{1}{2}$**
28. $1\frac{7}{8} \times 2\frac{2}{5}$ **$4\frac{1}{2}$**

I multiplied 1 × 8 and added 7 to get $\frac{15}{8}$; I multiplied 2 × 5 and added 2 to get $\frac{12}{5}$.

G Tell how you changed the mixed numbers to improper fractions in Exercise 28. **See above.**

H Explain how you could use the Distributive Property in Exercise 23. **$5\frac{5}{7} \times 7$ becomes $(5 \times 7) + (\frac{5}{7} \times 7) = 35 + 5 = 40$.**

Item Analysis for Diagnosis and Intervention

Objective	Review Items	Diagnostic Checkpoint Items	Student Book Pages*	Intervention System
Multiply a fraction and a whole number.	1–6	1, 3–6	248–251	H37
Multiply fractions.	7–12	2, 7–12	252–255	H39
Estimate products and quotients with fractions and mixed numbers.	13–20	13–16, 25	256–257	H38
Multiply mixed numbers.	21–28	17–24, 26	258–259	H40

*For each lesson, there is a *Reteaching* activity in *Reaching All Learners* and a *Reteaching* master.

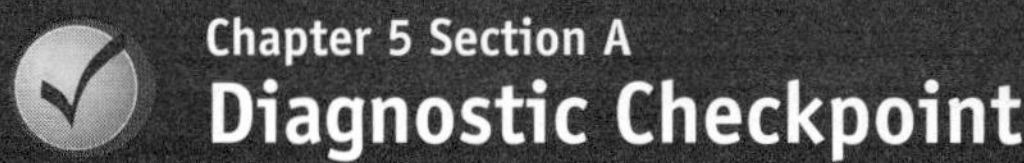

Chapter 5 Section A

Diagnostic Checkpoint

MULTIPLE CHOICE

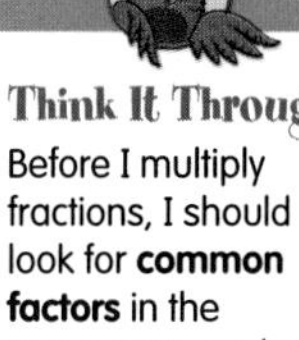

Think It Through
Before I multiply fractions, I should look for **common factors** in the numerators and denominators.

1. Which is $\frac{4}{7} \times 28$? (5-1)

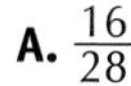

A. $\frac{16}{28}$ **B.** $\frac{16}{7}$ **(C.)** 16 **D.** 49

2. Which is the product $\frac{2}{3} \times \frac{6}{7}$? (5-2)

(A.) $\frac{4}{7}$ **B.** $\frac{14}{18}$ **C.** $\frac{9}{7}$ **D.** $\frac{7}{4}$

FREE RESPONSE

Find the product. (5-1)

3. $\frac{3}{5} \times 20$ **12** **4.** $18 \times \frac{5}{6}$ **15** **5.** $40 \times \frac{7}{8}$ **35** **6.** $\frac{1}{2} \times 40$ **20**

Find each product. Simplify if possible. (5-2)

7. $\frac{2}{3} \times \frac{9}{14}$ $\mathbf{\frac{3}{7}}$ **8.** $\frac{3}{5} \times \frac{10}{27}$ $\mathbf{\frac{2}{9}}$ **9.** $\frac{1}{2} \times \frac{4}{5}$ $\mathbf{\frac{2}{5}}$

10. $\frac{3}{8} \times \frac{4}{5}$ $\mathbf{\frac{3}{10}}$ **11.** $\frac{1}{3} \times \frac{1}{2}$ $\mathbf{\frac{1}{6}}$ **12.** $\frac{3}{4} \times \frac{8}{9}$ $\mathbf{\frac{2}{3}}$

Estimate each product or quotient. (5-3)
Sample answers are given.

13. $2\frac{3}{7} \times 13$ **26** **14.** $3\frac{5}{6} \times 24$ **100** **15.** $25 \div 4\frac{3}{8}$ **6** **16.** $19\frac{7}{8} \div 3\frac{1}{3}$ **7**

Find each product. Simplify if possible. (5-4)

17. $1\frac{3}{5} \times 1\frac{3}{8}$ $\mathbf{2\frac{1}{5}}$ **18.** $5\frac{1}{5} \times 1\frac{1}{2}$ $\mathbf{7\frac{4}{5}}$ **19.** $6 \times 3\frac{1}{2}$ **21**

20. $9\frac{1}{3} \times 18$ **168** **21.** $4\frac{2}{3} \times 2\frac{1}{2}$ $\mathbf{11\frac{2}{3}}$ **22.** $4\frac{1}{5} \times 2\frac{3}{11}$ $\mathbf{9\frac{6}{11}}$

23. A ride on the roller coaster takes $2\frac{3}{4}$ minutes. Mario rode 6 times. For how many minutes did he ride? **$16\frac{1}{2}$ minutes**

24. A coin is $\frac{3}{4}$ copper and $\frac{1}{4}$ nickel. It weighs $8\frac{1}{2}$ grams. How many grams of copper are in the coin?
$6\frac{3}{8}$ grams

Writing in Math

25. Is 120 a reasonable estimate for $120 \div 1\frac{2}{3}$? Explain. (5-3) **No. $1\frac{2}{3}$ is closer to 2 than 1. $120 \div 2 = 60$ would be a better estimate.**

26. Explain how to use the distributive property to find $2\frac{1}{2} \times 8$. (5-4) **Write $2\frac{1}{2}$ as $(2 + \frac{1}{2})$. Multiply 2 by 8 and multiply $\frac{1}{2} \times 8$. Then add both products.**

Sample student work for Exercise 25

No. A good estimate for
$120 \div 1\frac{2}{3}$ is about 60.
$120 \div 1 = 120$.

The rubric below is a scoring guide that shows how many points to give an answer to Exercise 25. Many teachers would assign a score of 3 points to this explanation. Discuss the sample response shown and compare it to papers produced by students.

Scoring Rubric

4 Full credit: 4 points
The answer is correct; understands estimating quotients with mixed numbers; explanation is complete.

3 Partial credit: 3 points
The answer is correct; understands estimating quotients with mixed numbers; explanation is incomplete.

2 Partial credit: 2 points
The answer is incorrect; understands estimating quotients with mixed numbers; gives a good explanation.

1 Partial credit: 1 point
The answer is correct; gives no explanation.

0 No credit
The answer is incorrect; does not know how to estimate quotients.

Reading for Math Success

Purpose Reinforce reading skills and strategies to use in math. *Understand Graphic Sources: Lists* helps prepare students for the problem-solving strategy lesson, *Make an Organized List,* which follows.

Using Student Pages 262–263

In reading, students sometimes are expected to read and understand information they find in organized lists. In mathematics, students can use their knowledge of organized lists to solve certain kinds of problems. They do this either by making sense of lists they are given or by creating their own lists.

Model the Process Explain that to make sense of organized lists, students should begin by noting the types or categories of items a list includes. Generally the labels at the top of a list will make this clear. Students then need to note how many different combinations from those categories the list contains. **In order to make sense of an organized list, I find out the types of items included in each combination in the list. Generally this information is given in the labels at the top of the list. Next, I look at the number of rows in the list. Since each row shows a different combination, counting the rows tells me how many different combinations are possible.**

Reading For Math Success

Understand Graphic Sources: Lists

Understanding graphic sources such as lists when you read in math can help you use the **problem-solving strategy,** ***Make an Organized List,*** in the next lesson.

In reading, understanding lists can help you understand what you read. In math, understanding lists can help you solve problems.

Vera made an organized list to show all the combinations of quarters, dimes, and nickels that make 55¢.

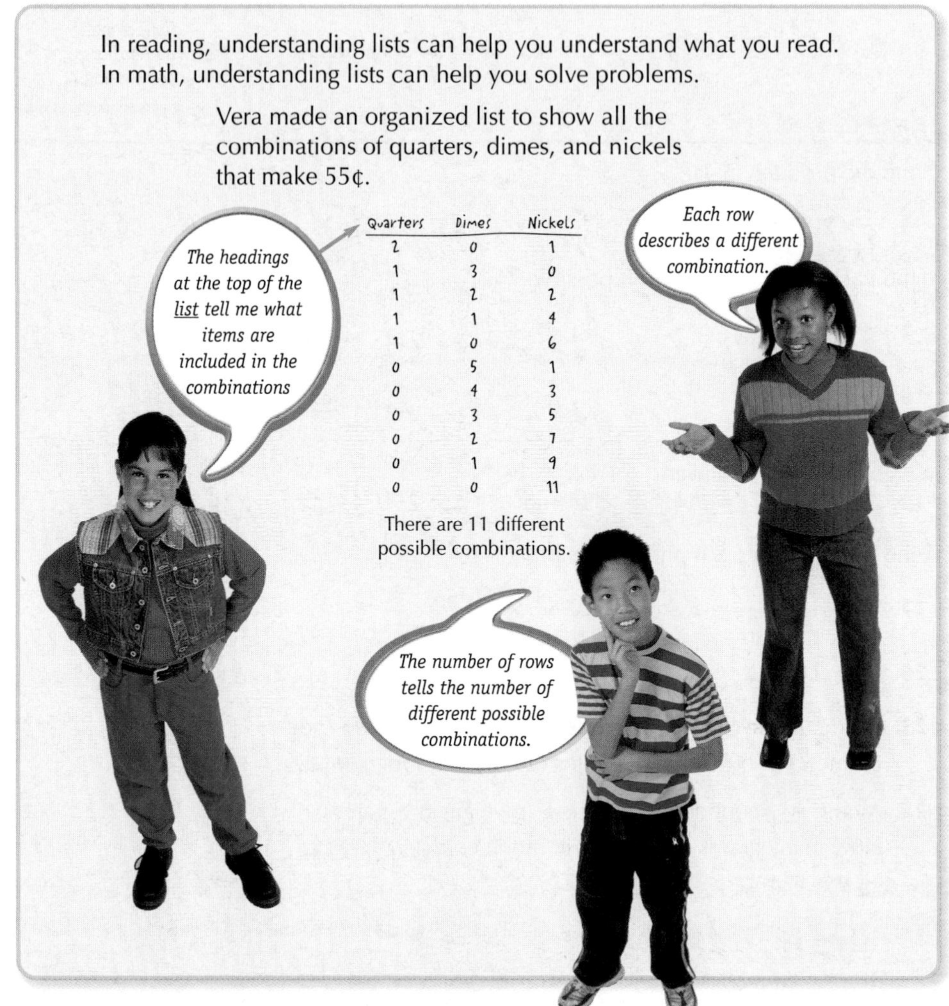

The headings at the top of the list tell me what items are included in the combinations
Each row describes a different combination.
The number of rows tells the number of different possible combinations.

Quarters	Dimes	Nickels
2	0	1
1	3	0
1	2	2
1	1	4
1	0	6
0	5	1
0	4	3
0	3	5
0	2	7
0	1	9
0	0	11

There are 11 different possible combinations.

1. How many different kinds of coins are used in the combinations of 55¢? **3**
2. How many combinations have no quarters? **6**
3. How could Vera have organized her list in a different way? **Sample answer: Start with nickels in first column.**

262

For 4–7, use the problem below and the list at the right.

Bill made an organized list to show the different outfits he could wear on vacation.

Pants	Shirt	Shoes
shorts	red shirt	sneakers
shorts	red shirt	sandals
shorts	blue shirt	sneakers
shorts	blue shirt	sandals
shorts	white shirt	sneakers
shorts	white shirt	sandals
jeans	red shirt	sneakers
jeans	red shirt	sandals
jeans	blue shirt	sneakers
jeans	blue shirt	sandals
jeans	white shirt	sneakers
jeans	white shirt	sandals

4. What items are in an outfit?
   Pants, shirt, shoes
5. How many different types of shoes are there to choose from? 2
6. How many combinations include a blue shirt and sneakers? 2
7. **Writing in Math** How could Bill have organized his list in a different way?
   Sample answer: List jeans before shorts.

For 8–10, use the problem below and the list at the right.

Ms. Von Helms began an organized list to show the different possible orders of 4 students who are going to perform in a talent show.

First	Second	Third	Fourth
Mark	Eric	Jessica	Tina
Mark	Eric	Tina	Jessica
Mark	Jessica	Eric	Tina
Mark	Jessica	Tina	Eric
Mark	Tina	Eric	Jessica
Mark	Tina	Jessica	Eric
Jessica	Mark	Eric	Tina
Jessica	Mark	Tina	Eric
Jessica	Eric	Mark	Tina
Jessica	Eric	Tina	Mark
Jessica	Tina	Mark	Eric
Jessica	Tina	Eric	Mark

8. Does the list show all the different orders that are possible if Mark is first? Yes
9. How many orders are possible if Mark performs first? if Jessica performs first? 6; 6
10. **Writing in Math** How many more rows will Ms. Von Helms need to write to complete the list? Explain.
    12; for any given student there are 6 rows to show the possible orders with that student first, so, there would be $2 \times 6 = 12$ more rows with Eric or Tina first.

For 11–12, use the problem below and the list at the right.

Cal wants to buy 3 caps in different colors. His choices are red, blue, black, and gray.

Cap 1	Cap 2	Cap 3
red	blue	black
red	blue	gray
red	black	gray
blue	black	gray

11. How many combinations do not include blue? 1
12. **Writing in Math** Why doesn't this list show a row that starts with black?
    It has already been combined with every possible pair of other colors.

Guide the Activity Direct students' attention to the organized list. **What types of items does this list contain?** *(Quarters, dimes, and nickels)* **How are the items combined in each row?** *(Each row shows a combination of coins that add up to 55 cents.)* **How many rows are in the list?** *(11)* **What does this tell you about the possible combinations that add up to 55 cents?** *(There are eleven possible combinations.)* Discuss Exercises 1–3 as a class, and ask students to come up with several possible answers for Exercise 3. Then assign Exercises 4–12. Tell students that one list is partially complete and that they will have to use what they've already learned in order to add the missing data.

Error Intervention

If students have trouble understanding organized lists,

then tell them to put the information into a different format—for example, into a drawing or diagram.

Journal Idea Have students look again at the list in Exercises 8–10. Have students write all the different orders that are possible if Eric were first.

Lesson Organizer

Quick Lesson Overview

Objective Solve word problems by making organized lists.

Math Understanding Making an organized list can help to represent what you know in solving a problem.

How Children Learn Math Visual learners will benefit from making and manipulating a diagram to record each possible arrangement. Cooperative learners will help each other organize their thinking in list form. Mathematical/logical learners will be able to create the list using logical thinking and patterns.

NCTM Standards

- Data Analysis and Probability

(For a complete correlation to the NCTM Standards and Grades 6–8 Expectations, see pages 246G–H.)

Getting Started

Spiral Review

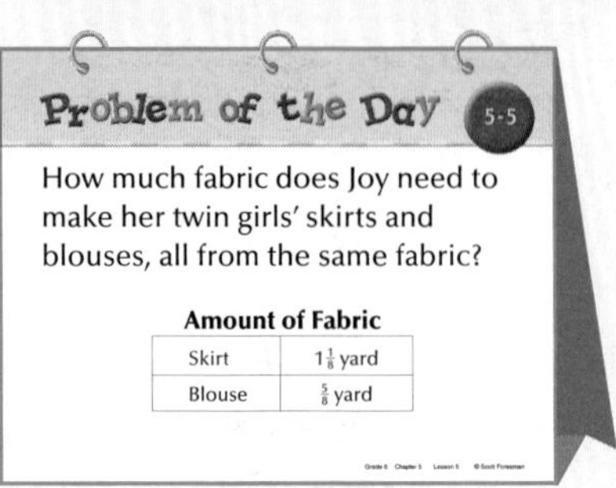

Problem of the Day 5-5

How much fabric does Joy need to make her twin girls' skirts and blouses, all from the same fabric?

Amount of Fabric

Skirt	$1\frac{1}{8}$ yard
Blouse	$\frac{5}{8}$ yard

Grade 6 Chapter 5 Lesson 5

Topics Reviewed

- Adding and multiplying mixed numbers
- Problem-Solving Skill: Multiple-Step Problem

Answer Joy needs $3\frac{1}{2}$ yd of fabric.

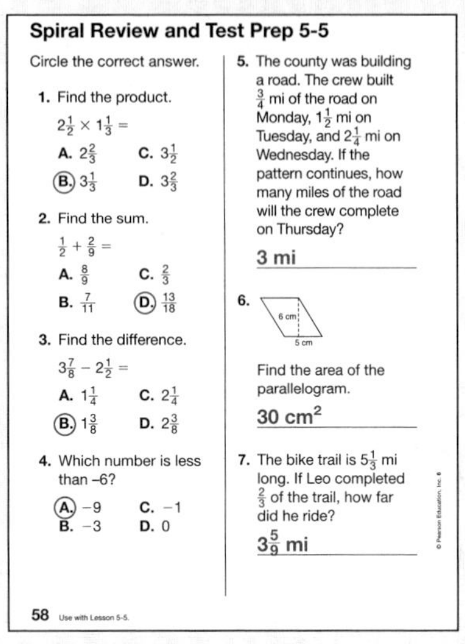

Spiral Review and Test Prep 5-5

Circle the correct answer.

1. Find the product.
$2\frac{1}{2} \times 1\frac{1}{3} =$
A. $2\frac{2}{3}$ C. $3\frac{1}{2}$
(B.) $3\frac{1}{3}$ D. $3\frac{2}{3}$

2. Find the sum.
$\frac{1}{2} + \frac{2}{9} =$
A. $\frac{8}{9}$ C. $\frac{2}{3}$
B. $\frac{7}{11}$ (D.) $\frac{13}{18}$

3. Find the difference.
$3\frac{7}{8} - 2\frac{1}{2} =$
A. $1\frac{1}{4}$ C. $2\frac{1}{4}$
(B.) $1\frac{3}{8}$ D. $2\frac{3}{8}$

4. Which number is less than –6?
(A.) –9 C. –1
B. –3 D. 0

5. The county was building a road. The crew built $\frac{3}{4}$ mi of the road on Monday, $1\frac{1}{2}$ mi on Tuesday, and $2\frac{1}{4}$ mi on Wednesday. If the pattern continues, how many miles of the road will the crew complete on Thursday?
3 mi

6.

Find the area of the parallelogram.
30 cm^2

7. The bike trail is $5\frac{1}{3}$ mi long. If Leo completed $\frac{2}{3}$ of the trail, how far did he ride?
$3\frac{5}{9}$ mi

58 Use with Lesson 5-5.

Available as a transparency and as a blackline master

Topics Reviewed

1., 7. Multiplying mixed numbers; **2.–3.** Adding and subtracting fractions with unlike denominators; **4.** Using integers; **5.** Look for a pattern; **6.** Areas of parallelograms

Investigating the Concept

Making a List

10–15 MIN **Kinesthetic**

Materials Sheets of paper labeled 1, 2, and 3

What to Do

- **The problem is to arrange three students in a line in as many ways as possible**. Give three volunteers the numbers 1, 2, and 3. **How can you find out how many ways there are to arrange these three students?** *(Sample answer: Move them around.)*
- Encourage students to share their ideas about how to ensure that all the possibilities are listed. They should suggest making a list.
- As a class activity, make an organized list. Have students find the arrangements with 1 first, then 2 first, then 3 first.

1	2	3
1	3	2
2	1	3
2	3	1
3	1	2
3	2	1

Ongoing Assessment

- **Reasoning If Students 1 and 2 are not allowed to stand next to each other, in how many ways can the three students be arranged?** *(2 ways: 1-3-2 or 2-3-1)*

 EC NTL 12 11 10 9 8 7 6

Reaching All Learners

Writing in Math

Creating a Problem

 15–20 MIN **Linguistic** 

Materials *(per pair)* Index card containing related words such as *blouse* and *skirt*

- **Choose an index card. Work with your partner to write a problem using the words on your card that could be solved by making a list.**
- Have pairs exchange cards and solve.

> Maria has a white blouse, a green blouse, a black blouse, and a blue blouse. She has a grey skirt, a black skirt, and a white skirt. How many different outfits can she make?

Activate Prior Knowledge/Build Background

English Language Learners

Lists

 10–15 MIN **Verbal/Logical/Mathematical** 

- **Before class, I make a list of topics to cover. What lists have you made?**
- Write on the board the grocery list shown here. Ask volunteers to list the foods under the headings dairy, meat, vegetables, and fruits.
- Demonstrate writing a possible food combination with one food from each group, such as milk, chicken, lettuce, and apple. Have a volunteer list another combination.
- Have pairs talk through a few more food combinations and dictate them to add to the list on the board. This is called an organized list.

milk
chicken
lettuce
apples
tuna
grapes
potatoes
yogurt

Reteaching

Totals and Products

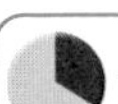 15–20 MIN **Social/Cooperative** 

Materials *(per pair)* Spinners or Teaching Tool 4: labeled 1–3

- **How many different sums are possible if you spin these two spinners? How many different products are possible? Work with your partner to model and make a list of the possibilities.**
- **What are the possible pairs of numbers?**

1, 1 *2, 1* *3, 1*
1, 2 *2, 2* *3, 2*
1, 3 *2, 3* *3, 3*

- **How many different sums are there?** *(5 different sums: 2, 3, 4, 5, and 6)* **How many different products?** *(6 different products: 1, 2, 3, 4, 6, and 9)*

Students with Special Needs

Making Connections

 10–15 MIN **Kinesthetic** 

Materials *(per group)* Six 6-foot-long pieces of string, rope, or similar material

- **Mary, Bill, José, and Sally want to play each other in tennis. How many matches will they need to play?**
- Have four students stand in a square. Have them use their pieces of string to connect with each other so everyone is connected with everyone else one time. As each connection is made, write it in a list on the board.
- **How many connections are there?** *(6 connections)* **How many matches will you need?** *(6 matches)*

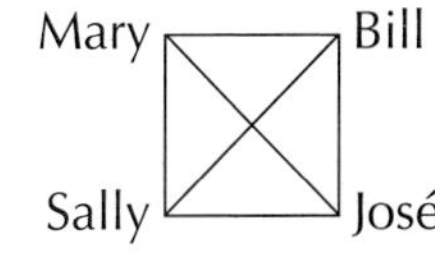

Objective Solve word problems by making organized lists.

1 Warm Up

Activate Prior Knowledge Review the basic problem-solving steps: *Read and Understand, Plan and Solve,* and *Look Back and Check.*

2 Teach

LEARN Explain the example on page 264 or present the problem using these teaching actions.

BEFORE Read and Understand

Which numbers did the class use to make the 3-digit combinations? *(5, 7, and 9)* How many students need locker combinations? *(30 students)*

DURING Plan and Solve

How many combinations start with the number 5? *(9 combinations)*
With the number 7? *(9 combinations)*
With the number 9? *(9 combinations)*

AFTER Look Back and Check

If the teacher handed out 27 locker combinations, how many students would be without a locker combination? *(3 students)*

Problem-Solving Strategy

Key Idea
Learning how and when to make an organized list can help you solve problems.

Reading Helps!
Understanding graphic sources such as lists
can help you with...
the problem-solving strategy, *Make an Organized List.*

Make an Organized List

LEARN

How can you make an organized list to solve problems?

Locker Combinations A class was given the numbers 5, 7, and 9 to use for 3-digit locker combinations. Can they make enough different combinations for the 30 students in the class?

Read and Understand

What do you know? Three numbers are available—5, 7, and 9. Each combination must have 3 digits. The digits can be repeated in a combination.

What are you trying to find? How many different locker combinations using the digits 5, 7, and 9 can be made?

Plan and Solve

What strategy will you use? **Strategy: Make an Organized List**

How to Make an Organized List

Step 1 Identify the items to be combined.

Step 2 Choose one of the items. Find combinations keeping that item fixed.

Step 3 Repeat Step 2 as often as needed.

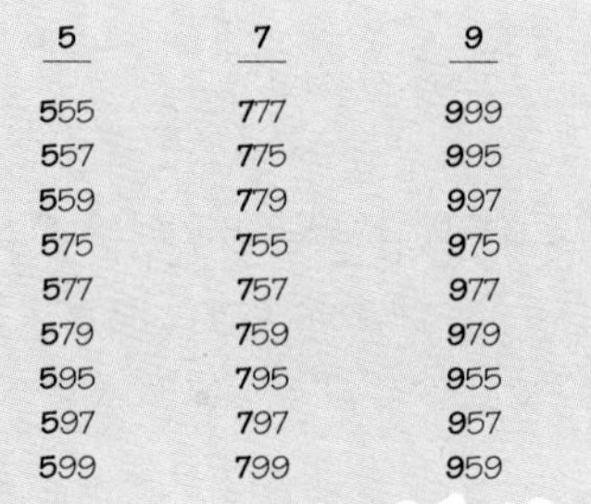

5	7	9
555	777	999
557	775	995
559	779	997
575	755	975
577	757	977
579	759	979
595	795	955
597	797	957
599	799	959

Answer: There are 27 combinations possible. So, there are not enough for the 30 students.

Look Back and Check

Is your answer reasonable? Yes, no combinations are repeated. There are 3 sets of 9 ways.

Reteaching — Below Level

PROBLEM-SOLVING STRATEGY R 5-5

Make an Organized List

Standing in Line How many different ways can Jose, Sumi, and Tina be arranged in a straight line?

Read and Understand

Step 1: What do you know?
There are 3 different people who must be arranged in a straight line: Jose, Sumi, and Tina.

Step 2: What are you trying to find?
How many different ways they can be arranged?

Plan and Solve

Step 3: What strategy will you use? **Strategy:** Make an organized list

Jose first	Sumi first	Tina first
Jose, Sumi, Tina	Sumi, Jose, Tina	Tina, Jose, Sumi
Jose, Tina, Sumi	Sumi, Tina, Jose	Tina, Sumi, Jose

Answer: The students can be arranged 6 different ways.

Look Back and Check

Is your answer reasonable? Yes, no combinations are repeated.

1. How many different four-digit combinations can be made using the digits 2, 3, 6, and 9? No digit combinations can be repeated. Complete the chart.

2	3	6	9
2369	3269	6239	9236
2396	3296	6293	9263
2693	3692	6392	9362
2639	3629	6329	9326
2936	3926	6923	9623
2963	3962	6932	9632

24 different combinations

Practice — On Level

PROBLEM-SOLVING STRATEGY P 5-5

Make an Organized List

Solve by making an organized list.

1. Ernest is planting flowers, four to a row. He is planting red, purple, yellow, and white flowers. Each row must contain all four colors and be in a different order from right to left. How many rows can Ernest plant?

Ernest can plant 24 rows.

2. Sandra is buying tickets for a play. There are shows on Friday, Saturday, and Sunday. Each day has a show at 6:00 P.M., 8:00 P.M., and 10:00 P.M. How many possible choices for a day and a time are there?

Sandra has 9 choices for a day and a time.

3. Tanya has to wear a cap and a T-shirt for her job at the amusement park. She can wear a red, blue, or yellow cap and a red or green shirt. How many different shirt and hat combinations can Tanya wear?

Tanya can wear 6 different combinations.

4. **Writing in Math** Explain how you would find the number of three-letter arrangements that can be made with the letters L, G, and F if no repetition of letters is allowed.

L	G	F
LGF	GFL	FLG
LFG	GLF	FGL

Make an organized list.
There are 6 different arrangements.

✓ Talk About It

1. Suppose digits cannot be repeated in the Locker Combinations problem. How many combinations are possible?
6 combinations
2. **Patterns** Explain how patterns were used to organize the Locker Combinations list.
First, all the combinations that started with 55 were listed, then 57 and 59.

CHECK ✓

For another example, see Set 5-5 on p. 293.

Solve by making an organized list. The lists have been started for you.

M	A	T	H

MAT
MAH
MTA
MTH
MHA
MHT

1. How many different arrangements of 3 letters can be made from the letters in the word MATH if no repetition of letters is allowed? **24 arrangements**
2. In how many ways can you make $0.60 using at least one quarter? You cannot use half dollars or pennies. **6 ways**

Q	D	N
2	1	0

3.

Middle Bricks	3	4	5	6	7
Total Bricks	9	16	25	36	49

PRACTICE

For more practice, see Set 5-5 on p. 296.

Solve by making an organized list.

3. Fumiko wants to lay out a patio in a design like the one shown at right. She has 50 bricks to use. How many bricks should she place in the middle row to use the greatest number of bricks? Draw a diagram or make a table, then look for a pattern. **7 bricks. See above.**

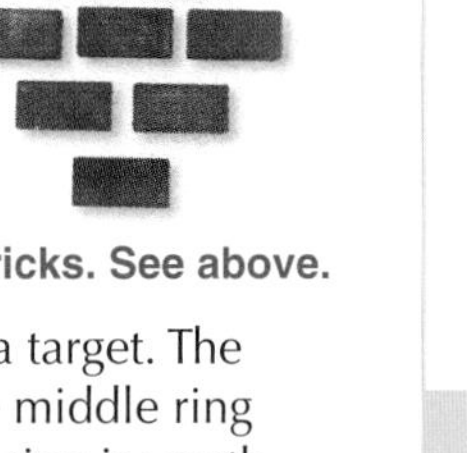

STRATEGIES

- **Show What You Know**
  Draw a Picture
  Make an Organized List
  Make a Table
  Make a Graph
  Act It Out or Use Objects
- **Look for a Pattern**
- **Try, Check, and Revise**
- **Write an Equation**
- **Use Logical Reasoning**
- **Solve a Simpler Problem**
- **Work Backward**

Choose a tool
Mental Math

4. Three darts are thrown at and hit a target. The center ring is worth 10 points, the middle ring is worth 6 points, and the outside ring is worth 3 points. How many different total points are possible? **10 different total points**
5. The chess club has 4 senior members. They are planning a special tournament in which every member plays every other member just once. How many games will be played? **6 games**
6. **Writing in Math** Explain how you would find the number of different ways to arrange Marcus, Norio, Catana, and Alfons in a row. **I would list all the possibilities if Marcus was first, then if Norio was first then if Catano was first, then if Alfons was first.**

CHECK ✓

Error Intervention

If students list options more than once or forget to list options,

then have them work with partners to make a plan for an organized list. Once they have made a plan, have them use manipulatives to represent the objects being arranged and record the list. *(Also see* Reteaching, *p. 264B.)*

3 Practice

TEST TALK

Exercise 6 It may help students to use the first letter of each name and then make a list using the letter combinations.

Leveled Practice

Below Level Ex. 3–6

On Level Ex. 3–6

Above Level Ex. 3–6

Early Finishers Have pairs of students list three lunch entrees, two drinks, and two desserts they like. Then have them find how many different lunches they could create consisting of one entree, one drink, and one dessert.

4 Assess

Journal Idea Have students describe how to find the number of ways to arrange the letters of MATH.

Enrichment — Above Level

Keep to the Schedule

E 5-5
DECISION MAKING

Kaya is the manager of the city volleyball league. She has to make a game schedule that meets the following requirements.

- There are 6 teams: Robins, Orioles, Cardinals, Bluebirds, Hawks, and Eagles.
- Each team must play each other team at least twice.
- The Cardinals cannot play during Week 2.
- The Bluebirds cannot play during Week 4.
- Each team can play up to 2 games per week.
- There are 4 games per week.

Make a game schedule for Kaya that meets all of the requirements. Use these abbreviations: R = Robins, O = Orioles, C = Cardinals, B = Bluebirds, H = Hawks, E = Eagles. The first week is done for you.

Sample answers are given.

City Volleyball League Schedule

Week	Games			
1	R-O	E-C	C-B	B-H
2	H-E	B-E	O-H	O-B
3	E-C	B-R	H-B	C-O
4	O-E	R-H	E-R	O-C
5	R-O	C-B	H-C	H-E
6	B-E	C-H	B-O	R-C
7	R-B	O-H	C-R	E-O
8	H-R	R-E	C-B	H-O

58 Use with Lesson 5-5.

Problem Solving

PROBLEM-SOLVING STRATEGY
PS 5-5

Make an Organized List

Football Scoring The Wescott High School football team scored three times in a recent game. They scored one touchdown. Each time they scored, it was a different type of scoring. How many different combinations are there, and what possible point totals could they have at the end of the game?

Types of Scoring—Football	
Touchdown	6 points
Field goal	3 points
Safety	2 points
2-point conversion	2 points
Extra point	1 point

Read and Understand

1. What do you need to find? **Sample answer: How many different combinations there were and what possible point totals they could have had**

Plan and Solve

2. Complete the organized list.

Touchdown 6	Field Goal 3	Safety 2	Conversion 2	Extra Point 1	Total Points
X	X	X			11
X	X		X		11
X	X			X	10
X		X	X		10
X		X		X	9
X			X	X	9

3. Solve the problem, and write your answer in a complete sentence.
The team could have ended the game with 9, 10, or 11 points. There were 6 possible combinations.

Look Back and Check

4. Is your answer reasonable? **Sample answer: Yes, since the team must have scored a touchdown, the only possible added points are 3, 4, or 5.**

58 Use with Lesson 5-5.

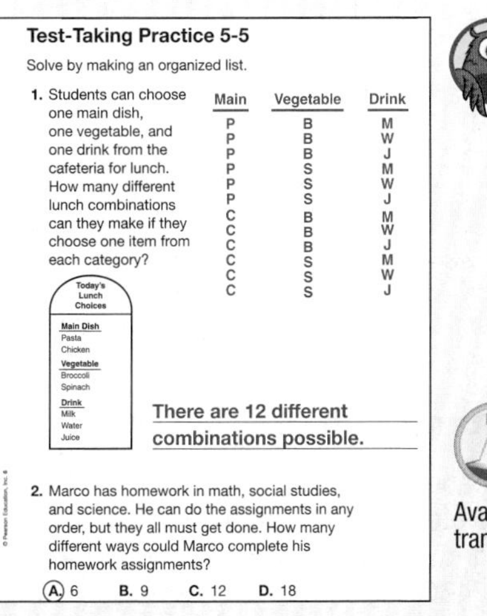

Test-Taking Practice 5-5

Solve by making an organized list.

1. Students can choose one main dish, one vegetable, and one drink from the cafeteria for lunch. How many different lunch combinations can they make if they choose one item from each category?

Main	Vegetable	Drink
P	B	M
P	B	W
P	B	J
P	S	M
P	S	W
P	S	J
C	B	M
C	B	W
C	B	J
C	S	M
C	S	W
C	S	J

There are 12 different combinations possible.

2. Marco has homework in math, social studies, and science. He can do the assignments in any order, but they all must get done. How many different ways could Marco complete his homework assignments?

(A.) 6 B. 9 C. 12 D. 18

Available as a transparency

5-6 Dividing Fractions

Lesson Organizer

Quick Lesson Overview

Objective Divide fractions.

Math Understanding When we divide by a fraction that is less than 1, the quotient is greater than the number being divided (the dividend).

Vocabulary Reciprocal, multiplicative inverse

Professional Development Note

Research Base

Huinker's research (1998, 2002) consistently points to the necessity of having students develop a meaningful understanding of the operations for fractions. The measurement meaning is suggested for division–the meaning that is developed in this lesson.

NCTM Standards

- Numbers and Operations

(For a complete correlation to the NCTM Standards and Grades 6–8 Expectations, see pages 246G–H.)

Getting Started

Spiral Review

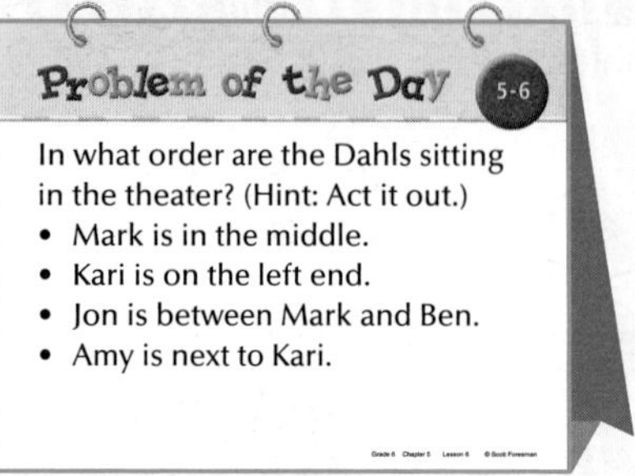

Problem of the Day 5-6

In what order are the Dahls sitting in the theater? (Hint: Act it out.)
- Mark is in the middle.
- Kari is on the left end.
- Jon is between Mark and Ben.
- Amy is next to Kari.

Topics Reviewed
- Problem-Solving Strategy: Act It Out

Answer The correct order, from left to right, is Kari, Amy, Mark, Jon, and Ben.

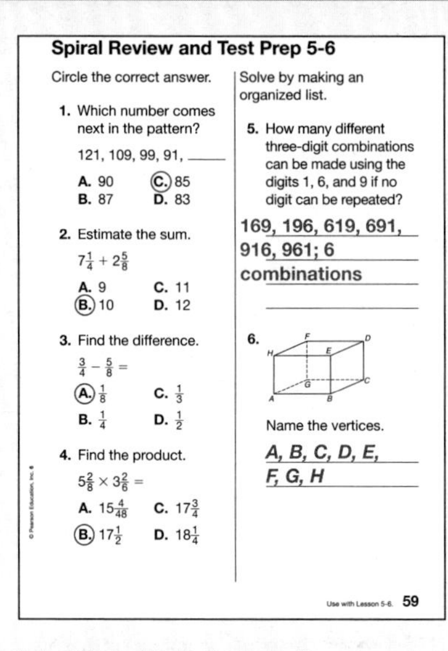

Spiral Review and Test Prep 5-6

Circle the correct answer.

1. Which number comes next in the pattern?
121, 109, 99, 91, ____
A. 90 (C.) 85
B. 87 D. 83

2. Estimate the sum.
$7\frac{1}{4} + 2\frac{5}{8}$
A. 9 C. 11
(B.) 10 D. 12

3. Find the difference.
$\frac{3}{4} - \frac{5}{8} =$
(A.) $\frac{1}{8}$ C. $\frac{1}{3}$
B. $\frac{1}{4}$ D. $\frac{1}{2}$

4. Find the product.
$5\frac{2}{8} \times 3\frac{2}{6} =$
A. $15\frac{4}{48}$ C. $17\frac{3}{4}$
(B.) $17\frac{1}{2}$ D. $18\frac{1}{4}$

Solve by making an organized list.

5. How many different three-digit combinations can be made using the digits 1, 6, and 9 if no digit can be repeated?
169, 196, 619, 691, 916, 961; 6 combinations

6.

Name the vertices.
A, B, C, D, E, F, G, H

Use with Lesson 5-6. 59

Available as a transparency and as a blackline master

Topics Reviewed

1. Look for a pattern; **2.** Adding mixed numbers; **3.** Subtracting fractions with unlike denominators; **4.** Multiplying mixed numbers; **5.** Make an organized list; **6.** Solid figures

Investigating the Concept

Using a Number Line

10–15 MIN **Visual/Spatial**

What to Do

- **Start with a line 3 units long. To divide 3 by $\frac{1}{4}$, divide each unit into fourths. How many fourths are there?**
(12 fourths) Write $3 \div \frac{1}{4} = 12$ on the board. Next to it write $3 \times \frac{4}{1} = 12$.
- **Using the same line, divide 3 by $\frac{3}{4}$ by circling groups of $\frac{3}{4}$. How many groups are there?** *(4 groups)* **What is $3 \div \frac{3}{4}$?** *(4)* Write $3 \div \frac{3}{4} = 4$ on the board. Next to it write $3 \times \frac{4}{3} = 4$.
Notice that when you divide by $\frac{1}{4}$, you get the same results as when you multiply by $\frac{4}{1}$. The same is true for $\frac{3}{4}$ and $\frac{4}{3}$. $\frac{1}{4}$ and $\frac{4}{1}$ are *reciprocals.* $\frac{3}{4}$ and $\frac{4}{3}$ are also reciprocals. Dividing by a number produces the same result as multiplying by its reciprocal.

Ongoing Assessment

- **Reasoning What is $4 \div \frac{1}{16}$?** *(64)*
- **What is $5 \div \frac{5}{6}$?** *(6)*

Reaching All Learners

Math and Literature

Math Curse

 15–20 MIN **Auditory** 

Materials *Math Curse* by Jon Scieszka and Lane Smith (Viking, 1995)

- This funny book tells the story of a young girl who is afflicted with a "math curse." Read part of this book to the students.
- At one point, the book asks how many quarts there are in a gallon. Tell students, **One quart equals $\frac{1}{4}$ of a gallon. How many quarts are there in one gallon?** *(4 quarts)* **Write that situation as a division problem.** *($1 \div \frac{1}{4} = 1 \times 4 = 4$)*

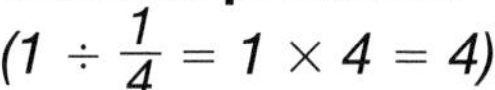

English Language Learners

Activate Prior Knowledge/Build Background

Dividing the Pizza

10–15 MIN **Visual/Spatial/Kinesthetic**

- Have one student in the group draw a large pizza on a sheet of paper. Have another student draw a line to divide the pizza in half. Model asking: **What is one half of one whole?** *($\frac{1}{2}$)*
- Have a student divide the pizza into 4 equal parts while another asks: "What is one half of $\frac{1}{2}$?" *($\frac{1}{4}$)*
- Have a third student divide one of the slices in half while another asks: "What is one half of $\frac{1}{4}$?". *($\frac{1}{8}$)*
- Have groups discuss: **Were you multiplying or dividing the fractions of the pizza? How do you know?**

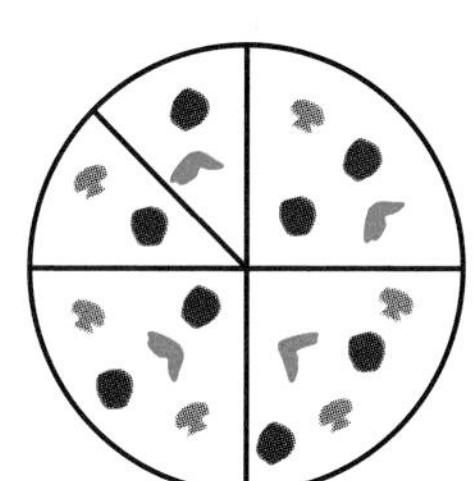

Reteaching

Using Fraction Strips

 5–10 MIN **Social/Cooperative** 

Materials *(per pair)* Fraction Strips or Teaching Tool 15

- Write $2 \div \frac{1}{3}$ on the board.
- Have students work with partners to represent the exercise using fraction strips.
- **Divide 2 into thirds. How many thirds are in 2?** *(6 thirds)* **What is $2 \div \frac{1}{3}$?** *(6)* **What multiplication has the same answer?** *(2×3)*
- **What is $4 \div \frac{1}{2}$? Use fraction strips to help.** *($4 \div \frac{1}{2} = 8$)*

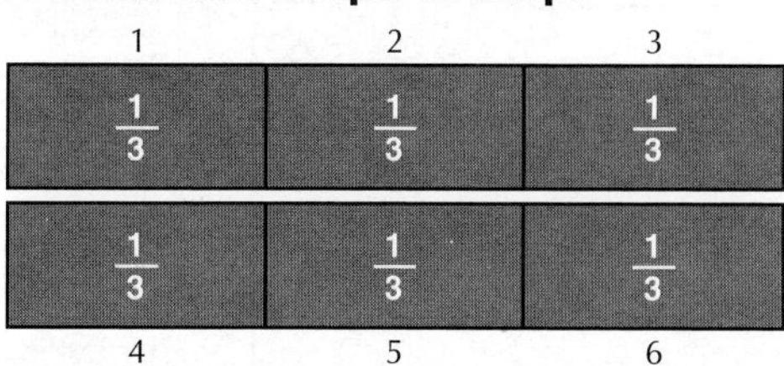

Math and Technology

Using a Calculator to Divide

 5–10 MIN **Social/Cooperative** 

Materials *(per student)* Calculator

- Write a division exercise with mixed numbers on the board, such as $5\frac{1}{3} \div \frac{2}{9}$. Have both partners write the reciprocal of $\frac{2}{9}$. *($\frac{9}{2}$)*
- Have Partner 1 write a sequence of keystrokes to solve $5\frac{1}{3} \div \frac{2}{9}$. Have Partner 2 write and use a sequence of keystrokes to find $5\frac{1}{3} \times \frac{9}{2}$.
- Then have partners compare answers, exchange roles, and solve another exercise.

Objective Divide fractions.

1 Warm Up

Activate Prior Knowledge Review multiplication of fractions.

2 Teach

LEARN Have the students use the models to explain why $5 \div \frac{1}{2}$ must be greater than 5 but $\frac{3}{4} \div 4$ must be less than $\frac{3}{4}$.

Some students need many examples to discover the patterns in the activity. Encourage students to use models to show the division and multiplication.

Lesson 5-6

Key Idea
You can use multiplication to divide fractions.

Vocabulary
- reciprocal
- multiplicative inverse

Think It Through
- I can **use models** to show division of fractions.
- I can **look for a pattern** to understand how division and multiplication are related.

Dividing Fractions

WARM UP

1. $8 \times \frac{5}{4}$ 10
2. $12 \times \frac{7}{3}$ 28
3. $\frac{5}{6} \times \frac{3}{2}$ $1\frac{1}{4}$
4. $\frac{3}{8} \times \frac{4}{3}$ $\frac{1}{2}$

LEARN

How can you model division of fractions?

Example A

Mr. Wagner makes wooden coasters for glasses. He cuts small round posts into $\frac{1}{2}$-inch thick slices. How many slices can he get from a 5-inch post?

Find $5 \div \frac{1}{2}$.

Think: "How many halves are in 5?"

Divide 5 inches into $\frac{1}{2}$-inch sections.

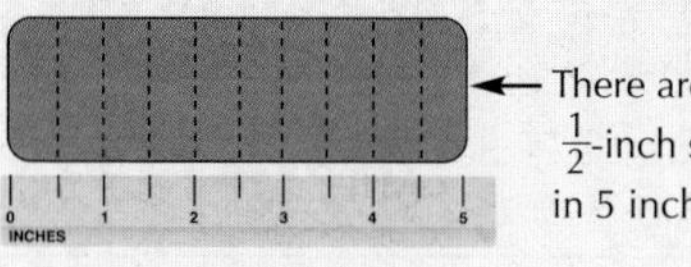

There are ten $\frac{1}{2}$-inch slices in 5 inches.

So, $5 \div \frac{1}{2} = 10$.

Mr. Wagner can get 10 slices from a 5-inch post.

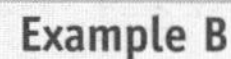

Example B

Find $\frac{3}{4} \div 4$.

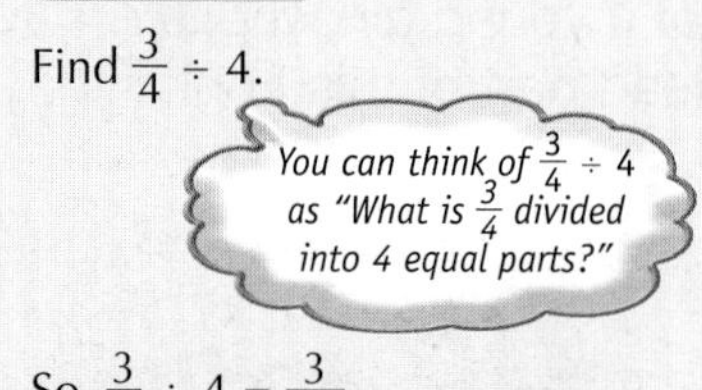

You can think of $\frac{3}{4} \div 4$ as "What is $\frac{3}{4}$ divided into 4 equal parts?"

Show $\frac{3}{4}$.

Divide $\frac{3}{4}$ into 4 equal parts.

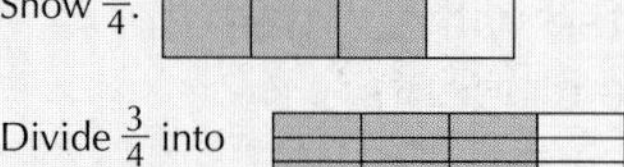

Each of the four equal parts contains 3 sixteenths.

So, $\frac{3}{4} \div 4 = \frac{3}{16}$.

How can you divide fractions?

Activity

a. Study the patterns below. Compare the first and second columns.

Pattern 1	
$6 \div \frac{3}{1} = 2$	$6 \times \frac{1}{3} = 2$
$3 \div \frac{4}{1} = \frac{3}{4}$	$3 \times \frac{1}{4} = \frac{3}{4}$
$4 \div \frac{1}{2} = 8$	$4 \times \frac{2}{1} = 8$

Pattern 2	
$\frac{3}{4} \div \frac{2}{1} = \frac{3}{8}$	$\frac{3}{4} \times \frac{1}{2} = \frac{3}{8}$
$\frac{1}{4} \div \frac{1}{12} = 3$	$\frac{1}{4} \times \frac{12}{1} = 3$
$\frac{3}{4} \div \frac{3}{8} = 2$	$\frac{3}{4} \times \frac{8}{3} = 2$

b. What do you notice about the divisors in the first column and the factors in the second column of each pattern?
The numerators and denominators are reversed.

c. How does the quotient compare to the dividend when the divisor is a fraction less than 1? **The quotient is greater than the dividend.**

Reteaching — Below Level

Dividing Fractions

R 5-6

Dividing by a fraction is the same as multiplying by its reciprocal. The product of a number and its reciprocal is 1. For example:

Number	×	Reciprocal	=	Product
3	×	$\frac{1}{3}$	=	1
$\frac{1}{8}$	×	$\frac{8}{1}$	=	1
$\frac{2}{3}$	×	$\frac{3}{2}$	=	1

Find $\frac{4}{5} \div \frac{3}{10}$.

Step 1	Step 2
Rewrite the problem as a multiplication problem. Rewrite the divisor as its reciprocal.	Simplify if possible. Multiply. If your answer is an improper fraction, change it to a mixed number.
The reciprocal of $\frac{3}{10}$ is $\frac{10}{3}$. $\frac{4}{5} \times \frac{10}{3}$	$\frac{4}{5} \times \frac{10}{3} = \frac{8}{3}$ (5 and 10 cancelled to 1 and 2) $\frac{8}{3} = 2\frac{2}{3}$

Write the reciprocal of each fraction or number.

1. $\frac{2}{5}$ $\frac{5}{2}$
2. $\frac{1}{7}$ 7, or $\frac{7}{1}$
3. 9 $\frac{1}{9}$
4. 15 $\frac{1}{15}$

Find each quotient. Simplify if possible.

5. $6 \div \frac{1}{4} =$ 24
6. $\frac{2}{3} \div \frac{1}{2} =$ $\frac{4}{3}$, or $1\frac{1}{3}$
7. $\frac{4}{5} \div 10 =$ $\frac{2}{25}$
8. $\frac{1}{3} \div \frac{8}{9} =$ $\frac{3}{8}$
9. $12 \div \frac{3}{8} =$ 32
10. $\frac{7}{10} \div \frac{3}{4} =$ $\frac{14}{15}$
11. $\frac{11}{12} \div \frac{1}{3} =$ $2\frac{3}{4}$
12. $\frac{5}{8} \div 6 =$ $\frac{5}{48}$
13. Marcus is making tea for his friends. He has 6 tbsp of honey. If he puts $\frac{1}{2}$ tbsp of honey in each cup of tea, how many cups can he make?
Marcus can make 12 cups of tea.

Use with Lesson 5-6. 59

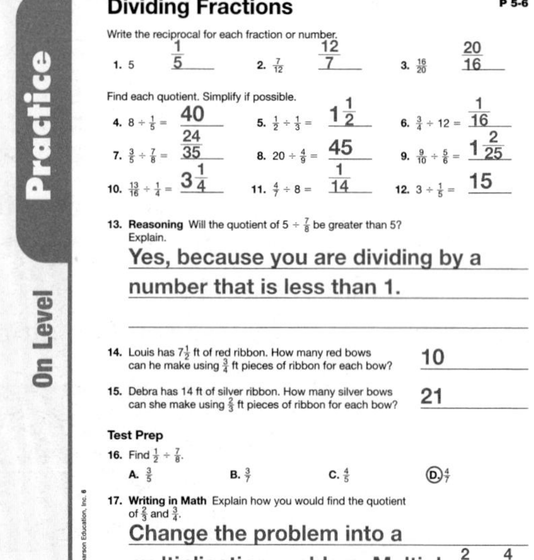

Practice — On Level

Dividing Fractions

P 5-6

Write the reciprocal for each fraction or number.

1. 5 $\frac{1}{5}$
2. $\frac{7}{12}$ $\frac{12}{7}$
3. $\frac{16}{20}$ $\frac{20}{16}$

Find each quotient. Simplify if possible.

4. $8 \div \frac{1}{5} =$ 40
5. $\frac{1}{2} \div \frac{1}{3} =$ $1\frac{1}{2}$
6. $\frac{3}{4} \div 12 =$ $\frac{1}{16}$
7. $\frac{3}{5} \div \frac{7}{8} =$ $\frac{24}{35}$
8. $20 \div \frac{4}{9} =$ 45
9. $\frac{9}{10} \div \frac{5}{6} =$ $1\frac{2}{25}$
10. $\frac{13}{16} \div \frac{1}{4} =$ $3\frac{1}{4}$
11. $\frac{4}{7} \div 8 =$ $\frac{1}{14}$
12. $3 \div \frac{1}{5} =$ 15
13. **Reasoning** Will the quotient of $5 \div \frac{7}{8}$ be greater than 5? Explain.
Yes, because you are dividing by a number that is less than 1.
14. Louis has $7\frac{1}{2}$ ft of red ribbon. How many red bows can he make using $\frac{3}{4}$ ft pieces of ribbon for each bow? 10
15. Debra has 14 ft of silver ribbon. How many silver bows can she make using $\frac{2}{3}$ ft pieces of ribbon for each bow? 21

Test Prep

16. Find $\frac{1}{2} \div \frac{7}{8}$.
A. $\frac{3}{5}$ B. $\frac{3}{7}$ C. $\frac{4}{5}$ (D.) $\frac{4}{7}$
17. **Writing in Math** Explain how you would find the quotient of $\frac{2}{3}$ and $\frac{3}{4}$.
Change the problem into a multiplication problem. Multiply $\frac{2}{3} \times \frac{4}{3}$. The quotient is $\frac{8}{9}$.

Use with Lesson 5-6. 59

Dividing by a fraction is the same as multiplying by its **reciprocal.** The product of a number and its reciprocal is 1. For example, $\frac{3}{4} \times \frac{4}{3} = 1$, so $\frac{3}{4}$ and $\frac{4}{3}$ are reciprocals. Reciprocals are also called **multiplicative inverses.**

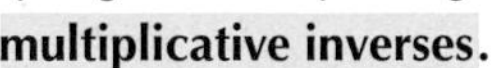

The reciprocal of $\frac{1}{4}$ is $\frac{4}{1}$.

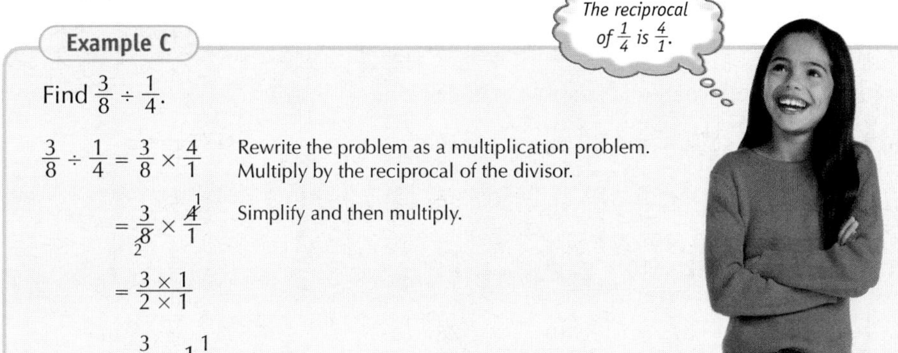

Example C

Find $\frac{3}{8} \div \frac{1}{4}$.

$\frac{3}{8} \div \frac{1}{4} = \frac{3}{8} \times \frac{4}{1}$ Rewrite the problem as a multiplication problem. Multiply by the reciprocal of the divisor.

$= \frac{3}{\not{8}_2} \times \frac{\not{4}^1}{1}$ Simplify and then multiply.

$= \frac{3 \times 1}{2 \times 1}$

$= \frac{3}{2} = 1\frac{1}{2}$

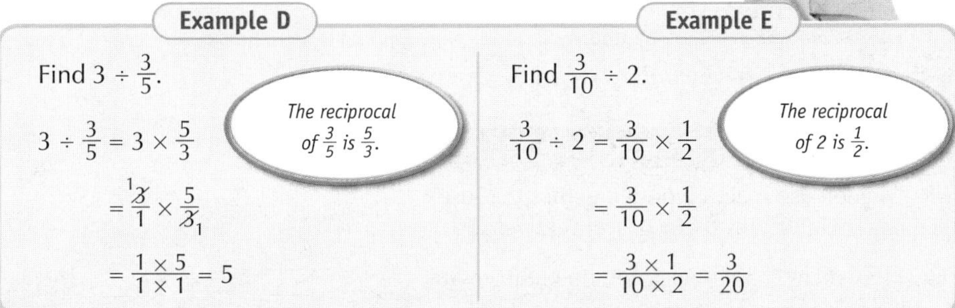

Example D

Find $3 \div \frac{3}{5}$.

The reciprocal of $\frac{3}{5}$ is $\frac{5}{3}$.

$3 \div \frac{3}{5} = 3 \times \frac{5}{3}$

$= \frac{^1\not{3}}{1} \times \frac{5}{\not{3}_1}$

$= \frac{1 \times 5}{1 \times 1} = 5$

Example E

Find $\frac{3}{10} \div 2$.

The reciprocal of 2 is $\frac{1}{2}$.

$\frac{3}{10} \div 2 = \frac{3}{10} \times \frac{1}{2}$

$= \frac{3}{10} \times \frac{1}{2}$

$= \frac{3 \times 1}{10 \times 2} = \frac{3}{20}$

Talk About It

1. How can you think of $3 \div \frac{1}{4}$? $\frac{1}{4} \div 3$? **See above.**
   1. How many fourths are in 3? What is $\frac{1}{4}$ divided into 3 equal parts?
2. How is dividing 5 by $\frac{1}{2}$ different from multiplying 5 by $\frac{1}{2}$?
   2. Dividing 5 by $\frac{1}{2}$ is finding how many halves are in 5. Multiplying 5 by $\frac{1}{2}$ is finding $\frac{1}{2}$ of 5.
3. Write and solve $36 \div 9$ as a multiplication problem.
   $36 \div 9 = 36 \times \frac{1}{9} = 4$

CHECK

For another example, see Set 5-6 on p. 293.

Write the reciprocal of each fraction or number.

1. $\frac{8}{9}$ **$\frac{9}{8}$**
2. $\frac{7}{10}$ **$\frac{10}{7}$**
3. 12 **$\frac{1}{12}$**
4. $\frac{4}{3}$ **$\frac{3}{4}$**

Find each quotient. Simplify if possible.

5. $8 \div \frac{2}{3}$ **12**
6. $\frac{2}{3} \div \frac{3}{4}$ **$\frac{8}{9}$**
7. $\frac{5}{8} \div \frac{7}{12}$ **$1\frac{1}{14}$**
8. $\frac{5}{12} \div 3$ **$\frac{5}{36}$**
9. **Number Sense** When you divide a whole number by a fraction less than 1, is the quotient greater or less than the whole number? **Greater than the whole number**

Examples C and D Before discussing these examples, have students practice finding the reciprocals of fractions. Have them check each pair by verifying that the product is 1.

Ongoing Assessment

Talk About It: Question 2

If students feel the two exercises are the same,

then tell them to look at the model for $5 \div \frac{1}{2}$ in Example A. **If you divide 5 inches into $\frac{1}{2}$-inch pieces, how many do you have?** *(10 pieces)* **If instead you take $\frac{1}{2}$ of 5 inches, how much do you have?** *($2\frac{1}{2}$ inches)*

CHECK

Error Intervention

If students find the reciprocal of the first number or both numbers,

then write the steps in finding the quotient of two fractions: "1. Write the first fraction. 2. Write a times sign and the reciprocal of the second fraction. 3. Multiply." Have students follow the steps for each division problem. *(Also see* Reteaching, *p. 266B.)*

Enrichment — Above Level

Fraction Figures

E 5-6 PATTERNS

Divide the square into fourths.

1. How many fourths do you see? **4**

Divide one of the fourths into fourths.

2. How many total sections are there? **7**
3. Continue the pattern three more times. Each time you divide a new section into fourths, tell how many total sections you have. **10, 13, 16**
4. What pattern do you see in the number of sections? **Add 3**
5. Divide the rectangle into thirds. Divide one of the thirds into thirds. Continue the pattern three more times.
6. What pattern do you see in the number of sections? **Add 2**

Use with Lesson 5-6. 59

Problem Solving

Dividing Fractions

PS 5-6

Flag Line In parades, the members of the flag line march in front of the band and perform with beautifully decorated flags. Each year, the members of the flag line design new flags to match their uniforms.

1. The flag line decided to use some green flags. The fabric that was purchased was 8 yd long. Each flag required $\frac{3}{4}$ of a yard. How many green flags were cut from this fabric? **$10\frac{2}{3}$ flags**
2. Some of the flags will be blue. Blue flags must be cut from fabric that is 10 yd long. Each blue flag is $\frac{4}{5}$ of a yard long. How many blue flags can be cut from the fabric? **$12\frac{1}{2}$ flags**
3. The flagpoles are cut from lengths of wood. Each flagpole is $\frac{7}{8}$ of a yard long. How many flagpoles can be cut from a wooden pole that is 6 yd long? **$6\frac{6}{7}$ flagpoles**

Family-Fun Relay At the school picnic, one of the activities is the family-fun relay. The route is 3 mi long. Each member of the family can participate.

4. Each member of the Lee family will run exactly $\frac{3}{5}$ of a mile. How many members of the Lee family are participating in the relay? **5 members of the Lee family**
5. The members of the Mendez family will each run $\frac{6}{8}$ of a mile to complete the relay. How many members of the Mendez family must be participating in the relay? **4 members of the Mendez family**
6. **Writing in Math** The Pindar family has 7 members. Leo figured that 4 of them could each run $\frac{3}{5}$ of a mile in the relay. Was he correct? Explain your reasoning. **No; Sample answer: Four members could each run $\frac{3}{4}$ of a mile because $3 \div 4$ is $\frac{3}{4}$. Five members could each run $\frac{3}{5}$ of the race.**

Use with Lesson 5-6. 59

3 Practice

Exercises 14–29 Begin by asking students to circle the number whose reciprocal is needed. Then have them write the reciprocal and, finally, rewrite the division exercise as a multiplication exercise.

Exercise 35 For some students, after they identify an error in one explanation they may assume that the other explanation is correct. Be sure students read both explanations with a critical eye.

Reading Assist Make Predictions In Exercise 33, have students discuss whether they think the answer will be greater or less than 32. *(Less than 32, because they are dividing by a number greater than $\frac{1}{2}$)*

PRACTICE For more practice, see Set 5-6 on p. 296.

A Skills and Understanding

Write the reciprocal of each fraction or number.

10. $\frac{3}{10}$ **$\frac{10}{3}$** **11.** $6\frac{1}{6}$ **12.** $\frac{1}{15}$ **15** **13.** $3\frac{1}{3}$

Find each quotient. Simplify if possible.

14. $9 \div \frac{3}{5}$ **15** **15.** $\frac{5}{7} \div 20$ **$\frac{1}{28}$** **16.** $\frac{2}{9} \div \frac{1}{3}$ **$\frac{2}{3}$** **17.** $\frac{4}{5} \div 6$ **$\frac{2}{15}$**

18. $24 \div \frac{2}{3}$ **36** **19.** $\frac{8}{9} \div 12$ **$\frac{2}{27}$** **20.** $\frac{3}{10} \div \frac{5}{6}$ **$\frac{9}{25}$** **21.** $\frac{11}{12} \div \frac{3}{4}$ **$1\frac{2}{9}$**

22. $\frac{3}{8} \div 5$ **$\frac{3}{40}$** **23.** $10 \div \frac{5}{9}$ **18** **24.** $\frac{7}{8} \div \frac{1}{8}$ **7** **25.** $\frac{9}{14} \div \frac{3}{7}$ **$1\frac{1}{2}$**

26. $\frac{11}{13} \div \frac{13}{11}$ **$\frac{121}{169}$** **27.** $6 \div \frac{6}{10}$ **10** **28.** $\frac{1}{2} \div \frac{2}{3}$ **$\frac{3}{4}$** **29.** $\frac{6}{7} \div \frac{1}{3}$ **$2\frac{4}{7}$**

30. Reasoning Will $3 \div \frac{2}{5}$ have a whole number answer? Explain. **No. $3 \times \frac{5}{2}$ will be an odd number divided by 2.**

31. Number Sense Explain how to use decimals to find $6 \div \frac{3}{4}$. **$6 \div \frac{3}{4}$ is the same as $6 \div 0.75 = 8$.**

B Reasoning and Problem Solving

Math and Everyday Life

Mr. Wagner also makes wooden games that use peg markers. He cuts the pegs from dowel rods.

32. How many $\frac{1}{2}$-inch pegs can he cut from an 18-inch dowel rod? **36 pegs**

33. How many $\frac{3}{4}$-inch pegs can he cut from a 16-inch dowel rod? **$21\frac{1}{3}$ pegs**

34. How long a dowel rod would he need to make 24 pegs that are each $\frac{1}{2}$ inch? **12-inch dowel rod**

35. **Writing in Math** Are the explanations correct? If not, tell why and write a correct response.

Find $4 \div \frac{2}{5}$.
I can rewrite this problem as $\frac{1}{4} \times \frac{5}{2}$ because dividing by a fraction is the same as multiplying by its reciprocal. $\frac{1}{4} \times \frac{5}{2} = \frac{5}{8}$.
No. The dividend does not change. It should be $4 \times \frac{5}{2} = 10$.

Find $4 \div \frac{2}{5}$.
I can rewrite this problem as $\frac{4}{1} \times \frac{2}{5}$ because dividing by a fraction is the same as the reciprocal of the answer. $\frac{4}{1} \times \frac{2}{5} = \frac{8}{5}$, and the reciprocal of $\frac{8}{5}$ is $\frac{5}{8}$.
No. This student did not multiply by the reciprocal. It should be $\frac{4}{1} \times \frac{5}{2} = 10$.

Test-Taking Practice

Test-Taking Practice, Item 1, p. 269 There are two parts to the question; the answer and explanation are each worth two points. remind students that they should answer as much as they can since partial credit is given for this type of problem.

Discuss the sample responses shown and compare them to papers produced by your students.

4-point answer Answer is correct; shows complete understanding of dividing fractions.

18; Change 10 to $\frac{10}{1}$.
Change $\frac{5}{9}$ to its reciprocal, $\frac{9}{5}$.
Simplify and multiply the fractions.

PRACTICE

C Extensions

36. **Number Sense** Which number is its own reciprocal? Explain. One. It can also be written as $\frac{1}{1}$, so its reciprocal is the same.

37. **Number Sense** Is there any number that does not have a reciprocal? Explain. See above.

37. Yes; zero can be written $\frac{0}{1}$, but the reciprocal is $\frac{1}{0}$, which is impossible.

Mixed Review and Test Prep

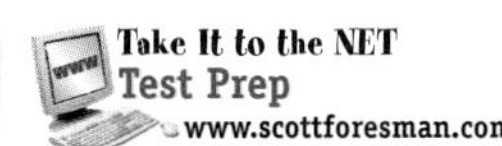

38. Without computing, is $3.05 \div 0.75$ more than or less than 3.05? Explain how you know. More than 3.05; When you divide a number by a number less than 1, the quotient is greater than the dividend.

Find each product. Simplify if possible.

39. $4\frac{5}{6} \times \frac{3}{4}$ $3\frac{5}{8}$

40. $7\frac{1}{2} \times 1\frac{1}{5}$ 9

41. $16 \times 2\frac{1}{4}$ 36

42. Which is the prime factorization of 576?

A. $8^2 \times 9$ B. $4^3 \times 3^2$ C. $2^4 \times 3^2 \times 4$ (D.) $2^6 \times 3^2$

43. Which is $\frac{2}{5}$ written as a decimal?

A. 2.5 (B.) 0.4 C. 0.25 D. 0.04

Discover Math in Your World

2. 800 bees-per-pound

Not-So-Sweet Honeybee

While "killer bees" look like domestic honeybees, they are much more quick-tempered and aggressive.

1. When threatened, a "killer bee" will pursue an intruder up to $\frac{1}{12}$ mile. A domestic bee will chase an intruder up to $\frac{1}{35}$ mile. How many times farther is the chase distance of a "killer bee?" $2\frac{11}{12}$ times farther
2. About 60,000 domestic bees produce 100 pounds of honey. An equal number of "killer bees" produces $\frac{3}{4}$ that amount. Calculate the bees-per-pound production of the "killer bee." See above.

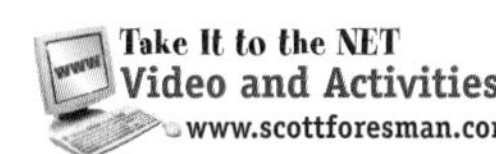

Take It to the NET
Video and Activities
www.scottforesman.com

 All text pages available online and on CD-ROM.

Leveled Practice

Below Level Ex. 10–17, 18–32 even, 35, 38–43

On Level Ex. 11–27 odd, 28–35, 38–43

Above Level Ex. 21–43

Early Finishers Have students refer to Exercises 20–25 on page 254. Have them rewrite the exercises, replacing each × symbol with a ÷ symbol. Then have them find each quotient.

Discover Math in Your World To help students determine whether to divide or multiply to solve each problem, suggest they start by drawing a diagram to illustrate the problem.

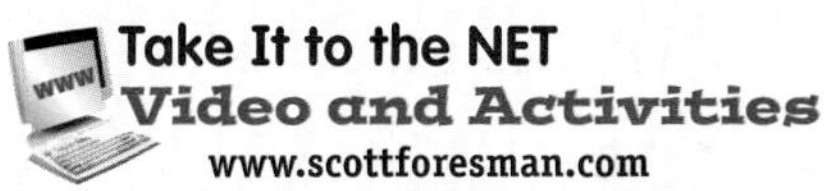

The video includes pre-viewing and post-viewing questions. A Discovery Channel Blackline Master is also provided.

4 Assess

Journal Idea Have students describe how to model $\frac{2}{3} \div 2$ and then draw a model to show the steps for finding the quotient.

3-point answer Answer is correct; explanation shows incomplete understanding of dividing fractions.

18; Change 10 to $\frac{10}{1}$.
Change $\frac{5}{9}$ to its reciprocal.

3-point answer Answer is incomplete; explanation shows understanding of dividing fractions.

$\frac{90}{5}$; Change 10 to $\frac{10}{1}$.
Change $\frac{5}{9}$ to its reciprocal, $\frac{9}{5}$.
Multiply the fractions.

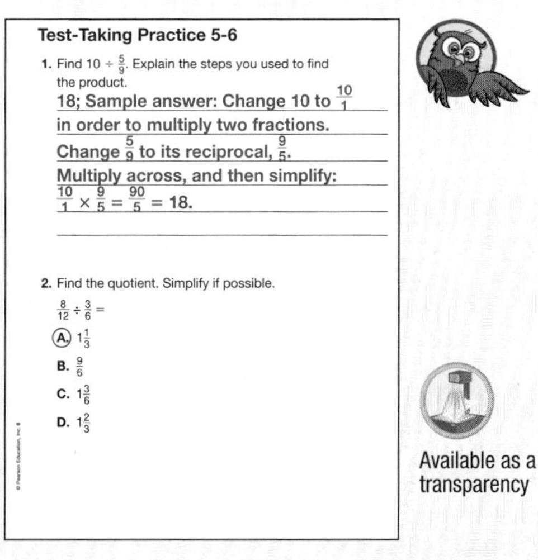

Test-Taking Practice 5-6

1. Find $10 \div \frac{5}{9}$. Explain the steps you used to find the product.
18; Sample answer: Change 10 to $\frac{10}{1}$ in order to multiply two fractions. Change $\frac{5}{9}$ to its reciprocal, $\frac{9}{5}$. Multiply across, and then simplify: $\frac{10}{1} \times \frac{9}{5} = \frac{90}{5} = 18$.

2. Find the quotient. Simplify if possible.
$\frac{8}{12} \div \frac{3}{6} =$
(A) $1\frac{1}{3}$
B. $\frac{9}{6}$
C. $1\frac{3}{6}$
D. $1\frac{2}{3}$

Available as a transparency

5-7 Dividing Mixed Numbers

Lesson Organizer

Quick Lesson Overview 

Objective Find the quotients of divisions with mixed numbers.

Math Understanding Mixed numbers can be expressed as improper fractions, or they can be broken apart into their whole-number and fractional parts. This provides a basis for estimating and doing operations with two mixed numbers, with a mixed number and a whole number, and with a mixed number and a fraction.

How Children Learn Math Help students verbalize their thinking about the steps used to divide mixed numbers. Talking about their ideas will clarify and solidify their knowledge.

NCTM Standards

- Number and Operations

(For a complete correlation to the NCTM Standards and Grades 6–8 Expectations, see pages 246G–H.)

Getting Started

Spiral Review

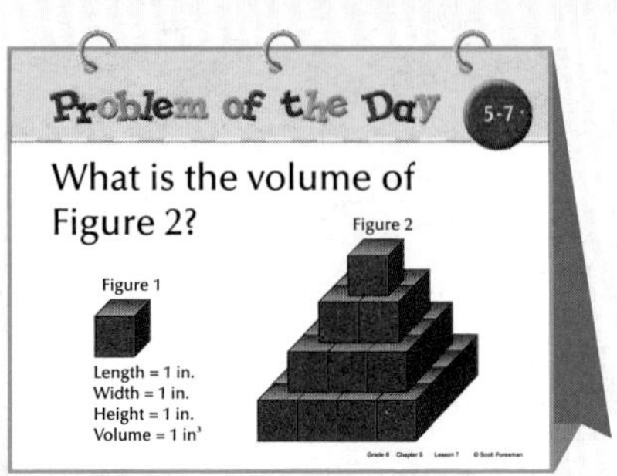

Topics Reviewed

- Volume
- Problem-Solving Strategy: Use Objects

Answer The volume of Figure 2 is 30 cubic inches.

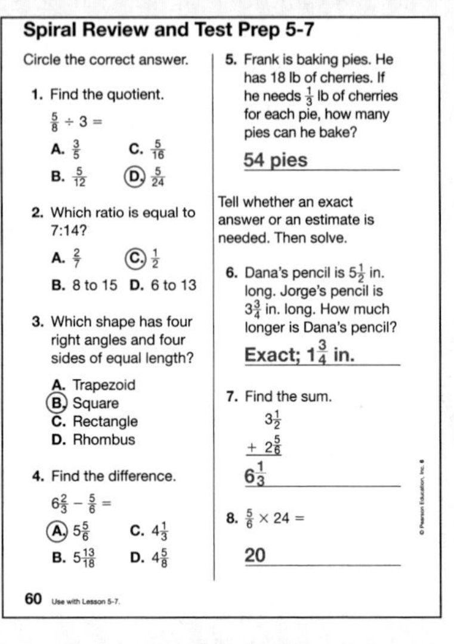

Spiral Review and Test Prep 5-7

Circle the correct answer.

1. Find the quotient.
   $\frac{5}{8} \div 3 =$
   A. $\frac{3}{5}$ C. $\frac{5}{16}$
   B. $\frac{5}{12}$ (D.) $\frac{5}{24}$

2. Which ratio is equal to 7:14?
   A. $\frac{2}{7}$ (C.) $\frac{1}{2}$
   B. 8 to 15 D. 6 to 13

3. Which shape has four right angles and four sides of equal length?
   A. Trapezoid
   (B.) Square
   C. Rectangle
   D. Rhombus

4. Find the difference.
   $6\frac{2}{3} - \frac{5}{6} =$
   (A.) $5\frac{5}{6}$ C. $4\frac{1}{3}$
   B. $5\frac{13}{18}$ D. $4\frac{5}{8}$

5. Frank is baking pies. He has 18 lb of cherries. If he needs $\frac{1}{3}$ lb of cherries for each pie, how many pies can he bake?
   54 pies

Tell whether an exact answer or an estimate is needed. Then solve.

6. Dana's pencil is $5\frac{1}{2}$ in. long. Jorge's pencil is $3\frac{3}{4}$ in. long. How much longer is Dana's pencil?
   Exact; $1\frac{3}{4}$ in.

7. Find the sum.
   $3\frac{1}{2} + 2\frac{5}{6}$
   $6\frac{1}{3}$

8. $\frac{5}{6} \times 24 =$
   20

60 Use with Lesson 5-7.

Available as a transparency and as a blackline master

Topics Reviewed

1. Dividing fractions; **2.** Equal ratios **3.** Classifying quadrilaterals; **4., 7.** Subtracting and adding mixed numbers; **5.** Dividing fractions; **6.** Exact or estimate; **8.** Multiplying fractions

Investigating the Concept

Measure It

 10–15 MIN **Kinesthetic** 

Materials *(per pair)* Ruler or Teaching Tool 19; string; scissors

What to Do

- Direct Partner 1 to draw a line $6\frac{3}{4}$ inches long. Have Partner 2 measure a piece of string $1\frac{1}{8}$ inches long. **Work together to find out how many $1\frac{1}{8}$-in. lengths are in $6\frac{3}{4}$ in.** *(6 lengths)* **Is your answer reasonable?** *(Yes; it is close to an estimate of 7 ÷ 1 = 7.)* **What is the improper fraction for $6\frac{3}{4}$?** *($\frac{27}{4}$)* **For $1\frac{1}{8}$?** *($\frac{9}{8}$)* Write $\frac{27}{4} \div \frac{9}{8}$ on the board.

1 2 3 4 5 6
0 1 2 3 4 5 6 7
INCHES $6\frac{3}{4}$

- **When we divided with fractions, we rewrote the problem as multiplying by the reciprocal. What should we write for $\frac{27}{4} \div \frac{9}{8}$?** *($\frac{27}{4} \times \frac{8}{9}$)* Write that multiplication problem under the division problem. **What do you get after you simplify and multiply?** *(6)*

Ongoing Assessment

- **Show how to find the quotient $6\frac{3}{4} \div 2\frac{1}{4}$.** *($\frac{27}{4} \div \frac{9}{4} = \frac{27}{4} \times \frac{4}{9} = 3$)*

Reaching All Learners

Math Vocabulary

Expression Match

 10–15 MIN **Linguistic** 

Materials *(per student)* 5 index cards

- Have students make cards showing $\frac{1}{2} + 5$, $5 - \frac{1}{2}$, $\frac{1}{2} \times 5$, $5 \div 1\frac{1}{2}$, and $\frac{1}{2} \div 5$.

 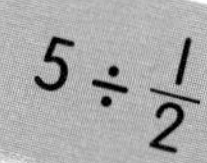

- Write the following on the board.

one half divided by 5	the quotient of 5 and $1\frac{1}{2}$
one half of 5	the sum of 5 and $\frac{1}{2}$
5 divided by $1\frac{1}{2}$	5 decreased by $\frac{1}{2}$
$\frac{1}{2}$ less than 5	the product of 5 and $\frac{1}{2}$
5 more than $\frac{1}{2}$	the quotient of $\frac{1}{2}$ and 5

- **As I write each expression, hold up the correct card.**

Activate Prior Knowledge/Build Background

English Language Learners

Cutting the Pipe

 10–15 MIN **Visual/Spatial** 

Materials *(per pair)* Ruler, paper

- **Have you ever had to divide something up for three people? Were the parts equal? Why or why not?**
- A plumber has a $3\frac{1}{2}$-foot pipe that he wants cut into three 1–foot pieces.
- Model drawing the pipe on the board. Write $3\frac{1}{2}$ ft.
- Have each pair use their ruler to draw the pipe on paper, using $3\frac{1}{2}$ inches to represent the $3\frac{1}{2}$ feet.
- Partners talk through dividing the pipe into the three pieces and determine how much is left over. *($\frac{1}{2}$ foot)*

Reteaching

Proper or Improper?

 10–15 MIN **Visual/Spatial** 

Materials *(per group)* Index cards showing mixed numbers such as $4\frac{3}{4}$ and $5\frac{1}{8}$

- Give each group enough index cards so everyone has one.
- On the board, show the steps for writing a mixed number as an improper fraction.

1. Multiply the denominator times the whole number.
2. Add the numerator.
3. Write the result over the denominator.

- Have each student explain the steps in writing his or her mixed number as an improper fraction, for example: Multiply: $4 \times 4 = 16$. Add the numerator: $16 + 3 = 19$. Write the result over the denominator: $\frac{19}{4}$.

Math and Social Studies

How Many Teachers?

 5–10 MIN **Logical/Mathematical** 

Materials *(per student)* Calculator

- Show students the following table.
- **Suppose a school in Arizona has 500 students. About how many teachers would it have? Use your calculator.** *(About 25 teachers)*
- **If a school in Washington has 1,100 students, about how many teachers would it have?** *(About 55 teachers)*

State	Students per Teacher
Washington	$19\frac{9}{10}$
Oregon	$19\frac{3}{5}$
Nevada	$18\frac{7}{10}$
Arizona	$19\frac{2}{5}$

1999–2000 school year

Objective Find the quotients of divisions with mixed numbers.

1 Warm Up

Activate Prior Knowledge Review division of fractions.

2 Teach

LEARN Ask students how multiplying mixed numbers is similar to multiplying fractions. Then ask if they think dividing mixed numbers will be similar to dividing fractions.

Ongoing Assessment

Talk About It: Question 2

If students feel the Commutative Property works,

then have them estimate two quotients such as $6\frac{1}{2} \div 2\frac{3}{4}$ and $2\frac{3}{4} \div 6\frac{1}{2}$. They should see that the first quotient will be greater than 1 and the second quotient will be less than 1, so the two quotients cannot be equal.

Answers

2. No. Sample answer: $2\frac{1}{2} \div 1\frac{1}{3} = \frac{5}{2} \times \frac{3}{4} = \frac{15}{8}$, but $1\frac{1}{3} \div 2\frac{1}{2} = \frac{4}{3} \times \frac{2}{5} = \frac{8}{15}$.

Lesson 5-7

Key Idea
You can use the same methods to divide mixed numbers that you used to divide fractions.

Think It Through
I should **make an estimate** before using a calculator.

Dividing Mixed Numbers

WARM UP

1. $\frac{5}{6} \div \frac{2}{3}$ $1\frac{1}{4}$
2. $\frac{3}{8} \div \frac{3}{10}$ $1\frac{1}{4}$
3. $\frac{3}{4} \div 6$ $\frac{1}{8}$
4. $3 \div \frac{3}{10}$ 10

LEARN

How can you find the quotient of mixed numbers?

Example A

Find $4\frac{1}{2} \div 3\frac{3}{4}$. Estimate: $5 \div 4 = \frac{5}{4} = 1\frac{1}{4}$

STEP 1 Write each mixed number as an improper fraction.	$4\frac{1}{2} \div 3\frac{3}{4} = \frac{9}{2} \div \frac{15}{4}$
STEP 2 Find the reciprocal of the divisor. Rewrite as a multiplication problem.	$= \frac{9}{2} \times \frac{4}{15}$
STEP 3 Look for common factors, simplify, and then multiply.	$= \frac{\cancel{9}^{3}}{\cancel{2}_{1}} \times \frac{\cancel{4}^{2}}{\cancel{15}_{5}}$ $= \frac{6}{5} = 1\frac{1}{5}$ $1\frac{1}{5}$ is close to $1\frac{1}{4}$, so the answer is reasonable.

Example B

Find $26 \div 1\frac{5}{8}$.

Estimate: $26 \div 2 = 13$

$26 \div 1\frac{5}{8} = \frac{26}{1} \div \frac{13}{8}$

$= \frac{26}{1} \times \frac{8}{13}$

$= \frac{\cancel{26}^{2}}{1} \times \frac{8}{\cancel{13}_{1}}$

$= 16$

16 is close to 13, so the answer is reasonable.

Example C

Find $17\frac{8}{9} \div 3$ using a calculator.

Estimate: $18 \div 3 = 6$

Press: 17 [Unit] 8 [/] 9 [÷] 3 [=]

Display: 161/27

Press: [Ab/c]

Display: 5u26/27

Since $5\frac{26}{27}$ is close to 6, the answer is reasonable.

Talk About It

1. Explain how to estimate and then find $3\frac{2}{5} \div 8$ using paper and pencil. **Round $3\frac{2}{5}$ down to 3, then divide by 8 to get an estimate; $\frac{17}{5} \times \frac{1}{8} = \frac{17}{40}$, which is close to $\frac{3}{8}$.** See above.
2. **Reasoning** Does the commutative property work for division of mixed numbers? Explain using an example. **See margin.**

Below Level — Reteaching

Dividing Mixed Numbers R 5-7

You can follow these steps to find $5\frac{1}{3} \div 1\frac{1}{3}$ and $21 \div 2\frac{1}{3}$.

Step 1 First estimate. Then write each number as an improper fraction.	Step 2 Find the reciprocal of the divisor. Rewrite as a multiplication problem.	Step 3 Look for common factors. Simplify, then multiply.
Find $5\frac{1}{3} \div 1\frac{1}{3}$. Estimate $5 \div 1 = 5$. $5\frac{1}{3} \div 1\frac{1}{3} =$ $\downarrow \quad \downarrow$ $\frac{16}{3} \div \frac{4}{3}$	$\frac{16}{3} \div \frac{4}{3} =$ $\frac{16}{3} \times \frac{3}{4}$	$\frac{16}{3} \times \frac{3}{4} =$ $\frac{\cancel{16}^{4}}{\cancel{3}_{1}} \times \frac{\cancel{3}^{1}}{\cancel{4}_{1}} = \frac{4}{1} = 4$ 4 is close to 5, so the answer is reasonable.
Find $21 \div 2\frac{1}{3}$. Estimate $21 \div 2 = 10\frac{1}{2}$. $21 \div 2\frac{1}{3}$ $\downarrow \quad \downarrow$ $\frac{21}{1} \div \frac{7}{3}$	$\frac{21}{1} \div \frac{7}{3} =$ $\frac{21}{1} \times \frac{3}{7}$	$\frac{21}{1} \times \frac{3}{7} =$ $\frac{\cancel{21}^{3}}{1} \times \frac{3}{\cancel{7}_{1}} = \frac{9}{1} = 9$ 9 is close to $10\frac{1}{2}$, so the answer is reasonable.

Find each quotient. Simplify if possible.

1. $2\frac{2}{3} \div 3\frac{1}{4} =$ $\frac{32}{39}$
2. $1\frac{3}{4} \div 4\frac{1}{8} =$ $\frac{14}{33}$
3. $2\frac{1}{5} \div 2\frac{1}{3} =$ $\frac{33}{35}$
4. $5\frac{1}{4} \div 3 =$ $1\frac{3}{4}$
5. $10 \div 3\frac{1}{4} =$ $3\frac{1}{13}$
6. $7\frac{1}{4} \div 2\frac{1}{8} =$ $3\frac{7}{17}$
7. **Writing in Math** Paper needs to be cut for voting ballots. Each piece of paper is $10\frac{1}{2}$ in. long. Each ballot should be $1\frac{3}{4}$ in. long. How many ballots can be cut from one piece of paper?. **Six ballots can be cut.**

On Level — Practice

Dividing Mixed Numbers P 5-7

Find each quotient. Simplify if possible.

1. $1\frac{1}{2} \div 2\frac{1}{3} =$ $\frac{9}{14}$
2. $4\frac{1}{4} \div 3\frac{1}{8} =$ $1\frac{9}{25}$
3. $2\frac{1}{4} \div 5\frac{1}{2} =$ $\frac{9}{22}$
4. $3\frac{1}{2} \div 2\frac{1}{4} =$ $1\frac{5}{9}$
5. $3\frac{3}{4} \div 2 =$ $1\frac{7}{8}$
6. $1\frac{1}{2} \div 2\frac{1}{4} =$ $\frac{2}{3}$
7. $8 \div 2\frac{3}{4} =$ $2\frac{10}{11}$
8. $2\frac{1}{2} \div 1\frac{3}{8} =$ $1\frac{9}{11}$
9. $4\frac{2}{3} \div 1\frac{3}{4} =$ $2\frac{2}{3}$
10. **Reasoning** Is it possible to divide 15 by a mixed number and get a quotient that is greater than 15? Explain. **No, because you are dividing by a number that is greater than 1.**

Room	Gallons of Paint
Kitchen	$2\frac{1}{2}$
Bedroom	$3\frac{3}{4}$
Living room	$4\frac{1}{3}$

Max is painting the inside of an apartment complex. The table shows how many gallons of paint are needed to paint each type of room.

11. How many kitchens can Max paint with 20 gal? **8 kitchens**
12. How many living rooms can Max paint with 26 gal? **6 living rooms**
13. How many bedrooms can Max paint with 60 gal? **16 bedrooms**

Test Prep

14. Find $4\frac{1}{2} \div 2\frac{1}{4}$.
    A. 1 (B.) 2 C. 3 D. 4
15. **Writing in Math** Explain how you would find $4\frac{1}{5} \div 2\frac{1}{3}$. **Sample answer: Write each mixed number as an improper fraction. Find the reciprocal of the second term and multiply the two fractions. Simplify the answer.**

CHECK ✓

For another example, see Set 5-7 on p. 294.

Find each quotient. Simplify if possible.

1. $2\frac{3}{8} \div 4\frac{2}{5}$ $\frac{95}{176}$
2. $4\frac{1}{2} \div 2\frac{7}{10}$ $1\frac{2}{3}$
3. $2\frac{2}{3} \div 1\frac{1}{2}$ $1\frac{7}{9}$
4. $3 \div 6\frac{1}{4}$ $\frac{12}{25}$
5. **Number Sense** When you divide a whole number by a mixed number, is the quotient greater or less than the dividend? Explain. **Less than the dividend; A whole number divided by any number greater than 1 is always smaller than the whole number.**

PRACTICE

For more practice, see Set 5-7 on p. 297.

A Skills and Understanding

14. $7 \div \frac{x}{3} = 7 \times \frac{x}{3}$. If $\frac{3}{x} = \frac{x}{3}$, then x must be 3.

Find each quotient. Simplify if possible.

6. $4\frac{1}{2} \div 1\frac{4}{9}$ $3\frac{3}{26}$
7. $1\frac{1}{3} \div 1\frac{1}{6}$ $1\frac{1}{7}$
8. $3\frac{4}{5} \div 1\frac{9}{10}$ 2
9. $2\frac{5}{8} \div 3$ $\frac{7}{8}$
10. $3\frac{1}{9} \div 1\frac{7}{12}$ $1\frac{55}{57}$
11. $8\frac{1}{4} \div 3\frac{2}{3}$ $2\frac{1}{4}$
12. $11\frac{1}{4} \div 1\frac{5}{6}$ $6\frac{3}{22}$
13. $14\frac{3}{8} \div 3\frac{1}{3}$ $4\frac{5}{16}$
14. **Algebra** If $7 \div \frac{x}{3} = 7 \times \frac{x}{3}$, what is the value of x? Explain. **See above.**

B Reasoning and Problem Solving

Robin makes wooden bird feeders and houses. The table at the right shows the amount of lumber needed for each item.

Data File

Item	Lumber
Feeder	$2\frac{1}{2}$ ft
Wren house	$3\frac{1}{3}$ ft
Bluebird house	$4\frac{1}{2}$ ft
Martin house	32 ft

15. How many feeders can Robin make from an 8-ft board? **3 feeders**
16. How many wren houses can be made from the amount of lumber needed for a martin house? **9 wren houses**
17. **Writing in Math** Explain why $5\frac{1}{2} \div \frac{1}{2}$ has a greater quotient than $5\frac{1}{2} \times \frac{1}{2}$. **$5\frac{1}{2} \div \frac{1}{2}$ is asking how many halves are in $5\frac{1}{2}$. $5\frac{1}{2} \times \frac{1}{2}$ is asking for one half of $5\frac{1}{2}$.**

C Extensions

18. **Representations** Draw a model to show $3\frac{1}{2} \div 2$.
19. **Algebra** Simplify the expression $\frac{5}{6} \times \frac{2}{3} \div 2\frac{1}{4}$. $\frac{20}{81}$

Mixed Review and Test Prep

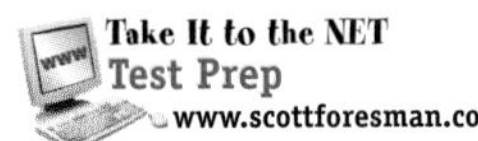

Find each quotient. Simplify if possible.

20. $\frac{7}{10} \div \frac{3}{8}$ $1\frac{13}{15}$
21. $3 \div \frac{5}{6}$ $3\frac{3}{5}$
22. $\frac{5}{6} \div \frac{2}{3}$ $1\frac{1}{4}$
23. Which is 0.0000021 written in scientific notation?

A. 21×10^{-6} B. 0.21×10^{-6} C. 2.1×10^{6} **(D.)** 2.1×10^{-6}

All text pages available online and on CD-ROM.

CHECK ✓

Error Intervention

If students multiply by the reciprocal of the wrong number,

then have them circle the divisor in each problem and determine its reciprocal before they begin the division process. *(Also see Reteaching, p. 270B.)*

3 Practice

TEST TALK **Exercise 17** Stress the importance of clear and complete explanations. If students describe the expressions as "the number of halves in $5\frac{1}{2}$" and "half of $5\frac{1}{2}$," that may help them explain their answers.

Leveled Practice

Below Level Ex. 6–15, 17, 20–23

On Level Ex. 8–18, 20–23

Above Level Ex. 9–23

Early Finishers Have students look at Exercises 6–10. In each exercise, they should switch the divisor and dividend and then calculate the new quotient.

4 Assess

Journal Idea Have students explain the steps used to divide one mixed number by another.

Test-Taking Practice 5-7

1. When you divide one mixed number by another mixed number, is the quotient larger or smaller than the dividend? Explain. **Sample answer: The quotient is smaller than the dividend, because a mixed number is greater than one.**

2. Find the quotient. Simplify if possible.

$3\frac{6}{7} \div 4\frac{1}{2} =$

A. $\frac{3}{5}$
(B.) $\frac{6}{7}$
C. $\frac{27}{7}$
D. $17\frac{5}{14}$

Available as a transparency

Above Level — Enrichment

A Fraction Operation

E 5-7 NUMBER SENSE

Fill in the empty boxes in the puzzles below so that all rows are true number sentences. Remember the order of operations: multiply and divide from left to right, then add and subtract from left to right.

Write +, −, ×, or ÷ in each empty box.

1. $4\frac{1}{2} \times 2 \times \frac{1}{3} = 3$
2. $\frac{1}{4} + \frac{1}{8} \div \frac{1}{2} = \frac{1}{2}$
3. $3\frac{2}{3} \div 1\frac{1}{3} + 1\frac{1}{2} = 4\frac{1}{4}$
4. $6\frac{1}{4} \times \frac{1}{4} - \frac{1}{32} = 1\frac{17}{32}$
5. $3\frac{1}{4} + 7\frac{2}{3} - 9\frac{5}{12} = 1\frac{1}{2}$
6. $4\frac{1}{3} \div \frac{2}{3} + 1\frac{2}{3} = 8\frac{1}{6}$
7. $\frac{7}{11} \times 2\frac{1}{2} + 2\frac{7}{22} = 3\frac{10}{11}$
8. $\frac{7}{64} \div \frac{1}{4} \times 3\frac{1}{7} = 1\frac{3}{8}$
9. $4\frac{7}{8} \times 2\frac{1}{4} - 3 = 7\frac{31}{32}$
10. $1\frac{9}{10} \div 3\frac{1}{4} + 7 = 7\frac{38}{65}$

60 Use with Lesson 5-7.

Problem Solving

Dividing Mixed Numbers

PS 5-7

Grocery List Gregory wrote down a list of ingredients that he had in the house so that he could make muffins for his class.

Groceries on Hand
$5\frac{1}{2}$ lb of flour
$3\frac{1}{2}$ lb of sugar
$1\frac{1}{2}$ dozen eggs
$3\frac{3}{4}$ c berries

1. Each batch of muffins requires $1\frac{1}{4}$ lb of flour. How many full batches could Gregory make with the flour he has? How much flour would he have left over? **4 batches, $\frac{1}{2}$ lb of flour left over**
2. Each batch of muffins requires $1\frac{1}{8}$ lb of sugar. How many full batches of muffins could Gregory make with the sugar he has in the house? What fraction of a batch could he still make? **3 batches, $\frac{1}{9}$ of a batch**
3. Each batch of muffins takes $1\frac{1}{2}$ c of berries. How many full batches of muffins could Gregory make with the berries he has? If he wanted to make another full batch, how many additional cups of berries would he need? **2 batches, $\frac{3}{4}$ c of berries**
4. Each batch of muffins takes $\frac{1}{4}$ of a dozen eggs. How many batches of muffins could Gregory make with the eggs he has? **6 batches**
5. Consider your answers for Exercises 1–4. What is the greatest number of complete batches of muffins that Gregory can make with the ingredients he has? **2 batches**
6. **Writing in Math** If Gregory made $3\frac{1}{2}$ dozen muffins, and his muffin containers could each hold $1\frac{1}{4}$ dozen muffins, how many containers could Gregory fill with muffins? How many muffins would there be in the container that is not completely full? Explain. **Sample answer: Two full containers would hold 15 muffins each. The other container would hold 12 muffins or $\frac{4}{5}$ of a container.**

60 Use with Lesson 5-7.

Review

Purpose Help students review content learned in Section B.

Using Student Pages 272–273

Do You Know How? exercises are appropriate for written work.

Do You Understand? questions are designed for whole-class discussion or small-group discussion followed by a report to the whole class.

Vocabulary Review

You may wish to review these terms before assigning the page.

reciprocal *(p. 267)*

multiplicative inverse *(p. 267)*

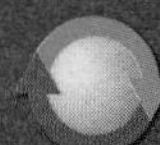

Section B: Lessons 5-5 through 5-7

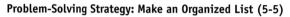

Review

Do You Know How?

Do You Understand?

Problem-Solving Strategy: Make an Organized List (5-5)

Solve by making an organized list.

1. There are 5 pitchers and 3 catchers on the intramural baseball team. From how many pitcher-catcher pairs can the coach choose? **15 pairs**
2. A spinner has 4 colors—red, yellow, blue, and green. If you spin two times, how many color pairs can you get? **16 color pairs**

A Explain how you identified the pitchers and catchers in Exercise 1. **See below.**

B Discuss why you should carefully organize your list. **Lists should be organized so combinations are not duplicated or missed.**

A. Sample answer: I labeled the pitchers A–E and the catchers 1–3. Then I made sure each listed item had 1 letter and 1 number paired.

Dividing Fractions (5-6)

Write the reciprocal of each fraction or number.

3. $\frac{3}{7}$ **$\frac{7}{3}$** 4. 5 **$\frac{1}{5}$** 5. 1 **$\frac{1}{1}$**

Find each quotient.

6. $21 \div \frac{3}{7}$ **49**
7. $\frac{1}{6} \div 4$ **$\frac{1}{24}$**
8. $\frac{6}{7} \div 9$ **$\frac{2}{21}$**
9. $\frac{5}{9} \div \frac{5}{6}$ **$\frac{2}{3}$**
10. $\frac{2}{3} \div \frac{1}{3}$ **2**
11. $6 \div \frac{1}{2}$ **12**
12. $\frac{9}{2} \div \frac{1}{6}$ **27**
13. $\frac{18}{25} \div \frac{12}{15}$ **$\frac{9}{10}$**

C Tell how you can think of $8 \div \frac{1}{4}$ and $\frac{2}{3} \div 4$. **See below.**

D Explain how to write and solve $56 \div 7$ as a multiplication problem.

Multiply 56 by the reciprocal of 7, which is $\frac{1}{7}$. The GCF of 56 and 7 is 7. After simplification, $8 \times \frac{1}{1} = 8$.

C. How many one-fourths are in 8? How can $\frac{2}{3}$ be divided into 4 equal amounts?

Dividing Mixed Numbers (5-7)

Find each quotient. Simplify if possible.

14. $1\frac{1}{2} \div 1\frac{1}{4}$ **$1\frac{1}{5}$**
15. $16 \div 2\frac{3}{4}$ **$5\frac{9}{11}$**
16. $5\frac{2}{9} \div 1\frac{2}{3}$ **$3\frac{2}{15}$**
17. $9\frac{3}{8} \div 3\frac{9}{10}$ **$2\frac{21}{52}$**
18. $20\frac{4}{5} \div 4\frac{9}{10}$ **$4\frac{12}{49}$**
19. $19 \div 1\frac{1}{5}$ **$15\frac{5}{6}$**
20. $1\frac{4}{9} \div 2\frac{2}{3}$ **$\frac{13}{24}$**
21. $3\frac{21}{25} \div 1\frac{2}{5}$ **$2\frac{26}{35}$**

E. Sample answer: I would use pencil and paper because $24\frac{1}{4} \div \frac{1}{4}$ becomes $\frac{97}{4} \times \frac{4}{1} = 97$.

E Tell which method you would choose for $24\frac{1}{4} \div \frac{1}{4}$ and why. **See above.**

F How is dividing with mixed numbers different from dividing with fractions? **In most cases, when you divide by a mixed number, you must express the mixed number as an improper fraction before multiplying.**

Item Analysis for Diagnosis and Intervention

Objective	Review Items	Diagnostic Checkpoint Items	Student Book Pages*	Intervention System
Make an organized list to solve a problem.	1–2	3	264–265	M28
Divide fractions.	3–13	1, 4–15, 27–28	266–269	H42
Divide mixed numbers.	14–21	16–26	270–271	H43

*For each lesson, there is a *Reteaching* activity in *Reaching All Learners* and a *Reteaching* master.

Chapter 5 Section B

Diagnostic Checkpoint

MULTIPLE CHOICE

Think It Through
Before I divide mixed numbers, I should **estimate** the quotient.

1. Which is $\frac{1}{6} \div \frac{3}{8}$? (5-6)

   A. $\frac{1}{16}$ (B.) $\frac{4}{9}$ C. $2\frac{1}{4}$ D. $2\frac{7}{8}$

2. Which is the quotient $4\frac{2}{3} \div 7$? (5-7)

   A. $\frac{3}{98}$ (B.) $\frac{2}{3}$ C. $1\frac{1}{2}$ D. $32\frac{2}{3}$

FREE RESPONSE

Solve by making an organized list. (5-5)

3. A spinner has 3 colors—red, yellow, and blue. If you spin two times, how many color pairs can you get? **9 color pairs**

Give the reciprocal of each fraction or number. (5-6)

4. $\frac{4}{7}$ **$\frac{7}{4}$** 5. 6 **$\frac{1}{6}$** 6. $\frac{8}{3}$ **$\frac{3}{8}$** 7. 12 **$\frac{1}{12}$**

Find each quotient. Simplify if possible. (5-6)

8. $\frac{5}{6} \div 20$ **$\frac{1}{24}$** 9. $18 \div \frac{6}{11}$ **33** 10. $\frac{1}{6} \div \frac{8}{3}$ **$\frac{1}{16}$** 11. $\frac{1}{5} \div \frac{14}{15}$ **$\frac{3}{14}$**

12. $\frac{2}{9} \div \frac{4}{81}$ **$4\frac{1}{2}$** 13. $\frac{3}{4} \div \frac{5}{16}$ **$2\frac{2}{5}$** 14. $\frac{7}{19} \div 14$ **$\frac{1}{38}$** 15. $48 \div \frac{16}{21}$ **63**

Find each quotient. Simplify if possible. (5-7)

16. $2\frac{1}{3} \div 1\frac{1}{14}$ **$2\frac{8}{45}$** 17. $5\frac{2}{5} \div 1\frac{5}{9}$ **$3\frac{33}{70}$** 18. $6\frac{2}{3} \div 4\frac{1}{5}$ **$1\frac{37}{63}$**

19. $24 \div 1\frac{8}{9}$ **$12\frac{12}{17}$** 20. $18 \div 2\frac{4}{15}$ **$7\frac{16}{17}$** 21. $2\frac{3}{4} \div 1\frac{5}{11}$ **$1\frac{57}{64}$**

22. $7\frac{3}{7} \div 3\frac{1}{5}$ **$2\frac{9}{28}$** 23. $4\frac{4}{9} \div 7\frac{2}{3}$ **$\frac{40}{69}$** 24. $98 \div 4\frac{5}{12}$ **$22\frac{10}{53}$**

25. Elka bought a 12-ft length of ribbon from which she wants to cut $\frac{3}{4}$-ft pieces. How many pieces can she cut? (5-7) **16 pieces**

26. To make 11 puppets, Kevin used $5\frac{1}{2}$ yards of material. How much material did he use for each puppet? **$\frac{1}{2}$ yard**

Writing in Math

27. Sample answer: $6 \div \frac{1}{3}$ means finding how many thirds are in 6. $6 \times \frac{1}{3}$ means finding $\frac{1}{3}$ of 6.

27. How is dividing 6 by $\frac{1}{3}$ different from multiplying 6 by $\frac{1}{3}$. (5-6) **See above.**

28. Explain why when you divide a whole number other than zero by a proper fraction, the quotient is always greater than the whole number. (5-7) **Sample answer: The quotient shows how many parts of a whole are in the whole number, so the quotient will always be greater than the original whole number.**

Sample student work for Exercise 27

For $6 \div \frac{1}{3}$, you want to know how many tiny $\frac{1}{3}$s are in 6. If you had 6 pies cut into $\frac{1}{3}$ pieces, there would be 18 pieces of pie. But $6 \times \frac{1}{3}$ is $\frac{1}{3}$ of 6 or $6 \div 3$, and $6 \div 3 = 2$. $\frac{1}{3}$ of 6 pieces of pie is 2 pieces.

The rubric below is a scoring guide that shows how many points to give an answer to Exercise 27. Many teachers would assign a score of 4 points to this explanation. Discuss the sample response shown and compare it to papers produced by students.

Scoring Rubric

4 — Full credit: 4 points
The answer is correct; knows how to multiply and divide fractions; explanation is complete.

3 — Partial credit: 3 points
The answer is correct; knows how to multiply and divide fractions; explanation is incomplete.

2 — Partial credit: 2 points
The answer shows understanding of multiplying and dividing fractions; contains computational errors.

1 — Partial credit: 1 point
The answer consists of correct computations with no explanation.

0 — No credit
The answer is incorrect; does not know how to multiply and divide fractions.

Lesson Organizer

Quick Lesson Overview

Objective Write word phrases as, and evaluate, algebraic expressions with fractions.

Math Understanding Word phrases that express mathematical situations can be translated into specific expressions using numbers and operations, and expressions can be evaluated by substituting given values for the variable.

Professional Development Note

Research Base

Kleiman (1998) presents a general framework for modeling real situations in middle school algebra. Kleiman emphasizes that information should be extracted from real situations and expressed in mathematical form. These mathematical expressions are evaluated to produce a solution that can then be returned to the original situation. In this lesson, students translate real situations into expressions involving fractions. In the next lesson they learn to use fractions to solve the equations.

NCTM Standards

- Algebra

(For a complete correlation to the NCTM Standards and Grades 6–8 Expectations, see pages 246G–H.)

Getting Started

Spiral Review

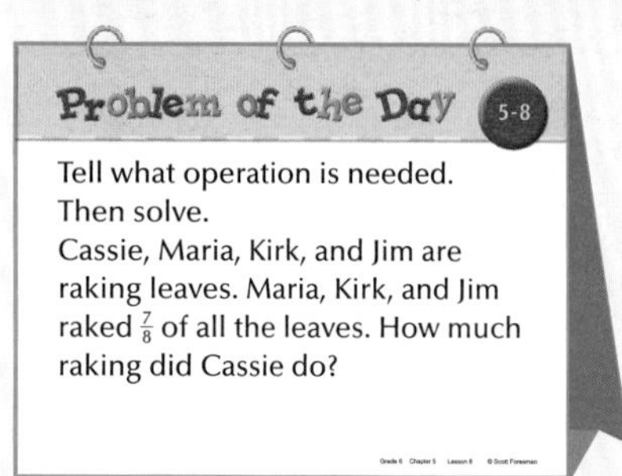

Problem of the Day 5-8

Tell what operation is needed. Then solve.
Cassie, Maria, Kirk, and Jim are raking leaves. Maria, Kirk, and Jim raked $\frac{7}{8}$ of all the leaves. How much raking did Cassie do?

Topics Reviewed

- Problem-solving Skill: Choose an Operation

Answer The operation needed is subtraction. Cassie raked $\frac{1}{8}$ of all the leaves.

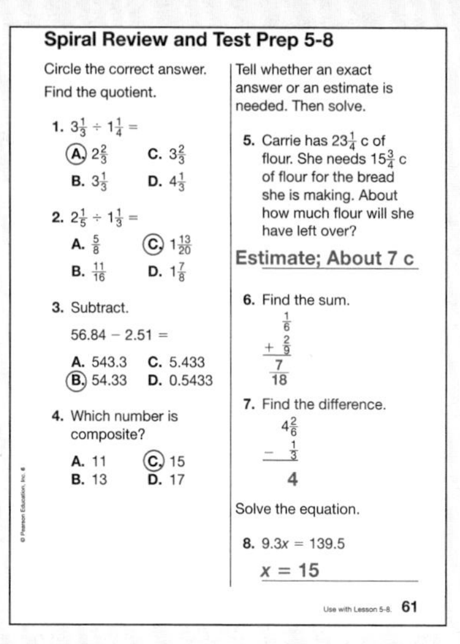

Spiral Review and Test Prep 5-8

Circle the correct answer.
Find the quotient.

1. $3\frac{1}{3} \div 1\frac{1}{4} =$
   (A.) $2\frac{2}{3}$ C. $3\frac{2}{3}$
   B. $3\frac{1}{3}$ D. $4\frac{1}{3}$
2. $2\frac{1}{5} \div 1\frac{1}{3} =$
   A. $\frac{5}{8}$ (C.) $1\frac{13}{20}$
   B. $\frac{11}{16}$ D. $1\frac{7}{8}$
3. Subtract.
   $56.84 - 2.51 =$
   A. 543.3 C. 5.433
   (B.) 54.33 D. 0.5433
4. Which number is composite?
   A. 11 (C.) 15
   B. 13 D. 17

Tell whether an exact answer or an estimate is needed. Then solve.

5. Carrie has $23\frac{1}{4}$ c of flour. She needs $15\frac{3}{4}$ c of flour for the bread she is making. About how much flour will she have left over?
   Estimate; About 7 c
6. Find the sum.
   $\frac{1}{6} + \frac{2}{9}$
   $\frac{7}{18}$
7. Find the difference.
   $4\frac{2}{6} - \frac{1}{3}$
   4

Solve the equation.

8. $9.3x = 139.5$
   $x = 15$

Use with Lesson 5-8. 61

Available as a transparency and as a blackline master

Topics Reviewed

1.–2., 7. Dividing and subtracting mixed numbers; **3.** Subtracting decimals; **4.** Prime and composite numbers; **5.** Exact or estimate; **6.** Adding fractions with unlike denominators; **8.** Solving equations with decimals

Investigating the Concept

Express Yourself

5–10 MIN **Auditory**

What to Do

- On the board, write this problem: A crate contains books. The crate weighs $1\frac{1}{2}$ pounds and each book weighs $2\frac{3}{4}$ pounds. **Write an expression for the combined weight of the books and crate. What is the variable?** *(The number of books in the crate)* **If you know there are 2 books, how can you find the combined weight?** *(Multiply 2 by $2\frac{3}{4}$ and add $1\frac{1}{2}$.)*
- **What expression describes the problem?** *($2\frac{3}{4}n + 1\frac{1}{2}$)*
- **How can you find the value of the expression when $n = 5$?** *(Substitute 5 for n in $2\frac{3}{4}n + 1\frac{1}{2}$.)* **What is that value?** *($15\frac{1}{4}$)* **What does the answer tell you?** *(The weight of the crate with 5 books is $15\frac{1}{4}$ pounds.)*

Ongoing Assessment

- **Number Sense What values can n have in this problem?** *(Whole numbers)*
  What is the value of the expression for $n = 8$? *($23\frac{1}{2}$)*

$2\frac{3}{4}(5) + 1\frac{1}{2}$

$13\frac{3}{4} + 1\frac{1}{2} = 15\frac{1}{4}$

Reaching All Learners

Writing in Math

Write a Riddle

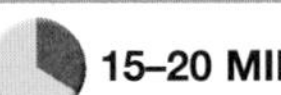
15–20 MIN **Linguistic**

- Have students write a riddle like the one below.
- Ask students to exchange papers and solve each others' riddles by writing an algebraic expression and evaluating it for the given number.

I multiplied my height by $1\frac{2}{3}$ and then I added $3\frac{3}{8}$. What's the result if my height is 60 inches?

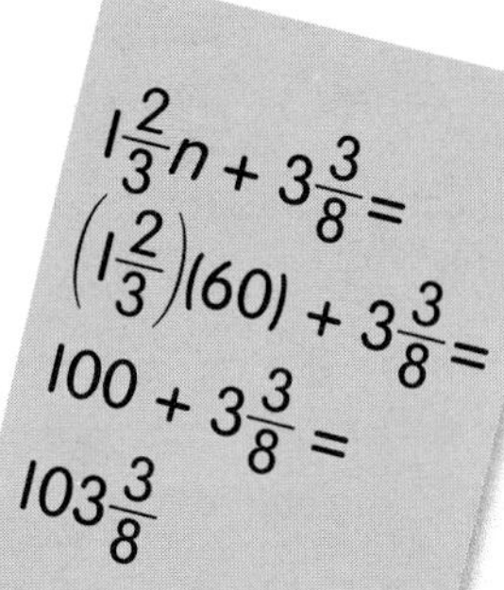

Extend Language

English Language Learners

Words into Numbers

10–15 MIN **Linguistic**

- Read the Key Idea on page 274. Then have a volunteer read the problem in Example A.
- Work with students to chart the algebraic expression and the words that explain it.

Words	Algebraic Expressions
number of hours Miguel worked	$\frac{1}{2}d$

- Have small groups each write a similar word problem.
- Have groups exchange word problems. Then have each group talk through making a chart showing the words and the algebraic expression.

Reteaching

Match Up

10–15 MIN **Logical/Mathematical**

Materials *(per pair)* Cards containing word phrases and the related algebraic expressions

- Have students turn the word phrase cards face down. Have partner 1 draw a word phrase. **Read the phrase.** *(sample answer: 4 less than $\frac{2}{3}$ of a number)* Have partner 2 look through the algebraic expressions to find the matching card and explain why they are the same.
- **What is the value of that expression for $n = 6$?** *(0)*

4 less than $\frac{2}{3}$ of a number

$\frac{2}{3}n - 4$

Advanced Learners

Input/Output Table

5–10 MIN **Logical/Mathematical**

- Have students use algebraic expressions to complete an input/output table like the following:

Input	$\frac{2x-1}{x}$	Output
1	$\frac{2 \times 1 - 1}{1}$	*(1)*
2	$\frac{2 \times 2 - 1}{2}$	*($1\frac{1}{2}$)*
3	$\frac{2 \times 3 - 1}{3}$	*($1\frac{2}{3}$)*

- **Look at the pattern. What is the output if $x = 9$?** *($1\frac{8}{9}$)* **Do you think the output will ever be equal to 2? Explain.** *(No, the whole-number part is always 1, and the numerator of the fraction will always be 1 less than the denominator.)*
- Challenge students to make their own tables.

Objective Write word phrases as, and evaluate, algebraic expressions with fractions.

1 Warm Up

Activate Prior Knowledge Review evaluating algebraic expressions containing whole numbers.

2 Teach

LEARN Students have written and evaluated algebraic expressions using whole numbers. They can extend those skills to algebraic expressions that contain fractions.

Ongoing Assessment

Talk About It: Question 1

If students cannot think of another way,

then have them start with a simpler problem. Ask: **What is another way to write $\frac{1}{2}$ or $\frac{1}{3}$?** *(Sample answer: 0.5 or 0.333. . .)*

CHECK

Error Intervention

If students evaluate the expressions incorrectly,

then suggest they first evaluate each expression with a whole number and then follow the same steps to evaluate the expressions with the fraction and then with the mixed number. *(Also see* Reteaching, *p. 274B.)*

Lesson 5-8

Algebra

Key Idea
Relationships among fractional quantities can be written using algebra.

Think It Through
I need to use **order of operations** to simplify expressions.

Expressions with Fractions

WARM UP

Evaluate for $x = 4$ and $x = 12$.

1. $3x$ 12; 36
2. $2.5x$ 10; 30
3. $x \div 2$ 2; 6
4. $12 \div x$ 3; 1

LEARN

How can you write algebraic expressions with fractions?

Example A

At the bowling alley, Miguel works half the number of hours that Damaris works.

Write an algebraic expression for the number of hours Miguel works.

Let d equal the number of hours Damaris works.

Then $\frac{1}{2}d$ is the number of hours Miguel works.

Example B

Carlote's salary is \$4 more than $\frac{1}{3}$ the salary of the bowling alley's manager.

Write an algebraic expression for Carlote's salary.

Let s equal the manager's salary.

Then $\frac{1}{3}s + 4$ is Carlote's salary.

How can you evaluate algebraic expressions with fractions?

Example C

Brett is half as old as Victor.

Find Brett's age if Victor is 14 years old.

Evaluate the expression $\frac{1}{2}v$ when $v = 14$.

$\frac{1}{2}v$ Substitute 14 for v.

$\frac{1}{2}(14) = 7$ Simplify.

Brett is 7 years old.

Example D

Evaluate $\frac{1}{5}m + 7$ when $m = 4\frac{1}{6}$.

$\frac{1}{5}\left(4\frac{1}{6}\right) + 7$ Substitute $4\frac{1}{6}$ for m.

$\frac{1}{5}\left(\frac{25}{6}\right) + 7$ Use order of operations and simplify.

$\frac{1}{\cancel{5}_1}\left(\frac{\cancel{25}^5}{6}\right) + 7$

$\frac{5}{6} + 7$

$7\frac{5}{6}$

Talk About It 1. $\frac{d}{2}$; $0.5d$; $\frac{s}{3}$; $0.\overline{3}s$

1. What is another way to write $\frac{1}{2}d$ and $\frac{1}{3}s$?

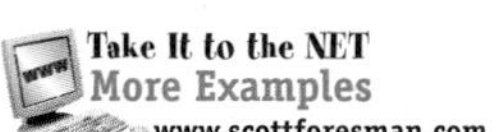

274

Reteaching — Below Level

Expressions with Fractions R 5-8

Writing an Algebraic Expression

Yesterday the temperature in Portland, Oregon, was 10° more than half the temperature in Phoenix, Arizona. Write an algebraic expression for the temperature in Portland.

Let m = the temperature in Phoenix.

The temperature in Portland was $\frac{1}{2}m + 10$.

Evaluating an Algebraic Expression

If the temperature in Phoenix was 80° yesterday, what was the temperature in Portland?

Substitute 80 for m.

Use order of operations to simplify.

$\frac{1}{2}(80) + 10$

$40 + 10 = 50$

It was 50° in Portland.

Write each word phrase as an algebraic expression.

1. 1 more than $\frac{3}{5}f$ $\frac{3}{5}f + 1$
2. $\frac{2}{3}$ Tom's weight $\frac{2}{3}m$
3. 5 fewer than $\frac{5}{6}$ the amount $\frac{5}{6}n - 5$
4. **Number Sense** Write a word phrase that represents $\frac{1}{2}n + 4$. Four more than $\frac{1}{2}$ the number n

Evaluate each expression for $n = \frac{1}{3}$ and $n = 1\frac{1}{4}$.

5. $\frac{7}{8}n$ $\frac{7}{24}$; $1\frac{3}{32}$
6. $2\frac{1}{3}n$ $\frac{7}{9}$; $2\frac{11}{12}$
7. $3 + \frac{1}{2}n$ $3\frac{1}{6}$; $3\frac{5}{8}$
8. $10n - 3$ $\frac{1}{3}$; $9\frac{1}{2}$

Use with Lesson 5-8. 61

Practice — On Level

Expressions with Fractions P 5-8

Write each word phrase as an algebraic expression.

1. 2 more than $\frac{2}{3}d$ $\frac{2}{3}d + 2$
2. $\frac{7}{8}$ Amanda's age $\frac{7}{8}n$
3. 10 fewer than $\frac{1}{2}$ the number $\frac{1}{2}n - 10$
4. **Number Sense** How do the word phrases representing $\frac{5}{6}x + 4$ and $\frac{5}{6}x - 4$ differ? The word phrase for $\frac{5}{6}x + 4$ is 4 more than $\frac{5}{6}$ of a number. The word phrase for $\frac{5}{6}x - 4$ is 4 less than $\frac{5}{6}$ of a number.

Evaluate each expression for $n = \frac{1}{4}$ and $n = 1\frac{5}{6}$.

5. $\frac{9}{10}n$ $\frac{9}{40}$; $1\frac{13}{20}$
6. $4\frac{1}{8}n$ $1\frac{1}{32}$; $7\frac{9}{16}$

Evaluate each expression for $n = 2\frac{1}{3}$ and $n = 3\frac{3}{4}$.

7. $\frac{3}{5}n$ $1\frac{2}{5}$; $2\frac{1}{4}$
8. $5\frac{1}{2}n$ $12\frac{5}{6}$; $20\frac{5}{8}$
9. You can calculate Aaron's age using the expression $\frac{1}{2}n + 5$. If n = Beth's age and Beth is 16, how old is Aaron? 13

Test Prep

10. Evaluate $5\frac{1}{4}n$ for $n = \frac{2}{3}$.
    A. $1\frac{1}{2}$ B. $2\frac{1}{5}$ C. $2\frac{3}{4}$ (D.) $3\frac{1}{2}$
11. **Writing in Math** Martha's teacher gave her a phrase and asked her to write an expression for the phrase. The expression Martha wrote was $\frac{3}{8}n$. What could the phrase have been? Explain how you know. The phrase could have been $\frac{3}{8}$ of a number. $\frac{3}{8}n$ means $\frac{3}{8}$ times n.

Use with Lesson 5-8. 61

CHECK

For another example, see Set 5-8 on p. 294.

Write each word phrase as an algebraic expression.

1. two thirds Josh's age **$\frac{2}{3}j$**
2. 6 less than $\frac{1}{9}k$ **$\frac{1}{9}k - 6$**
3. 4 more than $\frac{1}{8}x$ **$\frac{1}{8}x + 4$**

Evaluate each expression for $n = \frac{3}{4}$ and $n = 2\frac{1}{2}$.

4. $8n$ **6; 20**
5. $\frac{1}{2}n$ **$\frac{3}{8}$; $1\frac{1}{4}$**
6. $2\frac{1}{2}n + 3\frac{1}{8}$ **5; $9\frac{3}{8}$**
7. **Number Sense** How do the word phrases representing $\frac{1}{4}x + 5$ and $\frac{1}{4}(x + 5)$ differ? **See below right.**

PRACTICE

For more practice, see Set 5-8 on p. 297.

7. $\frac{1}{4}x + 5$ is, "5 more than $\frac{1}{4}x$", while $\frac{1}{4}(x + 5)$ is, "$\frac{1}{4}$ the sum of x + 5."

A Skills and Understanding

Write each word phrase as an algebraic expression.

8. $\frac{5}{6}$ Yuri's height **$\frac{5}{6}h$**
9. 3 more than $\frac{1}{4}c$ **$\frac{1}{4}c + 3$**
10. 8 fewer than $\frac{1}{3}$ the amount **$\frac{1}{3}a - 8$**
11. 5 less than r **$r - 5$**
12. p decreased by 12 **$p - 12$**
13. 8 more than 3 times a number **$3n + 8$**

Evaluate each expression for $n = \frac{5}{6}$ and $n = 1\frac{1}{4}$.

14. $2\frac{1}{5}n$ **$1\frac{5}{6}$; $2\frac{3}{4}$**
15. $2 + \frac{3}{10}n$ **$2\frac{1}{4}$; $2\frac{3}{8}$**
16. $24n - 8$ **12; 22**
17. **Number Sense** How do the word phrases representing $3 - \frac{2}{3}y$ and $\frac{2}{3}y - 3$ differ? **$3 - \frac{2}{3}y$ is $\frac{2}{3}y$ less than 3, while $\frac{2}{3}y - 3$ is 3 less than $\frac{2}{3}y$.**

B Reasoning and Problem Solving

18. A bowler's handicap is calculated using the expression $\frac{4}{5}(200 - a)$, where a is the bowler's average score. What is the handicap for a bowler whose average is 140? 180? **48 handicap; 16 handicap**
19. **Writing in Math** When given the phrase, "$\frac{1}{3}$ of two times a number," Callista wrote the expression $\frac{2}{3}x$. Is she correct? Explain. **Yes. Sample answer: $\frac{1}{3}(2x) = \frac{1}{3}\left(\frac{2}{1}\right)(x) = \frac{2}{3}x$**

Mixed Review and Test Prep

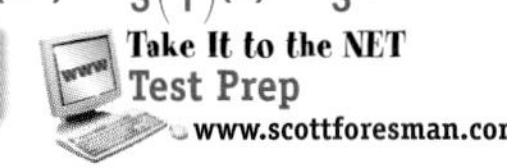

Take It to the NET Test Prep www.scottforesman.com

20. How long will it take to walk $3\frac{1}{2}$ miles at a rate of $2\frac{1}{2}$ miles per hour? **$1\frac{2}{5}$ hours**
21. How many $\frac{3}{4}$-pound servings are in 15 pounds? **20 servings**
22. $5\frac{1}{2} \div 3\frac{2}{3}$ equals

A. $\frac{6}{121}$ B. $\frac{2}{3}$ **(C.)** $1\frac{1}{2}$ D. $20\frac{1}{6}$

All text pages available online and on CD-ROM.

3 Practice

Exercise 19 Once students have written an expression for the word phrase, remind them they can use properties of multiplication to change or simplify what they have written.

Leveled Practice

Below Level	Ex. 8–15, 17, 19–22
On Level	Ex. 8–15, 18–22
Above Level	Ex. 8–10, 13–22

Early Finishers Have each student write an algebraic expression that contains a fraction and a value for the variable. Then students should exchange papers and evaluate each others' algebraic expression.

4 Assess

Journal Idea Have students explain how to evaluate $4\frac{2}{3} + 1\frac{5}{6}n$ for $n = 1\frac{1}{2}$.

Enrichment — Above Level

Set the Table

E 5-8 ALGEBRA

1. Complete the table by evaluating each expression. Use the values given for n. The first row has been completed for you.

	$n = \frac{1}{2}$	$n = 2\frac{1}{4}$	$n = 3\frac{2}{5}$
$2n$	1	$4\frac{1}{2}$	$6\frac{4}{5}$
$1\frac{3}{4}n$	$\frac{7}{8}$	$3\frac{15}{16}$	$5\frac{19}{20}$
$1\frac{5}{16}n$	$\frac{21}{32}$	$2\frac{61}{64}$	$4\frac{37}{80}$
$\frac{7}{8}n$	$\frac{7}{16}$	$1\frac{31}{32}$	$2\frac{39}{40}$

2. Create your own table. Use 4 expressions and 3 values for n. The expressions and values should all be fractions.

Sample answer:

	$n = 1\frac{1}{4}$	$n = 2\frac{3}{4}$	$n = 4\frac{1}{4}$
$n + \frac{1}{2}$	$1\frac{3}{4}$	$3\frac{1}{4}$	$4\frac{3}{4}$
$n - \frac{3}{4}$	$\frac{1}{2}$	2	$3\frac{1}{2}$
$\frac{5}{6}n$	$1\frac{1}{24}$	$2\frac{7}{24}$	$3\frac{13}{24}$
$n \div \frac{2}{3}$	$1\frac{7}{8}$	$4\frac{1}{8}$	$6\frac{3}{8}$

Use with Lesson 5-8. 61

Problem Solving

Expressions with Fractions

PS 5-8

Skyscrapers The number of floors that are in some of the world's tallest buildings is shown. Use this data for 1–3.

Building	Number of Floors
Sears Tower, Chicago	110
Sciotia Plaza, Toronto	68
Bank of America Plaza, Atlanta	55
Empire State Building, New York	102
Peachtree Tower, Atlanta	50
Chase Tower, Houston	75

1. Which skyscraper is described as having $\frac{1}{2}$ the number of floors as the Sears Tower? **Bank of America Plaza**
2. The number of floors of which skyscraper is described by the expression $\frac{2}{3}$(number of floors in Empire State Building)? **Sciotia Plaza**
3. The number of floors of which skyscraper is described by the expression $1\frac{1}{2}$(number of floors in Peachtree Tower)? **Chase Tower**

Measurements Some commonly used measurements are listed in the chart.

Measurements	
12 inches	= 1 foot
3 feet	= 1 yard

4. Write a number expression for the number of yards in a certain number of feet. Let f = ft. **$\frac{f}{3}$**
5. Write a number expression for the number of feet in a certain number of inches. Let i = in. **$\frac{i}{12}$**
6. **Writing in Math** Are the expressions four-fifths of x and $\frac{4x}{5}$ equal? Write a complete sentence to explain why or why not. **Sample answer: Yes, these expressions are equivalent because in each case the variable x is multiplied by 4 and divided by 5.**

Use with Lesson 5-8. 61

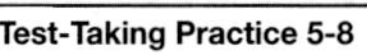

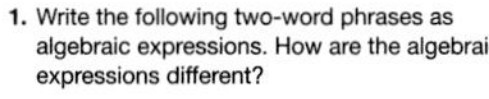

Test-Taking Practice 5-8

1. Write the following two-word phrases as algebraic expressions. How are the algebraic expressions different?

$1\frac{2}{3}$ Stephanie's height

$1\frac{2}{3}$ more than Stephanie's height

Sample answer: $1\frac{2}{3}n$; $n + 1\frac{2}{3}$; The first expression shows multiplication, while the second shows addition.

2. Evaluate the expression for $n = \frac{2}{3}$ and $n = 4\frac{2}{5}$.

$\frac{1}{2}n =$

(A.) $\frac{1}{3}$, $2\frac{1}{5}$

B. $\frac{1}{4}$, $2\frac{1}{4}$

C. $\frac{2}{6}$, $2\frac{2}{5}$

D. $\frac{1}{3}$, $1\frac{2}{5}$

Available as a transparency

Solving Equations with Fractions

Lesson Organizer

Quick Lesson Overview

Objective Solve one-step equations in one variable with fractions.

Math Understanding Using inverse operations and properties of equality can help you solve for the variable in an equation.

Professional Development Note

Effective Questioning Techniques Ask students to specify the operation in each equation and explain how they would solve these equations. Encourage all their answers and have students discuss those answers.

NCTM Standards

- Number and Operations
- Algebra

(For a complete correlation to the NCTM Standards and Grades 6–8 Expectations, see pages 246G–H.)

Getting Started

Spiral Review

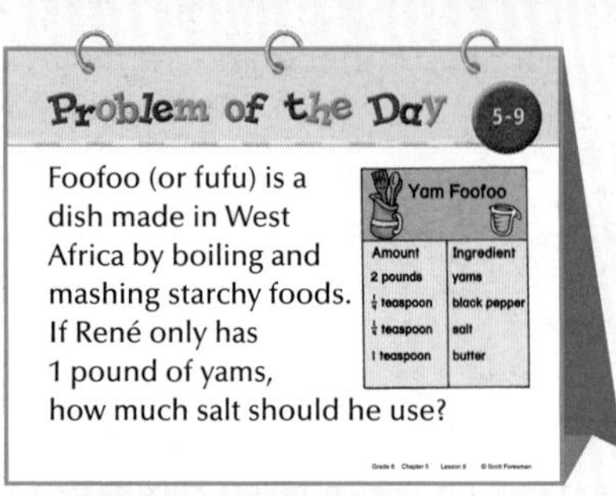

Problem of the Day 5-9

Foofoo (or fufu) is a dish made in West Africa by boiling and mashing starchy foods. If René only has 1 pound of yams, how much salt should he use?

Yam Foofoo

Amount	Ingredient
2 pounds	yams
$\frac{1}{4}$ teaspoon	black pepper
$\frac{1}{4}$ teaspoon	salt
1 teaspoon	butter

Grade 6 Chapter 5 Lesson 9 © Scott Foresman

Topics Reviewed

- Multiplying fractions
- Problem-Solving Skill: One-Step Problem

Answer René should use $\frac{1}{8}$ teaspoon of salt.

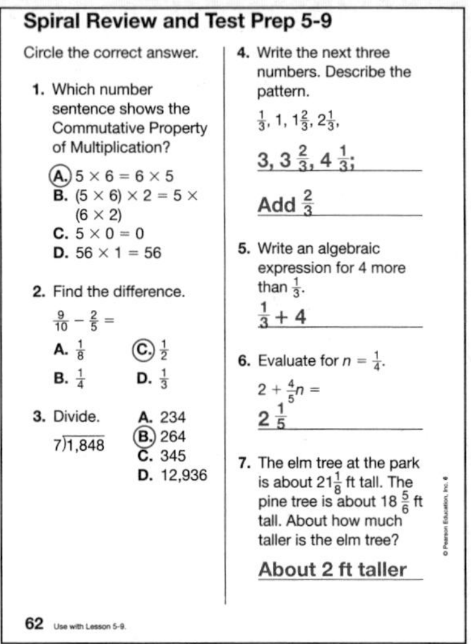

Spiral Review and Test Prep 5-9

Circle the correct answer.

1. Which number sentence shows the Commutative Property of Multiplication?
   (A.) $5 \times 6 = 6 \times 5$
   B. $(5 \times 6) \times 2 = 5 \times (6 \times 2)$
   C. $5 \times 0 = 0$
   D. $56 \times 1 = 56$

2. Find the difference.
   $\frac{9}{10} - \frac{2}{5} =$
   A. $\frac{1}{8}$ (C.) $\frac{1}{2}$
   B. $\frac{1}{4}$ D. $\frac{1}{3}$

3. Divide. $7\overline{)1,848}$
   A. 234
   (B.) 264
   C. 345
   D. 12,936

4. Write the next three numbers. Describe the pattern.
   $\frac{1}{3}, 1, 1\frac{2}{3}, 2\frac{1}{3},$
   $3, 3\frac{2}{3}, 4\frac{1}{3};$
   Add $\frac{2}{3}$

5. Write an algebraic expression for 4 more than $\frac{1}{3}$.
   $\frac{1}{3} + 4$

6. Evaluate for $n = \frac{1}{4}$.
   $2 + \frac{4}{5}n =$
   $2\frac{1}{5}$

7. The elm tree at the park is about $21\frac{1}{8}$ ft tall. The pine tree is about $18\frac{5}{6}$ ft tall. About how much taller is the elm tree?
   About 2 ft taller

© Pearson Education, Inc. 6

62 Use with Lesson 5-9.

Available as a transparency and as a blackline master

Topics Reviewed

1. Properties of operations; **2.** Subtracting fractions with unlike denominators; **3.** Dividing larger numbers; **4.** Look for a pattern; **5.–6.** Expressions with fractions; **7.** Estimating sums and differences of fractions and mixed numbers

Investigating the Concept

Solving the Equation

10–15 MIN **Kinesthetic**

Materials *(per group)* Centimeter Grid Paper (Teaching Tool 18)

What to Do

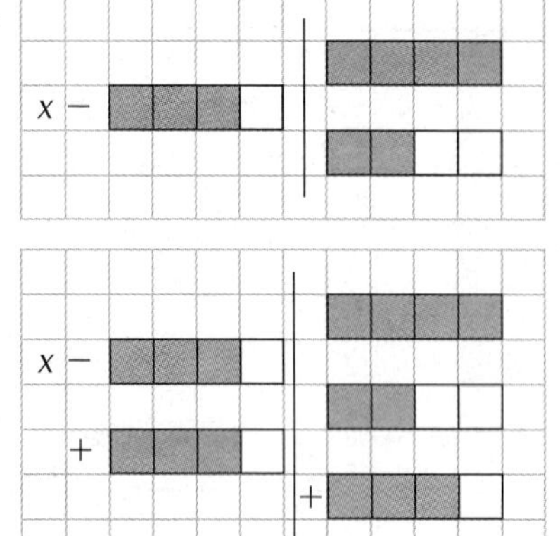

- Have students model the equation $x - \frac{3}{4} = 1\frac{1}{2}$ by drawing and shading rectangles on grid paper.
- **What should you do to undo subtracting $\frac{3}{4}$?** *(Add $\frac{3}{4}$.)* Model adding $\frac{3}{4}$ to the sketch.
- **What is the value of x?** *($2\frac{1}{4}$)*
- **Model $n + 1\frac{1}{4} = 2$. What will you do to both sides of the equation to undo adding $1\frac{1}{4}$?** *(Subtract $1\frac{1}{4}$.)* **What is the value of n?** *($\frac{3}{4}$)*

Ongoing Assessment

- **Number Sense For the equation $x + 2\frac{3}{4} = 4\frac{2}{3}$, is x less than or greater than $4\frac{2}{3}$? Explain.** *(Less, because you subtract $2\frac{3}{4}$ from both sides to solve)*
- **Solve $\frac{1}{3}x = 2\frac{2}{3}$.** *($x = 8$)*

Reaching All Learners

Reading in Math

Solving an Equation

15–20 MIN **Linguistic**

- Write the following problem on the board:

  Jane bought $3\frac{3}{8}$ yd of material today. With the material she bought yesterday, she now has $12\frac{1}{4}$ yd. How much material did she buy yesterday?
- **Summarize the main idea of this problem.** *($3\frac{3}{8}$ plus some number is a total of $12\frac{1}{4}$.)*
- Have partners work together to write an equation to solve. Then have them take turns solving the equation.

$$3\frac{3}{8} + n = 12\frac{1}{4}$$
$$3\frac{3}{8} + n - 3\frac{3}{8} = 12\frac{1}{4} - 3\frac{3}{8}$$
$$n = 8\frac{7}{8}$$

Access Content

English Language Learners

Left Equals Right

10–15 MIN **Logical/Mathematical/Verbal**

- Write $7\frac{1}{3} + \frac{2}{3} = 8$ on the board: **Note that the sum of the numbers on the left of the equation sign is the same as the value of the number on the right. Just check by adding.**
- Display the following on the board:
- Ask pairs to correctly match the expression on the left with one on the right and explain their computation. *(1. is 14; 2. is 2; 3. is $1\frac{1}{2}$; 4. is 7)*

1. $2\frac{1}{3} \div \frac{1}{6}$	$1\frac{1}{2}$
2. $\frac{3}{4} + 1\frac{1}{4}$	7
3. $3\frac{1}{2} - 2$	14
4. $5 \times 1\frac{2}{5}$	2

Reteaching

What Does It Mean?

15–20 MIN **Social/Cooperative**

Materials *(per group)* Index cards labeled *Undo addition by subtracting $2\frac{1}{2}$, Undo subtraction by adding $2\frac{1}{2}$, Undo multiplication by dividing by $2\frac{1}{2}$,* and *Undo division by multiplying by $2\frac{1}{2}$*

- Give each group the equation $x - 2\frac{1}{2} = 6\frac{1}{4}$. Have Student 1 read the equation. Then ask students to work together. **What operation is done in the equation?** *(Subtraction)* **Which direction for solving should you use?** *(Undo subtraction by adding $2\frac{1}{2}$.)*
- **What is your solution?** *($x = 8\frac{3}{4}$)*
- Repeat with the equations $x + 2\frac{1}{2} = 6\frac{1}{4}$, $(2\frac{1}{2})x = 6\frac{1}{4}$, and $x \div 2\frac{1}{2} = 6\frac{1}{4}$. *($x = 3\frac{3}{4}$; $x = 2\frac{1}{2}$; $x = 15\frac{5}{8}$)*

Math and History

Egyptian Measurements

5–10 MIN **Logical/Mathematical**

- Tell students about modern equivalents for ancient Egyptian measurements.

Measure	Derivation	Modern Measure
cubit	elbow to fingertips	$1\frac{1}{2}$ ft
span	tip of little finger to tip of thumb with hand stretched out	$\frac{3}{4}$ ft
hand	width of hand	$\frac{1}{3}$ ft

- **What is the number of spans in 5 cubits? Write and solve an equation.** *($\frac{3}{4}n = 5(1\frac{1}{2})$; 10 spans)*
- **Write a problem using these terms. Exchange problems and solve.**

Objective Solve one-step equations in one variable with fractions.

1 Warm Up

Activate Prior Knowledge Review solving equations with whole numbers and decimals.

2 Teach

LEARN Be sure students are familiar with how to undo operations in equations. It may be helpful to ask students what number they could multiply a specific fraction by to get a product of 1. (*The fraction's reciprocal*)

Ongoing Assessment

Talk About It: Question 1

If students have difficulty checking the answers,

then have them write the solution on a small piece of paper and lay it over the variable. Then they can simplify the left side, $4\frac{1}{3} \div \frac{2}{3}$.

$$\boxed{4\tfrac{1}{3}} \div \frac{2}{3} = 6\frac{1}{2}$$

CHECK

Error Intervention

If students multiply both sides of a multiplication equation by the fraction itself instead of by its reciprocal,

then ask: **Do you get b if you simplify $(\frac{5}{6})(\frac{5}{6})b$?** *(No)* They should see that they have to multiply by the reciprocal. *(Also see* Reteaching, *p. 276B.)*

Lesson 5-9

Algebra

Key Idea
You can solve equations with fractions using inverse operations, just as with whole numbers and decimals.

Think It Through
I know that **dividing by a fraction** is the same as **multiplying by its reciprocal.**

Solving Equations with Fractions

WARM UP

Solve.

1. $8.2 + x = 10$
   $x = 1.8$
2. $x - 18 = 19$
   $x = 37$
3. $32 = 175 - x$
   $x = 143$
4. $1.8 = x - 8.6$
   $x = 10.4$

LEARN

How can you solve equations involving fractions and mixed numbers?

Example A

Solve $x + \frac{2}{3} = 8$.

$$x + \frac{2}{3} = 8$$
$$x + \frac{2}{3} - \mathbf{\frac{2}{3}} = 8 - \mathbf{\frac{2}{3}}$$
$$x = 7\frac{1}{3}$$

Check: $x + \frac{2}{3} = 8$

$7\frac{1}{3} + \frac{2}{3} = 8$

$8 = 8$

Example B

Solve $n - 4\frac{1}{2} = 6\frac{3}{8}$.

$$n - 4\frac{1}{2} = 6\frac{3}{8}$$
$$n - 4\frac{1}{2} + \mathbf{4\frac{1}{2}} = 6\frac{3}{8} + \mathbf{4\frac{1}{2}}$$
$$\mathbf{n} = 6\frac{3}{8} + 4\frac{4}{8}$$
$$n = 10\frac{7}{8}$$

Check: $n - 4\frac{1}{2} = 6\frac{3}{8}$

$10\frac{7}{8} - 4\frac{1}{2} = 6\frac{3}{8}$

$6\frac{3}{8} = 6\frac{3}{8}$

Example C

Solve $\frac{4}{5}y = 32$.

$$\frac{4}{5}y = 32$$
$$\left(\mathbf{\frac{5}{4}}\right)\frac{4}{5}y = 32\left(\mathbf{\frac{5}{4}}\right)$$
$$y = \frac{\overset{8}{\cancel{32}}}{1} \times \frac{5}{\cancel{4}_1}$$
$$y = 40$$

Check: $\frac{4}{5}y = 32$

$\frac{4}{5}(40) = 32$

$32 = 32$

Example D

Solve $a \div \frac{2}{3} = 6\frac{1}{2}$.

$$a \div \frac{2}{3} = 6\frac{1}{2}$$
$$a \times \frac{3}{2} = 6\frac{1}{2} \qquad 6\frac{1}{2} = \frac{13}{2}$$
$$a \times \frac{3}{2}\left(\mathbf{\frac{2}{3}}\right) = \frac{13}{2}\left(\mathbf{\frac{2}{3}}\right)$$
$$a = \frac{13}{3}$$
$$a = 4\frac{1}{3}$$

Talk About It

1. How would you check the answer to the equation in Example D? Substitute $4\frac{1}{3}$ for a in the original equation. Then evaluate $4\frac{1}{3} \div \frac{2}{3}$. See above.

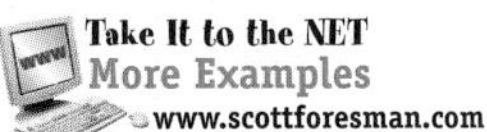

Take It to the NET
More Examples
www.scottforesman.com

276

Reteaching — Below Level

Solving Equations with Fractions

R 5-9

Here is how to solve addition, subtraction, multiplication, and division equations with fractions.

Addition	Subtraction
Solve $n + \frac{3}{5} = 9$. $n + \frac{3}{5} = 9$ $n + \frac{3}{5} - \mathbf{\frac{3}{5}} = 9 - \mathbf{\frac{3}{5}}$ $n = 8\frac{2}{5}$	Solve $x - 2\frac{1}{3} = 6\frac{1}{9}$. $x - 2\frac{1}{3} = 6\frac{1}{9}$ $x - 2\frac{1}{3} + \mathbf{2\frac{1}{3}} = 6\frac{1}{9} + \mathbf{2\frac{1}{3}}$ $x = 6\frac{1}{9} + 2\frac{3}{9}$ $x = 8\frac{4}{9}$
Multiplication	**Division**
Solve $\frac{5}{8}y = 1\frac{2}{3}$. $\frac{5}{8}y = 1\frac{2}{3}$ $\left(\mathbf{\frac{8}{5}}\right)\frac{5}{8}y = \frac{5}{3}\left(\mathbf{\frac{8}{5}}\right)$ $y = \frac{\overset{1}{\cancel{5}}}{3} \times \frac{8}{\cancel{8}_1}$ $y = \frac{8}{3} = 2\frac{2}{3}$	Solve $a \div \frac{1}{4} = 3\frac{1}{2}$. $a \div \frac{1}{4} = 3\frac{1}{2}$ $a \times \frac{4}{1} = 3\frac{1}{2}$ $a \times \frac{4}{1}\left(\mathbf{\frac{1}{4}}\right) = \frac{7}{2}\left(\mathbf{\frac{1}{4}}\right)$ $a = \frac{7}{8}$

Solve each equation and check your answer.

1. $z + 2\frac{1}{3} = 3\frac{1}{6}$ $\quad\frac{5}{6}$
2. $6n = \frac{3}{4}$ $\quad\frac{1}{8}$
3. $x - 1 = 4\frac{2}{3}$ $\quad 5\frac{2}{3}$
4. $y \div \frac{1}{2} = 2\frac{1}{8}$ $\quad 1\frac{1}{16}$
5. $\frac{3}{8} + n = 10$ $\quad 9\frac{5}{8}$
6. $2\frac{2}{9} \div 5 = x$ $\quad\frac{4}{9}$
7. **Algebra** The rainfall total for June is $4\frac{9}{10}$ in. Yesterday it rained $2\frac{1}{10}$ in. Use the equation $n + 2\frac{1}{10} = 4\frac{9}{10}$ to calculate how much rainfall was received before yesterday. $2\frac{4}{5}$ in.

Practice — On Level

Solving Equations with Fractions

P 5-9

Solve each equation and check your answer.

1. $y + 1\frac{1}{4} = 2\frac{3}{8}$ $\quad y = \frac{9}{8}$ or $1\frac{1}{8}$
2. $w - 2 = 3\frac{1}{2}$ $\quad w = \frac{11}{2}$ or $5\frac{1}{2}$
3. $z \div \frac{3}{4} = 4\frac{1}{4}$ $\quad z = 3\frac{3}{16}$
4. $\frac{1}{3} = \frac{7}{8}q$ $\quad q = \frac{8}{21}$
5. $6\frac{1}{2} = \frac{5}{6}b$ $\quad b = 7\frac{4}{5}$
6. $2\frac{1}{4} = p - \frac{3}{8}$ $\quad p = 2\frac{5}{8}$
7. $2\frac{1}{4} = x \div \frac{1}{2}$ $\quad x = \frac{9}{8}$ or $1\frac{1}{8}$
8. **Number Sense** Is the solution of $m \div \frac{2}{3} = 9$ greater than or less than the solution of $m \div \frac{1}{4} = 9$? Explain. Sample answer: $m \div \frac{2}{3} = 9$ is greater because you are dividing by a larger number.
9. The bakery used $42\frac{1}{3}$ c of flour. There were $10\frac{1}{3}$ c left in the flour bin. Use the equation $x - 42\frac{1}{3} = 10\frac{1}{3}$ to find out how many cups of flour the bakery had to start with. $52\frac{2}{3}$ c
10. Alex had a ball of string. He cut the string into 26 equal pieces. Each piece measured $3\frac{1}{4}$ in. Use the equation $m \div 26 = 3\frac{1}{4}$ to find the length of the ball of string. $84\frac{1}{2}$ in.

Test Prep

11. Solve $12y = 2\frac{1}{4}$.
    A. $1\frac{1}{2}$ B. $1\frac{1}{8}$ C. $\frac{7}{36}$ **(D.)** $\frac{9}{48}$
12. **Writing in Math** Write the steps you would use to solve the equation $z + 3\frac{1}{5} = 6\frac{3}{5}$. Solve. Change the mixed numbers to improper fractions and write $z + \frac{16}{5} = \frac{33}{5}$. Then subtract $\frac{16}{5}$ from both sides of the equation. So, $z = \frac{17}{5}$, or $3\frac{2}{5}$.

CHECK

For another example, see Set 5-9 on p. 294.

Solve each equation and check your answer.

1. $c + 4 = 7\frac{1}{2}$ **$c = 3\frac{1}{2}$**
2. $m - \frac{5}{6} = 4\frac{2}{3}$ **$m = 5\frac{1}{2}$**
3. $\frac{5}{6}b = 7\frac{1}{2}$ **$b = 9$**
4. $w \div \frac{3}{4} = 4\frac{1}{2}$ **$w = 3\frac{3}{8}$**
5. **Number Sense** Is the solution of $\frac{5}{4}x = 20$ greater than or less than 20? **Less than 20**

PRACTICE

For more practice, see Set 5-9 on p. 297.

A Skills and Understanding

Solve each equation and check your answer.

6. $x + 2\frac{2}{3} = 5\frac{1}{6}$ **$x = 2\frac{1}{2}$**
7. $b - 5 = 6\frac{3}{8}$ **$b = 11\frac{3}{8}$**
8. $2p = \frac{5}{8}$ **$p = \frac{5}{16}$**
9. $x \div \frac{6}{7} = 1\frac{1}{6}$ **$x = 1$**
10. $\frac{1}{3} + m = 4\frac{1}{4}$ **$m = 3\frac{11}{12}$**
11. $7\frac{6}{7} = p - 2\frac{1}{5}$ **$p = 10\frac{2}{35}$**
12. $\frac{1}{2} = \frac{5}{6}y$ **$y = \frac{3}{5}$**
13. $4\frac{3}{4} = w \div \frac{1}{5}$ **$w = \frac{19}{20}$**
14. **Number Sense** Is the solution of $y \div \frac{4}{3} = 15$ greater than or less than 15? **Greater than 15**

B Reasoning and Problem Solving

15. After completing $36\frac{3}{4}$ miles of a bike race, Kimi still has $8\frac{3}{4}$ miles to go. Use the equation $b - 36\frac{3}{4} = 8\frac{3}{4}$ to find the total length of the race. **$45\frac{1}{2}$ miles**

16. Tyrell divided a spool of ribbon into 12 pieces of the same length shown below. Use the equation $r \div 12 = 2\frac{1}{2}$ to find the number of feet of ribbon the spool held. **30 feet**

17. **Writing in Math** Marta said, "I'm thinking of a fraction. If I divide it by $\frac{1}{2}$, I get $\frac{7}{12}$." Describe how you would determine what fraction Marta was thinking of; then solve the problem. **I would write the equation $f \div \frac{1}{2} = \frac{7}{12}$, then solve for f; Marta was thinking of $\frac{7}{24}$.**

Mixed Review and Test Prep

Take It to the NET Test Prep www.scottforesman.com

Choose a variable and write an expression for each phrase.

18. five more than $\frac{1}{3}$ Jill's score **$\frac{1}{3}s + 5$**
19. three less than $\frac{7}{8}$ a number **$\frac{7}{8}n - 3$**
20. Choose the expression with the greatest quotient.
    A. $5\frac{1}{2} \div \frac{1}{4}$ B. $3\frac{1}{3} \div \frac{1}{4}$ **(C.)** $7 \div \frac{1}{4}$ D. $\frac{1}{10} \div \frac{1}{4}$

All text pages available online and on CD-ROM.

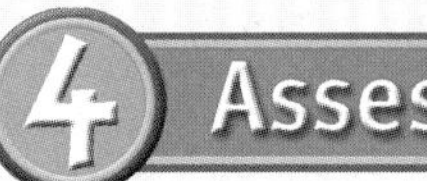

3 Practice

Test Talk **Exercise 17** Suggest that students start with the algebraic expression that represents "divide a fraction by $\frac{1}{2}$." Once they have written the expression, they can complete the equation and solve.

Leveled Practice

- **Below Level** Ex. 6–14, 16–20
- **On Level** Ex. 6–14, 16–20
- **Above Level** Ex. 7–20

Early Finishers Have students use Exercises 8–10 in Lesson 5–8. Have them write each expression as one side of an equation and any whole number greater than 2 as the other side of the equation and then solve.

4 Assess

Journal Idea Have students explain how to solve an equation that contains fractions.

Above Level — Enrichment

Make the Right Choice

E 5-9 REASONING

In each of these problems, some numbers are missing. Read each problem. Then circle the letter of the correct way to solve the problem.

1. You are buying books at the bookstore. Each book you buy costs the same amount. You know how much money you started with and also how much you have already spent. How many books can you buy and still have enough for a set of bookends?
   (A.) Add the cost of the bookends to what you have already spent. Subtract that amount from the amount of money you started with. Divide that number by the price of a book.
   B. Subtract what you have already spent from the amount of money you started with. Add the cost of the bookends. Divide that answer by the price of a book.
   C. Subtract the cost of the bookends from the amount of money you started with. Multiply that number by the price of a book.
2. You are making lasagna for your friends. You know how many people your recipe serves and the amount of each ingredient you need. More people will be eating than the recipe serves. How will you change the recipe to make enough?
   A. Divide the recipe ingredients by the number of people who will be eating.
   B. Multiply the amount of each ingredient by the number of people who will be eating.
   (C.) Divide the number of people who will be eating by the number the recipe serves. Multiply that answer by the amount of each ingredient.
3. You know how many hours you have between the end of school and bedtime. You also know how many minutes you spend doing homework. How can you find what fraction of the time after school you spend doing homework?
   A. Multiply to change the after-school time to minutes. Divide by the minutes of homework time.
   (B.) Multiply to change the after-school time to minutes. Divide the number of minutes of homework time by that product.
   C. Divide the hours of after-school time by the minutes of homework time.

62 Use with Lesson 5-9.

Problem Solving

Solving Equations with Fractions

PS 5-9

Temperature Two common ways to measure and express temperature are Celsius and Fahrenheit. Use the equation $c = \frac{5}{9}(f - 32)$ when the Fahrenheit temperature is known. Use the equation $f = \frac{9}{5}c + 32$ when the Celsius temperature is known.

1. Jennifer was told that the average temperature for her vacation destination was 77°F. She was used to temperature expressions in Celsius. What is the average temperature in Celsius? **25°C**
2. Stephan was traveling from the United States to Canada and was told to expect temperatures of 30°C. He did not know whether to bring snow skis or a bathing suit. Convert the temperature to Farenheit, and write what Stephan should bring. **86°F, a bathing suit**

American History Club The students in the American history club are preparing a display for the spring open house at school.

3. Michael is using a large roll of paper to make an American history time line for the display. He has used $1\frac{1}{3}$ rolls of paper. He will use another $2\frac{1}{3}$ rolls to complete the time line. Solve the equation $p - 1\frac{1}{3} = 2\frac{1}{3}$ to find the total number of rolls of paper Michael will use. **$3\frac{2}{3}$ rolls of paper**

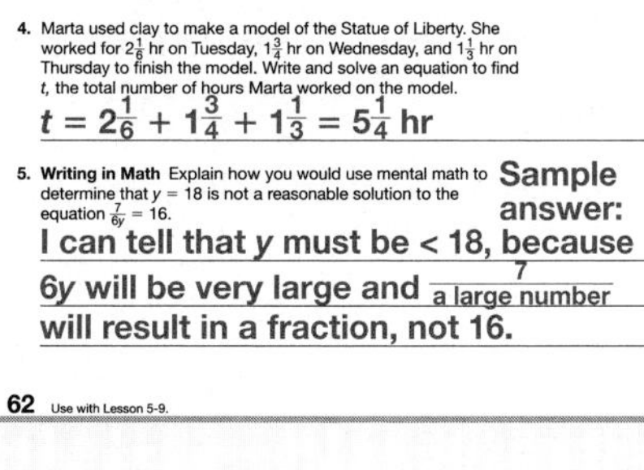

4. Marta used clay to make a model of the Statue of Liberty. She worked for $2\frac{1}{6}$ hr on Tuesday, $1\frac{3}{4}$ hr on Wednesday, and $1\frac{1}{3}$ hr on Thursday to finish the model. Write and solve an equation to find t, the total number of hours Marta worked on the model. **$t = 2\frac{1}{6} + 1\frac{3}{4} + 1\frac{1}{3} = 5\frac{1}{4}$ hr**
5. **Writing in Math** Explain how you would use mental math to determine that $y = 18$ is not a reasonable solution to the equation $\frac{7}{6y} = 16$. **Sample answer: I can tell that y must be < 18, because $6y$ will be very large and $\frac{7}{\text{a large number}}$ will result in a fraction, not 16.**

62 Use with Lesson 5-9.

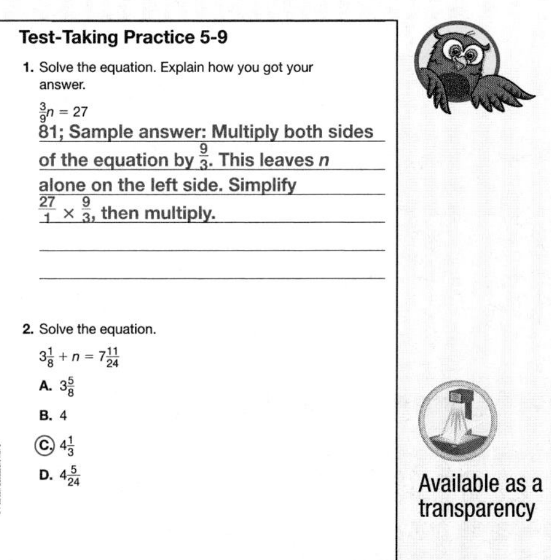

Test-Taking Practice 5-9

1. Solve the equation. Explain how you got your answer.
   $\frac{3}{9}n = 27$
   81; Sample answer: Multiply both sides of the equation by $\frac{9}{3}$. This leaves n alone on the left side. Simplify $\frac{27}{1} \times \frac{9}{3}$, then multiply.
2. Solve the equation.
   $3\frac{1}{8} + n = 7\frac{11}{24}$
   A. $3\frac{5}{8}$
   B. 4
   (C.) $4\frac{1}{3}$
   D. $4\frac{5}{24}$

Available as a transparency

PROBLEM-SOLVING SKILL 5-10

Writing to Explain

Lesson Organizer

Quick Lesson Overview 

Objective Explain solutions to word problems.

Math Understanding An explanation of the solution to a problem includes information that is known and how you have used this information.

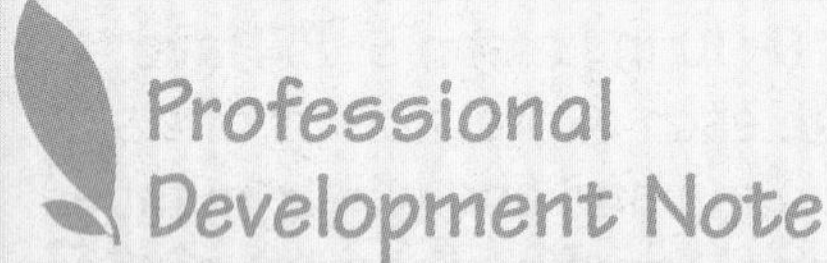

Managing Instruction Have students ask a family member to explain the steps they use in an activity. Tell the students to record the explanation as completely as possible. Point out that each step needs to be clear and complete, so another person could follow the steps and repeat the activity.

NCTM Standards

- Number and Operations

(For a complete correlation to the NCTM Standards and Grades 6–8 Expectations, see pages 246G–H.)

Getting Started

Spiral Review

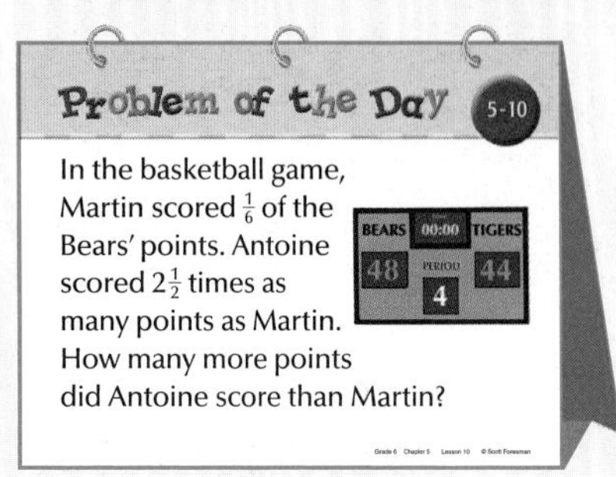

Problem of the Day 5-10

In the basketball game, Martin scored $\frac{1}{6}$ of the Bears' points. Antoine scored $2\frac{1}{2}$ times as many points as Martin. How many more points did Antoine score than Martin?

Grade 6 Chapter 5 Lesson 10 © Scott Foresman

Topics Reviewed

- Multiplying fractions and mixed numbers; subtracting whole numbers
- Problem-Solving Skill: Multiple-Step Problem

Answer Antoine scored 12 more points than Martin.

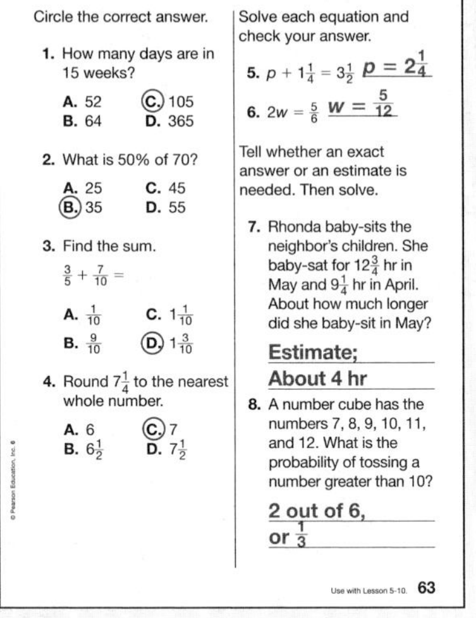

Spiral Review and Test Prep 5-10

Circle the correct answer.

1. How many days are in 15 weeks?
   A. 52 (C.) 105
   B. 64 D. 365
2. What is 50% of 70?
   A. 25 C. 45
   (B.) 35 D. 55
3. Find the sum.
   $\frac{3}{5} + \frac{7}{10} =$
   A. $\frac{1}{10}$ C. $1\frac{1}{10}$
   B. $\frac{9}{10}$ (D.) $1\frac{3}{10}$
4. Round $7\frac{1}{4}$ to the nearest whole number.
   A. 6 (C.) 7
   B. $6\frac{1}{2}$ D. $7\frac{1}{2}$

Solve each equation and check your answer.

5. $p + 1\frac{1}{4} = 3\frac{1}{2}$ $p = 2\frac{1}{4}$
6. $2w = \frac{5}{6}$ $w = \frac{5}{12}$

Tell whether an exact answer or an estimate is needed. Then solve.

7. Rhonda baby-sits the neighbor's children. She baby-sat for $12\frac{3}{4}$ hr in May and $9\frac{1}{4}$ hr in April. About how much longer did she baby-sit in May?
   Estimate; About 4 hr
8. A number cube has the numbers 7, 8, 9, 10, 11, and 12. What is the probability of tossing a number greater than 10?
   2 out of 6, or $\frac{1}{3}$

© Pearson Education, Inc. 6

Use with Lesson 5-10. 63

Available as a transparency and as a blackline master

Topics Reviewed

1. Time; **2.** Finding the percent of a number; **3.** Adding fractions with unlike denominators; **4.** Rounding mixed numbers; **5.–6.** Solving equations with fractions; **7.** Exact or estimate **8.** Probability

Investigating the Concept

Describing the Solution

15–20 MIN | **Linguistic**

What to Do

- Write this problem on the board: Mario is planting bushes in a $12\frac{1}{2}$-foot-long row. He starts at one end and plants them $2\frac{1}{2}$ feet apart. The bushes cost $15 each. How much did he spend?
- **Here are the steps Mario used. Write them in order.** *(C, A, B)* Write these steps below the problem.

  A. I drew a picture. It shows 6 bushes, with 1 at each end of the row.

  B. I multiplied 6 by $15. The bushes cost $90.

  C. I divided $12\frac{1}{2}$ by $2\frac{1}{2}$ to find out how many spaces there would be between bushes. I got 5.

Ongoing Assessment

- **Reasoning What did the solver learn from the first step?** *(The $12\frac{1}{2}$-foot-long row will be divided into 5 sections.)*
- **Why is 5 not the number of bushes?** *(Because there are bushes at each end of the row)*

 EC NTL 12 11 10 9 8 7 6

Reaching All Learners

Math Vocabulary

What Is a Good Explanation?

 15–20 MIN **Auditory** 

- To help students understand what writing a good explanation means, ask them to list the steps they would use to find the word *dog* in a dictionary.
- **Exchange papers. Follow the directions. Do they work or is something missing? What makes a good explanation?** *(Sample answer: The steps are clear and complete. When you follow them, you get from question to solution, step by step.)*

1. Get dictionary.
2. Open to the section that has words beginning with D.
3. Find the words with second letter "o."
4. Continue down that list until the third letter is "g."
5. Read the definition.

Extend Language

English Language Learners

Step By Step

 10–15 MIN **Verbal/Logical/Mathematical** 

- Model explaining how you got to school today, including the type of transportation and the order of the streets you took. Have students in small groups take turns explaining how they got to school today. Encourage them to tell the steps in order.
- Direct attention to the chart in the Check section on page 279. Have one group find the fraction of students who prefer Math, another group find the fraction of students who prefer Reading, and a third group find the fraction of students who prefer Social Studies.
- Ask students from each group to give a step-by-step explanation of their solution for the class.

Reteaching

Put the Steps in Order

 10–15 MIN **Social/Cooperative** 

Materials *(per pair)* 4 index cards with these steps, one step per card: Draw a diagram. Label the dimensions. Subtract. Answer the question.

- Write on the board: Mac had an 8-inch-by-10-inch sheet of paper. He cut a 1-inch square from each corner, folded up the sides, and made a box. How big is the box?
- Mix the cards. **Work together to put the cards in the order you would use to solve the problem. Use them to assist you in writing an explanation of how you solved the problem. Include the solution.** *(6" by 8" by 1")*

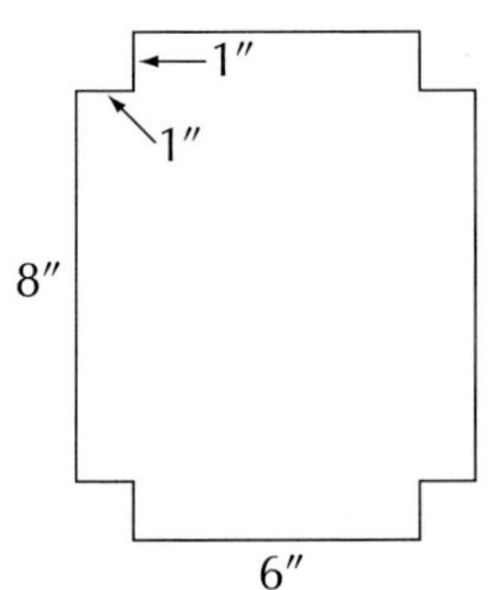

Advanced Learners

How Warm Is It?

 10–15 MIN **Logical/Mathematical** 

- Show students the body temperature information.
- **The difference between the body temperatures of the elephant and the bear is $\frac{1}{7}$ of the difference between the owl's and the gull's temperatures. What is the body temperature of the elephant? Write an explanation.** *(Subtract $93\frac{1}{5}$ from $104\frac{2}{5}$ and multiply by $\frac{1}{7}$. Because the elephant's temperature is less than the bear's, subtract $1\frac{3}{5}$ from $99\frac{1}{10}$ to get $97\frac{1}{2}°$.)*

94°F 96°F 98°F 100°F 102°F 104°F

Arctic Gull $93\frac{1}{5}$°F

African Elephant

Polar Bear $99\frac{1}{10}$°F

Owl $104\frac{2}{5}$°F

Objective Explain solutions to word problems.

1 Warm Up

Activate Prior Knowledge Ask students to brainstorm what makes a good explanation.

2 Teach

LEARN Encourage students to express and discuss their ideas about why a logical and clear description of the solution to a problem is important.

Ongoing Assessment

Talk About It: Question 1

If students do not identify the necessary information,

then suggest they begin by listing all the information shown in the diagram. They can then find each piece of information in the explanation and identify how it was used.

CHECK

Error Intervention

If students have difficulty finding the fractions,

then ask: **What part of a fraction would the numbers in the table represent?** *(The numerator)* **How would you find the denominator?** *(Add all four numbers.) (Also see* Reteaching, *p. 278B.)*

Lesson 5-10

Problem-Solving Skill

Reading Helps!

Identifying steps in a process can help you with... writing to explain.

Key Idea
There are specific things you can do to write a good explanation in math.

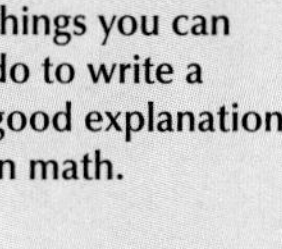

Think It Through
When you write to explain, it is important that you **describe each step** in the solution clearly.

Writing to Explain

LEARN

How do you write a good explanation?

Wooden Pegs Camille plans to make a wooden rack for hanging keys and purses by drilling 6 peg holes, each $\frac{7}{8}$ inch in diameter, in a piece of wood $16\frac{5}{8}$ inches long.

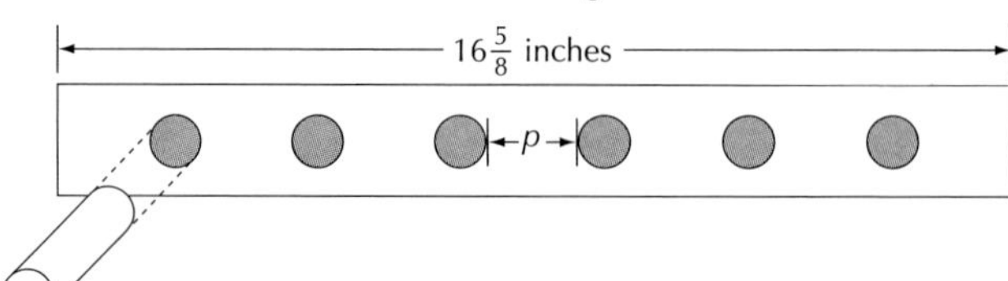

The space at each end of the rack is the same size as the space between any two pegs. What is the distance (*p*) between any two pegs? Show your work and explain in writing how you solved the problem.

To find the amount of space taken up by the peg holes, I multiplied the diameter of each hole by the number of peg holes $\left(\frac{7}{8} \times 6 = \frac{21}{4} = 5\frac{1}{4} \text{ in.}\right)$. I then subtracted this amount from $16\frac{5}{8}$ to find the amount of wood left between the holes (*p*) and at the ends $\left(16\frac{5}{8} - 5\frac{1}{4} = 11\frac{3}{8}\right)$. Using the picture, I counted the spaces between the holes and at the ends and got 7 spaces. Since all of these spaces are equal, I divided the $11\frac{3}{8}$ inches of wood space by 7; $\frac{91}{8} \div 7 = \frac{13}{8} = 1\frac{5}{8}$. So, the distance between any two pegs (*p*) is $1\frac{5}{8}$ inches.

Tips for Writing Good Explanations

- Include the work you did that led to that solution.
- Describe the steps and operations you used in the order you used them.
- Refer to any diagrams or data that provide important information or supporting details.

Reteaching — Below Level

PROBLEM-SOLVING SKILL R 5-10

Writing to Explain

Stanley and Mary are growing plants in science class. Stanley's plant is $1\frac{3}{8}$ in. tall. Mary's plant is 4 times as tall. How tall is Mary's plant?

When you are writing to explain your solution,

- include the work you did that led to that solution.
- describe the steps and operations you used in the order you used them.
- refer to any diagrams or data that provide important information or supporting details.

To find the height of Mary's plant, I multiplied the height of Stanley's plant by 4.

Before multiplying I estimated

$1\frac{3}{8} \times 4 \rightarrow 1 \times 4 = 4$

$1\frac{3}{8} \times 4 = \frac{11}{\cancel{8}_2} \times \frac{\cancel{4}^1}{1} = \frac{11}{2} = 5\frac{1}{2}$

$5\frac{1}{2}$ is close to 4, so my answer is reasonable.

So Mary's plant is $5\frac{1}{2}$ in. tall.

Explain your solution and show your work.

1. Paula is 12 years old. Tess is 4 more than $\frac{3}{4}$ Paula's age. How old is Tess?

Sample answer: Multiply Paula's age by $\frac{3}{4}$. Write $\frac{12}{1} \times \frac{3}{4}$. Simplify to get $\frac{3}{1} \times \frac{3}{1} = 9$. Then add 9 + 4 to find out how old Tess is. Tess is 13 years old.

Practice — On Level

PROBLEM-SOLVING SKILL P 5-10

Writing to Explain

Explain your solution and show your work.

1. Rita is riding in an 18 mi bike race. She takes a break every $4\frac{1}{2}$ mi. How many breaks will she take?

To find the number of breaks Rita takes, divide 18 by $4\frac{1}{2}$. The quotient is 4. Rita takes 4 breaks.

2. Frederick makes toy rocking horses. He needs $7\frac{1}{2}$ ft of wood to make a small horse and $9\frac{3}{4}$ ft of wood to make a large horse. How many feet of wood does he need to make 5 small horses and 7 large horses?

Multiply $7\frac{1}{2}$ by 5 to find the wood needed for the small horses ($7\frac{1}{2} \times 5 = \frac{15}{2} \times 5 = \frac{75}{2} = 37\frac{1}{2}$). Multiply $9\frac{3}{4}$ by 7 to find the wood needed for the large horses ($9\frac{3}{4} \times 7 = \frac{39}{4} \times 7 = \frac{273}{4} = 68\frac{1}{4}$). Frederick needs a total of $105\frac{3}{4}$ ft of wood ($37\frac{1}{2} + 68\frac{1}{4} = 105\frac{3}{4}$).

3. Sephina is baking bread for the school bake sale. She is planning on baking 15 small loaves and 5 large loaves. For each of the small loaves, she needs $1\frac{2}{3}$ c of flour. For each of the large loaves, she needs $4\frac{1}{5}$ c of flour. How many cups of flour does she need altogether?

Multiply $1\frac{2}{3}$ by 15 to find the number of cups of flour needed for the small loaves. Then multiply $4\frac{1}{5}$ by 5 to find the number of cups of flour needed for the large loaves. Simplify the products to 25 and 21 and add. Sephina needs a total of 46 c of flour.

Talk About It

1. What information from the diagram of the wooden rack was needed to solve the problem? How is the information used in the explanation? **The number of spaces between holes and at the ends, the length of the piece of wood. The information provides supporting details.**

2. **$\frac{3}{8}$ of 880 = 880 × $\frac{3}{8}$ = 110 × 3 = 330; Math accounts for $\frac{3}{8}$ of the preferences.**

CHECK

For another example, see Set 5-10 on p. 294.

Explain your solution and show your work.
Sample explanations are given. Check students' work.

A number of sixth graders were asked which of 4 subjects they prefer. The number of students who prefer each subject appears in the table at the right.

Subject	Number of 6th graders
Math	330
Science	255
Reading	190
Social Studies	105

1. What fraction of students prefer science? **Students who prefer science: 255; total students: 880; $\frac{255}{880} = \frac{51}{176}$**
2. Which subject accounts for $\frac{3}{8}$ of the preferences? **See above.**

PRACTICE

For more practice, see Set 5-10 on p. 297.

Explain your solution and show your work. **Sample explanations are given. Check students' work.**

3. Mr. Masong began planting his garden. The section marked on the diagram shows 18 plants with 3 plants in each square. If he continues the pattern, find the number of plants that he will need to finish planting his garden. **72 plants; Each square is 3 ft × 3 ft, so 24 more squares are needed: 24 × 3 = 72 plants.**

15 feet

18 feet

4. $\frac{8}{15}$ of the money; total money = (25 × 75) + (150 × 25) = 5,625; Patina won ($\frac{4}{5}$ × 1,875) + ($\frac{2}{5}$ × 3,750) = 3,000; $\frac{3{,}000}{5{,}625} = \frac{8}{15}$

4. Patina participated in an academic game show consisting of two 25-question rounds. Correct answers in the first round were worth \$75 each; in the second, they were worth \$150 each. Patina correctly answered $\frac{4}{5}$ of the first-round questions and $\frac{2}{5}$ of the second-round questions. What fraction of the total possible money did Patina win? **See above right.**

5. 72 yards; $4\frac{7}{8} + 1\frac{1}{8}$ = 6 yards per chorus member; 6 × 12 = 72 yards.

5. The 12 members of the chorus are wearing matching robes and hats for the evening performances. The seamstress needs $4\frac{7}{8}$ yards of material for each robe and $1\frac{1}{8}$ yards for each hat. Calculate the total number of yards of material needed to make robes and hats for the entire chorus. **See above.**

6. A truck driver started the year making $\frac{7}{20}$ dollar for each mile she drove. Halfway through the year, she received a raise and earned $\frac{19}{50}$ dollar per mile. She drove 48,000 miles in the first 6 months, and 45,000 miles in the last 6 months. Find her truck-driver earnings for the year.
\$33,900; 48,000 × $\frac{7}{20}$ = \$16,800 for the first half of the year; 45,000 × $\frac{19}{50}$ = \$17,100 for the second half of the year; \$16,800 + \$17,100 = \$33,900

All text pages available online and on CD-ROM.

3 Practice

Exercise 4 Ask students to tell what numbers they need in order to determine the fraction Patina won of the total possible money. *(The numerator will be the money Patina won; the denominator will be the total amount of money possible.)*

Leveled Practice

Below Level Ex. 3–6

On Level Ex. 3–6

Above Level Ex. 3–6

Early Finishers Have students select a problem from the textbook and write a clear explanation of the steps involved in the solution.

4 Assess

Journal Idea Have students explain why it is important to be able to write a logical and clear explanation of the solution to a problem.

Enrichment — Above Level

Tablecloth Tally

E 5-10 DATA

The craft club is making tablecloths to raise money for the class trip. The table shows how much fabric is needed for each type of tablecloth.

Tablecloth Fabric

Shape	Yards of Fabric
Round	$2\frac{1}{2}$
Rectangle	$4\frac{1}{3}$
Square	$3\frac{3}{4}$

1. How many round tablecloths can be made with $32\frac{1}{2}$ yd of fabric? **13 round tablecloths**
2. Is 38 yd of fabric enough to make 9 square tablecloths? Explain. **Yes; 9 square tablecloths use $33\frac{3}{4}$ yd of fabric, which is less than 38 yd.**
3. How much fabric is needed to make 6 round tablecloths, 12 rectangle tablecloths, and 8 square tablecloths? **97 yd**

The poster shows the prices for each of the tablecloths.

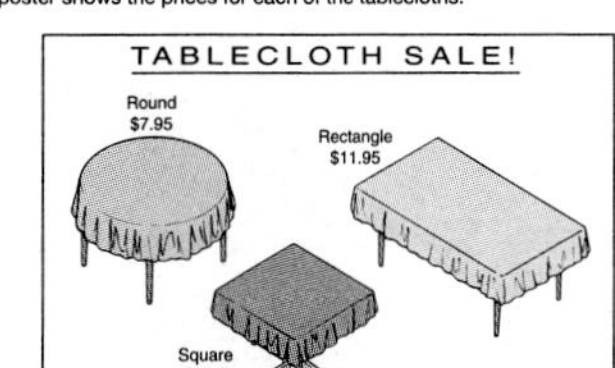

TABLECLOTH SALE!
Round
\$7.95
Rectangle
\$11.95
Square
\$9.95

4. Is \$80.00 enough to buy 3 of each kind of tablecloth? Explain. **No; 3 round tablecloths = \$23.85, 3 rectangle tablecloths = \$35.85, and 3 square tablecloths = \$29.85, for a total of \$89.55. That is greater than \$80.00.**

Problem Solving

PROBLEM-SOLVING SKILL

Writing to Explain

PS 5-10

Race Day The Middletown festival included three different events. The table shows the number of participants who finished each event. The participants in the adults' race finished how many more total miles than the participants in the kids' race?

Race	Length	Number of Participants
Kids'	$1\frac{1}{4}$ mi	132
Adults'	$3\frac{1}{2}$ mi	120
Cross town	$13\frac{2}{3}$ mi	51

Read and Understand

1. How many total participants were there in the kids' race? **132 kids**
2. How many total participants were there in the adults' race? **120 adults**

Plan and Solve

3. Write an equation for the total miles run by adults. **$a = 120 \times 3\frac{1}{2} = 420$**
4. Write an equation for the total miles run by the kids. **$k = 132 \times 1\frac{1}{4} = 165$**
5. Solve the problem. Write the answer in a complete sentence. **The total miles run in the adults' race was 255 more than the total miles run in the kids' race.**

Look Back and Check

6. Is your answer reasonable? How can you tell? **Yes; Sample answer: The number of participants is close, but the adults ran almost 3 times as far, so their distance run should be more than the kids'.**

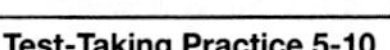

Test-Taking Practice 5-10

1. The marching band will march $3\frac{3}{4}$ mi in the parade. For each mile they march, they can play $1\frac{1}{3}$ songs. How many songs can they play in the parade? Explain your solution and show your work.
5 songs; Sample answer: Multiply $3\frac{3}{4}$ by $1\frac{1}{3}$. Change both mixed numbers to improper fractions. $\frac{15}{4} \times \frac{4}{3}$. Simplify, then multiply.

2. Louis asked his son Joe to paint $6\frac{1}{2}$ of his grocery store's display tables. Joe painted $\frac{1}{2}$ of them the first day. How many more must Joe still paint?
   A. $3\frac{1}{2}$
   (B.) $3\frac{1}{4}$
   C. $2\frac{1}{3}$
   D. $2\frac{3}{4}$

Available as a transparency

Beehive

Lesson Organizer

Quick Lesson Overview

Objective Review and apply key concepts, skills, and strategies learned in this and previous chapters.

Math Understanding Some real-world problems can be solved using known concepts, skills, and strategies.

How Children Learn Math If students have a difficult time making sense of multiplying and dividing fractions, then utilization of real-world situations and the use of modeling or drawing the situation can help students develop a conceptual understanding of these operations on fractions.

NCTM Standards

- Number and Operations

(For a complete correlation to the NCTM Standards and Grades 6–8 Expectations, see pages 246G-H.)

Getting Started

Spiral Review

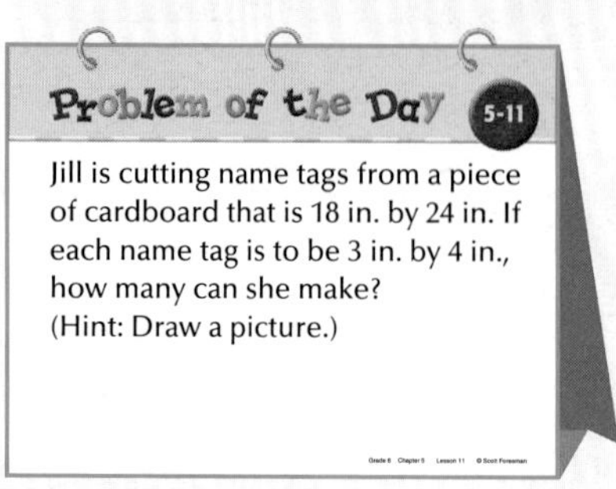
Problem of the Day 5-11

Jill is cutting name tags from a piece of cardboard that is 18 in. by 24 in. If each name tag is to be 3 in. by 4 in., how many can she make? (Hint: Draw a picture.)

Topics Reviewed

- Similarity; area
- Problem-Solving Strategy: Draw a Picture

Answer Jill can cut out 36 name tags.

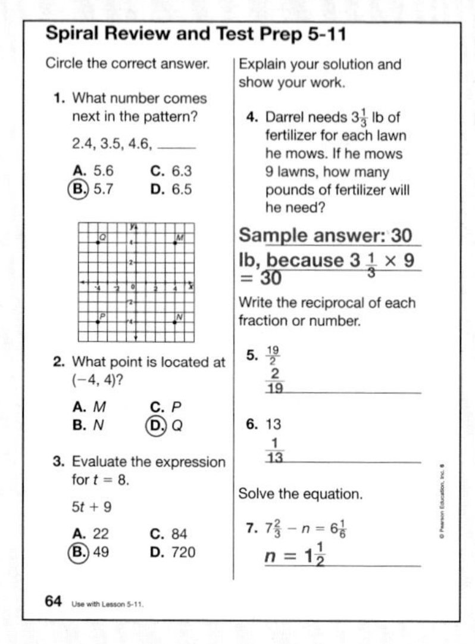
Spiral Review and Test Prep 5-11

Circle the correct answer.

1. What number comes next in the pattern?
   2.4, 3.5, 4.6, ____
   A. 5.6 C. 6.3
   (B.) 5.7 D. 6.5

2. What point is located at (−4, 4)?
   A. *M* C. *P*
   B. *N* (D.) *Q*

3. Evaluate the expression for $t = 8$.
   $5t + 9$
   A. 22 C. 84
   (B.) 49 D. 720

Explain your solution and show your work.

4. Darrel needs $3\frac{1}{3}$ lb of fertilizer for each lawn he mows. If he mows 9 lawns, how many pounds of fertilizer will he need?
   Sample answer: 30 lb, because $3\frac{1}{3} \times 9 = 30$

Write the reciprocal of each fraction or number.

5. $\frac{19}{2}$ $\frac{2}{19}$

6. 13 $\frac{1}{13}$

Solve the equation.

7. $7\frac{2}{3} - n = 6\frac{1}{6}$ $n = 1\frac{1}{2}$

64 Use with Lesson 5-11.

Available as a transparency and as a blackline master

Topics Reviewed

1. Look for a pattern; **2.** Coordinate points; **3.** Evaluating expressions; **4.** Writing to explain; **5.–6.** Dividing fractions; **7.** Solving equations with fractions

Investigating the Concept

Modeling Multiplication of Fractions

10-15 MIN **Kinesthetic/Visual/Spatial**

Materials *(per student)* Counters

What to Do

- Have students place 12 counters into 4 rows. **How many counters are in three rows?** *(9)* Explain that this is a way to find the product of the fraction $\frac{3}{4}$ times a whole number 12. Write $\frac{3}{4} \times 12 = 9$ on the board.
- Copy the following problems on the board. Have students solve them both with counters and by the standard algorithm. *($\frac{1}{6} \times 12 = 2$; $\frac{5}{6} \times 12 = 10$; $\frac{1}{3} \times 12 = 4$; $\frac{2}{3} \times 12 = 8$)*

Ongoing Assessment

- **Number Sense** **Explain how you could get the products in the bottom row by using the products in the top row.** *($\frac{5}{6} \times 12$ is 5 times $\frac{1}{6} \times 12$. Since $\frac{1}{6} \times 12$ is 2, $\frac{5}{6} \times 12$ is 5×2 or 10. Similarly, since $\frac{1}{3} \times 12$ is 4, $\frac{2}{3} \times 12$ is 2×4 or 8.)*

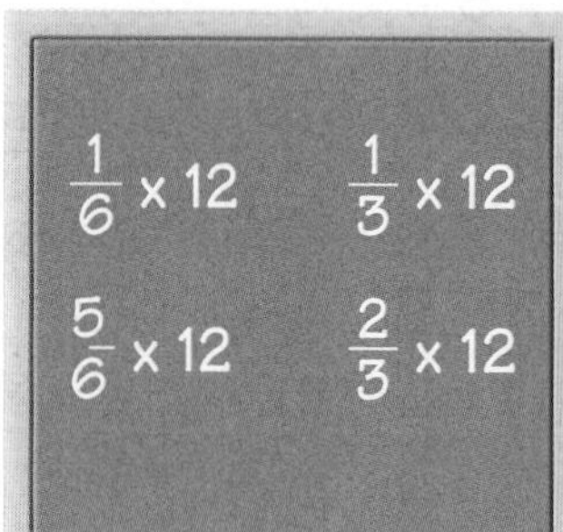

Reaching All Learners

Reading in Math

Summarize

 10-15 MIN **Auditory** 

- Have students read Exercise 1 on page 280 aloud.
- **What is the question asking?** *(How long it takes a worker bee to develop into an adult)*
- **What information is given?** *(It takes 24 days for a drone bee to develop into an adult and it takes $\frac{7}{8}$ of this time for the worker bee to develop into an adult.)*
- Have students solve the problem.
- Repeat for Exercise 3.

Access Content

English Language Learners

Questions About Key Facts

 15-20 MIN **Social/Cooperative/Linguistic** 

- Have volunteers read each Key Fact on page 281. Discuss any unfamiliar terms such as *colony, hives, cells,* and *nectar.*
- Have students read Exercise 5 on page 281.
- Using Exercise 5 as a model, have partners talk through creating questions and answers using each of the Key Facts.
- Have partners exchange and answer each other's questions.

If there are 5 hives,
about how many
cells would there be?

Reteaching

Multiplying Fractions

 10-15 MIN **Visual/Spatial** 

Materials *(per student)* Scrap paper

- Have students fold pieces of paper in half vertically, twice, and shade $\frac{1}{4}$ with diagonal lines.

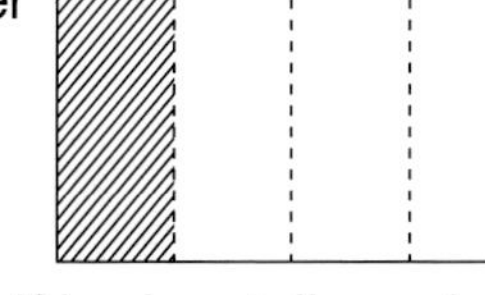

- Have students fold the paper in half horizontally and shade $\frac{1}{2}$ with diagonal lines going the opposite way.
- **The part shaded both directions is $\frac{1}{2}$ of $\frac{1}{4}$ or $\frac{1}{2}$ times $\frac{1}{4}$. What part of the whole paper is shaded both ways?** *($\frac{1}{8}$)* Write $\frac{1}{2} \times \frac{1}{4} = \frac{1}{8}$ on the board.
- Have students find $\frac{1}{2} \times \frac{3}{4}$ *($\frac{3}{8}$)*, $\frac{1}{3} \times \frac{1}{2}$ *($\frac{1}{6}$)*, and $\frac{1}{4} \times \frac{2}{3}$ *($\frac{2}{12}$ or $\frac{1}{6}$)*, similarly.

Advanced Learners

Missing Factor

 10-15 MIN **Logical/Mathematical** 

Materials *(per pair)* Index cards labeled as shown below.

- Place the six cards, face down. Have one student draw a card so that their partner cannot see it and read it aloud. The student could say, for example, $\frac{1}{2}$ of what number is 6?

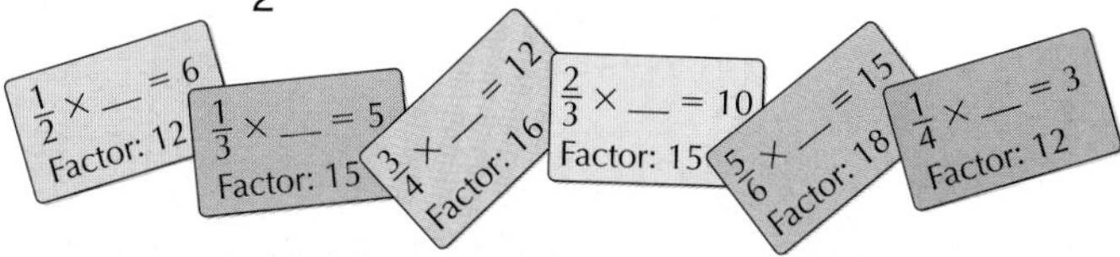

- Have the other student find the missing factor. Use your knowledge of students' abilities to decide whether to allow students to use paper and pencil or to require them to use mental math.
- Repeat until all cards have been used, with students switching roles each time.

Objective Review and apply key concepts, skills, and strategies learned in this and previous chapters.

Activate Prior Knowledge Ask students to find $\frac{3}{8}$ of 20. *($7\frac{1}{2}$)*

2 Teach

Explain to the students that they will use what they already know.

Ongoing Assessment

Talk About It: Exercise 1

- **What are we trying to find out?** *(The amount of time it takes a worker bee to develop)*
- **What do we know?** *(24 days for a drone to develop; $\frac{7}{8}$ of that time for a worker bee to develop)*
- **What operation/strategy would you use?** *(Multiplication)*

Error Intervention

If students are having difficulty with these exercises,

then have them begin each exercise by telling what they will do to find the answer.

Answers

6. Sample answer: I don't think hexagonal lockers would work well because coats would not hang well in them. Students with upper lockers would stand in the way of students with lower lockers.

Lesson 5-11

Problem-Solving Applications

Honeybees Bees gather pollen and nectar for food. From the nectar they make honey. The food is stored in the honeycomb's cells. These cells are also where bees grow from eggs into adults.

Trivia Honey is made by a bee sucking nectar into its honey stomach, regurgitating it, adding enzymes, then allowing the water to evaporate.

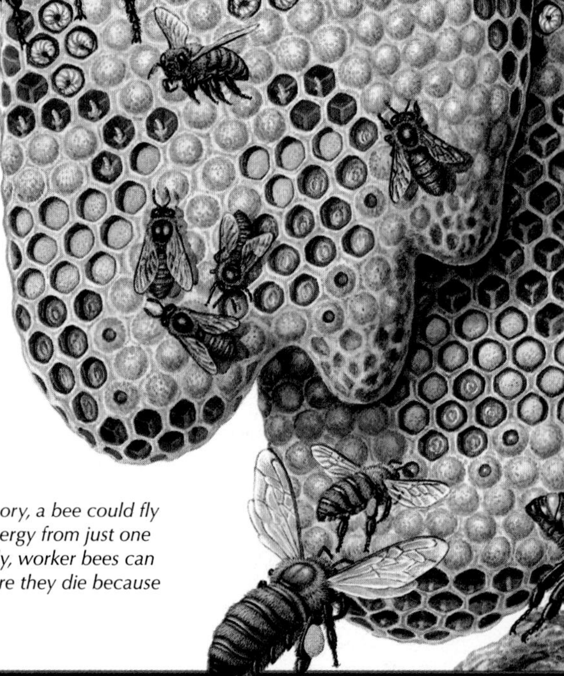

1. It takes 24 days for some drone bees to develop from an egg to an adult. Worker bees need $\frac{7}{8}$ of that time to develop. How long does it take a worker bee to develop?
   21 days

2. A bee spends $\frac{8}{20}$ of its development time as a larva or prepupa. If $\frac{1}{10}$ of the development time is in the prepupa stage, what fraction is spent as a larva? $\frac{3}{10}$

3. An average worker bee produces $\frac{1}{12}$ teaspoon of honey in its lifetime. About how many worker bees would it take to produce $\frac{1}{2}$ teaspoon of honey?
   6 bees

Good News/Bad News *In theory, a bee could fly around the world with the energy from just one ounce of honey. Unfortunately, worker bees can only fly about 500 miles before they die because their bodies simply wear out.*

280

Reteaching — Below Level

PROBLEM-SOLVING APPLICATIONS **R 5-11**

The Bridge

The Golden Gate Bridge in California is approximately $1\frac{7}{10}$ mi long and crosses the Golden Gate Strait.

How long would $2\frac{1}{2}$ times the length of the Golden Gate Bridge be?

$1\frac{7}{10} \times 2\frac{1}{2}$

$\frac{17}{10} \times \frac{5}{2}$ (10 and 5 crossed out and simplified to 2 and 1) Write the mixed numbers as improper fractions. Simplify if possible.

$\frac{17}{2} \times \frac{1}{2} = \frac{17}{4} = 4\frac{1}{4}$ Multiply. Write the product as a mixed number.

The bridge would be $4\frac{1}{4}$ mi long.

1. If you rode your bike halfway across the Golden Gate Bridge, how far would you have ridden? **$\frac{17}{20}$ mi**
2. If a man jogged from one end of the Golden Gate Bridge and back, how many miles would he have jogged? **$3\frac{2}{5}$ mi**
3. Suppose the first $\frac{5}{8}$ of the Golden Gate Bridge was repainted. How many miles of the bridge were repainted? **$1\frac{1}{16}$ mi**
4. Suppose a different bridge in California were $\frac{1}{3}$ the length of the Golden Gate Bridge. Write an algebraic expression for the length of this other bridge. Let d equal the length of the Golden Gate Bridge. **$\frac{1}{3}d$**
5. If the Golden Gate Bridge were divided into 5 equal sections, how long would each section be? **$\frac{17}{50}$ mi long**
6. How long would 5 times the length of the Golden Gate Bridge be? **$8\frac{1}{2}$ mi long**

Practice — On Level

PROBLEM-SOLVING APPLICATION **P 5-11**

Black Walnut Tree

The Institute of Agriculture and Natural Resources at the University of Nebraska published a study of the black walnut tree. The information in the published report is used by farmers and forestry experts to monitor and improve the growth of the black walnut tree in the Nebraska area.

Part of the study examined the growth of 10 different black walnut trees on 2 different sites. Site 1 was a shallow, hilly area that had some clay in the soil. Site 2 was a deep, well-drained area.

Tree 1 on Site 1 grew at a rate of about $1\frac{3}{4}$ ft per year.

1. At this rate, how tall would the tree be after $\frac{1}{3}$ year? **$\frac{7}{12}$ ft**
2. At this rate, how tall would the tree be after 6 years? After 8 years? **$10\frac{1}{2}$ ft; 14 ft**

Suppose the black walnut tree's growth changes every $3\frac{5}{12}$ years. As a result, the researchers make records of the tree's growth every $3\frac{5}{12}$ years. For the study, the researchers called every $3\frac{5}{12}$ years a "period." At a growth rate of $1\frac{3}{4}$ ft per year, the black walnut tree would grow about $5\frac{19}{20}$ ft every period of $3\frac{5}{12}$ years.

3. To find an estimate for how much the tree would grow in 3 periods, first round $5\frac{19}{20}$ to a compatible whole number. Then multiply your answer by 3 to get the estimate.
   6; about 18 ft in the first 3 periods
4. Now find exactly how much the tree would grow in 3 periods, based on the data given. **$17\frac{17}{20}$ ft**
5. How much would the tree grow in 12 periods? **$71\frac{2}{5}$ ft**
6. Suppose researchers found that Tree 7 on Site 2 grew $2\frac{1}{7}$ ft per year. How much would Tree 7 grow in 1 period of $3\frac{5}{12}$ years? **$7\frac{9}{28}$ ft**
7. How much would Tree 7 grow in 4 periods? **$29\frac{2}{7}$ ft**

Dorling Kindersley

Using Key Facts

4 Almost $\frac{95}{100}$ of all bees are worker bees. How many worker bees are in a typical colony?
52,250 workers

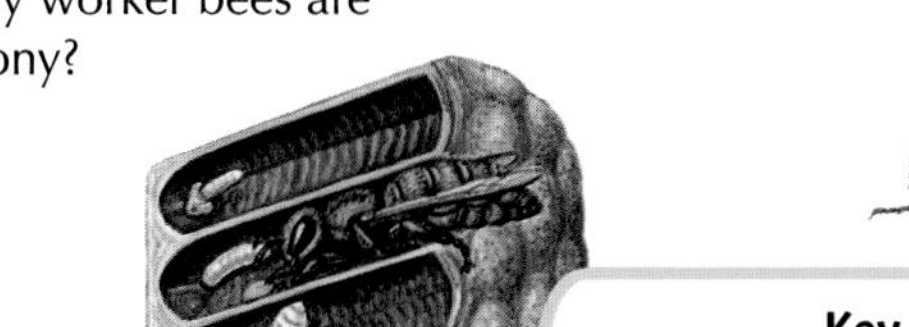

Key Facts
Honeybees

- A colony may have 55,000 bees.
- A queen can lay 200,000 eggs per year.
- Hives may have over 100,000 cells.
- The nectar from about 2,000,000 flowers is needed to make 1 pound of honey.

5 A typical hive needs to store at least 40 pounds of honey for winter food. How many flowers would a colony have to visit to make this much honey? **80,000,000 flowers**

6 **Writing in Math** Hexagonal cells are efficient shapes for honeycombs. They leave little wasted space between cells or around each larva. Do you think that school lockers should be hexagonal in shape? How efficient would a honeycomb-configuration of lockers be? Include a drawing in your explanation. **See margin.**

7 **Decision Making** Emma and Jon counted 274 cells in one cross-section of honeycomb. Emma used front-end estimation and predicted that there would be approximately 20,000 cells in 100 of these cross-sections. Jon used rounding and estimated there would be about 30,000 cells. Which method of estimation would you use to predict the number of cells? Explain your choice. **Sample answer: If you assume that on average, 100 cross-sections of a honeycomb would have a large number of cells, rounding would be the more appropriate method of estimation.**

Practice

Exercise 6 To help students draw hexagonal cells to support their explanations, have them trace around the hexagonal polygon, if available.

Exercise 7 Remind students that they have a choice of estimation methods. However, their choice must be justified.

Leveled Practice

Below Level Work alone on Ex. 1–3. Work on Ex. 4–7 with a partner.

On Level Work alone on Ex. 1–5. Work on Ex. 6 and 7 with a partner.

Above Level Work alone on Ex. 1–6. Work on Ex. 7 with a partner.

Early Finishers Have students estimate the number of teaspoons in a small jar of honey. Then have them figure out how many worker bees it would take to produce that amount of honey.

Assess

Journal Idea Have students use the information in this lesson to write a word problem that might be solved by multiplying with fractions, and then write the answer in a complete sentence.

Enrichment — **Above Level**

Bakers' Dozen — E 5-11 REASONING

The Baker family is making muffins. Each member of the family adds something to or subtracts something from the mixing bowl. Use the clues below to find the order in which each member adds to or subtracts from the mix. Write the numbers from 1 to 6 on the line to the left of each quotation.

6 "I poured the mix into baking cups and put them in the oven." **Mrs. Baker**

5 "I took $\frac{1}{4}$ of the mix out of the bowl to bring to school." **Ronald**

1 "I measured 2 c of flour and 2 tsp of baking powder and put them into a mixing bowl." **Mr. Baker**

2 "I added $\frac{1}{2}$ tsp of salt, $\frac{1}{2}$ c of butter, and 2 eggs before the blueberries were added." **Sierra**

3 "I added $\frac{3}{4}$ c of brown sugar and $1\frac{1}{4}$ tsp of vanilla." **Barbara**

4 "I added 2 c of blueberries right after the brown sugar was added." **Jane**

Read these clues, and then write the name of the family member who made each statement above in the blank that follows each statement.

- The members of the Baker family are Mr. and Mrs. Baker, Jane, Barbara, Ronald, and Sierra.
- Sierra added something to the mix before anyone added fruit or sugar.
- The mix was not started by a female.
- Jane did not put the muffins in the oven.
- Barbara added two items to the mix.
- Ronald was the fifth person to add or subtract something from the mix.

Problem Solving

PROBLEM-SOLVING APPLICATION — PS 5-11

Color Combinations

Each student in Mrs. Morgan's class needs two folders for homework. The folders must be different colors. The students have a choice of red, green, yellow, or blue folders. How many different possible color combinations are there if no color combination is repeated? (RG is the same as GR.)

Read and Understand

1. How many folders does each student need?
Two folders

2. What are the possible color choices listed?
Red, green, yellow, or blue folders

Plan and Solve

3. Make an organized list to solve the problem.
RG, RY, RB, GY, GB, YB

4. Write your answer in a complete sentence.
There are 6 possible color combinations.

Look Back and Check

5. Is your answer reasonable?
Sample answer: Yes, because the list shows that any other combination is a repeat.

Solve Another Problem

6. The choir teacher is organizing groups of four students to sing at the local retirement home. One of the groups will be Maria, Jasmine, Pete, and Sunil. In how many different orders could they stand in a row to sing?
24 possible ways

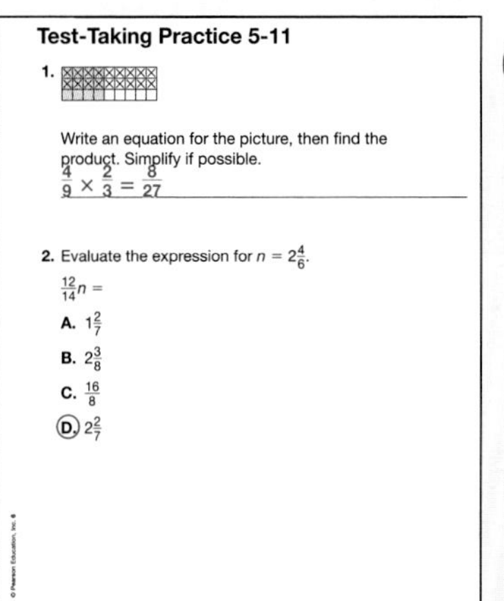

Test-Taking Practice 5-11

1. Write an equation for the picture, then find the product. Simplify if possible.
$\frac{4}{9} \times \frac{2}{3} = \frac{8}{27}$

2. Evaluate the expression for $n = 2\frac{4}{6}$.
$\frac{12}{14}n =$
A. $1\frac{2}{7}$
B. $2\frac{3}{8}$
C. $\frac{16}{8}$
(D.) $2\frac{2}{7}$

Available as a transparency

Review

Purpose Help students review content learned in Section C.

Using Student Pages 282–283

Do You Know How? exercises are appropriate for written work.

Do You Understand? questions are designed for whole-class discussion or small-group discussion followed by a report to the whole class.

Section C: Lessons 5-8 through 5-11

Review

Do You Know How?

Expressions with Fractions (5-8)

Write each word phrase as an algebraic expression.

1. $\frac{1}{5}$ Jasmine's age $\mathbf{\frac{1}{5}j}$
2. seven more than $\frac{1}{2}$ a number $\mathbf{\frac{1}{2}n + 7}$
3. 35 cents less than $\frac{3}{4}$ Cassie's allowance $\mathbf{\frac{3}{4}c - 35}$
4. 9 miles fewer than $\frac{7}{10}$ the distance **See above right.** **4.** $\mathbf{\frac{7}{10}d - 9}$

Evaluate each expression for $x = \frac{2}{5}$ and $x = 2\frac{2}{3}$.

5. $3x$ $\mathbf{1\frac{1}{5}; 8}$
6. $2\frac{1}{2}x + 3$ $\mathbf{4; 9\frac{2}{3}}$
7. $5x - 1$ $\mathbf{1; 12\frac{1}{3}}$
8. $\frac{2}{3}x$ $\mathbf{\frac{4}{15}; 1\frac{7}{9}}$

Do You Understand?

A. The only unknown amount is the distance and the first letter in that word is "d".

A Share how you decided what the variable would represent in Exercise 4. **See above.**

B Explain how you can mentally evaluate the expression in Exercise 5 for $x = 2\frac{2}{3}$. **Convert $2\frac{2}{3}$ to $\frac{8}{3}$ in your head. Then simplify, so the answer is 8.**

Solving Equations with Fractions (5-9)

Solve each equation and check your answer.

9. $\frac{2}{3} + b = 3$ $\mathbf{b = 2\frac{1}{3}}$
10. $p - 2\frac{2}{3} = 5$ $\mathbf{p = 7\frac{2}{3}}$
11. $5\frac{1}{2} = 1\frac{3}{4} + m$ $\mathbf{m = 3\frac{3}{4}}$
12. $n - \frac{5}{6} = 1\frac{1}{3}$ $\mathbf{n = 2\frac{1}{6}}$
13. $\frac{3}{5}g = 27$ $\mathbf{g = 45}$
14. $d \div \frac{1}{5} = \frac{7}{10}$ $\mathbf{d = \frac{7}{50}}$
15. $4c = \frac{2}{7}$ $\mathbf{c = \frac{1}{14}}$
16. $\frac{1}{2} = w \div \frac{3}{4}$ $\mathbf{w = \frac{3}{8}}$

C Share how you solved the equation in Exercise 11. **See below.**

D Explain how to check your answer in Exercise 14. **Substitute your answer for *d* and simplify to make sure the equation is balanced.**

C. I subtracted $1\frac{3}{4}$ from both sides to get *m* alone. Then I simplified the left side of the equation.

Problem-Solving Skill: Writing to Explain (5-10)

Explain your solution and show your work.

17. A tile setter is tiling a floor with tiles that measure $\frac{3}{4}$ ft on each side. If he uses 17 tiles along a wall, how long is the wall? **$12\frac{3}{4}$ ft long; Multiply $17 \times \frac{3}{4}$ to get $\frac{51}{4}$, then rewrite to $12\frac{3}{4}$.**

E What information from the problem is needed to solve the problem? **The length of each tile and the number of tiles**

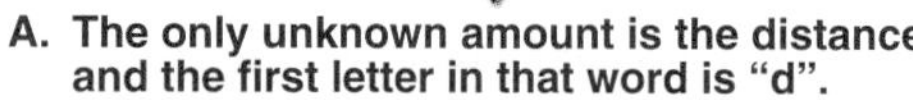

282 Chapter 5 Section C Review

Item Analysis for Diagnosis and Intervention

Objective	Review Items	Diagnostic Checkpoint Items	Student Book Pages*	Intervention System
Write and evaluate algebraic expressions with fractions and mixed numbers.	1–8	3–8	274–275	J33
Solve equations with fractions and mixed numbers.	9–16	1–2, 9–20, 22–23	276–277	J33
Write to explain a solution.	17	21–23	278–279	M18

*For each lesson, there is a *Reteaching* activity in *Reaching All Learners* and a *Reteaching* master.

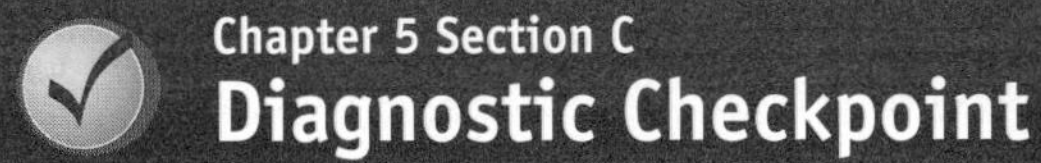

Chapter 5 Section C
Diagnostic Checkpoint

MULTIPLE CHOICE

Think It Through
For multiple-choice items, first **eliminate any unreasonable answers.**

1. Which is the solution to $p - 2\frac{1}{9} = 2\frac{2}{3}$? (5-9)

A. $\frac{1}{6}$ **B.** $\frac{5}{9}$ **C.** $4\frac{1}{4}$ **(D.)** $4\frac{7}{9}$

2. Which is the solution to $\frac{5}{7}m = 10$? (5-9)

A. $7\frac{1}{7}$ **B.** $9\frac{2}{7}$ **C.** $10\frac{5}{7}$ **(D.)** 14

FREE RESPONSE

Write each word phrase as an algebraic expression. (5-8)

3. $\frac{4}{5}$ Luis' height **$\frac{4}{5}h$**

4. 5 inches more than $\frac{2}{3}$ the width **$\frac{2}{3}w + 5$**

Evaluate each expression for $n = \frac{7}{8}$. (5-8)

5. $16n$ **14** **6.** $\frac{1}{7}n + 4$ **$4\frac{1}{8}$** **7.** $4n - 1$ **$2\frac{1}{2}$** **8.** $1\frac{1}{2} + n$ **$2\frac{3}{8}$**

Solve each equation and check your answer. (5-9, 5-11)

9. $p - \frac{4}{9} = 2$ **$p = 2\frac{4}{9}$** **10.** $2\frac{1}{5} = r + 1\frac{1}{3}$ **$r = \frac{13}{15}$** **11.** $d - 3\frac{4}{5} = 8$ **$d = 11\frac{4}{5}$**

12. $6\frac{2}{3} + g = 10$ **$g = 3\frac{1}{3}$** **13.** $\frac{4}{7} = b + \frac{1}{6}$ **$b = \frac{17}{42}$** **14.** $y - 1\frac{5}{9} = 2\frac{2}{3}$ **$y = 4\frac{2}{9}$**

15. $\frac{5}{8}p = 12$ **$p = 19\frac{1}{5}$** **16.** $m \div \frac{2}{5} = 8$ **$m = 3\frac{1}{5}$** **17.** $18 = \frac{3}{7}a$ **$a = 42$**

18. $1\frac{3}{4}t = 3\frac{2}{7}$ **$t = 1\frac{43}{49}$** **19.** $p \div 4 = 5\frac{5}{7}$ **$p = 22\frac{6}{7}$** **20.** $2\frac{2}{5} = j \div 1\frac{1}{5}$ **$j = 2\frac{22}{25}$**

Explain your solution and show your work. (5-10, 5-11)

21. Samuel wants to cover the top of a square table with a pattern made from assorted glass pieces. A bag of assorted glass contains about 300 pieces. Samuel has calculated that the shaded section of the tabletop, shown in the diagram at right, will require $\frac{3}{4}$ of one bag. Estimate the number of bags of glass Samuel will need to cover the entire tabletop. **About 6 bags; I figured out that it would take about 8 triangles to cover the square, so I multiplied $8 \times \frac{3}{4}$ to get 6 bags of glass.**

Writing in Math

22. What ideas are used in solving equations regardless of whether they contain whole numbers, decimals, or fractions? (5-9) **Sample answer: using inverse operations to solve equations**

23. Explain why the solution of $\frac{7}{8}x = 43$ is more than 43. (5-9) **A portion of a number x is 43, so the number x must be greater than 43.**

Sample student work for Exercise 22

To solve an equation, you have to do the same thing to both sides to keep them balanced. If you add on one side, you have to add on the other.

$$x - \frac{3}{4} = 2 - \frac{1}{4}$$
$$+ \frac{3}{4} \qquad + \frac{3}{4}$$
$$x + 0 = 2 - \frac{1}{4} + \frac{3}{4} \qquad x = 3$$

The rubric below is a scoring guide that shows how many points to give an answer to Exercise 22. Many teachers would assign a score of 3 points to this explanation. Discuss the sample response shown and compare it to papers produced by students.

Scoring Rubric

4 Full credit: 4 points
The answer states principles correctly; understands how to solve equations; explanation is complete.

3 Partial credit: 3 points
The answer states principles correctly; understands how to solve equations; explanation is incomplete.

2 Partial credit: 2 points
The answer states principles only partially or vaguely and does not clarify them with examples.

1 Partial credit: 1 point
The answer has good examples but no theory or explanation; shows some understanding of solving equations.

0 No credit
The answer is incorrect; does not understand how to solve equations.

Test Talk

Purpose Promote focused instruction on test-taking strategies.

Using Student Pages 284–285

The intent of these pages is to help students formulate clear written answers when test questions call for them. Students examine two kinds of problems calling for written explanations, one involving estimation and the other including several steps and operations.

Direct students' attention to Exercise 1 and the first three strategies following it. Mention that information they get as they apply these strategies will be used in their written explanations. Then focus on the *Use writing in math* strategy. Read to the class the three points about how to apply the strategy. Then ask a student to read the written explanation aloud and evaluate whether it followed those points. For Exercise 2, use *Think It Through* to help students recognize the steps needed to solve the problem and the best order to explain them in.

In Exercise 3, students' estimate should be 3,200 yards. Their written explanations should follow the pattern from Exercise 1. For Exercise 4, students should explain that they multiplied $12\frac{1}{2} \times 5$ and 5×2, and that they added the products, $62\frac{1}{2} + 10$, to get a total length of $72\frac{1}{2}$ inches.

Test-Taking Strategies

- Understand the question.
- Get information for the answer.
- Plan how to find the answer.
- Make smart choices.
- ➡ **Use writing in math.**
- Improve written answers.

Use Writing in Math

Sometimes a test question asks for a written answer, such as an explanation, a description, or a comparison. See how one student followed the steps below to answer this test item by writing in math.

1. Ethan is planting petunias in a circular garden. He has determined that he needs about 125 petunias for Section 1 of the garden, shown in the drawing below.

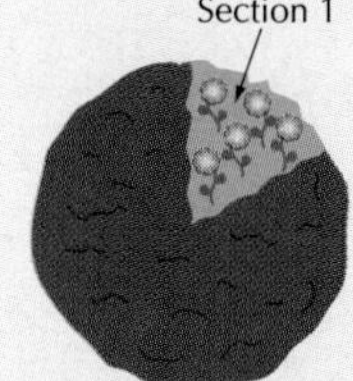

ESTIMATE the number of petunias Ethan needs for the entire garden.

Estimated number of petunias: ________

Show your work or explain in words how you found your estimate.

Understand the question.

I need to *estimate the number of petunias Ethan needs for the entire garden.*

Get information for the answer.

I'll need to get information from the text and the picture.

Plan how to find the answer.

Each section of the garden will have about the same number of petunias. So, I can use multiplication.

Use writing in math.

- Make your answer brief but complete.
- Use words from the problem and use math terms accurately.
- Describe steps in order.

Estimated number of petunias: 750

Show your work or explain in words how you found your estimate.

First, I estimated that Section 1 is about $\frac{1}{6}$ the entire garden. Then I multiplied 125 x 6. I got the estimate of 750.

- Is the question completely answered?
- Is the answer clear?
- Are the steps explained in order?

284

2. Lorenzo is building a shelving unit with 5 shelves, as shown below. Each shelf is $\frac{3}{4}$ inch thick, and there is a space of 14 inches between the shelves.

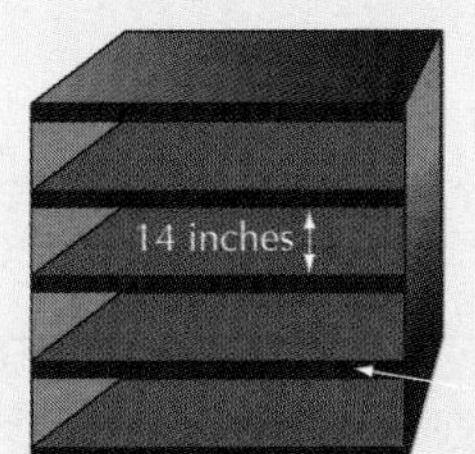

Think It Through

I have found the total height of $59\frac{3}{4}$ inches. Now I need to explain how I found my answer.

I should describe the steps I used in order. I will begin by explaining how I found the total height of the 5 shelves. Next I'll tell how I found the total height of the 4 spaces. Then I'll explain how I added together the results to get the total height.

Find the total height in inches of the shelving unit.

$59\frac{3}{4}$ inches

Show or explain in words how you found your answer.

First I multiplied $5 \times \frac{3}{4}$. Next I multiplied 4×14. Then I added together the two products $3\frac{3}{4} + 56$. I got $59\frac{3}{4}$ inches for the total height.

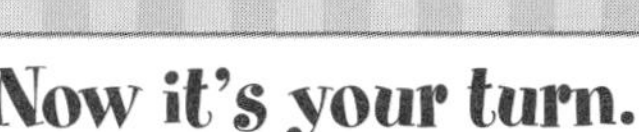

Now it's your turn.

For each problem, give a complete response.

3. Inez is hooking a rug. She used about 800 yards of yarn to complete section 1.

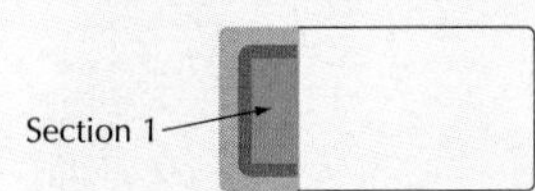

ESTIMATE the number of yards of yarn Inez needs for the entire rug. **Sample answer: 3,200**

Estimated number of yards: ________

Show your work or explain in words how you found your estimate. **See margin.**

4. Lee knit a winter scarf that had 5 diamonds, as shown below. Each diamond is $12\frac{1}{2}$ inches long, and there is a 5-inch fringe at each end.

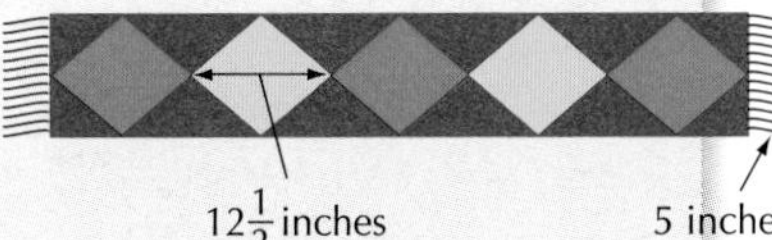

Find the total length of the scarf. Then show or explain in words how you found your answer. **$72\frac{1}{2}$ inches. See margin for explanation.**

Test-Taking Strategies

Understand the Question

- Look for important words.
- Turn the question into a statement: "I need to find out . . ."

Get Information for the Answer

- Get information from text.
- Get information from pictures, maps, diagrams, tables, graphs.

Plan How to Find the Answer

- Think about problem-solving skills and strategies.
- Choose computation methods.

Make Smart Choices

- Eliminate wrong answers.
- Try working backward from an answer.
- Check answers for reasonableness; estimate.

Use Writing in Math

- Make your answer brief but complete.
- Use words from the problem and use math terms accurately.
- Describe steps in order.
- Draw pictures if they help you explain your thinking.

Improve Written Answers

- Check if your answer is complete.
- Check if your answer is clear and easy to follow.
- Check if your answer makes sense.

Answers:

3. Sample explanation: First, I estimated that section 1 is about $\frac{1}{4}$ the entire rug. Then I multiplied 800×4. My estimate was 3,200 yards.

4. Sample explanation: First I found the length of the row of diamonds by multiplying $12\frac{1}{2} \times 5$. Next I multiplied 5×2 to get the total fringe length. Then I added the two products $62\frac{1}{2} + 10$. My answer was $72\frac{1}{2}$ inches for the total length.

Key Vocabulary and Concept Review

Using Student Pages 286–287

Purpose Provide students with a review of vocabulary and concepts in Chapter 5 through worked-out examples, vocabulary tips, and self-checking exercises.

Key Vocabulary and Concept Review focuses on the vocabulary of the chapter. It provides real-life connections to strengthen students' understanding of mathematical terms.

In addition, it reviews the concepts studied in the chapter. Exercises allow students to show they understand the meanings of words and they can apply the concepts.

Answers are printed upside down in red, so students can check their own work. Lesson references are given, so students can look back at any time.

MindPoint Quiz Show CD-ROM Use *MindPoint Quiz Show* for additional practice on Chapter 5.

Chapter 5

Key Vocabulary and Concept Review

GCF stands for greatest common factor.

*The **greatest common factor** of two numbers is the largest number that divides into both evenly. (pp. 150, 252)*

Multiply fractions and mixed numbers. (Lessons 5-1, 5-2, 5-3, 5-4)

There are different ways to multiply by fractions and mixed numbers. One way is to write each factor as a fraction. Then multiply the numerators and multiply the denominators.

$30 \times \frac{5}{6} = \frac{30}{1} \times \frac{5}{6}$ Simplify.

$= \frac{\overset{5}{\cancel{30}}}{1} \times \frac{5}{\underset{1}{\cancel{6}}}$ Divide 30 and 6 by the **GCF,** 6.

$= 25$

$\frac{1}{6} \times \frac{3}{4} = \frac{1}{\underset{2}{\cancel{6}}} \times \frac{\overset{1}{\cancel{3}}}{4}$

$= \frac{1}{8}$

$3\frac{1}{4} \times 2\frac{2}{3} = \frac{13}{\underset{1}{\cancel{4}}} \times \frac{\overset{2}{\cancel{8}}}{3}$ Estimate: $3 \times 3 = 9$

$= \frac{26}{3}$ Since $8\frac{2}{3}$ is close to 9, the answer is reasonable.

$= 8\frac{2}{3}$

1. Find $\frac{7}{8} \times 48$, $\frac{3}{5} \times \frac{15}{16}$, and $3\frac{1}{8} \times 4\frac{3}{5}$.

After I've baked a cake, I invert the cake pan to remove the cake.

*I can find the **multiplicative inverse,** or **reciprocal,** by turning a fraction upside down. (p. 266)*

You can use multiplication to divide fractions. (Lessons 5-6, 5-7)

Multiply by the **reciprocal** of the divisor. The reciprocal is also called the **multiplicative inverse.**

$\frac{9}{10} \div \frac{3}{5} = \frac{9}{10} \times \frac{5}{3}$

$= \frac{\overset{3}{\cancel{9}}}{\underset{2}{\cancel{10}}} \times \frac{\overset{1}{\cancel{5}}}{\underset{1}{\cancel{3}}}$ Simplify and then multiply.

$= \frac{3}{2}$

$= 1\frac{1}{2}$

$17\frac{1}{2} \div 2\frac{1}{2} = \frac{35}{2} \div \frac{5}{2}$ Estimate: $18 \div 3 = 6$

$= \frac{35}{2} \times \frac{2}{5}$

$= \frac{\overset{7}{\cancel{35}}}{\underset{1}{\cancel{2}}} \times \frac{\overset{1}{\cancel{2}}}{\underset{1}{\cancel{5}}}$

$= 7$ Since 7 is close to 6, the answer is reasonable.

2. Find $\frac{3}{4} \div \frac{7}{8}$, $2\frac{2}{5} \div 6$, and $4\frac{1}{4} \div 1\frac{2}{3}$.

286

"Equation" sounds like it contains the word "equal."

Remember, an ***equation*** *has an equal sign, but an* ***expression*** *doesn't.* *(p. 276)*

Algebraic expressions and equations may contain fractions. (Lessons 5-8, 5-9)

Iyo's age is 3 years older than $\frac{3}{4}$ Michael's age.

Write an algebraic expression for Iyo's age.

Let m equal Michael's age.

Then $\frac{3}{4}m + 3$ is Iyo's age.

Evaluate $\frac{1}{6}n + 8$ when $n = 24$.

Substitute 24 for n. Then use order of operations.

$\frac{1}{6}(24) + 8$

$4 + 8$

12

Solve $\frac{2}{5}y = 8$.

$\frac{2}{5}y = 8$

$\left(\frac{5}{2}\right)\frac{2}{5}y = 8\left(\frac{5}{2}\right)$

$y = \frac{\overset{4}{\cancel{8}}}{1} \times \frac{5}{\cancel{2}_1}$

$y = 20$

3. Evaluate $\frac{7}{8}w - 5$ when $w = 40$, and solve $\frac{2}{3}p = 18$.

Make an organized list and write to explain how to solve problems. (Lessons 5-5, 5-10)

Pamela's 4-digit locker combination uses all four of the digits 1, 3, 4, and 5. How many different locker combinations are possible? Explain your answer.

To make an organized list:

Step 1: Identify the items to be combined.

Step 2: Choose one of the items. Find combinations keeping that item fixed.

Step 3: Repeat Step 2 as often as needed.

1	3	4	5
1345	3145	4135	5134
1354	3154	4153	5143
1435	3415	4315	5314
1453	3451	4351	5341
1534	3514	4513	5413
1543	3541	4531	5431

I made an organized list. First I showed all the combinations starting with 1, then starting with 3, then 4, and then 5. There are 24 different locker combinations.

4. In how many ways can you make 30¢ without using pennies?

Answers: 1. 42; $\frac{9}{16}$; $14\frac{3}{8}$ 2. $\frac{6}{7}$; $\frac{2}{5}$; $2\frac{11}{20}$ 3. 30; $p = 27$ 4. 5 ways

287

Chapter Test

Using Student Pages 288–289

Purpose Assess students' progress by checking their understanding of the concepts and skills in Chapter 5. Use as a review, practice test, or chapter test.

Sample student work for Exercise 29

To find the reciprocal of $2\frac{3}{4}$, change it to an improper fraction.
$2\frac{3}{4} = \frac{11}{3}$
Then flip over the improper fraction.
The reciprocal of $\frac{11}{3}$ is $\frac{3}{11}$.

The score for this paper is 4. The student's answer is correct and demonstrates how to find the reciprocal of a mixed number.

Scoring Rubric

4 Full credit: 4 points
The answer is correct; understands how to find a reciprocal of a mixed number; explanation is complete.

3 Partial credit: 3 points
The answer is correct; understands how to find a reciprocal of a mixed number; explanation is incomplete.

2 Partial credit: 2 points
The answer contains elements of the proper method, but examples are worked out incorrectly.

1 Partial credit: 1 point
The answer contains valid examples but no explanation.

0 No credit
The answer is incorrect; does not understand how to find a reciprocal.

CHAPTER 5

Chapter Test

MULTIPLE CHOICE

Choose the correct letter for each answer.

1. What is $\frac{7}{8} \times 72$?

A. 9 **(C.)** 63
B. 56 **D.** 70

2. Mandy has a garden in which $\frac{3}{5}$ of the plants are tomato plants. Of the tomato plants, $\frac{1}{3}$ are cherry tomato plants. What fraction of the plants in Mandy's garden are cherry tomato plants?

A. $\frac{1}{3}$ **C.** $\frac{3}{5}$
(B.) $\frac{1}{5}$ **D.** $\frac{1}{15}$

3. Estimate $\frac{2}{5} \times 36$ using compatible numbers.

A. 7 **(C.)** 14
B. 10 **D.** 72

4. Find $4\frac{1}{6} \times 2\frac{3}{5}$.

(A.) $10\frac{5}{6}$ **C.** $8\frac{1}{10}$
B. $10\frac{1}{8}$ **D.** $4\frac{23}{30}$

5. Carol is $1\frac{1}{3}$ times as tall as her younger brother. Her younger brother is 48 inches tall. How tall is Carol?

A. 16 inches **(C.)** 64 inches
B. 56 inches **D.** 66 inches

6. Find $3\frac{1}{3} \div 1\frac{1}{9}$.

(A.) 3
B. $3\frac{1}{27}$
C. $3\frac{1}{9}$
D. 9

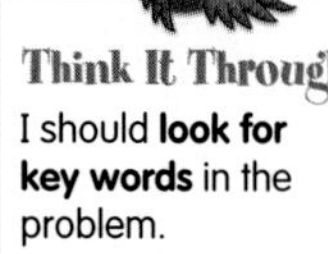

Think It Through
I should **look for key words** in the problem.

7. Which is the reciprocal of $2\frac{1}{7}$?

A. $2\frac{7}{1}$ **C.** $\frac{7}{10}$
B. $1\frac{5}{7}$ **(D.)** $\frac{7}{15}$

8. Kiko has 6 boxes. This is only $\frac{2}{3}$ of the number she needs. How many boxes does she need?

A. 4 boxes
B. 8 boxes
(C.) 9 boxes
D. 10 boxes

9. Which expression represents three more than $\frac{2}{7}$ of a number, n?

A. $\frac{2}{7}n \times 3$ **C.** $3n + \frac{2}{7}$
(B.) $3 + \frac{2}{7}n$ **D.** $n \div \frac{2}{7} + 3$

10. Solve $x \div \frac{4}{5} = 3$.

A. $x = \frac{4}{15}$ **C.** $x = 3\frac{3}{4}$
(B.) $x = 2\frac{2}{5}$ **D.** $x = 3\frac{4}{5}$

288

Item Analysis for Diagnosis and Intervention

Objective	Items	Student Book Pages*	Intervention System
Multiply a fraction and a whole number.	1, 14	248–251	H37
Multiply fractions.	2, 12	252–255	H39
Estimate products and quotients with fractions and mixed numbers.	3, 17–18	256–257	H38
Multiply mixed numbers.	4–5, 11, 13–14	258–259	H40
Make an organized list to solve a problem.	26	264–265	M28

*For each lesson, there is a *Reteaching* activity in *Reaching All Learners* and a *Reteaching* master.

For 11–12, use the ingredient list below.

Custard Pie Filling
Ingredients

4 eggs	$\frac{1}{4}$ teaspoon nutmeg
$\frac{2}{3}$ cup sugar	$2\frac{2}{3}$ cups milk
$\frac{1}{2}$ teaspoon salt	1 teaspoon vanilla

11. If you doubled the recipe, how much milk would you need?

A. $4\frac{1}{3}$ cups **(C.)** $5\frac{1}{3}$ cups

B. $4\frac{2}{3}$ cups **D.** $5\frac{2}{3}$ cups

12. Justin wants to make a custard pie that is $\frac{1}{4}$ the size of the pie that the recipe makes. How much sugar will he need for his pie?

A. $\frac{1}{3}$ cup **(C.)** $\frac{1}{6}$ cup

B. $\frac{1}{4}$ cup **D.** $\frac{1}{12}$ cup

FREE RESPONSE

Find each product. Simplify if possible.

13. $2\frac{3}{8} \times 6\frac{1}{4}$ **$14\frac{27}{32}$** **14.** $3\frac{1}{9} \times 4$ **$12\frac{4}{9}$**

Write the reciprocal of each.

15. $\frac{6}{7}$ **$\frac{7}{6}$** **16.** 12 **$\frac{1}{12}$**

Estimate. **Sample answers are given.**

17. $\frac{5}{7} \times 33$ **25** **18.** $7\frac{4}{5} \div 2\frac{1}{4}$ **4**

For 19–20 find each quotient. Simplify if possible.

19. $7\frac{3}{4} \div 1\frac{2}{3}$ **$4\frac{13}{20}$** **20.** $\frac{3}{7} \div 6$ **$\frac{1}{14}$**

21. Write 6 fewer than $\frac{5}{6}$ a number h as an algebraic expression. **$\frac{5}{6}h - 6$**

22. Evaluate $\frac{1}{8}n + 2\frac{1}{4}$ for $n = \frac{3}{4}$. **$2\frac{11}{32}$**

Solve each equation and check your answer.

23. $3\frac{3}{5}p = \frac{2}{5}$ **$p = \frac{1}{9}$** **24.** $y + \frac{4}{5} = 3\frac{1}{10}$ **$y = 2\frac{3}{10}$**

Writing in Math

25. Explain how to find the reciprocal of a mixed number. **See below.**

26. The digits 0, 1, 2, and 4 are in the 4-digit combination for a lock. Each number is used only once. How many different combinations are possible? Solve by making an organized list. **24 combinations**

27. To make a border around her room, Erica painted balloons that were $2\frac{4}{5}$ inches wide. Leaving a space at each end, she painted 15 evenly spaced balloons along a 150-inch wall. What was the distance between any two balloons? Explain your solution and show your work.

Think It Through
- I need to make sure I **describe the steps and operations I used in the order I used them.**
- I can **draw a diagram or make a model** to help describe my work.

25. Convert the mixed number to an improper fraction then invert it.

27. $6\frac{3}{4}$ in.; I multiplied $2\frac{4}{5}$ by 15 to get 42 inches. Then I subtracted 150 − 42 = 108 and divided by 16 to get $6\frac{3}{4}$ in. spaces.

Assessment Sourcebook

Additional assessment options may be found in the *Assessment Sourcebook.*
- Chapter 5 Test (Forms A and B)
- Chapter 5 Performance Assessment
- Chapters 1–6 Cumulative Test (Use after Chapter 6.)

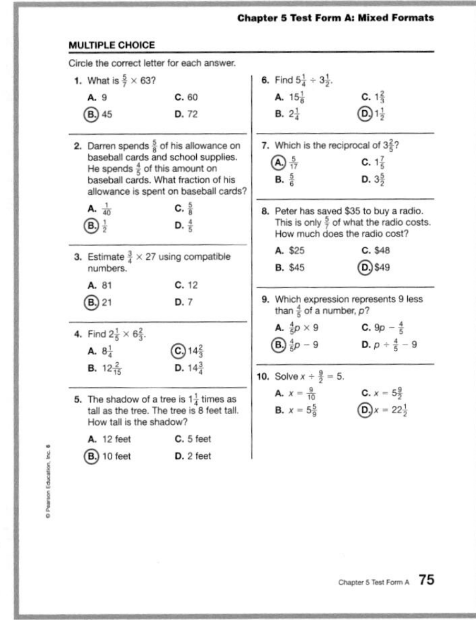

Chapter 5 Test Form A: Mixed Formats

MULTIPLE CHOICE

Circle the correct letter for each answer.

1. What is $\frac{5}{7} \times 63$?
A. 9 **C.** 60 **(B.)** 45 **D.** 72

2. Darren spends $\frac{5}{8}$ of his allowance on baseball cards and school supplies. He spends $\frac{4}{5}$ of this amount on baseball cards. What fraction of his allowance is spent on baseball cards?
A. $\frac{1}{40}$ **C.** $\frac{5}{8}$ **(B.)** $\frac{1}{2}$ **D.** $\frac{4}{5}$

3. Estimate $\frac{3}{4} \times 27$ using compatible numbers.
A. 81 **C.** 12 **(B.)** 21 **D.** 7

4. Find $2\frac{1}{5} \times 6\frac{2}{3}$.
A. $8\frac{1}{4}$ **(C.)** $14\frac{2}{3}$ **B.** $12\frac{2}{15}$ **D.** $14\frac{3}{4}$

5. The shadow of a tree is $1\frac{1}{4}$ times as tall as the tree. The tree is 8 feet tall. How tall is the shadow?
A. 12 feet **C.** 5 feet **(B.)** 10 feet **D.** 2 feet

6. Find $5\frac{1}{4} \div 3\frac{1}{2}$.
A. $15\frac{1}{8}$ **C.** $1\frac{2}{3}$ **B.** $2\frac{1}{4}$ **(D.)** $1\frac{1}{2}$

7. Which is the reciprocal of $3\frac{2}{5}$?
(A.) $\frac{5}{17}$ **C.** $1\frac{7}{5}$ **B.** $\frac{5}{6}$ **D.** $3\frac{5}{2}$

8. Peter has saved \$35 to buy a radio. This is only $\frac{5}{7}$ of what the radio costs. How much does the radio cost?
A. \$25 **C.** \$48 **B.** \$45 **(D.)** \$49

9. Which expression represents 9 less than $\frac{4}{5}$ of a number, p?
A. $\frac{4}{5}p \times 9$ **C.** $9p - \frac{4}{5}$ **(B.)** $\frac{4}{5}p - 9$ **D.** $p \div \frac{4}{5} - 9$

10. Solve $x \div \frac{9}{2} = 5$.
A. $x = \frac{9}{10}$ **C.** $x = 5\frac{9}{2}$ **B.** $x = 5\frac{5}{9}$ **(D.)** $x = 22\frac{1}{2}$

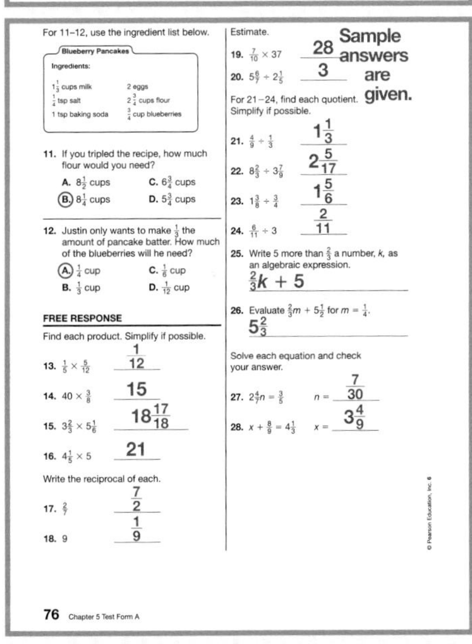

For 11–12, use the ingredient list below.

Blueberry Pancakes
Ingredients:

$1\frac{1}{3}$ cups milk	2 eggs
$\frac{1}{4}$ tsp salt	$2\frac{3}{4}$ cups flour
1 tsp baking soda	$\frac{3}{4}$ cup blueberries

11. If you tripled the recipe, how much flour would you need?
A. $8\frac{1}{2}$ cups **C.** $6\frac{3}{4}$ cups **(B.)** $8\frac{1}{4}$ cups **D.** $5\frac{3}{4}$ cups

12. Justin only wants to make $\frac{1}{3}$ the amount of pancake batter. How much of the blueberries will he need?
(A.) $\frac{1}{4}$ cup **C.** $\frac{1}{6}$ cup **B.** $\frac{1}{3}$ cup **D.** $\frac{1}{12}$ cup

FREE RESPONSE

Find each product. Simplify if possible.

13. $\frac{1}{5} \times \frac{5}{12}$ **$\frac{1}{12}$**

14. $40 \times \frac{3}{8}$ **15**

15. $3\frac{2}{3} \times 5\frac{1}{6}$ **$18\frac{17}{18}$**

16. $4\frac{1}{5} \times 5$ **21**

Write the reciprocal of each.

17. $\frac{2}{7}$ **$\frac{7}{2}$**

18. 9 **$\frac{1}{9}$**

Estimate.

19. $\frac{7}{10} \times 37$ **28**

20. $5\frac{6}{7} \div 2\frac{1}{5}$ **3**

Sample answers are given.

For 21–24, find each quotient. Simplify if possible.

21. $\frac{4}{9} \div \frac{1}{3}$ **$1\frac{1}{3}$**

22. $8\frac{2}{3} \div 3\frac{7}{9}$ **$2\frac{5}{17}$**

23. $1\frac{3}{8} \div \frac{3}{4}$ **$1\frac{5}{6}$**

24. $\frac{6}{11} \div 3$ **$\frac{2}{11}$**

25. Write 5 more than $\frac{2}{3}$ a number, k, as an algebraic expression.
$\frac{2}{3}k + 5$

26. Evaluate $\frac{2}{3}m + 5\frac{1}{2}$ for $m = \frac{1}{4}$.
$5\frac{2}{3}$

Solve each equation and check your answer.

27. $2\frac{4}{7}n = \frac{3}{5}$ $n =$ **$\frac{7}{30}$**

28. $x + \frac{8}{9} = 4\frac{1}{3}$ $x =$ **$3\frac{4}{9}$**

WRITING IN MATH

29. Explain why $\frac{3}{7}$ and $2\frac{1}{3}$ are reciprocals.
Their product is one.
$\frac{3}{7} \times 2\frac{1}{3} = \frac{3}{7} \times \frac{7}{3} = 1$

30. A computer password uses the letters A, B, C, and D. Each letter is used only once. How many different combinations are possible? Solve by making an organized list.
24 combinations

31. In a parking garage, each parking space is $6\frac{1}{4}$ ft wide. There are 20 spaces along a 132-foot wall of the garage. Each space is separated by a line of equal width. There is also a line of the same width at both ends. What is the width of each line? Explain your solution and show your work.
$\frac{1}{3}$ ft; I multiplied $6\frac{1}{4}$ by 20 to get 125 ft. Then, I subtracted 132 − 125 = 7 and divided by 21 to get $\frac{1}{3}$ ft.

Item Analysis for Diagnosis and Intervention

Objective	Items	Student Book Pages*	Intervention System
Divide fractions.	8, 15–16, 21, 24	266–269	H42
Divide mixed numbers.	6–7, 23	270–271	H43
Write and evaluate algebraic expressions with fractions and mixed numbers.	9, 21–22	274–275	J33
Solve equations with fractions and mixed numbers.	8, 10, 23–24, 27	276–277	J33
Write to explain a solution.	25, 27	278–279	M18

*For each lesson, there is a *Reteaching* activity in *Reaching All Learners* and a *Reteaching* master.

Cumulative Review and Test Prep

Using Student Pages 290–291

Purpose Provide students with a review of math concepts from Chapters 1–5 and previous grades.

For intervention, use the resources listed below.

Answers

11. I would convert $2\frac{3}{5}$ to the improper fraction $\frac{13}{5}$. Next, I would find a common denominator that is the GCF of 5 and 7 and rewrite the fractions using a denominator of 35. Then I would add, and write my answer as the mixed number $2\frac{26}{35}$.

Chapters 1–5

Cumulative Review and Test Prep

Number and Operation

MULTIPLE CHOICE

1. What is the product $\frac{2}{3} \times \frac{4}{5}$?
   - A. $\frac{2}{5}$
   - C. $\frac{3}{4}$
   - (B.) $\frac{8}{15}$
   - D. $\frac{5}{6}$
2. Estimate 1.47 + 2.8 to the nearest whole number.
   - A. 5
   - C. 3
   - (B.) 4
   - D. 2
3. Which is the LCM of 28 and 36?
   - (A.) 252
   - C. 4
   - B. 126
   - D. 2

12. Sample answer: Because 36 is divisible by 4, round to 3,600 and use 40 for the divisor. 3,600 ÷ 40 = 90

FREE RESPONSE

4. Aurora walks $3\frac{3}{4}$ miles each week. At this pace, how many weeks will it take her to walk 30 miles? **8 weeks**
5. $4\frac{1}{7} \times 3\frac{2}{5}$ **$14\frac{3}{35}$**
6. $5\frac{3}{5} \div \frac{7}{8}$ **$6\frac{2}{5}$**
7. $3.4 + 2.08 + 6\frac{1}{5}$ **11.68**
8. $\frac{2}{3} \times 45$ **30**
9. $76 \div 3\frac{1}{4}$ **$23\frac{5}{13}$**
10. $5\frac{1}{4} + 11\frac{3}{15}$ **$16\frac{9}{20}$**

TEST TALK

Think It Through

I should **describe steps in order.**

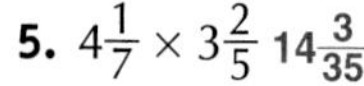

Writing in Math

11. Explain how you would add $2\frac{3}{5}$ and $\frac{1}{7}$. **See margin.**
12. Describe how to estimate 3,624 ÷ 38 using compatible numbers. **See above.**

Geometry and Measurement

MULTIPLE CHOICE

13. The side of a square measures 2.3 cm. What is its perimeter?
    - A. 4.6 cm
    - C. 6.93 cm
    - B. 5.29 cm
    - (D.) 9.2 cm
14. How many feet are in $3\frac{1}{3}$ yards?
    - A. 7 feet
    - C. $13\frac{1}{3}$ feet
    - (B.) 10 feet
    - D. 40 feet
15. Which polygon below has more than six sides?
    - A. quadrilateral
    - (C.) octagon
    - B. pentagon
    - D. hexagon

FREE RESPONSE

16. Find the area of a rectangle with length $5\frac{1}{6}$ ft and width $8\frac{3}{4}$ ft. **$45\frac{5}{24}$ ft²**
17. What is the name of a quadrilateral with no right angles and four sides of equal length? **Rhombus**
18. Name a quadrilateral that is NOT a parallelogram. **Trapezoid**
19. Find the perimeter of a rectangle with length $14\frac{5}{16}$ in. and width 11 in. **$50\frac{5}{8}$ in.**
20. Write an expression for the perimeter of a regular pentagon with side s. **5s**

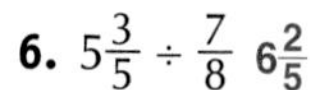

Writing in Math

21. Maria cut 12 feet of ribbon into 16 pieces of equal length. Explain how to find the length of each piece. **Divide 12 by 16, which is $\frac{12}{16}$, or $\frac{3}{4}$ feet when reduced. $\frac{3}{4} \times \frac{12}{1} = 9$ inches.**

290

Item Analysis for Diagnosis and Intervention

Objective	Items	Student Book Pages*	Intervention System
Multiply fractions.	1, 8	252–255	H39
Estimate decimal sums.	2	82–83	I12
Find least common multiple.	3	152–153	H5
Divide mixed numbers.	4, 6, 9	270–271	H43
Multiply mixed numbers.	5	258–259	H40
Convert between fractions and decimals; add decimals.	7	86–89, 172–175	H21, I15, I16
Add mixed numbers and fractions.	10–11	218–219	H34
Estimate quotients of whole numbers.	12	18–19	G56, G65
Compute perimeter.	13, 19–20	Grade 5	K26
Understand customary units of length.	14	Grade 5	K2
Identify and analyze attributes of two-dimensional shapes.	15, 17–18	Grade 5	K51

*For each lesson, there is a *Reteaching* activity in *Reaching All Learners* and a *Reteaching* master.

Data Analysis and Probability

MULTIPLE CHOICE

22. Kristi has 4 nickels, 2 dimes, and 7 quarters. She pulls out one coin. What is the probability that the coin she pulls out is a quarter?

A. $\frac{7}{4}$ **(C.)** $\frac{7}{13}$

B. $\frac{7}{6}$ **D.** $\frac{1}{7}$

23. What is the median of this data set?

3, 5, 9, 7, 5, 8, 7, 11, 3, 4, 4

(A.) 5 **C.** 7

B. 6 **D.** 8

FREE RESPONSE

For 24–26, use the bar graph.

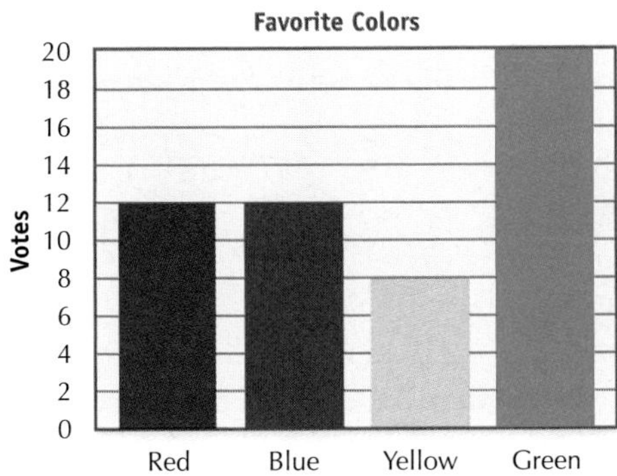

24. How many more people chose green than chose red? **8 more people**

25. How many people chose red, yellow, or blue? **32 people**

26. How many votes are represented in the graph? **52 votes**

Writing in Math

27. What is meant by the probability of an event? Give an example.
See margin.

Algebra

MULTIPLE CHOICE

28. Solve $y + 3\frac{1}{5} = 11$.

A. $y = 13\frac{1}{5}$ **C.** $y = 7\frac{1}{5}$

(B.) $y = 7\frac{4}{5}$ **D.** $y = 6\frac{4}{5}$

29. Which expression represents five more than two-thirds a number, m?

A. $\frac{2}{3}m - 5$ **C.** $5m + \frac{2}{3}$

(B.) $5 + \frac{2}{3}m$ **D.** $5 \div \frac{2}{3}m$

FREE RESPONSE

Write a rule for each table.

30.

x	2	3	6	10	16
y	$\frac{1}{2}$	$\frac{3}{4}$	$\frac{3}{2}$	$\frac{5}{2}$	4

Divide by 4

31.

x	$\frac{1}{4}$	$\frac{1}{2}$	$\frac{3}{4}$	1
y	1	2	3	4

Multiply by 4

32.

x	60	50	40	30	20
y	49	39	29	19	9

Subtract 11

33. Write an algebraic expression for 6 less than twice Matt's age. Then, find the value if Matt is 18 years old.
$2a - 6$; 30

34. Write an algebraic expression for \$12 more than $\frac{1}{5}$ Quincy's salary. Then, find the value if Quincy's salary is \$25,000. **$\frac{1}{5}q + 12$; \$5,012**

Writing in Math

35. Write an equation that includes a variable and a fraction on one side and can be solved by multiplying both sides by a fraction.
Sample answer: $\frac{3}{2}b = \frac{9}{10}$; multiply both sides of the equation by $\frac{2}{3}$ to isolate the variable.

Answers

27. Sample answer: The number of ways an event can happen in relation to the total number of possible outcomes. The probability of tossing a coin one time and getting heads is $\frac{1}{2}$.

Item Analysis for Diagnosis and Intervention

Objective	Items	Student Book Pages*	Intervention System
Compute area of a rectangle.	16	Grade 5	K28
Write to explain a solution.	21	278–279	M18
Determine the probability of an event.	22	Grade 5	L18
Find the median of a set of data.	23	Grade 5	L26
Interpret bar graphs to solve problems.	24–26	Grade 5	L3
Define probability of an event.	27	Grade 5	L18
Solve equations with fractions and mixed numbers.	28	276–277	J33
Write algebraic expressions with fractions.	29, 35	274–275	J33
Write a rule for a table.	30–32	Grade 5	J13
Write algebraic expressions.	33–34	40–43	J30

*For each lesson, there is a *Reteaching* activity in *Reaching All Learners* and a *Reteaching* master.

Reteaching

Using Student Pages 292–294

Purpose Provide students with more examples and practice for each lesson in the chapter.

- Use *Reteaching* pages for students having difficulty with *Check* exercises.
- For additional practice, use *More Practice* exercises starting on page 295.
- For intervention, use the resources listed below.

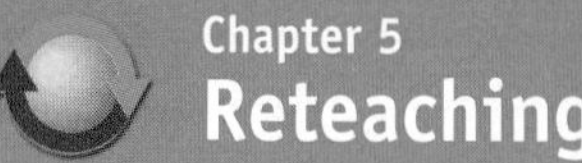

Chapter 5

Reteaching

Set 5-1 (pages 248–251)

Find $\frac{2}{5} \times 15$.

$15 \div 5 = 3$, so $\frac{1}{5} \times 15 = 3$

Since $\frac{2}{5}$ is 2 times $\frac{1}{5}$,

$\frac{2}{5} \times 15 = 2 \times (\frac{1}{5} \text{ of } 15) = 2 \times 3 = 6.$

$\frac{2}{5} \times 15 = 6$

Remember if the denominator is a factor of the whole number, you can use division and mental math.

1. $10 \times \frac{3}{5}$ **6**

2. $\frac{3}{4} \times 12$ **9**

3. $\frac{5}{7} \times 28$ **20**

4. $18 \times \frac{8}{9}$ **16**

5. $32 \times \frac{5}{8}$ **20**

6. $\frac{2}{3} \times 45$ **30**

7. $144 \times \frac{1}{6}$ **24**

8. $\frac{7}{12} \times 108$ **63**

Set 5-2 (pages 252–255)

Find $\frac{3}{4}$ of $\frac{2}{5}$. Simplify if possible.

Multiply the numerators and denominators.

$\frac{3}{4} \times \frac{2}{5} = \frac{3 \times 2}{4 \times 5} = \frac{6}{20}$

Simplify if possible.

$\frac{6}{20} = \frac{6 \div 2}{20 \div 2} = \frac{3}{10}$ Divide both the numerator and denominator by 2, the GCF of 6 and 20.

Remember you can also use the greatest common factor to simplify the fractions before multiplying.

1. $\frac{1}{4} \times \frac{5}{6}$ $\mathbf{\frac{5}{24}}$

2. $\frac{6}{7} \times \frac{14}{15}$ $\mathbf{\frac{4}{5}}$

3. $\frac{2}{9} \times \frac{3}{10}$ $\mathbf{\frac{1}{15}}$

4. $\frac{2}{3} \times \frac{3}{7}$ $\mathbf{\frac{2}{7}}$

5. $\frac{4}{9} \times \frac{5}{8}$ $\mathbf{\frac{5}{18}}$

6. $\frac{9}{10} \times \frac{5}{6}$ $\mathbf{\frac{3}{4}}$

7. $\frac{8}{11} \times \frac{1}{6}$ $\mathbf{\frac{4}{33}}$

8. $\frac{12}{13} \times \frac{39}{44}$ $\mathbf{\frac{9}{11}}$

Set 5-3 (pages 256–257)

Estimate $2\frac{5}{6} \times 31\frac{1}{3}$ using rounding.

$2\frac{5}{6} \times 31\frac{1}{3} \approx 3 \times 31 = 93$ Round each fraction to the nearest whole number.

$2\frac{5}{6} \times 31\frac{1}{3} \approx 93$

Estimate $18\frac{9}{10} \div 2\frac{3}{10}$.

$18\frac{9}{10} \div 2\frac{3}{10}$

$19 \div 2$ Round each mixed number to the nearest whole number.

$20 \div 2 = 10.$ Use compatible numbers to divide.

$18\frac{9}{10} \div 2\frac{3}{10} \approx 10$

Remember you can also use benchmark fractions to estimate a product or quotient. **Sample answers are given.**

1. $9\frac{1}{3} \times 2\frac{4}{5}$ **27**

2. $35 \times \frac{7}{8}$ **28**

3. $28 \div 3\frac{1}{4}$ **9**

4. $5\frac{1}{6} \times 4\frac{7}{9}$ **25**

5. $3\frac{3}{5} \div 2\frac{1}{8}$ **2**

6. $16\frac{11}{12} \div 7\frac{3}{10}$ **2**

7. $4\frac{1}{2} \times 11\frac{1}{3}$ **55**

8. $2\frac{5}{8} \div 7$ $\mathbf{\frac{3}{7}}$

9. $100 \times 5\frac{3}{10}$ **525**

10. $16 \times 1\frac{5}{8}$ **24**

292

Item Analysis for Diagnosis and Intervention

Objective	Review Items	Student Book Pages*	Intervention System
Multiply a fraction and a whole number.	Set 5–1	248–251	H37
Multiply fractions.	Set 5–2	252–255	H39
Estimate products and quotients with fractions and mixed numbers.	Set 5–3	256–257	H38
Multiply mixed numbers.	Set 5–4	258–259	H40
Make an organized list to solve a problem.	Set 5–5	264–265	M28
Divide fractions.	Set 5–6	266–269	H42
Divide mixed numbers.	Set 5–7	270–271	H43
Write and evaluate algebraic expressions with fractions and mixed numbers.	Set 5–8	274–275	J33
Solve equations with fractions and mixed numbers.	Set 5–9	276–277	J33
Write to explain a solution.	Set 5–10	278–279	M18

*For each lesson, there is a *Reteaching* activity in *Reaching All Learners* and a *Reteaching* master.

Take It to the NET
More Practice
www.scottforesman.com

Set 5-7 (pages 270–271)

Find each quotient. Simplify if possible.

1. $3\frac{4}{5} \div 1\frac{9}{10}$ **2**
2. $\frac{2}{3} \div 10\frac{1}{3}$ **$\frac{2}{31}$**
3. $4\frac{1}{2} \div 1\frac{4}{9}$ **$3\frac{3}{26}$**
4. $5\frac{1}{5} \div 6\frac{1}{6}$ **$\frac{156}{185}$**
5. $9\frac{7}{10} \div 3\frac{1}{3}$ **$2\frac{91}{100}$**
6. $8\frac{7}{8} \div 2\frac{3}{4}$ **$3\frac{5}{22}$**
7. Mona has a $6\frac{3}{4}$-yard length of ribbon that she wants to cut into $1\frac{1}{8}$-yard pieces. How many pieces will she have? **6 pieces**

Set 5-8 (pages 274–275)

Write each word phrase as an algebraic expression.

1. $\frac{5}{8}$ of the blue markers **$\frac{5}{8}m$**
2. 5 less than $\frac{2}{5}$ Ed's height **$\frac{2}{5}h - 5$**
3. $1\frac{2}{5}$ miles more than $\frac{1}{2}$ Jack's distance **$\frac{1}{2}d + 1\frac{2}{5}$**
4. \$25 plus \$6 per hour for x hours **\$25 + \$6x**

Evaluate each expression for $n = \frac{3}{4}$ and $n = 1\frac{1}{6}$.

5. $3\frac{1}{5}n$ **$2\frac{2}{5}$; $3\frac{11}{15}$**
6. $4 + \frac{7}{8}n$ **$4\frac{21}{32}$; $5\frac{1}{48}$**
7. $5n - 2$ **$1\frac{3}{4}$; $3\frac{5}{6}$**
8. $n \div 4$ **$\frac{3}{16}$; $\frac{7}{24}$**
9. $2\frac{5}{8}n + 3$ **$4\frac{31}{32}$; $6\frac{1}{16}$**
10. $1\frac{1}{3}n - n$ **$\frac{1}{4}$; $\frac{7}{18}$**

Set 5-9 (pages 276–277)

Solve each equation and check your answer.

1. $\frac{7}{8}p = 14$ **$p = 16$**
2. $m - 2\frac{5}{8} = 1\frac{3}{7}$ **$m = 4\frac{3}{56}$**
3. $3 + w = 9\frac{2}{7}$ **$w = 6\frac{2}{7}$**
4. $k \div 1\frac{1}{4} = 12$ **$k = 15$**
5. $\frac{2}{7}a = 4\frac{5}{6}$ **$a = 16\frac{11}{12}$**
6. $\frac{5}{6} = z - 4\frac{2}{3}$ **$z = 5\frac{1}{2}$**
7. $3\frac{1}{2} + 4\frac{1}{3} = d$ **$d = 7\frac{5}{6}$**
8. $x \div \frac{3}{4} = 3\frac{1}{9}$ **$x = 2\frac{1}{3}$**
9. $n - 2\frac{1}{5} = \frac{14}{5}$ **$n = 5$**
10. Jerome wants to walk $5\frac{1}{3}$ miles. In the morning, he walked $1\frac{7}{8}$ miles. How much farther does he have to walk to reach his goal? **$3\frac{11}{24}$ miles**

Set 5-10
1. Row A: $\frac{3}{8} \times 16 = 6$ Row B: $\frac{3}{4} \times 16 = 12$ Row C: $\frac{7}{8} \times 16 = 14$
6 + 12 + 14 = 32 plants

Set 5-10 (pages 278–279)

Explain your solution and show your work.

1. Hayley planted 3 rows of flowers. She planted 16 flowers in each row. In Row A, $\frac{3}{8}$ of the flowers blossomed. In Row B, $\frac{3}{4}$ of the flowers blossomed, and in Row C, $\frac{7}{8}$ of the flowers blossomed. How many plants blossomed? **See above.**

CHAPTER 6

Lesson Planner

Ratio, Rates, and Proportion

Suggested Pacing: 12 days

Section A Ratio and Rates

6-1 pp. 300–301	6-2 pp. 302–305	6-3 pp. 306–309	6-4 pp. 312–313
Understanding Ratios **Objective** Express comparisons as ratios in three ways. **Math Understanding** There are different types of comparisons that can be expressed as ratios. The order in which the quantities are compared is important (3 to 2 is not the same as 2 to 3). **Focus Question** • What is a mathematical way to compare quantities? **Vocabulary** Ratio, terms	**Equal Ratios** **Objective** Create equal ratios. **Math Understanding** Equal ratios, like equivalent fractions, can be generated using multiplication or division. **Focus Question** • How can you find equal ratios? **Enrichment: The Golden Ratio, p. 305**	**Rates and Unit Rates** **Objective** Find the unit rate for a given rate, and use rates to identify the better buy or the lower rate. **Math Understanding** Rates are a special type of ratio where unlike quantities are compared. A unit rate has 1 for its second term. **Focus Questions** • *Activity* Can you compare ratios? • Are there special kinds of ratios? • How can unit rates help you make comparisons? **Vocabulary** Rate, unit rate Discovery Channel School **Discover Math in Your World: The Not-So-Mammoth Mastodon, p. 309** Reading For Math Success pp. 310–311	Problem-Solving Strategy **Use Objects** **Objective** Find, and write in sentences, solutions to word problems involving rates. **Math Understanding** Using objects can help to represent what you know in solving a problem. **Focus Question** • How can you use objects to solve a problem? **Section A Review, p. 314** **Section A Diagnostic Checkpoint, p. 315**

Diagnosing Readiness, pp. 298–299

Resources in the Student Book

Ongoing Assessment and Test Prep *Also see pp. 298G–298H.*

Instant Check System™
- **Diagnosing Readiness** start of chapter
- **Warm Up** start of lessons
- **Talk About It** after examples
- **Check** before Practice
- **Diagnostic Checkpoint** end of sections

Test Prep
- **Test Talk: Think It Through** in lessons
- **Mixed Review and Test Prep** in lessons
- **Test Talk** end of chapter
- **Cumulative Review and Test Prep** end of chapter

Daily Real-World Problem Solving plus ...

Problem-Solving Applications lesson on pp. 334–335 uses data from Dorling Kindersley literature.

Discover Math in Your World on p. 309 uses data from a topic in the Discovery Channel School Video Library, Segment 6.

EC NTL 12 11 10 9 8 7 6 5 4 3 2

Section B Proportions

6-5 pp. 316–317

Understanding Proportions

Objective Identify ratios that form proportions.

Math Understanding A proportion is a statement that two ratios are equal.

Focus Question

- What is a proportion?

Vocabulary Proportion, vary proportionally, cross products

6-6 pp. 318–321

Solving Proportions

Objective Solve proportions whose terms are whole numbers or money.

Math Understanding Two methods of solving proportions are to use the unit amount and to use a common factor.

Focus Questions

- *Activity* How can you use ratio tables to solve proportions?
- What are other methods for solving proportions?

Enrichment: Dimensional Analysis, p. 321

6-7 pp. 322–323

Solving Proportions Using Cross Products

Objective Use cross products to solve proportions.

Math Understanding You can use cross products to solve proportions. Cross products are derived by multiplying both sides of a proportion by the product of the second terms.

Focus Question

- How can you use cross products to solve proportions?

Vocabulary Cross products (p. 316)

6-8 pp. 324–325

Problem-Solving Skill

Writing to Explain

Objective Solve word problems and explain how the solution was obtained.

Math Understanding An explanation of the solution to a problem includes information that is known and how you have used this information.

Focus Question

- How do you write a good explanation?

Section B Review, p. 326

Section B Diagnostic Checkpoint, p. 327

eading and Writing in Math *Throughout*

his feature shows how reading skills nd strategies can help with problem-olving skills and strategies in math. lso, **Reading Assists** are in the eacher's Edition.

Writing in Math

All lessons include **Writing in Math** exercises. Also, daily **Journal Ideas** are in the Teacher's Edition.

Technology Resources for Students *Also see p. T20.*

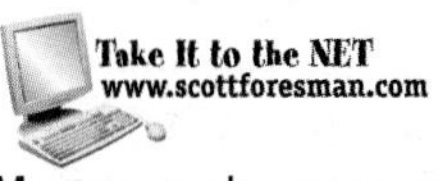

More examples, more practice, test prep, Discovery Channel School Video Library, and Math eTools

Math eTools: electronic manipulatives online, on CD-ROM, and in the Online Student's Edition

All text pages are available online and on CD-ROM. The Online Student's Edition includes Math eTools plus glossary links for vocabulary.

Ratio, Rates, and Proportion (continued)

Section C Similarity and Scale Drawings

6-9 pp. 328–329

Algebra Using Formulas

Objective Use formulas to solve problems involving rates.

Math Understanding Many formulas involve unit rates.

Focus Questions
- What is a formula?
- How do you use a formula to solve a problem?

Vocabulary Formula

6-10 pp. 330–333

Scale Drawings and Maps

Objective Solve word problems based on scale drawings.

Math Understanding Scale drawings involve similar figures, and corresponding parts of similar figures are proportional.

Focus Questions
- What is a scale drawing?
- *Activity* How do you make a scale drawing?
- How can you use scale drawings?
- How can you use the scale on a map?

Vocabulary Scale drawing, scale

Materials for Student Pages Ruler, centimeter grid paper or tools

Learning with Technology: The Geometry Drawing eTool, p. 333

6-11 pp. 334–335

DK Problem-Solving Applications

The Stars and Stripes

Objective Review and apply key concepts, skills, and strategies learned in this and previous chapters.

Math Understanding Some real-world problems can be solved using known concepts, skills, and strategies.

Section C Review, p. 336

Section C Diagnostic Checkpoint, p. 337

Wrap Up

pp. 338–351

Test Talk: Improve Written Answers, pp. 338–339

Key Vocabulary and Concept Review, pp. 340–341

Chapter 6 Test, pp. 342–343

Cumulative Review and Test Prep, pp. 344–345

Reteaching, pp. 346–348

More Practice, pp. 349–351

Additional Resources for...

Reaching All Learners

- **Practice** Masters/Workbook, every lesson
- **Reteaching** Masters/Workbook, every lesson
- **Enrichment** Masters/Workbook, every lesson
- **Every Student Learns** A teacher resource with daily suggestions for helping students overcome language barriers to learning math
- **Spiral Review and Test Prep** Transparencies and Masters/Workbook, every lesson
- **Math Games** Use *Strike or Spare* anytime after Lesson 6-7.
- **Investigation** See pp. 298I–298J.

Problem Solving

- **Problem Solving** Masters/Workbook, every lesson
- **Problem of the Day** Flipchart/Transparencies, every lesson
- **Discovery Channel** Masters, follow-up to Segment 6 in the Discovery Channel School Video Library

Notes

Reading in Math

- **Vocabulary Kit** Word Cards plus transparencies and activities for instructional word walls and for small groups
- **Dorling Kindersley Literature Library** Books with interesting data

Assessment, Intervention, and Test Prep

- **Assessment Sourcebook** See pp. 298G–298H.
- **Math Diagnosis and Intervention System** See pp. 298G–298H.
- **Test-Taking Practice** Transparencies, every lesson
- **SAT 9, SAT 10, TerraNova, ITBS Practice and Test Prep** Includes practice tests, correlations, and more.
- **Benchmark Tests** Multiple-choice tests on content in Chapters 1-2, 3-4, 5-6, 7-8, 9-10 and in the National Assessment of Educational Progress.

Teacher Support

- **Teaching Tools** Masters: paper manipulatives and more
- **Home-School Connection** Masters, use Chapter 6 Family Letter at the start of the chapter. Use Study Buddies 11 and 12 after Lessons 6-3 and 6-7.
- **Professional Development Resources** See p. T18.
- **Technology Resources** TE and more; see p. T20.

CHAPTER 6

Professional Development

Skills Trace - Ratio, Rates, and Proportion

BEFORE Chapter 6	DURING Chapter 6	AFTER Chapter 6
Grade 5 introduced the concepts of ratios, rates, equal ratios, and proportions and developed using equal ratios to solve problems related to scale drawings. **Chapter 3 in Grade 6** reviewed the fraction concepts related to finding equal ratios.	**Chapter 6** extends concepts of ratios, rates, equal ratios, and proportions to include unit rates and solving proportions using the cross-product method. The chapter applies the concepts in solving problems related to scale drawings, maps, and similar figures.	**Chapter 7 in Grade 6** applies the concept of ratio to percent. Grade 7 applies proportional reasoning in solving problems about similar figures, scale drawings, and percent, and extends ratio and proportion concepts to include dimensional analysis.

Math Background and Teaching Tips

Section A

Ratio and Rates pp. 300–315

A **ratio** is a comparison of quantities. Ratios in different settings or contexts have different meanings as illustrated below.

Example 1 A comparison of part of a set to the whole set

There are 12 males out of 30 people in the room.

Example 2 A comparison of part of a set to another part of a set

There are 12 males and 18 females in the room.

Example 3 A comparison of two different quantities of the same variable

Carmen bought 25 gallons of gasoline last week. She bought 30 gallons of gasoline this week.

Example 4 A comparison of two different variables measured in the same units

The recipe calls for 3 cans of orange juice for every 1 can of water.

Example 5 A comparison of unlike quantities; this is called a **rate**. A rate that has a denominator of 1 unit is called a **unit rate**.

The car is traveling at a rate of 55 miles per hour.

There are 12 girls in a room. There 18 boys in the room. What is the ratio of girls to boys?

12 to 18 12:18 $\frac{12}{18}$

Math Understandings

- There are different types of comparisons that can be expressed as ratios. The order in which the quantities are compared is important (3 to 2 is not the same as 2 to 3).
- Equal ratios, like equivalent fractions, can be generated using multiplication or division.
- Rates are a special type of ratio where unlike quantities are compared. A unit rate has 1 for its second term.
- Using objects can help to represent what you know in solving a problem.

Ratios can be written in three forms:

a to *b* *a*:*b* $\frac{a}{b}$

All ratios can be written using $\frac{a}{b}$ notation, but not all ratios are fractions, a comparison of a part to a whole. Here are some key points about ratios and fractions.

- A ratio places two or more quantities in a multiplicative comparison.
- All fractions are ratios, but not all ratios are fractions.
- All rates are ratios, but not all ratios are rates.

TIP! Make Connections *Be sure students see how ratios and fractions are alike and how they are different. Example 1 can be used to show a ratio that is a fraction (part to whole). Example 2 shows a ratio that is not a fraction (part to part).*

Section B

Proportions pp. 316–327

A **proportion** is a statement that two ratios are equal. The ratio table below shows ratios that are equal to the ratio $\frac{4}{\$2}$. Any two equal ratios found in the table can be used to write a proportion.

$$\frac{4}{\$2} = \frac{12}{\$6}$$

The rule for the table can be expressed as the ratio $\frac{n}{c} = 2$ for all values of *n* and *c*. If $\frac{n}{c} = 2$ then $n = 2c$. Notice how this ratio matches the form $y = ax$, the basic form for a linear equation. This is why the graph of equal ratios is a straight line, and the slope of the line is a constant ratio, 2 in this example.

Number of balloons (*n*)	4	8	12	16	20
Cost (*c*)	\$2	\$4	\$6	\$8	\$10

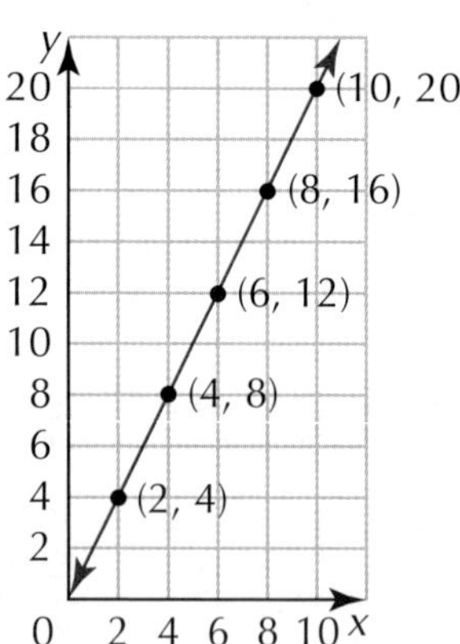

TIP! Make Connections *Be sure students understand that there is more than one way to solve a proportion. For example, the problem on the next page can be solved in a variety of ways.*

Math Understandings

- A proportion is a statement that two ratios are equal.
- Two methods of solving proportions are to use the unit amount and to use a common factor.
- You can use cross products to solve proportions. Cross products are derived by multiplying both sides of a proportion by the product of the second terms.
- An explanation of the solution to a problem includes information that is known and how you have used this information.

A clown can buy 4 helium-filled balloons for $2. How many can she buy if her balloon budget is $10?

Solve using a ratio table.

Look for the entry above $10 in the ratio table on the previous page. It shows 20 balloons.

Solve by finding the unit rate.

$4 \div 2 = 2$

Unit rate: 2 balloons for $1

So, 10×2 or 20 balloons can be bought for $10.

Solve using a common denominator.

$\frac{4}{2} = \frac{n}{10}$ Think $2 \times 5 = 10$

Multiply 4 by 5

$\frac{4 \times 5}{2 \times 5} = \frac{20}{10}$

So, $n = 20$.

Solve using cross products.

$\frac{4}{2} = \frac{n}{10}$

$4(10) = 2n$

$40 = 2n$

$20 = n$

Section C

Similarity and Scale Drawings pp. 328–337

Similar figures are figures that have the same shape but not necessarily the same size. Congruent figures have the same shape and size. Thus, all congruent figures are also similar, but two similar figures may or may not be congruent.

In similar figures, corresponding angles have the same measure and corresponding sides are proportional. Therefore, proportions can be used to solve problems involving similar figures.

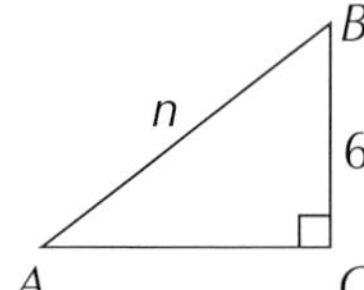

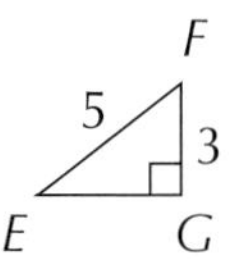

Solve for n using cross products.

$\frac{3}{5} = \frac{6}{n}$

$3 \times n = 5 \times 6$

$3n = 30$

$n = 10$

TIP! Assess Understanding *Students should understand that a proportion can be written in different ways. The key is that the two sides of the proportion compare the quantities in the same order.*

The following proportions can be written for the side lengths of these figures.

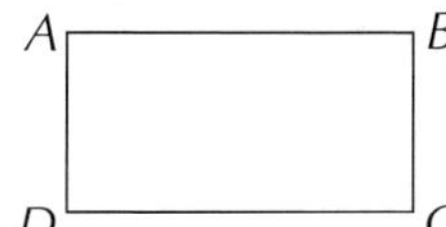

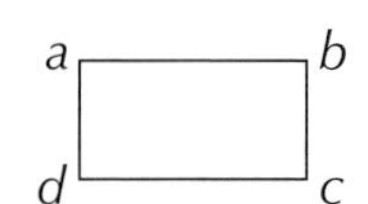

$\frac{AB}{CD} = \frac{ab}{cd}$ $\frac{CD}{AB} = \frac{cd}{ab}$ $\frac{AB}{ab} = \frac{CD}{cd}$ $\frac{ab}{AB} = \frac{cd}{CD}$

Math Understandings

- Many formulas involve unit rates.
- Scale drawings involve similar figures, and corresponding parts of similar figures are proportional.

A scale drawing shows a figure that is similar to another larger figure. If the scale and an actual length are known, the scale length can be found using a proportion. If the scale and a scale length are known, the actual length can be determined.

The scale of a drawing is 1 in.: 3 ft.
Find the scale length needed to represent 12 feet.
Let n = scale length

scale length (in.) ⟶ / actual length (ft) ⟶ $\frac{1}{3} = \frac{n}{12}$

$3n = 12$

$n = 4$

The scale length needed to represent 12 feet is 4 inches.

Find the actual length represented by a scale length of 6 inches.

Let n = actual length

scale length (in.) ⟶ / actual length (ft) ⟶ $\frac{1}{3} = \frac{6}{n}$

$n = 3 \times 6$

$n = 18$

The actual length represented by a scale length of 6 inches is 18 feet.

TIP! Assess Understanding *When using the $\frac{a}{b}$ form of a proportion, ask students if this is the same as a fraction; for example, whether $\frac{1\text{ in.}}{3\text{ ft}}$ is the same as $\frac{1}{3}$. This will help determine whether students are confused by the notation for proportion.*

Assessment, Intervention, Test Prep

Assessment Resources

DIAGNOSING READINESS

Start of Year Diagnosing Readiness for Grade 6, Assessment Sourcebook, pp. 43–46 and in Online Intervention

✓ **Start of Chapter** Diagnosing Readiness for Chapter 6, Student Book pp. 298–299 and in Online Intervention

✓ **Start of Lesson** Warm Up, Student Book pp. 300, 302, 306, 316, 318, 322, 324, 328, 330

✓ Instant Check System™

ONGOING ASSESSMENT

✓ **During Instruction** Talk About It, Student Book, every lesson

✓ **Before Independent Practice** Check, Student Book, every lesson

✓ **After a Section** Diagnostic Checkpoint, pp. 315, 327, 337 and in Online Intervention

Basic-Facts Timed Test 6 Assessment Sourcebook, p. 32

FORMAL EVALUATION

Chapter Tests Chapter 6 Test, Student Book pp. 342–343; Assessment Sourcebook Forms A and B pp. 81–86, Form C Performance Assessment p. 11; Multiple-Choice Chapter Test in Online Intervention

Cumulative Tests Chapters 1-3, 1-6, 1-9, 1-12; Assessment Sourcebook, pp. 65–68, 87–90, 109–112, 131–134; Online Intervention

Test Generator Computer-generated tests; can be customized

Correlation to Assessments, Intervention, and Standardized Tests

	Assessments		Intervention	Standardized Tests				
Lessons	Diagnostic Checkpoint	Chapter Test	Math Diagnosis and Intervention System	SAT 9/10	ITBS	CTBS	CAT	MAT
6-1 Understanding Ratios	p. 315: Ex. 3–6, 21	Ex. 1, 12–14	Booklet I: I30	/•	•	•		
6-2 Equal Ratios	p. 315: Ex. 1, 7–15, 21	Ex. 2, 3, 15–20, 28	Booklet I: I31	/•	•			
6-3 Rates and Unit Rates	p. 315: Ex. 2, 16–19, 22	Ex. 4, 8, 9, 19, 20, 25	Booklet I: I33, I38	/•	•	•		
6-4 Problem-Solving Strategy: Use Objects	p. 315: Ex. 20	Ex. 30	Booklet M: M33	•/•	•			•
6-5 Understanding Proportions	p. 327: Ex. 1, 3–14	Ex. 6, 21, 22	Booklet I: I39	/•				
6-6 Solving Proportions	p. 327: Ex. 2, 15–29	Ex. 5, 7, 23, 24, 26, 29	Booklet I: I39	/•				
6-7 Solving Proportions Using Cross Products	p. 327: Ex. 2, 15–29	Ex. 5, 7, 23, 24, 26, 29	Booklet I: I40	/•				
6-8 Problem-Solving Skill: Writing to Explain	p. 327: Ex. 27–29	Ex. 28–30	Booklet M: M18	/•				
6-9 Using Formulas	p. 337: Ex. 1, 3–4	Ex. 10, 25	Booklet J: J34					
6-10 Scale Drawings and Maps	p. 337: Ex. 2, 4–8	Ex. 11, 27	Booklet I: I34	•/•		•		•

KEY: **SAT 9** Stanford Achievement Test; **SAT 10** Stanford Achievement Test; **ITBS** Iowa Test of Basic Skills; **CAT** California Achievement Test; **CTBS** Comprehensive Test of Basic Skills (TerraNova); **MAT** Metropolitan Achievement Test

Intervention and Test Prep Resources

INTERVENTION

During Instruction Helpful "If... Then..." suggestions in the Teacher's Edition in Ongoing Assessment and Error Intervention.

During Practice "Reteaching" and "More Practice" sets at the back of the chapter, referenced under "Check" and "Practice" in the lessons.

Math Diagnosis and Intervention System Diagnostic tests, individual and class record forms, two-page Intervention Lessons (example, practice, test prep), and one-page Intervention Practice (multiple choice), all in cross-grade strand booklets (Booklets A-E for Grades 1–3, Booklets F-M for Grades 4–6).

Online Intervention Diagnostic tests; individual, class, school, and district reports; remediation including tutorials, video, games, practice exercises.

 TEST PREP

Test Talk: Think It Through within lessons and tests

Mixed Review and Test Prep end of lessons

Test Talk before the chapter test, pp. 338–339

Cumulative Review and Test Prep after each chapter, pp. 344–345

Test-Taking Strategies, pp. xv-xix before Chapter 1

Pacing for Test Success, pp. T36-T-47

Test-Taking Practice Transparencies for every lesson

Spiral Review and Test Prep for every lesson

SAT 9, SAT 10, ITBS, TerraNova Practice and Test Prep section quizzes, practice tests

Take It to the Net: Test Prep www.scottforesman.com, referenced in lessons

Correlation to NCTM Standards and Grades 6–8 Expectations

Number and Operations

Understand numbers, ways of representing numbers, relationships among numbers, and number systems.

Grades 6–8 Expectations

- Understand and use ratios and proportions to represent quantitative relationships. *Lessons 6-1, 6-2, 6-3, 6-5*

Understand meanings of operations and how they relate to one another.

Grades 6–8 Expectations

- Understand the meaning and effects of arithmetic operations with fractions, decimals, and integers. *Lesson 6-4*

Compute fluently and make reasonable estimates.

Grades 6–8 Expectations

- Develop, analyze, and explain methods for solving problems involving proportions, such as scaling and finding equivalent ratios. *Lessons 6-6, 6-7, 6–8, 6-10, 6-11*

Algebra

Represent and analyze mathematical situations and structures using algebraic symbols.

Grades 6–8 Expectations

- Use symbolic algebra to represent situations and to solve problems, especially those that involve linear relationships. *Lessons 6-6, 6-7, 6–8, 6-9, 6-10*

Use mathematical models to represent and understand quantitative relationships.

Grades 6–8 Expectations

- Model and solve contextualized problems using various representations, such as graphs, tables, and equations. *Lessons 6-6, 6-7, 6–8, 6-9, 6-10*

Measurement

Apply appropriate techniques, tools, and formulas to determine measurements.

Grades 6–8 Expectations

- Solve problems involving scale factors, using ratio and proportion. *Lesson 6-10*
- Solve simple problems involving rates and derived measurements for such attributes as velocity and density. *Lessons 6-3, 6-6, 6-9*

The NCTM 2000 Pre-K through Grade 12 Content Standards are Number and Operations, Algebra, Geometry, Measurement, and Data Analysis and Probability. The Process Standards (Problem Solving, Reasoning and Proof, Communication, Connections, and Representation) are incorporated throughout lessons.

Investigation

Ratio, Rates, and Proportion

Activity 1

Use in place of the Investigating the Concept activity before Lesson 6-2.

Using Equal Ratios

Overview Students solve a problem using equal ratios, before learning ways to write equal ratios in Lesson 6-2.

Materials (per small group) Power Polygons: 20 triangles and 20 hexagons

The Task

- Distribute materials.
- **Suppose you plan to make a pattern using 30 triangles and hexagons in all. The ratio of triangles to hexagons in your pattern will be 3 to 2. Use any procedure that you want to find how many of each shape you will need. Write to explain how you solved this problem.**

Observing and Questioning

- Observe how students approach this problem. If needed, ask the following questions to spur further thinking.
- **What does the ratio 3 to 2 mean in this situation?**
- **How can you use Power Polygons to solve this problem?**
- **Would making a table help you? How?**
- Watch for students who are writing incorrect numbers in their tables. Have them show each number of shapes with the Power Polygons and check that they have 3 triangles for every 2 hexagons.

Sharing and Summarizing

- After students show their work, summarize the different methods used. For example, below Alex repeated the ratio until he had used a total of 30 shapes. Shamika made a table showing the number of each different shape she would use in all each time she repeated the pattern of 3 triangles and 2 hexagons.
- If no students made a table such as Shamika's, have students help you construct one on the chalkboard based on their work. Have volunteers write a ratio of triangles to hexagons for each column in the table. Ask, **Are these ratios equal? How do you know? What patterns do you see in the first terms of the ratios? In the second terms?**
- **Key Idea** As students share their observations, summarize the different patterns found. Listen for students who recognize that the first terms are multiples of 3 and the second terms are multiples of 2. Lesson 6-2 presents using multiplication and division to find equal ratios.

Follow-Up

- Have students make their own pattern using a different ratio of triangles to hexagons and find how many of each shape they would need if they were to use about 30 shapes in all.

Alex

△△△ △△△ △△△
⬡⬡ ⬡⬡ ⬡⬡
△△△ △△△ △△△
⬡⬡ ⬡⬡ ⬡⬡

I repeated the ratio until I had used 30 shapes. I used 18 triangles and 12 hexagons in all.

Shamika

I made a table.

Triangles	3	6	9	12	15	18
Hexagons	2	4	6	8	10	12
Shapes	5	10	15	20	25	30

18 triangles and 12 hexagons make 30 shapes in all.

Activity 2

Use in place of the Investigating the Concept activity before Lesson 6-5.

Equal Ratios

Overview Students look for patterns in pairs of equal ratios, which are defined as proportions in Lesson 6-5.

Materials Patterns in Ratios (Teaching Tool 44)

The Task

- Write $\frac{4}{5} = \frac{8}{10}$ on the chalkboard and distribute Teaching Tool 44
- Review with students how they know that the ratios $\frac{4}{5}$ and $\frac{8}{10}$ are equal.
- **Complete the statements for the first set of ratios using $\frac{4}{5}$ and $\frac{8}{10}$ on Teaching Tool 44. Then write two more pair of equal ratios in the next two sets of boxes and complete the equations for those ratios. Look for patterns in the completed equations. Write descriptions of them.**

Observing and Questioning

- Observe how students are completing the equations. To check students' understanding, ask them to explain how they found each number.
- Watch for students who are having difficulty writing their own pairs of equal ratios. Ask, **What operations can you use to write equal ratios? How do you use them?**

Sharing and Summarizing

- After students share their work, summarize the patterns they found. For example, the student work pictured below includes the patterns students are likely to find.
- **Key Idea** Point out that pairs of equal ratios are known as proportions. Relate the patterns among the top and bottom terms of a proportion to the operations students use to find equal ratios. Introduce the term "cross products" and point out the pattern in them.

Follow-Up

- Have students use the patterns they found to determine whether each pair of ratios forms a proportion: $\frac{2}{3}, \frac{6}{9}$; $\frac{3}{5}, \frac{9}{10}$; and $\frac{12}{15}, \frac{8}{10}$.

Patterns in Equal Ratios

Both terms on the left are multiplied by the same number to get the terms on the right. Both terms on the right are multiplied by the same number to get the terms on the left.

The number the terms on the left are multiplied by and the number the terms on the right are multiplied by are reciprocals.

The product of the top term on the left side and the bottom term on the right side equals the product of the top term on the right side and the bottom term on the left side.

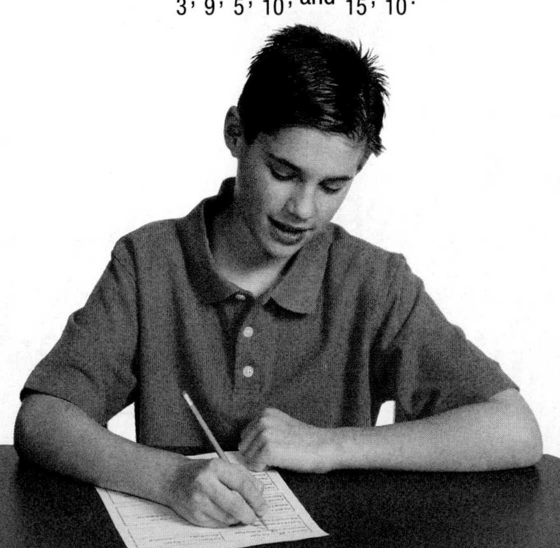

CHAPTER 6

Ratio, Rates, and Proportion

Chapter 6 focuses on understanding rates, ratios, and proportions and solving proportions. Proportions are used to solve problems involving scale drawings. Formulas are used to solve problems involving rates.

Vocabulary

Also, see Glossary, *pp. 742–748.*

ratio *(p. 300)*

terms *(p. 300)*

rate *(p. 306)*

unit rate *(p. 306)*

proportion *(p. 316)*

cross products *(p. 316)*

formula *(p. 328)*

scale drawing *(p. 330)*

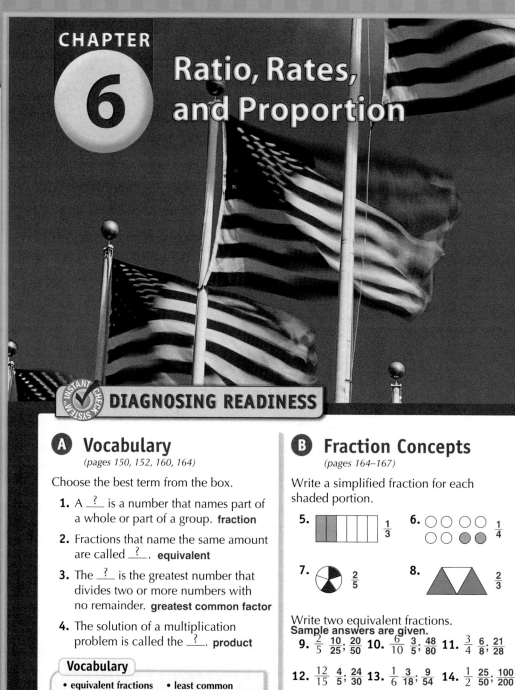

scale *(p. 330)*

CHAPTER 6

Ratio, Rates, and Proportion

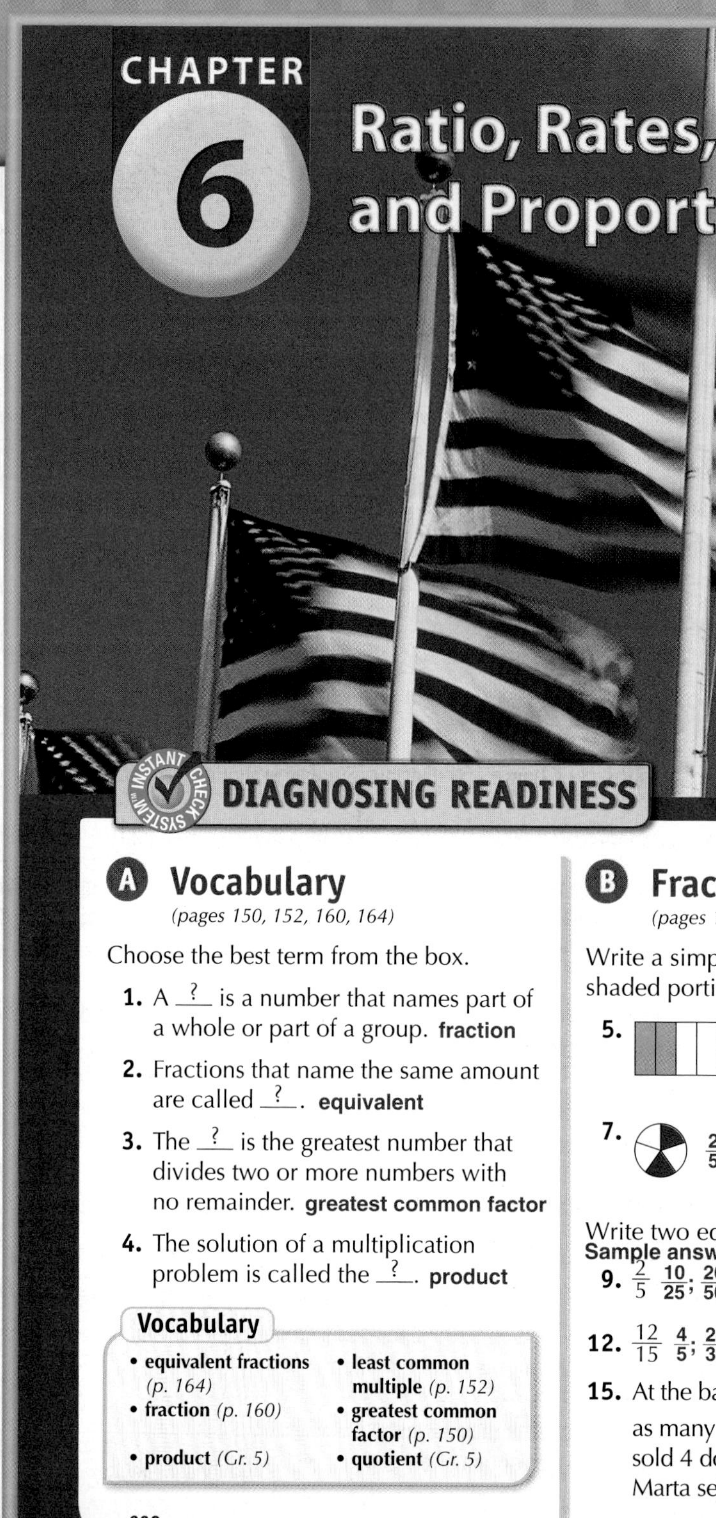

INSTANT CHECK SYSTEM

DIAGNOSING READINESS

A Vocabulary

(pages 150, 152, 160, 164)

Choose the best term from the box.

1. A __?__ is a number that names part of a whole or part of a group. **fraction**
2. Fractions that name the same amount are called __?__. **equivalent**
3. The __?__ is the greatest number that divides two or more numbers with no remainder. **greatest common factor**
4. The solution of a multiplication problem is called the __?__. **product**

Vocabulary

- **equivalent fractions** *(p. 164)*
- **fraction** *(p. 160)*
- **product** *(Gr. 5)*
- **least common multiple** *(p. 152)*
- **greatest common factor** *(p. 150)*
- **quotient** *(Gr. 5)*

B Fraction Concepts

(pages 164–167)

Write a simplified fraction for each shaded portion.

5. $\frac{1}{3}$
6. $\frac{1}{4}$
7. $\frac{2}{5}$
8. $\frac{2}{3}$

Write two equivalent fractions.
Sample answers are given.

9. $\frac{2}{5}$ **$\frac{10}{25}$; $\frac{20}{50}$**
10. $\frac{6}{10}$ **$\frac{3}{5}$; $\frac{48}{80}$**
11. $\frac{3}{4}$ **$\frac{6}{8}$; $\frac{21}{28}$**
12. $\frac{12}{15}$ **$\frac{4}{5}$; $\frac{24}{30}$**
13. $\frac{1}{6}$ **$\frac{3}{18}$; $\frac{9}{54}$**
14. $\frac{1}{2}$ **$\frac{25}{50}$; $\frac{100}{200}$**
15. At the bake sale, Marta sold $1\frac{1}{4}$ times as many muffins as Tina did. If Tina sold 4 dozen muffins, how many did Marta sell? **5 dozen**

298

Math Vocabulary Kit

Every vocabulary word is written on a card with the definition of the word printed on the back. Vocabulary activities are provided in the *Math Vocabulary Kit Teacher's Guide.*

Add the words from the *Vocabulary* list at the left to your Math Word Wall.

formula

ratio

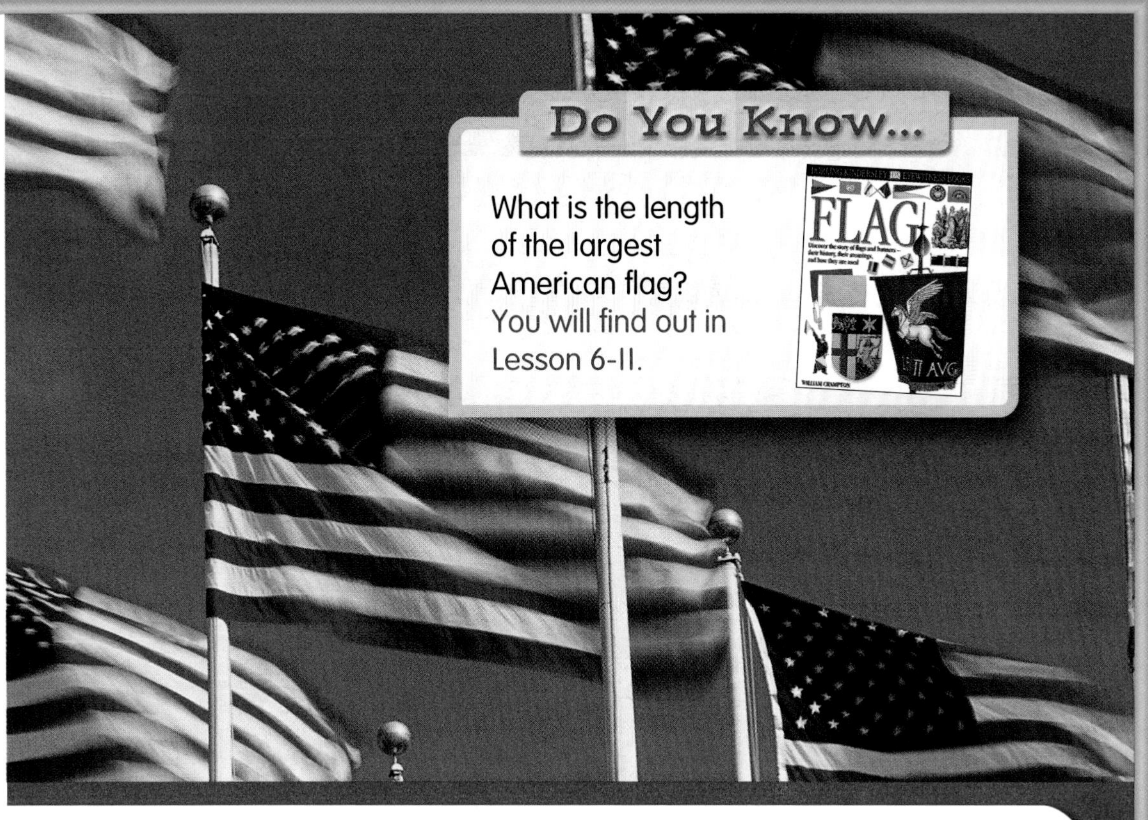

Do You Know...
What is the length of the largest American flag? You will find out in Lesson 6-11.

C Multiplication & Division (pages 30, 32, 94)

Multiply.

16. 23×9 **207**

17. 18×12 **216**

18. 16×23 **368**

19. 67×28 **1,876**

Divide.

20. $108 \div 9$ **12**

21. $126 \div 14$ **9**

22. $210 \div 25$ **8.4**

23. $782 \div 34$ **23**

24. Becky wants to buy 4 T-shirts. Each shirt costs $12.98, including tax. What will be the total cost? **$51.92**

25. Tonya bought 3 bracelets for a total of $54, excluding tax. How much did each bracelet cost? **$18**

D Solving Equations (pages 44–47)

Solve for the variable.

26. $24 + c = 53$ **$c = 29$**

27. $y - 15 = 129$ **$y = 144$**

28. $5b = 45$ **$b = 9$**

29. $\frac{v}{4} = 8$ **$v = 32$**

30. $3g = 123$ **$g = 41$**

31. $x + 14 = 37$ **$x = 23$**

32. $\frac{t}{8} = 9$ **$t = 72$**

33. $27 = m - 9$ **$m = 36$**

34. The area of a rectangle is 18 ft^2. If the width is 3 ft, what is the length? (Area = length × width) **6 ft.**

35. The height of a triangle is $\frac{3}{8}$ the length of the base. Find the height of the triangle if the base measures 16 inches. **6 inches**

299

Literature: Dorling Kindersley and Other Sources

The Atlas of Archaeology
Mick Aston and Tim Taylor. New York: Dorling Kindersley Publishing, Inc., 1998.

Use with Lesson 6-10 The drawings of archaeological sites, as sites would have appeared originally, provide a real-world use of scale and proportion.

What's Faster than a Speeding Cheetah?
Robert E. Wells. Morton Grove, IL: Albert Whitman & Company, 1997.

Use with Lesson 6-3
This book compares the speeds of various animals to faster things like rockets and meteoroids in miles per hour.

Gulliver's Travels
Jonathan Swift, retold by Raymond James. Mahwah, NJ: Troll Associates, 1990.

Use with Lesson 6-6 An Englishman finds himself wrecked on an island where people are only six inches tall.

Math Leveled Literature Library

Baseball's Greatest Games
(Challenging)
Dan Gutman. New York: Puffin Books, 1994.

This book offers facts and statistics about baseball's greatest ever games.

DIAGNOSING READINESS

Purpose Diagnose students' readiness by assessing prerequisite content.

- Assign each set of exercises and go over the answers.
- Check to see which students did not get at least 66% of the exercises correct in a section.

  Section A: 3 out of 4
  Section B: 8 out of 11
  Section C: 7 out of 10
  Section D: 7 out of 10

- For intervention, use the resources listed at the right.

Item Analysis for Diagnosis and Intervention

Objective	Items	Student Book Pages*	Intervention System
Recall the definitions of equivalent fractions, product, least common multiple, greatest common factor, and quotient.	1–4	100, 150, 152, 160, 164	H4, H5, H12 H14, H24 I28
Understand fractions and equivalent fractions.	5–15	160–167	H12, H14, H24
Multiply and divide with whole numbers and money.	16–25	90–97	H15, I20 I27
Solve equations with whole numbers and fractions.	26–35	48–51, 276–277	J31, J33

*For each lesson, there is a *Reteaching* activity in *Reaching All Learners* and a *Reteaching* master.

Lesson Organizer

Quick Lesson Overview

Objective Express comparisons as ratios in three ways.

Math Understanding There are different types of comparisons that can be expressed as ratios. The order in which the quantities are compared is important (3 to 2 is not the same as 2 to 3).

Vocabulary Ratio, terms

Research Base

Fractions can be interpreted as a measure, a quotient or indicated division, a ratio, and as an operator (Kieren, 1980). Ratio is a comparison of two numbers. This section includes lessons involving ratio, rates, and unit rates.

NCTM Standards

- Number and Operations

(For a complete correlation to the NCTM Standards and Grades 6–8 Expectations, see pages 298G–H.)

Getting Started

Spiral Review

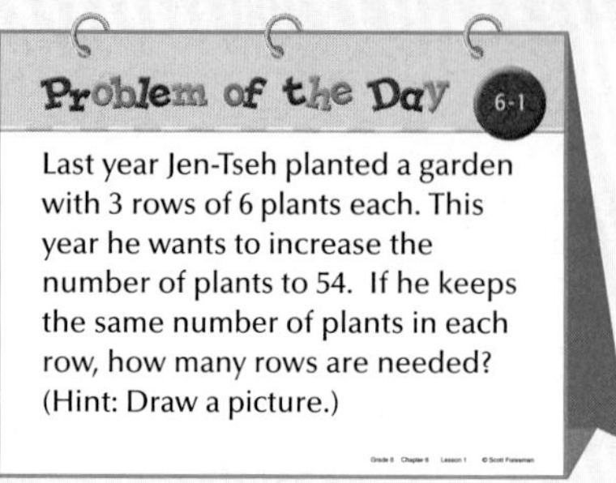

Problem of the Day 6-1

Last year Jen-Tseh planted a garden with 3 rows of 6 plants each. This year he wants to increase the number of plants to 54. If he keeps the same number of plants in each row, how many rows are needed? (Hint: Draw a picture.)

Topics Reviewed

- Multiplication; arrays
- Problem-Solving Strategy: Draw a Picture

Answer Jen-Tseh will need 9 rows of 6 plants.

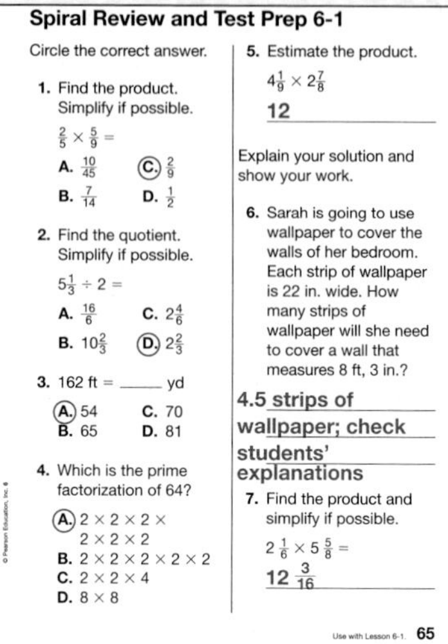

Spiral Review and Test Prep 6-1

Circle the correct answer.

1. Find the product. Simplify if possible.
   $\frac{2}{5} \times \frac{5}{9} =$
   A. $\frac{10}{45}$ (C.) $\frac{2}{9}$
   B. $\frac{7}{14}$ D. $\frac{1}{2}$
2. Find the quotient. Simplify if possible.
   $5\frac{1}{3} \div 2 =$
   A. $\frac{16}{6}$ C. $2\frac{4}{6}$
   B. $10\frac{2}{3}$ (D.) $2\frac{2}{3}$
3. 162 ft = _____ yd
   (A.) 54 C. 70
   B. 65 D. 81
4. Which is the prime factorization of 64?
   (A.) $2 \times 2 \times 2 \times 2 \times 2 \times 2$
   B. $2 \times 2 \times 2 \times 2 \times 2$
   C. $2 \times 2 \times 4$
   D. 8×8
5. Estimate the product.
   $4\frac{1}{9} \times 2\frac{7}{8}$
   12

Explain your solution and show your work.

6. Sarah is going to use wallpaper to cover the walls of her bedroom. Each strip of wallpaper is 22 in. wide. How many strips of wallpaper will she need to cover a wall that measures 8 ft, 3 in.?
   4.5 strips of wallpaper; check students' explanations
7. Find the product and simplify if possible.
   $2\frac{1}{6} \times 5\frac{5}{8} =$
   $12\frac{3}{16}$

Use with Lesson 6-1. 65

Available as a transparency and as a blackline master

Topics Reviewed

1., 2., 7. Multiplying and dividing fractions and mixed numbers; **3.** Customary units of length; **4.** Factors and multiples; **5.** Estimating with fractions and mixed numbers; **6.** Writing to explain

Investigating the Concept

Find the Ratio

10–15 MIN **Social/Cooperative**

Materials *(per group)* 7 triangles, 5 squares, and 3 pentagons cut from construction paper

What to Do

- Ask groups to work together with their polygons. **A *ratio* is a comparison of two quantities. Show the ratio of triangles to squares. You can write that ratio in three ways.** Write 7:5, $\frac{7}{5}$, and 7 to 5 on the board. **The numbers 7 and 5 are called the *terms* of the ratio.**
- **Model the ratio of pentagons to squares, and write the ratio in three ways:** *(3:5, $\frac{3}{5}$, 3 to 5)*
- **Describe and write a ratio that compares a part to the whole.** *(Sample answer: The ratio of triangles to all shapes is 7:15.)*
- Have students work together to model and write other ratios.

Ongoing Assessment

- **Reasoning How can you use your shapes to model the ratio 8:7?** *(8:7 is the ratio of squares and pentagons to triangles.)*

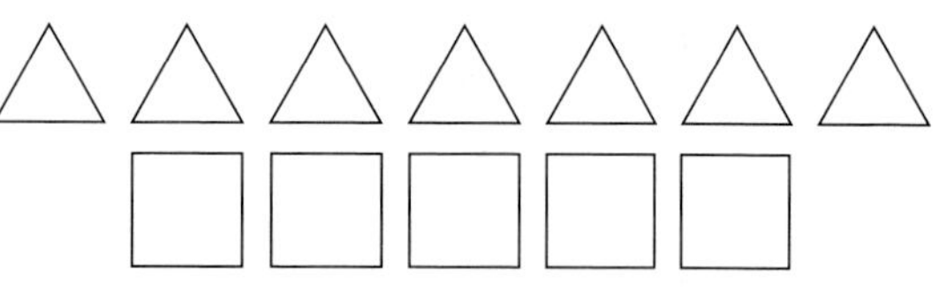

Reaching All Learners

Writing in Math

Ratios—Part-to-Part or Part-to-Whole?

 10–15 MIN **Linguistic** 

- On the board, write 3 ratios such as those shown.
- **Write a story problem for each ratio.**
- **Trade stories with your partner. Have your partner decide if each of your stories shows a part-to-part or a part-to-whole relationship.**

$\frac{7}{6}$ 2:12

8 to 5

Extend Language

English Language Learners

Ratios and Terms

 10–15 MIN **Verbal/Linguistic** 

- Have each group of students talk through creating ratios about their own group or class, such as the number of students from a specific country to the total number of students.
- Encourage students to explain how they know which number should be the first term of the ratio and which should be the second.
- Ask students to talk through defining *ratio* and *term* without looking at their books. Discuss other meanings of *term*: "a length of time, such as a school term" and "a word used in a subject, such as a science term."

Reteaching

Modeling Ratios

 10–15 MIN **Kinesthetic** 

Materials *(per group)* Counters or Teaching Tool 9

- **Use different colored counters to model the ratio of boys to girls in your group. How many boys are there?** *(Sample answer: 3 boys)* **How many girls?** *(Sample answer: 2 girls)* **What is the ratio of boys to girls?** *(Sample answer: 3:2)*
- **What is the ratio of boys to students in your group?** *(Sample answer: 3:5)*
- **What is the ratio of students to girls?** *(Sample answer: 5:2)*

 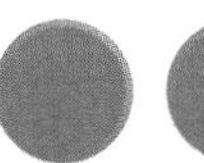 

Math and Physical Education

Fitness Ratios

 10–15 MIN **Logical/Mathematical** 

- Show students Mario's workout log for last week.
- **What is the ratio of pushups to sit-ups for Monday?** $(\frac{30}{25})$ **For Tuesday?** $(\frac{32}{20})$ **For the week?** $(\frac{131}{102})$
- Have students use the table to find other ratios.

Day	Number of Pushups	Number of Sit-Ups
Monday	30	25
Tuesday	32	20
Thursday	40	30
Friday	29	27

Objective Express comparisons as ratios in three ways.

1 Warm Up

Activate Prior Knowledge Review how to write a fraction to represent part of a whole.

2 Teach

LEARN Help students understand that a ratio is not a measure of how many items there are, but instead a comparison of two quantities.

Ongoing Assessment

Talk About It: Question 1

If students do not write the terms of the ratio in the proper order,

then have them write a ratio using words, and then write it in numbers.

$$\frac{\text{Total number of birthdays}}{\text{January birthdays}} = \frac{28}{4}$$

Answers

8. A fraction compares a part to a whole. The whole can never be zero. A ratio can compare a part to a part. A part can be zero.

Key Idea
You can compare two amounts using a ratio.

Vocabulary
• ratio

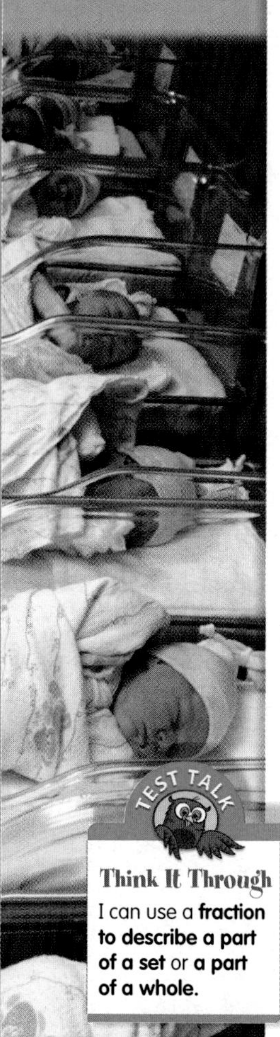

Understanding Ratios

LEARN

What is a mathematical way to compare quantities?

Ms. Aeriko surveyed her students to find out the number of students who celebrate a birthday each month.

A **ratio** is a comparison of two quantities that can be written as a to b, $a:b$, or $\frac{a}{b}$.

The quantities in the ratio are called **terms.** The first term in the ratio above is a, and the second term is b.

WARM UP

Write a fraction for each shaded portion.

1. [bar with 3 of 4 parts shaded] $\frac{3}{4}$
2. [circle with 5 of 7 parts shaded] $\frac{5}{7}$

Data File

Birthdays

Month	Number of Students
January	4
February	5
April	7
May	1
June	5
August	2
September	1
October	3

Example A

Write a ratio comparing the students with August birthdays to the students with April birthdays.

There are 2 students who have August birthdays and 7 students who have April birthdays.

The ratio is 2 to 7, 2:7, or $\frac{2}{7}$.

Example B

Write a ratio comparing the students with October birthdays to the total number of students.

There are 3 students who have October birthdays. The total number of students is $4 + 5 + 7 + 1 + 5 + 2 + 1 + 3 = 28$.

The ratio is 3 to 28, 3:28, or $\frac{3}{28}$.

TEST TALK

Think It Through
I can use a **fraction to describe a part of a set** or **a part of a whole.**

1. 28 to 4, 28:4, $\frac{28}{4}$
2. The first term is compared to the second term, so it is the first given number.

Talk About It

1. What is the ratio comparing the total number of students to students with January birthdays? **See above.**
2. How do you decide which number to give as the first term of a ratio? **See above.**
3. **Number Sense** A fraction compares a part to a whole. Which ratios in the examples compare a part to a whole? Do all ratios compare a part to a whole?
3 to 28, 3:28, $\frac{3}{28}$; No. Some ratios compare a part to a part.

300

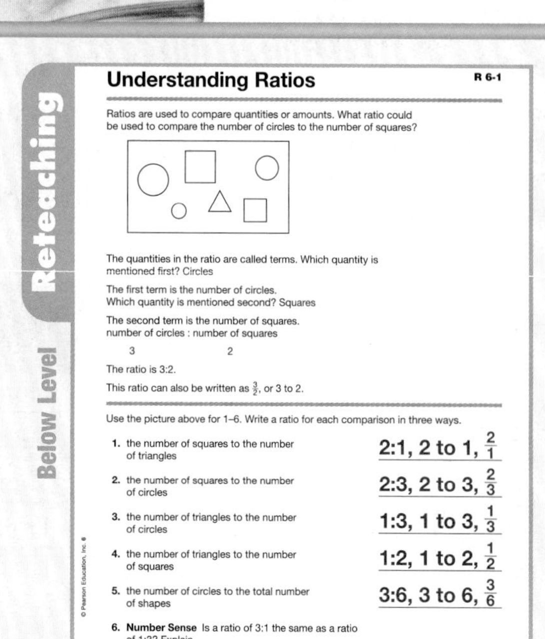

Reteaching — Below Level

Understanding Ratios
R 6-1

Ratios are used to compare quantities or amounts. What ratio could be used to compare the number of circles to the number of squares?

The quantities in the ratio are called terms. Which quantity is mentioned first? Circles

The first term is the number of circles.
Which quantity is mentioned second? Squares

The second term is the number of squares.
number of circles : number of squares

3 2

The ratio is 3:2.

This ratio can also be written as $\frac{3}{2}$, or 3 to 2.

Use the picture above for 1–6. Write a ratio for each comparison in three ways.

1. the number of squares to the number of triangles **2:1, 2 to 1, $\frac{2}{1}$**
2. the number of squares to the number of circles **2:3, 2 to 3, $\frac{2}{3}$**
3. the number of triangles to the number of circles **1:3, 1 to 3, $\frac{1}{3}$**
4. the number of triangles to the number of squares **1:2, 1 to 2, $\frac{1}{2}$**
5. the number of circles to the total number of shapes **3:6, 3 to 6, $\frac{3}{6}$**
6. **Number Sense** Is a ratio of 3:1 the same as a ratio of 1:3? Explain.
No, the terms are not in the same order.

Use with Lesson 6-1. 65

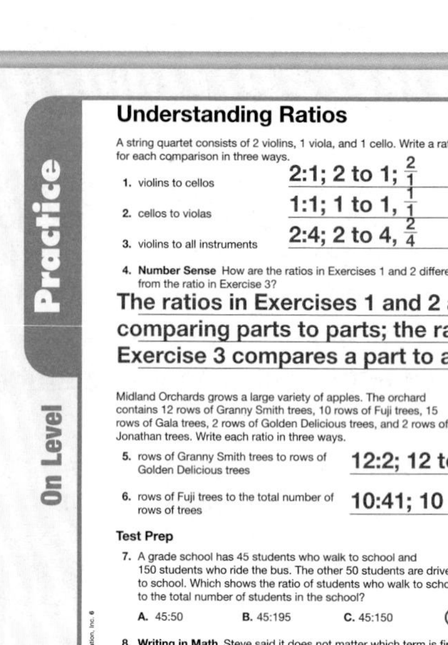

Practice — On Level

Understanding Ratios
P 6-1

A string quartet consists of 2 violins, 1 viola, and 1 cello. Write a ratio for each comparison in three ways.

1. violins to cellos **2:1; 2 to 1; $\frac{2}{1}$**
2. cellos to violas **1:1; 1 to 1, $\frac{1}{1}$**
3. violins to all instruments **2:4; 2 to 4, $\frac{2}{4}$**
4. **Number Sense** How are the ratios in Exercises 1 and 2 different from the ratio in Exercise 3?
The ratios in Exercises 1 and 2 are comparing parts to parts; the ratio in Exercise 3 compares a part to a whole.

Midland Orchards grows a large variety of apples. The orchard contains 12 rows of Granny Smith trees, 10 rows of Fuji trees, 15 rows of Gala trees, 2 rows of Golden Delicious trees, and 2 rows of Jonathan trees. Write each ratio in three ways.

5. rows of Granny Smith trees to rows of Golden Delicious trees **12:2; 12 to 2; $\frac{12}{2}$**
6. rows of Fuji trees to the total number of rows of trees **10:41; 10 to 41; $\frac{10}{41}$**

Test Prep

7. A grade school has 45 students who walk to school and 150 students who ride the bus. The other 50 students are driven to school. Which shows the ratio of students who walk to school to the total number of students in the school?

A. 45:50 B. 45:195 C. 45:150 (D.) 45:245

8. **Writing in Math** Steve said it does not matter which term is first and which term is second in a ratio, since ratios are different than fractions. Is he correct? Explain why or why not.
No; It does matter. If the terms are reversed, then a different comparison is being made.

Use with Lesson 6-1. 65

CHECK

For another example, see Set 6-1 on p. 346.

A person's blood type is denoted with the letters A, B, and O and the symbols + and −. The blood type A+ is read *A positive*. The blood type B− is read *B negative*. Write a ratio for each comparison in three different ways.

Data File

Blood Donors	
Type	Donors
A+	60
B+	25
AB+	9
O+	120
A−	27
B−	0
AB−	6
O−	12
Total	259

1. O+ donors to A+ donors **See below.**
2. AB− donors to total donors **See below.**
3. What does the ratio $\frac{120}{12}$ represent in the table? Explain.
4. **Number Sense** How are the ratios $\frac{9}{25}$ and $\frac{25}{9}$ different? Explain. **The ratio $\frac{9}{25}$ compares the number of AB^+ donors to the number of B^+ donors. The ratio $\frac{25}{9}$ compares the number of B^+ donors to the number of AB^+ donors.**

1. 120 to 60, 120:60, $\frac{120}{60}$ 2. 6 to 259, 6:259, $\frac{6}{259}$

PRACTICE

For more practice, see Set 6-1 on p. 349.

3. O^+ blood to O^- blood; 120 donors have type O^+; 12 donors have type O^-.

A Skills and Understanding

5. 6 to 2, 6:2, $\frac{6}{2}$ 6. 6 to 11, 6:11, $\frac{6}{11}$

A recipe for Vegetable Tossed Salad calls for the ingredients pictured. Write a ratio for each comparison in three different ways.

Vegetable Tossed Salad	
Ingredients:	
6 tomatoes	1 onion
2 peppers	2 cucumbers

5. tomatoes to peppers **See above right.**
6. tomatoes to all ingredients **See above right.**
7. Suppose you added 3 stalks of celery to the mix. What would be the ratio of stalks of celery to tomatoes? Stalks of celery to the total number of vegetables? **3 to 6; 3 to 14**
8. **Number Sense** Explain why the denominator of a fraction can never be zero but any term of a ratio can be zero. **See Margin.**

B Reasoning and Problem Solving

Janice is making a quilt with different colored squares—12 green, 9 rose, and 4 white. Write each ratio in three different ways. **9–12. See below.**

9. green to rose
10. white to green
11. rose to all colors
12. green to other colors
13. **Writing in Math** Give an example of a ratio that compares a part to a part and explain how it is different from a fraction. **Sample answer: 2 boys to 3 girls. This is different from a fraction because a fraction represents part of a whole.**

Mixed Review and Test Prep

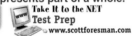

Take It to the NET Test Prep www.scottforesman.com

9. 12 to 9, 12:9, $\frac{12}{9}$ 10. 4 to 12, 4:12, $\frac{4}{12}$ 11. 9 to 25, 9:25, $\frac{9}{25}$ 12. 12 to 13, 12:13, $\frac{12}{13}$

Solve.

14. $\frac{3}{2} \times n = 12$ **$n = 8$**
15. $\frac{x}{2} = 12$ **$x = 24$**
16. $b \div 8 = 6$ **$b = 48$**
17. What is the sum $2\frac{3}{5} + 7\frac{1}{8}$ written in simplest form?

A. $9\frac{1}{20}$ B. $9\frac{1}{10}$ C. $9\frac{4}{13}$ **(D.)** $9\frac{29}{40}$

Enrichment — Above Level

Take a Picture E 6-1 VISUAL THINKING

Draw a picture to represent each of the ratios below. Your picture can show the ratio as the comparison of two parts, or as the comparison of a part to a whole. Be creative, and use a different picture for each ratio. Write a sentence that describes your picture. Here is an example.

Ratio: $\frac{6}{11}$

There are six baseballs in the group of sports equipment.

Sample answers are given.

1. 4:5 **There are 4 triangles and 5 squares.**
2. 9 to 1 **There are 9 shaded circles and 1 unshaded circle.**
3. $\frac{3}{3}$ **There are 3 stars and 3 bells.**

Use with Lesson 6-1. 65

Problem Solving

Understanding Ratios PS 6-1

School Band The list at the right shows the number of band members who play each type of instrument. The school band also has one conductor.

School Band Members	
Brass	42
Woodwinds	35
Percussion	12

1. What is the ratio of brass players to woodwind players? **42:35**
2. What is the ratio of band members to conductors? **89:1**
3. If 3 woodwind players switched to become percussion players, what would the ratio of woodwind to percussion players be? **32:15**

Fifty States There are 50 states in the United States. The states joined the United States at different times. The list at the right shows the total number of states in each given year.

Year	Number of States
1750	0
1800	16
1850	31
1900	45
1950	48
2000	50

4. What is the ratio of the number of states in 1800 to the number of states in 2000? **16:50**
5. What is the ratio of the number of states in 1900 to the number of states in 1850? **45:31**
6. What is the ratio of the number of states in 1950 to the number of states today? **48:50**
7. **Writing in Math** Sarah says the ratio of the number of states from 1900 to 2000 is 50:45. Why is she incorrect? **Sample answer: Sarah is giving the ratio in the wrong order. It should be 1900 to 2000, but she gave it as 2000 to 1900.**

Use with Lesson 6-1. 65

CHECK

Error Intervention

If students have difficulty distinguishing between part-to-whole ratios and part-to-part ratios,

then have them look back at Example A and ask if 2 and 7 were being compared as a part-to-part or a part-to-whole ratio. *(Also see* Reteaching, *p. 300B.)*

3 Practice

TEST TALK **Exercise 13** Suggest that students draw and label a diagram such as colored marbles in a bag and refer to the diagram in their explanation.

Leveled Practice

Below Level Ex. 5–17

On Level Ex. 5–17

Above Level Ex. 5–17

Early Finishers Have students use the data in the Blood Donors table at the top of page 301 and make up five problems involving ratios. Then have them exchange problems and solve.

4 Assess

Journal Idea Have students explain how to find the ratio of consonants to vowels in the word *parallelogram*.

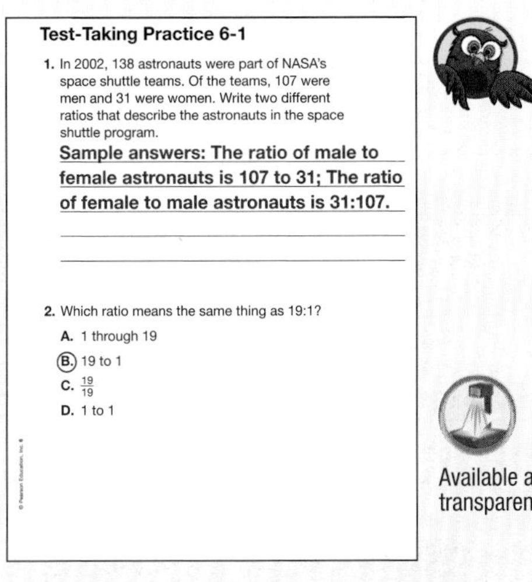

Test-Taking Practice 6-1

1. In 2002, 138 astronauts were part of NASA's space shuttle teams. Of the teams, 107 were men and 31 were women. Write two different ratios that describe the astronauts in the space shuttle program. **Sample answers: The ratio of male to female astronauts is 107 to 31; The ratio of female to male astronauts is 31:107.**
2. Which ratio means the same thing as 19:1?
   A. 1 through 19
   (B.) 19 to 1
   C. $\frac{19}{19}$
   D. 1 to 1

Available as a transparency

6-2 Equal Ratios

Lesson Organizer

Quick Lesson Overview

Objective Create equal ratios.

Math Understanding Equal ratios, like equivalent fractions, can be generated using multiplication or division.

Professional Development Note

How Children Learn Math Help students build on their knowledge of fractions by having them express, discuss, and compare their ideas about equal ratios and equivalent fractions, as well as writing ratios and fractions in simplest form. Ask students to listen to others' ideas and to put them into their own words.

NCTM Standards

- Number and Operations

(For a complete correlation to the NCTM Standards and Grades 6–8 Expectations, see pages 298G–H.)

Getting Started

Spiral Review

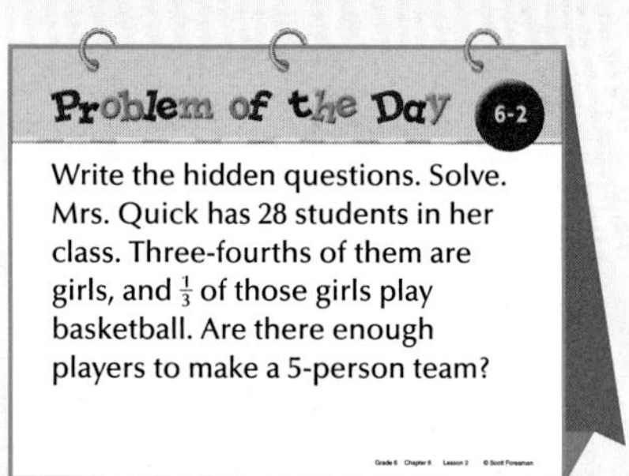

Problem of the Day 6-2

Write the hidden questions. Solve. Mrs. Quick has 28 students in her class. Three-fourths of them are girls, and $\frac{1}{3}$ of those girls play basketball. Are there enough players to make a 5-person team?

Topics Reviewed

- Multiplying whole numbers and fractions
- Problem-Solving Skill: Multiple-Step Problem

Answer Hidden Question 1: How many girls are in Mrs. Quick's class?

Hidden Question 2: How many girls play basketball?

There are enough players for a 5-person team.

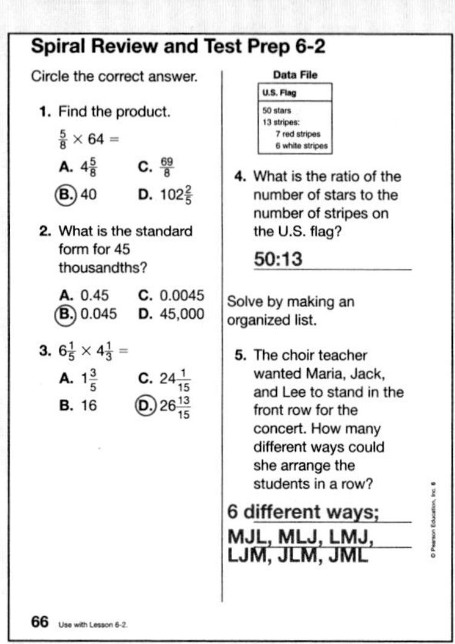

Spiral Review and Test Prep 6-2

Circle the correct answer.

1. Find the product.

$\frac{5}{8} \times 64 =$

A. $4\frac{5}{8}$ C. $\frac{69}{8}$
(B.) 40 D. $102\frac{2}{5}$

2. What is the standard form for 45 thousandths?

A. 0.45 C. 0.0045
(B.) 0.045 D. 45,000

3. $6\frac{1}{5} \times 4\frac{1}{3} =$

A. $1\frac{3}{5}$ C. $24\frac{1}{15}$
B. 16 (D.) $26\frac{13}{15}$

Data File

U.S. Flag
50 stars 13 stripes: 7 red stripes 6 white stripes

4. What is the ratio of the number of stars to the number of stripes on the U.S. flag?

50:13

Solve by making an organized list.

5. The choir teacher wanted Maria, Jack, and Lee to stand in the front row for the concert. How many different ways could she arrange the students in a row?

6 different ways; MJL, MLJ, LMJ, LJM, JLM, JML

© Pearson Education, Inc. 6

66 Use with Lesson 6-2.

Available as a transparency and as a blackline master

Topics Reviewed

1. Multiplying a fraction and a whole number; **2.** Place value; **3.** Multiplying mixed numbers; **4.** Ratios; **5.** Make an organized list

Investigating the Concept

Making a Quilt

10–15 MIN **Kinesthetic**

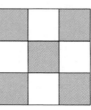

Materials *(per student)* 3-by-3 grid of squares; marker

What to Do

- Ask each group to fill in the pattern shown below with 5 blue squares and 4 white ones. **In each grid, what is the ratio of blue squares to white squares?** *($\frac{5}{4}$)* **Put two grids together. What is the ratio of blue squares to white squares?** *($\frac{10}{8}$)*
- Ask for the blue-to-white ratios for groups of three, four, and five grids. *($\frac{15}{12}$, $\frac{20}{16}$, $\frac{25}{20}$)* **The ratios $\frac{5}{4}$, $\frac{10}{8}$, $\frac{15}{12}$, $\frac{20}{16}$, and $\frac{25}{20}$ are equal ratios. How can you change the ratio $\frac{5}{4}$ to $\frac{15}{12}$?** *(Multiply both terms of $\frac{5}{4}$ by 3.)* **How can you change $\frac{20}{16}$ to $\frac{10}{8}$?** *(Divide both terms of $\frac{20}{16}$ by 2.)*

Ongoing Assessment

- **Reasoning For any number of grids, can you tell the ratio of blue squares to white squares?** *(Yes)* **What is it?** *($\frac{5}{4}$)*
- **Find a ratio equal to $\frac{2}{3}$.** *(Sample answer: $\frac{4}{6}$)*

Reaching All Learners

Math and Literature

The Yellowstone Fire

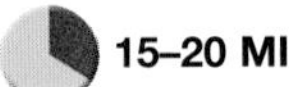 15–20 MIN **Auditory** 

Materials *Summer of Fire: Yellowstone 1988* by Patricia Lauber (Orchard Books, 1991)

- Read parts of this short (64-page) book to students and show them the photos. The text and photos describe the ecological effects of a fire.
- **The fire burned 733,333 acres of the 2,200,000 acres in the park. Estimate the ratio of acres burned to total acres.** *(Sample answer: About 7:22 or 1:3)*

YELLOWSTONE 1988
SUMMER OF FIRE
BY PATRICIA LAUBER

Activate Prior Knowledge/Build Understanding

English Language Learners

Two to One

 10–15 MIN  **Kinesthetic/Social/Cooperative** 

Materials: *(per pair)* Pennies or Teaching Tool 5; bags

- Give each pair 6 pennies and 2 bags. Direct pairs to bag their pennies so that one bag has twice as many as the other. Have students share their results and explain their thinking.
- Ask a pair to demonstrate how to do the same thing with 12 pennies. Encourage students to "think aloud" as they do their bagging. Repeat with 18 pennies.

Reteaching

Group En-Counter

 15–20 MIN **Visual/Spatial** 

Materials *(per pair)* 20 Counters or Teaching Tool 9

- **Use your counters to model the ratio $\frac{8}{4}$.**
- **Now divide each set of counters into two equal groups. Write a ratio for each new set of counters.** *($\frac{4}{2}$)*
- **Divide each new set of counters into two equal groups. Write a ratio for each of these new sets of counters.** *($\frac{2}{1}$)*
- Repeat with other ratios, such as $\frac{12}{8}$.

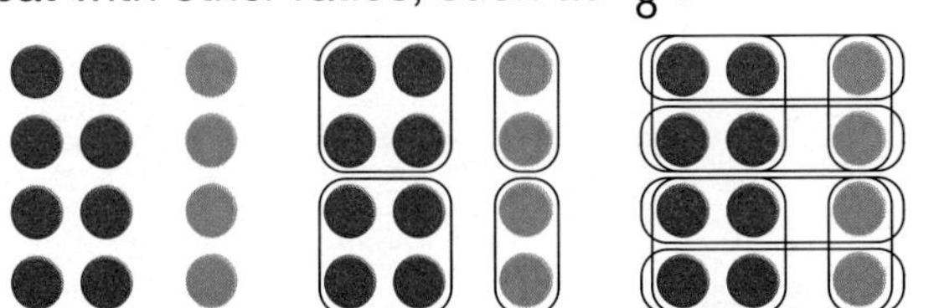

Math and Social Studies

A Game in New Guinea

 15–20 MIN **Social/Cooperative** 

- **On the island of New Guinea, children play a game with 5 balls, 4 hoops, and 1 rope.**
- **What is the ratio of balls to hoops?** *($\frac{5}{4}$)* **Find three ratios equal to that ratio.** *(Sample answer: $\frac{10}{8}$, $\frac{15}{12}$, $\frac{20}{16}$)*
- Have pairs work together to write other ratios to represent the balls, hoops, and rope. For each ratio, they should write two equal ratios.

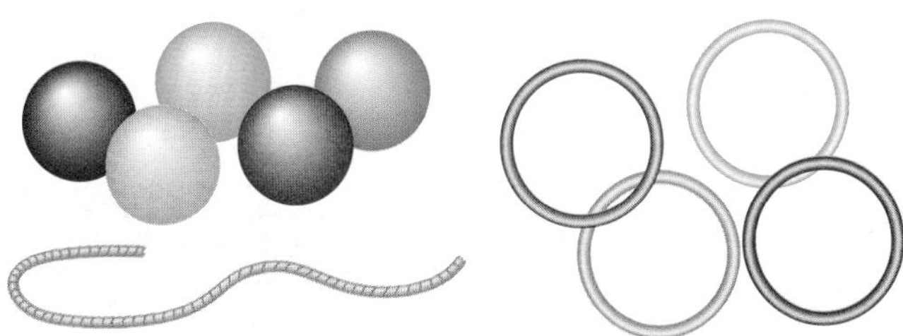

Objective Create equal ratios.

1 Warm Up

Activate Prior Knowledge Review divisibility rules for 2, 3, 4, 5, 6, 9, and 10.

2 Teach

LEARN Point out that ratios are useful for summarizing data. Finding and using equal ratios will help students describe and compare aspects of the data.

Example A Point out that when students multiply, they can select any nonzero number, but when they divide they must select a number by which both terms are divisible.

Example B Explain to students that they could have multiplied both terms of $\frac{3}{27}$ by the same nonzero number (40) and both terms of $\frac{5}{40}$ by the same nonzero number (27) to find equal ratios with the same second term. They would see that $\frac{120}{1,080}$ is not equal to $\frac{135}{1,080}$, but it would be a lot more work.

Key Idea
You can use multiplication or division to find equal ratios.

Think It Through
- I know that **multiplying and dividing by 1** does not change the amount.
- I can use **divisibility rules** to help me choose numbers that are easy to divide by.

Equal Ratios

WARM UP

Tell whether the number is divisible by 2, 3, 4, 5, 6, 9, or 10.

1. 483 3
2. 648 2, 3, 4, 6, 9
3. 108 2, 3, 4, 6, 9
4. 3,540 2, 3, 4, 5, 6, 10

LEARN

How can you find equal ratios?

In the survey, the ratio of left-handed tourists to the total number of tourists is $\frac{24}{60}$.

Sometimes you need to find ratios that are equal to a known ratio. You can create equal ratios by multiplying and dividing both terms of the ratio by the same nonzero amount.

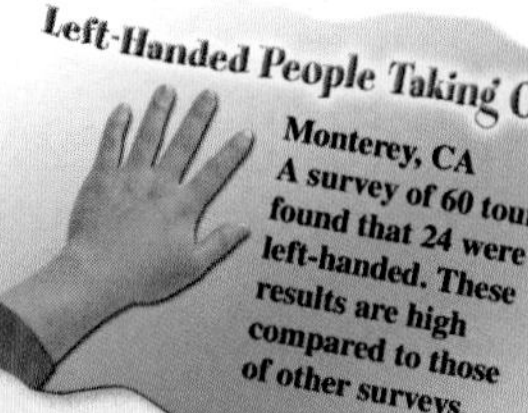

Left-Handed People Taking Over!
Monterey, CA
A survey of 60 tourists found that 24 were left-handed. These results are high compared to those of other surveys.

Example A

Find three ratios that are equal to $\frac{24}{60}$.

One Way	*Another Way*
Use multiplication.	Use division.
Multiply both terms by the same nonzero number.	Divide both terms by the same nonzero number.
$\frac{24 \times 2}{60 \times 2} = \frac{48}{120}$	$\frac{24 \div 12}{60 \div 12} = \frac{2}{5}$
$\frac{24 \times 3}{60 \times 3} = \frac{72}{180}$	$\frac{24 \div 6}{60 \div 6} = \frac{4}{10}$
$\frac{24 \times 4}{60 \times 4} = \frac{96}{240}$	$\frac{24 \div 4}{60 \div 4} = \frac{6}{15}$

So, $\frac{2}{5}$, $\frac{4}{10}$, $\frac{6}{15}$, $\frac{24}{60}$, $\frac{48}{120}$, $\frac{72}{180}$, and $\frac{96}{240}$ are all equal ratios.

Example B

Decide whether the ratios $\frac{3}{27}$ and $\frac{5}{40}$ are equal.

Divide by the GCF of 3 and 27.

$$\frac{3}{27} = \frac{3 \div 3}{27 \div 3} = \frac{1}{9}$$

Divide by the GCF of 5 and 40.

$$\frac{5}{40} = \frac{5 \div 5}{40 \div 5} = \frac{1}{8}$$

Since $\frac{1}{9} \neq \frac{1}{8}$, $\frac{3}{27}$ is not equal to $\frac{5}{40}$.

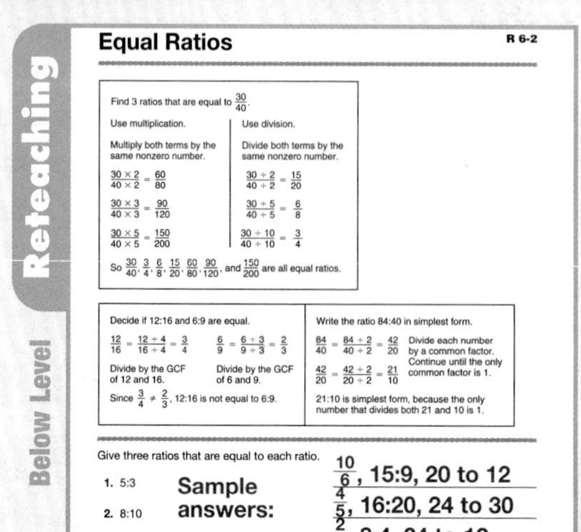

Reteaching — Below Level

Equal Ratios R 6-2

Find 3 ratios that are equal to $\frac{30}{40}$.

Use multiplication.	Use division.
Multiply both terms by the same nonzero number.	Divide both terms by the same nonzero number.
$\frac{30 \times 2}{40 \times 2} = \frac{60}{80}$	$\frac{30 \div 2}{40 \div 2} = \frac{15}{20}$
$\frac{30 \times 3}{40 \times 3} = \frac{90}{120}$	$\frac{30 \div 5}{40 \div 5} = \frac{6}{8}$
$\frac{30 \times 5}{40 \times 5} = \frac{150}{200}$	$\frac{30 \div 10}{40 \div 10} = \frac{3}{4}$

So $\frac{30}{40}$, $\frac{3}{4}$, $\frac{6}{8}$, $\frac{15}{20}$, $\frac{60}{80}$, $\frac{90}{120}$, and $\frac{150}{200}$ are all equal ratios.

Decide if 12:16 and 6:9 are equal.

$\frac{12}{16} = \frac{12 \div 4}{16 \div 4} = \frac{3}{4}$ Divide by the GCF of 12 and 16.

$\frac{6}{9} = \frac{6 \div 3}{9 \div 3} = \frac{2}{3}$ Divide by the GCF of 6 and 9.

Since $\frac{3}{4} \neq \frac{2}{3}$, 12:16 is not equal to 6:9.

Write the ratio 84:40 in simplest form.

$\frac{84}{40} = \frac{84 \div 2}{40 \div 2} = \frac{42}{20}$

$\frac{42}{20} = \frac{42 \div 2}{20 \div 2} = \frac{21}{10}$

Divide each number by a common factor. Continue until the only common factor is 1.

21:10 is simplest form, because the only number that divides both 21 and 10 is 1.

Give three ratios that are equal to each ratio. Sample answers:

1. 5:3 $\frac{10}{6}$, 15:9, 20 to 12
2. 8:10 $\frac{4}{5}$, 16:20, 24 to 30
3. $\frac{4}{2}$ $\frac{2}{1}$, 8:4, 24 to 12

Tell whether the ratios in each pair are equal.

4. $\frac{5}{6}$ and $\frac{25}{30}$ Yes
5. 9:5 and 5 to 9 No
6. **Number Sense** Dale says that the ratios 3:5 and 2:10 are equal. Is he correct? Explain.
   No, 2:10 is the same as $\frac{1}{5}$, and $\frac{1}{5}$ is not equal to $\frac{3}{5}$.

66 Use with Lesson 6-2.

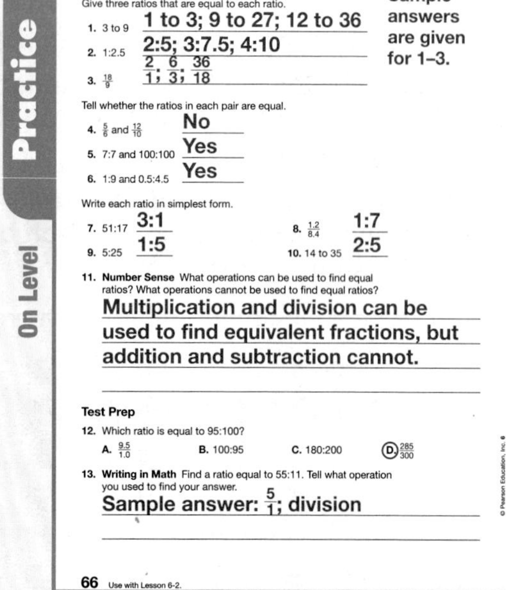

Practice — On Level

Equal Ratios P 6-2

Give three ratios that are equal to each ratio. Sample answers are given for 1–3.

1. 3 to 9 1 to 3; 9 to 27; 12 to 36
2. 1:2.5 2:5; 3:7.5; 4:10
3. $\frac{18}{9}$ $\frac{2}{1}$; $\frac{6}{3}$; $\frac{36}{18}$

Tell whether the ratios in each pair are equal.

4. $\frac{5}{6}$ and $\frac{12}{10}$ No
5. 7:7 and 100:100 Yes
6. 1:9 and 0.5:4.5 Yes

Write each ratio in simplest form.

7. 51:17 3:1
8. $\frac{1.2}{8.4}$ 1:7
9. 5:25 1:5
10. 14 to 35 2:5
11. **Number Sense** What operations can be used to find equal ratios? What operations cannot be used to find equal ratios?
    Multiplication and division can be used to find equivalent fractions, but addition and subtraction cannot.

Test Prep

12. Which ratio is equal to 95:100?
    A. $\frac{9.5}{1.0}$ B. 100:95 C. 180:200 (D.) $\frac{285}{300}$
13. **Writing in Math** Find a ratio equal to 55:11. Tell what operation you used to find your answer.
    Sample answer: $\frac{5}{1}$; division

66 Use with Lesson 6-2.

Example C

For any class field trip, a school requires every 10 students to have one chaperone. Do all the ratios in the table equal 10:1?

Number of Students	30	50	80	100
Number of Chaperones	3	5	8	10

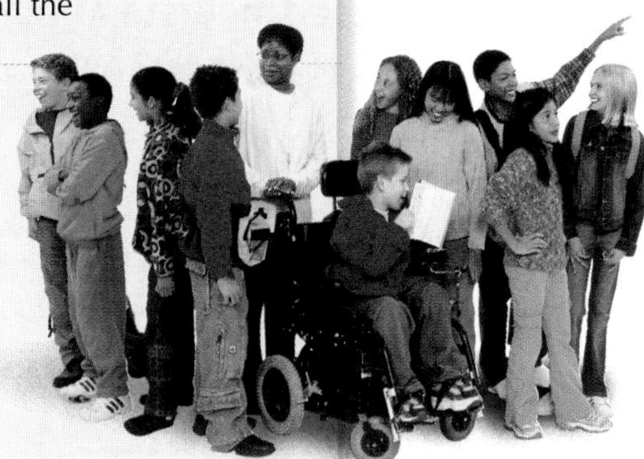

10:1 = 10 ÷ 1 = 10

30:3 = 30 ÷ 3 = 10

50:5 = 50 ÷ 5 = 10

80:8 = 80 ÷ 8 = 10

100:10 = 100 ÷ 10 = 10

Because the quotients are the same, the ratios are equal.

Example D

Write the ratio 96:60 in simplest form.

$\frac{96}{60} = \frac{96 \div 3}{60 \div 3} = \frac{32}{20}$ This is not in simplest form because both 32 and 20 have 4 as a factor.

$\frac{32}{20} = \frac{32 \div 4}{20 \div 4} = \frac{8}{5}$

8:5 is in simplest form because the only number that divides both 8 and 5 is 1.

Think It Through
I can **use the GCF** of 96 and 60.
$\frac{96}{60} = \frac{96 \div 12}{60 \div 12} = \frac{8}{5}$

Talk About It

1. Which ratio in Example C is in simplest form? Explain how you know. **10:1; Since the GCF of 10 and 1 is 1, the ratio is in simplest form.**
2. Are the ratios 5:2 and 35:14 equal? Tell how you decided. **Yes. Written in simplest form, 35:14 is 5:2. So the ratios are equal.**
3. Can you find an equal ratio by adding the same nonzero amount to each term in the ratio? Why or why not? **See above.**

3. No. Adding the same nonzero amount to each term will change the value of the ratio. Multiplying or dividing each term by the same nonzero number will give an equal ratio without changing the ratio's value.

Take It to the NET
More Examples
www.scottforesman.com

CHECK

For another example, see Set 6-2 on p. 346.

Give three ratios that are equal to each ratio.

1. $\frac{4}{9}$ **$\frac{8}{18}$, $\frac{12}{27}$, $\frac{16}{36}$**
2. 8 to 5 **16:10, 24 to 15, 32:20**
3. 6:10 **$\frac{3}{5}$, $\frac{12}{20}$, $\frac{18}{30}$**
4. $\frac{8}{3}$ **16:6, 24 to 9, 32 to 12**
5. $\frac{12}{60}$ **$\frac{1}{5}$, $\frac{2}{10}$, $\frac{4}{20}$**

Tell whether the ratios in each pair are equal.

6. $\frac{20}{12}$ and $\frac{15}{9}$ **Yes**
7. 3 to 5 and 12 to 15 **No**
8. $\frac{24}{3}$ and $\frac{16}{3}$ **No**
9. Write the ratio 52 to 4 in simplest form. **13 to 1**
10. **Number Sense** Are the ratios 5 to 1 and 6 to 1 equal? Explain. **See above.**

10. No. You cannot multiply 5 by any whole number to get 6.

Example C Students may suggest other ideas for solving this example, such as multiplying both terms of 10:1 by 3 to get 30:3, and so on. Encourage their suggestions.

Ongoing Assessment

Talk About It: Question 1

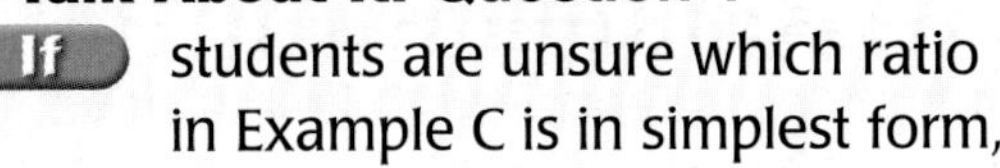

If students are unsure which ratio in Example C is in simplest form,

then have them reread Example D, discussing simplest form. Ask them to identify the GCF for each ratio in Example C.

CHECK

Error Intervention

If students do not multiply or divide both terms by the same number when finding equal ratios,

then use examples such as $\frac{1}{2} \neq \frac{2}{6}$ to show that multiplying the first and second terms by different numbers does *not* give an equal ratio. *(Also see* Reteaching, *p. 302B.)*

Enrichment — Above Level

What's My Rule?

E 6-2 PATTERNS

Determine the pattern in each set of equal ratios. Write the next three ratios for each set. Write the rule.

1. 3:6, 6:12, 12:24, **24:48**, **48:96**, **96:192**
   Multiply both numbers by 2.
2. $\frac{4,000}{2,400}$, $\frac{2,000}{1,200}$, $\frac{1,000}{600}$, **$\frac{500}{300}$**, **$\frac{250}{150}$**, **$\frac{125}{75}$**
   Divide both numbers by 2.
3. 5:3, 15:9, 45:27, **135:81**, **405:243**, **1,215:729**
   Multiply both numbers by 3.
4. 6 to 2, 30 to 10, 150 to 50, **750 to 250**, **3,750 to 1,250**, **18,750 to 6,250**
   Multiply both numbers by 5.
5. 200:160, 100:80, 50:40, **25:20**, **$12\frac{1}{2}$:10**, **$6\frac{1}{4}$:5**
   Divide both numbers by 2.
6. $\frac{5}{1}$, $\frac{20}{4}$, $\frac{80}{16}$, **320:64**, **1,280:256**, **5,120:1,024**
   Multiply both numbers by 4.
7. 2,500 to 3,125, 500 to 625, 100 to 125, **20 to 25**, **4 to 5**, **$\frac{4}{5}$ to 1**
   Divide both numbers by 5.

Problem Solving

Equal Ratios

PS 6-2

School Buses Jefferson Elementary has 1 school bus for every 45 students who ride the bus. Every year the school principal checks the number of bus riders to make sure there are enough buses.

1. In 2000, 315 students at Jefferson Elementary rode the bus. How many buses were required? **7 buses**
2. In 2001, only 225 students at Jefferson Elementary rode the bus. How many buses were required in 2001? **5 buses**
3. In 2002, the number of students who rode the bus increased to 360. How many buses were required? **8 buses**

Amusement Park An amusement park has 20 entrance booths. The number of booths that are open depends on the number of people coming into the amusement park. The manager knows that the ratio is 1 booth for every 300 people who enter in an hour.

4. The manager has predicted that 2,100 people will arrive at the entrance each hour on a Saturday. How many entrance booths should the manager open? **7 booths**
5. If the weather suddenly turns rainy, and only 1,200 people arrive at the amusement park each hour, how many entrance booths should the manager open? **4 booths**
6. On a holiday weekend, the manager expects 4,200 people to arrive at the amusement park each hour. How many admission booths should the manager plan to open? **14 booths**
7. **Writing in Math** Explain how you can use mental math to decide if 3:9 and 6:18 are equivalent ratios.
   Sample answer: I know that 6 is twice 3, and 18 is twice 9, so I can see that these are equivalent ratios.

3 Practice

Exercises 19–22 Point out that one or both terms of a ratio can be a decimal. In this way, a ratio is different from a fraction.

Exercise 34 Suggest students multiply both terms by 10 first to have whole numbers, and then simplify.

TEST TALK **Exercise 39** Students' answers should include both a general rule and the specific case, such as: *You can compare ratios if they have the same first terms, so 30:128 and 30:108 are not equal ratios.*

Reading Assist Vocabulary Use drawings or manipulatives to help students understand the meaning of *ratio, terms,* and *equal ratios.* Have students compare ratios in part-to-part and part-to-whole situations.

PRACTICE For more practice, see Set 6-2 on p. 349.

A Skills and Understanding

Give three ratios that are equal to each ratio. **Sample answers are given.**

11. $\frac{5}{6}$ **11.–16. See below.** **12.** 8 to 3 **13.** 7:8 **14.** $\frac{8}{6}$ **15.** 7 to 10 **16.** $\frac{20}{10}$

17. 12:36 **1:3, 6:18, 3:9** **18.** $\frac{42}{28}$ **$\frac{3}{2}, \frac{6}{4}, \frac{21}{14}$** **19.** 0.5 to 2 **1 to 4, 2 to 8, 3 to 12** **20.** 1:0.25 **4:1, 8:2, 100:25** **21.** $\frac{1.2}{3.6}$ **$\frac{1}{3}, \frac{2}{6}, \frac{12}{36}$** **22.** 4.5 to 9 **1 to 2, 2 to 4, 9 to 18**

Tell whether the ratios in each pair are equal.

23. $\frac{18}{36}$ and $\frac{3}{6}$ **Yes** **24.** 5 to 7 and 7 to 9 **No** **25.** 6:4 and 30:20 **Yes** **26.** $\frac{9}{32}$ and $\frac{3}{8}$ **No**

27. $\frac{30}{75}$ and $\frac{4}{10}$ **Yes** **28.** 14 to 7 and 12 to 5 **No** **29.** 45:54 and 60:72 **Yes** **30.** $\frac{15}{24}$ and $\frac{7}{12}$ **No**

Write each ratio in simplest form.

31. $\frac{75}{15}$ **$\frac{5}{1}$** **32.** 42 to 21 **2 to 1** **33.** 15:87 **5:29** **34.** $\frac{4.5}{90}$ **$\frac{1}{20}$**

35. Number Sense Are the ratios $\frac{12}{3}$ and 24:3 equal? How can you tell by just looking at them? **No. There is no nonzero number by which you can multiply both terms of the ratio 12:3 to get 24:3.**

B Reasoning and Problem Solving

Math and Science

The Data File shows bone counts for an adult human.

36. Express the number of bones in the skull to the total number of bones as a ratio. **22 to 206**

37. Find the ratio of the number of bones in the arms to the number of bones in the ears. Give two ratios that are equal to this ratio. **60 to 6; 10 to 1, 20 to 2**

38. The ratio of the number of bones in the hip to the number of bones in the sternum is 2:3. Is there another ratio in the table that is 2:3? **Yes, pectoral girdle bones to bones of the ear**

39. **Writing in Math** Is the explanation below correct? Explain. **Yes. $\frac{5 \times 6}{18 \times 6} = \frac{30}{108}$, not $\frac{30}{128}$.**

Are the ratios 5:18 and 30:128 equal?

I made a table of ratios equal to 5:18. When I got to 30:108, I stopped, because 30:108 is not equal to 30:128. The ratios are not equal.

	x2	x3	x4	x5	x6
5	10	15	20	25	30
18	36	54	72	90	108

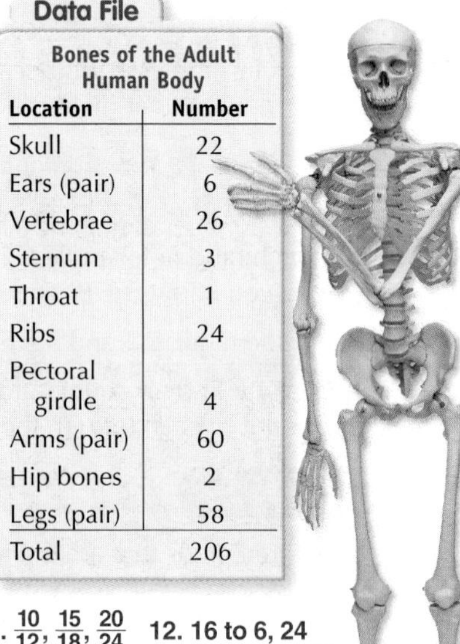

Data File

Bones of the Adult Human Body

Location	Number
Skull	22
Ears (pair)	6
Vertebrae	26
Sternum	3
Throat	1
Ribs	24
Pectoral girdle	4
Arms (pair)	60
Hip bones	2
Legs (pair)	58
Total	206

11. $\frac{10}{12}, \frac{15}{18}, \frac{20}{24}$ **12.** 16 to 6, 24 to 9, 32 to 12

13. 14:16, 21:24, 28:32 **14.** $\frac{4}{3}, \frac{12}{9}, \frac{16}{12}$

15. 14 to 20, 21 to 30, 28 to 40 **16.** $\frac{2}{1}, \frac{4}{2}, \frac{10}{5}$

304

Test-Taking Practice

Test-Taking Practice, Item 1, p. 305
There are four parts to the problem; each ratio is worth one point and the correct format is worth one point for a total of four points. Remind students that they should answer as much as they can since partial credit is given for this type of problem.

Discuss the sample responses shown and compare them to papers produced by your students.

4-point answer Ratios are correct and written properly; shows complete understanding of equal ratios.

$\frac{6}{14}$, 30:70, 15:35

PRACTICE

C Extensions

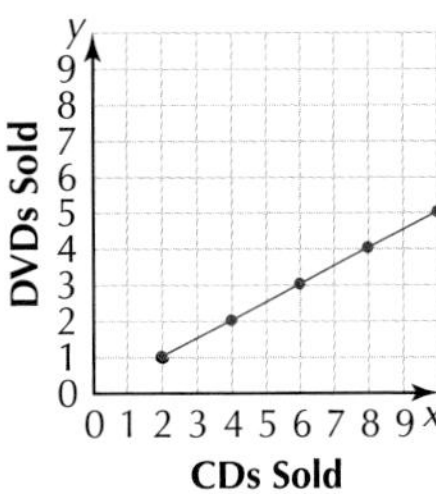

40. Algebra Copy the grid at the right. Then graph the ratios from the table and connect the points. The first ratio has been graphed for you. Describe any patterns you notice. **Sample answer: For each DVD sold, there were 2 CDs sold.**

Data File

Number of CDs Sold	2	4	6	8	10
Number of DVDs Sold	1	2	3	4	5

Mixed Review and Test Prep

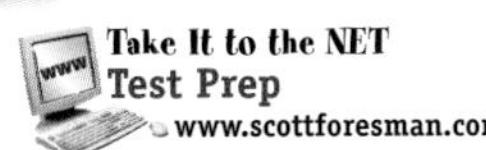

41. Six buses took 425 students to a state capital. Four adults were on each bus. What was the ratio of adults to students? **24 to 425**

42. Algebra Which shows 29,345 written in scientific notation?

A. 2.9345×10^3 **(B.)** 2.9345×10^4 **C.** 29.354×10^3 **D.** 29.345×10^4

Enrichment

The Golden Ratio

The ancient Greeks believed that rectangles with a length to width ratio of approximately $\frac{1.618}{1}$ were most pleasing to the eye. They called this ratio the *Golden Ratio* and used it to design the Parthenon.

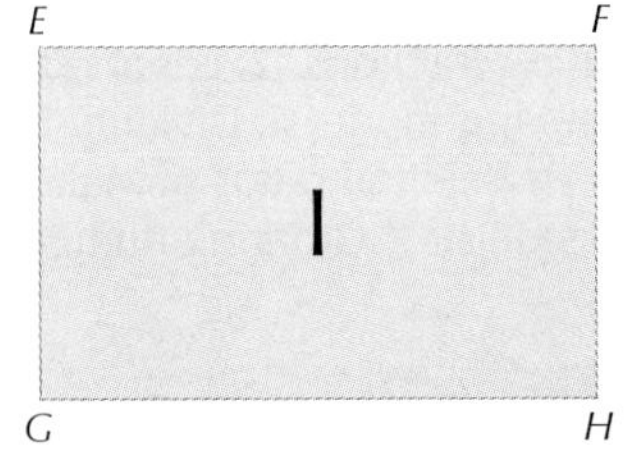

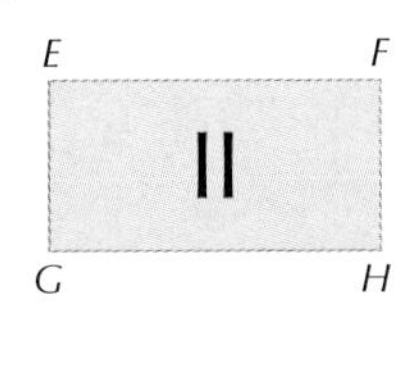

1. Which rectangle above appeals most to you?
Answers will be either Rectangle I or Rectangle II
2. Measure the sides of rectangles I and II to the nearest millimeter and then express the ratio $\frac{EF}{EG}$ for each rectangle as a decimal. Which rectangle has a length to width ratio closest to the *Golden Ratio*? Was this the rectangle you chose as most appealing? **Rectangle I: $\frac{50}{31}$; Rectangle II: $\frac{30}{15}$; Rectangle I; Answers will vary**

3-point answer One ratio is incorrect; answer shows understanding of equal ratios.

6:10, 30:70, 15:35

3-point answer All ratios are correct; written in incorrect format; shows understanding of equal ratios.

6, 14
30, 70
15, 35

Leveled Practice

Below Level Ex. 11–18, 23–26, 31–36, 39, 41, 42

On Level Ex. 15–28, 31–39 odd, 41, 42

Above Level Ex. 18–22, 27–42

Early Finishers Have students write a ratio that compares numbers of their family members, for example, sisters to siblings, and then write three ratios that are equal to that ratio.

Enrichment Have students begin by comparing the two rectangles and describing why they prefer the one they find more appealing. See if they can find any objects in the classroom that have a length-to-width ratio close to the Golden Ratio.

4 Assess

Journal Idea Have students explain how to use both multiplication and division to find ratios that are equal to $\frac{10}{12}$.

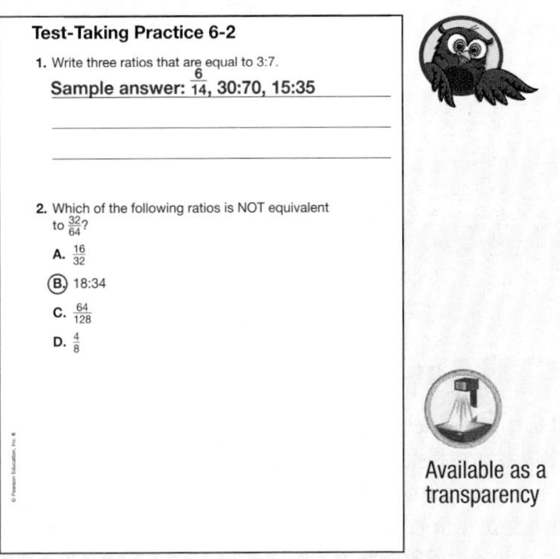

Test-Taking Practice 6-2

1. Write three ratios that are equal to 3:7.
Sample answer: $\frac{6}{14}$, 30:70, 15:35

2. Which of the following ratios is NOT equivalent to $\frac{32}{64}$?
A. $\frac{16}{32}$
(B) 18:34
C. $\frac{64}{128}$
D. $\frac{4}{8}$

Available as a transparency

Lesson Organizer

Quick Lesson Overview

Objective Find the unit rate for a given rate, and use rates to identify the better buy or the lower rate.

Math Understanding Rates are a special type of ratio where unlike quantities are compared. A unit rate has 1 for its second term.

Vocabulary Rate, unit rate

Professional Development Note

Managing Instruction Encourage students to go food shopping with their parents and look at the unit rate pricing for some of their favorite foods. Have them discuss how this helps shoppers decide what is a good buy. Ask them to report their findings to the class.

NCTM Standards

- Number and Operations
- Measurement

(For a complete correlation to the NCTM Standards and Grades 6–8 Expectations, see pages 298G–H.)

Getting Started

Spiral Review

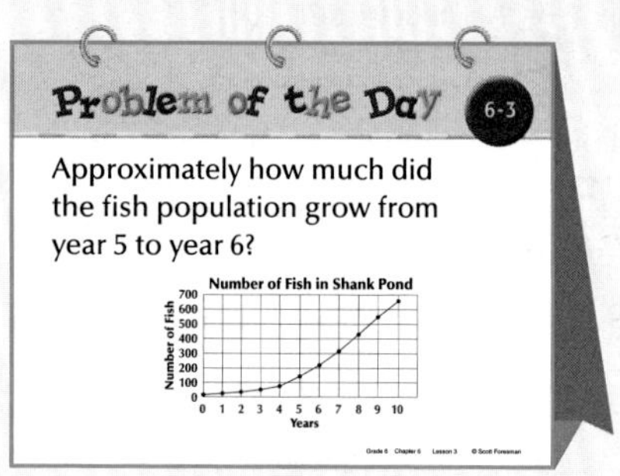

Problem of the Day 6-3

Approximately how much did the fish population grow from year 5 to year 6?

Topics Reviewed

- Reading line graphs; estimation
- Problem-Solving Skill: One-Step Problem

Answer Sample: Approximately 70 fish

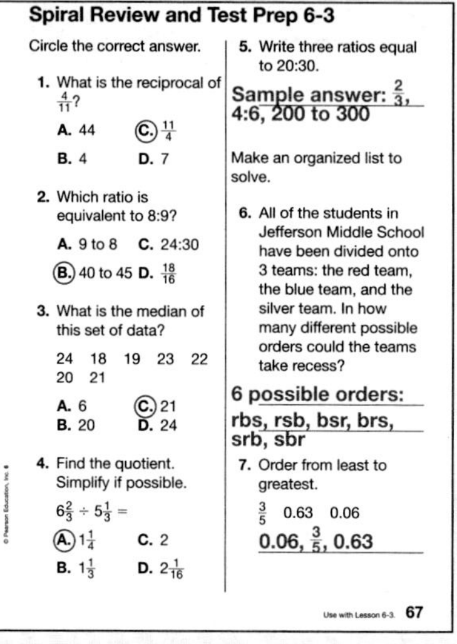

Spiral Review and Test Prep 6-3

Circle the correct answer.

1. What is the reciprocal of $\frac{4}{11}$?
   A. 44   (C.) $\frac{11}{4}$
   B. 4   D. 7
2. Which ratio is equivalent to 8:9?
   A. 9 to 8   C. 24:30
   (B.) 40 to 45   D. $\frac{18}{16}$
3. What is the median of this set of data?
   24 18 19 23 22 20 21
   A. 6   (C.) 21
   B. 20   D. 24
4. Find the quotient. Simplify if possible.
   $6\frac{2}{3} \div 5\frac{1}{3} =$
   (A.) $1\frac{1}{4}$ C. 2
   B. $1\frac{1}{3}$ D. $2\frac{1}{16}$
5. Write three ratios equal to 20:30.
   Sample answer: $\frac{2}{3}$, 4:6, 200 to 300

Make an organized list to solve.

6. All of the students in Jefferson Middle School have been divided onto 3 teams: the red team, the blue team, and the silver team. In how many different possible orders could the teams take recess?
   6 possible orders: rbs, rsb, bsr, brs, srb, sbr
7. Order from least to greatest.
   $\frac{3}{5}$ 0.63 0.06
   0.06, $\frac{3}{5}$, 0.63

Use with Lesson 6-3. 67

Available as a transparency and as a blackline master

Topics Reviewed

1. Dividing fractions; **2.** Equal ratios; **3.** Mean, median, and mode; **4.** Dividing mixed numbers; **5.** Equal ratios **6.** Make an organized list; **7.** Ordering numbers

Investigating the Concept

Counters per Person

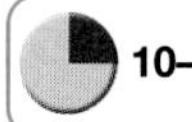

10–15 MIN   **Visual/Spatial**

Materials *(per group)* Counters or Teaching Tool 9

What to Do

- Ask each group of 4 students to write the ratio of counters to students. *(20:4)* **A *rate* compares different kinds of measurements. In this case, it is comparing 20 counters to 4 students.** Have students distribute their counters equally to group members. **Now, what is the rate of counters to 1 student?** *(5:1)* **When the second term in a rate is 1, the rate is called a *unit rate*. What is the unit rate of counters to students?** *(5:1)*
- **Suppose 3 students have 12 counters. What is the rate of counters to students?** *(12:3)* **What is the unit rate?** *(4:1)*
- **Is it easier to compare the rates 8:2 and 15:3 or to compare the rates 4:1 and 5:1?** *(4:1 and 5:1)* **Why are unit rates easier to compare?** *(Sample answer: When the second term of each rate is 1, you can compare the first terms of each rate.)*

Ongoing Assessment

- **Number Sense If you have a rate of 16 counters to 8 students, how can you find the unit rate?** *(Divide both terms by 8.)*

Reaching All Learners

Math Vocabulary

Pick a Term

 5–10 MIN **Auditory** 

- Write on the board:

  ratio rate unit rate

- Read each sentence and have students choose the term that best completes the sentence.

A _____ always has a second term that is 1. *(Unit rate)*

The _____ of girls to boys is 3:2. *(Ratio)*

A _____ always includes units of measure. *(Rate)*

The _____ for the cereal is 54¢ per 1 ounce. *(Unit rate)*

The _____ Cindy runs is 4 miles in 30 minutes. *(Rate)*

Activate Prior Knowledge/Build Background

English Language Learners

What's in Store?

 10–15 MIN **Visual/Spatial/Verbal** 

Materials *(per group)* Empty food packages

- Ask students to tell about their experiences shopping for food.
- Display the packages. Help students identify how much or how many each contains.
- Have students assign prices to the packages. For each one, ask: **Does the price seem reasonable? Why or why not?**
- Ask which foods students would buy, and why.

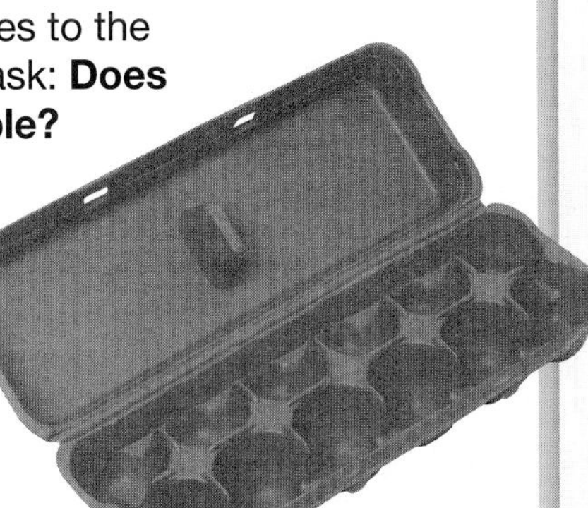

Reteaching

Bounce the Ball

 15–20 MIN **Kinesthetic** 

Materials *(per group)* Timer or watch with second hand; small rubber or tennis ball

- Have Student 1 bounce a ball for 30 seconds. Have Student 2 time the 30 seconds. Others in the group count the bounces in the 30 seconds.
- Repeat until each student in the group has an opportunity to bounce the ball.
- **The comparison of the number of bounces to 30 seconds is a rate. How could you calculate the number of bounces in 1 second?** *(Divide both terms by 30.)*
  The number of bounces per 1 second is called a *unit rate.*
- Have each student find his or her unit rate.

Advanced Learners

Breakfast Bargains

 10–15 MIN **Social/Cooperative** 

- Copy the information below on the board.
- **How can you decide which box of cereal is the best buy?** *(Find the unit price for each kind.)* **Find the unit prices.** *($0.30/oz, $0.32/oz, $0.28/oz, $3.52/lb)*
- **How can you compare all four?** *(Change so that all are rates per ounce.)*
- **What is the price per ounce for the last box?** *($0.22)* **Which is the best buy?** *(The cereal that costs $7.04 for 2 pounds)*

$4.50 for 15 ounces

$5.60 for 17.5 ounces

$4.48 for 16 ounces

$7.04 for 2 pounds

Objective Find the unit rate for a given rate, and use rates to identify the better buy or the lower rate.

1 Warm Up

Activate Prior Knowledge Review how to compare ratios.

2 Teach

LEARN Ask students to think how the ratio $\frac{\$1.25}{20\text{ oz}}$ and $\frac{9}{5}$ are alike and how they are different. Help them see that both compare two quantities. The difference is that the first one compares dollars to ounces, while the second one compares two numbers that have the same unit.

Example A Have students explain how the rate of 4 gallons per minute is calculated in the *One Way* and *Another Way* methods.

Example B Before they study the solution to this example, ask students how they would compare Willie's and Ben's rates.

Lesson 6-3

Key Idea
A rate is a special kind of ratio.

Vocabulary
- rate
- unit rate

TEST TALK

Think It Through
I can **use logical reasoning** to compare rates.

Rates and Unit Rates

WARM UP

Tell whether the ratios in each pair are equal.

1. $\frac{23}{24}$; 99:100 **No**
2. $\frac{5}{15}$; $\frac{7}{21}$ **Yes**
3. 9:5; $\frac{81}{45}$ **Yes**

LEARN

Activity

Can you compare ratios?

a. One ratio for the orange juice is $\frac{\$1.25}{20\text{ oz}}$. The first term is expressed in dollars. What unit of measure is used to express the second term? Write a ratio for the larger bottle of orange juice that includes units of measure. **ounces; $125 to 24 oz.**

b. Compare the two orange juice ratios. Are they equal? Is there a way to decide which ratio is greater? **No; Since they have the same first terms, the ratio with the smaller second term is greater.**

c. Write and compare the two cereal ratios. Then, write and compare the two ratios for the rolls. **$1.75 to 20 oz and $1.95 to 20 oz; $1.80 to 6 rolls and $2.50 to 10 rolls**

d. For which pair of items was it easiest to compare? For which pair was it hardest to compare? Explain. **Sample answer: It was easier to compare the cereal because the one with the larger first term is the larger ratio.; For the roll ratios, no terms are equal.**

Are there special kinds of ratios?

A **rate** is a ratio that compares two quantities with different units of measure. A common rate you already know is miles per hour. Some other examples of rates are shown at the right.

If the comparison is to 1 unit, the rate is called a **unit rate.** All of the common rates at the right are unit rates. Notice that 22 miles per gallon, $1.50 per pound, and 72 heartbeats per minute could also be given as 22 miles per 1 gallon, $1.50 per 1 pound, and 72 heartbeats per 1 minute.

Data File

Some Common Rates
- 22 miles per gallon
- 3 cups of water to 1 can of lemonade mix
- $1.50 per pound
- 72 heartbeats per minute

306

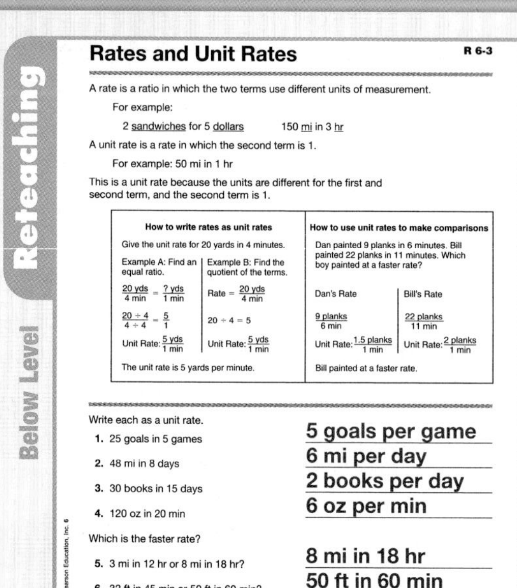

Reteaching — Below Level

Rates and Unit Rates

R 6-3

A rate is a ratio in which the two terms use different units of measurement.

For example:

2 sandwiches for 5 dollars   150 mi in 3 hr

A unit rate is a rate in which the second term is 1.

For example: 50 mi in 1 hr

This is a unit rate because the units are different for the first and second term, and the second term is 1.

How to write rates as unit rates		How to use unit rates to make comparisons	
Give the unit rate for 20 yards in 4 minutes.		Dan painted 9 planks in 6 minutes. Bill painted 22 planks in 11 minutes. Which boy painted at a faster rate?	
Example A: Find an equal ratio.	Example B: Find the quotient of the terms.	Dan's Rate	Bill's Rate
$\frac{20\text{ yds}}{4\text{ min}} = \frac{?\text{ yds}}{1\text{ min}}$	Rate = $\frac{20\text{ yds}}{4\text{ min}}$	$\frac{9\text{ planks}}{6\text{ min}}$	$\frac{22\text{ planks}}{11\text{ min}}$
$\frac{20 \div 4}{4 \div 4} = \frac{5}{1}$	$20 \div 4 = 5$	Unit Rate: $\frac{1.5\text{ planks}}{1\text{ min}}$	Unit Rate: $\frac{2\text{ planks}}{1\text{ min}}$
Unit Rate: $\frac{5\text{ yds}}{1\text{ min}}$	Unit Rate: $\frac{5\text{ yds}}{1\text{ min}}$		
The unit rate is 5 yards per minute.		Bill painted at a faster rate.	

Write each as a unit rate.

1. 25 goals in 5 games **5 goals per game**
2. 48 mi in 8 days **6 mi per day**
3. 30 books in 15 days **2 books per day**
4. 120 oz in 20 min **6 oz per min**

Which is the faster rate?

5. 3 mi in 12 hr or 8 mi in 18 hr? **8 mi in 18 hr**
6. 32 ft in 45 min or 50 ft in 60 min? **50 ft in 60 min**
7. **Number Sense** If a car goes 350 mi in 5 hr, what is its rate per hour? **70 mi per hour**

Use with Lesson 6-3. 67

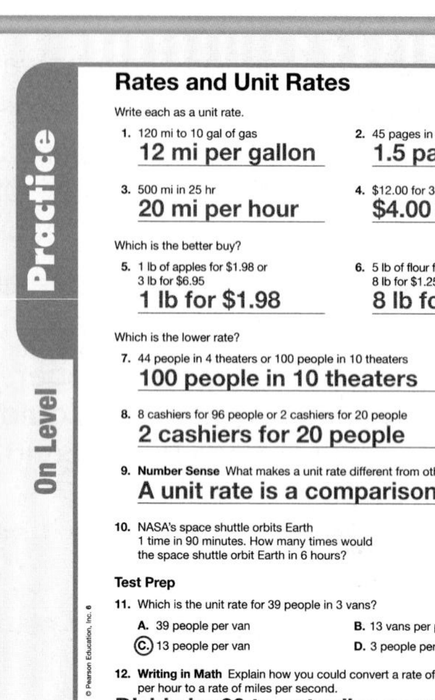

Practice — On Level

Rates and Unit Rates

P 6-3

Write each as a unit rate.

1. 120 mi to 10 gal of gas **12 mi per gallon**
2. 45 pages in 30 min **1.5 pages per minute**
3. 500 mi in 25 hr **20 mi per hour**
4. $12.00 for 3 lb **$4.00 per pound**

Which is the better buy?

5. 1 lb of apples for $1.98 or 3 lb for $6.95 **1 lb for $1.98**
6. 5 lb of flour for $0.90 or 8 lb for $1.25 **8 lb for $1.25**

Which is the lower rate?

7. 44 people in 4 theaters or 100 people in 10 theaters **100 people in 10 theaters**
8. 8 cashiers for 96 people or 2 cashiers for 20 people **2 cashiers for 20 people**
9. **Number Sense** What makes a unit rate different from other rates? **A unit rate is a comparison to one unit.**
10. NASA's space shuttle orbits Earth 1 time in 90 minutes. How many times would the space shuttle orbit Earth in 6 hours? **4 times**

Test Prep

11. Which is the unit rate for 39 people in 3 vans?
    A. 39 people per van
    B. 13 vans per person
    (C.) 13 people per van
    D. 3 people per van
12. **Writing in Math** Explain how you could convert a rate of miles per hour to a rate of miles per second. **Divide by 60 to get miles per minute, then divide by 60 again to get miles per second.**

Use with Lesson 6-3. 67

 EC NTL 12 11 10 9 8 7 6 5 4 3 2

Example A

Give the unit rate for 12 gallons of water in 3 minutes.

One Way

Find an equal ratio.

$\frac{12 \text{ gallons}}{3 \text{ minutes}} = \frac{x \text{ gallons}}{1 \text{ minute}}$

$\frac{12 \div 3}{3 \div 3} = \frac{4}{1}$

Unit rate: $\frac{4 \text{ gallons}}{1 \text{ minute}}$

Another Way

Find the quotient of the terms.

Rate $= \frac{12 \text{ gallons}}{3 \text{ minutes}}$

$12 \div 3 = 4$

Unit rate: $\frac{4 \text{ gallons}}{1 \text{ minute}}$

The unit rate is 4 gallons per minute.

✓ Talk About It

$\frac{\$0.30}{1 \text{ roll}}$ and $\frac{\$0.25}{1 \text{ roll}}$; The 10 pack is the better buy.

1. What are the unit rates for the rolls on the previous page? Which package of rolls is the better buy? **See above.**

How can unit rates help you make comparisons?

Example B

Jim ran 7 laps of a track in 5 minutes. Ben ran 11 laps of the same track in 8 minutes. Which boy ran at a faster rate?

Jim's Rate

$\frac{7 \text{ laps}}{5 \text{ minutes}}$ — *7 ÷ 5 = 1.4*

Unit rate $= \frac{1.4 \text{ laps}}{1 \text{ minute}}$

Ben's Rate

$\frac{11 \text{ laps}}{8 \text{ minutes}}$ — *11 ÷ 8 = 1.375*

Unit rate $= \frac{1.375 \text{ laps}}{1 \text{ minute}}$

Jim ran at a faster rate.

✓ Talk About It

2. How could you find Jim's rate in laps per hour?
I could multiply the unit rate by 60.

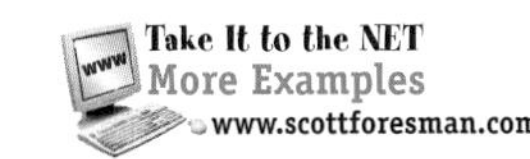

Take It to the NET
More Examples
www.scottforesman.com

For another example, see Set 6-3 on p. 346.

CHECK ✓

Write each as a unit rate.

1. 300 miles in 5 hours **$\frac{60 \text{ miles}}{1 \text{ hour}}$**
2. 250 calories in 10 crackers **$\frac{25 \text{ calories}}{1 \text{ cracker}}$**

Which is the better buy?

3. 6 T-shirts for \$31.50, or 5 T-shirts for \$27.50 **6 T-Shirts for \$31.50**
4. 3 boxes for \$6.89, or 5 boxes for \$10.93 **5 boxes for \$10.93**
5. **Number Sense** Ken runs 4 laps in 6 minutes. What is his rate for 1 hour? **$\frac{40 \text{ laps}}{1 \text{ hour}}$**

Ongoing Assessment

Talk About It: Question 1

If students set up the ratios incorrectly,

then tell them to start by writing what they want to find. In the case of the rolls, they want to find cost per roll. Write:

$\frac{\text{cost}}{\text{roll}} = \frac{\$1.80}{6 \text{ rolls}}$ and

$\frac{\text{cost}}{\text{roll}} = \frac{\$2.50}{10 \text{ rolls}}$

before they begin to find the unit rate.

CHECK ✓

Error Intervention

If students do not label the rates with units,

then remind students that a rate is a ratio with different units. Make a diagram, as shown here, to help. *(Also see* Reteaching, *p. 306B.)*

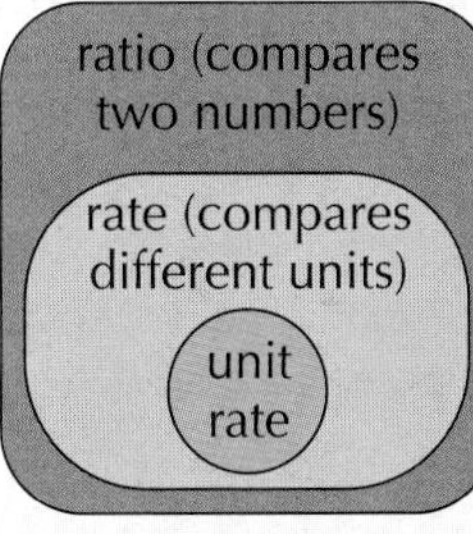

Above Level — Enrichment

Rates of Rhythm

E 6-3
DECISION MAKING

Franklin wants to begin taking drum lessons after basketball practice. Practice begins tomorrow, November 1, and lasts until 4:30 P.M. every school day. He found information for local music instruction centers.

	The Music School	Melody Maker	New Notes
Start Date	November 24	Anytime	November 15
Lesson Times	Mondays and Wednesdays 4:00–5:30 P.M.	Tuesdays 5:00–6:00 P.M. and Saturdays 10:00–11:00 A.M.	Monday, Wednesday, and Friday 5:00–5:45 P.M.
Number of Lessons	15	20	12
Cost	\$12 per lesson	\$200 for 20 lessons	\$27 per week

1. What is the unit rate for each lesson?
A. The Music School **\$12**
B. Melody Maker **\$10**
C. New Notes **\$9**

2. How would you answer Exercise 1 if you were to write the unit rate in cost per hour?

	Hours per payment	Cost per hour
A. The Music School	**$1\frac{1}{2}$ hr**	**\$8**
B. Melody Maker	**20 hr**	**\$10**
C. New Notes	**$2\frac{1}{4}$ hr**	**\$12**

3. What other factors should Franklin consider before choosing a music instruction center?
Sample answer: The start date, and the time the lessons start

4. Which instruction center do you think Franklin should choose? Explain.
Sample answer: Melody Maker; The start date is at any time, the time is convenient, and it costs the least per lesson.

Problem Solving

Rates and Unit Rates

PS 6-3

Wing Beats Different types of birds beat their wings at different rates. The rate of wing beats of several types of birds is shown.

Wing Beats	
Crow	20 wing beats/10 sec
Robin	23 wing beats/10 sec
Eagle	25 wing beats/10 sec
Owl	35 wing beats/10 sec
Chickadee	270 wing beats/10 sec
Hummingbird	700 wing beats/10 sec

1. Express the wing beat rate of the hummingbird as a unit rate of wing beats per second.
70 wing beats per second

2. Express the wing beat rate of the crow as a unit rate of wing beats per minute.
120 wing beats per minute

3. Express the wing beat rate of the robin as a unit rate of wing beats per hour.
8,280 wing beats per hour

Book Reading Each of the 22 students in Ms. Campbell's class has decided to read 3 books for each week of the school year. There are 40 weeks in the school year.

4. Express the number of books read by the entire class as a unit rate of books per week.
66 books per week

5. Express the number of books read by the entire class as a unit rate of books per school year.
2,640 books per school year

6. **Writing in Math** If yogurt shakes were \$2.48 for an 8-oz shake and \$4.48 for a 14-oz shake, which is the better buy? Explain how you used unit rates to figure out your answer.
Sample answer: The 8 oz shake is the better buy. The unit rate for the 8 oz shake is \$2.48 ÷ 8 = \$0.31 an ounce. The unit rate for the 14 oz shake is \$4.48 ÷ 14, which is \$0.32 an ounce.

3 Practice

Exercise 16 Students may think they should compare units in the order they are given, but it is usually easier to express the ratio as *price per ounce.*

Exercise 26 Be sure students know that their answers must include the reasons why the given explanation is not correct as well as provide a correct explanation.

Exercise 27 Suggest students start with three simple statements, such as $4 \times 3 = 12$, $\frac{12}{4} = 3$, and $\frac{12}{3} = 4$. Have them study the patterns in those statements and then apply those patterns to write the ratio for time.

Reading Assist Make Judgments In Exercises 6–13, have students make a judgment about which item will be the first term in each rate and which will be the second. Ask them to explain their decisions.

PRACTICE

For more practice, see Set 6-3 on p. 349.

A Skills and Understanding

Write each as a unit rate.

6. 120 students to 6 teachers **20 students per teacher**
7. 9 lb for $13.50 **$1.50 per pound**
8. 260 miles to 13 gallons of gas **20 miles per gallon of gas**
9. 8 ounces every 4 hours **2 ounces per hour**
10. 300 miles in 5 hours **60 miles per hour**
11. 18 marbles for 6 boys **3 marbles per boy**
12. $12 for 3 books **$4 per book**
13. $375 for working 30 hours **$12.50 per hour**

Which is the better buy?

14. one gallon of milk for $1.99, or $\frac{1}{2}$ gallon of milk for $0.98 **$\frac{1}{2}$ gallon of milk for $0.98**
15. $3.96 for 36 oz of cheese, or $6.30 for 42 oz of cheese **$3.96 for 36 oz of cheesea**
16. 16 oz of sour cream for $1.50, or 32 oz of sour cream for $2.75 **32 oz of sour cream for $2.75**

Which is the lower rate?

17. 2,133 km in 6 hours, or 1,498 km in 7 hours **1,498 km in 7 hours**
18. 144 students on 3 buses, or 208 students on 4 buses **144 students on 3 buses**
19. **Number Sense** Cristy runs 3 miles in 30 minutes. What is her rate per hour? **6 miles per hour**

B Reasoning and Problem Solving

Math and Science

Give three different rates that describe the speed of the following land animals.

For 20-22, See above.

20. lion 21. zebra 22. grizzly bear

20. $\frac{150 \text{ miles}}{3 \text{ hours}}$; $\frac{25 \text{ miles}}{0.5 \text{ hour}}$; $\frac{0.83 \text{ miles}}{1 \text{ minute}}$

21. 40 miles per hour; 20 miles per $\frac{1}{2}$ hour; $3.\overline{3}$ miles per 5 minutes

22. 15 miles per $\frac{1}{2}$ hour; 0.5 miles per minute; 30 miles per hour

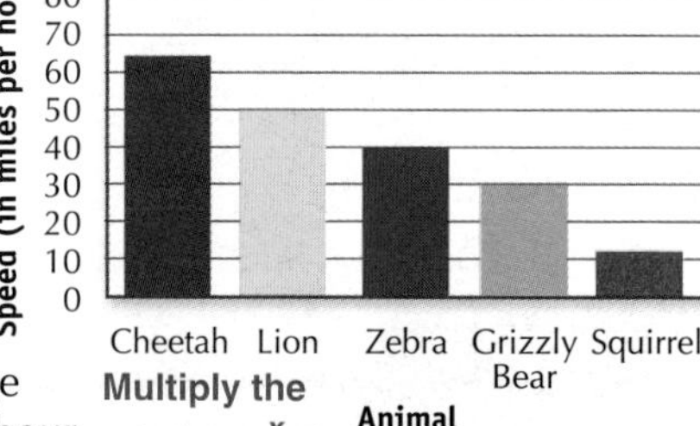

23. A cheetah runs 64 mph. How far can a cheetah run in 15 minutes? **16 miles**
24. The speed of a squirrel is 12 mph. If a squirrel could maintain this speed for 5 minutes, how far would it run? **1 mile**
25. **Connections** Describe how you could change a rate of feet per second to a rate of feet per hour. **Multiply the rate by $\frac{x}{3,600}$ seconds.**
26. **Writing in Math** Is the explanation below correct? If not, tell why not, and write the correct response. **They are equal because $1,240 × 52 = $64,480 for 1 year, not because they are both unit rates.**

Explain why $64,480 per year and $1,240 per week are equal rates.

They are equal rates because they are both unit rates.
One rate is $64,480 for 1 year, and the other is $1,240 for 1 week.

308

Test-Taking Practice

Test-Taking Practice, Item 1, p. 309 There are two parts to the problem; the answer and the explanation are each worth two points. Remind students that they should answer as much as they can since partial credit is given for this type of problem.

Discuss the sample responses shown and compare them to papers produced by your students.

4-point answer Answer is correct; explanation shows complete understanding of equal rates.

Yes, the rates are equal.

Find 60 mph x 24 hours per day.
60 x 24 = 1,440 mi per day

PRACTICE

C Extensions

Speed is a type of rate. It is calculated by evaluating the ratio $\frac{\text{distance}}{\text{time}}$. For example, 60 mph = $\frac{300 \text{ miles}}{5 \text{ hours}}$.

27. What ratio can you use to calculate the time it takes to cover 500 miles at a rate of 40 mph? **$\frac{\text{Distance}}{\text{speed}}$**

28. If the speed limit on a highway is 65 miles per hour, what is the shortest time a person can drive 410 miles on this highway without exceeding the speed limit? Express your answer in hours and minutes. **$6.\overline{3}$ hours; 6 hours 19 minutes**

Mixed Review and Test Prep

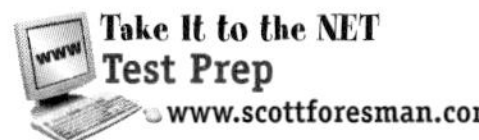

Take It to the NET
Test Prep
www.scottforesman.com

Give three ratios that are equal to each ratio. **Sample answers are given.**

29. $\frac{8}{24}$ **$\frac{1}{3}, \frac{2}{6}, \frac{4}{12}$**   **30.** $\frac{5}{12}$ **$\frac{10}{24}, \frac{15}{36}, \frac{20}{48}$**   **31.** $\frac{10}{16}$ **$\frac{5}{8}, \frac{15}{24}, \frac{20}{32}$**   **32.** $\frac{30}{10}$ **$\frac{3}{1}, \frac{6}{2}, \frac{60}{20}$**

33. Which is the expanded form for 5.072?

A. (5 × 0) + (7 × 0.1) + (2 × 0.01)

B. (5 × 1) + (7 × 0.1) + (2 × 0.01)

(C.) (5 × 1) + (7 × 0.01) + (2 × 0.001)

D. (5 × 10) + (7 × 0.01) + (2 × 0.001)

Discovery Channel School

Discover Math in Your World

The Not-So-Mammoth Mastodon

Often confused as being synonymous, the mastodon and the mammoth were two different animals. Standing at a maximum height of 10 feet and weighing up to 13,228 pounds, the mastodon was shorter and heavier than today's Asian elephants.

1. Express the weight of a mastodon in pounds per foot and pounds per inch. **1,322 pounds per foot; 110.2 pounds per inch**
2. Suppose the tusk of a male mastodon was about 9 feet long and weighed about 135 pounds. What was the weight of a tusk in pounds per foot? Pounds per inch? **15 pounds per foot; 1.25 pounds per inch**

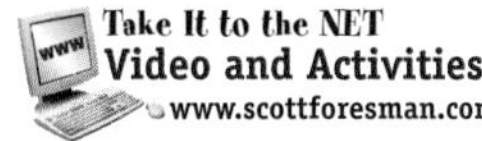

Take It to the NET
Video and Activities
www.scottforesman.com

All text pages available online and on CD-ROM.

Leveled Practice

Below Level Ex. 6–16, 17–23 odd, 26, 29–33

On Level Ex. 6–16 even, 17–26, 29–33

Above Level Ex. 7–19 odd, 20–33

Early Finishers Have students write some rates, such as $4.80 for 32 ounces or 800 miles in 20 hours. Then have them exchange papers and calculate each unit rate.

Discover Math in Your World Ask students to describe the steps in finding a pounds-per-inch-of-height rate if they are given measurements in pounds and feet. Then have students work with partners to answer the questions.

Take It to the NET
Video and Activities
www.scottforesman.com

The video includes pre-viewing and post-viewing questions. A Discovery Channel Blackline Master is also provided.

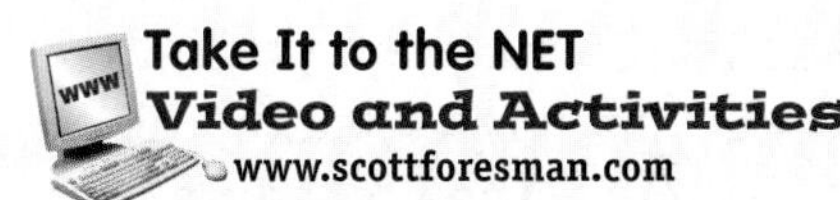

4 Assess

Journal Idea Have students explain how they could use unit rates to compare the prices of two different kinds and sizes of cereal.

-point answer Answer is correct; ncomplete explanation; shows nderstanding of equal ratios.

Yes, the rates are equal.
60 x 24 = 1,440

1-point answer Answer is incorrect; explanation shows little understanding of equal ratios.

No, they are not the same because 1,464 is larger than 1, 440.
Find 60 mph x3 24 hr in a day.
60 x 24 = 1,464

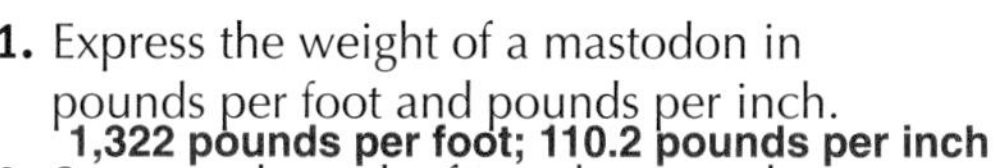

Test-Taking Practice 6-3

1. A car moving at a constant speed of 60 mi per hour will travel 1 mi every minute. Are 60 mi per hour and 1,440 mi per day equal rates? Explain how you know.
Yes, the rates are equal. This can be determined by multiplication: 60 mph × 24 hr in a day; 60 × 24 = 1,440.

2. Which of the following pay rates is equivalent to $8 per hour?
A. $80 for 8 hr worked
B. $55 for 7 hr worked
(C) $24 for 3 hr worked
D. $48 for 4 hr worked

Available as a transparency

Reading for Math Success

Purpose Reinforce reading skills and strategies to use in math. *Visualize* helps prepare students for the problem-solving strategy lesson, *Use Objects*, which follows.

Using Student Pages 310–311

Sometimes in reading, students are told to think about portions of a story or article and try to form mental pictures of what they've read. Through this sort of visualizing, students can put themselves into a text and appreciate it more fully. Visualizing in mathematics helps students solve certain problems, such as ones that involve geometric shapes or patterns. The procedure is to form a mental picture of what the problem asks for and then use objects to act it out.

Model the Process Tell students that a good strategy for solving some problems is to visualize, or "see," what the problems ask for. Using objects such as cut-out or plastic shapes will help them act out what they have visualized and in this way solve the problem. **When I start to solve a problem, I see if it deals with objects that have to cover something or are arranged in some pattern. With problems of this sort, first I visualize what the problem asks for, then describe what I see. I use objects, such as paper or plastic shapes, to act out the problem and figure out a solution to it.**

Visualize

Visualizing when you read in math can help you use the **problem-solving strategy, *Use Objects,*** in the next lesson.

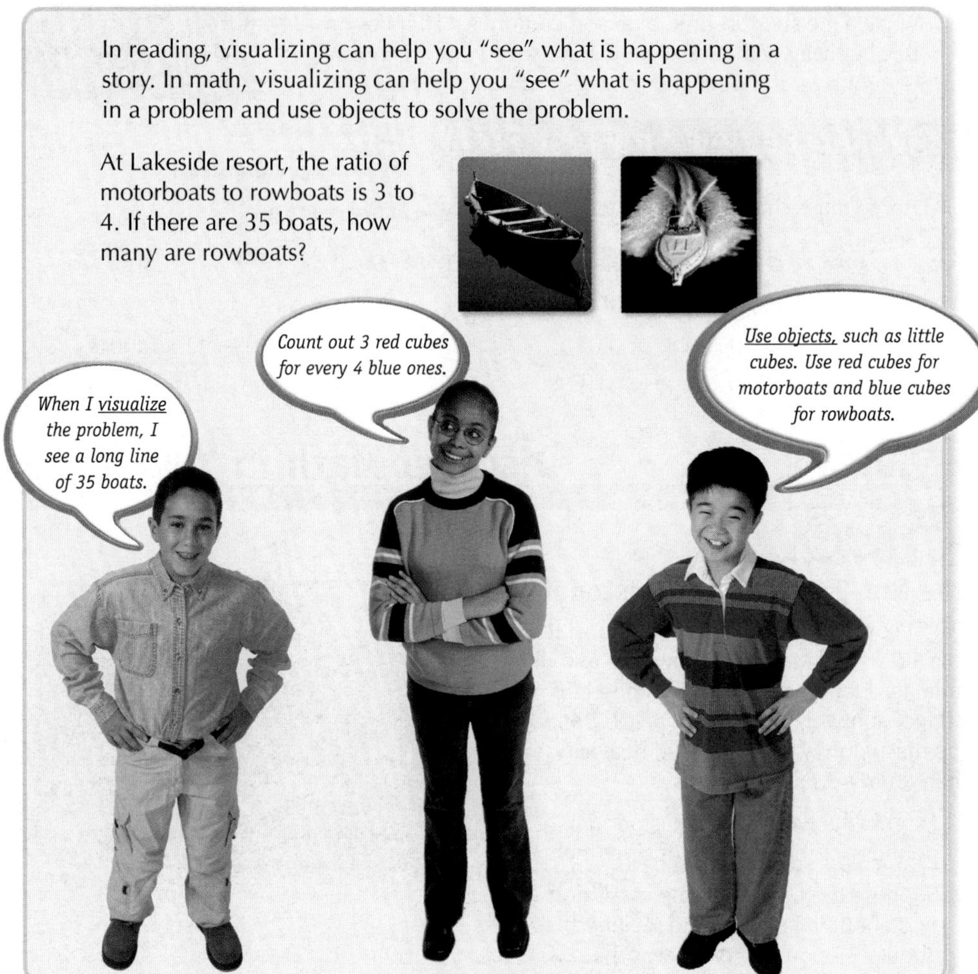

In reading, visualizing can help you "see" what is happening in a story. In math, visualizing can help you "see" what is happening in a problem and use objects to solve the problem.
At Lakeside resort, the ratio of motorboats to rowboats is 3 to 4. If there are 35 boats, how many are rowboats?
When I visualize the problem, I see a long line of 35 boats.
Count out 3 red cubes for every 4 blue ones.
Use objects, such as little cubes. Use red cubes for motorboats and blue cubes for rowboats.

1. How many cubes are needed to represent all the boats? **35**
2. What fraction of all the boats are rowboats? $\frac{4}{7}$

310

For 3–5, use the problem below.

At the puppet show, the ratio of adults' tickets sold to children's tickets was 3 to 5. In all, 56 tickets were sold. How many tickets sold were children's tickets?

Blue Haven Puppet Show Sunday Oct. 11 2:30 P.M. ADULT $6.50

Blue Haven Puppet Show Sunday Oct. 11 2:30 P.M. CHILD $4.00

3. Visualize the problem. Describe what you see.
   A collection of 56 tickets
4. Now act it out and use objects by representing the problem with small pieces of colored paper.
5. **Writing in Math** Could fewer than 28 children's tickets have been sold? Explain.
   No; more than half of the tickets sold were children's tickets, but 28 is exactly half of 56.

For 6–8, use the problem below.

Ned planted a border of 48 petunias in a single line around the perimeter of his square garden. He started in one corner with a white petunia and evenly spaced them all the way around, alternating between white and red petunias. What is the color of the flowers in the other 3 corners?

6. Visualize the problem. Describe what you see.
   A square with flowers along the perimeter
7. Now act it out and use small colored objects to represent the problem.
8. **Writing in Math** How many flowers are on each side? Explain how you found your answer. **13; I acted out the problem and then counted the objects along 1 side.**

For 9–12, use the problem and picture below.

Helen put up a wallpaper border of ballerinas on a wall of her dance studio. Each repeat of the pattern shows the same 4 ballerinas. If the length of the wall is 308 inches, how many of the ballerinas are pink?

9. Visualize the problem. Describe what you see
   A long line of ballerinas
10. **Writing in Math** How many repeats of the pattern were needed? Explain.
   14; divide 308 by 22.
11. Now use small colored objects to act out the problem.
12. How many objects did you need to represent the problem?
   56

Wallpaper Border #217 Height: 7″ Repeat: 22″

Guide the Activity Tell the class to look at the problem. **What does the student visualize in this problem?** *(A line of 35 boats)* **What objects will the student use to represent the boats?** *(Red cubes for motorboats and blue cubes for rowboats)* **How can this problem be acted out to find out how many rowboats there are?** *(Count out 3 red cubes for every 4 blue ones, until you get to 35.)* Have volunteers give answers for Exercises 1 and 2; then assign Exercises 3–12. You may want to have small colored objects available for students to use when they act out the exercises.

Error Intervention

If students have trouble visualizing and acting out problems,

then suggest that they diagram what the problem asks for and make additional notes as needed.

Journal Idea Have students look again at Exercises 9–12. Tell them to rewrite the problem using a different wall length, and write new answers for Exercises 10 and 12.

Answers

3. The arrangement and prices of seats at Blue Haven Outdoor Theater

Use Objects

Lesson Organizer

Quick Lesson Overview 

Objective Find, and write in sentences, solutions to word problems involving rates.

Math Understanding Using objects can help to represent what you know in solving a problem.

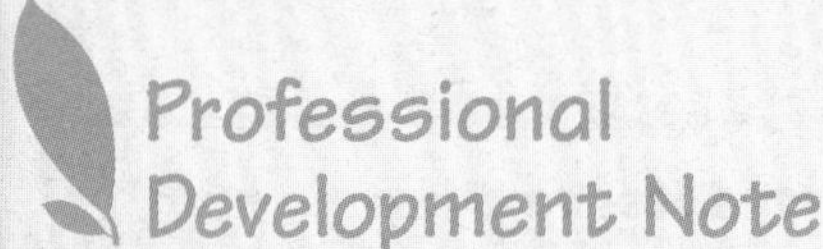

Managing Instruction Allowing students to work together to model problems gives them the opportunity to create useful models, discuss the models, and solve the problems. Encourage them to suggest other models that they could use to solve the Brass Section problem on page 312.

NCTM Standards

- Number and Operations

(For a complete correlation to the NCTM Standards and Grades 6–8 Expectations, see pages 298G–H.)

Getting Started

Spiral Review

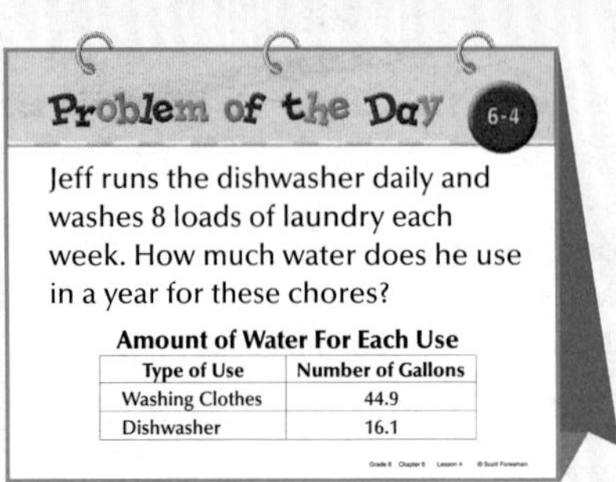

Problem of the Day 6-4

Jeff runs the dishwasher daily and washes 8 loads of laundry each week. How much water does he use in a year for these chores?

Amount of Water For Each Use

Type of Use	Number of Gallons
Washing Clothes	44.9
Dishwasher	16.1

Topics Reviewed

- Adding and multiplying whole numbers and decimals
- Problem-Solving Skill: Mutiple-Step Problem

Answer Jeff uses 24,554.9 gal of water in one year for the two chores.

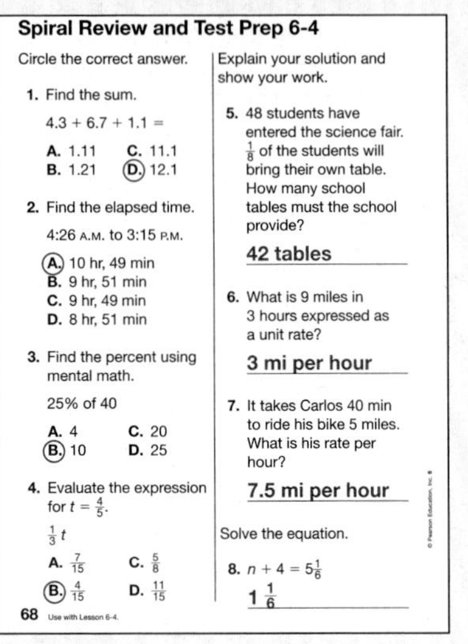

Spiral Review and Test Prep 6-4

Circle the correct answer.

1. Find the sum.
   4.3 + 6.7 + 1.1 =
   A. 1.11 C. 11.1
   B. 1.21 (D.) 12.1
2. Find the elapsed time.
   4:26 A.M. to 3:15 P.M.
   (A.) 10 hr, 49 min
   B. 9 hr, 51 min
   C. 9 hr, 49 min
   D. 8 hr, 51 min
3. Find the percent using mental math.
   25% of 40
   A. 4 C. 20
   (B.) 10 D. 25
4. Evaluate the expression for $t = \frac{4}{5}$.
   $\frac{1}{3}t$
   A. $\frac{7}{15}$ C. $\frac{5}{8}$
   (B.) $\frac{4}{15}$ D. $\frac{11}{15}$

Explain your solution and show your work.

5. 48 students have entered the science fair. $\frac{1}{8}$ of the students will bring their own table. How many school tables must the school provide?
   42 tables
6. What is 9 miles in 3 hours expressed as a unit rate?
   3 mi per hour
7. It takes Carlos 40 min to ride his bike 5 miles. What is his rate per hour?
   7.5 mi per hour

Solve the equation.

8. $n + 4 = 5\frac{1}{6}$
   $1\frac{1}{6}$

68 Use with Lesson 6-4.

Available as a transparency and as a blackline master

Topics Reviewed

1. Adding decimals; **2.** Elapsed time; **3.** Mental math: percent of a number; **4.** Expressions with fractions; **5.** Writing to explain; **6.–7.** Rates and unit rates; **8.** Solving equations with fractions

Investigating the Concept

Bowl It Over

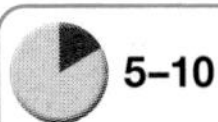 5–10 MIN **Visual/Spatial** 

Materials *(per pair)* 10 Counters or Teaching Tool 9

What to Do

- Present this problem: **Cara and Jack are setting up 10 bowling pins. They decided 1 pin out of 5 pins should be red. How many will be red?**
- **How can you solve this problem?** *(Sample answer: Use counters to model the bowling pins.)* **How can you show the different colored pins?** *(Let red counters represent the red pins and yellow counters represent the other pins.)*
- **Show 1 out of 5. How many identical groups do you need to represent 10 pins?** *(2 groups)* **How many of the pins are red?** *(2 pins)*

1 out of 5 is red.

Ongoing Assessment

- **Reasoning How did you decide you needed 2 groups?** *(There were 10 pins, and 2 groups of 5 make 10.)*
- **If 1 pin out of 2 pins is red, how many pins out of 10 pins are red?** *(5 pins)*

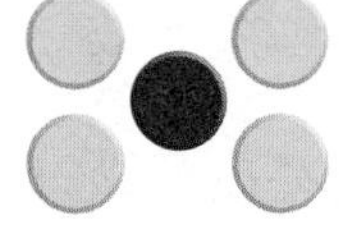 

Reaching All Learners

Writing in Math

Make Up a Story

 10–15 MIN **Linguistic** 

- Draw the five stars, as shown below, on the board.
- **Write a story that you could solve by using these stars.** *(Sample answer: The ratio of red stars to white stars is 3:2. If there are 25 stars in all, how many are white?)*
- Have pairs read their problem and explain how they would use the stars. *(Sample answer: They could use 5 sets of stars like these to represent the 25 stars.)* Ask others in the class to solve the problem. *(10 stars)*

Activate Prior Knowledge/Build Understanding

English Language Learners

Let's Model

 10–15 MIN **Verbal/Auditory** 

- Ask students who have made models (cars, planes, and so on) to share their experiences. If needed, show how to model with clay.
- Tell students that a model is a small copy of something. Ask them to name models in the classroom. *(Sample answers: Globe, map)*
- Ask students to suggest how they might use objects to make a model showing how many in the group are boys and how many are girls.

Reteaching

One Square, Two Square, Red Square, Blue Square

 10–15 MIN **Social/Cooperative** 

Materials *(per group)* 18 squares of paper, red and blue pencils or crayons

- **Maria is going to make a design that uses 18 squares. She decided that 2 of every 3 squares will be blue and the others red. How many red squares will she need?**
- Have students take turns coloring groups of 2 blue squares and 1 red square until 18 squares are colored. **How many squares are red?** *(6 squares)* Have each group make a design with its squares.

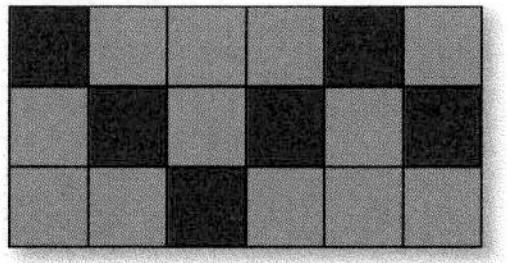

Students with Special Needs

Little League

 5–10 MIN **Kinesthetic** 

- On the board, draw the table shown below without tally marks.
- **In a volleyball league, all teams have 4 girls and 2 boys. There are 18 players in all. How many players are girls?**
- Ask Student 1 to draw tally marks for 4 girls and 2 boys. **Is this enough players?** *(No)*
- Have Student 2 and Student 3 draw tally marks. **Is this enough?** *(Yes)* **How many players are girls?** *(12 are girls.)*

Girls	Boys
////	//
////	//
////	//

Objective Find, and write in sentences, solutions to word problems involving rates.

1 Warm Up

Activate Prior Knowledge Review how to use multiplication and division to find equal ratios.

2 Teach

LEARN Explain the example on p. 312 or present the problem using these teaching actions.

BEFORE Read and Understand

What do you know? *(There are 20 members in the brass section; 3 out of every 5 members are new.)*

DURING Plan and Solve

Can you write a multiplication formula to solve the exercise? *(Yes; $\frac{3}{5} \times 20 = n$)*

AFTER Look Back and Check

Name another strategy you can use to solve the exercise. *(Draw a Picture; Make a Table; Use Logical Reasoning; Write a Number Sentence)*

Problem-Solving Strategy

Reading Helps!
Visualizing
can help you with...
the problem-solving strategy, Use Objects.

Key Idea
Learning how and when to use objects can help you solve problems.

Use Objects

LEARN

How can you use objects to solve a problem?

Brass Section There are 20 members in the brass section of an orchestra. Three out of every five musicians in the brass section are new to the orchestra. How many members of the brass section are new to the orchestra?

Read and Understand

What do you know? There are 20 members in the brass section. Three out of every five are new.

What are you trying to find? How many members out of the 20 in the brass section are new to the orchestra?

Plan and Solve

What strategy will you use? **Strategy: Use Objects**

How to Use Objects
Step 1 Choose objects.
Step 2 Show the known information.
Step 3 Use the objects to solve the problem.

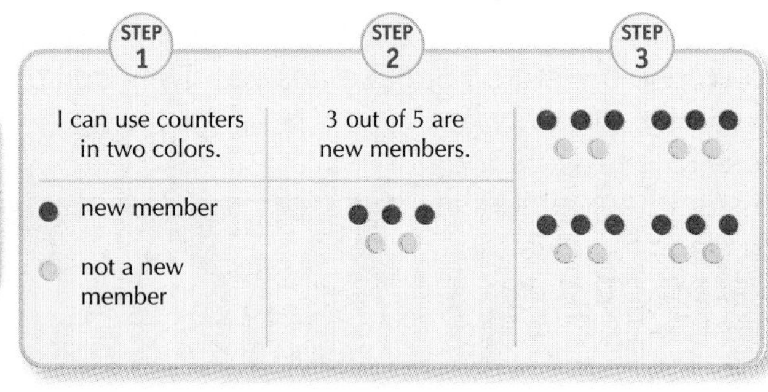

STEP 1
STEP 2
STEP 3
I can use counters in two colors.
3 out of 5 are new members.
new member
not a new member

Answer: There are 12 new members in the brass section.

Look Back and Check

Is your work correct? Yes. The model shows 20 members and that 3 out of every 5 are new.

Talk About It

1. The red counters show new members, the yellow counters show old members.

1. What do the red and yellow counters show in Step 2?

312

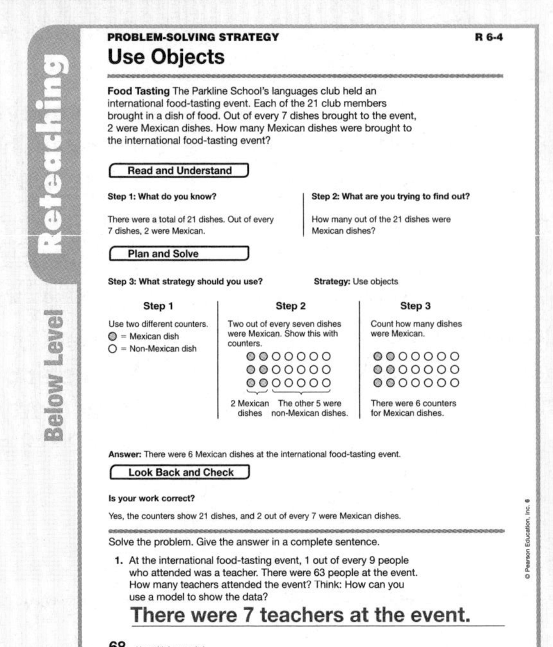

Reteaching — Below Level

PROBLEM-SOLVING STRATEGY R 6-4

Use Objects

Food Tasting The Parkline School's languages club held an international food-tasting event. Each of the 21 club members brought in a dish of food. Out of every 7 dishes brought to the event, 2 were Mexican dishes. How many Mexican dishes were brought to the international food-tasting event?

Read and Understand

Step 1: What do you know?
There were a total of 21 dishes. Out of every 7 dishes, 2 were Mexican.

Step 2: What are you trying to find out?
How many out of the 21 dishes were Mexican dishes?

Plan and Solve

Step 3: What strategy should you use? **Strategy:** Use objects

Step 1	Step 2	Step 3
Use two different counters. ◉ = Mexican dish ○ = Non-Mexican dish	Two out of every seven dishes were Mexican. Show this with counters. 2 Mexican dishes; The other 5 were non-Mexican dishes.	Count how many dishes were Mexican. There were 6 counters for Mexican dishes.

Answer: There were 6 Mexican dishes at the international food-tasting event.

Look Back and Check

Is your work correct?
Yes, the counters show 21 dishes, and 2 out of every 7 were Mexican dishes.

Solve the problem. Give the answer in a complete sentence.

1. At the international food-tasting event, 1 out of every 9 people who attended was a teacher. There were 63 people at the event. How many teachers attended the event? Think: How can you use a model to show the data?
There were 7 teachers at the event.

68 Use with Lesson 6-4.

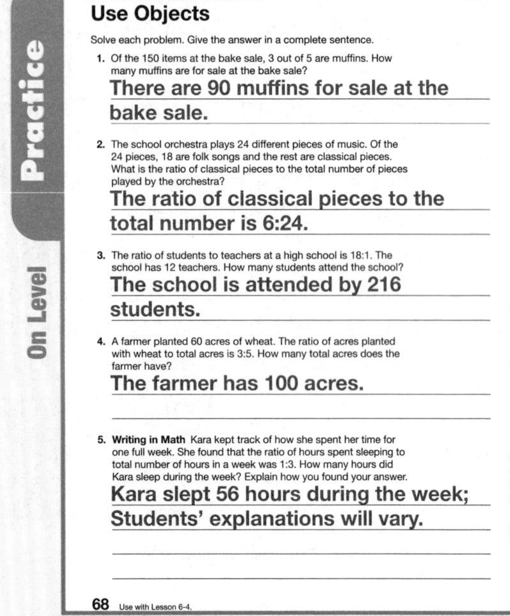

Practice — On Level

PROBLEM-SOLVING STRATEGY P 6-4

Use Objects

Solve each problem. Give the answer in a complete sentence.

1. Of the 150 items at the bake sale, 3 out of 5 are muffins. How many muffins are for sale at the bake sale?
There are 90 muffins for sale at the bake sale.

2. The school orchestra plays 24 different pieces of music. Of the 24 pieces, 18 are folk songs and the rest are classical pieces. What is the ratio of classical pieces to the total number of pieces played by the orchestra?
The ratio of classical pieces to the total number is 6:24.

3. The ratio of students to teachers at a high school is 18:1. The school has 12 teachers. How many students attend the school?
The school is attended by 216 students.

4. A farmer planted 60 acres of wheat. The ratio of acres planted with wheat to total acres is 3:5. How many total acres does the farmer have?
The farmer has 100 acres.

5. **Writing in Math** Kara kept track of how she spent her time for one full week. She found that the ratio of hours spent sleeping to total number of hours in a week was 1:3. How many hours did Kara sleep during the week? Explain how you found your answer.
Kara slept 56 hours during the week; Students' explanations will vary.

68 Use with Lesson 6-4.

CHECK

For another example, see Set 6-4 on p. 347.

Use objects to solve each problem. Give the answer in a complete sentence.

1. There are 24 players on a baseball team. Two out of every three players were on the team last year. How many players were on the team last year. **16 players were on the team last year.**
2. Erik has 30 tomato plants. One out of every 5 plants has yellow tomatoes. How many plants have yellow tomatoes? **6 plants have yellow tomatoes**

PRACTICE

For more practice, see Set 6-4 on p. 350.

Solve each problem. Give the answer in a complete sentence.

3. Cathy has a large aquarium containing 50 fish. Three out of every 5 fish are guppies. How many fish are guppies? The green color tiles represent guppies. The blue tiles represent other fish. Use the color tiles pictured below to solve the problem.

Cathy has 30 fish that are guppies.

4. Of the 120 members in the Trevian marching band, 2 out of every 5 members are girls. How many girls are in the band? **There are 48 girls in the band.**
5. A rock band needed 250 hours of studio work to record 45 minutes of music. What is the ratio of minutes of music to minutes of studio work? **The ratio of minutes of music to minutes of studio work is 3:1000.**
6. Lisa is older than Susan. Glenn is younger than Susan. Rodney's age is between Glenn's and Susan's. What is the order of the four children from youngest to oldest? **The order of children from youngest to oldest is Glenn, Rodney, Susan, Lisa.**
7. How many boys are in a class of 32 students if the ratio of boys to girls is 3:5? **There are 12 boys in the class.**
8. **Reasoning** Pets, Incorporated has 36 kittens and puppies. Two out of every 3 of these young animals are kittens. How many of the animals are puppies? **Pets, Incorporated has 12 puppies.**
9. **Writing in Math** A math test had 24 items. For every 5 correct answers, Carrie had 1 incorrect answer. Explain how to find how many items Carrie had correct. **Sample answer: Draw groups of 6 objects with 5 shaded to represent correct answers and 1 not shaded to represent incorrect answers. Draw groups until there are 24 objects and then count the number of shaded objects.**

STRATEGIES

- **Show What You Know**
  - Draw a Picture
  - Make an Organized List
  - Make a Table
  - Make a Graph
  - Act It Out or Use Objects
- **Look for a Pattern**
- **Try, Check, and Revise**
- **Write an Equation**
- **Use Logical Reasoning**
- **Solve a Simpler Problem**
- **Work Backward**

Choose a tool Mental Math

TEST TALK — Think It Through

Stuck? I won't give up. I can:
- Reread the problem.
- Tell what I know.
- Identify key facts and details.
- Tell the problem in my own words.
- Show the main idea.
- Try a different strategy.
- Retrace my steps.

CHECK

Error Intervention

If students do not understand how to use a ratio model to solve a problem,

then have them start with enough counters (30) to model each problem and then group the objects so each group represents the ratio given in the problem. *(Also see* Reteaching, *p. 312B.)*

3 Practice

TEST TALK **Exercise 9** The key to this problem is to realize that the given information is a part-to-part ratio rather than a part-to-whole ratio.

Leveled Practice

Below Level	Ex. 3–9
On Level	Ex. 3–9
Above Level	Ex. 3–9

Early Finishers Have students look at Exercises 3 and 4 and rewrite the problems using different numbers. Then students should exchange problems and solve.

4 Assess

Journal Idea Have students explain how they used objects to model Exercise 7.

Test-Taking Practice 6-4

1. Scientists believe that about 1 in 10 Americans is left-handed. This means that about 9 out of 10 Americans are right-handed. In a group of 30 people, about how many people will be left-handed? Draw objects to solve the problem.

Sample answer: About 3 out of 30 would be left-handed.

2. Out of every 5 members of a school math club, 2 are in fourth grade. There are 30 members in the club. How many are in fourth grade?
   - A. 6
   - B. 8
   - C. 10
   - (D) 12

Available as a transparency

Above Level — Enrichment

On the Blocks E 6-4 VISUAL THINKING

Count the blocks in each structure. Each block sits on top of another, unless the picture shows differently.

1.  10
2.  16
3.  12
4.  15
5.  40
6.  32
7.  25
8.  48
9. 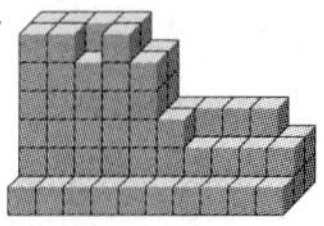 92

68 Use with Lesson 6-4.

Problem Solving

PROBLEM-SOLVING STRATEGY PS 6-4

Use Objects

Pizzeria On a Thursday evening, a local pizzeria sold 56 pizzas. Out of every 8 pizzas sold, 7 pizzas had one or more vegetables as a topping. How many pizzas sold on Thursday night had at least one vegetable as a topping?

Read and Understand

1. How many pizzas were sold on Thursday? **56**
2. For every 8 pizzas sold, how many had vegetable toppings? **7 pizzas**

Plan and Solve

3. Make a model showing 7 out of 8.

Check students' work; Any model with 8 counters showing 7 of one color and one of another color is correct.

4. How many groups of 8 are there in 56 pizzas? **7 groups of 8**
5. Solve the problem. Write the answer in a complete sentence. **Sample answer: There were 49 pizzas with vegetable toppings.**

Look Back and Check

6. What is one other problem-solving strategy you could use to solve this problem? **Sample answer: I could have made a table listing 8, 16, 24, 32, 40, 48, and 56 pizzas, and 7, 14, 21, 28, 35, 42, and 49 veggie pizzas.**

68 Use with Lesson 6-4.

Review

Purpose Help students review content learned in Section A.

Using Student Pages 314–315

Do You Know How? exercises are appropriate for written work.

Do You Understand? questions are designed for whole-class discussion or small-group discussion followed by a report to the whole class.

Vocabulary Review

You may wish to review these terms before assigning the page.

ratio *(p. 300)*

terms *(p. 300)*

rate *(p. 306)*

unit rate *(p. 306)*

Section A: Lessons 6-1 through 6-4

Review

Do You Know How?

Understanding Ratios (6-1)

Write a ratio for each comparison in three ways.

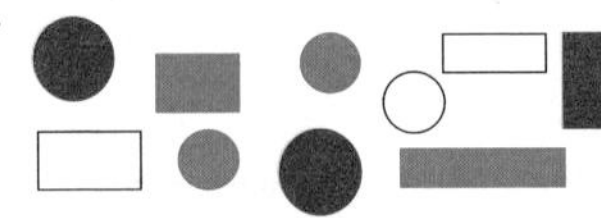

1. red circles to blue circles **2 to 2, 2:2, $\frac{2}{2}$**
2. circles to rectangles **5 to 5, 5:5, $\frac{5}{5}$**
3. red shapes to all shapes **3 to 10, 3:10, $\frac{3}{10}$**

Equal Ratios (6-2)

4. 6 to 8, 9 to 12, 12 to 16 5. 5:3, 15:9, 20:12 6. $\frac{6}{4}, \frac{9}{6}, \frac{12}{8}$

Give three ratios that are equal to each ratio. **Sample ratios are given. 4–6 See above.**

4. 3 to 4
5. 10:6
6. $\frac{3}{2}$

Tell whether the ratios in each pair are equal.

7. $\frac{10}{8}, \frac{15}{12}$ **Yes**
8. $\frac{6}{2}, \frac{8}{2}$ **No**
9. $\frac{3}{12}, \frac{4}{1}$ **No**

Rates and Unit Rates (6-3)

Write each as a unit rate.

10. \$2.67 for 3 liters **\$0.89 per liter**
11. 8 meters in 10 seconds **0.8 meters per second**
12. 164 miles on 8 gallons of gas **20.5 miles per gallon**

Use Objects (6-4)

13. There were 21 guests who chose chicken.

Use objects to solve the problem. Give the answer in a complete sentence.

13. At a dinner, the guests could choose between beef or chicken. Of the 35 guests, 3 out of 5 chose chicken. How many guests chose chicken?

Do You Understand?

A. I compared what was asked for first to what was asked for second; Yes, because the order must correspond to what is being asked.

A Explain how you found each ratio. Is the order of the terms in the ratio important? Tell why or why not. **See above.**

B How is a ratio similar to a fraction? How is it different? **They can both compare a part to a whole; a ratio can compare a part to a part, whereas a fraction must compare a part to a whole.**

C. Multiply or divide both terms of the ratio by the same non-zero number to create equivalent ratios.

C Explain how to use multiplication and division to find equal ratios. **See above.**

D Describe two methods that you can use to tell whether two ratios are equal. **Multiply both terms of the ratio by the same non-zero number, or divide the first term of each ratio by the second term and compare the quotients.**

E. A rate compares 2 quantities, a unit rate is the comparison of a given quantity to 1 unit.

E What is the difference between a rate and a unit rate? **See above.**

F Explain how to use unit rates to decide which is a better buy: 5 lb for \$5.60 or 7 lb for \$8.05. **See below.**

F. Divide \$5.60 by 5 and \$8.05 by 7 to find the unit costs, and select the lesser unit cost.

G What other strategies could you use to find the number of guests who chose chicken? **Sample answer: Draw a Picture**

Item Analysis for Diagnosis and Intervention

Objective	Review Items	Diagnostic Checkpoint Items	Student Book Pages*	Intervention System
Understand ratios.	1–3	3–6, 21	300–301	I30
Find equivalent ratios.	4–9	1, 7–15, 21	302–305	I31
Understand rates and unit rates.	10–12	2, 16–19, 22	306–309	I33, I38
Make a model to solve a problem.	13	20	312–313	M33

*For each lesson, there is a *Reteaching* activity in *Reaching All Learners* and a *Reteaching* master.

Chapter 6 Section A
Diagnostic Checkpoint

MULTIPLE CHOICE

1. Which ratio is equal to 3 to 5? (6-2)

   A. $\frac{5}{3}$ **C.** 3:10

   (B.) $\frac{12}{20}$ **D.** 12:15

2. Which is the best buy? (6-3)

   A. $9.95 for 5 lb **C.** $6.15 for 3 lb

   (B.) $13.23 for 7 lb **D.** $8.60 for 4 lb

TEST TALK

Think It Through
I know that **the order of the terms in a ratio** is important.

FREE RESPONSE

T-shirts Galore recorded the number of each color T-shirt they sold. Write a ratio for each comparison in three ways. (6-1)

Data File

T-shirt Sales

Color	Amount
red	15
blue	9
black	12
white	28
purple	8

3. red T-shirts to white T-shirts **15 to 28, 15:28, $\frac{15}{28}$**
4. black T-shirts to purple T-shirts **12 to 8, 12:8, $\frac{12}{8}$**
5. blue T-shirts to all other T-shirts **9 to 63, 9:63, $\frac{9}{63}$**
6. white T-shirts to all T-shirts **28 to 72, 28:72, $\frac{28}{72}$**

Give three ratios that are equal to each ratio. (6-2) **Sample ratios are given.**

7. $\frac{6}{5}$ **$\frac{12}{10}$, $\frac{18}{15}$, $\frac{24}{20}$** **8.** 12 to 8 **3 to 2, 6 to 4, 9 to 6** **9.** 36:48 **3:4, 6:8, 12:16** **10.** 3 to 1 **6 to 2, 9 to 3, 12 to 4** **11.** $\frac{2}{7}$ **$\frac{4}{14}$, $\frac{6}{21}$, $\frac{8}{28}$**

Write each ratio in simplest form. (6-2)

12. 54 to 16 **27 to 8** **13.** $\frac{64}{88}$ **$\frac{8}{11}$** **14.** 33 to 270 **11 to 90** **15.** 96:8 **12:1**

Write each as a unit rate. (6-3)

16. 171 miles in 3 hours **57 miles per hour**
17. $290 for 25 hours of work **$11.60 per hour of work**
18. 2 cups of flour for 4 dozen cookies **$\frac{1}{2}$ cup of flour per 1 dozen cookies**
19. $2.88 for 32 oz **$0.09 per ounce**
20. Mrs. McGregor has 12 rose bushes around her house. Two out of every 3 rose bushes have red flowers. How many rose bushes have red flowers? (6-4) **8 rose bushes have red flowers**

Writing in Math

21. Yvette did 30 sit ups and 18 push ups. She wrote the ratio 3:5 to compare the number of sit ups to the number of push ups. Is this correct? Explain your answer. (6-1, 6-2)
No. Yvette reversed the ratio. The number of sit ups to the number of push ups is 5:3.
22. Explain how to decide if 5 cans for $3.25 or 12 cans for $8.16 is the better buy.
Find the unit rate of each ratio. The unit rate with the lesser value is the better buy.

Sample student work for Exercise 22

$3.25 / 5 cans $3.25 ÷ 5 = $0.65

$8.16 / 12 cans $8.16 ÷ 12 = $0.68

If I divide the price by the number of cans, I get the price of one can. 65¢ is less than 68¢, so the better buy is 5 cans for $3.25.

The rubric below is a scoring guide that shows how many points to give an answer to Exercise 22. Many teachers would assign a score of 4 points to this explanation. Discuss the sample response shown and compare it to papers produced by students.

Scoring Rubric

4 Full credit: 4 points
The answer is correct; understands how to use rates to make comparisons; explanation is complete.

3 Partial credit: 3 points
The answer is correct; understands how to use rates to make comparisons; explanation is incomplete.

2 Partial credit: 2 points
The answer is incorrect; understands how to use rates to make comparisons; gives a good explanation.

1 Partial credit: 1 point
The answer is correct; gives no explanation.

0 No credit
The answer is incorrect; shows no understanding of comparing rates.

Lesson Organizer

Quick Lesson Overview

Objective Identify ratios that form proportions.

Math Understanding If two ratios are equal, they form a proportion.

Vocabulary Proportion, cross products

Professional Development Note

Research Base

The ability to reason about comparisons is closely tied to proportional reasoning (Lamon, 1993), arguably the gateway between arithmetic and higher mathematics. This section focuses on understanding and solving problems involving proportions.

NCTM Standards

- Number and Operations

(For a complete correlation to the NCTM Standards and Grades 6–8 Expectations, see pages 298G–H.)

Getting Started

Spiral Review

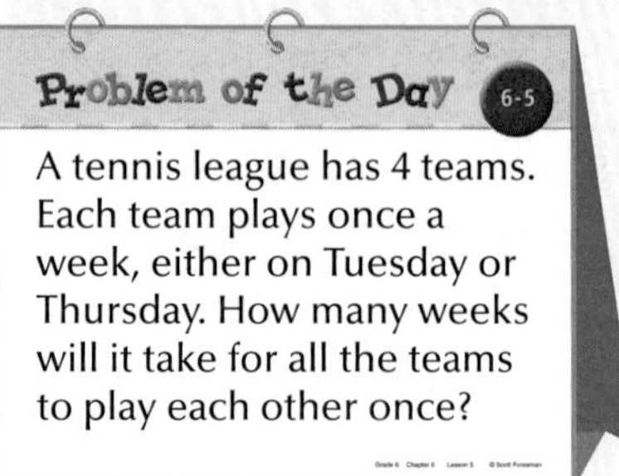

Problem of the Day 6-5

A tennis league has 4 teams. Each team plays once a week, either on Tuesday or Thursday. How many weeks will it take for all the teams to play each other once?

Topics Reviewed

- Listing outcomes
- Problem-Solving Strategy: Make an Organized List

Answer It will take 3 weeks for each team to play the other teams one time.

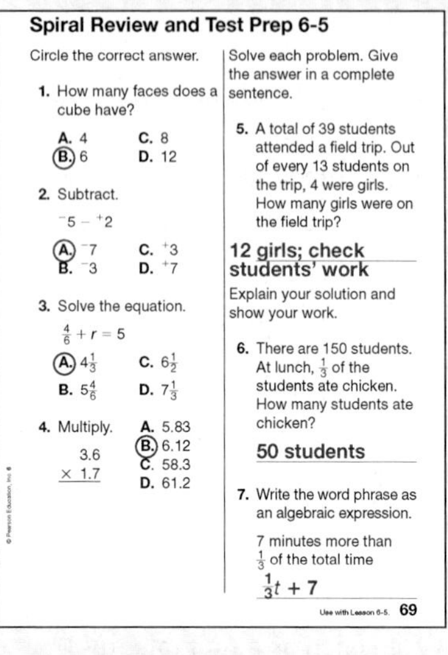

Spiral Review and Test Prep 6-5

Circle the correct answer.

1. How many faces does a cube have?
   A. 4 (B.) 6 C. 8 D. 12
2. Subtract. $^{-}5 - {}^{+}2$
   (A.) $^{-}7$ B. $^{-}3$ C. $^{+}3$ D. $^{+}7$
3. Solve the equation. $\frac{4}{6} + r = 5$
   (A.) $4\frac{1}{3}$ B. $5\frac{4}{6}$ C. $6\frac{1}{2}$ D. $7\frac{1}{3}$
4. Multiply. 3.6×1.7
   A. 5.83 (B.) 6.12 C. 58.3 D. 61.2

Solve each problem. Give the answer in a complete sentence.

5. A total of 39 students attended a field trip. Out of every 13 students on the trip, 4 were girls. How many girls were on the field trip?
   12 girls; check students' work

Explain your solution and show your work.

6. There are 150 students. At lunch, $\frac{1}{3}$ of the students ate chicken. How many students ate chicken?
   50 students
7. Write the word phrase as an algebraic expression.
   7 minutes more than $\frac{1}{3}$ of the total time
   $\frac{1}{3}t + 7$

© Pearson Education, Inc. 6

Use with Lesson 6-5. 69

Available as a transparency and as a blackline master

Topics Reviewed

1. Solid figures; **2.** Subtracting integers; **3.** Solving equations with fractions; **4.** Multiplying decimals; **5.** Use objects; **6.** Writing to explain; **7.** Expressions with fractions

Investigating the Concept

Proportional Thinking

10–15 MIN | **Visual/Spatial**

What to Do

- Write the ratios on the board. Omit the equal signs. **Which pairs of ratios are equal?** *(The first and second; the third and fourth)* Write the equal signs.
- **An equation that states that two ratios are equal is called a *proportion* and the ratios are said to *vary proportionally.* Look at the units in the proportions. Describe them.** *(The units are the same either right and left or up and down.)*
- Point to the cross products. **What is true about 1 × 12 and 3 × 4?** *(They both equal 12.)* **We call these *cross products.* The cross products in a proportion are always equal.**

Ongoing Assessment

- **Number Sense Do the ratios $\frac{2}{3}$ and $\frac{5}{9}$ form a proportion? Explain.** *(No; $\frac{2 \times 3}{3 \times 3} = \frac{6}{9}$, not $\frac{5}{9}$.)* **Are the cross products equal?** *(No; $2 \times 9 = 18 \neq 3 \times 5 = 15$)*

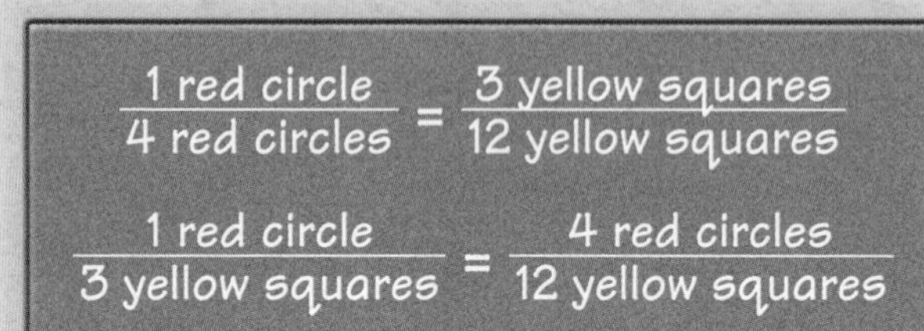

1 red circle / 4 red circles = 3 yellow squares / 12 yellow squares
1 red circle / 3 yellow squares = 4 red circles / 12 yellow squares

Reaching All Learners

Reading in Math

Puppies and People

 15–20 MIN **Logical/Mathematical** 

- Display the table shown below. **One dog year is often considered to be equivalent to 7 human years. Here are the actual equivalents. Do you think the $\frac{1}{7}$ ratio is correct?**

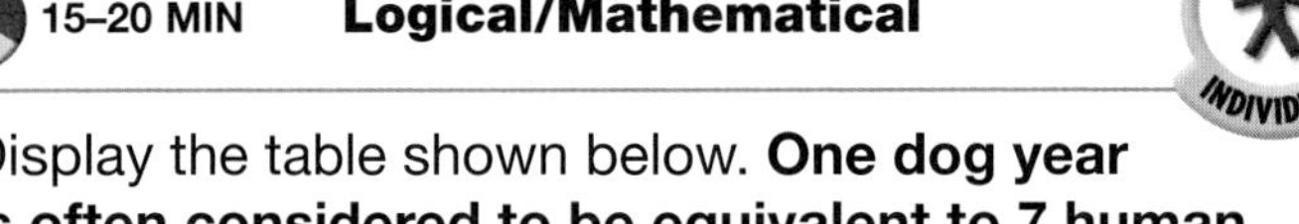

Dog Years	$\frac{2}{3}$	1	3	5	9
People Years	13	16	28	36	52

- **What does the problem tell you?** *(The common idea is that 1 dog year is equivalent to 7 human years; the actual relationships are given in the table.)*
- **Are the ratios in the table equivalent to $\frac{1}{7}$ and each other? Explain.** *(No; for example, $\frac{1}{7} \neq \frac{1}{16} \neq \frac{3}{28}$)*

Access Content

English Language Learners

Money Matters

 10–15 MIN **Verbal/Logical/Mathematical**

Materials: Play Money or Teaching Tool 5

- Direct attention to the tables on page 316. Model acting out renting a Value Vehicle car for 1 day, using play money. Have pairs repeat the activity of acting out renting a Value Vehicle for 2 or 3 days and then for a What-A-Deal Wheels car.
- Have pairs discuss: **Which car-rental company has the better deal? Why?** *(What-A-Deal Wheels; the rate for 3 days is less than Value Vehicle's rate for 3 days.)*
- Read the first paragraph on page 316 to the class. **Can you use the same two entries in the table for What-A-Deal Wheels to write a proportion? Why or why not?** *(No; $\frac{1}{20} \neq \frac{2}{35}$)*

Reteaching

Fractions and Proportions

 10–15 MIN **Social/Cooperative** 

Materials *(per group)* Fraction Strips or Teaching Tool 15

- **Use the fraction strips to model $\frac{3}{4}$. What ratio corresponds to $\frac{3}{4}$?** *(3:4)*
- **Now use twelfths strips to model a fraction equal to $\frac{3}{4}$. How many twelfths are there?** *(9 twelfths)* **What ratio corresponds to $\frac{9}{12}$?** *(9:12)*
- **Do $\frac{3}{4}$ and $\frac{9}{12}$ form a proportion? Find the cross product to check.** *(Yes; $3 \times 12 = 36 = 4 \times 9$)*
- Have students use fraction strips to model other pairs of equal ratios and find cross products to verify that the ratios form a proportion.

Math and Technology

Cross Product Calculation

 5–10 MIN **Auditory** 

Materials *(per student)* Calculator

- **You can use a calculator to determine if two ratios form a proportion. If two numbers are equal, what is their difference?** *(0)* Write these two ratios.

$$\frac{657 \text{ mi}}{3 \text{ hr}} \qquad \frac{2{,}409 \text{ mi}}{11 \text{ hr}}$$

- **How can you use memory keys to decide if the ratios are equal?** *(Enter one cross product into memory. Subtract the other cross product, and check that the memory is 0.)*

Objective Identify ratios that form proportions.

1 Warm Up

Activate Prior Knowledge Review how to compare two ratios.

2 Teach

LEARN Remind students that a rate is a special kind of ratio, so a proportion can be a statement that two rates are equal or that two ratios are equal. For two rates to be proportional, the units across the top and bottom of both rates must be the same. Two ratios may be proportional even if their units differ.

Ongoing Assessment

Talk About It: Question 1

If students think that the two ratios do not form a proportion because they have different units,

then point out that each cross product will be 72 ft × sec. The cross products will be equal and have the same units, so the ratios form a proportion.

Key Idea
A proportion is a statement that two ratios are equal.

Vocabulary
- proportion
- cross products

Understanding Proportions

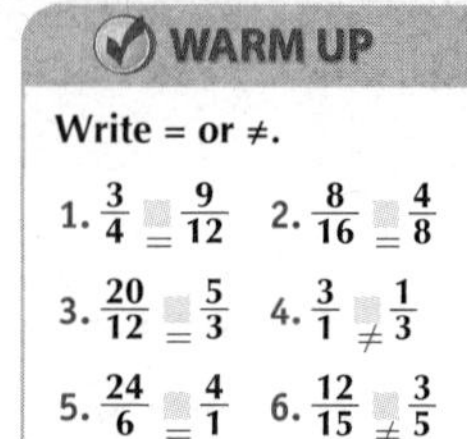
WARM UP

Write = or ≠.

1. $\frac{3}{4} = \frac{9}{12}$ 2. $\frac{8}{16} = \frac{4}{8}$
3. $\frac{20}{12} = \frac{5}{3}$ 4. $\frac{3}{1} \neq \frac{1}{3}$
5. $\frac{24}{6} = \frac{4}{1}$ 6. $\frac{12}{15} \neq \frac{3}{5}$

LEARN

What is a proportion?

A **proportion** states that two ratios are equal. You can use the first two Value Vehicle ratios to write a proportion: $\frac{1 \text{ day}}{\$20} = \frac{2 \text{ days}}{\$40}$.

In a proportion, the units must be the same across the top and bottom, or down the left and right sides. In this case, days are across the top and dollars across the bottom.

For Value Vehicle, the ratios of days to the cost of renting a car are all equal. We say that these quantities **vary proportionally.** The What-A-Deal Wheels ratios are NOT all equal, so these quantities do NOT vary proportionally.

In the proportion $\frac{1}{20} = \frac{2}{40}$, 1 × 40 and 20 × 2 are cross products. The **cross products** of the terms in a proportion are equal.

Value Vehicle

Days	Cost
1	$20
2	$40
3	$60
4	$80

What-A-Deal Wheels

Days	Cost
1	$20
2	$35
3	$48
4	$59

Example

Decide if the ratios $\frac{3 \text{ ft}}{8 \text{ sec}}$ and $\frac{9 \text{ ft}}{24 \text{ sec}}$ form a proportion.

What You Do

Look at the units.

$\frac{3 \text{ ft}}{8 \text{ sec}} \stackrel{?}{=} \frac{9 \text{ ft}}{24 \text{ sec}}$ The units are the same across the top and bottom.

Look at the cross products.

$3 \times 24 \stackrel{?}{=} 8 \times 9$ ← The cross products are equal.

$72 = 72$

Why It Works

Multiply both sides of the proportion by 24 × 8 and simplify.

$\frac{24 \times \cancel{8} \times 3}{\cancel{8}} = \frac{9 \times \cancel{24} \times 8}{\cancel{24}}$

$24 \times 3 = 9 \times 8$ ← cross products

$72 = 72$

Since the units are the same and the cross products are equal, the ratios form a proportion.

Talk About It

1. Do the ratios $\frac{4 \text{ ft}}{6 \text{ ft}}$ and $\frac{12 \text{ sec}}{18 \text{ sec}}$ form a proportion? Why or why not?
Yes, the units are consistent and the cross products are equal.

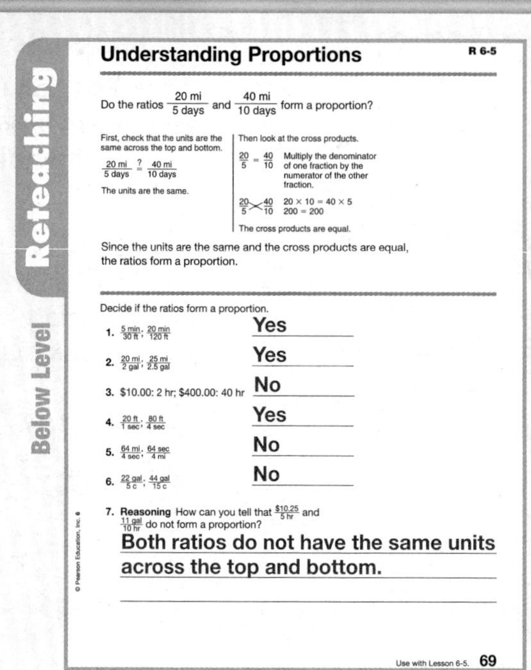
Reteaching — Below Level

Understanding Proportions R 6-5

Do the ratios $\frac{20 \text{ mi}}{5 \text{ days}}$ and $\frac{40 \text{ mi}}{10 \text{ days}}$ form a proportion?

First, check that the units are the same across the top and bottom.

$\frac{20 \text{ mi}}{5 \text{ days}} \stackrel{?}{=} \frac{40 \text{ mi}}{10 \text{ days}}$

The units are the same.

Then look at the cross products.

$\frac{20}{5} = \frac{40}{10}$ Multiply the denominator of one fraction by the numerator of the other fraction.

$20 \times 10 = 40 \times 5$
$200 = 200$

The cross products are equal.

Since the units are the same and the cross products are equal, the ratios form a proportion.

Decide if the ratios form a proportion.

1. $\frac{5 \text{ min}}{30 \text{ ft}}; \frac{20 \text{ min}}{120 \text{ ft}}$ **Yes**
2. $\frac{20 \text{ mi}}{2 \text{ gal}}; \frac{25 \text{ mi}}{2.5 \text{ gal}}$ **Yes**
3. $10.00: 2 hr; $400.00: 40 hr **No**
4. $\frac{20 \text{ ft}}{1 \text{ sec}}; \frac{80 \text{ ft}}{4 \text{ sec}}$ **Yes**
5. $\frac{64 \text{ mi}}{4 \text{ sec}}; \frac{64 \text{ sec}}{4 \text{ mi}}$ **No**
6. $\frac{22 \text{ gal}}{5 \text{ c}}; \frac{44 \text{ gal}}{15 \text{ c}}$ **No**
7. **Reasoning** How can you tell that $\frac{\$10.25}{5 \text{ hr}}$ and $\frac{11 \text{ gal}}{10 \text{ hr}}$ do not form a proportion?
Both ratios do not have the same units across the top and bottom.

Use with Lesson 6-5. 69

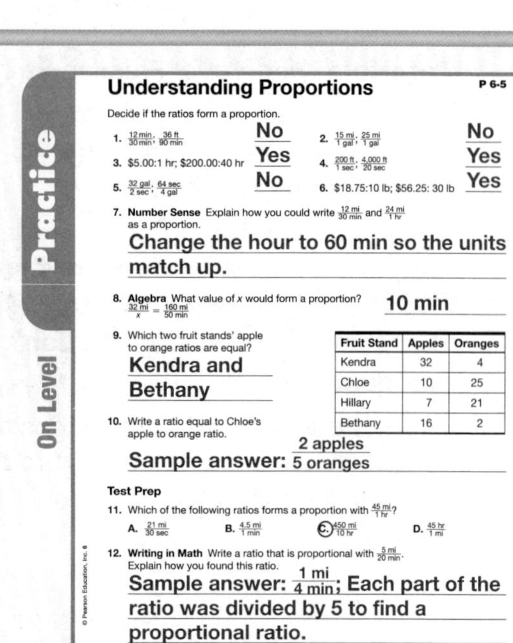
Practice — On Level

Understanding Proportions P 6-5

Decide if the ratios form a proportion.

1. $\frac{12 \text{ min}}{30 \text{ min}}; \frac{36 \text{ ft}}{90 \text{ min}}$ **No**
2. $\frac{15 \text{ mi}}{1 \text{ gal}}; \frac{25 \text{ mi}}{1 \text{ gal}}$ **No**
3. $5.00:1 hr; $200.00:40 hr **Yes**
4. $\frac{200 \text{ ft}}{1 \text{ sec}}; \frac{4{,}000 \text{ ft}}{20 \text{ sec}}$ **Yes**
5. $\frac{32 \text{ gal}}{2 \text{ sec}}; \frac{64 \text{ sec}}{4 \text{ gal}}$ **No**
6. $18.75:10 lb; $56.25: 30 lb **Yes**
7. **Number Sense** Explain how you could write $\frac{12 \text{ mi}}{30 \text{ min}}$ and $\frac{24 \text{ mi}}{1 \text{ hr}}$ as a proportion.
Change the hour to 60 min so the units match up.
8. **Algebra** What value of x would form a proportion? $\frac{32 \text{ mi}}{x} = \frac{160 \text{ mi}}{50 \text{ min}}$ **10 min**
9. Which two fruit stands' apple to orange ratios are equal?
Kendra and Bethany

Fruit Stand	Apples	Oranges
Kendra	32	4
Chloe	10	25
Hillary	7	21
Bethany	16	2

10. Write a ratio equal to Chloe's apple to orange ratio.
Sample answer: $\frac{2 \text{ apples}}{5 \text{ oranges}}$

Test Prep

11. Which of the following ratios forms a proportion with $\frac{45 \text{ mi}}{1 \text{ hr}}$?
A. $\frac{21 \text{ mi}}{30 \text{ sec}}$ B. $\frac{4.5 \text{ mi}}{1 \text{ min}}$ **(C.)** $\frac{450 \text{ mi}}{10 \text{ hr}}$ D. $\frac{45 \text{ hr}}{1 \text{ mi}}$
12. **Writing in Math** Write a ratio that is proportional with $\frac{5 \text{ mi}}{20 \text{ min}}$. Explain how you found this ratio.
Sample answer: $\frac{1 \text{ mi}}{4 \text{ min}}$**; Each part of the ratio was divided by 5 to find a proportional ratio.**

Use with Lesson 6-5. 69

CHECK

For another example, see Set 6-5 on p. 347.

Decide if the ratios form a proportion.

1. $\frac{2 \text{ tbs}}{1 \text{ oz}}, \frac{4 \text{ oz}}{8 \text{ tbs}}$ **No**
2. $\frac{100 \text{ mi}}{4 \text{ h}}, \frac{125 \text{ mi}}{5 \text{ h}}$ **Yes**
3. $\frac{5 \text{ ft}}{8 \text{ s}}, \frac{10 \text{ s}}{6 \text{ ft}}$ **No**
4. **Number Sense** Which proportion is written correctly? Explain. **See below.**
   a. 12 inches:1 foot = 4 feet:48 inches **b.** 12 inches:1 foot = 48 inches:4 feet

PRACTICE

For more practice, see Set 6-5 on p. 350.

A Skills and Understanding

4. b. is written correctly because the units on the left of each ratio remain the same and the units on the right of each ratio remain the same.

Decide if the ratios form a proportion.

5. $\frac{14 \text{ in.}}{10 \text{ min}}, \frac{70 \text{ in.}}{50 \text{ s}}$ **No**
6. $\frac{6 \text{ mi}}{10 \text{ mi}}, \frac{15 \text{ yd}}{25 \text{ yd}}$ **Yes**
7. $\frac{8 \text{ oranges}}{\$5}, \frac{11 \text{ oranges}}{\$7}$ **No**
8. \$75:5 h; \$35:2 h **No**
9. 1ft:8 s; 4 ft:33 s **No**
10. 3:25; 6:50 **Yes**
11. **Number Sense** Explain why $\frac{\$1.25}{5 \text{ oz}}$ and $\frac{20 \text{ oz}}{\$5}$ do not form a proportion.

11. The units are not the same across the top, across the bottom, or down the left or right sides. Also, the cross products are not equal.

B Reasoning and Problem Solving

12. Which two boys' successes to attempts ratios are equal? **Nate and Tomas**
13. **Reasoning** How can you tell by looking at the graph whether Nate or Anthony was more successful? **See below right.**
14. **Algebra** Find three *x*- and *y*-values for $\frac{5 \text{ tickets}}{\$40} = \frac{x \text{ tickets}}{\$y}$. **Sample answers:** $\frac{10 \text{ tickets}}{\$80}, \frac{15 \text{ tickets}}{\$120}, \frac{20 \text{ tickets}}{\$160}$
15. **Writing in Math** Some standard sizes for photographs are 3.5-by-5 inches, 4-by-6 inches, 5-by-7 inches, and 8-by-10 inches. Do the ratios of the dimensions vary proportionally? Explain how you know when quantities vary proportionally. **See below right.**

Tournament Field Goals

Player: Anthony, Nate, Nick, Tomas, Travis

Successes / Attempts

0 12 16 20 24 28 32 36 40 44

Number of Successes/Attempts

13. Nate is more successful because they each have the same number of attempts, but Nate has more successes.

Mixed Review and Test Prep

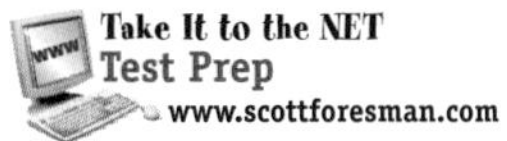

16. Kevin successfully completed 5 out of 6 serves at the volleyball game. If he served 30 times, how many serves did he complete successfully? **25 serves**

15. No; you know quantities vary proportionally when the cross products are equal.

17. Which is the GCF of 12 and 18?
    A. 3 **(B.)** 6 **C.** 36 **D.** 216
18. Which is the LCM of 54 and 72?
    A. 9 **B.** 18 **(C.)** 216 **D.** 972

All text pages available online and on CD-ROM.

Enrichment — Above Level

Circling Proportions

E 6-5 NUMBER SENSE

Look at the following sets of ratios. In each ◯, write = if the ratios form a proportion and ≠ if the ratios do not form a proportion. Then circle the proportions and put an "X" through the ratios that are not proportions.

1. $\frac{\$5.00}{10 \text{ days}} = \frac{\$25.00}{50 \text{ days}}$
2. $\frac{12 \text{ days}}{5 \text{ days}} \neq \frac{44 \text{ years}}{8 \text{ years}}$
3. $\frac{2 \text{ ft}}{30 \text{ sec}} \neq \frac{3 \text{ ft}}{40 \text{ sec}}$
4. $\frac{6 \text{ m}}{50 \text{ m}} = \frac{27 \text{ sec}}{225 \text{ sec}}$
5. $\frac{20 \text{ mi}}{50 \text{ mi}} = \frac{2 \text{ hr}}{5 \text{ hr}}$
6. $\frac{15 \text{ lb}}{180 \text{ ft}^2} \neq \frac{6 \text{ lb}}{35 \text{ ft}^2}$
7. $\frac{3 \text{ in.}}{1 \text{ week}} = \frac{9 \text{ in.}}{3 \text{ weeks}}$
8. $\frac{49 \text{ ft}}{63 \text{ rolls}} = \frac{77 \text{ ft}}{99 \text{ rolls}}$
9. $\frac{30 \text{ oz}}{\$4.00} \neq \frac{60 \text{ oz}}{\$6.00}$
10. $\frac{21 \text{ hr}}{51 \text{ hr}} = \frac{49 \text{ weeks}}{119 \text{ weeks}}$
11. $\frac{90 \text{ mi}}{2 \text{ hr}} = \frac{270 \text{ mi}}{6 \text{ hr}}$
12. $\frac{20 \text{ cm}}{45 \text{ sec}} = \frac{24 \text{ cm}}{54 \text{ sec}}$
13. $\frac{5 \text{ books}}{2 \text{ weeks}} = \frac{20 \text{ books}}{8 \text{ weeks}}$
14. $\frac{5 \text{ g}}{8 \text{ mL}} = \frac{60 \text{ g}}{96 \text{ mL}}$
15. $\frac{\$7.00}{1 \text{ hr}} \neq \frac{\$21.00}{2 \text{ hr}}$
16. $\frac{100 \text{ mi}}{6 \text{ days}} \neq \frac{40 \text{ mi}}{2 \text{ days}}$
17. $\frac{2 \text{ laps}}{20 \text{ min}} = \frac{3 \text{ laps}}{30 \text{ min}}$
18. $\frac{6 \text{ wins}}{9 \text{ games}} \neq \frac{64 \text{ wins}}{81 \text{ games}}$
19. $\frac{6 \text{ m}}{8 \text{ min}} \neq \frac{8 \text{ min}}{4 \text{ m}}$
20. $\frac{7 \text{ days}}{1 \text{ week}} = \frac{42 \text{ days}}{6 \text{ weeks}}$
21. $\frac{225 \text{ km}}{3 \text{ hr}} = \frac{450 \text{ km}}{6 \text{ hr}}$
22. $\frac{27 \text{ kg}}{180 \text{ bags}} = \frac{12 \text{ kg}}{80 \text{ bags}}$
23. $\frac{4 \text{ CDs}}{\$45.00} \neq \frac{8 \text{ CDs}}{\$60.00}$
24. $\frac{72 \text{ birds}}{20 \text{ trees}} = \frac{54 \text{ birds}}{15 \text{ trees}}$

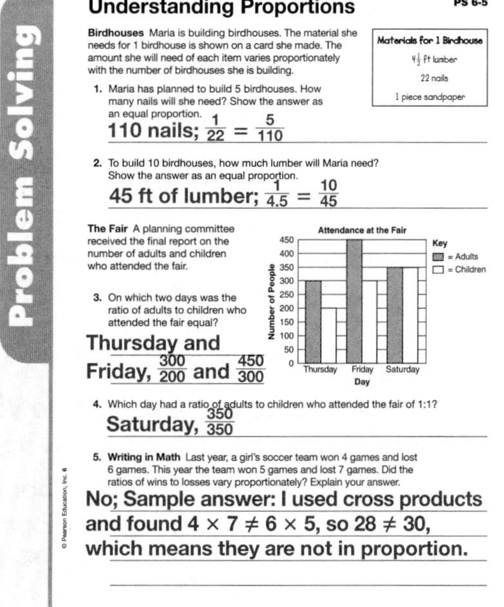

Problem Solving

Understanding Proportions

PS 6-5

Birdhouses Maria is building birdhouses. The material she needs for 1 birdhouse is shown on a card she made. The amount she will need of each item varies proportionately with the number of birdhouses she is building.

Materials for 1 Birdhouse
$4\frac{1}{2}$ ft lumber
22 nails
1 piece sandpaper

1. Maria has planned to build 5 birdhouses. How many nails will she need? Show the answer as an equal proportion.
   110 nails; $\frac{1}{22} = \frac{5}{110}$
2. To build 10 birdhouses, how much lumber will Maria need? Show the answer as an equal proportion.
   45 ft of lumber; $\frac{1}{4.5} = \frac{10}{45}$

The Fair A planning committee received the final report on the number of adults and children who attended the fair.

Attendance at the Fair
Number of People: 0 50 100 150 200 250 300 350 400 450
Day: Thursday Friday Saturday
Key: = Adults, = Children

3. On which two days was the ratio of adults to children who attended the fair equal?
   Thursday and Friday, $\frac{300}{200}$ and $\frac{450}{300}$
4. Which day had a ratio of adults to children who attended the fair of 1:1?
   Saturday, $\frac{350}{350}$
5. **Writing in Math** Last year, a girl's soccer team won 4 games and lost 6 games. This year the team won 5 games and lost 7 games. Did the ratios of wins to losses vary proportionately? Explain your answer.
   No; Sample answer: I used cross products and found $4 \times 7 \neq 6 \times 5$, so $28 \neq 30$, which means they are not in proportion.

CHECK

Error Intervention

If students multiply top terms and bottom terms instead of finding cross products,

then have them use a marker to show the numbers to be multiplied.

(*Also see* Reteaching, *p. 316B*.)

3 Practice

Exercise 15 Help students see that each photograph size can be written as a ratio. Review the definition of *vary proportionally*. Point out that for quantities to vary proportionally, *all* ratios must be equal.

Leveled Practice

Below Level Ex. 5–13, 15–18

On Level Ex. 6–18

Above Level Ex. 6–18

Early Finishers Have students find two photograph sizes whose dimensions vary proportionally with each of the four sizes in Exercise 15.

4 Assess

Journal Idea Have students explain how to tell when two ratios form a proportion.

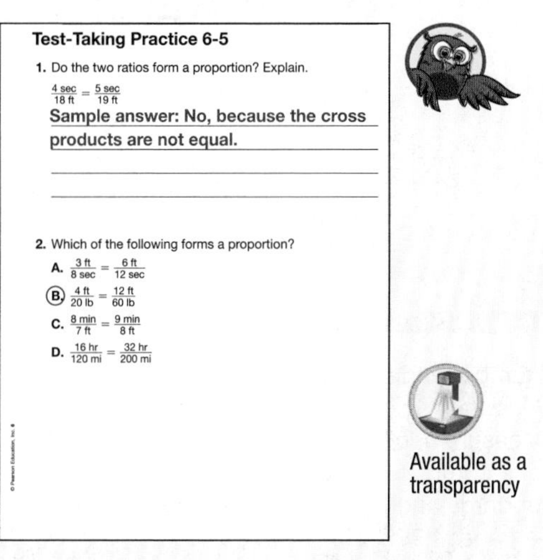

Test-Taking Practice 6-5

1. Do the two ratios form a proportion? Explain.
   $\frac{4 \text{ sec}}{18 \text{ ft}} = \frac{5 \text{ sec}}{19 \text{ ft}}$
   Sample answer: No, because the cross products are not equal.
2. Which of the following forms a proportion?
   A. $\frac{3 \text{ ft}}{8 \text{ sec}} = \frac{6 \text{ ft}}{12 \text{ sec}}$
   (B.) $\frac{4 \text{ ft}}{20 \text{ lb}} = \frac{12 \text{ ft}}{60 \text{ lb}}$
   C. $\frac{8 \text{ min}}{7 \text{ ft}} = \frac{9 \text{ min}}{8 \text{ ft}}$
   D. $\frac{16 \text{ hr}}{120 \text{ mi}} = \frac{32 \text{ hr}}{200 \text{ mi}}$

Available as a transparency

6-6 Solving Proportions

Lesson Organizer

Quick Lesson Overview

Objective Solve proportions whose terms are whole numbers or money.

Math Understanding Two methods of solving proportions are to use the unit amount and to use a common factor.

Managing Instruction As you discuss the solution to one example, have a student reproduce a ratio table on the board for the next example. To assist students in completing the activity, have them work together to complete each ratio table.

NCTM Standards

- Number and Operations
- Algebra
- Measurement

(For a complete correlation to the NCTM Standards and Grades 6–8 Expectations, see pages 298G–H.)

Getting Started

Spiral Review

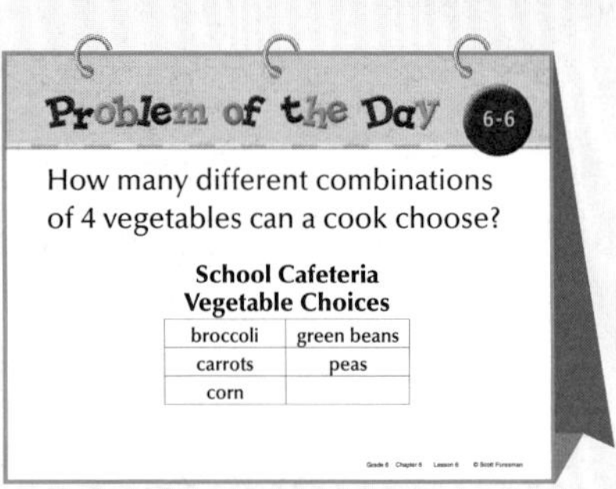

Problem of the Day 6-6

How many different combinations of 4 vegetables can a cook choose?

School Cafeteria Vegetable Choices

broccoli	green beans
carrots	peas
corn	

Topics Reviewed

- Listing outcomes
- Problem-Solving Strategy: Make an Organized List

Answer There are 5 ways to choose 4 vegetables from the list of 5 choices.

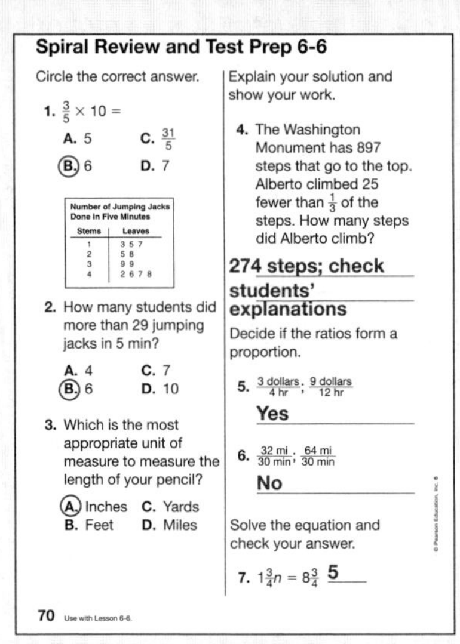

Spiral Review and Test Prep 6-6

Circle the correct answer.

1. $\frac{3}{5} \times 10 =$

A. 5 (B.) 6 C. $\frac{31}{5}$ D. 7

Number of Jumping Jacks Done in Five Minutes

Stems	Leaves
1	3 5 7
2	5 8
3	9 9
4	2 6 7 8

2. How many students did more than 29 jumping jacks in 5 min?

A. 4 (B.) 6 C. 7 D. 10

3. Which is the most appropriate unit of measure to measure the length of your pencil?

(A.) Inches B. Feet C. Yards D. Miles

Explain your solution and show your work.

4. The Washington Monument has 897 steps that go to the top. Alberto climbed 25 fewer than $\frac{1}{3}$ of the steps. How many steps did Alberto climb?

274 steps; check students' explanations

Decide if the ratios form a proportion.

5. $\frac{3 \text{ dollars}}{4 \text{ hr}}, \frac{9 \text{ dollars}}{12 \text{ hr}}$ Yes

6. $\frac{32 \text{ mi}}{30 \text{ min}}, \frac{64 \text{ mi}}{30 \text{ min}}$ No

Solve the equation and check your answer.

7. $1\frac{3}{4}n = 8\frac{3}{4}$ 5

70 Use with Lesson 6-6.

Available as a transparency and as a blackline master

Topics Reviewed

1. Multiplying a fraction and a whole number; **2.** Stem-and-leaf plots; **3.** Customary units of length; **4.** Writing to explain; **5.–6.** Understanding proportions; **7.** Solving equations with fractions

Investigating the Concept

Make a Ratio Table

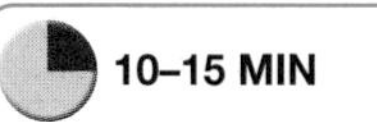

10–15 MIN **Kinesthetic**

What to Do

- Tell students the ratio of boys to girls on a committee is 2:3. Show students the table below. **This is called a *ratio table,* and we will use it to find the number of boys for 12 girls.**

Number of Boys	2	?	?	?
Number of Girls	3	6	9	12

- Have 3 girls come to the front of the class. **How many boys do we need?** *(2 boys)* Bring up 2 boys. Bring up more 3-girl groups and 2-boy groups. **Complete the table. How many boys are needed for 6 girls? For 9 girls? For 12 girls?** *(4 boys; 6 boys; 8 boys)*

Ongoing Assessment

- **Reasoning How many girls do you need for 10 boys? How do you know? Explain.** *(15 girls; The ratio 10 to 15 is equivalent to 2 to 3.)*
- **Number Sense Will the number of boys ever be greater than the number of girls? Explain.** *(No; The number of boys is less than the number of girls in the original ratio.)*

Reaching All Learners

Math and Literature

Building a Totem Pole

 15–20 MIN **Auditory** 

Materials: *Totem Pole* by Diane Hoyt-Goldsmith (Holiday House, 1994)

- Read the book to the class. In the story, a boy tells about his father's building a totem pole.
- **We learn that 6 feet of the pole is buried underground and 40 feet of carving stands above ground. If you made a model in which $\frac{1}{2}$ inch = 1 foot, how much of the model would be below ground?** *(3 in.)* **Above ground level?** *(20 in.)*

Activate Prior Knowledge/Build Background

English Language Learners

Cats and Dogs

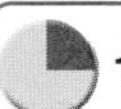 10–15 MIN **Logical/Mathematical** 

- Poll students to find out who prefers cats and who prefers dogs.
- Chart responses in a table like the one below.
- Ask students what they think would happen if you polled a larger group. Double the number of students preferring cats. Add that number to the chart. Have students predict how many of the larger group would then prefer dogs.

Students Preferring Cats	4
Students Preferring Dogs	3

Reteaching

Ratio Tables

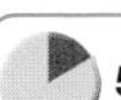 5–10 MIN **Social/Cooperative** 

- **Make a ratio table for the ratio of pencils to pens. Student 1, write the ratio of 5 pencils to 3 pens.** *($\frac{5}{3}$)* **The rest of the group, take turns writing equivalent ratios to complete the table.**
- **Use your ratio table to find how many pencils correspond to 12 pens. Which ratio can you use?** *($\frac{20}{12}$)* **How many pencils correspond to 12 pens?** *(20 pencils)*

Pencils	5	10	15	20	25
Pens	3				

Math and Science

Light and Sound

 5–10 MIN **Logical/Mathematical** 

- **Light travels 372,464 miles in 2 seconds and sound travels 2,232 feet in 2 seconds. How far does sound travel in 5 seconds?** *(5,580 ft)* **About how many miles is this?** *(About 1 mile)*
- **About how many times faster than sound does light travel?** *(Sample answer: About 880,000 times)*
- **Since sound travels 1 mile in 5 seconds, how can you estimate your distance, in miles, from a thunderstorm?** *(Sample answer: Divide 5 into the number of seconds between seeing lightning and hearing thunder.)*

Objective Solve proportions whose terms are whole numbers or money.

1 Warm Up

Activate Prior Knowledge Review how to find the cross products in a proportion.

2 Teach

LEARN Discuss all three ways presented to solve proportions. Visual learners may prefer using ratio tables, while logical/mathematical learners may prefer using unit rates or equivalent ratios. You may want to have students work in pairs to share their thinking.

Example In *Another Way,* students find an equivalent ratio by multiplying, but first they divide the second term of the second ratio (12) by the second term of the first ratio (5) to find an exact value with which to multiply. Some students may intuitively "jump" to using cross products to solve the proportion. Assure them that the next lesson will focus on this method.

Key Idea
There are different methods for solving proportions.

Think It Through
I can **make a table** and **look for a pattern** to solve proportions.

Solving Proportions

WARM UP

Find each pair of cross products.

1. $\frac{2}{3} = \frac{8}{12}$ 2. $\frac{18}{6} = \frac{15}{5}$
3. $\frac{24}{36} = \frac{4}{6}$ 4. $\frac{5}{10} = \frac{7}{14}$

1. $2 \times 12 = 3 \times 8 = 24$
2. $18 \times 5 = 6 \times 15 = 90$
3. $24 \times 6 = 36 \times 4 = 144$
4. $5 \times 14 = 10 \times 7 = 70$

LEARN

Activity

How can you use ratio tables to solve proportions?

Solve these problems by copying and completing the ratio tables. In each problem, the quantities vary proportionally.

a. For every 3 CD-of-the-month club subscriptions sold to men, 8 subscriptions are sold to women. At this rate, how many subscriptions would be sold to women if 18 are sold to men? Look at the pattern. **48 subscriptions**

The yellow counters below show the number of CD subscriptions sold to men. The red counters show the number sold to women.

Subscriptions Sold to Men	3	6	9	12	15	18
Subscriptions Sold to Women	8	16	?	?	?	?

24 32 40 48

b. Of the last 100 vehicles sold at a particular dealership, 60 were sport utility vehicles (SUVs). At this rate, how many SUVs would be sold out of the next 40 vehicles sold? **24 SUVs**

Total Vehicles Sold	100	10	20	30	40
Total SUVs Sold	60	6	?	?	?

c. In Problem a, how did you know what numbers to write in the row titled Subscriptions Sold to Women? **The numbers were multiples of 8.**

d. In Problem b, $\frac{100}{60}$ was first simplified to $\frac{10}{6}$. Then what was done to complete the table?

$\frac{10}{6}$ was multiplied by $\frac{2}{2}$, then $\frac{3}{3}$, then $\frac{4}{4}$.

Below Level **Reteaching**

Solving Proportions R 6-6

The Deejay A radio deejay plays 2 min of commercials for every 10 min of music he plays. If he has played 60 min of music, how many minutes of commercials does he need to play?

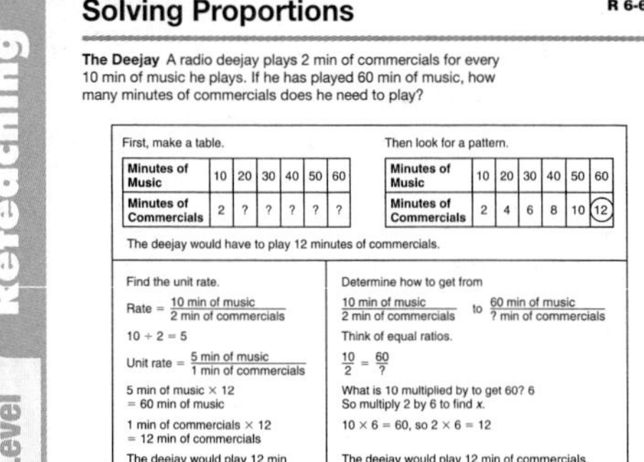

First, make a table.

Minutes of Music	10	20	30	40	50	60
Minutes of Commercials	2	?	?	?	?	?

Then look for a pattern.

Minutes of Music	10	20	30	40	50	60
Minutes of Commercials	2	4	6	8	10	12

The deejay would have to play 12 minutes of commercials.

Find the unit rate.

Rate = $\frac{\text{10 min of music}}{\text{2 min of commercials}}$

$10 \div 2 = 5$

Unit rate = $\frac{\text{5 min of music}}{\text{1 min of commercials}}$

5 min of music × 12
= 60 min of music

1 min of commercials × 12
= 12 min of commercials

The deejay would play 12 min of commercials.

Determine how to get from $\frac{\text{10 min of music}}{\text{2 min of commercials}}$ to $\frac{\text{60 min of music}}{\text{? min of commercials}}$

Think of equal ratios.

$\frac{10}{2} = \frac{60}{?}$

What is 10 multiplied by to get 60? 6
So multiply 2 by 6 to find x.

$10 \times 6 = 60$, so $2 \times 6 = 12$

The deejay would play 12 min of commercials.

Solve each proportion using any method.

1. $\frac{2\text{ ft}}{6\text{ hr}} = \frac{x\text{ ft}}{18\text{ hr}}$ **$x = 6$ ft**
2. $\frac{15\text{ ft}}{t\text{ hr}} = \frac{60\text{ ft}}{4\text{ hr}}$ **$t = 1$ hr**
3. $\frac{5\text{ in.}}{2\text{ weeks}} = \frac{b\text{ in.}}{1\text{ week}}$ **$b = 2.5$ in.**
4. $\frac{65\text{ mi}}{\text{hr}} = \frac{455\text{ mi}}{r\text{ hr}}$ **$r = 7$ hr**
5. $\frac{w\text{ ft}}{2\text{ hr}} = \frac{600\text{ ft}}{10\text{ hr}}$ **$w = 120$ ft**
6. $\frac{\$125}{\text{week}} = \frac{\$1{,}000}{s\text{ weeks}}$ **$s = 8$ weeks**
7. **Number Sense** Movies are filmed as a series of pictures called frames. Usually movies are shown at a rate of 24 frames, or pictures, per second. How many frames are in 8 sec of a movie? **192 frames**

On Level **Practice**

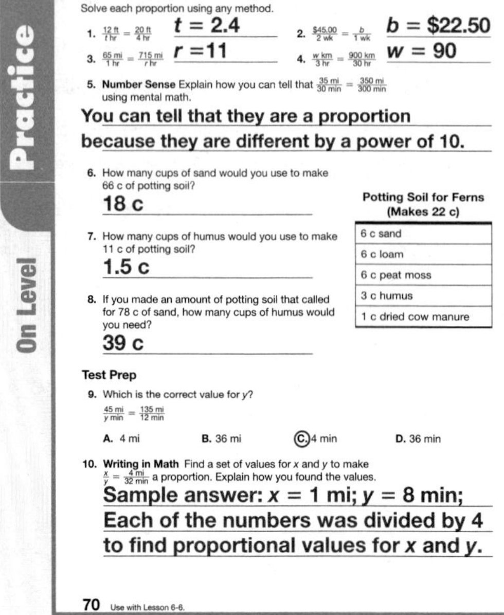

Solving Proportions P 6-6

Solve each proportion using any method.

1. $\frac{12\text{ ft}}{t\text{ hr}} = \frac{20\text{ ft}}{4\text{ hr}}$ **$t = 2.4$**
2. $\frac{\$45.00}{2\text{ wk}} = \frac{b}{1\text{ wk}}$ **$b = \$22.50$**
3. $\frac{65\text{ mi}}{1\text{ hr}} = \frac{715\text{ mi}}{r\text{ hr}}$ **$r = 11$**
4. $\frac{w\text{ km}}{3\text{ hr}} = \frac{900\text{ km}}{30\text{ hr}}$ **$w = 90$**
5. **Number Sense** Explain how you can tell that $\frac{35\text{ mi}}{30\text{ min}} = \frac{350\text{ mi}}{300\text{ min}}$ using mental math.
You can tell that they are a proportion because they are different by a power of 10.

Potting Soil for Ferns (Makes 22 c)

6 c sand
6 c loam
6 c peat moss
3 c humus
1 c dried cow manure

6. How many cups of sand would you use to make 66 c of potting soil? **18 c**
7. How many cups of humus would you use to make 11 c of potting soil? **1.5 c**
8. If you made an amount of potting soil that called for 78 c of sand, how many cups of humus would you need? **39 c**

Test Prep

9. Which is the correct value for y?
$\frac{45\text{ mi}}{y\text{ min}} = \frac{135\text{ mi}}{12\text{ min}}$
A. 4 mi B. 36 mi **C.** 4 min D. 36 min
10. **Writing in Math** Find a set of values for x and y to make $\frac{x}{y} = \frac{4\text{ mi}}{32\text{ min}}$ a proportion. Explain how you found the values.
Sample answer: $x = 1$ mi; $y = 8$ min; Each of the numbers was divided by 4 to find proportional values for x and y.

What are other methods for solving proportions?

Sometimes it is not easy to make a table to solve a proportion.

Example

Karla paid \$60 for 5 CDs. What would it cost to buy a dozen CDs?

Write a proportion, letting x represent the cost of a dozen CDs: $\frac{\$60}{5\text{ CDs}} = \frac{x}{12\text{ CDs}}$.

Then, solve the proportion for x.

One Way

Find the unit rate.

It costs \$60 for 5 CDs, so divide to find the price for 1 CD.

$5\overline{)\$60}$ = \$12 Unit rate: $\frac{\$12}{1\text{ CD}}$

One CD costs \$12, so 12 CDs would cost 12 × \$12 = \$144.

Another Way

Determine how to get from $\frac{\$60}{5\text{ CDs}}$ to $\frac{x}{12\text{ CDs}}$.

Think of equal ratios.

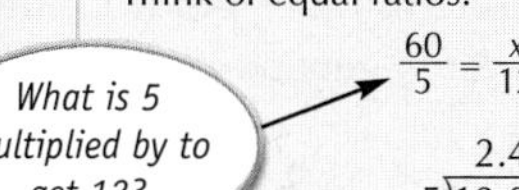

$\frac{60}{5} = \frac{x}{12}$

$5\overline{)12.0}$ = 2.4

5 × 2.4 = 12, and 60 × 2.4 = 144.

Multiply 60 by the same number to find x.

It would cost \$144 to buy 12 CDs.

Talk About It

1. In the first method in the Example, what two numbers were used to find the unit price? **\$60 and 5**
2. In the second method in the Example, would you use the same operation if you wrote the proportion $\frac{5\text{ CDs}}{\$60} = \frac{12\text{ CDs}}{x}$? **Yes**
3. **Estimation** How could you have estimated a value for x in the proportion above? **Since 12 is more than twice as much as 5, x should be a little more than 2 × \$60 = 120.**

CHECK

For another example, see Set 6-6 on p. 347.

Solve each proportion using any method.

1. $\frac{\$25}{4\text{ hours}} = \frac{x}{12\text{ hours}}$ **x = \$75**
2. $\frac{16\text{ ft}}{5\text{ s}} = \frac{48\text{ ft}}{x}$ **x = 15 s**
3. $\frac{5\text{ gal}}{20\text{ qt}} = \frac{x}{6\text{ qt}}$ **x = 1.5 gal**
4. Lauren's car averages 24 miles for each gallon of gasoline. How many gallons are needed for a trip of 216 miles? **9 gallons**
5. If rent for 2 weeks is \$750, how much rent is paid for 5 weeks? **\$1,875**
6. **Estimation** Melinda earned \$380 working 40 hours. Use *estimation* to decide if she earned between \$8 and \$9 an hour or between \$9 and \$10 an hour. Tell how you decided. **Between \$9 and \$10 an hour because 40 × \$9 = \$360 and 40 × \$10 = \$400.**

Ongoing Assessment

Talk About It: Question 1

If students think the two numbers 12 (the CDs) and 60 (dollars) should be used to determine the unit rate,

then suggest that they draw a picture to help them visualize the problem and write the ratios. They can use their diagram to see that \$60 corresponds to 5 CDs.

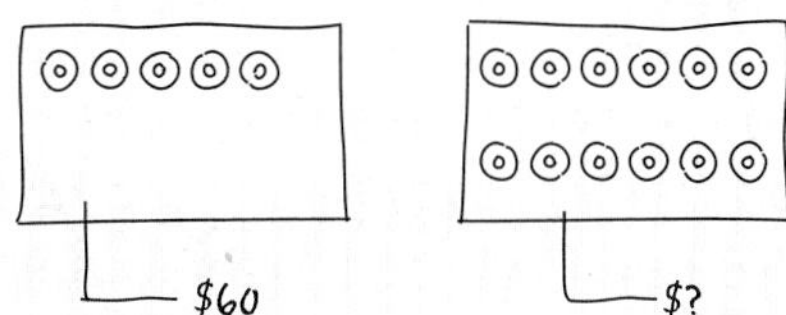

CHECK

Error Intervention

If students do not multiply or divide both terms of the ratio by the same number when completing a ratio table,

then remind students that all the entries in a ratio table are equivalent ratios, and if they multiply or divide the terms of the ratio by different numbers, they will not get an equivalent ratio. *(Also see* Reteaching, *p. 318B.)*

Enrichment — Above Level

Proper Proportions

E 6-6 REASONABLENESS

The proportions in the left column are missing a term. Find the term in the right column that will complete the proportion. Write the letter of the missing term in the space provided.

M 1. $\frac{\$3.00}{5\text{ hr}} = \frac{\$7.20}{x}$

H 2. $\frac{x}{9\text{ min}} = \frac{12\text{ oz}}{18\text{ oz}}$

B 3. $\frac{7\text{ ft}}{2\text{ sec}} = \frac{x}{90\text{ sec}}$

E 4. $\frac{75\text{ mi}}{100\text{ mi}} = \frac{3\text{ hr}}{x}$

C 5. $\frac{x}{65\text{ sec}} = \frac{6\text{ m}}{32.5\text{ m}}$

G 6. $\frac{17\text{ cm}}{2\text{ min}} = \frac{x}{4\text{ min}}$

I 7. $\frac{14\text{ mi}}{7\text{ days}} = \frac{36\text{ mi}}{x}$

P 8. $\frac{\$500}{x} = \frac{\$1{,}500}{3\text{ months}}$

Q 9. $\frac{45\text{ min}}{10\text{ pages}} = \frac{x}{50\text{ pages}}$

J 10. $\frac{90\text{ books}}{6\text{ weeks}} = \frac{x}{5\text{ weeks}}$

A. 7.5 days
B. 315 ft
C. 12 sec
D. 45 cm
E. 4 hr
F. 12 m
G. 34 cm
H. 6 min
I. 18 days
J. 75 books
K. \$12.00
L. 4 mi
M. 12 hr
N. 6 oz
O. 315 ft
P. 1 month
Q. 225 min

Problem Solving

Solving Proportions

PS 6-6

Measurements A local hardware store displayed some common measurements in their fence department.

Measurements
1 yd = 3 ft
1 mi = 1,760 yd
1 mi = 5,280 ft

1. A gardener measured his vegetable patch as 4 yd around, but garden fence was sold in feet. Use a ratio table to find the number of feet in 4 yd.

Feet	3	6	9	12
Yards	1	2	3	4

12 ft

2. Some stores sold garden fence cheaper by the yard. Solve an equation to find the correct proportion for 60 ft.
$\frac{1}{3} = \frac{x}{60}$, 60 = 3$x$, x = 20 yd

Minimum Wage The U.S. government sets a minimum wage that applies to many workers. In 2002, the minimum wage was \$5.15 per hour.

3. At the Mammoth Record Company, 20 out of every 160 workers are paid minimum wage. If the current workforce is 560, what is the payroll cost for minimum-wage workers for a 4-hr shift? Show your work.
$\frac{20}{160} = \frac{m}{560}$, 160$m$ = 20 × 560, m = 70 minimum-wage workers, 70 × 4 × \$5.15 = \$1,442.

4. If a worker received $1\frac{1}{2}$ times the hourly minimum wage for working on a holiday, how much would the worker receive for 4 hr of work on a holiday?
\$30.90; \$5.15 × 1.5 × 4 = \$30.90.

5. **Writing in Math** Solve $\frac{x\text{ laps}}{12\text{ min}} = \frac{18\text{ laps}}{54\text{ min}}$. Explain how you could find the number of laps run in 12 min using the unit method.
Sample answer: If 18 laps were run in 54 min, then 1 lap was run every 3 min. In 12 min, 4 laps were run.

3 Practice

Exercises 13 and 14 Before students begin work, suggest they decide what unit will be the first term and what unit will be the second term of each ratio. Then have them write each ratio using a variable to represent the unknown term.

Exercises 18 and 19 Suggest that students draw a diagram to help them picture what they know and what they need to find. In each case, have them decide which body part (hand or foot; toe or hand) will be longer to help them determine if their answers are reasonable.

TEST TALK **Exercise 21** Students' answers must reflect both parts of the question: Describe why the given explanation is correct or incorrect and, if incorrect, present a correct explanation.

Reading Assist Summarize Ask students to summarize the three methods in this lesson for solving a proportion and explain when they prefer to use each method.

PRACTICE *For more practice, see Set 6-6 on p. 350.*

A Skills and Understanding

Solve each proportion using any method.

7. $\frac{9 \text{ m}}{b \text{ s}} = \frac{6 \text{ m}}{8 \text{ s}}$ **b = 12 sec**

8. $\frac{\$31.50}{5 \text{ hours}} = \frac{f}{7 \text{ hours}}$ **f = $44.10**

9. $\frac{220 \text{ mi}}{4 \text{ h}} = \frac{82.5 \text{ mi}}{y \text{ h}}$ **y = 1.5 h**

10. $\frac{300 \text{ mi}}{p \text{ h}} = \frac{180 \text{ mi}}{6 \text{ h}}$ **p = 10 h**

11. $\frac{\$93.75}{y \text{ h}} = \frac{\$62.50}{10 \text{ h}}$ **y = 15 h**

12. $\frac{2.4 \text{ ft}}{4.5 \text{ s}} = \frac{p \text{ ft}}{1.8 \text{ s}}$ **p = 0.96 ft**

13. The local museum requires 3 chaperones for every 15 students. How many chaperones would be necessary for 125 students? **25 chaperones**

14. A model of a park has a length of 5 inches. The park has an actual length of 18 feet and a width of 27 feet. How wide is the model? **7.5 inches**

15. **Number Sense** Sol drove 440 miles in 8 hours. Calculate his speed by finding the unit rate of miles per hour (mph). Explain how you found your answer. **55 mph; I divided 440 by 8.**

B Reasoning and Problem Solving

16. At Happy Day Kiddie Kamp, the ratio of counselors to campers is 2 to 15. How many counselors should be hired if 120 children sign up for the camp? **16 counselors**

17. Chucky's Deli sells 60 salads for every 96 sandwiches. At this rate, how many salads will be sold for every 32 sandwiches? **20 salads**

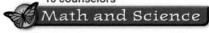

Math and Science

The famous scientist and artist Leonardo da Vinci felt that the parts of a perfect body should be related by certain ratios. His famous 1492 drawing, *Vitruvian Man,* is shown here. The armspan is equal to the man's height. Some of the other ratios are listed below the drawing.

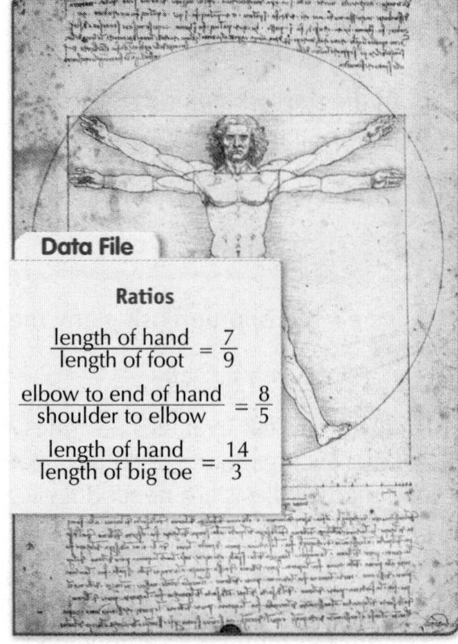

Data File

Ratios

$\frac{\text{length of hand}}{\text{length of foot}} = \frac{7}{9}$

$\frac{\text{elbow to end of hand}}{\text{shoulder to elbow}} = \frac{8}{5}$

$\frac{\text{length of hand}}{\text{length of big toe}} = \frac{14}{3}$

18. If the hand in a drawing measures 21 inches, how long should the foot be? **27 inches**

19. If the length of the big toe of a sculpture is 6 centimeters, how long should the hand be? **28 centimeters**

20. Suppose the distance from the elbow to the end of the hand on a statue measures 18 inches. How long should the distance from the shoulder to the elbow be? **$11\frac{1}{4}$ in.**

320

Test-Taking Practice

Test-Taking Practice, Item 1, p. 321 There are two parts to the problem; the answer and the explanation are each worth two points. Remind the students that they should answer as much as they can since partial credit is given to this type of problem.

Discuss the sample responses shown and compare them to papers produced by your students.

4-point answer Answer is correct; explanation shows complete understanding of solving proportions

Mia's agency will sell 3 opera tickets.

$\frac{21}{56} = \frac{x}{8}$

21×8 5 168; $\frac{168}{56} = 3$;

So, 3 opera tickets will be sold.

PRACTICE

21. **Writing in Math** Is the explanation below correct? If not, tell why and write the correct response.

Uma has 12 boys in her class of 20 students. Felix has 15 boys in his class of 24 students. Which class has the greater ratio of boys to students?

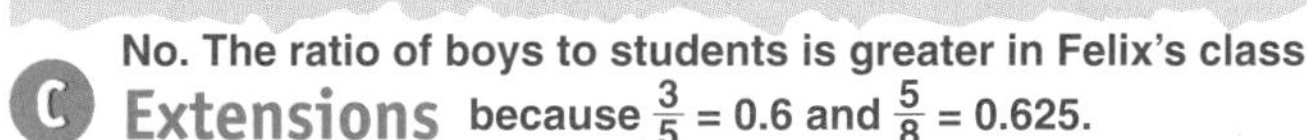

I need to look at the ratios $\frac{12 \text{ boys}}{20 \text{ students}}$ and $\frac{15 \text{ boys}}{24 \text{ students}}$.
When I simplify the ratio of boys to students in Uma's class, I get
$\frac{12 \div 4}{20 \div 4} = \frac{3 \text{ boys}}{5 \text{ students}}$. The simplified ratio for Felix's class is $\frac{5 \text{ boys}}{8 \text{ students}}$.

Since $\frac{3}{5} > \frac{5}{8}$, the ratio is greater in Uma's class.

Think It Through
I should ask myself if there is **another way to solve the problem** as a way to check my answer.

No. The ratio of boys to students is greater in Felix's class because $\frac{3}{5} = 0.6$ and $\frac{5}{8} = 0.625$.

C Extensions

22. **Algebra** Give four values for $\frac{x}{y}$ to make $\frac{50}{24} = \frac{x}{y}$ a proportion. Sample answer: $\frac{25}{12}, \frac{100}{48}, \frac{75}{36}, \frac{200}{96}$

Mixed Review and Test Prep

Take It to the NET
Test Prep
www.scottforesman.com

Decide if the ratios form a proportion.

23. $\frac{10 \text{ ft}}{4 \text{ sec}}, \frac{5 \text{ sec}}{2 \text{ ft}}$ No

24. $\frac{3}{4}, \frac{12}{16}$ Yes

25. $\frac{\$40}{8 \text{ hr}}, \frac{\$55}{11 \text{ hr}}$ Yes

26. Which is $\frac{2}{3} \div \frac{3}{5}$?

A. $\frac{2}{5}$ **(B.)** $\frac{10}{9}$ C. $\frac{9}{10}$ D. $\frac{5}{2}$

Enrichment

Dimensional Analysis

One way of changing units from one unit of measure to another is to use a formula. Another way is to analyze the units and use them to divide and simplify rates. This method is called **dimensional analysis.**

You can use dimensional analysis to calculate the number of times a person's heart beats in one hour, assuming it beats an average of 68 times per minute.

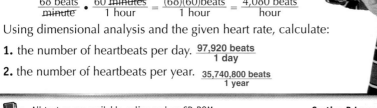

$$\frac{68 \text{ beats}}{\text{minute}} \cdot \frac{60 \text{ minutes}}{1 \text{ hour}} = \frac{(68)(60)\text{beats}}{1 \text{ hour}} = \frac{4{,}080 \text{ beats}}{\text{hour}}$$

Using dimensional analysis and the given heart rate, calculate:

1. the number of heartbeats per day. $\frac{97{,}920 \text{ beats}}{1 \text{ day}}$
2. the number of heartbeats per year. $\frac{35{,}740{,}800 \text{ beats}}{1 \text{ year}}$

3-point answer Answer is correct; explanation is incomplete; shows understanding of solving proportions.

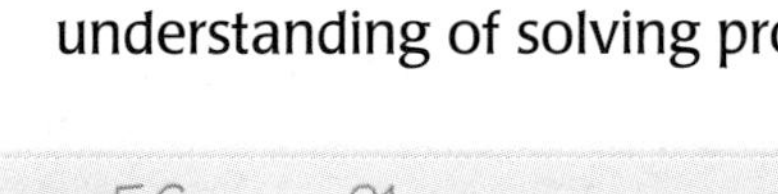

Mia's agency will sell 3 opera tickets.

Find the unit rate.

$\frac{21}{56} = 0.375; 0.375 \times 8 = 3$

1-point answer Incorrect answer; incomplete explanation; show little understanding of solving proportions.

$\frac{56}{8} = 7; \frac{21}{8} = 2.625$

So, 2.625 opera tickets will be sold.

Leveled Practice

Below Level Ex. 7–12, 13–21 odd, 23–26

On Level Ex. 7–15 odd, 16–21, 23–26

Above Level Ex. 12–26

Early Finishers Have students pick three exercises from Exercises 9–12. Then they should solve each exercise two more times, using each of the two methods that they did not already use.

Enrichment For Exercises 1 and 2, encourage students to write the product of every rate needed to convert beats per minute to beats per day or year. Ask them to describe how this method helps them get the correct answer.

4 Assess

Journal Idea Have students describe the method they used to solve Exercise 10 and explain why they chose that method.

Test-Taking Practice 6-6

1. Mia's ticket agency sells tickets to a variety of events. For every 56 tickets sold to the amusement park, Mia's agency sells 21 tickets to the opera. At this rate, how many tickets to the opera will be sold if Mia's agency sells 8 tickets to the amusement park? Explain how you solved the problem.
Sample answer: Mia's ticket agency will sell 3 tickets to the opera for every 8 tickets sold to the amusement park.
Sample explanation: I used this proportion: $\frac{21}{56} = \frac{x}{8}$; $21 \times 8 = 168$; $168 \div 56 = 3$; $x = 3$.

2. Solve the proportion. $\frac{12 \text{ in.}}{f \text{ sec}} = \frac{36 \text{ in.}}{6 \text{ sec}}$
(A) $f = 2$ sec
B. $f = 3$ sec
C. $f = 6$ sec
D. $f = 18$ sec

Available as a transparency

6-7 Solving Proportions Using Cross Products

Lesson Organizer

Quick Lesson Overview 

Objective Use cross products to solve proportions.

Math Understanding The cross-products method is an algorithm for solving proportions. It is based on properties of equality.

Vocabulary Cross products (p. 316)

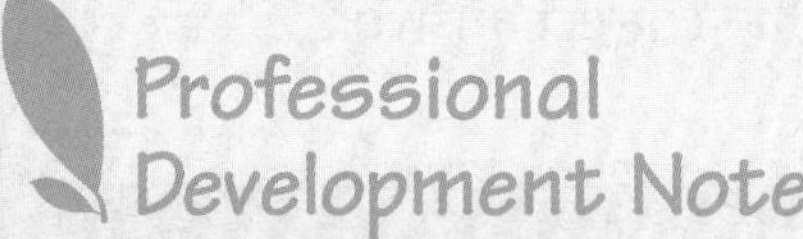

Math Background In the proportion $\frac{a}{b} = \frac{c}{d}$, with b and d not equal to 0, a and d are called the *extremes* of the proportion and b and c are called the *means.* Another way to say that cross products are equal is to say that the product of the means equals the product of the extremes.

NCTM Standards

- Number and Operations
- Algebra

(For a complete correlation to the NCTM Standards and Grades 6–8 Expectations, see pages 298G–H.)

Getting Started

Spiral Review

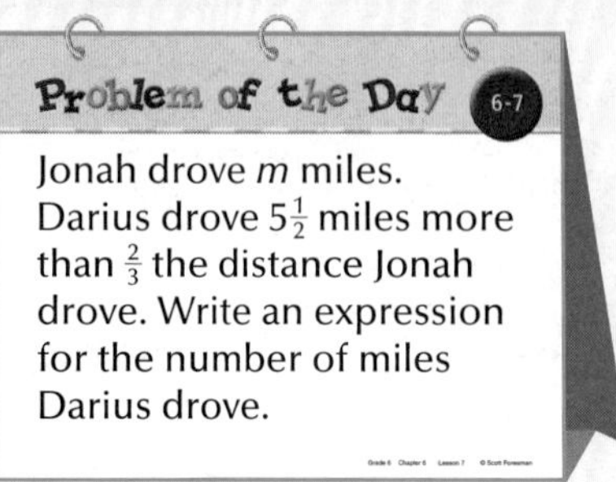

Problem of the Day 6-7

Jonah drove m miles. Darius drove $5\frac{1}{2}$ miles more than $\frac{2}{3}$ the distance Jonah drove. Write an expression for the number of miles Darius drove.

Topics Reviewed

- Expressions with fractions
- Problem-Solving Skill: Translating Words into Expressions

Answer $\frac{2}{3}m + 5\frac{1}{2}$

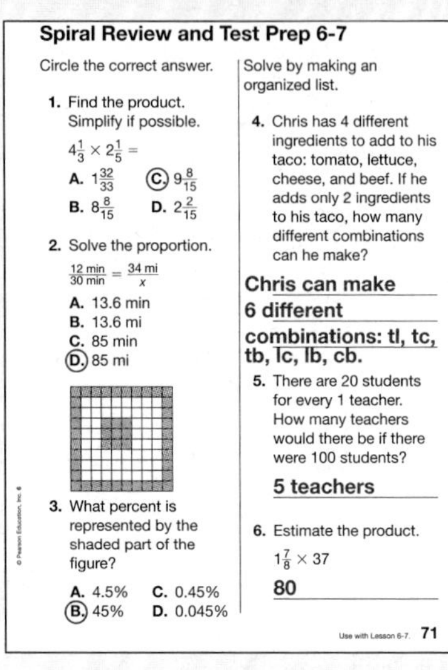

Spiral Review and Test Prep 6-7

Circle the correct answer.

1. Find the product. Simplify if possible.
$4\frac{1}{3} \times 2\frac{1}{5} =$
A. $1\frac{32}{33}$ (C.) $9\frac{8}{15}$
B. $8\frac{8}{15}$ D. $2\frac{2}{15}$

2. Solve the proportion.
$\frac{12 \text{ min}}{30 \text{ min}} = \frac{34 \text{ mi}}{x}$
A. 13.6 min
B. 13.6 mi
C. 85 min
(D.) 85 mi

3. What percent is represented by the shaded part of the figure?
A. 4.5% C. 0.45%
(B.) 45% D. 0.045%

Solve by making an organized list.

4. Chris has 4 different ingredients to add to his taco: tomato, lettuce, cheese, and beef. If he adds only 2 ingredients to his taco, how many different combinations can he make?
Chris can make 6 different combinations: tl, tc, tb, lc, lb, cb.

5. There are 20 students for every 1 teacher. How many teachers would there be if there were 100 students?
5 teachers

6. Estimate the product.
$1\frac{7}{8} \times 37$
80

Use with Lesson 6-7 71

Available as a transparency and as a blackline master

Topics Reviewed

1. Multiplying mixed numbers; **2.**, **5.** Introduction to solving proportions; **3.** Understanding percents; **4.** Make an organized list; **6.** Estimating with fractions and mixed numbers

Investigating the Concept

Using Cross Products

 10–15 MIN **Kinesthetic** 

Materials *(per pair)* 1 worksheet; 8 index cards with two each of 2, 3, 8, and r

What to Do

- Give each pair of students a worksheet containing the two forms shown below.
- Have students place their cards on the forms to show the proportion $\frac{2}{3} = \frac{8}{r}$. **What are the cross products?** *($2 \times r$ and 3×8)* **Show the cross products on the other form.** *($2 \times r = 3 \times 8$)*
- **How can you solve the cross-product equation for r?** *(Divide both sides by 2.)* **What is the solution?** *(12)*

Ongoing Assessment

- **Number Sense Will the unknown value in $\frac{8}{10} = \frac{r}{5}$ be greater than or less than 8? Explain.** *(Less than 8; sample answer: $5 < 10$, so $r < 8$ because they vary proportionally.)*

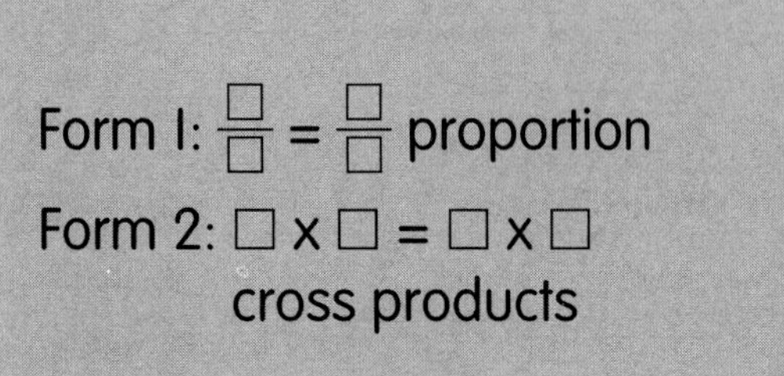

Reaching All Learners

Reading in Math

Step Right Up!

 10–15 MIN **Linguistic** 

- Write this problem on the board: In 1999 Manjit Singh did 4,135 step-ups in 60 minutes on an exercise bench. At that rate, about how many step-ups did Manjit do in 30 seconds?
- **What information is supplied?** *(Manjit did 4,135 step-ups in 60 minutes.)* **How can you use that information to solve the problem?** *(Write a proportion in which each ratio compares step-ups to minutes.)* **How many minutes are in 30 seconds?** *(0.5 or $\frac{1}{2}$ minute)* **How many step-ups did Manjit do in 30 seconds?** *(About 34 step-ups)*

Access Content

English Language Learners

Halves and Doubles

 10–15 MIN **Linguistic/Verbal**

- Ask students to describe their cooking experiences. **Did you follow a recipe when you cooked? How did that work out?**
- Direct attention to the recipe on page 322. Have students find the part that tells how many granola bars this recipe produces. Have groups think aloud as they answer these questions: **Suppose you wanted to make 2 dozen bars. What would you do?** *(Halve the recipe.)* **How many ounces of granola would you need?** *(6 oz)*
- Repeat for 8 dozen bars.

Reteaching

Highlighting the Cross Products

 5–10 MIN **Visual/Spatial** 

Materials *(per pair)* 20 Counters or Teaching Tool 9

- Write $\frac{6}{2} = \frac{9}{x}$ on the board. Show students how to highlight the cross products and write each cross product at the end of the "arrow."

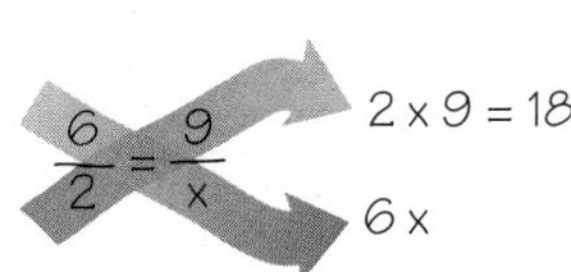

$6x = 18$

$\frac{6x}{6} = \frac{18}{6}$ Divide both sides by 6.

$x = 3$

- To check, have students model the proportion with counters, replacing the x with 3 red counters and then separating each side into groups of 1 yellow and 3 red counters.

Math and Technology

Solving Proportions

 10–15 MIN **Visual/Spatial** 

Materials Spreadsheet/Data/Grapher eTool

To solve proportions using cross products, set up a spreadsheet with the labels and equations shown.

- Enter numbers in cells B1–B3. Observe the proportion and cross products as the whole number, numerator, and denominator change.

	A	B	C	D
1	Enter a whole number here:			
2	Enter a numerator here:			
3	Enter a denominator here:			
4	Here's a proportion:	=B2		=B1
5		=B3		=B3*B1/B2
6	The cross products are:	=B4	x	=D5
7		=B5	x	=D4

Objective Use cross products to solve proportions.

1 Warm Up

Activate Prior Knowledge Review how to find the product of two whole numbers and the product of a whole number and a decimal.

2 Teach

LEARN After students have read the recipe, ask them if they will need to increase or decrease the ingredients to make 2 dozen bars *(decrease)* or to make 9 dozen bars *(increase)*.

Ongoing Assessment

Talk About It: Question 1

If students feel they should divide 6.2 by 2 to estimate,

then point out that if they start with $\frac{25}{6.2}$ and they multiply 25 by 2, then they must also multiply 6.2 by 2.

Lesson 6-7

Key Idea
Another method for solving proportions is to use cross products.

Vocabulary
- cross products (p. 316)

Think It Through
I can **draw a picture** to show the proportion.

Solving Proportions Using Cross Products

WARM UP

1. 8×5 40
2. 12×6 72
3. 7×20 140
4. 1.5×10 15
5. 5×2.4 12
6. 25×4 100

LEARN

How can you use cross products to solve proportions?

GRANOLA BARS
Sift together $1\frac{1}{4}$ cups flour, 1 tsp baking soda, $\frac{1}{2}$ tsp salt. Add 1 cup brown sugar 1 tsp vanilla, and 2 eggs. Beat until smooth. Stir in 12 oz of granola and cup chopped nuts. Spread into greased 9" x 13" pan and bake at 350 for about 25 minutes until brown.
Makes 4 dozen bars.

Example A

Granola Bars How many ounces of granola are needed to make 9 dozen bars?

The picture below shows the proportion.

12 oz	? oz
4 dozen	9 dozen

So, $\frac{12}{4} = \frac{x}{9}$, where x is the number of ounces of granola needed.

Solve $\frac{12}{4} = \frac{x}{9}$.

$12 \cdot 9 = 4x$	Write the cross products.
$108 = 4x$	Multiply.
$\frac{108}{4} = \frac{4x}{4}$	Solve for the variable.
$27 = x$	

For 9 dozen granola bars, 27 ounces of granola are needed.

Example B

Use a calculator to solve $\frac{58.5}{k} = \frac{25}{6.2}$.

Press: 58.5 [×] 6.2 [=] [÷] 25.

Display: 14.508

Why It Works

$\frac{58.5}{k} = \frac{25}{6.2}$

$(58.5)(6.2) = 25k$

$\frac{(58.5)(6.2)}{25} = k$ Round to the nearest tenth.

$14.5 \approx k$

Talk About It

1. **Estimation** In Example B, 58 is about 2 times 25. How can you use that fact to estimate the value of k?
It means that k should be a little more than 2 times 6.2 = 12.4.

322

Reteaching — Below Level

Solving Proportions Using Cross Products

R 6-7

Costumes Gena is making costumes for the school play. She knows that 4 costumes will require 16 yd of fabric. How many yards of fabric will she need for 10 costumes?

Step 1	Step 2	Step 3
Set up the proportion with the information in the problem. $\frac{4}{16} = \frac{10}{y}$	Write the cross products. $\frac{4}{16} \times \frac{10}{y}$ $4 \times y = 16 \times 10$ Then multiply: $4y = 160$	Solve for the variable. $4y = 160$ $\frac{4y}{4} = \frac{160}{4}$ $y = 40$ Gena will need 40 yards of fabric for 10 costumes.

Solve each proportion using cross products. Round to the nearest hundredth as needed.

1. $\frac{r}{50} = \frac{20}{80}$ **12.5**
2. $\frac{54}{h} = \frac{10.5}{21}$ **108**
3. $\frac{50}{60} = \frac{90}{g}$ **108**
4. $\frac{20}{y} = \frac{10}{100}$ **200**
5. $\frac{15}{w} = \frac{45}{120}$ **40**
6. $\frac{80}{75} = \frac{p}{90}$ **96**
7. **Number Sense** How can you tell that n is greater than 100 without solving $\frac{85}{150} = \frac{n}{375}$?
Sample answer: You can look at the bottom numbers and see that to get 375, you will have to multiply by at least 2. If you multiply 85 by at least 2, the number will be more than 100.

Use with Lesson 6-7. 71

Practice — On Level

Solving Proportions Using Cross Products

P 6-7

Solve each proportion using cross products. Round to the nearest hundredth as needed.

1. $\frac{r}{45} = \frac{90}{270}$ **15**
2. $\frac{32}{h} = \frac{5.9}{12}$ **65.08**
3. $\frac{45}{60} = \frac{81}{g}$ **108**
4. $\frac{78}{y} = \frac{98}{100}$ **79.59**
5. **Number Sense** Are the two ratios that make up a proportion always, sometimes, or never equivalent? **always**

The weight of objects on Earth would vary on other planets. This is due to the different gravitational force on each planet. The weight of objects on other planets can be determined by solving proportions.

6. An object that weighs 10 lb on Earth weighs 9 lb on Venus. What would an object that weighs 90 lb on Earth weigh on Venus? **81 lb**
7. An object that weighs 100 lb on Earth weighs 112.5 lb on Neptune. What would an object that weighs 50 lb on Earth weigh on Neptune? **56.25 lb**
8. An object that weighs 234 lb on Jupiter weighs 100 lb on Earth. What would an object that weighs 400 lb on Jupiter weigh on Earth? (Round your answer to the nearest hundredth.) **170.94 lb**

Test Prep

9. Cecelia has read 12 books this summer and has collected 72 tokens from the library's summer reading program. Which of the following shows how to solve for the number of tokens rewarded for each book?
A. $\frac{12}{72} = \frac{t}{1}$ B. $\frac{12}{1} = \frac{t}{72}$ **(C.)** $\frac{12}{72} = \frac{1}{t}$ D. $\frac{1}{12} = \frac{72}{t}$
10. **Writing in Math** Explain how you would use mental math to solve the proportion $\frac{75}{w} = \frac{1}{2}$.
Sample answer: First, multiply 75 by 2 to get 150. Then, divide 150 by 1 to get 150. $w = 150$

Use with Lesson 6-7. 71

 EC NTL 12 11 10 9 8 7 6

CHECK

For another example, see Set 6-7 on p. 347.

Solve each proportion using cross products. Round to the nearest hundredth as needed.

1. $\frac{6}{8} = \frac{p}{12}$ **p = 9**
2. $\frac{g}{6} = \frac{1}{4}$ **g = 1.5**
3. $\frac{4}{m} = \frac{20}{36}$ **m = 7.2**
4. $\frac{2.4}{4.5} = \frac{d}{1.8}$ **d = 0.96**
5. **Number Sense** How can you tell without solving $\frac{45}{20} = \frac{h}{50}$ that h is greater than 100? **45 is more than twice as much as 20 so h must be more than twice as much as 50 = 100.**

PRACTICE

For more practice, see Set 6-7 on p. 350.

A Skills and Understanding

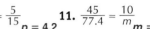

Solve each proportion using cross products. Round to the nearest hundredth as needed.

6. $\frac{b}{3} = \frac{8}{4}$ **b = 6**
7. $\frac{3}{5} = \frac{14}{c}$ **c = 23.33**
8. $\frac{8.4}{h} = \frac{11.2}{6.8}$ **h = 5.1**
9. $\frac{3}{10} = \frac{k}{60}$ **k = 18**
10. $\frac{p}{12.6} = \frac{5}{15}$ **p = 4.2**
11. $\frac{45}{77.4} = \frac{10}{m}$ **m = 17.2**
12. $\frac{w}{24} = \frac{0.875}{6}$ **w = 3.5**
13. $\frac{35}{8} = \frac{27}{j}$ **j = 6.17**
14. **Number Sense** Franci can read 40 pages in 30 minutes. How can you mentally calculate the number of pages she can read in 45 minutes? **45 is 30 plus $\frac{1}{2}$ of 30. Since I added half of 30 to 30, I should add half of 40 to 40 to get 60 pages.**

17. 24 chaperones; 120 = 6 × 20, so 6 × 4 = 24 since there are 6 groups that each need 4 chaperones.

B Reasoning and Problem Solving

The table at the right gives the ratio of pedal turns to rear-wheel turns for each gear of a 5-speed bicycle.

Data File

5-speed Bicycle

Gear	Pedal Turns: Rear-wheel Turns
First	9:14
Second	4:7
Third	1:2
Fourth	3:7
Fifth	5:14

15. On Miguel's bike, the rear wheel turns 770 times per mile. How many times would he have to pedal to travel 1 mile in first gear? fifth gear? **495 pedal turns; 275 pedal turns**
16. If Miguel pedals 385 times to go 1 mile, what gear is the bicycle in? **Third gear**
17. **Writing in Math** For a bike trip, there are to be 4 chaperones for every 20 students. How many chaperones are needed for 120 students? Explain how you found your answer. **see above data file.**

Mixed Review and Test Prep

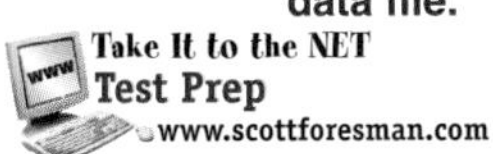

Solve each proportion.

18. $\frac{\$3}{4 \text{ oz}} = \frac{m}{6 \text{ oz}}$ **m = $4.50**
19. $\frac{\$14}{4 \text{ hr}} = \frac{\$35}{v \text{ hr}}$ **v = 10 hr**
20. $\frac{165 \text{ mi}}{3 \text{ hr}} = \frac{r \text{ mi}}{2 \text{ hr}}$ **r = 110 mi**
21. Which is 6.54 × 18.9?

A. 25.44 B. 117.72 **(C.)** 123.606 D. 123.66

 All text pages available online and on CD-ROM.

CHECK

Error Intervention

If students are multiplying the correct terms to find cross products, but have trouble solving for the variable,

then remind them that they will need to divide by the multiplier of the variable to solve the proportion. *(Also see* Reteaching, *p. 322B.)*

3 Practice

TEST TALK

Exercise 17 Suggest that students start by identifying the two categories that are being compared and then deciding which category will be the first term in each ratio and which category will be the second term.

Leveled Practice

Below Level Ex. 6–14, 17–21

On Level Ex. 8–21

Above Level Ex. 8–21

Early Finishers Have students make up two questions using the Data File in Section B. Then they should exchange papers and solve.

4 Assess

Journal Idea Have students explain how to use cross products to find the missing number in a proportion.

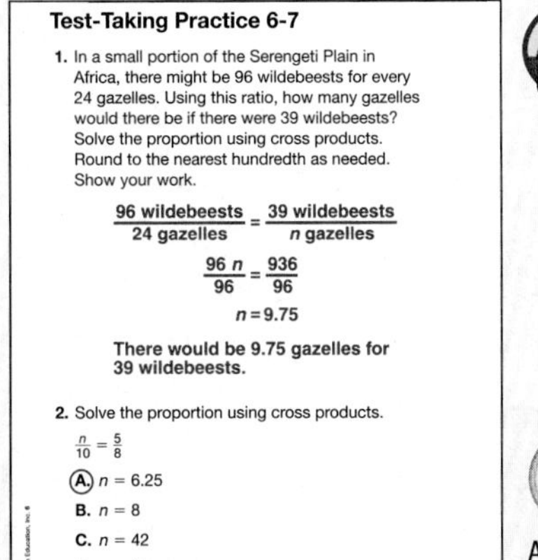
Test-Taking Practice 6-7

1. In a small portion of the Serengeti Plain in Africa, there might be 96 wildebeests for every 24 gazelles. Using this ratio, how many gazelles would there be if there were 39 wildebeests? Solve the proportion using cross products. Round to the nearest hundredth as needed. Show your work.

$$\frac{96 \text{ wildebeests}}{24 \text{ gazelles}} = \frac{39 \text{ wildebeests}}{n \text{ gazelles}}$$
$$\frac{96n}{96} = \frac{936}{96}$$
$$n = 9.75$$

There would be 9.75 gazelles for 39 wildebeests.

2. Solve the proportion using cross products.

$\frac{n}{10} = \frac{5}{8}$

(A.) $n = 6.25$
B. $n = 8$
C. $n = 42$
D. $n = 58$

Available as a transparency

Enrichment — Above Level

Complex Cross Products

E 6-7 ALGEBRA

Proportions can also be written with fractions and mixed numbers. Using cross products to solve for missing numbers works the same way as with whole numbers.

Find the missing number in the proportion $\frac{x}{4} = \frac{(\frac{2}{5})}{(\frac{1}{8})}$.	
Find the cross products.	$x \times \frac{1}{8} = 4 \times \frac{2}{5}$
Multiply each side.	$\frac{x}{8} = \frac{8}{5}$
Multiply by the reciprocal.	$8 \times \frac{x}{8} = \frac{8}{5} \times 8$
Simplify.	$x = \frac{64}{5}$ or $12\frac{4}{5}$

Find the missing number in each proportion.

1. $\frac{(\frac{1}{2})}{(\frac{3}{4})} = \frac{j}{24}$ $j =$ **16**
2. $\frac{(\frac{1}{4})}{(\frac{1}{6})} = \frac{18}{t}$ $t =$ **12**
3. $\frac{(\frac{1}{3})}{14} = \frac{r}{36}$ $r =$ **$\frac{6}{7}$**
4. $\frac{(\frac{5}{6})}{x} = \frac{18}{72}$ $x =$ **$3\frac{1}{3}$**
5. $\frac{p}{12} = \frac{(5\frac{1}{2})}{(27\frac{1}{2})}$ $p =$ **$2\frac{2}{5}$**
6. $\frac{(\frac{1}{3})}{(\frac{1}{4})} = \frac{m}{48}$ $m =$ **64**
7. $\frac{(\frac{2}{3})}{(\frac{5}{8})} = \frac{24}{b}$ $b =$ **$22\frac{1}{2}$**
8. $\frac{a}{60} = \frac{(\frac{1}{2})}{(\frac{9}{10})}$ $a =$ **$33\frac{1}{3}$**
9. $\frac{8}{w} = \frac{(\frac{11}{12})}{(1\frac{1}{2})}$ $w =$ **$13\frac{1}{11}$**
10. $\frac{(\frac{8}{9})}{(\frac{6}{7})} = \frac{56}{y}$ $y =$ **54**

Use with Lesson 6-7. 71

Problem Solving

Solving Proportions Using Cross Products

PS 6-7

Ice Skating Sarah and Tom went ice skating. They skated 66 laps around the rink in 2 hr.

1. How many laps could Sarah and Tom have skated around the rink in 3 hr? **99 laps**
2. Write a unit rate that describes the laps per hour that Sarah and Tom skated. **33 laps per hour**
3. How many times could Sarah and Tom have skated around the rink in 5 hr? **165 laps**

Planet Earth Earth rotates on its axis about once every 24 hr. It also revolves around the Sun about once every 365 days.

4. Write and solve a proportion to find the number of hours it would take Earth to rotate 3 times. **$\frac{1}{24} = \frac{3}{h}$; 72 hr**
5. Write and solve a proportion to find the number of days it would take Earth to revolve around the Sun $1\frac{1}{2}$ times. **$\frac{1}{365} = \frac{1.5}{r}$; 547.5 days**
6. Write and solve a proportion to find the number of hours it would take Earth to rotate 12 times. **$\frac{1}{24} = \frac{12}{h}$; 288 hr**
7. **Writing in Math** A bakery bakes 4 bran muffins for every 12 fruit muffins they bake. If they baked 54 fruit muffins, how many bran muffins did they bake? Explain your answer. **They baked 18 bran muffins. I used cross products. $\frac{4}{12} = \frac{b}{54}$; $4 \times 54 = 12b$; $\frac{216}{12} = b = 18$. (The numbers could be reduced prior to cross multiplying, $\frac{4}{12} = \frac{1}{3}$)**

Use with Lesson 6-7. 71

Writing to Explain

Lesson Organizer

Quick Lesson Overview

Objective Solve word problems and explain how the solution was obtained.

Math Understanding An explanation of the solution to a problem includes information that is known and how you have used this information.

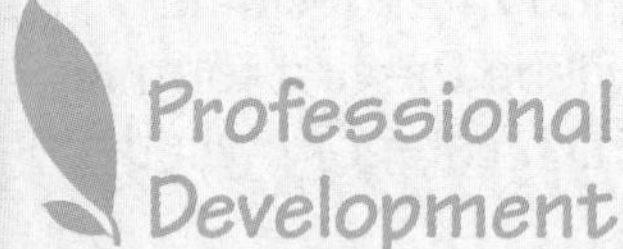

How Children Learn Math
Kinesthetic students may want to use counters to represent art. Logical/mathematical students may see other ways to answer the lesson's questions. Linguistic students who find explanations easy to write can be paired with students who find writing more difficult.

NCTM Standards

- Number and Operations
- Algebra

(For a complete correlation to the NCTM Standards and Grades 6–8 Expectations, see pages 298G–H.)

Getting Started

Spiral Review

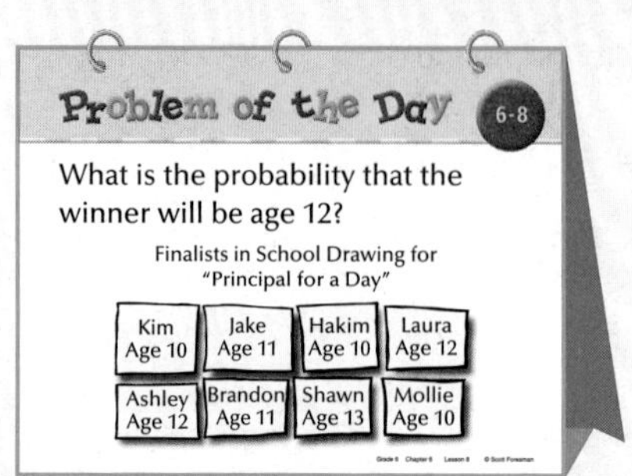

Topics Reviewed

- Probability
- Problem-Solving Skill: One-Step Problem

Answer The probability is $\frac{1}{4}$.

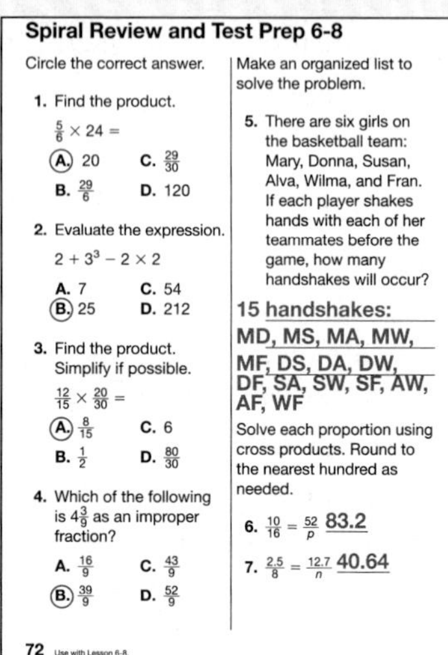

Spiral Review and Test Prep 6-8

Circle the correct answer.

1. Find the product.
   $\frac{5}{6} \times 24 =$
   (A.) 20 C. $\frac{29}{30}$
   B. $\frac{29}{6}$ D. 120

2. Evaluate the expression.
   $2 + 3^3 - 2 \times 2$
   A. 7 C. 54
   (B.) 25 D. 212

3. Find the product. Simplify if possible.
   $\frac{12}{15} \times \frac{20}{30} =$
   (A.) $\frac{8}{15}$ C. 6
   B. $\frac{1}{2}$ D. $\frac{80}{30}$

4. Which of the following is $4\frac{3}{9}$ as an improper fraction?
   A. $\frac{16}{9}$ C. $\frac{43}{9}$
   (B.) $\frac{39}{9}$ D. $\frac{52}{9}$

Make an organized list to solve the problem.

5. There are six girls on the basketball team: Mary, Donna, Susan, Alva, Wilma, and Fran. If each player shakes hands with each of her teammates before the game, how many handshakes will occur?
   15 handshakes: MD, MS, MA, MW, MF, DS, DA, DW, DF, SA, SW, SF, AW, AF, WF

Solve each proportion using cross products. Round to the nearest hundred as needed.

6. $\frac{10}{16} = \frac{52}{p}$ 83.2
7. $\frac{2.5}{8} = \frac{12.7}{n}$ 40.64

72 Use with Lesson 6-8.

Available as a transparency and as a blackline master

Topics Reviewed

1. Multiplying a fraction and a whole number; **2.** Order of operations; **3.** Multiplying fractions; **4.** Mixed numbers and improper fractions; **5.** Mak an organized list; **6.–7.** Solving proportions using cross products

Investigating the Concept

Is It a Match?

10–15 MIN | **Visual/Spatial** | INDIVIDUAL

What to Do

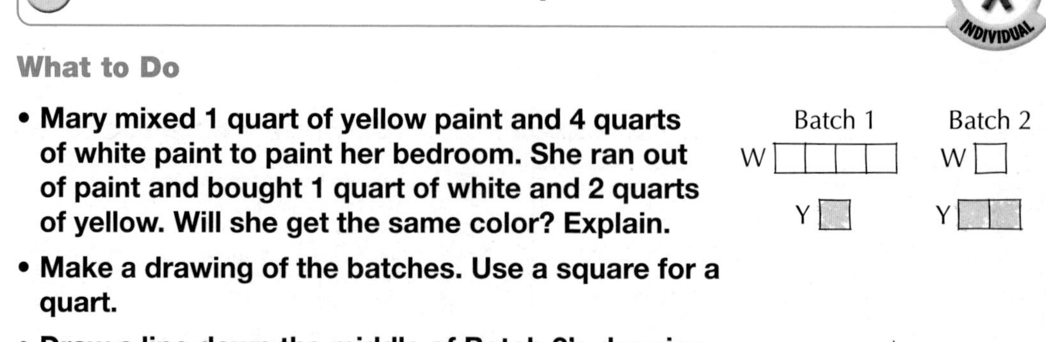

- **Mary mixed 1 quart of yellow paint and 4 quarts of white paint to paint her bedroom. She ran out of paint and bought 1 quart of white and 2 quarts of yellow. Will she get the same color? Explain.**
- **Make a drawing of the batches. Use a square for a quart.**
- **Draw a line down the middle of Batch 2's drawing, so you see how much white was used for 1 quart of yellow. Explain to Mary why she will or won't get the same color.** *(Sample answer: Batch 1 has more white than batch 2 has. So Batch 2 will be darker.)*

Ongoing Assessment

- **Reasoning Describe another way that you could solve the problem.** *(Sample answer: $\frac{4}{1} \neq \frac{1}{2}$.)*

Reaching All Learners

Writing in Math

Picture This

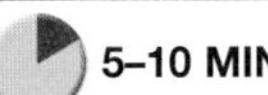 5–10 MIN **Linguistic** 

- Show the negative below. **Write a proportion problem about making a picture from the negative.** *(Sample answer: Martina is making a photo 140 mm long. How wide is it?)*
- **Trade problems. Solve and write an explanation.** *(Sample answer: I wrote the proportion $\frac{35}{23} = \frac{w}{140}$. Then I found cross products and solved to find $w = 213.04$. The width of the photo is 213.04 mm.)*

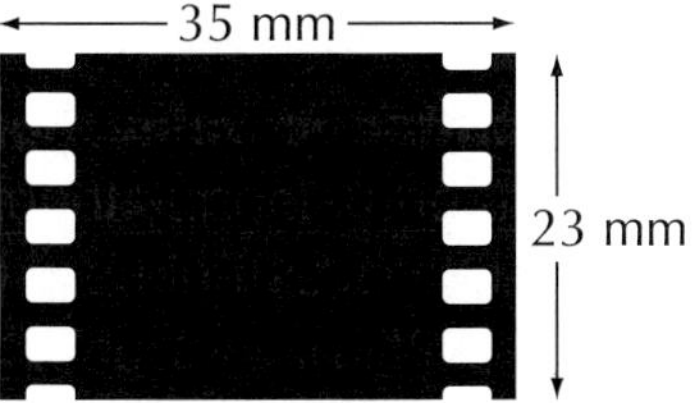

Extend Language

English Language Learners

Adding *-able*

 10–15 MIN **Auditory/Verbal** 

- Display the words *vary* and *variable.* Explain that the suffix *–able* adds the meaning "able to" or "likely to" to a base word. ***Variable* means "likely to vary", and *vary* means "change".**
- Invite students to name any other words they know that end in *–able*
- Have pairs of students read or reread aloud the problem and explanation on page 324, then discuss question 1 in the Talk About It section.
- Ask partners to explain what variable means in their own words. *(Example, A letter like Y or T is a variable because it represents a quantity whose value can vary, or change.)*

Reteaching

Bike Trip

 10–15 MIN **Kinesthetic** 

Materials *(per pair)* Copy of number line shown below

- **What does the number line show?** *(Sample answer: Someone traveled 15 mi in 3 hr.)* **How can you find out how long it will take the person to travel 45 miles?** *(Sample answer: Extend the top number line to 45 mi and the bottom one to 9 hr.)*
- **Solve and write an explanation.** *(Sample answer: Extending the top number line to 45 mi and the bottom one to 9 hr shows that the person should take 9 hr to ride 45 mi.)*

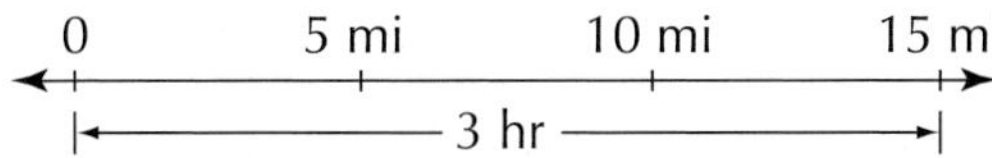

Students with Special Needs

How Many on a Bus?

 10–15 MIN **Auditory** 

- Read aloud Exercise 1 on page 325. **Draw and describe a picture.** *(There are 6 girls for every 5 boys.)*
- **What does the problem ask?** *(How many boys are there when there are 18 girls?)*
- **Solve and explain your solution.** *(Sample answer: I drew a long bus and labeled 6 girls for every 5 boys. When I reached 18 girls, I counted the boys. There were 15 boys.)*

Objective Solve word problems and explain how the solution was obtained.

1 Warm Up

Activate Prior Knowledge Review how to solve proportions and multiplication equations.

2 Teach

LEARN As students develop their skill in writing good explanations, they usually find that they are able to catch errors or identify missing steps in their own solutions.

Ongoing Assessment

Talk About It: Question 2

If students do not see another way to state the solution,

then write several ratios on the board, such as $\frac{1}{4}$, $\frac{2}{4}$, $\frac{2}{5}$, and $\frac{4}{5}$. Tell students that each fraction represents a ratio of concentrate to water. Ask which ratio they think indicates more orange flavor. Have them use their knowledge of ordering fractions to help them with this question.

Problem-Solving Skill

Reading Helps!
Identifying steps in a process can help you with... writing to explain.

Key Idea
There are specific things you can do to write a good explanation in math.

TEST TALK

Think It Through
I should make sure my explanations are clear and well organized so that others can understand them.

Writing to Explain

LEARN

How do you write a good explanation?

When you write to explain, it is important that you describe each step in the solution clearly.

Orange Drink Kimberley has the two recipes for orange drink shown below.

Orange-Drink Recipe 1
- 2 cans orange juice concentrate
- 3 cans of cold water

Orange-Drink Recipe 2
- 4 cans orange juice concentrate
- 8 cans of cold water

Which recipe do you think has more of an orange taste? Write and explain how you decided.

Writing a Math Explanation
- State your answer.
- Break your explanation into steps so it is easier to follow.
- Use pictures or diagrams, if they help in the explanation.
- If computation is part of the solution, show the computation.

I think that Recipe 1 has more of an orange taste. Here is why.

This shows Recipe 2. 4 circles show cans of juice and 8 circles show cans of water.

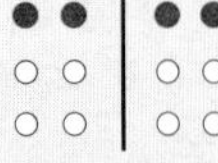

I drew the line to show equal groups. Each group has 2 cans of juice and 4 cans of water.

Recipe 2 uses 2 cans of juice for 4 cans of water. Recipe 1 uses 2 cans of juice for 3 cans of water. Recipe 1 has more juice per can of water, so Recipe 1 has more orange flavor.

✓ Talk About It

2. Yes, the ratio $\frac{2}{3}$ is greater than the ratio $\frac{1}{2}$, so Recipe 1 has more orange juice concentrate.

1. How does the picture help in the explanation? **The picture helps to show the ratio of cans of juice to cans of water for each recipe.**
2. Is there another way to explain the solution to the problem? Explain. **See above.**

Below Level — Reteaching

PROBLEM-SOLVING SKILL R 6-8

Writing to Explain

Chess Club The chess club has 16 members. Out of every 4 members, 1 is a fifth grader and the other members are sixth graders. How many of the chess-club members are fifth graders?

Gerry's explanation:

There are 4 fifth graders. Here is how I found out.

There are 16 members in the group. I drew a circle for each member. Since 1 out of every 4 is a fifth grader, I drew 16 circles in groups of 4. Then I colored in 1 circle out of each group of 4.

● = fifth graders
○ = other students

Then I counted up the number of dark circles. There are 4, so I know there are 4 fifth graders in the club.

To write a good explanation, you should write the steps in order and explain any symbols or drawings you used.

1. Ms. Chin's class recorded the weather conditions for 14 days. Out of every 7 days for which they recorded the data, 3 days were cloudy. Ms. Jensen's class recorded the weather for the next 10 days. Out of every 5 days for which they recorded the data, 4 days were cloudy. Which class recorded more cloudy days? Write and explain how you decided. Remember the steps for a good written explanation.
Ms. Jensen's class; Students' explanations should be written in order and logically explain how the problem was solved.

72 Use with Lesson 6-8.

On Level — Practice

PROBLEM-SOLVING SKILL P 6-8

Writing to Explain **Students' explanations will vary for 1–4.**

1. A school fundraiser was held to raise money for a new school playground. Of every \$20.00 raised, \$16.00 will be spent on playground equipment, \$2.00 on new walkways, and \$2.00 on a new fence. The fundraiser provided \$500.00 for playground equipment. What was the total amount of money raised? Explain how you found the answer.
The total amount raised was \$625.00.
2. Stephan planned a hiking trip at a national park. He planned to hike 22.5 mi per day and camp at night. After the fourth day of the trip, he had hiked a total of 90.5 mi. Is Stephan ahead of schedule, behind schedule, or right on schedule? Explain how you found the answer.
Stephan is $\frac{1}{2}$ mile ahead of schedule.
3. Marcos has a new odometer on his bike that records the distance he traveled in both miles and kilometers. After his bike ride, the odometer read 15 mi, or 24.15 km. How could Marcos use this information to find the number of kilometers equal to 1 mi?
Marcos could set up a proportion using the odometer reading; $\frac{15 \text{ mi}}{24.19 \text{ km}} = \frac{1 \text{ mi}}{x \text{ km}}$; $x \approx 1.61$ km.
4. Kara can run 3 mi in 25.5 min. At this pace, how long would it take her to run 2 mi? Explain how you found the answer.
At the same pace, Kara can run 2 mi in 17 min.

72 Use with Lesson 6-8.

CHECK

For another example, see Set 6-8 on p. 348.

1. For every 6 girls on a bus, there are 5 boys. If there are 18 girls on the bus, how many boys are on the bus? Write to explain how to find the answer. **See below.**

1. 15 boys; I solved the proportion $\frac{6}{5} = \frac{18}{b}$ for *b*.

PRACTICE

For more practice, see Set 6-8 on p. 351.

2. Perry goes for a walk every morning. Today he walked more miles than he did yesterday and in less time. On which day did he walk faster? Write to explain how to find the answer. **Today; If he walked further in less time he must have walked faster.**
3. Lynette earns $5 by delivering newspapers. She saves $3 and she spends the rest. If she saved $27 one month, how much money did she spend? Explain how to find the answer. **See below.**
4. Filipi and Junko are on a swim team. Their training swim is 200 meters and usually takes them 3 minutes. Explain how long, at this rate, it would take them to complete an 800-meter swim. **12 minutes**
5. Deliah's car travels 180 miles on 4 gallons of gas. Explain how far the car will travel on 7 gallons of gas. **315 miles**

3. $18; I set up the proportion $\frac{\$3 \text{ saved}}{\$2 \text{ spent}} = \frac{\$27 \text{ saved}}{x \text{ spent}}$ and solved for x.

Reasonableness For Problems 6–8, rewrite each problem so that it makes sense.

6. Jake walks 35 miles to school in one hour. **Jake walks 3.5 miles to school in one hour.**
7. Ben receives an allowance of $4 each week. At this rate, he will receive about $100 in allowance per month. **Ben receives an allowance of $4 each week. At this rate, he will receive about $16 in allowance per month.**
8. Janice knows that 1 kilometer is a little more than $\frac{1}{2}$ mile. If she runs 10 kilometers in 1 hour, then she runs at a rate of 4 miles per hour. **Janice runs at a rate of over half the number of kilometers or about 5 miles per hour.**

Model railroad hobbyists can collect toy trains and equipment that are precise replicas of the actual trains. There are four popular scales which appear in the table at the right.

Scale Name	Scale (inches) Model: Actual
H	$\frac{1}{24}$
HO	$\frac{1}{87}$
O	$\frac{1}{48}$
S	$\frac{1}{64}$

9. How many inches long is the actual locomotive if an O scale model is 18 inches long? **864 inches**
10. How long, in inches, would an S scale model of a 768-inch locomotive be? **12 inches**
11. Write a proportion to convert 13.5 inches to feet. **$\frac{13.5 \text{ inches}}{x \text{ ft}} = \frac{12 \text{ inches}}{1 \text{ ft}}$, $x = 1.125$ ft.**

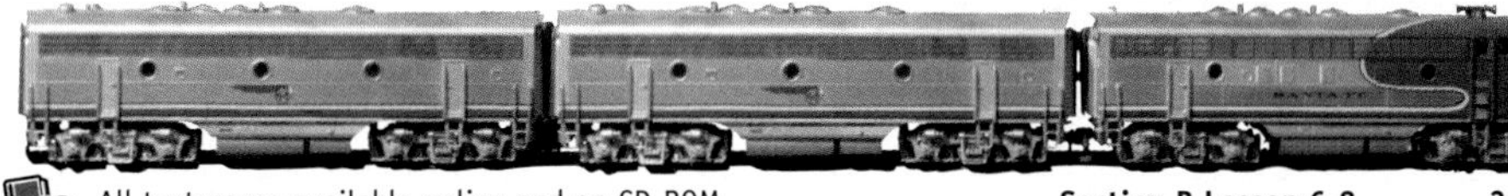

CHECK

Error Intervention

If students get the correct answer but write incomplete or careless explanations,

then tell them that learning to write good explanations is an important math skill. It helps organize their own thinking and makes their work understandable to others. *(Also see* Reteaching, *p. 324B.)*

3 Practice

Exercise 8 Students' answers should provide the conversion between kilometers and miles. Using this conversion, students can rewrite the problem to make sense.

Leveled Practice

Below Level Ex. 2–7, 9, 10

On Level Ex. 2–7, 9, 10

Above Level Ex. 2–4, 7–11

Early Finishers Have students choose a problem from another lesson and write a good explanation for its solution.

4 Assess

Journal Idea Have students explain how a drawing can be a part of a good explanation for a solution.

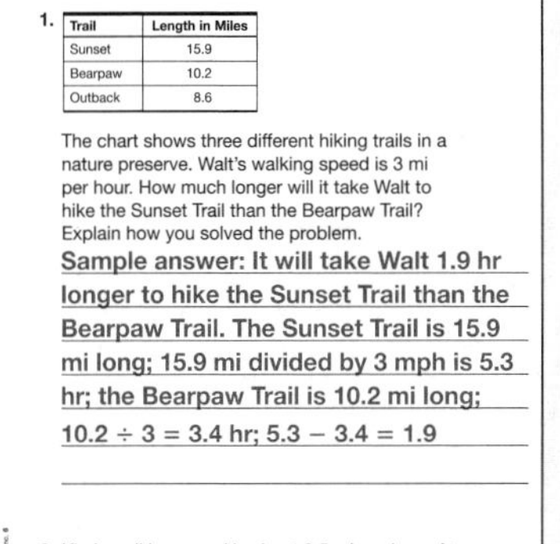

Test-Taking Practice 6-8

1.

Trail	Length in Miles
Sunset	15.9
Bearpaw	10.2
Outback	8.6

The chart shows three different hiking trails in a nature preserve. Walt's walking speed is 3 mi per hour. How much longer will it take Walt to hike the Sunset Trail than the Bearpaw Trail? Explain how you solved the problem.

Sample answer: It will take Walt 1.9 hr longer to hike the Sunset Trail than the Bearpaw Trail. The Sunset Trail is 15.9 mi long; 15.9 mi divided by 3 mph is 5.3 hr; the Bearpaw Trail is 10.2 mi long; 10.2 ÷ 3 = 3.4 hr; 5.3 − 3.4 = 1.9

2. Kim's walking speed is about 2.5 mi per hour. At this rate, about how long will it take Kim to hike the Outback Trail?

A. About 3 hr, 15 min
(B.) About 3 hr, 30 min
C. About 3 hr, 45 min
D. About 4 hr

Available as a transparency

Above Level — Enrichment

Making Plans

E 6-8 DECISION MAKING

Use the information in the diagram and the questions to plan a trip to one or more of the places shown. You can only travel on the paths shown. Remember to plan to spend some time at each place you visit.

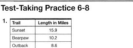

Home — Park: 2 mi; Park — Library: 1 mi; Home — Library: 4 mi; Home — Pizza shop: 2 mi; Pizza shop — Mall: $\frac{1}{2}$ mi; Home — Mall: 2 mi; Library — Mall: 3 mi

Sample answers are given.

1. Plan an outing that will take about 2 hr. You will be traveling by bike at a rate of 6 mi per hour. You must start and finish your trip at home. You must visit at least one location shown on the map. Where will you go? How much time will you spend riding your bike? How much time will you spend at each location? Exactly how long will your trip take?
I will go to the library. I will spend 1 hr 20 min riding my bike and 40 min at the library. My trip will take 2 hr.
2. Plan an outing that will take about 4 hr. This time, your little sister needs to tag along, so you can only bike 4 mi per hour. You must start and finish your trip at home. You must visit at least two locations shown on the map. Where will you go? How much time will you and your sister spend riding your bikes? How much time will you spend at each location? Exactly how long will your trip take?
We will go to the mall and the pizza shop. We will spend 1 hr $7\frac{1}{2}$ min riding our bikes, 1 hr 30 min at the mall, and 1 hr at the pizza shop. The trip will take exactly 3 hr $37\frac{1}{2}$ min.

72 Use with Lesson 6-8.

Problem Solving

PROBLEM-SOLVING SKILL PS 6-8

Writing to Explain

Hiking Philip and Jamal have planned a daylong hike. They plan to hike for the first 46 min of each hour, and rest for the last 14 min. If they have rested for 42 min, how many minutes have they hiked?

Read and Understand

1. How long will Philip and Jamal rest each hour? **14 min**
2. How long will Philip and Jamal hike each hour? **46 min**
3. What do you need to find? **How many minutes they have hiked if they rested 42 min**

Plan and Solve

4. What is the ratio of hiking to resting? **46:14**
5. Use a proportion to solve the problem. **The ratio of hiking to resting is 46:14, so the proportion is $\frac{46}{14 \text{ min}} = \frac{h}{42 \text{ min}}$; 138 min**

Look Back and Check

6. Is your answer reasonable? **Sample answer: Yes, since they hiked 3 times longer than they rested, my answer of 138 is slightly over 3 times 42 min of resting.**

Solve Another Problem

7. **Baseball** A baseball coach requires her team to practice for 3 hr each week. Of that time, $\frac{1}{2}$ hr is review of the rules and strategies, and $2\frac{1}{2}$ hr is practice on the field. So far this season, the team has spent 15 hr on the field. How long have they spent reviewing the rules and strategies? **3 hr**

72 Use with Lesson 6-8.

Review

Purpose Help students review content learned in Section B.

Using Student Pages 326–327

Do You Know How? exercises are appropriate for written work.

Do You Understand? questions are designed for whole-class discussion or small-group discussion followed by a report to the whole class.

Vocabulary Review

You may wish to review these terms before assigning the page.

proportion *(p. 316)*

cross products *(p. 316)*

Section B: Lessons 6-5 through 6-8

Review

Do You Know How?

Understanding Proportions (6-5)

Decide if the ratios form a proportion.

1. $\frac{25 \text{ mi}}{5 \text{ h}}, \frac{15 \text{ mi}}{3 \text{ h}}$ **Yes**
2. $\frac{3 \text{ in.}}{8 \text{ ft}}, \frac{6 \text{ ft}}{16 \text{ in.}}$ **No**
3. $\frac{10 \text{ cm}}{5 \text{ m}}, \frac{1 \text{ cm}}{2 \text{ m}}$ **No**
4. $\frac{9 \text{ lb}}{\$13.50}, \frac{4 \text{ lb}}{\$6.00}$ **Yes**

Solving Proportions (6-6)
Solving Proportions Using Cross Products (6-7)

Solve each proportion using any method.

5. $\frac{6 \text{ cans}}{\$4.50} = \frac{x \text{ cans}}{\$1.50}$ **x = 2**
6. $\frac{2 \text{ in.}}{5 \text{ ft}} = \frac{7 \text{ in.}}{y \text{ ft}}$ **y = 17.5**
7. $\frac{9.6 \text{ mi}}{2 \text{ h}} = \frac{24 \text{ mi}}{y \text{ h}}$ **y = 5**
8. $\frac{2 \text{ L}}{\$3.98} = \frac{5 \text{ L}}{x}$ **x = $9.95**

Solve each proportion using cross products.

9. $\frac{3 \text{ in.}}{120 \text{ mi}} = \frac{5 \text{ in.}}{t \text{ mi}}$ **t = 200**
10. $\frac{15}{b} = \frac{21}{7}$ **b = 5**
11. $\frac{5 \text{ h}}{\$53.25} = \frac{8 \text{ h}}{m}$ **m = $85.20**
12. $\frac{t}{90} = \frac{16}{100}$ **t = 14.4**

Writing to Explain (6-8)

13. Fly By Night Airlines keeps the ratio of discount-fare seats to full-fare seats at 2 to 15. How many discount-fare tickets should be sold for a 240 full-fare seat flight? **32 discount-fare tickets**
14. Four shovels of sand are used for every 5 shovels of concrete. How many shovels of sand are needed for 25 shovels of concrete? **20 shovels**
15. The ratio of weight on Earth to weight on the moon is 6:1. If you weigh 138 pounds on Earth, how much would you weigh on the moon? **23 pounds**

Do You Understand?

The units remained constant and the cross products are equal.

A Explain how you decided whether the ratios form a proportion. **See above.**

B How can you tell without calculating whether $\frac{4 \text{ in.}}{21 \text{ ft}}, \frac{1 \text{ ft}}{7 \text{ in.}}$ is a proportion? **See below.**

B. The units on top and bottom do not remain the same in both ratios so I know it is not a proportion.

C Explain what method you used to solve the proportion in Exercise 5. **See below.**

D Describe how to use cross products to find the missing value in a proportion. **Multiply the numerator and the denominator from opposite ratios. Then divide the product by the other known value.**

C. Sample answer: I used cross products.

E Describe how you could use proportions to solve each problem. **See below.**

F What should you include to write a good explanation to a math problem? **Write the steps in order and explain any special symbols, variables, or abbreviations.**

E. For 13, I solved the proportion $\frac{2}{15} = \frac{x}{240}$.
For 14, I solved the proportion $\frac{4}{5} = \frac{x}{25}$.
For 15, I solved the proportion $\frac{6}{1} = \frac{138}{x}$.

326 Chapter 6 Section B Review

Item Analysis for Diagnosis and Intervention

Objective	Review Items	Diagnostic Checkpoint Items	Student Book Pages*	Intervention System
Understand proportions.	1–4	1, 3–14	316–317	I39
Solve proportions using patterns in tables.	5–8	2, 15–29	318–321	I39
Solve proportions using cross products.	5–12	2, 15–29	322–323	I40
Write to explain your reasoning.	13–15	27–29	324–325	M18

*For each lesson, there is a *Reteaching* activity in *Reaching All Learners* and a *Reteaching* master.

Chapter 6 Section B
Diagnostic Checkpoint

MULTIPLE CHOICE

1. Which of the following is NOT a proportion? (6-5)

A. $\frac{3 \text{ in.}}{12 \text{ ft}} = \frac{1 \text{ in.}}{4 \text{ ft}}$ **B.** $\frac{\$9}{3 \text{ lb}} = \frac{\$6}{2 \text{ lb}}$ **(C.)** $\frac{360 \text{ mi}}{7.2 \text{ h}} = \frac{50 \text{ h}}{1 \text{ mi}}$ **D.** $\frac{4 \text{ laps}}{12 \text{ min}} = \frac{6 \text{ laps}}{18 \text{ min}}$

2. Jack runs 3 miles in 27 minutes. At this rate, how long will it take him to run 10 miles? (6-6, 6-7, 6-8)

A. 1.1 hours **(B.)** 90 minutes **C.** 81 minutes **D.** 57 minutes

FREE RESPONSE

Decide if the ratios form a proportion. (6-5)

3. $\frac{64 \text{ mi}}{2 \text{ h}}, \frac{160 \text{ mi}}{5 \text{ h}}$ **Yes**

4. $\frac{3 \text{ cm}}{15 \text{ km}}, \frac{5 \text{ cm}}{25 \text{ km}}$ **Yes**

5. $\frac{6 \text{ gal}}{\$3.48}, \frac{\$0.58}{1 \text{ gal}}$ **No**

6. $\frac{2 \text{ tsp}}{1 \text{ oz}}, \frac{4 \text{ oz}}{8 \text{ tsp}}$ **No**

7. $\frac{6 \text{ acres}}{10 \text{ acres}}, \frac{15 \text{ ft}}{25 \text{ ft}}$ **Yes**

8. $\frac{6 \text{ ft}}{10 \text{ s}}, \frac{9 \text{ ft}}{15 \text{ s}}$ **Yes**

9. $\frac{14}{17}, \frac{70}{55}$ **No**

10. $\frac{1 \text{ mi}}{7 \text{ min}}, \frac{7 \text{ mi}}{49 \text{ min}}$ **Yes**

11. $\frac{3}{8}, \frac{6}{9.5}$ **No**

12. $\frac{2 \text{ tsp}}{12 \text{ oz}}, \frac{1.5 \text{ tsp}}{9 \text{ oz}}$ **Yes**

13. $\frac{4}{6}, \frac{0.9}{1.3}$ **No**

14. $\frac{12.7 \text{ cm}}{20 \text{ m}}, \frac{8.9 \text{ cm}}{14.06 \text{ m}}$ **No**

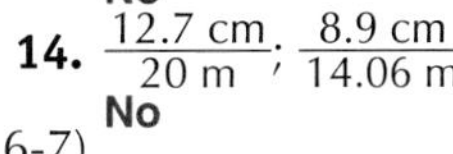

Think It Through
I can use what I know about **equal ratios** to solve a proportion.

Solve each proportion using any method. (6-6, 6-7)

15. $\frac{\$97.50}{13 \text{ h}} = \frac{\$y}{6 \text{ h}}$ **$y = \$45$**

16. $\frac{7 \text{ in.}}{35 \text{ ft}} = \frac{9 \text{ in.}}{n \text{ ft}}$ **$n = 45$ ft**

17. $\frac{2 \text{ cups}}{5 \text{ gal}} = \frac{x \text{ cups}}{8 \text{ gal}}$ **$x = 3.2$ cups**

18. $\frac{65 \text{ mi}}{4 \text{ h}} = \frac{130 \text{ mi}}{b \text{ h}}$ **$b = 8$ h**

19. $\frac{1 \text{ in.}}{2.54 \text{ cm}} = \frac{t \text{ in.}}{254 \text{ cm}}$ **$t = 100$ in.**

20. $\frac{3 \text{ tbsp}}{2 \text{ gal}} = \frac{x \text{ tbsp}}{15 \text{ gal}}$ **$x = 22.5$ tbsp**

21. $\frac{8.4}{y} = \frac{11.2}{6.8}$ **$y = 5.1$**

22. $\frac{2.4}{4.5} = \frac{w}{1.8}$ **$w = 0.96$**

23. $\frac{24 \text{ lb}}{12 \text{ ft}} = \frac{x \text{ lb}}{28 \text{ ft}}$ **$x = 56$ lb**

24. $\frac{4 \text{ lbs}}{\$89} = \frac{9 \text{ lbs}}{m}$ **$m = \$200.25$**

25. $\frac{\$13{,}500}{9 \text{ mos}} = \frac{x}{10 \text{ mos}}$ **$x = \$15{,}000$**

26. $\frac{160.95}{37} = \frac{26.10}{n}$ **$n = 6$**

28. No, this does not make a proportion. Set up the proportion $\frac{\$5}{\$20} = \frac{\$25}{x}$ and solve, $x = \$100$. Maggie needs to earn \$100 to put \$25 in her savings account.

Writing in Math

27. 4 lawns; I solved the proportion $\frac{\$7}{1 \text{ lawn}} = \frac{\$28}{n \text{ lawns}}$, where n is the number of lawns that Justin mowed yesterday.

27. Justin earns \$7 for each lawn he mows. If he earned \$28 yesterday, how many lawns did he mow? Explain how you found the answer. (6-8)
See above.

28. Maggie puts \$5 out of every \$20 she earns into her savings account. She says that to put \$25 in her savings account, she needs to earn \$220. Is this reasonable? Explain your answer. (6-8)
See above right.

29. Andrew drove 120 miles on 5 gallons of gas. He says his car uses 1 gallon to go 24 miles. Does this make sense? Explain your answer. (6-8)
Yes; according to the proportion, $\frac{120 \text{ miles}}{5 \text{ gallons}} = \frac{24 \text{ miles}}{1 \text{ gallon}}$

Sample student work for Exercise 28

Maggie should set up a proportion to find out how much money she needs to earn to save \$25.

$\frac{\$5}{\$20} = \frac{\$25}{m}$ $5m = 20 \times 25$ $5m = 500$ $m = \$100$

Maggie needs to earn \$100 to save \$25. She could also make a table.

The rubric below is a scoring guide that shows how many points to give an answer to Exercise 28. Many teachers would assign a score of 4 points to this explanation. Discuss the sample response shown and compare it to papers produced by students.

Scoring Rubric

4 — Full credit: 4 points
The answer is correct; understands how to write and solve proportions; explanation is complete.

3 — Partial credit: 3 points
The answer is correct; understands how to write and solve proportions; explanation is incomplete.

2 — Partial credit: 2 points
The answer is incorrect; understands how to write and solve proportions; explanation is complete.

1 — Partial credit: 1 point
The answer is correct; there is no explanation.

0 — No credit
The answer is incorrect; shows no understanding of proportions.

6-9 Using Formulas

Lesson Organizer

Quick Lesson Overview

Objective Use formulas to solve problems involving rates.

Math Understanding Many formulas involve unit rates.

Vocabulary Formula

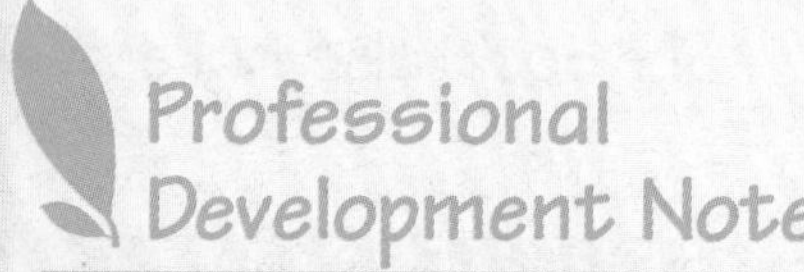

Professional Development Note

Research Base

Middle grade students would benefit from experiences with a rich variety of multiplicative situations. These would include proportionality, inverse variation, and exponentiation (Mathematical Learning Study Committee, 2001). This section includes lessons which link proportional reasoning to situations which involve similarity and scale drawings.

NCTM Standards

- Algebra
- Measurement

(For a complete correlation to the NCTM Standards and Grades 6–8 Expectations, see pages 298G–H.)

Getting Started

Spiral Review

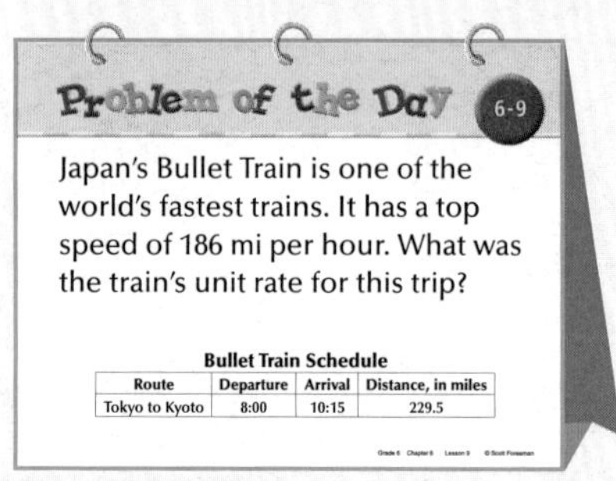

Problem of the Day 6-9

Japan's Bullet Train is one of the world's fastest trains. It has a top speed of 186 mi per hour. What was the train's unit rate for this trip?

Bullet Train Schedule

Route	Departure	Arrival	Distance, in miles
Tokyo to Kyoto	8:00	10:15	229.5

Topics Reviewed

- Elapsed time; rates; dividing decimals by decimals
- Problem-Solving Skill: Multiple-Step Problem

Answer The train traveled 102 mi per hour on this trip.

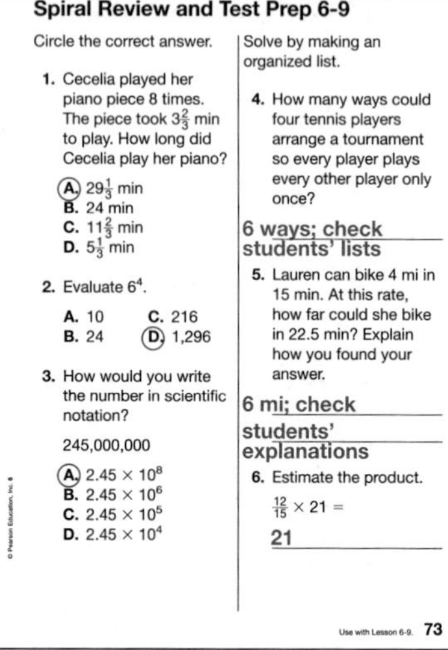

Spiral Review and Test Prep 6-9

Circle the correct answer.

1. Cecelia played her piano piece 8 times. The piece took $3\frac{2}{3}$ min to play. How long did Cecelia play her piano?
   (A) $29\frac{1}{3}$ min
   B. 24 min
   C. $11\frac{2}{3}$ min
   D. $5\frac{1}{3}$ min

2. Evaluate 6^4.
   A. 10 C. 216
   B. 24 (D) 1,296

3. How would you write the number in scientific notation?
   245,000,000
   (A) 2.45×10^8
   B. 2.45×10^6
   C. 2.45×10^5
   D. 2.45×10^4

Solve by making an organized list.

4. How many ways could four tennis players arrange a tournament so every player plays every other player only once?
   6 ways; check students' lists

5. Lauren can bike 4 mi in 15 min. At this rate, how far could she bike in 22.5 min? Explain how you found your answer.
   6 mi; check students' explanations

6. Estimate the product.
   $\frac{12}{15} \times 21 =$
   21

© Pearson Education, Inc. 6

Use with Lesson 6-9. 73

Available as a transparency and as a blackline master

Topics Reviewed

1. Multiplying mixed numbers; **2.** Exponents; **3.** Scientific notation; **4.** Make an organized list; **5.** Writing to explain; **6.** Estimating with fractions and mixed numbers

Investigating the Concept

Working and Earning

5–10 MIN **Visual/Spatial**

Materials *(per student)* 2 index cards, labeled *4 hours* and *$8.50/hour*

What to Do

- **A formula is a rule that uses symbols to relate two or more quantities. The formula $p = h \times r$ relates pay, hours worked, and hourly rate of pay.**
- **What do you need to know to find pay?** *(You need to know the number of hours worked and the rate of pay.)*
- **Which card indicates hours?** *(4 hours)* **Which card indicates the rate of pay?** *($8.50/hour)* **Write the formula $p = h \times r$. Place each index card over the variable it replaces.**
- **Since *hour* is in both the numerator and denominator, you can cross the unit off. What is the pay?** *($34)*

$$p = 4\ \text{hours} \times \frac{\$8.50}{\text{hour}}$$

Ongoing Assessment

- **Reasoning How would you find the rate of pay if you work 6 hours and earn a total of $54?** *(Divide $54 by 6.)*

Reaching All Learners

Math Vocabulary

Follow the Formula

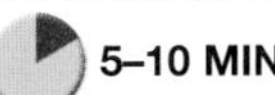 5–10 MIN **Auditory** 

- Write the following expressions on the board:
  a formula for success
  a formula racing car
  a baby's formula
- Discuss with students the meanings of *formula* in each phrase. Then write examples of math formulas like those shown below.
- **How are the first formulas related to a formula in math?** *(Sample answer: They provide a rule to follow or a procedure for the same result. In math, a formula provides a rule to follow to calculate an answer.)*
- **Ask students if they recognize any of the formulas.**

$C = \pi d$ $A = \pi r^2$

$A = lw$ $V = lwh$

$d = rt$

Activate Prior Knowledge/Build Background

English Language Learners

Seeing Symbols

 10–15 MIN **Verbal** 

- Talk with students about symbols they see every day.
- Ask students to name some symbols they use in school subjects.
- Write your initials on the board. Ask how initials are symbols for a person's name.
- Ask students what symbols they might use for math terms such as *rate, time,* and *distance.*

Reteaching

Go the Distance

 10–15 MIN **Logical/Mathematical** 

- Show students the chart below.
- **A plane travels 500 miles per hour.**
- **What pattern do you see in the chart?** *(Sample answer: If you multiply the rate in miles per hour by the time in hours you get the distance traveled.)*
- **A formula relates two or more quantities. What formula could you write to show the pattern?** *(Sample answer: Distance equals rate times time.)*

Distance d	Rate r	Time t
500 mi	500 mph	1 hr
1,000 mi	500 mph	2 hr
1,500 mi	500 mph	3 hr
2,500 mi	500 mph	5 hr

- **Express this answer as a formula.** *($d = r \times t$)*

Advanced Learners

Changing a Formula

 5–10 MIN **Social/Cooperative** 

- Write the distance formula $d = r \times t$ on the board.
- **How could you write this formula so it gives time when distance and rate are known?** *(Divide both sides by r. The result is $t = \frac{d}{r}$.)*
- **Use the formula to find the time need to travel 300 miles at 60 miles per hour.** *($t = \frac{300}{50} = 6$ hours)*
- **Rewrite the formula $c = 2.54i$ so i is alone.** *($i = \frac{c}{2.54}$)*

Objective Use formulas to solve problems involving rates.

1 Warm Up

Activate Prior Knowledge Review how to evaluate an expression and use inverse operations to solve an equation.

2 Teach

LEARN Help students differentiate between an *equation* and a *formula.* An equation is usually used to find the value of a variable in one particular situation. A formula is used to relate several quantities and applies to many situations.

Ongoing Assessment

Talk About It: Question 3

If students write a proportion for finding the number of centimeters in 1 inch,

then suggest that they draw a diagram to help them see the correct proportion.

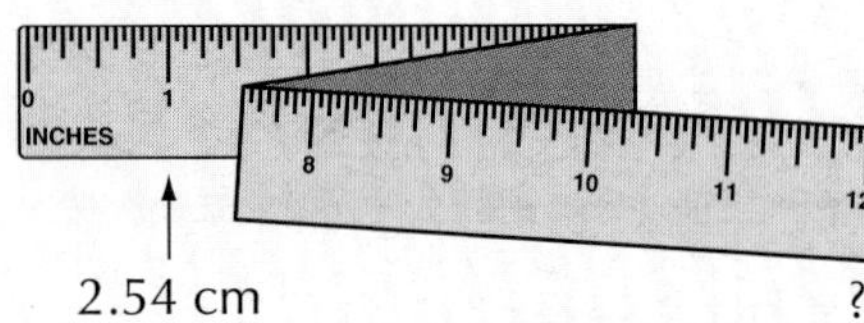

Lesson 6-9

Algebra

Key Idea
You can use formulas to solve problems involving unit rates.

Vocabulary
• formula

TEST TALK

Think It Through
I **substitute** the known values into a formula in order to find the missing value.

Using Formulas

WARM UP

Evaluate each expression for $x = 2, 4,$ and $5.$

1. $6x$ **12; 24; 30**
2. $\frac{20}{x}$ **10; 5; 4**

Solve for n.

3. $8n = 36$ **$n = 4.5$**
4. $\frac{n}{4} = 12$ **$n = 48$**

LEARN

What is a formula?

An airplane travels at a steady rate, *r,* and flies a specific distance, *d,* in *t* hours. How are rate, distance, and time related?

distance = rate × time

$d = r \times t$

3. $\frac{2.54 \text{ cm}}{1 \text{ inch}} = \frac{x \text{ cm}}{12 \text{ inches}}$; $x = 30.48$

A **formula** is a rule that uses symbols to relate two or more quantities. The formula above relates distance, rate, and time.

How do you use a formula to solve a problem?

Example A

A plane travels at a rate of 400 miles per hour. How far will the plane travel in 5 hours?

Use the formula that relates distance, rate, and time.

$d = r \times t$

$d = \frac{400 \text{ miles}}{\cancel{\text{hour}}} \times 5 \cancel{\text{ hours}}$

$d = 2{,}000$ miles

The plane will travel 2,000 miles.

Example B

The width of a box is 8 inches. How many centimeters wide is the box?

Use the formula that relates centimeters, *c,* to number of inches, *i*.

$c = 2.54i$

$c = 2.54\frac{\text{cm}}{\cancel{\text{inch}}} \bullet 8 \cancel{\text{ inches}}$

$c = 20.32$ cm

The box is 20.32 centimeters wide.

Talk About It

1. $\frac{400 \text{ miles}}{1 \text{ hour}} = \frac{d \text{ miles}}{5 \text{ hours}}$; $d = 2{,}000$

1. Use the rate $\frac{400 \text{ miles}}{1 \text{ hour}}$ in Example A to write a proportion that could be used to find the distance traveled in 5 hours. **See above.**
2. How long will it take a car traveling at a rate of 68 miles per hour to go 510 miles? **$510 = 68t$; $t = 7.5$ hours**
3. Write a proportion that you can use to find the number of centimeters in 1 foot. **See above.**

Take It to the NET
More Examples
www.scottforesman.com

328

Below Level **Reteaching**

Using Formulas

R 6-9

A formula is an equation that shows the way quantities relate to one another.

For example:

The formula $0.45p = k$ relates pounds to kilograms. The variable *p* stands for pounds and the variable *k* stands for kilograms.

How many kilograms does a 100 lb person measure?

First, substitute the information you know:

$0.45\,p = k$
$0.45\,(100 \text{ lb}) = k$

Then, solve the equation to find the answer.

$0.45 \times 100 = 45$ kg

Use the formula *total cost = unit price × ounces* to solve the exercises.

1. Orange juice costs $0.13 per ounce. How much do 8 oz of orange juice cost? **$1.04**
2. Cranberry juice costs $0.18 per ounce. How much do 6 oz of cranberry juice cost? **$1.08**
3. Grape juice costs $0.25 per ounce. How much do 7 oz of grape juice cost? **$1.75**
4. **Estimation** Carrot juice costs $0.32 per ounce. Durango purchased $1.92 worth of carrot juice. How many ounces of carrot juice did he purchase? **6 oz**

Use the formula *distance = rate × time* to solve the problems.

5. A car travels at a rate of 50 mi per hour. How far will the car travel in 4 hr? **200 mi**
6. A train travels at a rate of 110 mi per hour. How far will the train travel in 9 hr? **990 mi**
7. A truck traveled a total distance of 180 mi. It drove at a rate of 30 mi per hour. For how many hours did the truck travel? **6 hr**

On Level **Practice**

Using Formulas

P 6-9

Use the formulas to solve the problems.

Area Conversion
$a = \frac{s}{43.56}$
$s = 43.56 \times a$

a = acres
s = square feet

1. If the area is 5 acres, what is the area in square feet? **217.8 ft^2**
2. If the area is 500.94 ft^2, what is the area in acres? **11.5 acres**
3. If the area is 1,359.072 ft^2, what is the area in acres? **31.2 acres**
4. **Estimation** José says that a quick way to estimate the area in square feet is to multiply the number of acres by 40. Does his method make sense? Is it a good way to estimate? **Yes, this is a good method to estimate the area in square feet.**
5. Elise's science teacher had the students count their pulse for 10 seconds. They then used the formula *beats in 10 sec × 6 = beats per minute.* If Elise counted 12 beats in 10 sec, how many beats would she have in 1 minute? **72 beats**

Test Prep

6. If there are about 28.35 g in 1 oz, about how many grams are equal to 16 ounces?
   A. 0.56 g B. 1.77 g **(C.) 453.6 g** D. 4,356 g
7. **Writing in Math** Explain how you would use the data in Exercise 6 to find the number of ounces in a certain number of grams. ***Sample answer: Use the formula oz = 28.35 × g. Substitute the number of grams for g.***

CHECK ✓

For another example, see Set 6-9 on p. 348.

1. At Euro Furniture Design, all dimensions for custom orders must be given in centimeters. Use the formula $c = 2.54i$ to find the dimensions of a 9 ft by 5 ft dining room table in centimeters.
   274.32 cm by 152.4 cm
2. **Estimation** A car traveled 140 miles at a rate of 50 miles per hour. Estimate the number of hours the car traveled.
   About 3 hours

PRACTICE

For more practice, see Set 6-9 on p. 351.

A Skills and Understanding

At Veggies 'N' More, vegetables and fruits are sold by the pound. Use the formula *total cost* = *unit price* × *weight* to find the cost of each.

3. 4 lb of carrots **$7.56**
4. 8 lb of tomatoes **$17.52**
5. **Estimation** Jasmine purchased a bag of grapes for $6.30. Estimate how many pounds of grapes she purchased.
   About 3 pounds

B Reasoning and Problem Solving

Acceleration is the rate at which velocity changes with respect to time. To calculate acceleration, you divide the change in velocity by the amount of time. You can use the formula $a = \frac{v}{t}$ where a represents the acceleration (in meters per second squared), v is the change in velocity, and t is the time it takes to make the change.

6. The velocity of water flowing over Lara Falls is 12 meters per second. Before going over the falls, the velocity of the water is 6 meters per second. It takes 3 seconds to make the change in velocity. What is the acceleration of the water?
   2 meters per second squared
7. **Writing in Math** Can a car that gets 21 miles per gallon of gasoline travel 325 miles on 18 gallons of gasoline? Explain. **Yes. 21 × 18 = 378 miles, which is farther than 325.**

Mixed Review and Test Prep

Take It to the NET
Test Prep
www.scottforesman.com

Rewrite the problem so that it makes sense.

8. The president of a company earns $125,000 per year. At this salary, she will earn $1,000,000 in 6 years.
   She will earn $1,000,000 in 8 years.
9. Which is the solution for the proportion $\frac{6}{8} = \frac{15}{d}$?

   A. $d = 8$ **C.** $d = 17$
   B. $d = 10$ **(D.)** $d = 20$

CHECK ✓

Error Intervention

If students substitute the incorrect values into a formula,

then suggest that they write the general formula using a different color for each variable, write the value for each of the known variables using the same color scheme, and then substitute, matching colors. *(Also see* Reteaching, *p. 328B.)*

3 Practice

TEST TALK **Exercise 7** When a problem provides a lot of information, students can write each bit of information in a separate sentence before solving.

Leveled Practice

- **Below Level** Ex. 3–5, 7–9
- **On Level** Ex. 4–9
- **Above Level** Ex. 4–9

Early Finishers Have students write a formula for the perimeter of a square with side length *s*. Have them use the formula to find the perimeters of squares with side lengths 3 ft, 4 in., and 9 cm.

4 Assess

Journal Idea Have students describe the formula they used in Exercise 6 and explain how to use it.

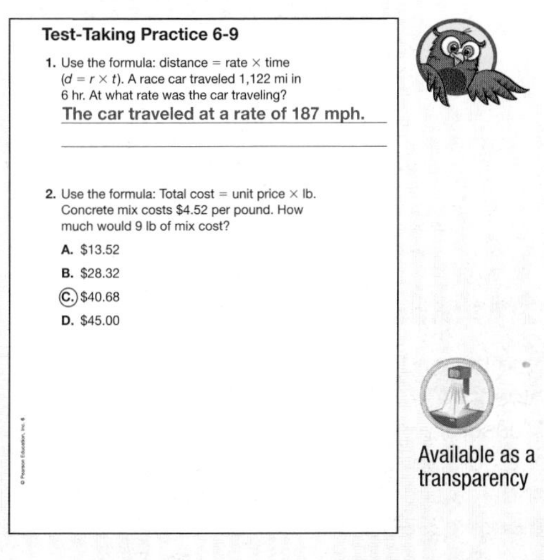

Test-Taking Practice 6-9

1. Use the formula: distance = rate × time ($d = r \times t$). A race car traveled 1,122 mi in 6 hr. At what rate was the car traveling?
   The car traveled at a rate of 187 mph.
2. Use the formula: Total cost = unit price × lb. Concrete mix costs $4.52 per pound. How much would 9 lb of mix cost?
   A. $13.52
   B. $28.32
   (C.) $40.68
   D. $45.00

Available as a transparency

Enrichment — Above Level

Fantastic Formulas E 6-9 DATA

Choose a formula from the chart to solve the problems below. There may be more than one formula that would work for each problem. Show your work.

Formula File	
inches × 2.54 = centimeters	pounds × 0.45 = kilograms
miles × 1.61 = kilometers	meters × 1.09 = yards
kilometers × 0.62 = miles	grams × 0.04 = ounces
ounces × 28.35 = grams	yards × 0.91 = meters
centimeters × 0.39 = inches	kilograms × 2.2 = pounds

1. How many centimeters long is this pencil?
   INCHES 0 1 2 3 4 5 6
   15.24 cm; 6 × 2.54 = 15.24
2. How many grams of cereal does this box measure?
   Wheaty Rounds Cereal 16.5 oz
   467.775 g; 16.5 × 28.35 = 467.775
3. How many kilograms does this dumbbell measure?
   Each = 50 lb.
   90 kg; 50 × 4 = 200 lb; 200 × 0.45 = 90

Use with Lesson 6-9. 73

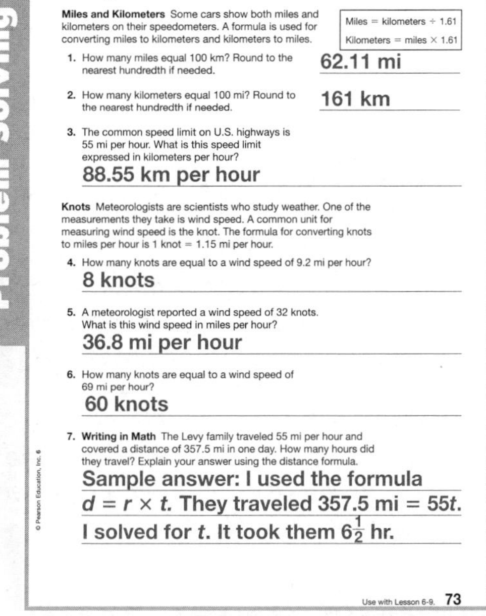

Problem Solving

Using Formulas PS 6-9

Miles and Kilometers Some cars show both miles and kilometers on their speedometers. A formula is used for converting miles to kilometers and kilometers to miles.

Miles = kilometers ÷ 1.61
Kilometers = miles × 1.61

1. How many miles equal 100 km? Round to the nearest hundredth if needed. 62.11 mi
2. How many kilometers equal 100 mi? Round to the nearest hundredth if needed. 161 km
3. The common speed limit on U.S. highways is 55 mi per hour. What is this speed limit expressed in kilometers per hour?
   88.55 km per hour

Knots Meteorologists are scientists who study weather. One of the measurements they take is wind speed. A common unit for measuring wind speed is the knot. The formula for converting knots to miles per hour is 1 knot = 1.15 mi per hour.

4. How many knots are equal to a wind speed of 9.2 mi per hour?
   8 knots
5. A meteorologist reported a wind speed of 32 knots. What is this wind speed in miles per hour?
   36.8 mi per hour
6. How many knots are equal to a wind speed of 69 mi per hour?
   60 knots
7. **Writing in Math** The Levy family traveled 55 mi per hour and covered a distance of 357.5 mi in one day. How many hours did they travel? Explain your answer using the distance formula.
   Sample answer: I used the formula $d = r \times t$. They traveled 357.5 mi = 55t. I solved for t. It took them $6\frac{1}{2}$ hr.

Use with Lesson 6-9. 73

6-10 Scale Drawings and Maps

Lesson Organizer

Quick Lesson Overview

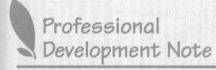

Objective Solve word problems based on scale drawings.

Math Understanding Scale drawings involve similar figures, and corresponding parts of similar figures are proportional.

Vocabulary Scale drawing, scale

Materials for Student Pages Ruler or Teaching Tool 19, Centimeter Grid Paper (Teaching Tool 18) or Geometry Drawing eTool

Managing Instruction Ask students to work with a family member to find examples of scale drawings such as maps, or to make scale drawings of rooms in their home. Ask students to share their findings by describing their scale drawings. Include a discussion of scale models as well.

NCTM Standards

- Number and Operations
- Algebra
- Measurement

(For a complete correlation to the NCTM Standards and Grades 6–8 Expectations, see pages 298G–H.)

Getting Started

Spiral Review

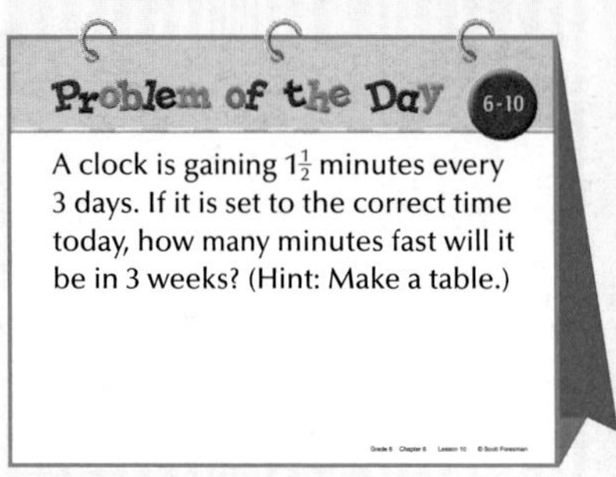

Problem of the Day 6-10

A clock is gaining $1\frac{1}{2}$ minutes every 3 days. If it is set to the correct time today, how many minutes fast will it be in 3 weeks? (Hint: Make a table.)

Topics Reviewed

- Adding mixed numbers
- Problem-Solving Strategy: Make a Table

Answer The clock will be $10\frac{1}{2}$ minutes fast in 3 weeks.

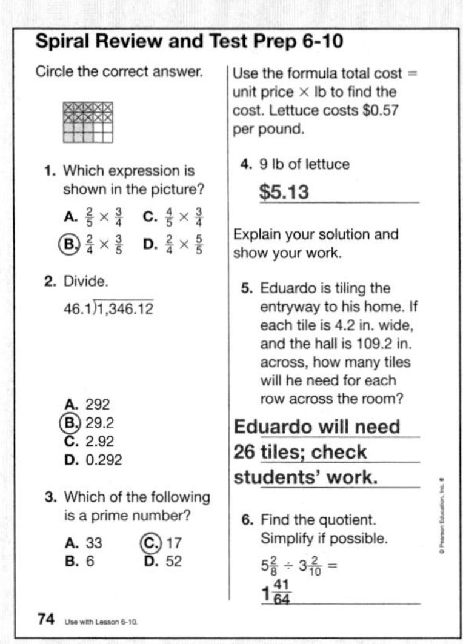

Spiral Review and Test Prep 6-10

Circle the correct answer.

1. Which expression is shown in the picture?
   A. $\frac{2}{5} \times \frac{3}{4}$ C. $\frac{4}{5} \times \frac{3}{4}$
   (B.) $\frac{2}{4} \times \frac{3}{5}$ D. $\frac{2}{4} \times \frac{5}{5}$
2. Divide.
   $46.1\overline{)1,346.12}$
   A. 292
   (B.) 29.2
   C. 2.92
   D. 0.292
3. Which of the following is a prime number?
   A. 33 (C.) 17
   B. 6 D. 52

Use the formula total cost = unit price × lb to find the cost. Lettuce costs $0.57 per pound.

4. 9 lb of lettuce
   $5.13

Explain your solution and show your work.

5. Eduardo is tiling the entryway to his home. If each tile is 4.2 in. wide, and the hall is 109.2 in. across, how many tiles will he need for each row across the room?
   Eduardo will need 26 tiles; check students' work.
6. Find the quotient. Simplify if possible.
   $5\frac{2}{8} \div 3\frac{2}{10} =$
   $1\frac{41}{64}$

74 Use with Lesson 6-10.

Available as a transparency and as a blackline master

Topics Reviewed

1. Multiplying fractions; **2.** Dividing decimals; **3.** Prime and composite numbers; **4.** Using formulas; **5.** Writing to explain; **6.** Dividing mixed numbers

Investigating the Concept

Tennis to Scale

15–20 MIN **Kinesthetic** SMALL GROUP

Materials *(per group)* Ruler or Teaching Tool 19; Centimeter Grid Paper (Teaching Tool 18); $\frac{1}{4}$-Inch Grid Paper (Teaching Tool 10)

What to Do

- Show a city or state map. Indicate distances on the map and use the terms *scale drawing* and *scale* as students view the map.
- Draw a tennis court on the board. **If you use the scale of 1 centimeter = 1 foot, will the drawing fit on a standard size sheet of paper?** *(No; The length of the drawing would be 78 cm, but the length of the paper, at 11 in., is only about 28 cm.)*

36 ft

78 ft

- **What scale might work?** *(Sample answer: 1 cm = 3 ft)* **Make a scale drawing using 1 centimeter = 3 feet. What are the dimensions of your drawing?** *(26 cm long and 12 cm wide)*

Ongoing Assessment

- **Number Sense Would a scale drawing using the scale 1 centimeter = 1 inch be useful?** *(Sample answer: No; The scale drawing would be very large, about 9 m by 4 m.)*

Reaching All Learners

Writing in Math

Map It Out

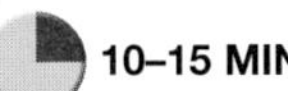 10–15 MIN **Linguistic** 

- **A map has scale 1 inch = 20 miles. The distance between two map points is 4.5 inches. What can you find?** *(You can find the actual distance between the two points.)*
- **Write a problem using that information. Exchange and solve.** *(Sample answer: On a map with scale 1 in = 20 mi, Maryville and Wilson are 4.5 in. apart. How far apart are they? Answer: 90 miles).*

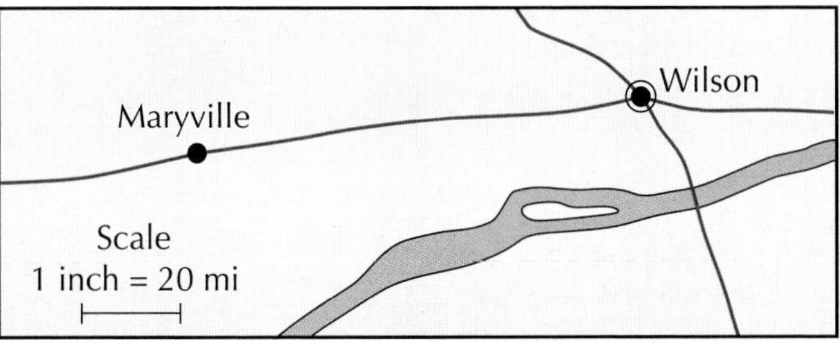

Activate Prior Knowledge/Build Background

English Language Learners

Changing Sizes

 10–15 MIN **Visual/Spatial** 

Materials *(per group)* Picture or photo; photocopy enlargement of picture or photo

- Display a picture or photo and an enlargement of it.
- Ask students to tell how the enlargement is similar to and different from the original.
- Have students in groups discuss: **When might you want to make something bigger but keep the same proportions? When might you want to make something smaller but proportional?** If necessary, refer students to the scale drawings on pages 330 or 332.

Reteaching

Copies by Design

 15–20 MIN **Visual/Spatial** 

Materials *(per student)* Centimeter Grid Paper (Teaching Tool 18); 1-inch Grid Paper (Teaching Tool 33)

- **Draw a design on inch grid paper. Then copy the design onto centimeter grid paper.**
- **Your second design is a scale drawing of the first one. What is the scale?** *(1 cm = 1 in.)* **If you draw a line 4 cm long on your second drawing, how long is the corresponding line on the first drawing?** *(4 in.)*

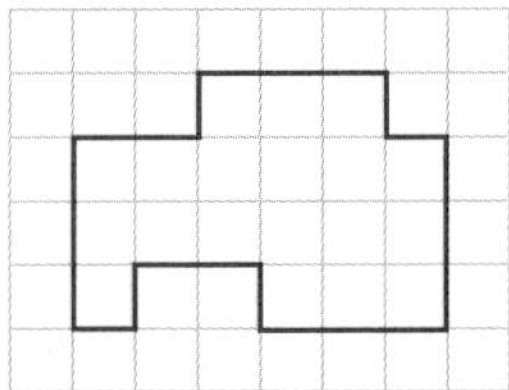

Math and Art

Big Rabbit

 5–10 MIN **Social/Cooperative** 

- Write the following problem on the board: Maria has a painting of a rabbit that is 21 centimeters high by 28 centimeters wide. She wants to enlarge the painting for a mural. If the mural is going to be 2.8 meters wide, find its height.
- **What is the scale?** *(1 cm = 0.1 m)* **How high is the mural?** *(2.1 m)*
- **Write other problems about the painting and solve them.**

Objective Solve word problems based on scale drawings.

1 Warm Up

Activate Prior Knowledge Review how to solve a proportion.

2 Teach

LEARN For problems involving scale drawings, as with any use of ratios and proportions, students need to set up the proportion so that like units correspond.

Examples A and B Before students look at the solutions, ask them to look at the unknown term in each proportion. **Will each unknown value be greater or less than the corresponding term in the first ratio?** *(Greater. Sample answer: The first term of the second ratio is greater than the first term of the first ratio, so the unknown value, the second term, will be greater than the second term of the first ratio.)*

Key Idea
Proportions are used to make scale drawings.

Vocabulary
- scale drawing
- scale

Materials
- ruler
- centimeter grid paper or

Think It Through
To make a scale drawing, I need to **draw a picture on grid paper.**

Scale Drawings and Maps

1. $n = 12$ 2. $x = 0.4$
3. $a = 2$ 4. $c = 6$

WARM UP

Solve each proportion.

1. $\frac{5}{n} = \frac{30}{72}$ 2. $\frac{x}{2} = \frac{10}{50}$
3. $\frac{16}{0.8} = \frac{40}{a}$ 4. $\frac{7}{14} = \frac{c}{12}$

See left.

LEARN

What is a scale drawing?

For a 1933 movie, a 24-inch poster of a gorilla was enlarged to make a building banner that was 50 feet high.

In a **scale drawing,** the dimensions of an object are reduced by the same ratio or **scale.** The dimensions of the scale drawing and the original figure are proportional. A house plan is a scale drawing. So is a map.

Activity

How do you make a scale drawing?

Step 1 Find the dimensions of your classroom.

Step 2 Decide what scale to use so that your drawing will fit on your piece of paper.

Step 3 Use a ruler to draw your classroom on grid paper. Convert the dimensions using the scale.

a–d. Answers will vary.

a. What scale did you use for your drawing? Explain your choice.

How is your scale drawing like your classroom? How is it different?

c. How many centimeters wide is your drawing? How does this compare to the actual width of your classroom?

d. Set up a proportion that shows the relationship between the scale drawing and the actual classroom.

Example:
Actual Length = 34 feet
Actual Width = 22 feet

Scale: 1 cm = 1 ft

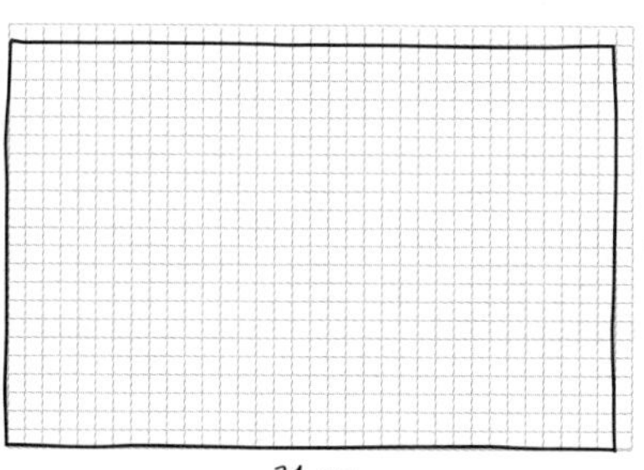

Reteaching — **Below Level**

Scale Drawings and Maps — R 6-10

On the drawing at the right, the scale tells us that 1 cm = 2 ft.

What is the actual length of the bedroom?

Let y be the actual length of the bedroom in feet. Use the scale to set up a proportion. Write the scale as the first ratio. The bedroom is 11 cm on the map. Use this information for the second ratio:

$\frac{1 \text{ cm}}{2 \text{ ft}} = \frac{11 \text{ cm}}{y \text{ ft}}$ ← scale length / ← actual length

Bedroom — Closet

Scale 1 cm = 2 ft

Solve the proportion to find the actual length of the bedroom. Use cross products.

$$\frac{1 \text{ cm}}{2 \text{ ft}} = \frac{11 \text{ cm}}{y \text{ ft}}$$

$$\frac{1y}{1} = \frac{22}{1}$$

$$y = 22 \text{ ft}$$

The actual length of the bedroom is 22 ft.

Use the scale drawing to answer 1–3.

Field — 4 in. — Store; Field — 3 in. — School; School — 2 in. — Library; Library — 2.5 in. — Store

Scale 1 in. = 2 mi

1. What is the actual distance from the school to the library?
   4 mi
2. What is the actual distance from the school to the field?
   6 mi
3. What is the actual distance from the field to the store?
   8 mi
4. **Reasoning** If a scale on a map is 1 in. = 300 mi, what would the map distance be if the actual distance between two places is 600 mi? Explain.
   2 in., because each inch equals 300 mi.

Practice — **On Level**

Scale Drawings and Maps — P 6-10

Scale: 1 in. = 20 ft

0.5 in. | 4.7 in. | 0.5 in. | Center line | 2.5 in. | 2.5 in. | 4.7 in. | Open space | 0.5 in.

1. What is the actual length and width of a college basketball court? 94 ft; 50 ft
2. How far should open space extend from each side of the court? 10 ft
3. What is the actual measurement from the end of the court to the center line? 47 ft
4. **Reasoning** What is the scale on a map that shows two cities that are 400 mi apart as 2.5 in. apart? 1 in. = 160 mi

Test Prep

5. If the scale of a drawing is 1 in. = 2.5 ft, which is the actual size of an object that is 2 in. long in the drawing?
   A. 1 in. B. 5 in. C. 2.5 ft (D.) 5 ft
6. **Writing in Math** Explain how you would choose a scale to use for a map. What things would you need to consider?
   Sample answer: You would need to consider how much area you need to show and how large the drawing can be.

How can you use scale drawings?

Example A

The scale in the drawing at the right is 1 cm:2 m. What is the actual length of the living room?

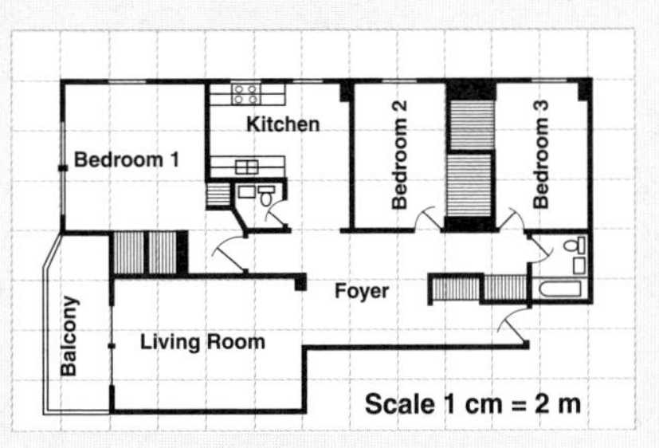

Let y be the actual length of the living room in meters. Use the scale to set up a proportion.

$\frac{1 \text{ cm}}{2 \text{ m}} = \frac{4 \text{ cm}}{y \text{ m}}$ ← scale length / ← actual length

$1(y) = 2(4)$ Solve the proportion.

$y = 8$

The actual length of the living room is 8 meters.

✓ Talk About It

1. Could the proportion in the example have been written as $\frac{2 \text{ m}}{1 \text{ cm}} = \frac{y}{4 \text{ cm}}$? Explain. **Yes, I still would have been able to use cross products to find y = 8 m.**
2. Find the length of the kitchen. **6 meters**

How can you use the scale on a map?

Example B

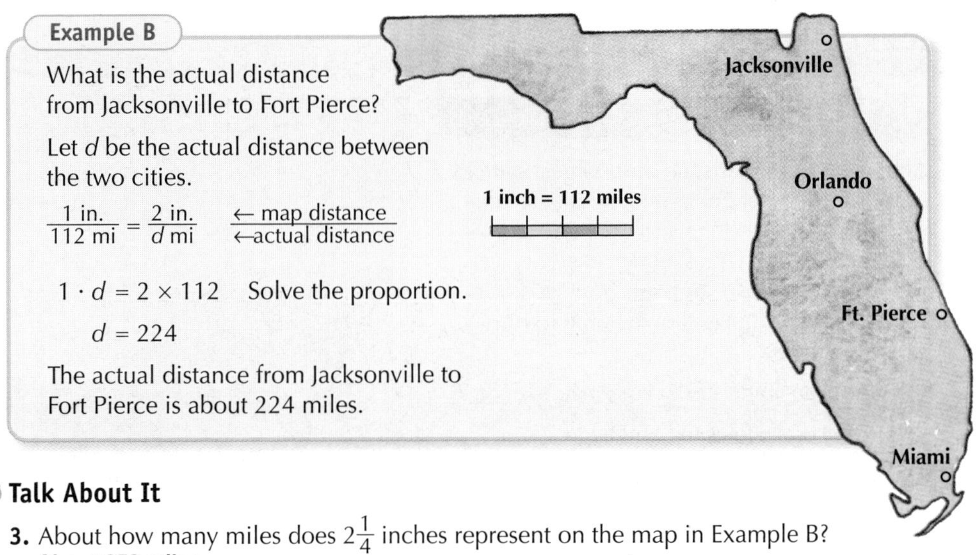

What is the actual distance from Jacksonville to Fort Pierce?

Let d be the actual distance between the two cities.

$\frac{1 \text{ in.}}{112 \text{ mi}} = \frac{2 \text{ in.}}{d \text{ mi}}$ ← map distance / ←actual distance

$1 \cdot d = 2 \times 112$ Solve the proportion.

$d = 224$

The actual distance from Jacksonville to Fort Pierce is about 224 miles.

✓ Talk About It

3. About how many miles does $2\frac{1}{4}$ inches represent on the map in Example B? **About 252 miles**

Ongoing Assessment

Talk About It: Question 1

If students think the only way to write a proportion is to compare scale to actual,

then remind them that the like units must correspond, but there are several ways to set up the ratios. Each of the ways will give them the same value for *y*.

Above Level **Enrichment**

Double Drawing

E 6-10 PATTERNS

Look at the two sets of drawings.

1. How are the two drawings alike? **Sample answers are given.** **The drawings have the same shapes.**
2. How are the two drawings different? **The drawings are different sizes.**
3. What pattern do you see in the two drawings? **The scale of the drawings is 2:1. Each line that takes 2 units in the larger drawing takes 1 unit in the smaller drawing.**

74 Use with Lesson 6-10.

Problem Solving

Scale Drawings and Maps

PS 6-10

School Map At Hoffman Elementary, new students and their families are given a school map. The map helps the students find their way around on their first day at school. The scale of the map is 1 in. = 20 ft.

1. On the map, the cafeteria is $4\frac{1}{2}$ in. from the library. What is the actual distance between the library and the cafeteria? **90 ft**
2. The actual distance between the office and the gym is 130 ft. How many inches apart do they appear on the map? **6.5 in.**
3. On the map, Mr. Pak's classroom is 6 in. from the office. What is the actual distance between the office and Mr. Pak's classroom? **120 ft**

Murals Murals are often designed with a scale drawing. A mural for a side of a building was drawn on small paper. The artist decided that every inch on the small drawing would equal 3 ft of that actual painting.

4. A flower in the actual mural is 6 ft high. How many inches high was the same flower on the small drawing? **2 in.**
5. On the small drawing, the Sun is shown as 4 in. wide. How wide will the Sun be in the actual mural? **12 ft**
6. The artist's signature is 2 in. long on the small drawing. How long will it be on the actual mural? **6 ft**
7. **Writing in Math** The scale on a map is 1 in. = 550 mi. How many miles are represented by 3 in.? Explain how you used proportion to solve the problem. **Sample answer: On the map, 3 in. = 1,650 mi. The proportion is $\frac{1}{550} = \frac{3}{m}$, $m = 3 \times 550$.**

74 Use with Lesson 6-10.

CHECK

Error Intervention

If students write incorrect proportions,

then have them label the terms in their proportions as actual and scale. *(Also see* Reteaching, *p. 330B.)*

3 Practice

Exercises 7–9 Students should recognize that they will have to measure the map distance for some of the terms in their proportions. Help students realize that the more carefully they measure, the more accurate their answers will be.

TEST TALK **Exercise 11** Remind students that a good explanation describes steps in order. Suggest they include a sketch of the map.

Reading Assist Vocabulary Make sure students understand that the word *scale,* as used in this lesson, is not the same as a *doctor's scale* or a *balance scale.* In this lesson, *scale* refers to reducing or enlarging drawings or models according to a given ratio.

CHECK

For another example, see Set 6-10 on p. 348.

1. On a map with scale 2 cm:25 km, what would be the dimensions of a 145 km by 80 km rectangle? **11.6 cm by 6.4 cm**
2. **Reasoning** If a scale on a map is 1 in. = 250 miles, what would be the map distance if the actual distance between two cities is 1,000 miles? **4 inches**

PRACTICE

For more practice, see Set 6-10 on p. 351.

A Skills and Understanding

Use the scale drawing to answer exercises 3–4.

Beach
3 in.
Marisa's house
4.5 in.
3.5 in.
Theater
Scale: 1.5 inches = 1 mile

3. Marisa left home and walked to the beach. What was the actual distance she walked? **2 miles**
4. It took Marisa 30 minutes to walk to the beach from home. If she walks at the same pace, how long will it take her to walk from her home to the theater? **35 minutes**
5. If Marisa were to walk from her house to the theater, from the theater to the beach, and from the beach to her house, what would be the total actual distance she walked? **$7\frac{1}{3}$ miles**
6. **Reasoning** If the actual distance between Chicago and Cincinnati is about 300 miles, what would the distance be on a map with a scale of 0.5 in. = 50 miles? **3 inches**

B Reasoning and Problem Solving

Math and Social Studies

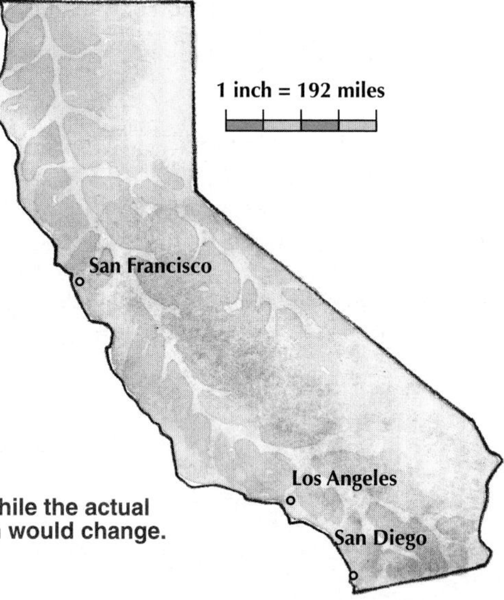

Although California is the third largest state by area, it is the most populated, with more than 33 million people! In fact, it contains four of the nation's 20 largest cities: Los Angeles, San Diego, San Jose, and San Francisco. A map of California is shown at the right. Find the distance

7. from San Francisco to Los Angeles. **about 384 mi**
8. from Los Angeles to San Diego. **about 120 mi**
9. from San Francisco to San Diego. **about 504 mi**
10. **Reasoning** If the map is enlarged, would the scale remain the same? Explain. **No, the distance on the map would be larger while the actual distance remained the same, so the proportion would change.**

Test-Taking Practice

Test-Taking Practice, Item 1, p. 333 There is one part to the problem; the scale is worth four points. Remind the students that they should answer as much as they can since partial credit is given for this type of problem.

Discuss the sample responses shown and compare them to papers produced by your students.

4-point answer Scale is correct; shows complete understanding of scale drawings and maps.

1 in. = 2.5 mi

PRACTICE

11. **Writing in Math** The scale on a map of Chicago's lakefront is 2.5 cm = 4 km. Rich wants to know how far it is from the Field Museum to the Museum of Science and Industry. Explain how Rich could calculate the actual distance between the two museums. **He could measure the distance from the Field Museum to the Museum of Science and Industry on the map and then set up a proportion with that distance and $\frac{2.5 \text{ cm}}{4 \text{ km}}$ to find the actual distance.**

C Extensions

12. **Reasoning** The Gateway Arch in St. Louis is 192 meters tall. Make a scale drawing of the arch that fits on one sheet of paper. Tell what scale you used to make your drawing. **Sample answer: 10 m = 1 cm**

Mixed Review and Test Prep

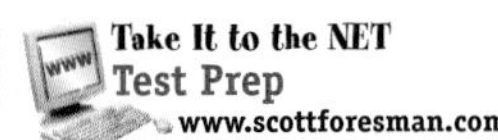

Use the formula $d = r \cdot t$ to solve each problem.

13. George drives at a rate of 30 miles per hour. How long will it take him to drive 150 miles? **5 hours**

14. Irene runs at a rate of 6 miles per hour. If she ran for 7 hours last week, how many total miles did she run? **42 miles**

15. Which ratio is equal to 4:10?

A. $\frac{5}{2}$ **B.** 10:4 **(C.)** $\frac{6}{15}$ **D.** 1 to 4

Learning with Technology

The Geometry Drawing eTool

1. Answers should be a proportion with a ratio of 1:3; yes

You can use the Geometry Drawing eTool to make scale drawings. Draw a small rectangle. Then, use the scale transformation tool to draw a new rectangle with sides that are three times as long as the sides of your small rectangle.

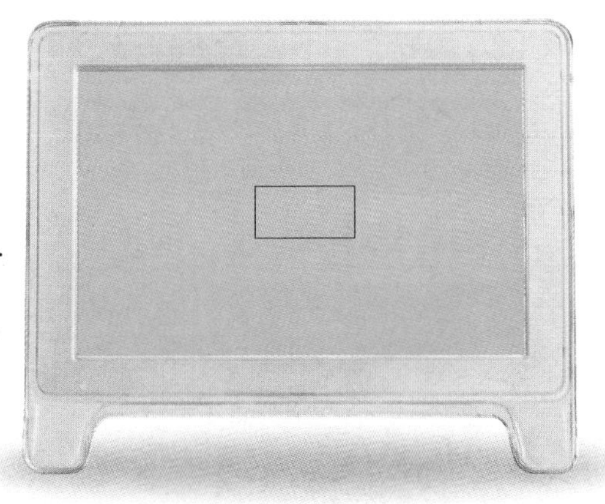

1. Measure the sides of each rectangle. Write ratios comparing the lengths of the shortest to longest sides of the 2 rectangles. Do the ratios form a proportion? **See above.**
2. Find the perimeters of each rectangle. How does the ratio of perimeters compare to the ratio of the length of the shortest sides? **It is the same.**

2-point answer Incorrect scale; shows some understanding of scale drawings and maps.

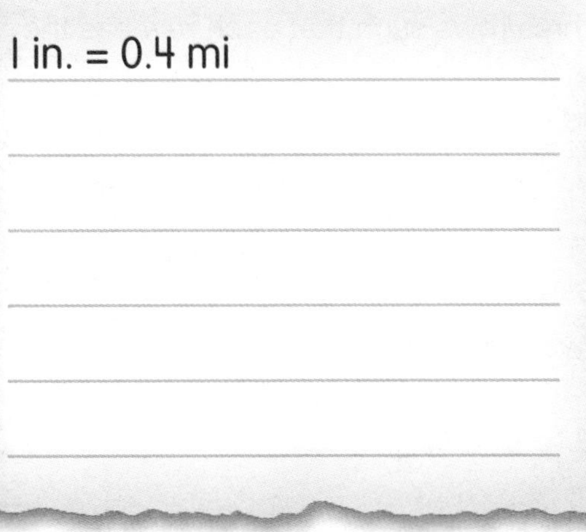

0-point answer Scale is incorrect; shows no understanding of scale drawings and maps.

1 in. = 1 mi

Leveled Practice

Below Level Ex. 3–8, 11, 13–15

On Level Ex. 5–11, 13–15

Above Level Ex. 4–7, 10–15

Early Finishers Working with a partner, students should use the map on page 332 and find the actual distances from Los Angeles to San Jose, from San Diego to San Jose, and from San Francisco to San Jose.

Learning with Technology Students need access to Geometry Drawing eTool.

Be sure that students understand how to use the features of the tool to draw, scale a figure, and measure. Students' understanding of ratio and proportion is extended to consider the relationship of perimeters of rectangles.

4 Assess

Journal Idea Have students explain how to find the actual distance between two towns if they know the map distance and the map's scale.

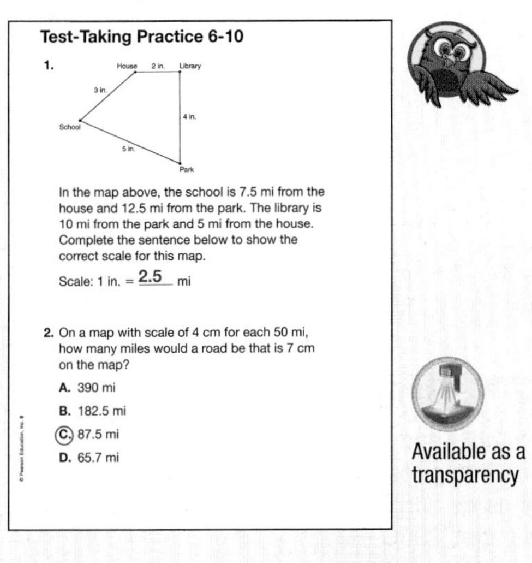

Test-Taking Practice 6-10

1. In the map above, the school is 7.5 mi from the house and 12.5 mi from the park. The library is 10 mi from the park and 5 mi from the house. Complete the sentence below to show the correct scale for this map.

Scale: 1 in. = **2.5** mi

2. On a map with scale of 4 cm for each 50 mi, how many miles would a road be that is 7 cm on the map?

A. 390 mi
B. 182.5 mi
(C) 87.5 mi
D. 65.7 mi

Available as a transparency

Stars and Stripes

Lesson Organizer

Quick Lesson Overview

Objective Review and apply key concepts, skills, and strategies learned in this and previous chapters.

Math Understanding Some real-world problems can be solved using known concepts, skills, and strategies.

How Children Learn Math During the middle grades, students are just beginning to develop proportional reasoning; therefore, it is important to use situations with familiar content.

NCTM Standards

- Number and Operations

(For a complete correlation to the NCTM Standards and Grades 6–8 Expectations, see pages 298G–H.)

Getting Started

Spiral Review

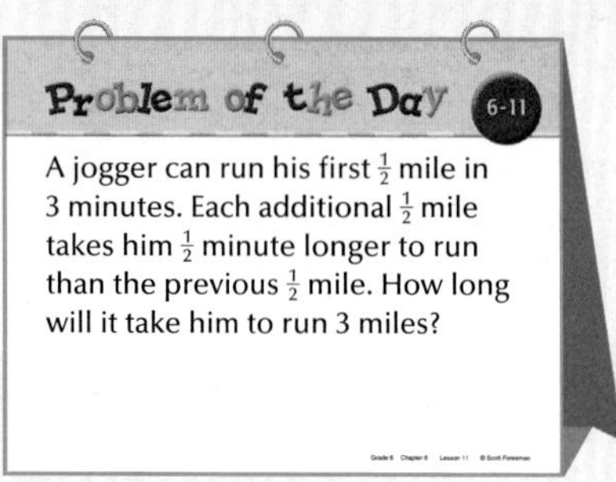

Problem of the Day 6-11

A jogger can run his first $\frac{1}{2}$ mile in 3 minutes. Each additional $\frac{1}{2}$ mile takes him $\frac{1}{2}$ minute longer to run than the previous $\frac{1}{2}$ mile. How long will it take him to run 3 miles?

Topics Reviewed

- Adding mixed numbers; time
- Problem-Solving Strategy: Make a Table

Answer It will take $25\frac{1}{2}$ minutes to jog 3 mi.

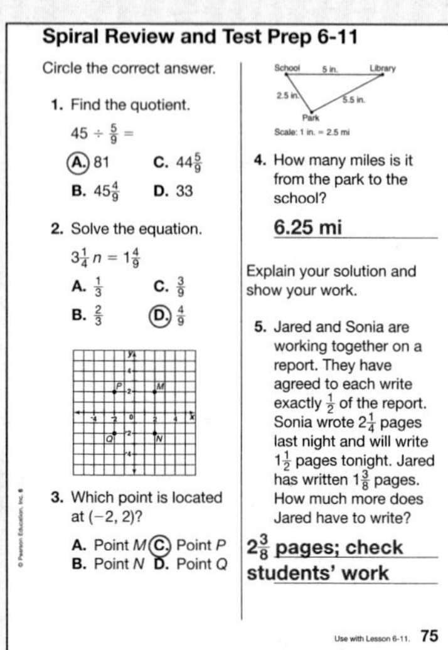

Spiral Review and Test Prep 6-11

Circle the correct answer.

1. Find the quotient.
$45 \div \frac{5}{9} =$
(A.) 81 C. $44\frac{5}{9}$
B. $45\frac{4}{9}$ D. 33

2. Solve the equation.
$3\frac{1}{4}n = 1\frac{4}{9}$
A. $\frac{1}{3}$ C. $\frac{3}{9}$
B. $\frac{2}{3}$ (D.) $\frac{4}{9}$

3. Which point is located at (−2, 2)?
A. Point M (C.) Point P
B. Point N D. Point Q

School 5 in. Library
2.5 in. 5.5 in.
Park
Scale: 1 in. = 2.5 mi

4. How many miles is it from the park to the school?
6.25 mi

Explain your solution and show your work.

5. Jared and Sonia are working together on a report. They have agreed to each write exactly $\frac{1}{2}$ of the report. Sonia wrote $2\frac{1}{4}$ pages last night and will write $1\frac{1}{2}$ pages tonight. Jared has written $1\frac{3}{8}$ pages. How much more does Jared have to write?
$2\frac{3}{8}$ pages; check students' work

© Pearson Education, Inc. 6

Use with Lesson 6-11. 75

Available as a transparency and as a blackline master

Topics Reviewed

1. Dividing fractions; **2.** Solving equations with fractions; **3.** The coordinate plane; **4.** Scale drawings and maps; **5.** Writing to explain

Investigating the Concept

Equal Ratios

5-10 MIN **Visual/Spatial/Kinesthetic**

Materials Counters or Teaching Tool 9

What to Do

- Have students line up 6 red counters and 3 yellow counters in a straight line as shown.

- **What is the ratio of yellow counters to red counters?** *(3 to 6)*
- Have student rearrange the counters into three rows such that each row has the same number of red and yellow counters.
- **What is the ratio of yellow counters to red counters within each row?** *(1 to 2)*
- **Are 3 to 6 and 1 to 2 equal ratios?** *(Yes)*

Ongoing Assessment

- **Reasoning What is another name that we could use to refer to a pair of equal ratios?** *(Proportion)*
- **State two other ways to write the ratio 3 to 6.** *(3:6; $\frac{3}{6}$)*

Reaching All Learners

Reading in Math

Show the Main Idea

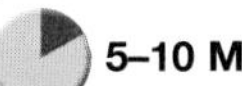 5–10 MIN **Visual/Spatial** 

Materials *(per student)* Centimeter Grid Paper (Teaching Tool 18)

- Have a volunteer read Exercise 4 on page 335.
- Have students use a scale of 1 cm to 1 foot to draw a picture on the grid paper that shows the main idea in the problem. *(Sample answer shown.)*
- **Write a proportion to find how wide the project flag should be and solve.** *($\frac{19}{10} = \frac{9\frac{1}{2}}{w}$; 5 feet)*

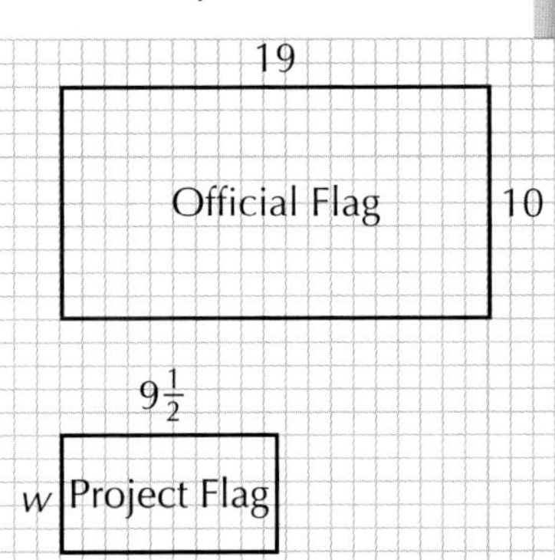

Access Content

English Language Learners

Fractions of Stars

 15–20 MIN **Visual/Spatial/Verbal** 

- Have a volunteer read item 2 on page 334. Ask students what steps they would take to solve the problem.
- Ask students what steps they would take if the problem referred to the second row of stars.
- Have partners each draw a flag of 50 stars with rows in a different configuration.
- Have partners ask each other what steps they would take to find the fraction of the stars in the top row.

Reteaching

Writing and Solving Proportions

 10–15 MIN **Logical/Mathematical** 

- Copy the following information onto the board.
- Explain how the proportion is set up. Have one student set up a proportion to determine how many liters of blue should be added to 6 liters of yellow to obtain the color green. *($\frac{\text{2 parts blue}}{\text{3 parts yellow}} = \frac{\text{b liters blue}}{\text{6 liters yellow}}$)*
- Have the other student solve the proportion. *(4 liters blue)*
- Have partners copy and complete the table, switching roles for each row. *(9 liters yellow; 15 liters yellow; 8 liters blue)*

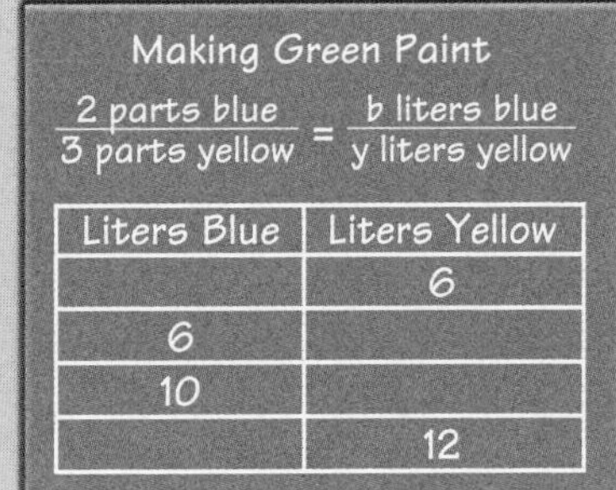

Making Green Paint

$\frac{\text{2 parts blue}}{\text{3 parts yellow}} = \frac{\text{b liters blue}}{\text{y liters yellow}}$

Liters Blue	Liters Yellow
	6
6	
10	
	12

Math and Technology

Solving Proportions on a Calculator

 5–10 MIN **Logical/Mathematical** 

Materials *(per pair)* Calculators

- Write the proportion $\frac{8}{32} = \frac{x}{200}$ on the board. Have students solve the proportion using pencil and paper. *(50)*
- Have students solve the proportion with the calculator, using one step. *($8 \times \frac{200}{32}$)*
- Have students check their answers to the problems in the lesson with a calculator.

$\frac{8\times200}{32}$ 50

Objective Review and apply key concepts, skills, and strategies learned in this and previous lessons.

Warm Up

Activate Prior Knowledge Ask students what is the ratio of length to width for a rectangle that is 24 feet long and 15 feet wide. *(8:5)*

Teach

Explain to the students that they will use what they already know.

Ongoing Assessment

Talk About It: Exercise 1

- **What are we trying to find out?** *(The number of years between two years mentally)*
- **What do we know?** *(The two years: 1777 and 1976)*
- **What strategy would you use?** *(Use the compensation mental-math strategy to subtract.)*

Error Intervention

If students are having difficulty interpreting some of the exercises,

then have them reread each exercise carefully and explain it in their own words to a partner.

Lesson 6-11

Problem-Solving Applications

The Stars and Stripes After the Revolutionary War, there were many versions of the American flag until President Taft, in 1912, set the first standards regarding the flag's proportions and arrangement of stars. The last change to the flag occurred on July 4, 1960, when a star was added to represent Hawaii, America's 50th state.

Trivia The rules of flag etiquette state that the flag should not be flown with the blue field down, except as a signal of distress in instances of extreme danger.

1. In 1777, the U.S. flag changed from the Grand Union flag, shown at the right, to the Stars and Stripes. One of the first styles of this flag, with 13 stars in a circle, is shown below. This early style of the flag was flown during the nation's bicentennial in 1976. Use mental math to find the number of years between 1777 and 1976. **199 years**

2. The current American flag is shown on the next page. What fraction of the stars are in the top row? Write your answer in simplest form. $\frac{3}{25}$

3. In 2002, the largest Stars and Stripes measured 255 feet wide, and had a width to length ratio of about 1 to 1.98. Find the length of this flag. **About 504.9 ft**

Good News/Bad News *You can still view the flag that inspired Francis Scott Key to write the poem that is used in the National Anthem. The bad news is that the flag is not in very good shape. Its original dimensions were 30 x 42 feet. It has been so battered and torn over time that, after restoration, it now measures only 30 x 34 feet.*

Reteaching — Below Level

PROBLEM-SOLVING APPLICATIONS — R 6-11

Outer Space

Data File

Distance from Earth to the moon:	238,900 mi
Time for Earth to rotate once:	24 hr
Number of planets that rotate clockwise:	1
Number of planets that rotate counterclockwise:	8

How many times does Earth rotate in 144 hr?

I know that Earth rotates 1 time in 24 hr. I can make a table to solve this problem. By looking for a pattern and filling in the table, I can see that in 144 hr, Earth will rotate 6 times.

Number of Hours	24	48	72	96	120	144
Number of Rotations	1	2	3	4	5	6

1. Write a ratio that compares the number of planets that rotate clockwise to the total number of planets. **1:9**
2. It takes the planet Mercury 88 days to revolve around the sun. The ratio for revolutions to days is 1:88. Write two other ratios that are equal to 1:88. **Sample answers: 2:176, 3:264**
3. Venus rotates on its axis once every 243 days. How many days would it take to rotate 4 times? **972 days**
4. Jason needed to make a scale drawing to show the distance between Earth and the moon. If the scale of his drawing was 1 in. = 60,000 mi, about how many inches apart would Earth and the moon be in Jason's drawing? **About 4 in.**

Use with Lesson 6-11. 75

Practice — On Level

PROBLEM-SOLVING APPLICATIONS — P 6-11

Sandwich Shop Hours

FRANK'S SANDWICH SHOP — Schedule — Week of Aug. 12

Name	Mon.	Tues.	Wed.	Thurs.	Fri.	Sat.	Sun.
Sasha	9–5	9–5	12–6	X	9–5	9–5	X
Miguel	5–8	5–8	X	5–8	X	X	X
Eric	X	X	5–8	X	5–8	5–8	12–6
Jen	10–6	X	9–12	9–5	X	X	12–6
Frank	9–6	9–6	9–6	X	12–5	9–6	12–4

1. What ratio describes the number of hours that Eric worked to the number of hours that Frank worked? **1:3**
2. What ratio describes the number of hours that Miguel worked to the number of hours that Frank worked? **1:5**
3. What ratio describes the number of hours that Jen worked to the number of hours all of the employees worked? **25:132**
4. Since everyone at the sandwich shop gets paid by the hour, the amount of pay is proportionate to the amount of work. If Sasha got paid $304.00 for the week of August 12, what would she have gotten paid for a week she worked 30 hr? **$240.00**
5. Using the information in Exercise 4, express Sasha's pay as a unit rate. **$ 8.00 per hour**
6. Frank gets paid twice as much as the other workers. Express Frank's pay as a unit rate. **$16.00 per hour**
7. If Miguel gets paid $9.00 per hour, how much did he earn the week of August 12? **$81.00**
8. Jen made $212.50 the week of August 12. Express her pay as a unit rate. **$8.50 per hour**

Use with Lesson 6-11. 75

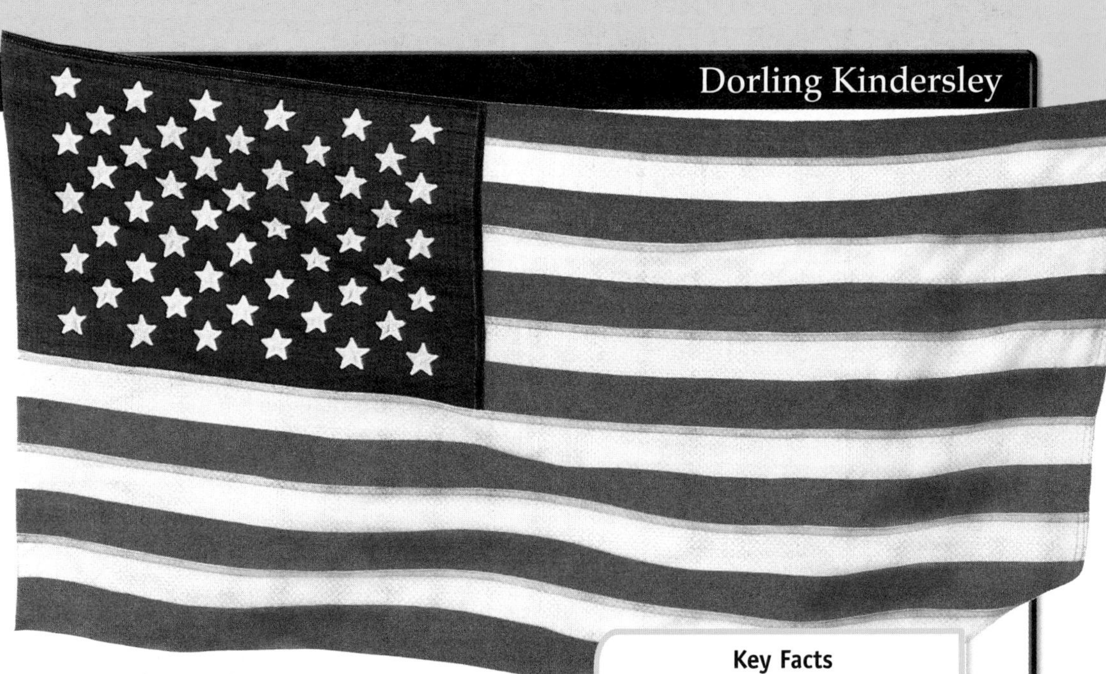

Using Key Facts

4 Suppose you need to make a U.S. flag for a school project. The flag's length must be $9\frac{1}{2}$ feet. How wide should the flag be? **5 ft**

5 The flag that was placed on the moon measured 5 feet long and 3 feet wide. Compare this length to width ratio to the official length to width ratio. Do the ratios form a proportion? **No**

Key Facts
Official Flag Ratios

Dimension	Ratio of Dimension to Flag's Width
• Length	19:10
• Blue field width	7:13
• Blue field length	76:100
• Stripe width	1:13

6 **Decision Making** Design your own flag. Record the colors and ratios of the design so that someone else could create a duplicate of your flag. **See margin.**

7 **Writing in Math** Using the pictures or information from this lesson, write your own word problem that involves ratios. Solve your problem and write the answer in a complete sentence. **Sample answer: What ratio of the stripes on today's flag extend across the flag's entire length? $\frac{6}{13}$ of the flag's stripes extend the entire length of the flag.**

3 Practice

Exercise 6 Students might find it helpful to trade papers with partners and try to recreate each other's flags.

TEST TALK **Exercise 7** Remind students there is a ratio in Exercise 3 in addition to those listed in the Key Facts chart.

Leveled Practice

Below Level Work alone on Ex. 1–3. Work on Ex. 4–7 with a partner.

On Level Work alone on Ex. 1–3 and Ex. 5–6. Work on Ex. 4 and 7 with a partner.

Above Level Work alone on Ex. 1–6. Work on Ex. 7 with a partner.

Early Finishers Have students draw a scale model of the current U.S. flag using the ratios in the Key Facts chart.

4 Assess

Journal Idea Have students explain how to find the length of a flag if it has a width of 15 feet and the ratio of length to width is 19:10.

Answers

6. Sample answer: The ratio of length to width is 2:1. The background color is green. Centered on the flag is a yellow circle. The ratio of the circle's diameter to the width of the flag is 2:3.

Enrichment — Above Level

Happy Trails

E 6-11 NUMBER SENSE

Simon wants to read a book, but he needs to finish his math homework first. To find out what the book Simon wants to read is about, shade the spaces in the puzzle below that are proportional to the ratios in 1–10. Unscramble the letters left unshaded to spell the subject of the book.

1. $\frac{14 \text{ min}}{72 \text{ min}}$
2. $\frac{108 \text{ cm}}{17 \text{ sec}}$
3. $\frac{9 \text{ quarters}}{\$2.25}$
4. \$6:2 books
5. $\frac{128 \text{ km}}{2 \text{ hr}}$
6. $\frac{8 \text{ oranges}}{18 \text{ apples}}$
7. $\frac{15 \text{ ft}}{3 \text{ ft}}$
8. $\frac{4 \text{ bags}}{34 \text{ oz}}$
9. 80 lb:4 boxes
10. $\frac{22 \text{ yd}}{71 \text{ yd}}$

11. Simon wants to read a book about **H I K I N G** the Appalachian Trail.

Problem Solving

PROBLEM-SOLVING APPLICATION PS 6-11

Fruit Juice

Laura has packed a cooler with cans of fruit juice for a class picnic. Out of every 6 cans of juice, 4 are grape juice, and the rest are apple juice. There are 8 cans of apple juice in the cooler. How many cans of juice are there in the cooler altogether?

Read and Understand

1. What is the ratio of grape juice to apple juice?
4 grape:2 apple
2. How many cans of apple juice are in the cooler?
8 cans of apple
3. What are you trying to find?
The total number of cans of juice in the cooler

Plan and Solve

4. Draw a model in the space at the right to show the proportion problem.
5. Add the number of grape juice cans to the apple juice cans. Write the answer in a complete sentence.
There are 24 total cans in the cooler.

Grape Juice | Apple Juice | 4 : 2 | 16 cans | 8 cans

Look Back and Check

6. Is your answer reasonable?
Sample answer: Yes, because there are twice as many cans of grape juice as apple juice.

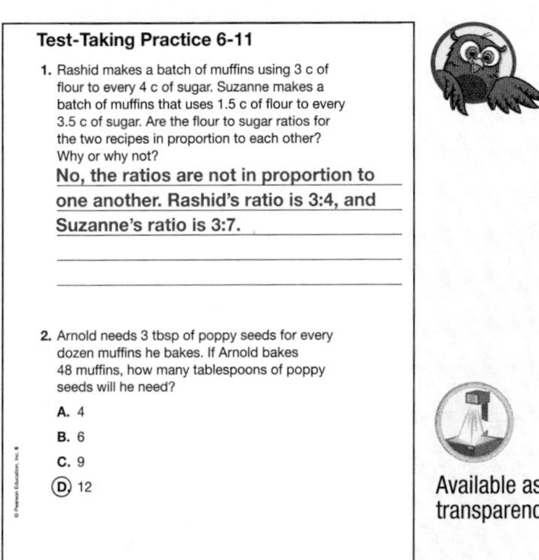
Test-Taking Practice 6-11

1. Rashid makes a batch of muffins using 3 c of flour to every 4 c of sugar. Suzanne makes a batch of muffins that uses 1.5 c of flour to every 3.5 c of sugar. Are the flour to sugar ratios for the two recipes in proportion to each other? Why or why not?
No, the ratios are not in proportion to one another. Rashid's ratio is 3:4, and Suzanne's ratio is 3:7.

2. Arnold needs 3 tbsp of poppy seeds for every dozen muffins he bakes. If Arnold bakes 48 muffins, how many tablespoons of poppy seeds will he need?
A. 4
B. 6
C. 9
(D) 12

Available as a transparency

Review

Purpose Help students review content learned in Section C.

Using Student Pages 336–337

Do You Know How? exercises are appropriate for written work.

Do You Understand? questions are designed for whole-class discussion or small-group discussion followed by a report to the whole class.

Vocabulary Review

You may wish to review these terms before assigning the page.

formula *(p. 328)*

scale drawing *(p. 330)*

scale *(p. 330)*

Do You Know How?

Using Formulas (6-9, 6-11)

1. A car traveled at a rate of 45 miles per hour for 3 hours. Use the formula $d = r \times t$ to find the distance the car traveled.
   135 miles
2. Myra's truck can travel 16 miles on 1 gallon of gasoline. How many gallons will Myra need to travel 296 miles? Use the formula $m = \frac{d}{g}$ where m represents miles per gallon, d is the distance traveled, and g is the number of gallons of gasoline used.
   18.5 gallons

Do You Understand?

When there is a constant proportion between two quantities.

A When can you use a formula?
See above.

B Use the rate $\frac{45 \text{ miles}}{3 \text{ hours}}$ to write a proportion that could be used to find the distance traveled in 1 hour.
$\frac{45 \text{ miles}}{3 \text{ hours}} = \frac{x \text{ miles}}{1 \text{ hour}}$

Garden

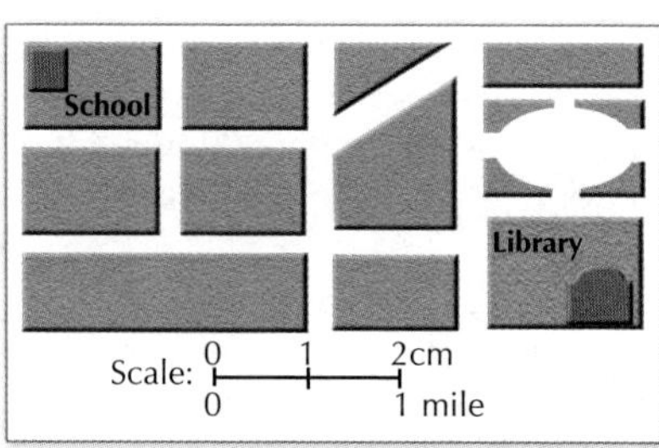

Map

Scale Drawings and Maps (6-10)

3. Express the length to width ratio of the garden pictured above in simplest form. **1.5 to 1**
4. The scale in the drawing of the garden above is 3 cm = 7 ft. Find the actual dimensions of the garden. **7 ft by 10.5 ft**
5. Use the map at the above right and a metric ruler to find the shortest distance between the school and the library.
   2.75 miles

C Describe how to use proportions to find the actual length of an object from a scale drawing.
See below.

D Explain what the scale on a map tells you.
See below.

C. Use the scale as the first ratio, and keeping the units of the top and bottom constant, create the second ratio.

D. It tells the proportion between the scale drawing and the actual size.

Item Analysis for Diagnosis and Intervention

Objective	Review Items	Diagnostic Checkpoint Items	Student Book Pages*	Intervention System
Use formulas to solve problems.	1–2	1, 3–4	328–329	J34
Use scale drawings to solve problems.	3–5	2, 4–8	330–333	I34

*For each lesson, there is a *Reteaching* activity in *Reaching All Learners* and a *Reteaching* master.

Chapter 6 Section C

Diagnostic Checkpoint

MULTIPLE CHOICE

Think It Through
In a **scale drawing,** the dimensions of the **scale drawing** and **the original figure are proportional.**

1. Apples are on sale for \$1.29 per pound. What is the cost of 4 pounds of apples? Use the formula *total cost* = *unit price* × *quantity.* (6-9)

   A. \$0.32 **C.** \$3.23
   (B.) \$5.16 **D.** \$5.96

2. The distance between two cities is 150 miles. On a map with a scale of 2 cm = 30 miles, how far apart are the two cities? (6-10)

   A. 3 cm **C.** 5 cm
   B. 7.5 cm **(D.)** 10 cm

FREE RESPONSE

3. Mr. Bruckner drove from his house to the beach without stopping. He drove at a rate of 55 miles per hour and it took him 5.5 hours. Use the formula *distance* = *rate* × *time* to find how far it is from Mr. Bruckner's house to the beach. (6-9)
   302.5 miles
4. In 11 seconds, a race car goes from 44 meters per second to 77 meters per second. Find the acceleration of the race car. Use the formula $a = \frac{f - s}{t}$ where a represents the acceleration (in meters per second squared), f is the final speed, s is the starting speed, and t is the time it took to make the change. (6-9, 6-11)
   3 meters per second squared.
5. On a blueprint of a house, the kitchen measures 5 in. long and 3 in. wide. The scale of the blueprint is 1 in. = 3 ft. What are the actual dimensions of the kitchen? (6-10)
   15 ft by 9 ft
6. Jessica looks on a map and finds that the amusement park is 3.5 cm from the hotel where she is staying. The scale of the map is 2 cm = 3 mi. How many miles away is the amusement park from the hotel? (6-10)
   5.25 miles

Writing in Math

7. What makes a drawing a scale drawing? (6-10, 6-11) **It must be proportional to the actual object.**
8. When you use a proportion to solve scale drawing problems, can the proportion be set up in more than one way? Explain. (6-10, 6-11)
   Yes, the proportion can be set up scale to actual = scale to actual or it can be set up actual to scale = actual to scale.

Sample student work for Exercise 7

A scale drawing is a reduced or enlarged size of the real thing. A map is a scale drawing of a place. It has to have a scale to tell you how the real size compares to the drawing. Everything is proportional.

The rubric below is a scoring guide that shows how many points to give an answer to Exercise 7. Many teachers would assign a score of 3 points to this explanation. Discuss the sample response shown and compare it to papers produced by students.

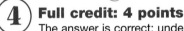

Scoring Rubric

4 Full credit: 4 points
The answer is correct; understands scale drawings; explanation is complete.

3 Partial credit: 3 points
The answer is correct; understands scale drawings; explanation is incomplete.

2 Partial credit: 2 points
The answer is correct; shows some understanding of scale drawings; very little explanation.

1 Partial credit: 1 point
The answer is incorrect; shows some understanding of scale drawings.

0 No credit
The answer is incorrect; does not understand scale drawings.

Test Talk

Purpose Promote focused instruction on test-taking strategies.

Using Student Pages 338–339

The purpose of these pages is to provide students with additional help in composing good written answers for test questions. Students are given a problem and then a written answer for it. They note what is good about the answer, as well as what is missing, and see how it would be scored on a rubric.

Have students read through Exercise 1; then discuss the three points under *Improve Written Answers*. Ask students what information must be included to make this answer complete. Point out also the importance of writing a clear answer that tells what is needed, but is not padded with extraneous information. Then have someone read aloud the sample answer. Use *Think It Through* to help them see what is wrong with this answer. Also have them read the Scoring Rubric so they can see why the answer receives only 3 points.

Have students do Exercise 2 on their own. After they finish, discuss the scores they gave the answer. Make sure they understand why the answer is incorrect and why it should receive a score of 2.

Test-Taking Strategies

- Understand the question.
- Get information for the answer.
- Plan how to find the answer.
- Make smart choices.
- Use writing in math.
- → Improve written answers.

Improve Written Answers

You can follow the tips below to learn how to improve written answers on a test. It is important to write a clear answer and include only information needed to answer the question.

1 The French Club is selling candles for a fundraiser. As a bonus, the club receives gift certificates for free pizzas. The table shows how many gift certificates the club might earn.

Number of boxes of candles sold	40	80	120	160
Number of pizza gift certificates	3	6	9	12

Use an equation, ratio, or rule to explain how the number of boxes of candles is related to the number of gift certificates. Then find the number of gift certificates the club would receive for selling 240 boxes of candles.

Improve Written Answers

- Check if your answer is complete.
  *In order to **get as many points as possible,** I must explain how the number of boxes of candles is related to the number of gift certificates and I must find the number of gift certificates the club would receive for selling 240 boxes of candles.*
- Check if your answer makes sense.
  I should check that my equation, ratio, or rule works for every pair of numbers in the table. Then I should check that it works for the number of gift certificates I said the club would earn for selling 240 boxes of candles.
- Check if your explanation is clear and easy to follow.
  *I should reread my explanation to be sure it is **accurate and clear.** I shouldn't include any unnecessary information.*

The rubric below is a scoring guide for Test Questions 1 and 2.

Scoring Rubric

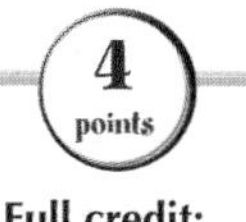

Full credit: 4 points
The answer and explanation are correct.

3 points
Partial credit: 3 points
The answer is correct, but the explanation does not fully describe the relationship.

2 points
Partial credit: 2 points
The answer is correct or the explanation is correct, but not both.

1 point
Partial credit: 1 point
The answer is incorrect. The explanation shows partial understanding.

0 points
No credit: 0 points
The answer and explanation are both incorrect or missing.

 EC NTL 12 11 10 9 8 7 6

Lourdes used the scoring rubric on page 338 to score a student's answer to Test Question 1. The student's paper is shown below.

As the number of boxes of candles increases, the number of pizza gift certificates also increases. The club would receive 18 pizza gift certificates for selling 240 boxes of candles.

Think It Through

The explanation seems incomplete. This would be a better way to describe the relationship: The ratio of the number of boxes of candles to the number of pizza gift certificates is $\frac{40}{3}$. The answer of 18 gift certificates is correct. Since the answer is correct, but the explanation does not fully describe the relationship, the score is 3 points.

Now it's your turn.

Score the student's paper. If it does not get 4 points, rewrite it so that it does.

2 Janie is planning to attend a summer music camp. The table shows how many music teachers will be at the camp.

Number of students	25	50	75	100
Number of music teachers	2	4	6	8

Use an equation, ratio, or rule to explain how the number of students is related to the number of music teachers. Then find the number of music teachers that would be at the camp if there are 225 students.

The ratio of students to music teachers is 25 to 2. For 225 students there would be 10 music teachers.

2 points; for 225 students there would be 18 music teachers.

Understand the Question
- Look for important words.
- Turn the question into a statement: "I need to find out . . ."

Get Information for the Answer
- Get information from text.
- Get information from pictures, maps, diagrams, tables, graphs.

Plan How to Find the Answer
- Think about problem-solving skills and strategies.
- Choose computation methods.

Make Smart Choices
- Eliminate wrong answers.
- Try working backward from an answer.
- Check answers for reasonableness; estimate.

Use Writing in Math
- Make your answer brief but complete.
- Use words from the problem and use math terms accurately.
- Describe steps in order.
- Draw pictures if they help you explain your thinking.

Improve Written Answers
- Check if your answer is complete.
- Check if your answer is clear and easy to follow.
- Check if your answer makes sense.

Key Vocabulary and Concept Review

Using Student Pages 340–341

Purpose Provide students with a review of vocabulary and concepts in Chapter 6 through worked-out examples, vocabulary tips, and self-checking exercises.

Key Vocabulary and Concept Review focuses on the vocabulary of the chapter. It provides real-life connections to strengthen students' understanding of mathematical terms.

In addition, it reviews the concepts studied in the chapter. Exercises allow students to show they understand the meanings of words and they can apply the concepts.

Answers are printed upside down in red, so students can check their own work. Lesson references are given, so students can look back at any time.

MindPoint Quiz Show CD-ROM
Use *MindPoint Quiz Show* for additional practice on Chapter 6.

Chapter 6

Key Vocabulary and Concept Review

We use special terms to help define things.

A ratio is defined by its ***terms,*** *the quantities in the ratio. (p. 300)*

Use ratios to compare amounts. (Lessons 6-1, 6-2)

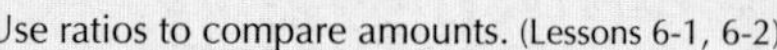

Write the **ratio** for the number of blue circles to the number of red circles.

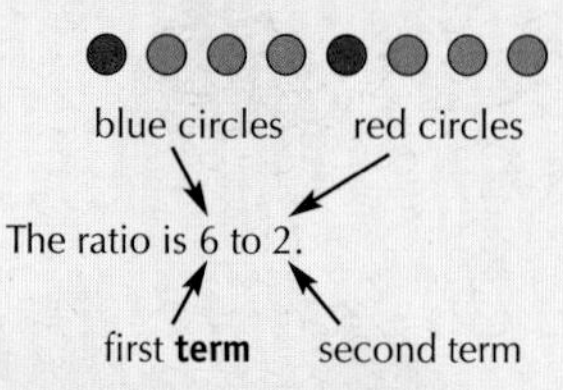

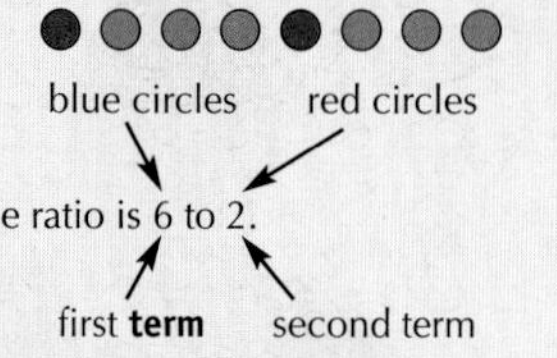

This can also be written as 6:2 or $\frac{6}{2}$.

Find three ratios that are equal to $\frac{16}{20}$.

Multiply or divide both terms by the same nonzero number.

$\frac{16 \times 2}{20 \times 2} = \frac{32}{40}$

$\frac{16 \div 2}{20 \div 2} = \frac{8}{10}$

$\frac{16 \div 4}{20 \div 4} = \frac{4}{5}$

$\frac{32}{40}$, $\frac{8}{10}$, and $\frac{4}{5}$ are equal ratios.

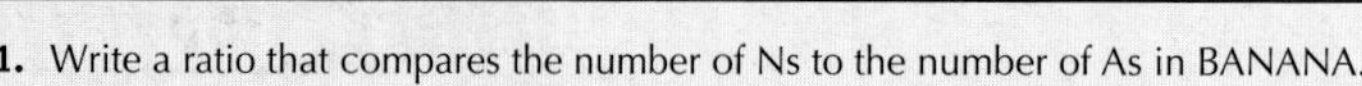

1. Write a ratio that compares the number of Ns to the number of As in BANANA.
2. Write three ratios equal to 18:24.

Unit means one.

A ***unit rate*** *is a comparison to 1 unit. (p. 306)*

Write unit rates and use formulas. (Lessons 6-3, 6-9)

Find the **unit rate** for 90 miles in 2 hours.

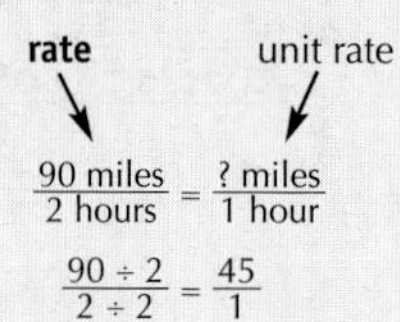

$\frac{90 \text{ miles}}{2 \text{ hours}} = \frac{? \text{ miles}}{1 \text{ hour}}$

$\frac{90 \div 2}{2 \div 2} = \frac{45}{1}$

Unit rate: 45 miles per hour

The **formula** $f = 5{,}280m$ gives the number of feet f in m miles. How many feet are in 3.4 miles?

$f = 5{,}280m$

$f = 5{,}280 \frac{\text{ft}}{\cancel{\text{mile}}} \cdot 3.4 \cancel{\text{miles}}$

$f = 17{,}952$ ft

3. Find the unit rate for $35 for 5 hours.
4. How many feet are in 7.5 miles?

340

When I cross something out, I draw an X over it.

When I find the ***cross products*** *in a proportion, I multiply like this.* *(p. 316)*

Use proportions. (Lessons 6-5, 6-6, 6-7, 6-10)

Do the ratios $\frac{6 \text{ gallons}}{\$9}$ and $\frac{10 \text{ gallons}}{\$15}$ form a **proportion?**

Check the **cross products.**

$$6 \times 15 \stackrel{?}{=} 9 \times 10$$

$$90 = 90$$

The units are the same and the cross products are equal, so the ratios form a proportion.

The **scale** on a **scale drawing** is 2 cm: 15 km. What is the actual distance represented by 5 cm on the drawing?

$\frac{2 \text{ cm}}{15 \text{ km}} = \frac{5 \text{ cm}}{x \text{ km}}$ ← scale length / ← actual length

$2x = 5(15)$ Write the cross products.

$2x = 75$ Multiply.

$\frac{2x}{2} = \frac{75}{2}$ Solve for x.

$x = 37.5$; The actual distance is 37.5 km.

5. Solve $\frac{12}{m} = \frac{24}{18}$.

Use objects or write to explain to solve problems. (Lessons 6-4, 6-8)

You can model some problems with objects.

Of the 12 kittens at the pet shop, 2 out of 3 have stripes. How many kittens have stripes.

● = striped ○ = not striped

●●○ ●●○ ●●○ ●●○

Eight kittens have stripes.

A drawing can help explain your thinking.

Would you rather be given 2 quarters every 6 days or 4 quarters every 10 days? Why?

I'd rather have 4 quarters every 10 days. Here's why.

My picture shows that 4 quarters in 10 days can be split into 2 equal groups of 2 quarters in 5 days. That's better than 2 quarters in 6 days.

6. There are 30 passengers. Four out of 5 are adults. How many are adults?

A grading scale compares a numerical test score to a letter grade.

The ***scale*** *in a* ***scale drawing*** *is a ratio that compares the dimensions in the drawing to the dimensions of the real object.* *(p. 330)*

Answers: 1. 2:3 2. Sample answer: 3:4, 9:12; 36:48 3. $7 per hour 4. 39,600 ft 5. m = 9 6. 24

Chapter Test

Using Student Pages 342–343

Purpose Assess students' progress by checking their understanding of the concepts and skills in Chapter 6. Use as a review, practice test, or chapter test.

Sample student work for Exercise 28

Make a table by multiplying 4 in. and 5 days by the same number.

in.	4	8	12	16	20	24
days	5	10	15	20	25	30

The values vary proportionally because each ratio can be reduced to $\frac{4}{5}$.

Many teachers would assign a score of 4 points to this explanation. The student's answer is correct and demonstrates an understanding of how to make a table of proportional values.

Scoring Rubric

4 Full credit: 4 points
The answer is correct; understands how to make a table of proportional values; explanation is complete.

3 Partial credit: 3 points
The answer is correct; understands how to make a table of proportional values; explanation is incomplete.

2 Partial credit: 2 points
The answer is incorrect; understands how to make a table of proportional values; explanation is complete.

1 Partial credit: 1 point
The answer is correct; there is no explanation.

0 No credit
The answer is incorrect; shows no understanding.

CHAPTER 6

Chapter Test

MULTIPLE CHOICE

Choose the correct letter for each answer.

1. Which ratio compares the number of circles to the number of diamonds?

A. 4 to 2 **C.** 4 to 3
(B.) 2 to 4 **D.** 2 to 3

2. Which ratio is equal to 8:2?

A. $\frac{1}{4}$ **(C.)** $\frac{20}{5}$
B. 3 to 12 **D.** 16:2

3. Which pair below are equal ratios?

A. $\frac{4}{6}$; 6:4 **C.** 4 to 3; 7 to 6
B. $\frac{6}{9}$; $\frac{1}{3}$ **(D.)** 12 to 10; $\frac{18}{15}$

4. Find the unit rate for 120 miles in 4 hours.

(A.) $\frac{30 \text{ mi}}{1 \text{ h}}$ **C.** $\frac{60 \text{ mi}}{2 \text{ h}}$
B. $\frac{1 \text{ mi}}{3 \text{ h}}$ **D.** $\frac{40 \text{ mi}}{1 \text{ h}}$

5. There are 35 students in Richard's class. Two out of every 7 students are wearing jeans. How many students in the class are wearing jeans?

A. 2 **(C.)** 10
B. 5 **D.** 14

6. Which proportion is written correctly?

A. $\frac{2 \text{ in.}}{5 \text{ ft}} = \frac{3 \text{ in.}}{72 \text{ in.}}$ **C.** $\frac{1 \text{ gal}}{4 \text{ qt}} = \frac{2 \text{ pints}}{1 \text{ quart}}$
(B.) $\frac{2 \text{ ft}}{5 \text{ ft}} = \frac{24 \text{ in.}}{60 \text{ in.}}$ **D.** $\frac{3 \text{ ft}}{1 \text{ yd}} = \frac{3 \text{ yd}}{9 \text{ ft}}$

7. Solve the proportion $\frac{42 \text{ mi}}{3 \text{ h}} = \frac{y \text{ mi}}{5 \text{ h}}$

A. $y = 2.8$ mi **(C.)** $y = 70$ mi
B. $y = 15$ mi **D.** $y = 84$ mi

8. Which is the best buy?

(A.) 20 oz for $4.60 **C.** 9 oz for $2.25
B. 16 oz for $4.00 **D.** 24 oz for $5.76

9. A car travels at a rate of 65 miles an hour. At this rate, how far will the car travel in 5 hours?

A. 13 miles **(C.)** 325 miles
B. 70 miles **D.** 845 miles

10. Ceila is 56 inches tall. Using the formula $c = 2.54i$, where c represents the number of centimeters, and i is the number of inches, find Ceila's height in centimeters.

A. 145.56 cm
(B.) 142.24 cm
C. 39.37 cm
D. 22.05 cm

TEST TALK — Think It Through
- I should **look for key words** in the problem.
- I can **eliminate** unreasonable answers.

11. What is the actual distance between Mathville and Fractiontown?

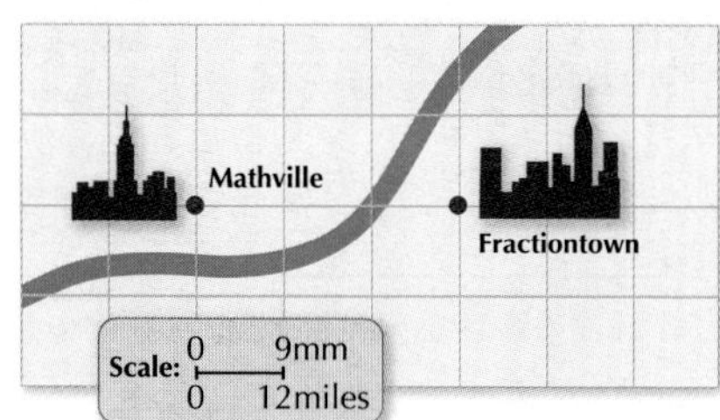

A. 3 miles **C.** 24 miles
B. 12 miles **(D.)** 36 miles

342

Item Analysis for Diagnosis and Intervention

Objective	Items	Student Book Pages*	Intervention System
Understand ratios.	1, 12–14	300–301	I30
Find equivalent ratios.	2–3, 15–20, 28	302–305	I31
Understand rates and unit rates.	4, 8–9, 19–20, 25	306–309	I38

*For each lesson, there is a *Reteaching* activity in *Reaching All Learners* and a *Reteaching* master.

FREE RESPONSE

Write a ratio for each comparison.

Color	red	blue	silver	white
Number of balloons	12	8	15	16

12. blue to red **8:12**

13. silver to all colors **15:51**

14. red to all other colors **12:39**

Give three ratios that are equal to each ratio. **Sample answers are given.**

15. 15:6 **5:2, 10:4, 20:8**

16. $\frac{12}{16}$ **$\frac{3}{4}$, $\frac{6}{8}$, $\frac{9}{12}$**

Write each ratio in simplest form.

17. 150:234 **25:39**

18. 3.5 to 0.5 **7:1**

Write each as a unit rate.

19. \$6.12 for 9 gal **\$0.68 per gallon**

20. 312 mi on 13 gal **24 mi per gallon**

Decide if the ratios form a proportion.

21. $\frac{5\text{ ft}}{8\text{ mi}}, \frac{15\text{ ft}}{18\text{ mi}}$ **No**

22. $\frac{9\text{ tbsp}}{3\text{ gal}}, \frac{12\text{ tbsp}}{4\text{ gal}}$ **Yes**

Solve each proportion.

23. $\frac{156\text{ mi}}{6\text{ gal}} = \frac{y\text{ mi}}{11\text{ gal}}$ **$y = 286$ mi**

24. $\frac{16}{22} = \frac{40}{w}$ **$w = 55$**

25. Patty drives at a rate of 42 miles per hour for 7 hours. How far does she drive? Use the formula $d = rt$. **294 miles**

26. There are 60.96 centimeters in 2 feet. How many centimeters are in 1 yard? **91.44 cm**

27. The scale on a map is 2.5 cm to 30 mi. If two cities are 8 cm apart on the map, what is the actual distance between the two cities? **96 miles**

Writing in Math

28. Beginning with the ratio $\frac{4\text{ in.}}{5\text{ days}}$ make a table of quantities that vary proportionally. Tell how you know that the values in the table vary proportionally. **See below.**

29. Travis is training for a duathlon. He bikes and runs each day. The ratio of miles biked to miles run is 4 to 1. If he runs 5 miles, how many miles does he bike? Solve and explain your reasoning. **See below.**

30. Explain how to use objects to solve the problem below. Give the answer in a complete sentence.

Loretta has 36 stuffed animals. Four out of every 9 stuffed animals are bears. How many bears are in Loretta's stuffed animal collection?

Use counters in two colors. Show 4 of one color for the bears and 5 of another color for the others. Keep adding groups until there are 36 counters in all.

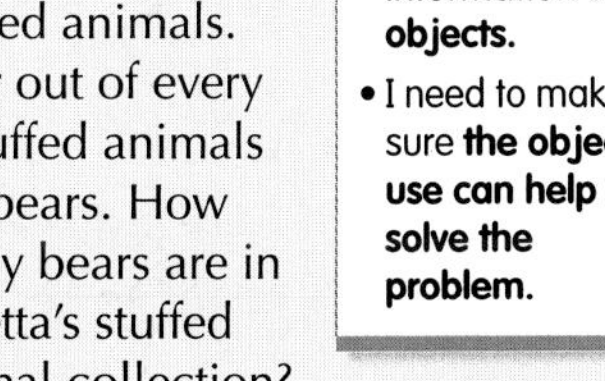

Think It Through

- Using objects involves **showing the known information with objects.**
- I need to make sure **the objects I use can help me solve the problem.**

28. Sample answer.

Inches	4	8	12	16	20
Days	5	10	15	20	25

The ratios in each column can be simplified to $\frac{4}{5}$.

29. 20 miles; I solved the proportion $\frac{4}{1} = \frac{x}{5}$; $x = 20$

Assessment Sourcebook

Additional assessment options may be found in the *Assessment Sourcebook.*

- Chapter 6 Test (Forms A and B)
- Chapter 6 Performance Assessment
- Chapters 1–6 Cumulative Test (Use after Chapter 6.)

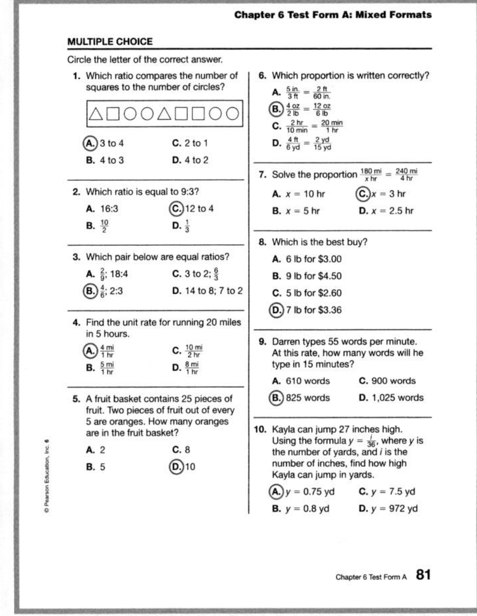

Chapter 6 Test Form A: Mixed Formats

MULTIPLE CHOICE

Circle the letter of the correct answer.

1. Which ratio compares the number of squares to the number of circles?
   (A.) 3 to 4 C. 2 to 1
   B. 4 to 3 D. 4 to 2
2. Which ratio is equal to 9:3?
   A. 16:3 (C.) 12 to 4
   B. $\frac{10}{2}$ D. $\frac{1}{3}$
3. Which pair below are equal ratios?
   A. $\frac{2}{9}$; 18:4 C. 3 to 2; $\frac{6}{3}$
   (B.) $\frac{4}{6}$; 2:3 D. 14 to 8; 7 to 2
4. Find the unit rate for running 20 miles in 5 hours.
   (A.) $\frac{4\text{ mi}}{1\text{ hr}}$ C. $\frac{10\text{ mi}}{2\text{ hr}}$
   B. $\frac{5\text{ mi}}{1\text{ hr}}$ D. $\frac{8\text{ mi}}{1\text{ hr}}$
5. A fruit basket contains 25 pieces of fruit. Two pieces of fruit out of every 5 are oranges. How many oranges are in the fruit basket?
   A. 2 C. 8
   B. 5 (D.) 10
6. Which proportion is written correctly?
   A. $\frac{5\text{ in.}}{3\text{ ft}} = \frac{2\text{ ft}}{60\text{ in.}}$
   (B.) $\frac{4\text{ oz}}{2\text{ lb}} = \frac{12\text{ oz}}{6\text{ lb}}$
   C. $\frac{2\text{ hr}}{10\text{ min}} = \frac{20\text{ min}}{1\text{ hr}}$
   D. $\frac{4\text{ ft}}{6\text{ yd}} = \frac{2\text{ yd}}{15\text{ yd}}$
7. Solve the proportion $\frac{180\text{ mi}}{x\text{ hr}} = \frac{240\text{ mi}}{4\text{ hr}}$
   A. $x = 10$ hr (C.) $x = 3$ hr
   B. $x = 5$ hr D. $x = 2.5$ hr
8. Which is the best buy?
   A. 6 lb for \$3.00
   B. 9 lb for \$4.50
   C. 5 lb for \$2.60
   (D.) 7 lb for \$3.36
9. Darren types 55 words per minute. At this rate, how many words will he type in 15 minutes?
   A. 610 words C. 900 words
   (B.) 825 words D. 1,025 words
10. Kayla can jump 27 inches high. Using the formula $y = \frac{i}{36}$, where y is the number of yards, and i is the number of inches, find how high Kayla can jump in yards.
   (A.) $y = 0.75$ yd C. $y = 7.5$ yd
   B. $y = 0.8$ yd D. $y = 972$ yd

© Pearson Education, Inc. 6

Chapter 6 Test Form A 81

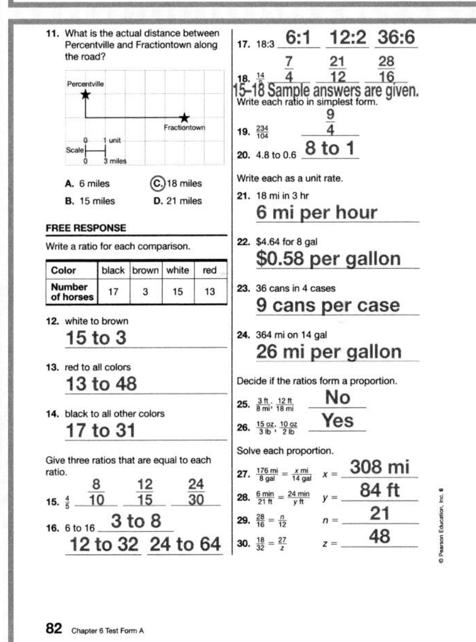

11. What is the actual distance between Percentville and Fractiontown along the road?

A. 6 miles (C.) 18 miles
B. 15 miles D. 21 miles

FREE RESPONSE

Write a ratio for each comparison.

Color	black	brown	white	red
Number of horses	17	3	15	13

12. white to brown **15 to 3**
13. red to all colors **13 to 48**
14. black to all other colors **17 to 31**

Give three ratios that are equal to each ratio.

15. $\frac{4}{5}$ **$\frac{8}{10}$ $\frac{12}{15}$ $\frac{24}{30}$**
16. 6 to 16 **3 to 8 12 to 32 24 to 64**
17. 18:3 **6:1 12:2 36:6**
18. $\frac{14}{8}$ **$\frac{7}{4}$ $\frac{21}{12}$ $\frac{28}{16}$**

15–18 Sample answers are given.

Write each ratio in simplest form.

19. $\frac{234}{104}$ **$\frac{9}{4}$**
20. 4.8 to 0.6 **8 to 1**

Write each as a unit rate.

21. 18 mi in 3 hr **6 mi per hour**
22. \$4.64 for 8 gal **\$0.58 per gallon**
23. 36 cans in 4 cases **9 cans per case**
24. 364 mi on 14 gal **26 mi per gallon**

Decide if the ratios form a proportion.

25. $\frac{3\text{ ft}}{8\text{ mi}}, \frac{12\text{ ft}}{18\text{ mi}}$ **No**
26. $\frac{15\text{ oz}}{3\text{ lb}}, \frac{10\text{ oz}}{2\text{ lb}}$ **Yes**

Solve each proportion.

27. $\frac{176\text{ mi}}{8\text{ gal}} = \frac{x\text{ mi}}{14\text{ gal}}$ $x =$ **308 mi**
28. $\frac{6\text{ min}}{21\text{ ft}} = \frac{24\text{ min}}{y\text{ ft}}$ $y =$ **84 ft**
29. $\frac{28}{16} = \frac{n}{12}$ $n =$ **21**
30. $\frac{18}{32} = \frac{27}{z}$ $z =$ **48**

© Pearson Education, Inc. 6

82 Chapter 6 Test Form A

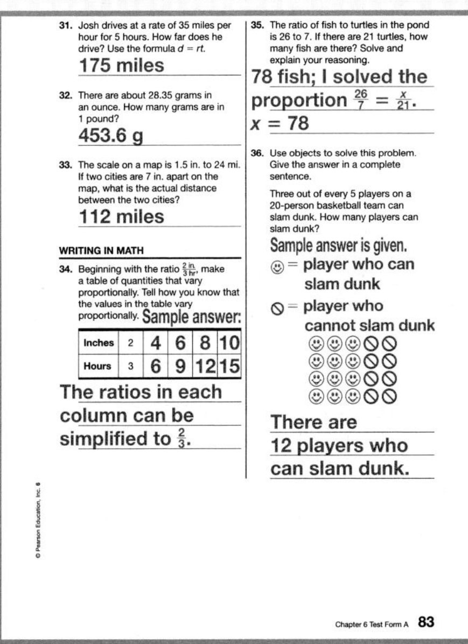

31. Josh drives at a rate of 35 miles per hour for 5 hours. How far does he drive? Use the formula $d = rt$. **175 miles**
32. There are about 28.35 grams in an ounce. How many grams are in 1 pound? **453.6 g**
33. The scale on a map is 1.5 in. to 24 mi. If two cities are 7 in. apart on the map, what is the actual distance between the two cities? **112 miles**

WRITING IN MATH

34. Beginning with the ratio $\frac{2\text{ in.}}{3\text{ hr}}$, make a table of quantities that vary proportionally. Tell how you know that the values in the table vary proportionally. **Sample answer:**

Inches	2	4	6	8	10
Hours	3	6	9	12	15

The ratios in each column can be simplified to $\frac{2}{3}$.

35. The ratio of fish to turtles in the pond is 26 to 7. If there are 21 turtles, how many fish are there? Solve and explain your reasoning. **78 fish; I solved the proportion $\frac{26}{7} = \frac{x}{21}$. $x = 78$**
36. Use objects to solve this problem. Give the answer in a complete sentence.

Three out of every 5 players on a 20-person basketball team can slam dunk. How many players can slam dunk?

Sample answer is given.

There are 12 players who can slam dunk.

© Pearson Education, Inc. 6

Chapter 6 Test Form A 83

Item Analysis for Diagnosis and Intervention

Objective	Items	Student Book Pages*	Intervention System
Use objects to solve problems.	30	312–313	M33
Understand proportions.	6, 21–22	316–317	I39
Solve proportions using patterns in tables.	5, 7, 23–24, 26, 29	318–321	I39
Solve proportions using cross products.	5, 7, 23–24, 26, 29	322–323	I40
Write to explain your reasoning.	28–30	324–325	M18
Use formulas to solve problems.	10, 25	328–329	J34
Use scale drawings to solve problems.	11, 27	330–333	I34

*For each lesson, there is a *Reteaching* activity in *Reaching All Learners* and a *Reteaching* master.

Cumulative Review and Test Prep

Using Student Pages 344–345

Purpose Provide students with a review of math concepts from Chapters 1–6 and previous grades.

For intervention, use the resources listed below.

Answers

9. The units on the top and bottom do not remain the same in each ratio.
10. They both compare a part to a whole. Ratios can compare a part to a part, fractions cannot.
22. Find all the sums possible by rolling 2 number cubes. Then count the number of ways to roll a sum of 5 and compare that to the total number of sums.
30. No; the scale of the map is represented by the ratio $\frac{3}{15}$. The proportion should have been $\frac{3 \text{ cm}}{15 \text{ mi}} = \frac{4 \text{ cm}}{y \text{ mi}}$ or $\frac{3 \text{ cm}}{4 \text{ cm}} = \frac{15 \text{ mi}}{y \text{ mi}}$ = 20 miles

Chapters 1–6

Cumulative Review and Test Prep

Number and Operation

MULTIPLE CHOICE

1. Find $6 + 4^2 \div 2$.

A. 5 **(C.)** 14
B. 11 **D.** 26

2. Which ratio is equal to 12:3?

A. 1 to 4 **(C.)** 8 to 2
B. 3:1 **D.** $\frac{8}{3}$

FREE RESPONSE

3. Which is the better buy? **14 oz for $2.52**

4. Find 5.2×9.36. **48.672**

5. What is the GCF of 8, 12, and 24? **4**

6. Find the LCM of 10, 30, and 45. **90**

7. Jeffrey is $6\frac{1}{5}$ feet tall. Christina is $5\frac{1}{4}$ feet tall. How much taller is Jeffrey? **$\frac{19}{20}$ feet taller**

8. Jon's grandfather needs $8\frac{1}{4}$ cups of raisins to make 2 fruitcakes. A 15-ounce box of raisins contains $2\frac{3}{4}$ cups. How many boxes should Jon's grandfather buy? **3 boxes**

Writing in Math

9. Explain why $\frac{4 \text{ lb}}{\$7.56}$ and $\frac{\$5.67}{3 \text{ lb}}$ do not form a proportion. **See margin.**

10. Compare fractions and ratios. How are they the same? How are they different? **See margin.**

Geometry and Measurement

MULTIPLE CHOICE

11. Which ratio is equal to $\frac{1 \text{ yard}}{91.44 \text{ centimeters}}$?

(A.) $\frac{5 \text{ yd}}{457.2 \text{ cm}}$ **C.** $\frac{3 \text{ ft}}{1 \text{ yd}}$
B. $\frac{457.2 \text{ cm}}{5 \text{ yd}}$ **D.** $\frac{3 \text{ ft}}{91.44 \text{ cm}}$

12. How many inches are in 4 feet?

A. 24 in. **C.** 40 in.
B. 36 in. **(D.)** 48 in.

17. I would divide $\frac{1}{2}$ inch by 12.

FREE RESPONSE

13. Find the circumference of a circle with a diameter of 7 cm. Use $\frac{22}{7}$ for π. **22 cm**

14. What is the name of a triangle with three angles that measure less than 90°? **acute triangle**

15. Find the area of a triangle with base 12 in. and height 8 in. Use the formula $A = \frac{1}{2}bh$. **48 in.²**

16. Use the proportion to find the number of centimeters in 1 foot. **30.48 cm**

$$\frac{2.54 \text{ cm}}{1 \text{ in.}} = \frac{x \text{ cm}}{12 \text{ in.}}$$

Writing in Math

17. An insect in a picture is $\frac{1}{2}$ inch long and a label says "enlarged 12 times." Explain how you would find the insect's actual length. **See above.**

18. Describe how to find the time elapsed between 11:46 A.M. and 2:13 P.M. **Count on from 11:46 A.M. Start by adding 2 hours to get 1:46 P.M. Then add 14 minutes to get 2:00 P.M. Then add 13 more minutes to get to 2:13 P.M. Time elapsed = 2 hours 27 minutes.**

344

Item Analysis for Diagnosis and Intervention

Objective	Items	Student Book Pages*	Intervention System
Use order of operations to evaluate numerical expressions.	1	24–27	J29
Find equivalent ratios.	2, 11	302–305	I31
Understand rates and unit rates.	3	306–309	I33
Multiply decimals.	4	90–93	I20
Find the greatest common factor of two or more numbers.	5	150–151	H4
Find the least common multiple.	6	152–153	H5
Subtract mixed numbers.	7	220–223	H35
Divide mixed numbers.	8	270–271	H43
Understand proportions.	9	316–317	I39
Understand ratios.	10	300–301	I30
Solve proportions.	12, 16, 23	318–321	I39
Compute circumference.	13	Grade 5	K27

*For each lesson, there is a *Reteaching* activity in *Reaching All Learners* and a *Reteaching* master.

Data Analysis and Probability

MULTIPLE CHOICE

19. What is the probability of spinning red?

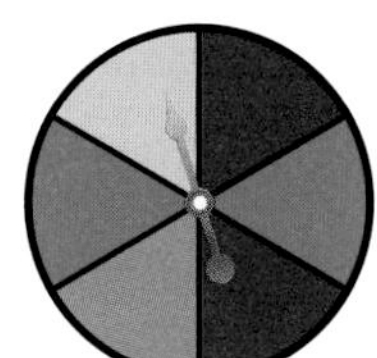

A. $\frac{2}{4}$ **B.** $\frac{1}{6}$ **C.** $\frac{6}{2}$ **(D.)** $\frac{1}{3}$

20. What is the median of the set of data below?

4, 10, 7, 4, 8, 1, 9, 6

A. 4 **B.** 6 **(C.)** 6.5 **D.** 8

FREE RESPONSE

21. Use the bar graph to write a comparison between the number of students who play baseball and the number of students who play tennis.

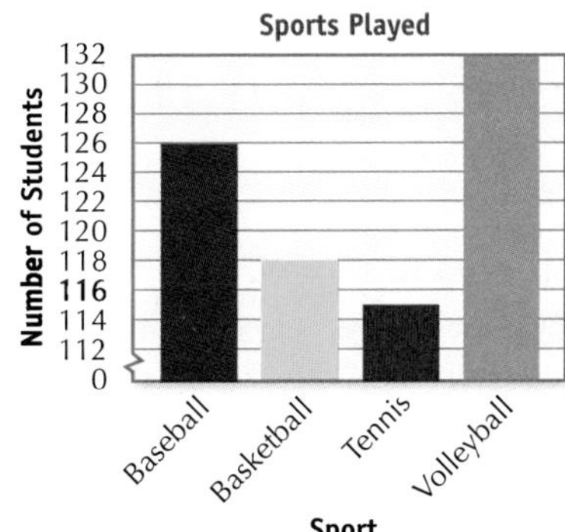

11 more students play baseball than play tennis.

Writing in Math

22. Explain how to find the probability of rolling a sum of 5 on two numbered cubes. **See margin.**

Algebra

MULTIPLE CHOICE

23. Solve the proportion. $\frac{3 \text{ in.}}{12 \text{ s}} = \frac{y \text{ in.}}{20 \text{ s}}$

A. $y = 1.8$ in. **(C.)** $y = 5$ in.

B. $y = 4$ in. **D.** $y = 6$ in.

24. Find $\frac{x}{2} + 8$ for $x = 10$.

A. 5 **(C.)** 13

B. 8 **D.** 17

FREE RESPONSE

25. Use the formula *distance* = *rate* × *time* to find how long it would take to travel 189 miles at a rate of 54 miles per hour.
3.5 hours

26. Evaluate the expression $\frac{3}{5}x - 4$ for $x = 10$, 15, and 20.
2; 5; 8

27. Write the word phrase as an algebraic expression.

24 less than a number

$n - 24$

28. Solve for the variable.

$\frac{3}{7}a = 9$

$a = 21$

29. Use the Distributive Property to find 4×109 mentally.
4(100 + 9) = 400 + 36 = 436

Writing in Math

30. A map has a scale of 3 cm = 15 mi. Carl measured the distance between two cities to be 4 cm. He set up and solved the following proportion. Is his answer correct? Explain. **See margin.**

$\frac{4}{15} = \frac{3}{y}$

$4y = 15 \times 3$

$y = 11.25$ miles

The two cities are 11.25 miles apart.

Item Analysis for Diagnosis and Intervention

Objective	Items	Student Book Pages*	Intervention System
Identify and analyze attributes of two-dimensional shapes.	14	Grade 5	K45
Use formulas to solve problems.	15, 25	328–329	J34
Use scale drawings to solve problems.	17, 30	330–333	I34
Find elapsed time.	18	Grade 5	K16
Determine the probability of an event.	19, 22	Grade 5	L16
Find the median of a set of data.	20	Grade 5	L26
Interpret bar graphs to solve problems.	21	Grade 5	L3
Evaluate algebraic expressions.	24, 26–27	40–43	J30
Use Properties of Equality to isolate the variable in an equation.	28	48–49	J31
Use the Distributive Property.	29	30–31	G64

*For each lesson, there is a *Reteaching* activity in *Reaching All Learners* and a *Reteaching* master.

Reteaching

Using Student Pages 346–348

Purpose Provide students with more examples and practice for each lesson in the chapter.

- Use *Reteaching* pages for students having difficulty with *Check* exercises.
- For additional practice, use *More Practice* exercises starting on page 349.
- For intervention, use the resources listed below.

Answers
Set 6-2

1. $\frac{2}{5}, \frac{6}{15}, \frac{8}{20}$
2. $\frac{6}{10}, \frac{9}{15}, \frac{12}{20}$
3. $\frac{44}{60}, \frac{66}{90}, \frac{88}{120}$
4. $\frac{2}{3}, \frac{4}{6}, \frac{16}{24}$
5. $\frac{5}{3}, \frac{10}{6}, \frac{40}{24}$
6. $\frac{2}{18}, \frac{3}{27}, \frac{4}{36}$
7. $\frac{5}{8}, \frac{50}{80}, \frac{500}{800}$
8. $\frac{6}{1}, \frac{12}{2}, \frac{720}{120}$
9. $\frac{39}{15}, \frac{26}{10}, \frac{13}{5}$

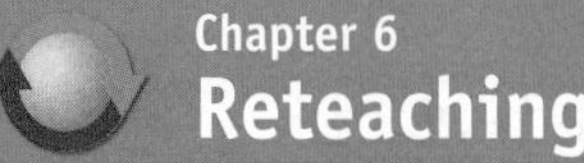

Chapter 6
Reteaching

Set 6-1 (pages 300–301)

Write a ratio for the comparison in three ways.

Stars to circles

There are 3 stars and 1 circle.

3:1 3 to 1 $\frac{3}{1}$

Remember that a ratio is a comparison of like or unlike quantities. The order of the terms is important.

Write a ratio for each comparison in three ways.

1. red shapes to blue shapes **1:1; 1 to 1; $\frac{1}{1}$**
2. squares to stars **2:3, 2 to 3, $\frac{2}{3}$**
3. white shapes to all shapes **1:6; 1 to 6; $\frac{1}{6}$**
4. blue stars to other stars **1:2; 1 to 2; $\frac{1}{2}$**

Set 6-2 (pages 302–305)

Find three ratios equal to $\frac{14}{24}$.

One Way Multiply.

$\frac{14 \times 2}{24 \times 2} = \frac{28}{48}$

$\frac{14 \times 3}{24 \times 3} = \frac{42}{72}$

Another Way Divide.

$\frac{14 \div 2}{24 \div 2} = \frac{7}{12}$

Write the ratio 48:15 in simplest form.

$\frac{48}{15} = \frac{48 \div 3}{15 \div 3} = \frac{16}{5}$ Divide by the GCF of 48 and 15.

Remember to find equal ratios, you must do the same operation to both terms.

Give three ratios that are equal to each ratio. **Sample ratios are given. See margin.**

1. $\frac{4}{10}$ 2. $\frac{3}{5}$ 3. $\frac{22}{30}$
4. $\frac{8}{12}$ 5. $\frac{20}{12}$ 6. $\frac{1}{9}$
7. $\frac{25}{40}$ 8. $\frac{36}{6}$ 9. $\frac{78}{30}$

Write each ratio in simplest form.

10. $\frac{224}{480}$ **$\frac{7}{15}$** 11. 42:68 **21:34** 12. 500 to 125 **4 to 1**

Set 6-3 (pages 306–309)

Write 25 miles in 5 hours as a unit rate.

One Way Use equivalent fractions.

$\frac{25}{5} = \frac{?}{1}$

$\frac{25 \div 5}{5 \div 5} = \frac{5}{1}$

Another Way Find the quotient of the terms.

$25 \div 5 = 5$

Unit rate = $\frac{5 \text{ miles}}{1 \text{ hour}}$

Remember that a unit rate is a comparison where the second term is 1 unit.

Write each as a unit rate.

1. $6.00 for 12 oranges **$0.50 per orange**
2. 336 miles on 12 gallons **28 miles per gallon**
3. 16 people to 4 pizzas **4 people per pizza**
4. $288 for 36 hours of work **$8 per hour of work**
5. 30 minutes for 15 laps **2 minutes per lap**
6. $7.17 for 3 pounds of meat **$2.39 per pound of meat**

346

Item Analysis for Diagnosis and Intervention

Objective	Review Items	Student Book Pages*	Intervention System
Understand ratios.	Set 6–1	300–301	I30
Find equivalent ratios.	Set 6–2	302–305	I31
Understand rates and unit rates.	Set 6–3	306–309	I38
Make a model to solve a problem.	Set 6–4	312–313	M33
Understand proportions.	Set 6–5	316–317	I39
Solve proportions using patterns in a table.	Set 6–6	318–321	I39
Solve proportions using cross products.	Set 6–7	322–323	I40
Write to explain your reasoning.	Set 6–8	324–325	M18
Use formulas to solve problems.	Set 6–9	328–329	J34
Use scale drawings to solve problems.	Set 6–10	330–333	I34

*For each lesson, there is a *Reteaching* activity in *Reaching All Learners* and a *Reteaching* master.

Set 6-4 (pages 312–313)

There are 12 books on the shelf. One out of every 4 books is a mystery book. How many books on the shelf are mystery books?

Use objects. 

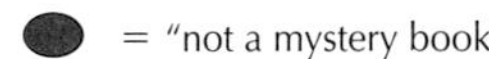

There are 3 mystery books on the shelf.

Remember to choose an object that you can use to represent known information. Write your answer in a complete sentence.

1. There are 24 girls on the team. Two out of every three girls are age 12. How many 12-year-old girls are on the team?
   There are sixteen 12-year-old girls.

Set 6-5 (pages 316–317)

Decide if the ratios form a proportion.

$\frac{2 \text{ mi}}{24 \text{ min}}; \frac{5 \text{ mi}}{60 \text{ min}}$ Find the cross products. $2 \times 60 = 120$ $24 \times 5 = 120$

The cross products are equal, so the ratios form a proportion.

Remember that in a proportion, the cross products are equal.

Decide if the ratios form a proportion.

1. $\frac{\$28}{7 \text{ h}}; \frac{\$45}{9 \text{ h}}$ **No**
2. $\frac{16 \text{ oz}}{2 \text{ tbsp}}; \frac{24 \text{ oz}}{3 \text{ tbsp}}$ **Yes**
3. $\frac{8}{10}; \frac{12}{15}$ **Yes**
4. $\frac{50}{24}; \frac{10}{6}$ **No**

Set 6-6 (pages 318–321)

Solve the proportion.

$\frac{\$132}{20 \text{ h}} = \frac{\$y}{40 \text{ h}}$

$\frac{\$132 \times 2}{20 \text{ h} \times 2} = \frac{\$264}{40 \text{ h}}$ Think of equal ratios.

Remember that ratios that form a proportion are equal ratios.

1. $\frac{312 \text{ mi}}{6 \text{ h}} = \frac{936 \text{ mi}}{x \text{ h}}$ **$x = 18$ h**
2. $\frac{\$7.96}{2 \text{ lb}} = \frac{\$n}{5 \text{ lb}}$ **$n = \$19.90$**
3. $\frac{4 \text{ in.}}{12 \text{ ft}} = \frac{3 \text{ in.}}{x \text{ ft}}$ **$x = 9$ ft**
4. $\frac{5 \text{ gal}}{2 \text{ days}} = \frac{y \text{ gal}}{8 \text{ days}}$ **$y = 20$ gal**

Set 6-7 (pages 322–323)

Solve $\frac{12}{3} = \frac{x}{5}$ using cross products.

$\frac{12}{3} = \frac{x}{5}$

$3x = 12 \times 5$ Write the cross products.

$3x = 60$ Multiply.

$x = 20$ Solve for x.

Remember that the cross products of the terms in a proportion are equal.

Solve each proportion using cross products.

1. $\frac{6}{8} = \frac{x}{12}$ **$x = 9$**
2. $\frac{12}{16} = \frac{9}{y}$ **$y = 12$**
3. $\frac{32}{6} = \frac{x}{9}$ **$x = 48$**
4. $\frac{21}{4} = \frac{x}{5}$ **$x = 26.25$**

Reteaching (continued)

Set 6-8 (pages 324–325)

Which is the better buy: 12 oz for $3.84 or 18 oz for $6.30? Tell how you decided.

12 oz for $3.84 is a better buy. I found the unit price for each and then compared.

12 oz for $3.84 unit price: $0.32 per oz
18 oz for $6.30 unit price: $0.35 per oz

Remember that you can draw pictures to explain your thinking.

1. Which is the better buy, 3 rolls for $3.57 or 8 rolls for $8.48? Tell how you decided. **8 rolls for $8.48; I compared the unit rates of each.**
2. Three out of every 7 students have blue eyes. If there are 28 students, how many students have blue eyes? Explain how you found the answer. **12 students; I solved the proportion $\frac{3}{7} = \frac{x}{28}$.**

Set 6-9 (pages 328–329)

Patricia bikes at a rate of 15 miles per hour. At this rate, how far will she bike in 2.5 hours?

Use the formula *distance* = *rate* × *time*.

$d = \frac{15 \text{ mi}}{1 \text{ h}} \times 2.5 \text{ h}$

$d = 37.5$ mi

Patricia can bike 37.5 miles in 2.5 hours.

Remember to insert the data into the formula and solve for the missing variable.

Use a formula to solve each problem.

1. A train traveled for 5 hours at a rate of 52 miles per hour. How far did the train travel? **260 miles**
2. Marcus earns $6.25 per hour. Use the formula *total earnings* = *pay rate* × *time* to find how much Marcus earns in 39 hours. **$243.75**

Set 6-10 (pages 330–333)

If a scale on a map is 2 cm = 125 mi, how long would the distance on the map be if the actual distance is 750 miles?

$\frac{2 \text{ cm}}{125 \text{ mi}} = \frac{y \text{ cm}}{750 \text{ mi}}$ Set up a proportion.

$750(2) = 125y$ Solve the proportion using cross products.

$\frac{1{,}500}{125} = \frac{125y}{125}$

$12 = y$

The distance on the map would be 12 cm.

Remember to check that the labels are the same for each ratio in the proportion.

1. The scale of a drawing is 1 in. = 7.5 ft. A building is 4 in. in the drawing. What is the actual height of the building? **30 feet**
2. Two cities are located 1.5 in. apart on a map. The scale of the map is 1 in. = 25 mi. How far apart are the two cities? **37.5 miles**
3. A model train is built using the scale 1:60. The actual length of the dining car is 2,100 cm. Find the length of the dining car of the model train. **35 cm**

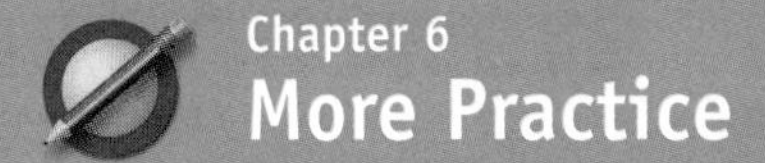

Chapter 6
More Practice

Take It to the NET
More Practice
www.scottforesman.com

Set 6-1 (pages 300–301)

The data at the right shows the number of students who play each type of sport. Write a ratio for each comparison in three ways.

Data File

Sport Participation

Sport	Number of Students
Baseball	42
Basketball	26
Tennis	18
Soccer	53
Swimming	20

1. basketball to soccer **26 to 53, 26:53, $\frac{26}{53}$**
2. swimming to tennis **20 to 18, 20:18, $\frac{20}{18}$**
3. baseball to all other sports **42 to 117, 42:117, $\frac{42}{117}$**
4. soccer to all sports **53 to 159, 53:159, $\frac{53}{159}$**
5. baseball to basketball **42 to 26, 42:26, $\frac{42}{26}$**
6. all sports to tennis **159 to 18, 159:18, $\frac{159}{18}$**
7. Of the students who play tennis, 12 are girls. Write a ratio comparing the number of girls that play tennis to the number of boys who play tennis. **12 to 6, 12:6, $\frac{12}{6}$**

Set 6-2 (pages 302–305)

Give three ratios that are equal to each ratio. **Sample ratios are given.**

1. 3 to 5 **6 to 10, 9 to 15, 12 to 20**
2. 12:6 **2:1, 4:2, 6:3**
3. 2 to 9 **4 to 18, 6 to 27, 8 to 36**
4. 7:11 **14:22, 21:33, 28:44**
5. $\frac{25}{14}$ **$\frac{50}{28}$, $\frac{75}{42}$, $\frac{100}{56}$**
6. $\frac{18}{30}$ **$\frac{3}{5}$, $\frac{6}{10}$, $\frac{9}{15}$**
7. 4 to 20 **1 to 5, 2 to 10, 3 to 15**
8. $\frac{21}{6}$ **$\frac{7}{2}$, $\frac{14}{4}$, $\frac{28}{8}$**

Tell whether the ratios in each pair are equal.

9. 4 to 6 and 12 to 8 **No**
10. 8:3 and 24:9 **Yes**
11. $\frac{7}{12}$ and $\frac{12}{7}$ **No**
12. $\frac{15}{5}$ and $\frac{3}{1}$ **Yes**
13. 9 to 11 and 27 to 33 **Yes**
14. 16:6 and 8:3 **Yes**

Write each ratio in simplest form.

15. 165 to 135 **11 to 9**
16. 126:495 **14:55**
17. $\frac{84}{248}$ **$\frac{21}{62}$**
18. The table shows the number of boys and girls in each class. Which classes have equal ratios of boys to girls? **Mrs. Alvarez and Mr. Collins' classes**

Teacher	Number of Boys	Number of Girls
Mrs. Alvarez	25	20
Mr. Collins	20	16
Ms. Cable	18	16

Set 6-3 (pages 306–309)

Write each as a unit rate.

1. 144 miles in 3 hours **48 mph**
2. 420 students to 20 teachers **21 students per teacher**
3. 5 cups for 8 servings **0.625 cups per serving**
4. $248.20 for 34 hours **$7.30 per hour**

Which is the better buy?

5. 2 liters of lemonade for $2.38, or 5 liters of lemonade for $5.80 **5 liters for $5.80**
6. 6 cans of juice for $3.90, or 24 cans of juice for $16.32 **6 cans for $3.90**
7. 12 oz box of cereal for $4.29, or 16 oz box of cereal for $5.89 **12 oz for $4.29**

More Practice

Using Student Pages 349–351

Purpose Provide students with additional practice for each lesson in the chapter.

- Use *More Practice* pages during each lesson or after the chapter as a review.
- For intervention, use the resources listed below.

Item Analysis for Diagnosis and Intervention

Objective	Review Items	Student Book Pages*	Intervention System
Understand ratios.	Set 6–1	300–301	I30
Find equivalent ratios.	Set 6–2	302–305	I31
Understand rates and unit rates.	Set 6–3	306–309	I38
Make a model to solve a problem.	Set 6–4	312–313	M33
Understand proportions.	Set 6–5	316–317	I39
Solve proportions using patterns in a table.	Set 6–6	318–321	I39
Solve proportions using cross products.	Set 6–7	322–323	I40
Write to explain your reasoning.	Set 6–8	324–325	M18
Use formulas to solve problems.	Set 6–9	328–329	J34
Use scale drawings to solve problems.	Set 6–10	330–333	I34

*For each lesson, there is a *Reteaching* activity in *Reaching All Learners* and a *Reteaching* master.

Chapter 6

More Practice (continued)

Set 6-4 (pages 312–313)

Use objects to solve each problem. Give the answer in a complete sentence.

1. Jasper's little league team won 3 out of every 4 games they played. If they played 12 games this season, how many did they win?
   Jasper's team won 9 games.
2. This year, 84 people attended the community fair. If 2 out of every 7 who attended were adults, how many children attended the fair?
   Sixty children attended the fair.

Set 6-5 (pages 316–317)

Decide if the ratios form a proposition.

1. $\frac{6 \text{ tbsp}}{10 \text{ cups}}, \frac{9 \text{ tbsp}}{15 \text{ cups}}$ **Yes**
2. $\frac{24 \text{ laps}}{30 \text{ min}}, \frac{4 \text{ laps}}{6 \text{ min}}$ **No**
3. $\frac{8 \text{ in.}}{24 \text{ ft}}, \frac{3 \text{ in.}}{9 \text{ ft}}$ **Yes**
4. $\frac{5 \text{ apples}}{\$4}; \frac{7 \text{ apples}}{\$9}$ **No**
5. $\frac{32}{6}; \frac{35}{9}$ **No**
6. $\frac{10}{45}; \frac{9}{2}$ **No**
7. Find a value for each variable to form the proportion $\frac{5 \text{ cups}}{6 \text{ tbsp}} = \frac{x}{y}$.
   Sample answer: x = 10 cups, y = 12 tbsp

Set 6-6 (pages 318–321)

Solve each proportion using any method.

1. $\frac{96 \text{ mi}}{3 \text{ h}} = \frac{x \text{ mi}}{5 \text{ h}}$
   x = 160 mi
2. $\frac{20 \text{ oz}}{5 \text{ servings}} = \frac{x \text{ oz}}{3 \text{ servings}}$
   x = 12 oz
3. $\frac{2 \text{ in.}}{5 \text{ min}} = \frac{8 \text{ in.}}{y \text{ min}}$
   y = 20 min
4. $\frac{4 \text{ buses}}{60 \text{ students}} = \frac{x \text{ buses}}{90 \text{ students}}$
   x = 6 buses
5. $\frac{\$75}{10 \text{ h}} = \frac{\$y}{21 \text{ h}}$
   y = $157.50
6. $\frac{3 \text{ qt}}{8 \text{ in.}} = \frac{5 \text{ qt}}{x \text{ in.}}$ **$x = 13\frac{1}{3}$ in.**
7. Kim uses 4 yards of ribbon to make 3 large bows. How many yards of ribbon will she need to make 24 large bows?
   32 yards of ribbon
8. Marc's car used 6 gallons of gasoline to travel 96 miles. How many gallons of gasoline will his car use to travel 152 miles?
   9.5 gallons

Set 6-7 (pages 322–323)

Solve each proportion using cross products.

1. $\frac{r}{35} = \frac{13}{5}$
   r = 91
2. $\frac{40}{8} = \frac{x}{3}$
   x = 15
3. $\frac{15}{y} = \frac{20}{11}$
   y = 8.25
4. $\frac{7}{28} = \frac{10}{n}$
   n = 40
5. $\frac{t}{18} = \frac{11}{12}$
   t = 16.5
6. $\frac{12}{7} = \frac{p}{28}$
   p = 48
7. At track practice, Nick ran 500 yards in 2.5 minutes. At this rate, how long will it take Nick to run 1 mile? [Hint: 1 mile = 1,760 yards]
   8.8 minutes
8. As a house painter, Tai works 6 hours and earns $71.70. If Tai works 8 hours, how much does he earn?
   $95.60

Take It to the NET
More Practice
www.scottforesman.com

Set 6-8 (pages 324–325)

For each problem, explain how you found your answer.

1. The ratio of an executive's expenses to income is 5 to 8. What are the executive's expenses for a month when the income is $9,800? **$6,125; I solved the proportion $\frac{5}{8} = \frac{\$x}{\$9,800}$**

2. In a package of colored balloons, 3 out of every 8 balloons are red. If there are 18 red balloons in the package, how many total balloons are there? **48 balloons; I solved the proportion $\frac{3 \text{ red}}{8 \text{ total}} = \frac{18 \text{ red}}{x \text{ total}}$**

3. Adams School orders 3 cartons of skim milk for every 7 students. If there are 581 students in the school, how many cartons of skim milk are ordered? **249 cartons of skim milk; I solved the proportion $\frac{3 \text{ cartons}}{7 \text{ students}} = \frac{x \text{ cartons}}{581 \text{ students}}$**

4. The ratio of teachers to students at a middle school is 1 to 36. If there are 720 students in the school, how many teachers are there? **20 teachers**

Set 6-9 (pages 328–329)

At Crafts Plus More, ribbon and fabric are sold by the yard. Use the formula *cost* = *unit price* × *quantity* to find the cost of each.

1. 4 yd red ribbon **$3.00**
2. 6.1 yd blue fabric **$10.86**
3. 2.3 yd patterned fabric **$4.88**
4. 3.5 yd lace **$3.43**

5. The new car Travis bought gets 33 miles to a gallon of gas. At this rate, how far can Travis travel on 12 gallons of gas? **396 miles**

6. Use the formula $d = r \times t$ to find the time it takes a train to travel 434 miles at a rate of 62 mph. **7 hours**

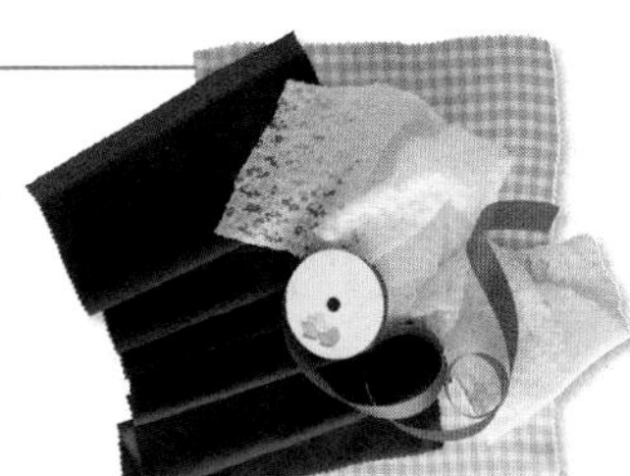

Red ribbon:	$0.75/yard
Lace:	$0.98/yard
Blue fabric:	$1.78/yard
Patterned fabric:	$2.12/yard

Set 6-10 (pages 330–333)

1. The scale in a drawing is 1 cm to 3 ft. In the drawing, the height of a flagpole is 3.5 cm. What is the actual height of the flagpole? **10.5 ft**

2. On a map, the scale is 2 inches to 15 miles. If two cities are 75 miles apart, how far apart are they on the map? **10 inches**

3. Jan's garden is 5 feet wide and 8 feet long. She wants to make a scale drawing of the garden. If she uses the scale 3 inches = 4 feet, what will be the dimensions of the garden in the scale drawing? **3.75 inches wide by 6 inches long**

4. The distance from *A* to *B* on the map is 4.2 cm. The distance from *B* to *C* is 1.4 cm. *B* is on a straight road from *A* to *C*. The scale on the map is 1 cm: 125 km. What is the actual distance from *A* to *C*? **700 km**

5. A map uses the scale 1 cm = 319 km. If South America is 27.7 cm long on the map, about what is the actual length of South America? **about 8,836 km**

Glossary and Table of Measures

GLOSSARY

absolute value The distance that a number is from zero on the number line. (p. 408)

acute angle An angle with a measure between 0° and 90°. (p. 477)

acute triangle A triangle with three acute angles. (p. 497)

adjacent angles A pair of angles with a common vertex and a common side but no common interior points. (p. 480)
Example:

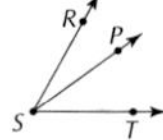

angle Two rays with the same endpoint. (p. 476)

angle bisector A ray that divides an angle into two adjacent angles that are congruent. (p. 485)

arc A part of a circle connecting two points on the circle. (p. 484) *Example:*

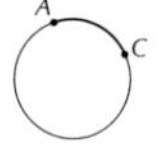

area The number of unit squares of the same size needed to cover a region. (p. 568)

associative properties Properties that state the way in which addends or factors are grouped does not affect the sum or product. (p. 28)

base (in geometry) A designated side of a polygon to which the height is drawn perpendicular (p. 572); one of the two parallel and congruent faces on a prism (p. 586); a particular flat surface of a solid, such as a cylinder or cone. (p. 586)

base (in numeration) A number multiplied by itself the number of times shown by an exponent. (p. 8) *Example:* $4^3 = 4 \times 4 \times 4 = 64$, where 4 is the base.

benchmark fraction Common fractions used for estimating, such as $\frac{1}{4}$, $\frac{1}{3}$, $\frac{1}{2}$, $\frac{2}{3}$, and $\frac{3}{4}$. (p. 170)

biased sample A sample which is not representative of the population from which it is drawn. (p. 621)

break apart Using the Distributive Property to compute mentally. (p. 30)

C

capacity The amount a container can hold. (p. 543)

Celsius (°C) A metric unit for measuring temperature. (p. 722)

center The interior point from which all points of a circle are equally distant. (p. 502)

centi- Prefix meaning $\frac{1}{100}$. (p. 546)

central angle An angle with its vertex at the center of a circle. (p. 502)
Example:

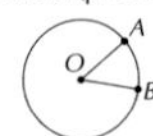

certain event An event that is sure to occur and has a probability of 1. (p. 662)

chord A line segment with both endpoints on a circle. (p. 502)

circle A closed plane figure with all points the same distance from a given point called the center. (p. 502)

circle graph A graph that represents a total divided into parts. (p. 642)

circumference The distance around a circle. (p. 576)

clustering An estimation method where numbers that are approximately equal are treated as if they were equal. (p. 16) *Example:* 26 + 24 + 23 is about 25 + 25 + 25, or 3 × 25.

combination Each possible arrangement of the outcomes of an event where order is not important. (p. 659)

common denominator A denominator that is the same in two or more fractions. (p. 204)

common factor A factor that is the same for two or more numbers. (p. 150)

common multiple A multiple that is the same for two or more numbers. (p. 152)

commutative properties The properties that state the order of the addends or factors does not affect the sum or product. (p. 28)

compatible numbers Numbers that are easy to compute mentally. (p. 18)

compensation Choosing numbers close to the numbers in a problem, and then adjusting the answer to compensate for the numbers chosen. (p. 33)

complementary angles Two angles with measures that add up to 90°. (p 480)

composite number A natural number greater than 2 that has more than two factors. (p. 147)

compound event A combination of two or more single events. (p. 655)

cone A three-dimensional figure that has one circular base. The points on this circle are joined to one point outside the base, sometimes called the vertex. (p. 586) *Example:*

congruent Having the same size and shape. (p. 472)

construction A geometric drawing that uses a limited set of tools, usually a compass and a straightedge. (p. 484)

coordinate plane A two-dimensional system in which a location is described by its distances from two perpendicular number lines called the *x*-axis and the *y*-axis. (p. 440)

Counting Principle If one choice can be made in *m* ways and a second choice can be made in *n* ways, then the two choices can be made together in *m* × *n* ways. (p. 655)

cross products The product of the first term of the first ratio and the second term of the second ratio, and the product of the second term of the first ratio and the first term of the second ratio. (p. 316)

cube A prism whose faces are all squares of the same size. (p. 586)

cubed A number that is multiplied by itself three times. (p. 9) *Example:* 2 cubed = 2^3 = 8

cubic unit A unit measuring volume, consisting of a cube with edges one unit long. (p. 594)

cylinder A three-dimensional figure that has two circular bases which are parallel and congruent. (p. 586) *Example:*

data Information that is gathered. (p. 620)

decagon A polygon with ten sides. (p. 494)

decimal A number with one or more numbers to the right of the decimal point. (p. 76)

degree (°) A unit for measuring angles. (p. 476)

denominator The number below the fraction bar in a fraction; the total number of equal parts in all. (p. 160)

dependent events Events for which the outcome of one affects the probability of the other. (p. 672)

diagonal A line segment that connects two vertices of a polygon and is not a side. (p. 494)
Example:

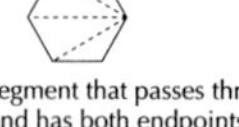

diameter A line segment that passes through the center of a circle and has both endpoints on the circle. (p. 502) *Example:*

discount The amount by which the regular price of an item is reduced. (p. 380)

disjoint Two or more events with no outcomes in common. (p. 669)

Distributive Property Multiplying a sum by a number produces the same result as multiplying each addend by the number and adding the products. (p. 30)
Example: 2 × (3 + 4) = (2 × 3) + (2 × 4)

dividend The number being divided by another number. (pp. 95,100) *Example:* In 12 ÷ 3, 12 is the dividend.

divisible A number is divisible by another number if its quotient is a whole number and the remainder is zero. (p. 142)

divisor The number used to divide another number. (pp. 100, 142) *Example:* In 12 ÷ 3, 3 is the divisor.

dot symbol for multiplication (·) The same meaning as the symbol × for multiplication. (p. 9)

dodecagon A polygon with 12 sides. (p. 494)

double-bar graph A graph that uses pairs of bars to compare information. (p. 636)

double-line graph A graph that uses pairs of lines to compare information. (p. 638)

edge The line segment where two faces of a polyhedron meet. (p. 586)

elapsed time Total amount of time that passes from the beginning time to the ending time. (p. 555)

equal additions Adding the same number to two numbers in a subtraction problem does not affect the difference. (p. 33)

equation A mathematical sentence stating that two expressions are equal. (p. 44)

equilateral triangle A triangle with three sides of the same length. (p. 497)

equivalent fractions Fractions that name the same amount. (p. 164)

estimate To find a number that is close to an exact answer. (p. 16)

evaluate To find the number that an algebraic expression names by replacing a variable with a given number. (p. 41) *Example:* Evaluate 2*n* + 5 when *n* = 3; 2(3) + 5 = 11.

event An outcome or set of outcomes of an experiment or situation. (p. 655)

expanded form A number written as the sum of the place values of its digits. (p. 5)

expanded form using exponents A number written in expanded form with the place values written in exponential form. (p. 9) *Example:* $3{,}246 = (3 \times 10^3) + (2 \times 10^2) + (4 \times 10^1) + (6 \times 10^0)$

experimental probability A probability based on the statistical results of an experiment. (p. 664)

exponent The number that tells how many times the base is being multiplied by itself. (p. 8) *Example:* $8^3 = 8 \times 8 \times 8$, where 3 is the exponent and 8 is the base.

exponential form A way of writing repeated multiplication of a number using exponents. (p. 8) *Example:* 2^5.

expression A mathematical phrase containing variables, constants, and operation symbols. (p. 40) *Example:* 12 − *x*.

F

face A flat surface of a polyhedron. (p. 586)

factor A number that divides another number without a remainder. (p. 142)

Fahrenheit (°F) A standard unit for measuring temperature. (p. 722)

flip (reflection) A mirror image of a figure. (p. 510)

formula A rule that uses symbols to relate two or more quantities. (p. 328)

fraction A number that can be used to describe a part of a whole, a part of a set, a location on a number line, or a division of whole numbers. (p. 160)

frequency table A table to organize data by showing the number of values that fall in particular groups. (p. 628)

front-end estimation A method of estimation using the first digits of each addend that have the same place value. (p. 16)

front-end estimation with adjusting A method of front-end estimation that adjusts the result based on the remaining digits of each addend. (p. 16)

function A relation in which each *x*-value is paired with exactly one *y*-value. (p. 444)

glide reflection Moving a figure by a slide (translation) followed by a flip (reflection). (p. 510)

gram (g) Metric unit of mass. (p. 546)

greatest common factor (GCF) The largest number that is a factor of two or more numbers. (p. 150)

height The segment from a vertex perpendicular to the line containing the opposite side (p. 572); the perpendicular distance between the bases of a solid. (p. 595)

heptagon A polygon with seven sides. (p. 494)

hexagon A polygon with six sides. (p. 494)

identity properties The properties that state the sum of any number and zero is that number and the product of any number and one is that number. (p. 28)

impossible event An event that will never occur and has a probability of 0. (p. 662)

improper fraction A fraction in which the numerator is greater than or equal to its denominator. (p. 168)

independent events Events for which the outcome of one does not affect the probability of the other. (p. 672)

inequality A statement that uses the symbols > (greater than), < (less than), ≥ (greater than or equal to), or ≤ (less than or equal to) to compare two expressions. (p. 698)

integers The set of positive whole numbers, their opposites, and zero. (p. 408)

interest A charge for the use of money, paid by the borrower to the lender. (p. 386)

intersecting lines Lines that have exactly one point in common. (p. 473)
Example:

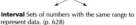

interval Sets of numbers with the same range to represent data. (p. 628)

inverse operations Operations that "undo" each other, such as addition and subtraction, or multiplication and division (except multiplication by 0). (p. 45)

isosceles triangle A triangle with at least two congruent sides. (p. 497)

kilo- Prefix meaning 1,000. (p. 546)

least common denominator (LCD) The least common multiple of the denominators of two or more fractions. (p. 164)
Example: 12 is the LCD of $\frac{1}{4}$ and $\frac{1}{6}$.

least common multiple (LCM) The smallest number, other than zero, that is a multiple of two or more numbers. (p. 152)

like denominators Denominators in two or more fractions that are the same. (p. 204)

line A straight path of points that goes on forever in two directions. (p. 472)

line graph A graph used to show changes over a period of time. (p. 638)

line plot A plot that shows the shape of a data set by stacking Xs above each value or interval on a number line. (p. 628)

line segment Part of a line that has two endpoints. (p. 472)

line of symmetry A line on which a figure can be folded into two congruent parts. (p. 514)

linear equation An equation whose graph is a straight line. (p. 448)

liter (L) Metric unit of capacity. (p. 546)

mass Measure of the amount of matter in an object. (p. 546)

maximum (in a data set) The greatest value in a set of numbers. (p. 624)

mean The sum of the values in a data set divided by the number of values. (p. 624)

median The middle value when a set of numbers is listed from least to greatest. (p. 624)

meter (m) Metric unit of length. (p. 546)

metric system (of measurement) A system using decimals and powers of 10 to measure length, mass, and capacity. (p. 546)

midpoint The point that divides the segment into two segments of equal length. (p. 472)

milli- Prefix meaning $\frac{1}{1{,}000}$. (p. 546)

minimum (in a data set) The least value in a set of numbers. (p. 624)

mixed number A number that combines a whole number and a fraction. (p. 168)

mode The number or numbers that occur most often in a set of data. (p. 624)

multiple The product of a number and a whole number greater than zero. (p. 142)

Multiplication Property of Zero Property that states the product of any number and zero is zero. (p. 28)

multiplicative inverse (reciprocal) Two numbers whose product is one. (p. 267) *Example:* The multiplicative inverse of $\frac{3}{4}$ is $\frac{4}{3}$ because $\frac{3}{4} \times \frac{4}{3} = 1$.

mutually exclusive Events that cannot occur at the same time. (p. 669)

negative power of ten A number in exponential form where the base is ten and the exponent is a negative integer. (p. 106)

net A plane figure pattern, which when folded, makes a solid. (p. 587)

nonagon A polygon with nine sides. (p. 494)

numerator The number above the fraction bar in a fraction; the number of objects or equal parts being considered. (p. 160)

O

obtuse angle An angle with a measure between 90° and 180°. (p. 477)

obtuse triangle A triangle with an obtuse angle. (p. 497)

octagon A polygon with eight sides. (p. 494)

opposite The integer on the opposite side of zero from a given number, but at the same distance from zero. (p. 408) *Example:* 7 and −7 are opposites.

order of operations A set of rules mathematicians use to determine the order in which operations are performed. (p. 24)

ordered pair A pair of numbers (*x*,*y*) used to locate a point on a coordinate plane. (p. 440)

origin The point (0,0), where the *x*- and *y*-axes of a coordinate plane intersect. (p. 440)

outcome The result in a probability experiment. (p. 655)

outlier A number very different from the other numbers in a data set. (p. 629)

P

parallel lines Lines in the same plane that do not intersect. (p. 473)

parallelogram A quadrilateral with both pairs of opposite sides parallel. (p. 500)

pentagon A polygon with five sides. (p. 494)

percent A ratio where the first term is compared to 100. (p. 354)

perimeter Distance around a figure. (p. 564)

permutation An arrangement of a group of things in a particular order. (p. 659)

perpendicular bisector A line, ray, or segment that intersects a segment at its midpoint and is perpendicular to it. (p. 484)
Example:

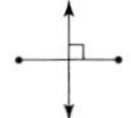

perpendicular lines Intersecting lines that form right angles. (p. 473)

pi (π) The ratio of the circumference of a circle to its diameter. Pi is approximately 3.14 or $\frac{22}{7}$. (p. 576)

plane A flat surface that extends forever in all directions. (p. 472)

point An exact location in space. (p. 472)

polygon A closed plane figure made up of three or more line segments. (p. 494)

polyhedron A three-dimensional figure made of flat surfaces that are polygons. (p. 586)

population The entire group of people or things that are being analyzed. (p. 620)

power The number of times a number is multiplied by itself. (p. 8)

prime factorization The set of primes whose product is a given composite. (p. 147) *Example:* $60 = 2^2 \times 3 \times 5$

prime number A whole number greater than 1 with exactly two whole positive factors, 1 and itself. (p. 147)

principal An amount of money borrowed or loaned. (p. 386)

prism A polyhedron with two congruent and parallel polygon-shaped faces. (p. 586)
Examples:

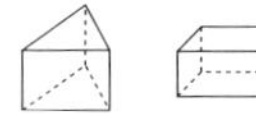

probability A ratio of the number of ways an event can happen to the total number of possible outcomes. (p. 662)

proper fraction A fraction less than 1; its numerator is less than its denominator. (p. 168)

properties of equality Properties that state performing the same operation to both sides of an equation keeps the equation balanced. (p. 44)

properties of inequality Properties that state adding or subtracting the same quantity or multiplying or dividing by the same positive quantity does not change the inequality. (p. 700)

proportion A statement that two ratios are equal. (p. 316)

pyramid A polyhedron whose base can be any polygon and whose faces are triangles. (p. 586)
Examples:

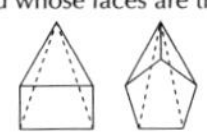

Q

quadrant One of the four regions into which the *x*- and *y*-axes divide the coordinate plane. The axes are not parts of the quadrant. (p. 440)

quadrilateral A polygon with four sides. (p. 494)

quotient The answer in a division problem. (p. 100) *Example:* In 45 ÷ 9 = 5, 5 is the quotient.

radius Any line segment that connects the center of the circle to a point on the circle. (p. 502)
Example:

random sampling Means of providing a representative sample, where each member of the population has an equal chance of being chosen. (p. 621)

range The difference between the greatest and least numbers in a set of data. (pp. 18, 624)

rate A ratio that compares two quantities with different units of measure. (p. 306)

ratio A pair of numbers that shows a comparison of two quantities and can be written as 9:4, $\frac{9}{4}$, or 9 to 4. (p. 300)

rational number Any number that can be written as fraction $\frac{a}{b}$, where *a* and *b* are integers and $b \neq 0$. (p. 412)

ray Part of a line with one endpoint, extending forever in only one direction. (p. 472)

reciprocal Two numbers whose product is one. (p. 267) *Example:* The reciprocal of $\frac{3}{4}$ is $\frac{4}{3}$ because $\frac{3}{4} \times \frac{4}{3} = 1$.

reflection (flip) The mirror image of a figure about a line of symmetry. (p. 510)

reflection symmetry Property of a figure that can be reflected onto itself. (p. 514)

regular polygon A polygon that has sides of equal length and angles of equal measure. (p. 494)

relation A set of ordered pairs (*x*,*y*). (p. 444)

repeating decimal A decimal in which a digit or digits repeat endlessly. (p. 173)

representative sample A sample which is representative of the population from which it is drawn. (p. 621)

rhombus A parallelogram with all four sides the same length. (p. 500)

right angle An angle which measures 90°. (p. 477)

right triangle A triangle with one right angle. (p. 497)

rotational symmetry Property of a figure that rotates onto itself in less than a full turn. (p. 514)

round To give an approximation for a number to the nearest one, ten, hundred, thousand, and so on. (p. 14)

S

sample Part of the population upon which an experiment or survey is conducted. (p. 620)

sample space The set of all possible outcomes of an experiment. (p. 655)

scale The ratio of the measurements in a drawing to the actual measurements of the object. (p. 330)

scale drawing A drawing made so that distances in the drawing are proportional to actual distances. (p. 330)

scalene triangle A triangle with no congruent sides. (p. 497)

scientific notation A number expressed as a product of a number greater than or equal to 1, but less than 10 and a power of 10. (p. 110) *Example:* $350 = 3.50 \times 10^2$

sector A region bounded by two radii and an arc. (p. 502) *Example:*

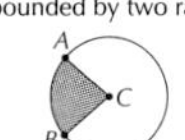

semicircle An arc that connects the endpoints of a diameter. (p. 502)

side A segment used to form a polygon (p. 494); a ray used to form an angle. (p. 476)

similar figures Figures that have the same shape, but not necessarily the same size. (p. 506)

simple interest Interest paid only on the principal, found by taking the product of the principal, rate, and time. (p. 386)

simplest form A fraction for which the greatest common factor of the numerator and denominator is 1; also, *lowest terms.* (p. 165)

skew lines Lines that lie in different planes that do not intersect and are not parallel. (p. 473)

slide (translation) The image of a figure that has been moved to a new position without flipping (reflecting) or turning (rotating). (p. 510)

sphere A three-dimensional figure such that every point is the same distance from the center. (p. 586) *Example:*

square A rectangle with all sides congruent. (p. 500)

squared A number that is multiplied by itself two times. (p. 9) *Example:* 5 squared = 5^2 = 25.

statistics Numerical data that have been collected and analyzed. (p. 621)

stem-and-leaf plot A frequency distribution that arranges data in order of place value. The leaves are the last digits of the numbers; the stems are the digits to the left of the leaves. (p. 632)

straight angle An angle which measures 180°. (p. 477)

supplementary angles Two angles with measures that add up to 180°. (p. 480)

surface area (SA) The sum of the areas of each face of a polyhedron. (p. 590)

survey Method to collect data from a sample to study some characteristic of the group. (p. 620)

T-table A table of *x*- and *y*-values used to graph an equation. (p. 448)

terminating decimal A decimal with a finite number of digits. (p. 173)
Example: 0.375

tessellation A pattern of congruent shapes covering a surface without gaps or overlaps. (p. 516)

theoretical probability Ratio of the favorable outcomes to the possible outcomes of an event. (p. 664)

translation (slide) The image of a figure that has been moved to a new position without flipping (reflecting) or turning (rotating). (p. 510)

trapezoid A quadrilateral with only one pair of opposite sides parallel. (p. 500)

tree diagram A diagram used to organize all the possible outcomes in a sample space. (p. 654)

trend A clear direction in a line graph suggesting how the data will behave in the future. (p. 638)

trial One of the instances of an experiment. (p. 664)

triangle A polygon with three sides. (p. 494)

turn (rotation) A transformation that turns a figure around a given point. (p. 510)

unit rate A rate in which the second number in the comparison is one unit. (p. 306)
Example: 25 feet per second

unlike denominators Denominators in two or more fractions that are different. (p. 206)

V

variable A quantity that can change or vary, often represented with a letter. (p. 40)

vertex (in an angle) The common endpoint of two rays that form an angle. (p. 476)

vertex (in a polygon) The point of intersection of two sides of a polygon. (p. 495)

vertex (in a polyhedron) The point of intersection of the edges of a polyhedron. (p. 586)

vertical angles A pair of angles formed by intersecting lines, the angles have no side in common. Vertical angles are congruent. (p. 480)
Example:

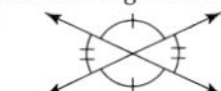

volume The number of cubic units that fit inside a space figure. (p. 594)

X

***x*-axis** The horizontal line on a coordinate plane. (p. 440)

***x*-coordinate** The first number in an ordered pair that tells the position left or right of the *y*-axis. (p. 440)

***y*-axis** The vertical line on a coordinate plane. (p. 440)

***y*-coordinate** The second number in an ordered pair that tells the position above or below the *x*-axis. (p. 440)

TABLES

Measures–Customary

Length	Weight	Capacity
1 foot (ft) = 12 inches (in.)	1 pound (lb) = 16 ounces (oz)	1 cup (c) = 8 fluid ounces (fl oz)
1 yard (yd) = 36 inches	1 ton (T) = 2,000 pounds	1 pint (pt) = 2 cups
1 yard = 3 feet		1 quart (qt) = 2 pints
1 mile (mi) = 5,280 feet		1 gallon (gal) = 4 quarts
1 mile = 1,760 yards		

Area

1 square foot (ft^2) = 144 square inches ($in.^2$)	1 acre = 43,560 square feet
1 square yard (yd^2) = 9 square feet	1 square mile (mi^2) = 640 acres

Measures–Metric

Length	Mass/Weight	Capacity
1 millimeter (mm) = 0.001 meter (m)	1 milligram (mg) = 0.001 gram (g)	1 milliliter (mL) = 0.001 liter (L)
1 centimeter (cm) = 0.01 meter	1 centigram (cg) = 0.01 gram	1 centiliter (cL) = 0.01 liter
1 kilometer (km) = 1,000 meters	1 kilogram (kg) = 1,000 grams	1 kiloliter (kL) = 1,000 liters
	1 metric ton (t) = 1,000 kilograms	

Area

1 square centimeter (cm^2) = 100 square millimeters (mm^2)	1 hectare (ha) = 10,000 square meters
1 square meter (m^2) = 10,000 square centimeters	1 square kilometer (km^2) = 1,000,000 square meters

Measures–*Customary and Metric Unit Equivalents*

Length	Weight and Mass	Capacity
1 in. = 2.54 cm	1 oz ≈ 28.35 g	1 L ≈ 1.06 qt
1 m ≈ 39.37 in.	1 kg ≈ 2.2 lb	1 gal ≈ 3.79 L
1 m ≈ 1.09 yd	1 metric ton (t) ≈ 1.102 tons (T)	
1 mi ≈ 1.61 km		

Symbols

=	is equal to	π	pi (approximately 3.14)	$\parallel$	is parallel to
≠	is not equal to	°	degree	2:5	ratio of 2 to 5
>	is greater than	°C	degree Celsius	10^2	ten to the second power
<	is less than	°F	degree Fahrenheit	+4	positive 4
≥	is greater than or equal to	$\overleftrightarrow{AB}$	line *AB*	−4	negative 4
≤	is less than or equal to	$\overline{AB}$	line segment *AB*	(3, 4)	ordered pair 3, 4
≈	is approximately equal to	$\overrightarrow{AB}$	ray *AB*	*P*(E)	probability of event E
≅	is congruent to	$\angle ABC$	angle *ABC*	⊥	is perpendicular to
~	is similar to	$\triangle ABC$	triangle *ABC*		
%	percent				

Formulas

$P = 2\ell + 2w$	Perimeter of a rectangle	$C = \pi \times d$	Circumference of a circle
$A = \ell \times w$	Area of a rectangle	$A = \pi \times r^2$	Area of a circle
$A = b \times h$	Area of a parallelogram	$V = \ell \times w \times h$	Volume of a rectangular prism
$A = \frac{1}{2} \times b \times h$	Area of a triangle	$I = p \times r \times t$	Simple interest

Credits

Cover

Illustration: Braldt Bralds

Photograph: ©Pal Hermansen/Getty Images

Text

Dorling Kindersley (DK) is an international publishing company specializing in the creation of high-quality reference content for books, CD-ROMs, online materials, and video. The hallmark of DK content is its unique combination of educational value and strong visual style. This combination allows DK to deliver appealing, accessible, and engaging educational content that delights children, parents, and teachers around the world. Scott Foresman is delighted to have been able to use selected extracts of DK content within this Scott Foresman Math program.

56–57: "Production" from *The World in One Day* by Russell Ash. Text copyright ©1997 by Russell Ash. Compilation and illustration copyright ©1997 by Dorling Kindersley Limited; 120–121: "The Toronto SkyDome" from *Amazing Buildings* by Philip Wilkinson. Text copyright ©1993 by Philip Wilkinson. Copyright ©1993 by Dorling Kindersley Limited; 188–189: "On the Surface" from *Incredible Comparisons* by Russell Ash. Copyright ©1996 by Dorling Kindersley Limited; 228–229: "Floating on Air" from *Machines and How They Work* by David Burnie. Copyright ©1991 by Dorling Kindersley; 280–281: "Beehive" from *Richard Orr's Nature Cross-Sections* by Moira Butterfield, illustrated by Richard Orr. Copyright ©1995 by Dorling Kindersley Limited; 334–335: "The United States of America" from *Flag* by William Crampton. Copyright ©2000 by Dorling Kindersley Limited; 388–389: "Airport" from *Stephen Biesty's Incredible Explosions* by Richard Platt, illustrated by Stephen Biesty. Copyright ©1996 by Dorling Kindersley Limited; 450–451: "Weather" from *Incredible Comparisons* by Russell Ash. Copyright ©1996 by Dorling Kindersley Limited; 520–521: "Neuschwanstein Castle" from *Amazing Buildings* by Philip Wilkinson. Text copyright ©1993 by Philip Wilkinson. Copyright ©1993 by Dorling Kindersley Limited; 598–599: "Beneath the Streets" from *Super Structures* by Philip Wilkinson. Copyright ©1996 by Dorling Kindersley Limited; 678–679: "Growth and Age" from *Incredible Comparisons* by Russell Ash. Copyright ©1996 by Dorling Kindersley Limited; 728–729: "The Summer Games" from *Olympics* by Chris Oxlade and David Ballheimer. Copyright ©2000 by Dorling Kindersley Limited.

Illustrations

331, 332, 436, 441, 442, 489 Phyllis Pollema-Cahill

Photographs

Every effort has been made to secure permission and provide appropriate credit for photographic material. The publisher deeply regrets any omission and pledges to correct errors called to its attention in subsequent editions.

Unless otherwise acknowledged, all photographs are the property of Scott Foresman, a division of Pearson Education.

Photo locators denoted as follows: Top (T), Center (C), Bottom (B), Left (L), Right (R), Background (Bkgd)

Chapter 1: 2 ©Joshua Ets-Hokin/Getty Images; 4 (L) David Nunuk/Photo Researchers, Inc., (BL) Daemmrich Photography; 6 ©Ken Usami/Getty Images; 7 (TC) Getty Images, (TR) Bridgeman Art Library International Ltd.; 10 (CR) The Granger Collection, (BR) ©Lester V. Bergman/Bettmann/Corbis; 12 ©Galen Rowell/Corbis; 14 Dembinsky Photo Associates; 16 Getty Images; 18 Joseph Sohm/Photo Researchers, Inc.; 19 Joseph Sohm/Photo Researchers, Inc.; 20 ©Chris Jones/Corbis; 21 ©G. K. and Vikki Hart/Getty Images; 28 Philip and Karen Smith/SuperStock; 29 ©Philippe Colombi/Getty Images; 30 H. Armstrong Roberts; 32 Paul Silverman/Fundamental Photographs; 34 (BC) Barry Runk/Grant Heilman Photography, (BR) Jessica Wecker/Photo Researchers, Inc., (BL) Getty Images, (B) Brock Optical Inc.; 36 Joe Atlas/Brand X Pictures; 40 (L) Photonica, (TR) ©Steve Cole/Getty Images; 42 ©AFP/Corbis; 43 ©Yann Arthus-Bertrand/Corbis; 46 ©Arthur Thévenart/Corbis; 48 Getty Images; 56 ©Dorling Kindersley; 59 Getty Images

Chapter 2: 74 ©Dorling Kindersley; 76 ©Charles O'Rear/Bettmann/Corbis; 77 Getty Images; 78 (L) ©Roger Ressmeyer/Bettmann/Corbis, (TL) ©Earth Imaging/Getty Images; 79 (BR) ©World Perspectives/Getty Images, (C) ©Photo Library International/Corbis, (TC) ©Roger Ressmeyer/Corbis; 80B (TL) Hemera Technologies; 80 (L) ©Tim Flach/Getty Images, (TR) ©Derek Berwin/Getty Images; 83 Burke/Triolo Productions/FoodPix; 86 ©R. W. Jones/Bettmann/Corbis; 88 (CR) ©G. K. and Vikki Hart/Getty Images, (CC, BR, BL) Getty Images; 90 Getty Images; 92 ©Craig Tuttle/Bettmann/Corbis; 96 Getty Images; 98 ©Galen Rowell/Bettmann/Corbis; 102 Eisenhut & Mayer/FoodPix; 103 GoodShoot/SuperStock; 106 ©Bettmann/Corbis; 108 Getty Images; 110 ©Dorling Kindersley; 112 ©Joseph Sohm/Bettmann/Corbis; 113 ©Bettmann/Corbis; 114 (CL) ©Ryan McVay/Getty Images, (C) Getty Images; 115 Getty Images; 116 ©Nancy R. Cohen/Getty Images; 117 Getty Images; 118 (BR) ©Robb Debenport/Getty Images, (T) ©Jules Frazier/Getty Images, (TR) Linda Holt Ayriss/Artville; 119 Getty Images; 120 ©Dorling Kindersley; 124 ©C Squared Studios/Getty Images; 125 ©Claire Hayden/Getty Images

Chapter 3: 142 (L) ©Jake Rajs/Getty Images, (T) digitalvisiononline.com; 143 Getty Images; 144 Lisette Le Bon/SuperStock; 149 ©Corbis Stock Market; 153 ©Corbis Stock Market; 160 (TR) Getty Images, (CC) ImageState, (CR) ©James P. Blair/Getty Images; 163 ©Bettmann/Corbis; 167 Getty Images; 168 (L) ©J. H. Pete Carmichael/Getty Images, (CR) ©Anthony Bannister/Corbis, (TR) Index Stock Imagery, (C) Joel MacGregor/Peter Arnold, Inc.; 170 ©Bob Torrez/Getty Images; 175 ©NASA/Corbis; 176 ©Jeff Hunter/Getty Images; 178 ©Amos Nachoum/Corbis; 180A (BR) Hemera Technologies; 182 ©Dorling Kindersley; 183 ©Dorling Kindersley; 186 Getty Images; 187 ©Larry Williams/Corbis; 188 ©Dorling Kindersley; 189 ©Dorling Kindersley

Chapter 4: 202 ©EMPICS; 208 ©Ron Chapple/Getty Images; 211 Corbis; 212 ©Reza Estakhrian/Getty Images; 215 Corbis; 218 ©Gavin Hellier/Getty Images; 220B (BR) Courtesy of CollectSource.com; 222 (CR, CC) Barbara Strnadova/Photo Researchers, Inc., (BC) Runk/Schoenberger/Grant Heilman Photography; 223 ©Nicholas DeVore/Getty Images; 225 ©Jake Martin/Getty Images; 226 ©Lori Adamski Peek/Getty Images; 228 ©Dorling Kindersley; 229 ©Dorling Kindersley; 231 Brand X Pictures; 245 Getty Images

Chapter 5: 246 digitalvisiononline.com; 252 ©Gary Cralle/Getty Images; 257 Getty Images; 258 (L) ©Tim Flach/Getty Images, (BL) ©Chris Rogers/Bettmann/Corbis; 263 Corbis; 265 (BR) ©Ryoichi Utsumi/Photonica, (BRR) ©Kei Muto/Photonica; 269 Scott Camazine/Photo Researchers, Inc.; 271 (L) ImageState, (CR) ©Steve Cole/Getty Images; 275 ©David Young-Wolff/PhotoEdit; 276 Charles Orrico/SuperStock; 279 ©Peter Walton/Index Stock Imagery; 280 Richard Orr/©Dorling Kindersley; 281 Richard Orr/©Dorling Kindersley

Chapter 6: 300 (L) ©Lori Adamski Peek/Getty Images, (T) Getty Images; 301 ©Paul Avis/Getty Images; 305 ©Antonio M. Rosario/Getty Images; 308 (CR) ©Alan Becker/Getty Images, (C) ©Stuart Westmorland/Corbis, (BR) ©James Balog/Getty Images, (BC) David L. Shirk/Animals Animals/Earth Scenes; 309 (BR) Corbis, (TR) Brand X Pictures; 310 (CR) ©Bill Bachmann/Index Stock Imagery, (CRB) Getty Images; 311 ©Dorling Kindersley; 312 (L) Getty Images, (CR) Corbis; 313 ©Bruce Ayres/Getty Images; 316 ©V.C.L./Getty Images; 318B (BR) Getty Images; 320 Bridgeman Art Library International Ltd.; 323 Kenneth McCray/SuperStock; 325 Gary Hoover; 328B (L, R) Getty Images; 328 (L) Roy Ooms/Masterfile Corporation, (BL) ©Doug Mazell/Index Stock Imagery, (CL) ©Greg Pease/Getty Images; 330B (BR) Getty Images; 330 (L) ©Bernard Roussel/Getty Images, (CR) ©Swim Ink/Corbis; 334 ©Dorling Kindersley; 335 (T) ©Dorling Kindersley, (BL) NASA

Chapter 7: 352 ©Andy Caulfield/Getty Images; 354 ©Kaz Mori/Getty Images; 355 ©Brian Hagiwara/FoodPix; 358 ©Sean Ellis/Getty Images; 360 Getty Images; 362 Getty Images; 368 ©Science Pictures Limited/Corbis; 369 ©Yorgos Nikas/Getty Images; 370 ©Kim Steele/Getty Images; 373 (C) Getty Images, (CR) ©Cathy Crawford/Corbis; 376 Corbis; 377 digitalvisiononline.com; 382 ©Doris De Witt/Getty Images; 383 ©Art Wolfe/Getty Images; 384 ©Christopher Gould/Getty Images; 386 ©Don Farrall/Getty Images; 388 ©Stephen Biesty; 392 Getty Images

Chapter 8: 406 digitalvisiononline.com; 408 Mark E. Gibson/Dembinsky Photo Associates; 409 ©Alan Schein Photography/Corbis; 410 Grant Heilman Photography; 411 Spencer Grant/PhotoEdit; 412 Rudi Von Briel/PhotoEdit; 414 ©Corbis Stock Market; 418 Grant Heilman Photography; 421 ©Steve Bronstein/Getty Images; 424 ©Bruce Heinemann/Getty Images; 426 Gala/SuperStock; 427 (CRC) ©Guido Alberto Rossi/Getty Images, (CR) ©H. W. Robison/Visuals Unlimited; 428 ©Galen Rowell/Corbis; 429 ©Jules Frazier/Getty Images; 430 ©Gary Braasch/Getty Images; 431 ©Roger Ressmeyer/Corbis; 434 digitalvisiononline.com; 444 ©World Perspectives/Getty Images; 448 Grant Heilman Photography; 450 ©Dorling Kindersley; 451 ©Dorling Kindersley; 467 ©World Perspectives/Getty Images

Chapter 9: 470 ©Josef Beck/Getty Images; 472 ©Mark E. Gibson/Mark E. Gibson Stock Photography; 479 The Granger Collection; 480 ©Denny Eilers/Grant Heilman Photography; 494 ©Gregg Mancuso/Stock Boston; 496 ©Gunter Marx Photography/Corbis; 498 Corbis; 499 Hemera Technologies; 500 ©Myrleen Cate/Index Stock Imagery; 502 (L) ©Grant Heilman/Grant Heilman Photography, (T) ©David R. Frazier Photolibrary; 503 Historic Hudson Valley, Tarrytown, NY; 508 Getty Images; 510 ©Mark E. Gibson/Mark E. Gibson Stock Photography; 513 (CR) Index Stock Imagery, (CL) ©Craig Newbauer/Peter Arnold, Inc.; 514 (L) ©Nicole Duplaix/NGS Image Collection, (CR) David Ball/Index Stock Imagery, (CL) ©Bill Varie/Corbis; 516 ©Gérard Degeorge/Corbis; 520 ©Josef Beck/Getty Images; 521 ©ZEFA/Masterfile Corporation

Chapter 10: 540 ©Lauree Feldman/Index Stock Imagery; 542 ©SIU Biomedical Communications/Photo Researchers, Inc.; 546B (BR) Getty Images; 546 ©Space Frontiers/Getty Images; 547 ©Scott Barrow, Inc./SuperStock; 550 ©Erich Lessing/Art Resource, NY; 553 ©Bill Wittman; 554 ©Georg Gerster/Photo Researchers, Inc.; 555 (TR) ©Jennifer Thermes/Getty Images, (CR) ©Mark E. Gibson Stock Photography, (T) Robert W. Ginn/PhotoEdit; 556 Corbis; 557 ©Earl and Nazima Kowall/Corbis; 559 (L, CR, R) Getty Images, (CC) digitalvisiononline.com; 560 ©Matthias Kulka/Corbis; 561 (BR) ©Scott Murphy/New York Stock Photo Agency, (R) ©Mitch Diamond/Index Stock Imagery, (B) ©Rob Crandall/Stock Boston, (BC) ©Corbis Stock Market; 564 ©Ron Chapple/Getty Images; 570 ©Mark E. Gibson Stock Photography; 572 Bill Aron/PhotoEdit; l577 ©David R. Frazier/Photo Researchers, Inc.; 578 ©Eric Roth/Index Stock Imagery; 580 ©Gregg Ozzo/Visuals Unlimited, (BR) ©Comstock Inc.; 583 ©Corbis Stock Market; 586 ©Yoshio Tomii/SuperStock; 589 Cluster of Four Cubes, Gift of George Rickey and Patrons' Permanent Fund, Image © 2004 Board of Trustees, National Gallery of Art, Washington, 1992, stainless steel. Photo by Philip A. Charles; 590 Getty Images; 596 ©Ken Cavanaugh/Photo Researchers, Inc.; 598 ©Dorling Kindersley

Chapter 11: 618 Digital Stock; 620 ©Tom Carter/PhotoEdit; 621 ©Tony Freeman/PhotoEdit; 624B (BR) ©Dorling Kindersley; 624 ©David Young-Wolff/PhotoEdit; 626 ©Cleve Bryant/PhotoEdit; 631 Getty Images; 632 ©Klaus Rose/Okapia/Photo Researchers, Inc.; 633 ©David Young-Wolff/PhotoEdit; 638 ©SW Productions/Getty Images; 645 ©Kevin Fleming/Corbis; 647 (TR) ©George Ranalli/Photo Researchers, Inc., (CR) ©Ryan McVay/Getty Images, (BR) Getty Images; 648 ©David Toase/Getty Images; 667 WGN TV; 670 (L) Getty Images, (CL) ©Arthur S. Aubry/Getty Images; 672 ©Stephen Frisch/Stock Boston; 674 ©Paul Gallaher/Index Stock Imagery; 676 (CL, B) ©Dorling Kindersley; 677 ©Dorling Kindersley; 678 ©Dorling Kindersley; 695 Getty Images

Chapter 12: 696 ©Pete Saloutos/Corbis; 698 ©David Carriere/Index Stock Imagery; 699 ©Barbara Leslie/Getty Images; 702 digitalvisiononline.com; 705 Getty Images; 707 ©Stuart Westmorland/Photo Researchers, Inc.; 709 Getty Images; 711 (CR) Getty Images, (T) ©David Madison Sports Images, Inc.; 712 ©A. Bartel/Getty Images; 714 Getty Images; 716 Getty Images; 718 ©Larry Mulvehill/Photo Researchers, Inc.; 721 ©Chuck Pefley/Stock Boston; 722 ©Gary Hush/Getty Images; 728 (T) ©Mike Hewitt/Getty Images, (CR) ©Mike Powell/Getty Images, (BL) ©Agence Vandystad/Bruno Bade/Getty Images, (BR) ©Pascal Rondeau/Getty Images; 729 ©Dorling Kindersley

Chapter 4

Page 213

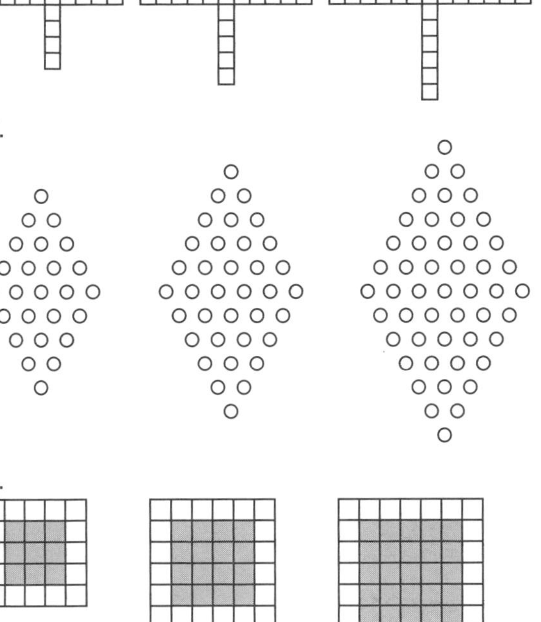

Page 225

6. $9\frac{3}{5}$; mental math

7. $3\frac{37}{40}$; paper and pencil

8. $9\frac{5}{12}$; paper and pencil

9. $\frac{5}{24}$; paper and pencil

0. $15\frac{23}{30}$; paper and pencil

4. Sample answer: $5\frac{3}{4} + 2\frac{3}{8}$: $\frac{3}{8} = \frac{1}{4} + \frac{1}{8}$ and the $\frac{1}{4}$ can be added to the $\frac{3}{4}$ making it a whole number, leaving only a fraction of $\frac{1}{8}$.

Notes

Index

Index

Index

 EC NTL 12 11 10 9 8 7 6 5 4 3 2

Notes

Notes

Notes

Notes

Notes

Notes

Notes

Notes

Notes

EC NTL 12 11 10 9 8 7 6